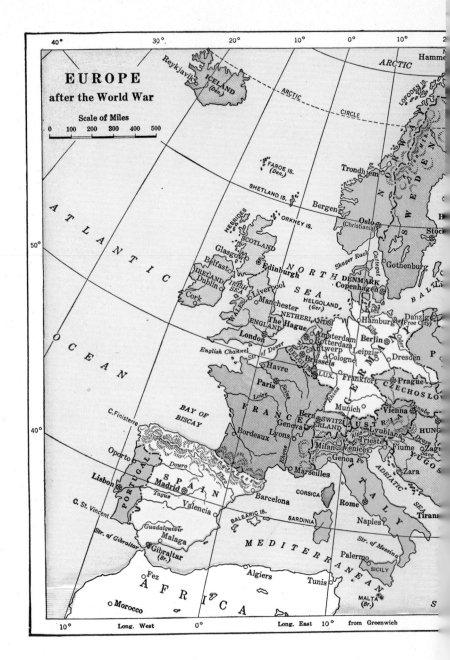

EUROPE
after the World War

Scale of Miles

0   100   200   300   400   500

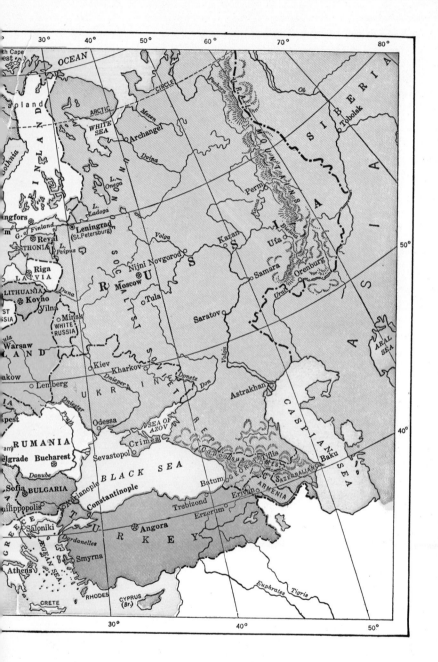

EUROPE SINCE 1870

BY

PRESTON WILLIAM SLOSSON, Ph.D.

ASSOCIATE PROFESSOR OF HISTORY, UNIVERSITY OF MICHIGAN
AUTHOR OF *Twentieth Century Europe, The Great Crusade and After*, etc.

WITH A FOREWORD BY

JAMES T. SHOTWELL, LL.D.

PROFESSOR OF HISTORY, COLUMBIA UNIVERSITY

HOUGHTON MIFFLIN COMPANY

BOSTON · NEW YORK · CHICAGO · DALLAS · ATLANTA · SAN FRANCISCO

The Riverside Press Cambridge

The Riverside Press
CAMBRIDGE · MASSACHUSETTS
PRINTED IN THE U.S.A.

EDITOR'S INTRODUCTION

THE field surveyed by this volume is one to which historians
will turn for many centuries to come. If Thucydides, the
wisest among the historians of the ancient world, could
regard the Peloponnesian War as the greatest theme in the
annals of mankind down to his day, because it was bound to
mark a turning point in the development of the Greek city
states, and if his judgment has been widely accepted by
Hellenists because those states were the repositories of a
culture without parallel, then what of the Peloponnesian
War of the Europe of modern times? Already it is receding
into the perspectives in which its magnitude may be measured against the skyline of the past; but it is also beginning
to lose some of that intimate sense of experience which it has
had for the generation that endured and carried it through.
Just at this turning point, from a contemporary event to
one that takes its place in the ages, the era of the World War
offers more to the historian than he is likely to find in it at
any time in the future. We are already aware of most of
the problems which it presents: why it happened when it
did; how much of the change wrought by it was fundamental, how much a mere arrangement of externals; why the
drift and current of events kept here and there to the old-
time channels, while elsewhere they swept away the institutions of the past like dikes of sand. These and many other
such questions are now in the crucible of history.

But the answers can only be molded in the hands of those
historians who conceive their task in the sense in which the
author of this volume conceives it. No mere listing of political and military events can throw light on these intricate
and elusive problems. Equally inadequate is that interest
in events which is satisfied when they are arranged in logical

order and sorted out for ready reference. To trace the pattern of the past according to an accepted scheme is not enough. Characters, actions, institutions must be studied in the light of their own time and environment, with reference to all the varied influences which played upon them. The history of an era of war is therefore also the history of the preceding years, conceived not merely as a prelude to the main event but as it appeared at the time, and must deal with the consequences as they developed under new and unforeseen conditions.

The present volume has been written with these major problems in mind. If it does not attempt to answer them all, it faces them with that thoughtfulness which stirs a similar response in the reader. It explores with sympathetic insight the quiet years of peace which make pre-war Europe seem now so far-off and unreal, and traces the shaping and reshaping of the issues of the post-war period with a growing sense of distance from 1918 and a growing emphasis upon those problems which mark the beginning of a new era.

The story of the unique experiment of Soviet Russia is complete in itself. Similarly the rise of dictatorships in central and eastern Europe is shown to have reached a second stage in which the original causes tend more and more to sink to the background and new policies arise to furnish the test of their strength for endurance. It is in keeping with the sobriety of the narrative that it ends, somewhat abruptly, at this point, without a prophetic forecast. The vision of future possibilities is hinted at in the closing words, but only in most general terms. The story deals with the tragic past of Europe, its inadequacies and its achievements rather than with the measure of its potentialities.

If, as I have said elsewhere, the World Depression may prove to be the last battle of the World War, the result of its impact upon that tenuous but all-pervading web of business relations that extends in time as in space and registers long afterwards and in distant places the effect of war and violence, then the period covered by this volume has an underlying unity in spite of its apparent contrasts and diversities of interest. The long peace of the Great Powers, from 1870 to 1914, is succeeded by the long crisis, from 1914 to the present. In the one we see the apparent close of the process of national state formation; in the other we see the anarchy which arises from the imperfection of that process, and the consequence of its maintenance of the right of sovereign states to use war as the instrument of national policy. The effort to reform the process, to substitute conference, conciliation and judicial settlement of disputes for war or the menace of war, grew naturally out of the con-ditions of 1918. The League of Nations emerges, not as an artificial and external creation, the product of utopian dreams, but as the embodiment of the hope of mankind that it could build an alternative to war.

But international relations are themselves the reflection of the political ideals and attitudes of the nations as wit-nessed in their internal development, and the peace of the world is again imperiled by a return of the old nationalism, intensified by resentment or frustration. The outstanding leaders of this trend are, or have been, demagogues whose pathway to power has been lit by the flames of animosities against other nations. American observers of this unlovely spectacle have hitherto pointed the finger of scorn at certain European countries whose liberties have been lost to those who denounced the wickedness of other peoples and held out the promise of emancipation from the evils of the day. But the millions who are listening today in the United States to the specious and often dishonest appeals to prejudice and trickery, whether under the guise of political debate or religion, may yet be faced with the same decisions as the peoples of Europe.

The best of training for that discipline of the mind which

is the only sure defense of the citizen against demagoguery lies in the study of history as here presented, dispassionate but not disinterested in the great issues that have confronted and still confront civilization. History does not offer a guide to the future in a world which no longer repeats itself but is eternally changing as it conquers the conditions of livelihood; but it can and should breed caution, prudence and sound judgment. By a paradox, universally accepted by historians, it can do this all the better if it is unconscious of any such aim, but concentrates, as Professor Slosson has so admirably done, upon the task of scholarship, the search for the truth about men and nations. It was Polybius, the most pragmatic of the historians of the ancient world, who said that "as a living creature is rendered wholly useless if deprived of its eyes, so if you take truth from History, what is left but an unprofitable tale?"

JAMES T. SHOTWELL

PREFACE

Europe Since 1870 is a political history of Europe since the Franco-Prussian War. Considerations of space made it impossible to include any systematic account of the economic, social and cultural development of the age, or a detailed analysis of battles and campaigns, or even the full political history of countries outside Europe. But the narrative is not narrowly political nor narrowly European. Equal weight is given to domestic politics and to international diplomacy, and the economic and cultural causes and effects of major political events are emphasized. The affairs of America, Asia and Africa come into the picture as often as they involve important European interests. As a really complete bibliography of that crowded period would be considerably larger than this volume, it has been necessary to limit references to a highly selected list, with preference to books written in English or available in translation.

The bibliography itself is an acknowledgment of my indebtedness to many other writers of our time, but I wish to thank particularly Professors James T. Shotwell of Columbia University, Laurence B. Packard of Amherst College, and Howard Ehrmann of the University of Michigan, who have had the patience and kindness to read the manuscript and offer suggestions of the utmost value. Those writers are fortunate who can count such friends among their critics.

PRESTON SLOSSON

Ann Arbor, Michigan

CONTENTS

MAPS AND CHARTS

CHAPTER I

NATIONS ON THE ANVIL

ON SEPTEMBER 4, 1870, France declared herself a republic, thus ending the Second Empire. On September 20, an Italian army marched into Rome, completing the *Three* unification of Italy. On January 18 of the fol- *landmarks* lowing year, the new German Empire was proclaimed at Versailles, completing the work of nation-building which Bismarck had snatched from the hands of German liberals and idealists.

Thus dramatically closed a period of war, revolution and political experiment. For more than forty-three years thereafter Europe was destined to enjoy the long- *An epoch of* est respite from armed conflict recorded in her *war replaced* annals. Wars continued but they were fought *by the "armed* far away from the centers of civilization: in *peace" of* Cuba, in South Africa, in Manchuria and in the *1871-1914* half-Asiatic Balkans. No frontier in western or central Europe was crossed by an invader, no industrial center threatened with siege or bombardment. Civil disturbance was also rare and the majority of political changes of the time were peacefully effected. Yet this unprecedented era of peace was filled with naval rivalries, colonial jealousies, hostile alliances and the ever-fiercer struggle of classes and nationalities for "a place in the sun." When the long-delayed explosion came at last in 1914, the keenest observers of international politics were surprised only that the general peace had endured for so many years.

Insecure though it proved to be, the peace enjoyed by the generation following the Franco-Prussian War is evidence that some, at least, of the major political problems of Europe had found solution, just as the continued unrest in the Balkans bore witness that other problems remained unsolved. The early nineteenth century witnessed the rise and partial triumph of certain powerful political forces which bear the labels "nationalism," "liberalism," "democracy" and "socialism." As these forces were to play an even greater rôle after 1870, a few words about their entrance upon the European stage may be needed as an introduction to our modern problems.

National patriotism has been by all odds the most powerful political force in modern times and yet it is not always *Nationalism* easy to see how it arises or wins its mastery over the souls of men. Of course, there is nothing deeper in human nature, not even the instinct of self-preservation, than the "consciousness of kind" which makes some people and institutions seem "kindred" and others "foreign." But the social group to which the individual may give his allegiance — and if need be his life — has not always been the same. The ancient Greek was a patriot for Athens or Sparta rather than for Greece; the city was his nation. Rome expanded from a city into a world empire without ever really halting at the halfway point of nationhood. In the Middle Ages loyalty was largely a personal matter, the knight served the overlord to whom he had sworn fealty. Even as late as the sixteenth century, Protestants and Catholics hated a rival church with a sincerity much greater than the hostility between the subjects of one king and those of another. National patriotism attained early development in England, Scotland and Scandinavia; it bloomed somewhat later in France, Holland and Spain, and scarcely influenced Germany, Italy and southeastern Europe until the nineteenth century. The factors that established nationhood varied. Usually a common language was the primary bond, but not always. The English-speaking Irishman, the German-speaking Alsatian were not invariably loyal Britons or Germans. Sometimes religion played a part; had not Ireland been Roman Catholic and Scotland Presbyterian, théy might more easily have merged their separate national identities with that of England. Occasionally, as in the case of Switzerland, the memory of common sufferings and triumphs welded a people into one in defiance of differences both of speech and creed. The particular form which a national movement will take depends on circumstances. A subject nationality demands either complete independence or local self-government (autonomy or "home rule"). A divided nationality desires union. A nation both free and united will usually seek to expand and extend its power, even at the expense of other countries.

Liberalism and nationalism have sometimes been allies and sometimes enemies. Where an oppressed nationality struggles for independence, it will usually win *Liberalism* liberal sympathy, but when the national state uses its power to repress minority groups, liberalism and nationalism part company. Liberalism is the doctrine of freedom — the "right to choose" — for individuals and for voluntary groups. In modern times it has demanded freedom of religious worship for all creeds; freedom of speech, press, public meeting and organization; constitutional guarantees and legal rights to protect the individual against arbitrary arrest and punishment. Though these freedoms can exist to some degree under an aristocratic or even an autocratic government (if the autocrat be a mild and tolerant ruler), in the main the liberal movement has historically been associated with the democratic movement, the cry for popular self-government.

Down to the French Revolution of 1789 most of the states of Europe had been hereditary monarchies, and the power of the kings seemed rather to increase than diminish as governments became more centralized and stable. There were a few exceptions to this rule, the outstanding one being England, where well-organized classes of merchants

The prob-
lem of pop-
ular sover-
eignty

and country squires, acting through a representative Parliament, had reduced the monarch
to little more than a figurehead.[1] But in France,
Spain, Portugal, Austria, Prussia, Russia, Denmark, Turkey, and most of the lesser German and Italian
states, the will of the sovereign had the force of law. The
king was not the only possessor of hereditary privilege. He
was surrounded by a class of nobles whose profession (at
least in theory) was war, whose wealth was mainly in land,
and whose social position was recognized by law. The clergy
of the established church usually enjoyed exceptional rights
and immunities. Below the privileged orders came the
"commoners," termed by the French the "third estate."
Even among these, however, many individuals rose to rank
and power as official servants of the king, and in some
countries the whole class of wealthy town dwellers (the
"bourgeoisie") had acquired considerable influence. The
more the real importance of this class increased, however,
the more impatient they became with the belated feudal
forms which had survived into the modern age. Their
leaders became the spokesmen for the hitherto inarticulate
masses, demanded the abolition of the special privileges of
the nobles and clergy and advocated constitutions to limit
the power of the kings.

The first great struggle on the continent of Europe between the old régime and the democratic movement took

The French
Revolution

place in France, not because the French people
were more oppressed than others but partly because the French monarchy had become extraordinarily
slack and inefficient in its conduct of the public business,[2]

[1] Other exceptions of importance were the Dutch and Swiss republics and the
disorderly elective monarchy of Poland. The United States of America was the
first really democratic government to cover a very extensive area.

[2] In contrast to Prussia, Austria and some other states where "enlightened
despots" of the type of Frederick the Great had tried to blend absolute monarchy
with the reform of abuses.

and partly because the champions of reform were unusually numerous and outspoken. Popular sovereignty was proclaimed, feudal privileges abolished by law, and, when King Louis XVI attempted feebly to stem the tide of radicalism, royalty itself was swept away. But the first French republic triumphed in arms over the "confederate kings" only to become subject to the dictatorship of its foremost captain. And when Emperor Napoleon was finally overthrown democracy was not restored in France nor established anywhere else. On the contrary, the leading diplomats at the Congress of Vienna in 1814–15 looked back with nostalgic longing to the institutions of the old régime.

The treaty of Vienna which marked the victory of the old order in Europe was not a bad one by the standards of past centuries. The spoils were distributed with *The Vienna* some approach to fairness, defeated France was *Congress,* permitted to keep her pre-revolutionary bound- *1814-15* aries, and the victorious powers organized an alliance which some have considered a far-off anticipation of the League of Nations. That there had been real progress in the moral sense of Europe is shown, to take one example, by the fact that England, which had made a particular point of demanding a share in the African slave trade at the Congress of Utrecht a century earlier, was now foremost in demanding the total abolition of that traffic. Where the peacemakers at Vienna erred was in ignoring completely the political ideals of the new day. In the old-fashioned way they divided territories to produce a "balance of power" among the ruling dynasties with no reference at all to the wishes of the governed. Finland was left to Russia to please one victorious power; Norway transferred from Denmark to Sweden to please another. Belgium was united with the former Dutch Republic into a common Netherlandish Kingdom to strengthen a frontier against the French, and Austria compensated for the loss of Belgium (formerly the "Austrian

Netherlands") by Lombardy and Venetia in Italy. Poland was redivided among Russia, Austria and Prussia. Hungary still remained subject to an Austrian ruler. Italy, still a mere "geographical expression," was partitioned among petty kings and dukes of varying degrees of incompetence. The hopes of German patriots for a real German nation were mocked by a loose confederation of German sovereigns under the presidency of Austria. The Diet of this Confederation or *Bund* resembled rather a congress of diplomatic delegates than the legislature of a national state, and there was no common flag, law of citizenship, representative assembly of the people, legal code, tariff union, army or navy. Even foreign princes who chanced to have territory within the confederation were given the right to meddle with its affairs.

If the treaty-makers of Vienna ignored nationality, the restored rulers still more definitely opposed liberalism and

"The age of Metternich," 1815-48

democracy. The French Revolution and the Napoleonic adventure had convinced most of them that popular government was a dragon of anarchy to be fought to the uttermost. Prince Metternich, the Austrian statesman who had been the most prominent figure at the Vienna Congress, turned the alliance of victorious powers from a mere agreement to keep the peace to an international police force for the repression of revolution. Most of the German rulers refused to honor their promises to grant constitutions within their realms, the Italian states continued despotic, and the King of Spain revoked the constitution written by the Spanish patriots who had helped replace him on his throne. The liberal Tsar Alexander I of Russia turned reactionary as age and Metternich mastered his mind. Even the two outstanding constitutional Powers in Europe, Great Britain and France, were governed under narrow franchise laws which denied the suffrage to the mass of the middle and working classes.

Metternich's policy of reaction and repression in continental Europe has been defended on the ground that at least it brought a long interval of peace to the war-torn continent. Until the revolutionary movements of 1848 shattered his "system," Metternich could boast that Europe was relatively free from war. To be sure, outbreaks occurred and some of them were successful. By the close of the third decade of the century Greece had won her freedom from Turkey, France had replaced the reactionary King Charles X by the relatively liberal Louis Philippe, Belgium had seceded from the Kingdom of the Netherlands, and the Spanish colonies one by one had become Spanish-American republics. But rebellions in Italy, Germany, Poland and Spain were put down, and no wars among the Great Powers took place. The fundamental weakness of the policy of negation pursued by most European statesmen from 1815 to 1848 was that while it might postpone war and revolution it could not solve the problems which bred them. The aspirations of nationality did not become less keen for being unsatisfied. The demand for popular government did not diminish with time. The industrial development which peace made possible concentrated the laboring class in factory towns where radical propaganda of every sort — nationalist, democratic and socialistic — could be promoted more easily than among the peasants of the countryside.

A change far more fundamental than any political overturn which the world has ever known was taking place in the economic life of Europe. After all, even the *The Industrial Revolution* most exacting government touches daily life at only a few points, while the problem of making a living is never far away from the life of humanity. During the latter part of the eighteenth century, Great Britain, fortunately situated because of the seas that held back foreign invasion, and wealthy in natural stores of coal and iron, developed new methods of manufacture which were copied and extended on the continent after the close of the Napoleonic wars. The change was threefold: ingenious new machines were invented, especially in the textile industry; water power and steam power were applied to the running of these machines; labor was organized in large factory units for the most economical use of the costly new tools of production. A still further development became general early in the nineteenth century, the application of steam power to locomotion. The age of the railroad and the steamboat had arrived. Large parts of Europe, such as Russia and the Balkan peninsula, remained still little affected by the new industrialism, but in France, Belgium, western Germany, northern Italy and, above all, Great Britain, the economic structure had been profoundly altered. It was futile to expect that political forms would remain unaffected.

It is significant of the new time that when rebellious Paris, weary of the uninspiring rule of Louis Philippe, pro-*The rise of* claimed the second French Republic, the old *Socialism* watchword of political "liberty, equality and fraternity" did not suffice. The radicals in the republican movement demanded "national workshops" for the unemployed. Some even favored the full program of Socialism; that is, the social rather than individual ownership of land, mines, factories, and other means of production and distribution. These ideas had long been discussed by isolated individual thinkers ("Utopian Socialists") such as Saint-Simon, Cabet and Fourier in France, and Robert Owen in Great Britain. But not until the French revolution of 1848 did they become the program of a great political movement.[1] Even more significant than the brief and unsuccessful experiments of moderate Socialists, such as Louis Blanc, in

[1] Of course communistic or collectivistic ideas were no new thing in the world. The peasant rebellions of the Middle Ages and some radical trends in the French Revolution of the eighteenth century aimed at economic as well as political equality. But the coming of the industrial revolution gave a new setting to the "class conflict" and made possible the socialist movement in the modern sense.

state-directed industry, was the publication of a *Communist Manifesto* by two German-Jewish economists, Karl Marx and Friedrich Engels. This professed to set forth a program based on "scientific" as opposed to Utopian Socialism. The chief doctrines of the new faith were that the course of history is determined by economic factors, often called the "economic" or, less accurately, the "materialist conception of history"; that one of the chief of these factors is the struggle between economic groups or classes with divergent interests; that in modern times, thanks to the industrial revolution, two main classes tend to emerge, the "bourgeoisie" who possess the means of production, and the "proletariat" who have no property and must live on the wages of their toil. When capital has been sufficiently concentrated in the hands of the few, the proletariat will seize it, peaceably or by force as circumstances might determine, and declare it the property of the whole people. "Workingmen of the world unite; you have nothing to lose but your chains and you have a world to gain!"

The Socialist movement which had its humble beginning in the revolution of 1848 was destined to become an ever-mightier power in Europe as industry advanced. But as it spread it broke into faction and schism. Even in the early days of the party Karl Marx had a bitter fight to prevent the capture of his "International" organization by the anarchists, the men who would abolish public government along with private property. At later periods there were schisms between the strict followers of Marx and the moderate "revisionists" (such as Eduard Bernstein in Germany and the Fabian Society in England) who believed that socialism might be brought about by piecemeal, evolutionary reforms. On the other hand, more impatient spirits accused the orthodox Marxians of succumbing to "parliamentarianism" and demanded the immediate seizure of private business by workers' syndicates ("Syndicalism")

or by a class dictatorship ("Communism"). The name
"socialist" was sometimes even borrowed by mild parties
of social reform which had nothing in common with Marxian
Socialism except the advocacy of factory laws, old-age pensions, government insurance and like humanitarian legislation.

Despite the appearance of socialism in the revolution of
1848, the main influences in the revolutions of that tur-
Revolutions bulent year were the older forces of nationalism,
of 1848 liberalism and democracy.   In France the liberal monarchists under the historian-politician Adolphe
Thiers had challenged the government, but the movement
soon got out of hand, as revolutions have the habit of doing,
and a republican provisional government, half Socialist
and half middle-class radical, assumed the power of the
exiled King Louis Philippe.   By 1848 news traveled rapidly.
Within a few months Metternich had been driven into exile
from Austria, new constitutions had been proclaimed in
most of the German states, Hungary and Bohemia demanded
home rule, Italian rulers coerced by their subjects marched
against the Austrians, a national convention was summoned to draw up a constitution for united Germany.   Even
England was thrown into a temporary panic by the radical
demand for a "People's Charter" granting universal manhood suffrage, and Switzerland seized the occasion to adopt
a more centralized national constitution.   It was the greatest effort which European liberalism had ever made and
for the moment paralyzed the "trades union of kings"
which had dominated continental European affairs ever
since Waterloo.   Metternich, indeed, never himself returned
to power.   But nowhere did the revolution take the favorable course which its authors had hoped.

Two events doomed the French Republic.   One was the
schism between the Socialists and the moderate Republicans.   The government had offered work to all the unem-

ployed, but the experiment of "national workshops" was
badly bungled by administrators who had little *France and*
sympathy with it, and as soon as the voice of the *the Second*
conservative peasants could be heard in Paris *Republic*
the whole plan was dropped.   The radical workingmen of
the capital rose in insurrection but were speedily repressed;
henceforth they cared little about a mere "bourgeois republic," while in turn the conservatives were frightened at
this bloody sequel of the downfall of monarchy.   Yet the
Second Republic might have endured for lack of an evident
alternative if Napoleon had not left to France a legend
and an ambitious nephew.   It was just long enough after
the Emperor's day for France to remember the glories of
his triumphs and forget the miseries they had cost the French
people.   The Bourbon monarchy had been rejected; the
Republic was discredited; the nation turned toward the
Bonapartist solution.   Louis Napoleon Bonaparte was
elected President in December, 1848, assumed dictatorial
power in December, 1851, and took the throne as Emperor
Napoleon III [1] in December, 1852.

Affairs went no better in Italy.   Of the Italian States
which joined in the national league to force Austria out of
Lombardy and Venetia only one threw itself *Reaction in*
into the struggle with wholehearted sincerity.   *Italy*
This was rocky Piedmont in the extreme northwestern part
of the peninsula, officially known as the Kingdom of Sardinia
because it possessed the Mediterranean island of that name.
But the Austrian government had recovered its power at
home and defeated the Sardinian army at Novara.   King
Charles Albert abdicated in favor of his son Victor Emmanuel.   The short-lived republic established at Rome by
the liberal idealist Giuseppe Mazzini was garrisoned by
French troops and the authority of Pope Pius IX restored
throughout the Papal States of central Italy.   The Pope

[1] Napoleon II, the son of the first Emperor, had never actually reigned.

himself was transformed by the experiences of the revolution from a moderate liberal to a resolute conservative; Italy could hope nothing from his aid henceforward. The petty dynasts climbed back to their thrones. Except that Sardinia now had a constitution and an energetic king everything in Italy seemed to be as it had been in the days of Metternich.

The very variety of the enemies of the House of Habsburg proved its salvation. Polish noble in Galicia, German *Reaction in* student in Vienna, Magyar squire in Hungary, *the Austrian* Slavic Bohemian at Prague, malcontent Italian *lands* in Milan or Venice might be all in insurrection against the Austrian government, but there was no concerted movement. The Austrian authorities could and did use the German Austrians against the Italians and the southern Slavs against the Hungarians. Moreover, Russia loaned an army, on the old Metternich principle that kings must stand together against revolution, to crush the Hungarian rebellion. The chief republican leader, Louis Kossuth, was driven into exile; some of his less fortunate colleagues were caught and hanged. The promise of a constitution was forgotten, young Francis Joseph (1848–1916) succeeded Ferdinand (1835–48) as Emperor, and the real power rested in the hand of the reactionary Prince Felix von Schwarzenberg, a successor to both the authority and the policy of Metternich.

The reaction in Austria doomed the prospect of union in Germany. After prolonged debate the German constituent *Reaction in* National Assembly decided to establish a federal *Germany* German Empire, exclusive of Austria (whose Slavic, Hungarian and Latin lands could hardly form part of a truly national German state) and under the headship of the King of Prussia. But Austria would permit no such program and the Prussian King Friedrich Wilhelm IV (1840–61) was a weak, romantic, irresolute ruler who would have liked to be the first Emperor of united Germany but feared to antagonize Austria and scorned to "take a crown from the gutter" by obtaining it from a revolutionary assembly without the concurrence of his fellow German princes. The old German Confederation was restored at Austria's dictation, and in their heart of hearts most of the German princes and nobles were content that it should be so.

Apparently the reaction had triumphed almost everywhere. A Bonaparte had replaced a Bourbon on the throne of France; Metternich had retired; Prussia, Sardinia and Switzerland had new constitutions — that was all. Yet the generation which succeeded 1848 was to be very different from that *The nation-builders of the new epoch* which had preceded the revolution. Though the radical reformers had lost their chance, even among the conservatives statesmen arose who had learned from the revolution that a policy of mere resistance to change would no longer serve; that some popular aspirations, at least, might well be realized on the basis of royal authority. Nationalism would go forward, even though democracy must halt. Three leaders of the age, who strove for a middle path between reaction and revolution, are of particular importance: Emperor Napoleon III of France; Count Camillo Benso di Cavour, the chief adviser to King Victor Emmanuel of Sardinia, and Count Otto von Bismarck-Schönhausen, a Prussian noble who first won prominence by his hostility to the liberal revolutionists of 1848. Sharply contrasted though they were in temperament and policy, these statesmen were alike in willingness to bring about great changes in Europe, even at the cost of war, and alike also in a common hostility toward Austria, whose unbending conservatism blocked the path to nation-building. Probably the least able of the three, but for many years the most prominent, was Napoleon III, "Emperor of the French."

Louis Napoleon is hard to estimate. As a young man he

was considered a mere doctrinaire intriguer, vainly trying
to breathe life into the dead Napoleonic Empire.
Napoleon III Europe smiled comfortably at his incessant plots
and propaganda.   But the discords which wrecked the
Second Republic gave him his opportunity.   He became
President by a large majority, staged an ingenious quarrel
with the politicians of the Assembly, appealed to the nation
(after sending to prison or exile every probable leader of
opposition), and upon winning a vote of confidence proceded
to make his power virtually absolute.   The bourgeoisie,
the peasantry, and even the old royalist aristocracy turned
to him willingly enough as the only evident alternative to
radicalism and socialism.   Only the urban workingmen and
such convinced republican idealists as Victor Hugo remained unreconciled.   He encouraged commerce, beauti-
fied the capital, and did his best to make prosperity and
national glory compensate for the loss of political freedom.
In foreign policy he showed some wisdom, seeking an alliance with Britain, the nation whose obstinate hostility
had done most to wreck the fortunes of his uncle, and striving to identify his policy with the new trend towards nationalism in various parts of Europe.   Yet, taken as a whole,
the Second Empire seems to have been a pretentious sham.
Few able statesmen served it, and the rigorous censorship
of criticism merely served to conceal inefficiency in the army
and other departments of government.   Even Napoleon's
foreign policy was marred by uncertainty of purpose.   In
alliance with Britain, Turkey and Sardinia he warred against
Russia though French interests were not very urgently
involved.[1]   He aided Sardinia to liberate northern Italy
from Austria, and then paused, his goal half-won, forfeiting
Italian gratitude to avoid a complete break with the Pope.
He sent a French army to bolster up an Austrian prince as
Emperor of Mexico, and then withdrew it to avoid compli-

---

[1] For the Crimean War see Chapter II.

cations with the United States. He permitted Prussia to rise to the leadership of the German States, and then lost his throne in a rash attempt to prevent the last steps in German national consolidation.

The only work of the French Emperor which seems to have borne lasting fruit was the aid which he extended, partial and hesitating though it was, toward the *The making* liberation of Italy. The unsuccessful national *of united* uprising of 1848 had demonstrated that the *Italy* Italians could not throw off the Austrian yoke without foreign aid. It was also necessary to find at least one Italian State able and willing to undertake the task of initiating an anti-Austrian alliance. The Pope, the King of the Two Sicilies (Naples and Sicily), the grand-ducal or ducal houses of Tuscany, Parma, Modena and Lucca were all too dependent on Austrian support to assume such leadership. Sardinia was the only Italian State in a position to oppose Austrian diplomatic policy. King Victor Emmanuel though a conservative was also a patriot. His great minister Count Cavour devoted his first efforts to building up the strength and prosperity of Sardinia and to making her parliamentary government a practical success, to the end that Italians in every part of the peninsula would see in his little country the natural leader of them all.

His second achievement was to buy the aid of some great foreign Power which could defeat Austria in pitched battle. France was the most convenient for his purpose. *The Franco-* Napoleon III was of Italian descent, he had *Austrian* sympathized in his youth with the Italian revo- *War of 1859* lutionary movement, the French people cherished the memory of victories won over the Austrians on the plains of north Italy in the time of the first Napoleon, and Sardinia had sided with France at the time of the Crimean War. Yet he did not go to war from altruistic motives alone; on the contrary he drove a hard bargain. Sardinia must appear to be on the defensive, so that France could justify an alliance with her against Austria. The city of Nice and the province of Savoy must be ceded to France. If this were done, he agreed to set Italy free "from Alps to Adriatic," adding Austria's Lombardo-Venetian Kingdom to the territory of Sardinia. In the war which resulted the French and Italian arms triumphed but Napoleon became alarmed by his own success. Suppose Prussia were to mobilize on the Rhine to aid her "German sister"? Suppose the Roman Catholics of France were to turn against his régime because the spirit of revolution, unchained by the French victory, swept over the Papal States? At Villafranca he agreed to an armistice concluded without the consent of his allies which resulted in the transfer of Lombardy, through his hands, from Austria to Sardinia but kept the Venetian territory Austrian.

The removal of Austrian pressure, however, had profound effects in central and southern Italy. Tuscany, Parma, *The annexa-* Modena and a portion of the Papal States voted *tion of the* by large majorities to join Sardinia to form the *south* new Kingdom of Italy, while the brave adventurer Giuseppe Garibaldi with a small army of volunteers conquered the Kingdom of the Two Sicilies. Save for Austrian Venice and Papal Rome the task of unification was essentially complete. Napoleon III now accepted Nice and Savoy; he had not, it is true, kept his promise of freeing Venice, but he had a new claim, "compensation" for the annexations which he had "permitted" Sardinia to make in central and southern Italy! Cavour had lived to see only the partial unification of Italy; he died before Venice and Rome were added, but he left a valuable legacy to the nation not only in his diplomatic work but in the new vitality which his commercial policy had brought to Italian industry and the liberal tradition of orderly constitutional government which he had established in Italian politics.

While Italy was in the making an even greater power took shape in northern Europe. Germany had certain initial advantages over Italy in the common task of nation-building which lay before them. The Italian States had been entirely independent of *The foundations of German unity* each other, whereas the German States had, alike under the old Holy Roman Empire and the later *Bund*, at least a formal and nominal tie. No Italian State had at its disposal a formidable military power, whereas two German States, Austria and Prussia, had long ranked among the Great Powers. Austria, however, was an enemy of German union since her domains included millions of Slavs, Hungarians, Italians and other non-Germans, and she preferred to play the leading part in a loose alliance of sovereign princes rather than risk disruption of the Habsburg family properties by merging them in a national Germany. The Kingdom of Prussia was a more promising candidate. Though Prussia had many Polish subjects, the great majority of her people were German. Her army was one of the best in Europe. She had bound most of the lesser German States to her in a customs union or *Zollverein* which made Germany at least an economic entity, if not as yet a political one. Perhaps her most important contribution· to German public life was a tradition of administrative efficiency. The Hohenzollern rulers had for the most part been hard-headed and thrifty, and the Prussian aristocracy were accustomed to diligent toil as servants of the State, alike in peace and war.

Yet Prussia failed to take early advantage of her chances. In an absolute monarchy nearly everything depends on the personality of the ruler, and the successors of Frederick the Great (Friedrich II, 1740–86) were temperamentally incapable of assuming leader- *Prussia and the Hohenzollerns* ship in Germany. Friedrich Wilhelm II (1786–97) was a mere self-indulgent waster; Friedrich Wilhelm III (1797–

1840) was a conscientious but timid man, distrustful of himself and of others; Friedrich Wilhelm IV (1840–61) was fitful and eccentric and we have noted already how he missed the opportunity which the revolution of 1848 had offered him.   But Wilhelm I (Regent, 1858; King, 1861; Emperor, 1871–88) was of a different stamp.   Not more brilliant than others, he had at least a firm and resolute personality; he could select able ministers and sustain them in office against criticism.   He was believed to be no great friend to constitutional government, and when the new Prussian legislature refused the army appropriations which he considered necessary he looked around for a minister who could build up the Prussian army even in defiance of votes and majorities.   In 1862 he chose for this duty Count Bismarck, a member of the old nobility who was wholly untainted by liberalism or democracy and had become a late and reluctant convert even to German unity.   Bismarck as minister-president of the Kingdom of Prussia entered upon his invidious task without fear or reluctance.   It should never be forgotten that his first victory, his first step in assuring Prussian predominance in German and European affairs, was a triumph over the representatives of the people.   The memory of this triumph erased from the mind of most Germans the liberal tradition of 1848, now discredited by failure, and replaced it by a belief in the value of "strong" government and autocratic authority.   Without legal authorization, Bismarck collected taxes and made possible the strengthened Prussian army which he and the king desired.

Bismarck, the obdurate monarchist and militarist who hurled at the wordy legislators the challenge, "It is not by

The archi- speeches and majority resolutions that the great
tect of Ger- questions of the time are to be decided... but
many   by blood and iron!", was not the whole of the man.   His was in truth a singularly complex character; a man of iron strength of body and will who was nevertheless

shaken by frequent storms of nervous excitement and liable
to moods of deep, almost suicidal, depression; a loyal servant
of the House of Hohenzollern who was free from illusions as
to the defects of its members and who often addressed his
sovereign in terms of stern rebuke; a hater of paper constitutions and of democracy who was to give Germany a constitution including manhood suffrage; a narrow "little Prussian" particularist who was destined to create united Germany; engaged in three wars and yet so little a lover of war
that he kept the sword sheathed for twenty years when
Chancellor of the German Empire. His greatest quality,
even more remarkable than his titanic force of will, was his
singularly clear sense of the realities of any situation. More
than most statesmen he saw the world as it was, not as he
wished it to be. He was never led astray by limitless ambition in the manner of Alexander or Napoleon, nor was he
duped by his own dogmas and prejudices after the fashion of
Metternich. His prejudices were, indeed, exceptionally
strong, but they rarely swayed his policy. He opposed or
allied with Austria as Prussian interests dictated; he made
use of French diplomacy and then broke the power of
France in war; he used all the forces of his day, press, parliaments, national patriotism, commercial expansion, even the
socialistic aspirations of the working class, to further his
constant aim of building up a strong and prosperous Kingdom of Prussia, dominant in the councils of Germany and
of Europe.

At one time Bismarck had regarded Austria as the natural
ally of Prussia in the struggle against the common foe of
revolutionary democracy. But experience in *The Schles-*
various diplomatic posts, and particularly at *wig-Holstein*
Frankfort where the Diet of the German Con- *question*
federation conducted its futile debates, con- *Danish War*
vinced him that Austria would never permit *of 1864*
Prussia to rival her own ascendancy in German affairs. Yet

Bismarck's first war was fought in alliance with Austria against Denmark. The pretext for war was that the Danish king had extended a constitution over two largely German duchies, Schleswig and Holstein, which were attached to Denmark only by the person of the monarch. Holstein, in fact, lay within the German *Bund*, and the German Duke of Augustenburg claimed both duchies on the ground that a different law of succession prevailed in them from that of Denmark proper. Bismarck managed to set aside the claims of the Duke of Augustenburg, to avoid invoking the formal intervention of the German *Bund* as a whole, and to induce Austria to combine with Prussia in a special alliance. The only possible chance for Denmark, a small nation assailed by two Great Powers, would have been the intervention of Great Britain or France. Both countries sympathized with Denmark but both hesitated to assume the risks of war.

Austria and Prussia proceeded, as Bismarck had foreseen, to quarrel over the spoils of victory. By the Convention of
The Austro- Gastein (1865) Austria took over the adminis-
Prussian tration of Holstein and Prussia of Schleswig,
War of 1866 while a third and much smaller duchy, Lauen-
burg, was sold outright to Prussia. This arrangement proved unsatisfactory to Austria and her government tried to bring the question before the whole *Bund*. Prussia denounced this as a breach of the agreement between the two monarchies and war followed, a single brief and decisive campaign, sometimes called the Seven Weeks' War. Most of south Germany supported Austria, but Prussia had found an ally in Italy, eager to complete the work which Napoleon III had left unfinished.

The sudden and overwhelming victory of the Prussian army, trained and disciplined to perfection under Helmuth von Moltke, astonished Europe. It more than astonished France, whose Emperor now regretted that he had let Bismarck persuade him not to intervene. The use Prussia

made of her victory was more alarming still. Bismarck
treated Austria with lenity as he did not wish
her to cherish lasting enmity toward Prussia. *Expansion and consolidation of Prussia*
Aside from withdrawing from the German Con-
federation and handing over Venetia to Italy,
Austria lost nothing. But the withdrawal of Austria permitted Prussia to rearrange the map of Germany in her own
interest. Prussia annexed Schleswig-Holstein as a matter of
course. In addition, certain of Austria's allies whose territories lay conveniently between separated portions of the
Prussian Kingdom were now directly incorporated into it:
the Kingdom of Hanover, the Duchies of Nassau and Hesse-
Cassel, and the city of Frankfort. Thus Prussia's territory
became more compact at the same time it was enlarged.
The states of northern Germany which were allowed to retain their independence were federated with Prussia into a
smaller but much closer union than the old Confederation.
Bavaria, Baden and Würtemberg, together with part of
Hesse-Darmstadt, remained outside the new North German
Confederation, but it seemed only a matter of time when
they would be added to the rest.

The North German Confederation was under the perpetual presidency of the King of Prussia. There were two
legislative organs, a Federal Council or *Bundesrat*, *The North German Confederation of 1867*
modeled after the old Diet, and a new *Reichstag*,
elected directly by universal manhood suffrage.
In the Bundesrat the constituent states were
represented on a scale roughly approximating their relative
importance; Prussia casting seventeen votes in accordance
with instructions of the royal government. In the Reichstag
representation was proportioned to population.[1] Austria,
exiled from Germany, was also forced to make new constitutional arrangements. Hungary was recognized as a self-

[1] For a more detailed account of the German and Austro-Hungarian constitutions see Chapters III and VIII.

governing constitutional monarchy united with Austria by
the rule of a common sovereign, Emperor of Austria and
Austria-   King of Hungary.   Each half of the Dual Mon-
Hungary   archy had its parliament of two chambers.   This
agreement was known as the *Ausgleich* or Compromise of
1867, since it terminated a dispute of many years' standing
between Austrian and Hungarian views as to the proper
organization of the common Imperial government.

France was the remaining obstacle to the completion of
German unity.   Napoleon's tentative plans for obtaining
The Spanish   compensation for permitting the union of Ger-
crown a   many, as he had obtained Nice and Savoy for
gage of   permitting Sardinia to augment her territories
battle   in Italy, had come to nothing.   Belgium was
not to become French, nor Luxemburg, nor any German
lands west of the Rhine.   Added to all other French grievances and disappointments came the news that Prince
Leopold of Hohenzollern-Sigmaringen, a distant relative of
the Prussian royal house, had been offered the Spanish
throne, recently left vacant by revolution.   Was France to
be held in a vise between a Hohenzollern Spain and a Hohenzollern Germany as in the seventeenth century she had been
hemmed in by a Habsburg Spain and a Habsburg Austria?
Surely it was time that France called a halt to Prussian ambition!   So argued the French court and the French press.
Much to Bismarck's disappointment Prince Leopold decided to withdraw his claims and here the matter should have
ended, with a distinct diplomatic victory for France.   But
the French government converted victory into defeat by
pushing it too far.   Urged by the Empress Eugénie, herself
of Spanish birth, by the ministry, by excited deputies in the
national legislature, Napoleon III pressed the demand that
Prussia give guarantees for all coming time that the Hohenzollern candidacy would not be renewed.

This was more than King Wilhelm could endure.   He refused to discuss the matter further with Benedetti, the French ambassador, and so informed Bismarck. *The Ems* Bismarck saw his opportunity. Without di- *telegram* rectly falsifying the communication from the king he "edited" it for the press in such a way as to leave the impression that all diplomatic negotiations had been abruptly broken off. There has been endless discussion of the significance of this "Ems despatch," opinions varying all the way from the view that Bismarck committed a forgery to create a war to the view that he merely gave honest publicity to the insolent demands of France. We have his own admission that he regarded war inevitable and hoped that his condensed edition of the despatch would force a crisis, and there is no need to defend Bismarck against himself. On the other hand, if Bismarck had laid a trap, Napoleon III had needlessly walked into it. The Ems "insult" was not so serious that it would have forced France to declare war had she not desired to do so for deeper reasons.

At all events, whatever may be said of the relative moral responsibility of the French and Prussian governments in 1870, France by her declaration of hostilities *The Franco-* assumed formal responsibility. Napoleon III *Prussian* had neglected to prepare the diplomatic situa- *War, 1870-* tion for such a contingency. Vaguely he hoped *71* that Austria and the South German States would join France — had they not fought Prussia four years earlier? — and that Italy would be grateful for the decisive French aid of 1859. But Bismarck better understood the real state of affairs. Southern Germany was bound to the North German Confederation by secret military alliances and also by the newly awakened national spirit of the people. Austria had recent memory of wars with France as well as with Prussia, and had been somewhat appeased by Bismarck's conciliatory policy after the Seven Weeks' War. In any case Austria could not move unless assured of Russia's neutrality and

Russia was openly friendly to Prussia. Italy had received aid from Prussia in 1866 as well as from France in 1859, and furthermore resented the presence of a French garrison to protect the sovereignty of the Pope at Rome. Russia remembered the Crimean War; Britain, Napoleon's intrigues in Belgium; the United States, his attempt to conquer Mexico. No nation was willing to move a man or a ship to extricate the French Emperor from the difficulties into which he had fallen.

Still had the French army been as strong as it was generally believed to be, France would not have needed foreign aid. France was in those days as populous as Germany, even counting the South German States, and had a brave army, able officers and modern artillery. Where Prussia excelled was in organization. Behind the first line of the French army stood an enthusiastic but untrained civilian public; behind the Prussian army, a drilled and disciplined reserve which had graduated from a youthful period of compulsory military instruction. Though French officers were individually often well schooled in strategy and tactics, the army had no central organization comparable in efficiency with the Prussian general staff. The mobilization of the French army was sadly at fault, whereas the concentration of the Prussian troops proceeded like clockwork. The topography of eastern France, where the war was fought, had been more thoroughly studied by German officers than by French. The Prussians from the seventeenth century onward had shown a peculiar aptitude for mastering the dull and prosaic details of administrative routine, which bore abundant fruit in an age when war had become largely an affair of mobilization and mechanism, a wholesale application of the principles of mathematics, chemistry, railroading and office management.

The decisive phase of the Franco-Prussian War was as brief as that of the lesser wars against Denmark and Austria.

France had hoped to begin with an invasion of south Germany, but her mobilization had been too slow and *The German* the campaign speedily took the form of a series *victory* of sieges of enveloped French fortresses. The fighting began in July, 1870. Within two months a series of shattering defeats had crippled the main French armies. Marshal Bazaine was beleaguered at Metz and the great fortress-city of Sedan had fallen. Napoleon III himself was a prisoner of war. The news of his capture caused a revolution at Paris, a provisional government assumed power and faced the prospect of a siege with undaunted but somewhat Quixotic valor, vowing not to surrender an inch of French territory nor a stone of the French fortresses. Armies, untrained and unready for action, were raised in the provinces in a vain endeavor to save the capital. In January, 1871, Paris surrendered, less to the Germans than to cold and hunger; the trees of the parks had been cut down for firewood, and cats and rats had served for meat. Negotiations for peace began, and of necessity they were on Bismarck's own terms.

Bismarck was usually inclined to treat a defeated foe with moderation and at first he had some doubts as to the expediency of extensive annexations. But his military *Diplomatic* advisers assured him that not only German- *results of* speaking Alsace but even a large part of French- *the war* speaking Lorraine must be annexed in order to place in German hands the frontier line of the Vosges mountains and the important fortress of Metz. He permitted the French to retain the fortress of Belfort in southern Alsace and certain mining areas in Lorraine, concessions which the Germans regretted having made later on. He imposed a war indemnity of five billion francs (about $1,000,000,000) and kept German armies in France until it was paid. With much pomp and ceremony the unity of the German Empire was proclaimed in the Hall of Mirrors in the French royal palace at Versailles. The South German States were now united with the North German Confederation to form a single Empire. As the French troops had been withdrawn from Rome, the Italian army occupied it in spite of the protests of the Pope, and the seat of Italian government shifted from Florence to the Imperial City. Russia, taking advantage of the preoccupation of other powers with the Franco-Prussian conflict, seized her opportunity and denounced the stipulation in the Treaty of Paris (1856) which debarred her from maintaining a navy on the Black Sea.

The remoter effects of the Franco-Prussian War were even more important than its immediate results. Germany *Lasting ef-* became and remained until 1918 the strongest *fects of the* power in continental Europe and replaced France *war* as the pivot of European diplomacy. France was left with a grievance which time did not allay. The cause of nationality and of popular government both gained and lost. The unification of Germany ended a political problem which had been a war breeder for generations, but the annexation of Alsace-Lorraine created a new national minority within Germany. Autocratic government had revealed its inefficiency in Napoleon III and its efficiency in Bismarck, so France naturally turned towards republicanism while Germany subordinated political liberty to national power and glory.

For the immediate future the omens were favorable to European peace. The questions of German and Italian *Why peace* national unity had found solution. There was *was possible* still discontent among the subject races of Rus- *after 1871* sia and Austria-Hungary, but they were held powerless by strong central governments. France needed time to recover from her reverses and solve her internal problems; and in any case could hardly expect to make a successful counterattack on the growing power of Germany. The lesser states of continental Europe, save in the ever restless Balkans, asked nothing better than to be let alone and freed from the menace of war. British diplomacy was dominated by the conviction that "peace is the greatest of British interests," since wars in continental Europe spoiled good markets. Never before had the map of Europe seemed so stable, and it is not without significance that statesmen increasingly turned their attention from purely European problems to the vexed questions of the colonial world. The Franco-Prussian War had sown the seeds of the World War, but it was long unto the harvest.

CHAPTER II

THE NEAR EASTERN QUESTION

THE most urgent diplomatic problem in the years immediately following the Franco-Prussian War was what was then

The "Eastern Question" in history

termed the "Eastern Question." In our own times that phrase might cause misunderstanding; to some it might suggest issues arising in the Far East — China, Japan, and the balance of power on the Pacific; so the twentieth century usually speaks of the "Near East" for the Ottoman Empire and the countries recently released from its rule. Wars and rumors of war arising in this region are no new thing; they were probably an old story when Homer chronicled the campaigns of the Greeks against the Trojans, but the question entered its modern phase when the Byzantine or East Roman Empire crumbled before the assaults of Turkish war bands and the cross gave place to the crescent on the walls of Constantinople. The crescent moon which waxes and wanes was no bad emblem for the Empire of the Ottoman Turks. They had no fatherland with fixed boundaries, no "nation" in the European sense, but extended their conquests over alien peoples until the tide of victory turned, and one by one their provinces broke away to form independent states or dependencies of the European powers.

In 1871 almost the whole of southeastern Europe was still subject, at least in name, to the Sultan of Turkey; western

The Ottoman Empire

Asia, as far as the Persian frontier, owned his sway; several states in northern Africa paid him tribute. But, even so, the waning Ottoman Empire was but the shadow of what it had been. During the seventeenth century the Austrians reconquered the central Hungarian plains; during the eighteenth century the Russians conquered the northern shore of the Black Sea, and throughout the nineteenth century there were movements for national independence on the part of the Christian nationalities in the Balkan peninsula. The southern part of Greece won independence in the eighteen-twenties, after a long series of insurrections had at last attracted the sympathy and aid of Britain, France and Russia, and was established as an independent kingdom in 1832. Even earlier, though less noticed by Europe at large, the Serbs along the Danube had risen against their Turkish lords. Turkish authority was weakened also among the Rumanians of the Danube, though the two Rumanian-speaking provinces of Wallachia and Moldavia remained still nominally part of the Empire. More significant than the loss of territory was the structural weakness of the government which transplanted into nineteenth-century Europe institutions better adapted to medieval Asia. It is not too much to say that at all times after the seventeenth century the Ottoman Empire existed only by permission of the European powers, who were jointly and sometimes even singly able to conquer it by force of arms, but were far too jealous of each other to permit the experiment to be tried. Many statesmen preferred to see a weak and decadent authority in possession of the Near East and, above all, of the key position of Constantinople where the land routes from Europe to Asia cross the sea route from the Black Sea to the Mediterranean. So strong a strategic position might become dangerous in strong hands!

The Ottoman Empire was a belated survival of the ecclesiastical state, bound together by the privileges of a creed rather than by race, language or national sentiment. The Turks were numerous enough to dominate, but too few to settle their Balkan provinces. Even the Turkish language, a central Asiatic tongue, prevailed only in Asia Minor and the immediate neighborhood of Constantinople, and it was spoken by many who had no claim to descent from the orig-

inal invaders.   Many students of the East have pointed out
that the average "Turk" of our day has no more true Turkish blood than the average Englishman has Norman blood
from William the Conqueror and his warriors.   The subject
"nations" of the Empire were grouped according to religious
denomination, and the Turk ruled them less as a conquering
race than as the champion of a dominant religion.   The form
of government was an absolute despotism of the reigning
Sultan, exercised through a bureaucracy of his personal de-
pendents.   The chief practical limit on his power was the
law of the Koran, embodying the religious injunctions of
Mohammed and interpreted by the scholars of Islam.   No
strong feudal aristocracy held the Sultan in check, as most of
his officials were palace slaves who held office at his pleasure,
but the combined effect of distance and administrative inefficiency forced most rulers to be content with a merely
nominal obedience in the outlying provinces of the Empire.
The Turks with contemptuous tolerance permitted the Christian peasants to worship as they pleased, to keep their local
traditions, and to conduct petty village politics.   The general government did not conceive its duty to include the
regulation of the daily routine of life; it was rather a machine
for taxing the submissive and terrorizing the insurgent than
for administering the public business.

The civilization of the Ottoman Empire owed little to its
Turkish founders.   In part it was borrowed from the con-
The Islamic quered Greeks, in part taken from the Arabs.
tradition   Islam, like Christianity, means more than a
theology.   It is also a civilization, a tradition, a way of life.
Just as the Christian missionary in China or the South Seas
brings to the people whom he reaches many elements of
European or American culture, so the Turks in adopting
Mohammedanism had become half Arabian in thought and
life.   The creed of Mohammed was, indeed, distinguished
by simplicity: "There is one God and Mohammed is his

THE DISMEMBERMENT OF TURKEY, 1815–1908

prophet"; and Islam aimed at simplicity in church as well as in creed. A separate priesthood, in the full European sense, hardly existed, although there were teachers of the Koran, custodians of the temples or mosques, and self-devoted hermits, prophets and missionaries. Four observances were enjoined by Mohammed on his followers: daily prayers, an annual fast, almsgiving, and a pilgrimage, at least once a lifetime, to Mecca, his birthplace. Many usages of Islamic countries have a religious origin, such as the ban on "graven images" and the use of human or animal forms in decoration, the prohibition of alcoholic drinks, and the dating of the calendar from the flight of Mohammed from Mecca to Medina (622 A.D.) which began the more active period of his ministry. But many secular elements of the Arab civilization have been carried along with Mohammedan influence which were less directly dependent on religion. Such were slavery, polygamy, the seclusion and subordination of women, the Arabic alphabet and a literary culture derived from Arabia and Persia, a characteristic architecture, examples of which are scattered from Spain to northern India, and Arabian science, particularly in mathematics, geography, medicine and chemistry.[1]

The balance of diplomatic forces which kept in being the decadent Ottoman power is well illustrated by the mid-century war in which Britain, France and even tiny Sardinia leagued themselves together to preserve the independence and integrity of the *The Crimean War, 1854-56* Sultan's dominions against the encroachments of Russia. It was a strange alignment which made the most autocratic monarchy in Europe the liberator of the oppressed Christian subjects of the Turk, while three of the most liberal European nations fought to keep them in subjection. The explanation of this seeming paradox was that an exaggerated dread of

[1] A partial idea of the Arabic contribution to our own civilization may be obtained by listing words in English which have the Arab article "al" (= the) as prefix, such as alchemy, algebra, alcove, alkali, almanac.

the political and military power of Russia obsessed the minds of European statesmen. Conservatives justified the war on the traditional ground of the "balance of power"; Russia must be prevented from dominating the eastern Mediterranean, seizing Constantinople and the Straits, and endangering the trade routes to British India. Even liberals for the most part consoled themselves with the reflection that if Russia were not a more odious tyranny than Turkey she was at all events a more formidable one. Austria, which owed Russia a signal debt of thanks for help in putting down the Hungarian revolution of 1849, permitted jealousy to overcome gratitude and instead of coming to Russia's aid maintained a most unfriendly neutrality.

The chief campaigns were fought in the neighborhood of the Black Sea and especially in that Crimean peninsula of southern Russia which gave its name to the whole conflict. Neither side gained many military laurels. Russia suffered defeat; on the whole to her ultimate advantage, since the exposure of her incompetent administration under the merciless searchlight of war discredited absolute government and prepared the way for reforms. Napoleon III, who had hoped to reap much military glory from the venture, was forced to be content with the empty name of victory. The British medical service broke down so hopelessly as to afford Florence Nightingale and her volunteer nurses an opportunity to substitute a new system of caring for the ill and wounded. *Treaty of Paris, 1856* Turkey gained a military respite for another generation; Russia ceded southern Bessarabia and renounced her claim to protect the Danubian principalities and the Christian subjects of Turkey generally; naval competition in the Black Sea was restricted; a new code of rules governing naval warfare was adopted; Sardinia was permitted to discuss the Italian question before a conference of the European powers.

A certain significant spirit of internationalism appeared

at the Peace Conference, but the treaty provisions were
small fruits for so great an effort and even such
as they were did not all prove lasting. Within
a very few years from the Treaty of Paris there
were important changes in southeastern Europe.

Reopening of the Near Eastern question

In 1859 the two Danubian principalities of Wallachia and
Moldavia, still nominally subject to the Sultan, chose the
same ruler, Prince Alexander Cuza.   From this union came
the modern nation of Rumania.   In 1870 Russia announced
that she regarded herself as free to build a new Black Sea
fleet.   In 1875 and 1876 the cruel repression of Christian
rebels in Herzegovina and Bulgaria by Turkish irregular
troops attracted the sympathy of all Europe and enlisted
the active aid of Russia. Abdul Hamid II (1876–1909), the
new Turkish Sultan, was an abler sovereign than his immediate predecessors, but his skill lay rather in the tortuous in-
sincerities of diplomacy than in excellence of administration.
His policy was the merciless repression of his discontented
subjects combined with fair promises of constitutional reform
for the deception of foreign powers who might be disposed to
intervene.   He well understood the mutual rivalries of the
Christian powers and trusted that once more the western
powers would protect him against the wrath of Russia. His
confidence was only partly justified.   The British and the
Austrian governments did indeed watch with uneasiness the
Russian preparations for a new war, but the Bulgarian atrocities had so struck the popular imagination that a new pro-
Turkish league was unthinkable.   France, no longer under
the rule of the adventure-seeking Louis Napoleon, had little
heart for another war so soon after her defeat at the hands
of Prussia.   Germany in the person of Bismarck was bent
on neutrality.   England was ringing with denunciations of
the "unspeakable Turk" and Gladstone, the powerful leader
of the opposition, urged that "the Turks carry away their
abuses in the only possible manner, namely by carrying off

themselves." The moment was propitious for Russia to strike.

The little Slavic nations of Serbia and Montenegro began the struggle in 1876. In the following spring Russia and *The Russo-* Rumania joined forces in their aid. The war *Turkish* was not as one-sided as might be inferred from *War of 1877* the disparity of the chief belligerents in numbers, equipment and discipline. The Turk, even at his lowest ebb of decadence as ruler, was a first-class fighter; tough, patient, enduring, with a real appetite for combat. The wild and rugged country of the Balkans makes slow campaigning. The fortress of Plevna, between the Danube and the main range of the Balkan mountains, held up the Russian advance from July to December, 1877. But with the fall of Plevna the Turkish resistance crumbled and in January, 1878, the Russian forces occupied Adrianople and the war was virtually at an end.

The Ottoman government bowed to the storm and accepted the peace which Russia imposed in the treaty of San *Treaty of* Stefano. By its terms a great Bulgaria was to be *San Stefano,* created, including not only the present country *March, 1878* of that name but also the region of Macedonia with its mixed population of Bulgars, Greeks and Serbs. Serbia, Montenegro and Rumania were to be recognized as independent in name as they already were in fact and were to be given additional territory, though Rumania had to hand over her part of Bessarabia to Russia as payment for aid received. Russia also was to receive a war indemnity and part of Armenia. The peace if carried out in its original form would speedily have reduced Turkey-in-Europe to the present little area of eastern Thrace; since the districts to the south and west of Bulgaria (Greek-speaking Southern Macedonia, Thessaly, Albania, Bosnia, Herzegovina) could no longer be readily defended from Constantinople and must soon have been partitioned among the Austrians, Serbs and

Greeks. Bulgaria herself, though nominally tributary to the Sultan, would be so nearly independent as to be able to throw off the forms of allegiance at will, or else (and this is what Europe really feared) exchange a Turkish master for a Russian.

As the Russian armies poured through the broken passes of the Balkans toward Constantinople, the diplomats of rival powers asked themselves if they had not permitted Russia to go too far. Austria-Hungary, nearest the seat of war, felt that the treaty *Demand for treaty revision* of San Stefano would make the entire region henceforth a Russian sphere of influence, much to the diminution of her own position in the world. British music halls resounded with "We don't want to fight, but, by Jingo, if we do, we've got the ships, we've got the men, we've got the money too!" Queen Victoria, moved to an un- *"Jingoism"* usual degree, bombarded her ministers with demands for prompt and vigorous action to check Russia. Lord Beaconsfield (Benjamin Disraeli), the Conservative Prime Minister, concentrated troops from India at Malta, as a double witness to Europe that Britain was in earnest in resisting Russia and that India's loyalty could be relied on in the event of war. The British fleet lay ready for action.

The crisis was serious enough, but there was an unreality about much of it. Bismarck, ostentatiously proclaiming that to his mind the whole Eastern question was *Bargaining* "not worth the bones of a Pomeranian grena- *behind the* dier" promised that if an international confer- *scenes* ence were held he would act as "honest broker," handling the commissions of others without thought of profit for Germany. France and Italy were pacific and relatively disinterested. Austria-Hungary, whose claims to the provinces of Bosnia and Herzegovina had been conditionally recognized by Russia as far back as 1876 (agreement of Reichstadt), was bribed to peace by renewed assurances. Turkey consented that Great Britain might occupy Cyprus the better to protect Asiatic Turkey against Russia. Even the Russians admitted that, according to a time-honored precedent, a general revision of the map of the Near East should be ratified by a conference of the Powers. Thus when a congress was summoned to meet at Berlin in June many of its chief problems were already on the way to solution as the result of direct negotiation among the governments concerned.

Bismarck presided and the German capital was the meeting place. This was itself a significant tribute to the position which the Iron Chancellor had won for himself and for his nation; previous international conferences, if held at the capital of any power, were apt to go to Paris, London or Vienna. Bismarck's presence would have made any diplomatic gathering seem significant, and here were also such other famous dignitaries as Count Andrassy of Austria-Hungary, Prince Gortchakov from Russia, the Earl of Beaconsfield and the Marquess of Salisbury representing Britain. The smaller states, except Turkey, were not represented, though the Rumanians and Greeks were allowed their "day in court" to present their claims. Of course every interested group tried to get the private ear of the diplomats. "Civil and military agents of all European powers have flocked hither from all parts of the East," wrote the correspondent of the London *Times*, "Greek, Servian, Roumanian, Armenian, Albanian, Bulgarian, Turkish and Jewish claimants, like so many minor planets, busily revolve round the greater lights of the diplomatic and consular service." With its brilliant gathering of princely diplomats, its secret bargains, its disregard for the principles of nationality, and its anxious concern for the balance of power among the greater states, the Congress of Berlin was like a smaller edition of the Congress of Vienna in 1814–15. Metternich or Talleyrand would have felt quite at home.

Congress of Berlin, 1878

One thing only was lacking: the old-world air of leisure. Bismarck was too nervously apprehensive to enjoy the occasion; to avoid a possible Austro-Russian or Anglo-Russian war he pressed hard for an early settlement. The business of the Congress was finished in a few sessions and the elaborate treaty which resulted fixed the main foundations of Near Eastern politics for the next thirty years.

The main features of the settlement reached at Berlin, partly through open agreement and partly by special direct negotiation, were: (1) the abandonment of the *The Treaty* plan for the "big Bulgaria" envisaged by Russia *of Berlin,* and the division of its territory into three parts; *July, 1878* (2) the establishment of the northernmost of these as a self-governing Principality of Bulgaria, paying tribute to the Sultan; (3) the erection of the central division, under the name of Eastern Rumelia, into an autonomous state under a Christian governor, but distinctly separate from Bulgaria; (4) the return of the southern or Macedonian section directly to Turkish rule; (5) formal confirmation of the independence of Serbia, Rumania and Montenegro; (6) slight territorial additions to Serbia and Montenegro; (7) the transfer of Rumanian Bessarabia to Russia; (8) compensation for this transfer by the addition to Rumania of a district between the Danube and the Black Sea called the Dobrudja; (9) a promised rectification of her northern frontier to Greece; (10) the award of Kars, Batum and Ardahan in Asiatic Turkey to Russia; (11) a British leasehold for the island of Cyprus; (12) the grant to Austria-Hungary of the right to administer Bosnia and Herzegovina and to police a narrow strip of territory between Serbia and Montenegro (the Sanjak of Novi-Bazar).

The delegates of the Great Powers left Berlin with different emotions. Disraeli was openly jubilant. "I have brought back peace with honor" he claimed, and certainly he had done at least as much to preserve the Ottoman

Empire, hold back Russia and strengthen British power
Diplomatic in the Near East without a war as the statesmen
results of of two decades earlier had achieved after costly
the settle- conflict. Austria-Hungary felt fairly well satis-
ment fied with the "compensation" of Bosnia-Herzegovina. Bismarck was much relieved at the vanishing of
another war cloud; but his satisfaction was mingled with apprehension at the resentment felt by Russia. The Russians
felt, unjustly in the main but very naturally, that Bismarck
must have thrown his influence against them or a conference
held under his auspices could not have ended so disappoint-
ingly. In vain he protested that he had been entirely friendly
to Russia throughout and even that he had acted almost as
though he were "the third Russian delegate"; he was simply
not credited. France and Italy turned their attention to
the race for empire in northern Africa. Each of the Balkan
states was left with half-satisfied ambitions and the tacit
resolution to make better use of the next crisis that might
arise. For the cardinal error of Berlin in 1878 was that of
Vienna in 1814; by ignoring the principle of nationality to
build peace on the sands, and treat as a settlement what was
at best only a postponement.

Though the greater part of the Berlin settlement remained
intact till 1908, parts of it collapsed very speedily. Abdul
Reaction in Hamid II, who under the influence of such lib-
Turkey eral advisers as Midhat Pasha had promised
constitutional rule in 1876, quietly dropped his pledged reforms as soon as Europe turned attention to other questions.
The old abuses reappeared and the hopes of a milder rule for
the Sultan's Christian subjects vanished. The two self-
governing portions of Bulgaria followed the earlier example
of the Rumanians and sought union by the choice of a com-
Bulgarian mon ruler. In 1885 Prince Alexander of Batten-
union, 1885 berg who already reigned in Bulgaria accepted
the almost unanimous demand of the kindred people of

Eastern Rumelia to become their head as well. Thus an important part of the Berlin settlement, the division of autonomous Bulgaria into two isolated portions, was annulled within less than a decade.

It cannot be said that the reunion of Bulgaria took Europe by surprise. As early as 1881 Germany, Austria-Hungary and Russia had entered a secret compact which *The Serbo-* envisaged the possibility of such a union.[1] The *Bulgarian* British government, much encouraged by the *War, 1885* independent spirit which the Bulgarian people were showing toward their too exacting Russian liberators, had abandoned almost entirely the time-honored policy of preserving at all costs "the integrity of the Ottoman Empire." That policy had always been based on the assumption that small Slavic states in the Balkans could not stand alone and would probably gravitate into the Russian orbit. Experience had demonstrated that Bulgarian nationalism was a reality and not a mere cover for Russian ambition; that Bulgaria would be a barrier to Russian advance rather than "just another Russian army corps." Of all the powers, Russia was most offended at Bulgaria's bold stroke, and showed her displeasure by removing her army officers from the Bulgarian service at the very moment when jealous Serbia in the name of the "balance of power" launched an attack. In the brief war which followed Bulgaria was successful and would have followed up the victorious battle of Slivnitza by a counterattack on Serbia had not Austria-Hungary intervened.[2] In March, 1886, peace was concluded at Bucharest without change in the Serbo-Bulgarian frontier. But the honors of war were all with the young Bulgarian nation and no one now thought of attempting to reverse the act of union.

Russia was, however, resolved that Bulgaria must be

---

[1] See Chapter III.

[2] The war is perhaps best known to the Anglo-Saxon world from Bernard Shaw's comedy *Arms and the Man*.

punished; if not in one way, then in another. Conspirators
in Russia's service kidnaped Prince Alexander
and carried him to Russian soil. Broken in
spirit, he abdicated in September, 1886. But
power passed into the hands of a native dictator,
the energetic Stambulov, who boldly defied Russian threats
and induced the Bulgarian Parliament (*Sobranje*) to select
Prince Ferdinand of Saxe-Coburg as the new ruler. Prince
Ferdinand (1887; "Tsar," 1908–18), in no way dismayed by
the temporary refusal of the powers, under Russia's direction, to recognize his government, was a shrewd diplomat
who was thoroughly at home in the game of international
politics. With such a prince, backed by a political "boss"
of the bulldog type — his admirers called Stambulov "the
Bulgarian Bismarck" — the principality soon became independent of Turkey in all but name and, what was still more
to the point, independent of Russia in diplomatic fact. This
is the more significant since Bismarck, dreading a possible
Austro-Russian war, announced that he would have nothing
to do with any attempt on the part of other powers to interfere with Russia's Bulgarian policy. "In Bulgaria I am
Russian," he said. "It is nothing to us who rules in Bulgaria, or even what becomes of Bulgaria." His own solution
of the Eastern problem seems to have been the division of
the Balkan area into an eastern section as a Russian "sphere
of influence," and a western part which similarly would have
been subject to the exclusive intervention of Austria-Hungary; neither power interesting itself in the regional policies
of the other. Possibly such an agreement might have
averted the World War in 1914; it would certainly have
sacrificed the Balkan nations to "Great Power" imperialism.
Bismarck would have rejoiced in the former result and cared
nothing about the latter.

The other Balkan states, though enjoying a more independent position than Bulgaria with respect to Turkey, were

Russia fails to coerce the Bulgarians

perhaps even more helpless in maintaining real freedom of action as against such powers as Russia or *Pawns of* Austria-Hungary. Greece, Bulgaria and Rumania *diplomacy* all had foreign dynasties, borrowed as a rule from Germany. Serbia in 1881 and Rumania in 1883 bound themselves to Austria-Hungary by treaties of alliance. Austria-Hungary held Serbia helpless by her military occupation of Bosnia-Herzegovina; prevented any union with the Serbs of Montenegro by her policing of the Sanjak of Novi-Bazar; and could put economic pressure on the Serbs at any time by halting Serbian exports at her frontier, since Serbia was a landlocked state and her other boundaries touched Bulgaria, Rumania and Turkey; countries not very wealthy and none too friendly. One of the chief Serbian articles of export was the pig, and the Austrians could discover a need for "quarantine" whenever they wished to coerce the Serbs, a policy appropriately enough called "pig politics" (*Schweinpolitik*). Greece was permitted a slight frontier adjustment immediately after the Congress of Berlin but her dreams of further expansion on the mainland and in the Aegean were halted by the unanimous desire of the "Concert of Europe" to prevent a new Turkish war. By 1871 all European nations outside the Balkan area had attained at least apparent political stability, either as part of some strong empire or as civilized little commonwealths that gave no cause of offense to their neighbors. Southeastern Europe was the danger zone of the continent. There were other chessboards of diplomacy, such as Africa and China, but the peculiar mischief of the Balkan situation lay in the fact that in this instance a backward and exploitable area lay in immediate contact with the frontiers of the interested powers. That is why the questions of Bosnia, Macedonia and Constantinople even more deeply imperiled the general peace than disputes over Manchuria or Morocco.

Serbia, though legally independent, and after 1882 a

"kingdom," was really less fortunate than the "autonomous
principality" of Bulgaria. Bulgarians and Serbs
were alike of Slavic speech [1] and Greek Orthodox
faith, but their rivalry was none the less keen for their similarity. Serbia had the advantages of an earlier start on the
road to national independence and a native line of rulers, but
both advantages proved illusory. Serbia's cramped inland
position, the hostility of jealous neighbors, the absence of important natural resources, forbade her to become a strong
and wealthy state. Even the blessing of stable government
was lacking. Two rival dynasties, descended from early
leaders of the wars for independence, contested the throne.
King Milan of the Obrenovitch line, discredited by many
errors of administration, and above all by the crowning
blunder of an unsuccessful war with Bulgaria, abdicated in
1889 in favor of his son Alexander. The change was no improvement. Alexander was accused of being a despot and
a tool of Austrian intrigue, and he weakened his hold on the
nation by a most unpopular marriage. In 1903 a bloody
palace conspiracy resulted in the murder of King Alexander,
Queen Draga and many of the queen's family. The Karageorgevitch ("Black George") dynasty now succeeded in
the person of King Peter (1903–21), but the new ruler though
not personally responsible for the assassinations which
cleared his way to the throne was long viewed with disfavor
by the European powers.

Serbia

Montenegro was a fragment of Serbian territory which
had remained virtually independent even in the high tide
of Ottoman power. The Black Mountain which
gave its name to the nation enabled a hardy
band of warlike mountaineers to exist in isolation under their
own native princes. Prince Nicholas (1860; king, 1910–18)

Montenegro

---

[1] The *original* Bulgar stock was central Asiatic in type, like the Turks and the
Magyars of Hungary. But by modern times the Bulgars had been pretty completely Slavicized.

governed his tiny realm in patriarchal fashion until the result of the World War swept Serbia and Montenegro together as parts of a greater Kingdom of the Southern Slavs (*Yugoslavia*).

Greece with a lengthy coastline was more favorably situated than Serbia. But millions of Greeks still lived under Ottoman rule in Thessaly, Epirus, Macedonia, Thrace, Asia Minor and the islands of the Aegean. *Greece* Constant absorption in dreams of a "Greater Greece" which might revive Byzantine glories and stretch even to Constantinople dominated the lively Greek imagination and led to some neglect of urgent problems of domestic reform.[1] Two foreign dynasties succeeded each other; King George (1863–1913), a Danish prince, following the luckless Otto of Bavaria. Parties and party leaders rose and fell with kaleidoscopic rapidity. Brigandage prevailed in the country districts, the ports were neglected, commerce languished. Only a few Greek statesmen, notably Trikoupis and Venizelos, ever learned the hard lesson that a nation must be well organized at home before it can hope to win victories abroad. With the fall of Trikoupis, Greece embarked on an adventurous foreign policy which brought about a renewal of the old struggle with Turkey. A revolt of the Christian Greeks of Crete in 1896 so played upon the sympathies of their fellow nationals of the kingdom that, though quite unprepared for war, Greece sent military aid. In the following year the Turkish government declared war and easily vanquished Greece in a single brief campaign. The powers intervened to check the tide of invasion but permitted Turkey to advance her frontier a little to the south and to collect a war indemnity. The Cretan question was settled, for the moment, by a compromise. Crete obtained local autonomy under a Greek governor but still remained separate from the kingdom and a part of the Ottoman Empire.

[1] "The Greek nation's present was overshadowed by its future, and its actions paralyzed by its hopes." (Arnold J. Toynbee.)

Rumania is not in geographical strictness a Balkan state. The country lies in the lower Danube valley, north of the *Rumania* Balkans, and the people are neither Slavs nor Greeks but speak a language derived from the Latin. But a common subjection to the Turk (though the Ottoman yoke was lighter in the Danubian provinces than in most parts of the old Empire), a common struggle for national liberation, a common political weakness and economic backwardness, caused Rumania to be considered for practical purposes one of the Balkan group. The Rumanians considered themselves badly treated at Berlin in being forced to exchange Bessarabia for the less valued region of the Dobrudja at the insistence of Russia. Rumania's unredeemed provinces were no longer in Turkish hands but subject to Russia (Bessarabia) or to Hungary (Transylvania), and there seemed little prospect that they could ever be liberated from such mighty empires. The native ruler Prince Alexander Cuza was deposed in 1866 and Prince Carol of Hohenzollern-Sigmaringen called from Germany to take his place. In 1881 he took the title of king and placed on his head a crown of steel made from Turkish guns captured at the siege of Plevna in the recent war of liberation. His reign lasted until his death in 1914, a tribute to the skill with which he navigated the troubled political waters of Rumanian parliamentary life.

The two chief internal problems of the nation were the land question and the position of the Jews. Until the reforms of *The agrarian and Jewish questions* Prince Cuza the Rumanian peasants lived in practical serfdom and down to the present time the tension between the great landlords and the impoverished farm laborers has been the most frequent source of political crises. The Jews were a numerous racial and religious minority who previous to the Congress of Berlin had been denied citizenship. The Congress forced the unwilling Christian majority to remove the religious barrier, but this promise, though kept in form, was evaded in spirit, and only a few Jews were naturalized and many others were left men without a country so that they would remain subject to all legal discriminations against "aliens."

The reign of Abdul Hamid II was marked, as he could not but realize, by a weakening of his authority in the European and African parts of the Ottoman Empire. The *Turkey-in-* increase of British influence in Egypt, French *Asia* influence in Tunis, Austrian influence in Bosnia; the autonomy of Crete, the rising nationalism of Bulgaria, the continued unrest in Macedonia, all portended a disruption of the Empire which he was more concerned to postpone than wholly to prevent. All the more he resolved that in any event he would strengthen his Asiatic dominion. Here lay the true homeland of the Ottoman Turkish nation since their westward migration in medieval times. But here also were national minorities: Mohammedan Arabs and Kurds; Christian Armenians, Syrians and Greeks; Jews, and other faiths. Geographically, Asiatic Turkey can be divided into three parts: the vast and rugged highland of Asia Minor or Anatolia; the "fertile crescent" of Palestine, Syria and Mesopotamia (Iraq), the seat of some of the most ancient civilizations known to history; the Arabian desert. Anatolia was mainly Turkish, but fringed on the coast with partly Grecian settlements, such as Smyrna, and with large Armenian and Kurdish elements in the east. South of Anatolia there were many races and religions, but the dominant majority almost everywhere was Arabic in speech and Mohammedan in faith. The arable lands were under Ottoman control, but the central deserts were a no man's land of wandering Bedouin tribes who lived as their ancestors had done when Mohammed was a troublesome young prophet, and the acceptance of his teachings was almost the last social change which they had known.

Armenia gave the Sultan most concern.   The Armenians
were the largest Christian minority in the Asiatic provinces
and many of them lived in Constantinople as a
trading middle class in competition with the
Greeks and the Jews.   The true Turk usually
had a warrior's scorn for commerce and left it to
be cultivated by subject races and alien creeds.   Especially
vexatious was the fact that an artificial line drawn through
mainly Armenian territory divided transcaucasian Russia
from eastern Turkey.   At any time Russia might use Armenian discontent, as she had before used Bulgarian, to split
new provinces from the Ottoman Empire.   So when the Moslem Kurds attacked the Armenians, the soldiers and police,
acting evidently under instruction though no doubt willingly enough, threw all the blame on the Armenians, and in
the name of "restoring order" continued the massacre in a
more official and effective way.   The number slaughtered was
probably much greater than the number of Bulgarian victims
whose deaths had provoked war with Russia twenty years
earlier.   But this time atrocity was safe!   Russia was resolved to do nothing; Germany, no longer indifferent to Near
Eastern affairs, was assiduously cultivating Ottoman favor;
France fell in with Russian policy, and Austria with German.
Only the British threatened the use of force, but dared not
risk another war by coercing Turkey without the approval
of the rest of the European Concert.

*The Arme-
nian massa-
cres of
1894-96*

While Europe might cynically ignore an Armenian massacre in Asia Minor or even in the streets of Constantinople,
a Macedonian crisis was another matter.   European Turkey after 1878 consisted, if we ignore
the purely nominal "suzerainty" of the Sultan
over Bosnia-Herzegovina and the principality of Bulgaria,
of three main parts: Albania, Macedonia and Thrace.   Albania, the westernmost portion, had its own native language
which was quite distinct from that of the Turks, Slavs, Greeks

*Divisions of
European
Turkey
after 1878*

or Rumanians. In religion the Albanians were curiously divided, some being Moslems, some Greek Orthodox, some Roman Catholic. Mixed in with the Albanians were large numbers of Serbs and Greeks. Thrace, the eastern portion of European Turkey, had a large Turkish element, especially in and around the capital, but also large numbers of Greeks, Bulgars and others. Between these two lay Macedonia, the most cosmopolitan of all. The substratum of the population was Slavic and probably more Bulgarian than anything else, though there are many transition dialects between the kindred Serbian and Bulgarian tongues.[1] Along the coast the majority were Greeks. Mingled with the Greek, Bulgarian, Serb and nondescript Slavic settlements were little patches of Albanian, Turkish, Rumanian (Vlach) and Jewish population.

The many nationalities of Macedonia were not content to follow the rule of "live and let live" nor would their neighbors have permitted them to do so had they wished. Bulgaria claimed all Macedonian Slavs within her sphere of influence and eagerly spread the national idea by means of their separate church organization, the national Bulgarian division of the Greek Orthodox faith (the "exarchate" organized in 1870); by the establishment of schools in which Bulgarian was the language of instruction; and, when moral persuasion failed, by terrorizing the Macedonians with bands of armed insurgents. Greeks, Serbs and Albanians imitated the Bulgarian example. The inefficient Turkish officials could not pacify the region, though they kept it from open rebellion by an impartial persecution of all the Christian inhabitants. The name of Macedonia became sinister in all civilized lands as the most disorderly of countries, where

"The most distracted country that ever yet was seen"

---

[1] "The well-known recipe for making a Macedonian Slav village Bulgar is to add -*ov* or -*ev* to the names... and to make it Serb it is only necessary to add further the syllable -*ich*; -*ov* and -*ovich* being respectively the equivalent in Bulgarian and in Serbian of our termination -*son*." (Nevill Forbes.)

the unwary traveler was liable to seizure by bandits —
half highwaymen and half patriots — and carried to the
mountains for ransom, and where the distracted peasantry
were constant victims of raids, village burning and unspeakable atrocities. "A dreadful underworld," as George
Young truly called it, "where the machinery of civilization
— the railway, the telegraph, the police — were instruments
for the destruction of all that makes for civilization: where
the only hope of progress lay in the success of dynamitards
and banditti."

Such conditions could not continue indefinitely without
provoking intervention. The most drastic solution, per-
European
intervention haps the only final one, would have been the
in Mace-   creation of an independent Macedonia or the
donia   partition of the region among the neighboring
Christian kingdoms. To attempt this would,
however, risk a Balkan war, perhaps even a general European war, and so the powers still ingeminated the formula,
"preserve the integrity of the Ottoman Empire" — or what
was left of it! Reforms from within would, it was hoped,
bring Macedonia into a condition of tolerable order. In
1903 Russia and Austria-Hungary, the powers most immediately interested in the Near East, agreed to the establishment of an international police force to keep the peace
of Macedonia (the Mürzsteg program). Hampered by
Turkish procrastination and the divergent policy of the
rival European powers, the little force of gendarmes in Macedonia failed to cope with the growing anarchy of the countryside, and the principal result of the experiment was to increase the fear of patriotic Turks that Macedonia was about
to follow the path already taken by Serbia, Rumania and
Bulgaria: first a Turkish province, then a protected district
under European tutelage, then an autonomous dependency,
and at last an independent nation.

Abdul Hamid II had perhaps no virtues except patience

and patriotism, but he used the one to support the other. If his fellow Ottomans could endure the apparent decadence of some portions of the Empire for a season at all events a war might be averted and territorial loss postponed. *The Young Turk revolution, 1908* A favorable diplomatic turn might ultimately enable him to reassert his authority as forcibly in Macedonia as he had in Armenia; in the meanwhile the best course was to play for time. He left out of his reckoning another sort of Turk, equally patriotic but more impatient and progressive, convinced that the Ottoman Empire must choose and that right speedily between becoming European through choice and being Europeanized by foreign conquest. These "Young Turks," stirred by rumors that the powers were planning complete autonomy for Macedonia, raised the standard of revolution in Macedonia. The success of a revolution in any modern country usually depends on the attitude of the army, and on this occasion the more capable Turkish officers, many of them trained in foreign military schools, sympathized completely with the aims of the Committee of Union and Progress which directed the insurrection. Abdul Hamid bent to the storm and in July, 1908, promised to restore the constitutional government promised early in his reign and call without delay a parliament of the whole Ottoman Empire. In the following year he attempted to restore absolute rule, but his reactionary *coup d'état* failed, and he was forced to abdicate in favor of his brother Mohammed V (1909–18). But the real authority was in the hands of the inexperienced young Ottoman patriots of the Committee.

The news that the Ottoman Turks, the most backward of the world's ruling races, had declared for constitutional government roused great enthusiasm throughout liberal circles in Europe and America. The *A false dawn* initiative for reform had come not from the oppressed Christians who might be understood to welcome almost any change as an improvement, but actually from the dominant Moslem minority. Some saw in the fact a coming awakening of all the Mohammedan peoples, in Persia, Africa and India as well as in Turkey. Others hoped for a regenerated Ottoman Empire in which a common spirit of national loyalty would transcend the differences of creed. The new parliament met in an atmosphere of immense good will. Few saw that the work of national regeneration could not be considered a hopeful enterprise while three great obstacles remained unremoved: the conservatism of the Mohammedan peasantry; the national ambitions cherished by the Christian peoples of the Balkans; the imperialistic aims of the European powers.

Not all Turks were "Young Turks." To the majority, with their Asiatic traditions, Turkey was not a nation but *New wine and old bottles* an embodiment of the faith of Islam. The Sultan was important less as a secular ruler than as Khalif, successor to Mohammed and political champion of his gospel. How could an infidel Christian be a fellow citizen? The creed which a man professed was to the average Mohammedan more important than the language in which he professed it. A European of the sixteenth century would have understood this; the exaltation of national differences above differences of creed is a very modern tendency. Many of the new leaders were rumored to be lax in the faith, favorable to such irreligious innovations as the unveiling of women and the drinking of wine. Even the new army discipline, based on the German principle of compulsory service for all subjects alike, suited badly with native military traditions. On the other the Young Turks with all the intolerance of youth pushed forward their program alike indifferent to the protests of Moslem and Christian.

If old-fashioned Turks were a little bewildered by the transformation of their ancient ecclesiastical state into a

garian army, to press Bulgarian propaganda in Macedonia more vigorously than ever, and to enter into negotiations with neighboring states for an alliance against the Turk.

A greater power than Bulgaria seized the same opportunity to wrest from the Ottoman Empire territory where *Annexation* dormant Turkish claims might again be revived. *of Bosnia-* Austria-Hungary had for thirty years treated *Herzegovina* the provinces of Bosnia and Herzegovina as if they were integral parts of her own dominion, regarding Turkish suzerainty as the mere legal fiction it had become. Why make haste to assume the form of sovereignty when so thoroughly possessed of the substance? But now the question was more urgent. Already the European police had been withdrawn from Macedonia, that half-detached province was once more firmly joined to the rest of the Ottoman Empire; perhaps if annexation were further delayed someone might hint that Austrian administration was no longer needed even in Bosnia. Of course there would be formal protests from various signatory powers of the Treaty of Berlin at this new violation of its provisions, but only Russia would be apt to threaten war on such an issue, and as early as 1881 Russia had given Austria a free hand to annex the provinces when she chose. To make assurance doubly sure, Count Aehrenthal the Austro-Hungarian Foreign Minister sounded out Foreign Minister Izvolski, representing Russia, and in conversations so secret that the diplomats concerned later published widely divergent accounts of them, reached a new agreement (the Buchlau conversations). Russia seems to have promised not to oppose annexation but to have expected in return strong Austrian diplomatic support for a proposal to open the Straits to Russian warships. On October 7, annexation was proclaimed. Russia protested that the annexation was premature, that the matter should have been more ripely considered and then laid before a conference of the powers.

The British, sympathizing not a little with the plight of the Turkish reformers whose new government had to sustain the double blow of losing Bulgaria and Bosnia as the very consequence of their reforms, opposed any suggestion that Russia might be "compensated" at Turkish expense by opening the Straits.

Turkish opposition was not, however, very sustained. Though no doubt feeling that they had been ungenerously treated by Europe, the Turks had practically given up both Bulgaria and Bosnia-Herzegovina as "lost provinces." The injury was more to national prestige than to vital interests. Austria-Hungary made yielding easier by evacuating the Sanjak of Novi-Bazar, which lay between Serbia and Montenegro.[1] Germany came to Austria's support, "in shining armor" as the Kaiser put it, and the powers agreed, as they generally do, to recognize the accomplished fact. Formal approval by the Concert of Europe and a small payment to Turkey glossed over the new violation of the Treaty of Berlin.

Of all the nations concerned Serbia had the most genuine grievance. Legally, she had no standing at all; she was neither a suzerain of the annexed territories, like *Ominous* Turkey, nor a signatory of the Berlin Treaty, *increase in* *Austro-* like Russia. But where Turkey lost a paper *Serbian* claim and Russia a dubious weight in the balance *hostility* of power, Serbia suffered a vital blow to her dearest hopes. The provinces in question were southern Slavic in population and the largest element was the Serb. So long as Bosnia and Herzegovina remained Turkish, even nominally, there remained the chance that another war of liberation might unite them with Serbia. But what chance to wrest them from a Great Power? Only in the remote possibility that

[1] This evacuation had the later important consequence of permitting the two Serb kingdoms to establish a common frontier after the Balkan wars of 1912–13. Another reason for Austria's self-denying policy was that it deprived Italy of a claim for "compensation" which might otherwise have been advanced.

war or revolution should blast asunder the entire structure of the Dual Monarchy. In the winter of 1908–09 a portion of the Austro-Hungarian army was mobilized on the Serbian frontier and in the following March the Serbian government accepted an ultimatum couched in most humiliating terms:

> Serbia recognizes that the situation created in Bosnia-Herzegovina does not involve any injury to the rights of Serbia. In consequence, Serbia will conform to the decision which the Powers are going to take in regard to article 25 of the Treaty of Berlin. Serbia, conforming to the advice of the Powers agrees to renounce the attitude of protest and opposition which she has taken since the month of October of last year. She agrees to modify the line of her political conduct in regard to Austria-Hungary and to live in the future on good terms with her.

Extorted promises have seldom much value. An old legend tells of Galileo, forced to recant his belief that the earth moves round the sun, whispering under his breath, "It does move for all that!" Many a Serbian patriot, while in the very act of promising to forget all ambition to unite the Serbs of Bosnia with those of the independent kingdom, whispered to himself, "We *will* move for all that!"

CHAPTER III

GERMANY AND THE TRIPLE ALLIANCE

BISMARCK, who had bulked so large in European history when he represented only the Kingdom of Prussia, occupied a still more prominent position as Chancellor of the German Empire. For twenty years in his new office he dominated the diplomacy of conti- nental Europe as thoroughly as ever Napoleon or Metternich had done in their day. Historians have aptly enough termed the seventies and eighties of the nineteenth century the "Age of Bismarck." He was the last central figure to dominate the diplomacy of a continent; neither in Germany or any other state did there appear a successor able to give his name to an epoch. Yet a word of caution is necessary. Useful as was the genius of Bismarck to Ger- many, the might of Germany was even more essential to the plans of Bismarck. Had he represented a small or a weak state he would have been constrained, as Cavour had been, to rely on foreign aid to carry out his constructive plans and at best he would have been only a national hero of Germany, not the diplomatic dictator of Europe. But as things were, Bismarck could speak with the authority of the strongest army in the world to back his words, and behind that army lay the great population, able administrative organization, growing industrial wealth and enthusiastic national spirit of the German people. After Bismarck's resignation, though the affairs of the Empire fell into much weaker hands, Ger- many continued to be the center of European diplomatic combinations, whether friendly or hostile. Diplomacy be- fore, during and since the World War has been mainly oriented with reference to the "German problem."

Before we examine, therefore, the intricate system of

"Age of Bismarck" or "Age of Germany"?

diplomatic alliances and understandings with which Bis-
Natural re- marck protected the interests of Germany, it
sources and may be well to give some consideration to the
advantages internal structure of the Empire and the sources
of its strength.   The German Empire was not very large
when measured on a world scale and compared with such
political mastodons as the British, Russian or Chinese
Empires or the United States of America; it was about the
size of France and considerably smaller than the state of
Texas.   But population, resources and geographical position count for more than size, and Germany was the very
heart of Europe, touching directly the highly civilized
states of France, Belgium, The Netherlands, Luxemburg,
Denmark, Switzerland, in the west, and the vast empires of
Russia and Austria-Hungary to the east and south.   Her
ports looked across narrow seas to Great Britain and Sweden.
From south to north the German plain was traversed by
great rivers, the Rhine in the west, and then the Elbe, the
Oder and the Vistula.   Along the Rhine the genial climate
permitted grapes to ripen, while in the colder eastern provinces bread meant rye or barley rather than wheat.   There
was variety of topography as well as of climate, the mountainous south contrasting with the flat Baltic plain of the
north.   Though the soil of most parts of Germany was far
from rich there was a smaller proportion of wholly unpro-
ductive land than in any other major European country.
A noble stand of forests covered a quarter of the land and
about half of this belonged to some public authority.   Mineral wealth was even more important than agricultural
resources.   No other European nation had such extensive
coal reserves; and iron, lead, zinc and potash were present
in large quantities.

   In population Germany ranked next to Russia among the
European states.[1]   At the time of the Franco-Prussian War

[1] Not including overseas colonies, such as the British.

the population of France and of Germany were not far apart, but while the number of Frenchmen re- *Population* mained almost stationary at some forty million the number of Germans increased by more than half between the two wars, reaching about sixty-seven million in 1914. Each year increased the relative advantage in man power which Germany held over her chief rival. The Kingdom of Prussia alone came to have a population almost equal to that of all France. This advantage was indirectly increased by the fact that outside Germany, mainly in Austria but also in parts of Switzerland, Hungary, Russian Poland and the Russian Baltic provinces, lived other millions of German speech who had a certain sympathy with their fellow Germans of the Empire. Far beyond Europe, especially in the United States and the temperate parts of South America, lived many German emigrants who had not wholly forgotten the Fatherland. Over such populous empires as Russia and Austria-Hungary Germany enjoyed the further advantage that most of her population was of a single nationality. The old Slavic, Lithuanian and other non-German elements east of the Elbe had long since been Germanized except in the Polish provinces. The Jews did not form, as in Russia or Rumania, a "state within the state" but merged (until the persecutions of 1933) in the general life of the nation. Only three alien elements of political significance existed in the Empire: the natives of Alsace-Lorraine, partly German and partly French in speech, but largely French in sympathy; the Danes of northern Schleswig, and the Poles of eastern Prussia.

The Germany of 1870 was still mainly agricultural with over three fifths of the population dwelling in small villages or in the open country. By 1910 this proportion *Industrial* was reversed; three fifths of the people living in *and urban* towns or cities of over two thousand inhabitants. *growth* But this does not measure the full extent of the change, as

the increase was most rapid in the largest cities. Berlin,
with its suburbs, became second to London among European
capitals. Industrial towns on the Rhine grew as rapidly as
in the American Middle West. In 1882 of every hundred
Germans forty-two lived by agriculture; in 1907 only twenty-
eight. In Bismarck's own day the growing German population was partly offset by heavy emigration to America,
but after 1890 this outflow greatly diminished. On the eve
of the World War Germany was gaining more by immigration (chiefly laborers from impoverished Russian Poland)
than she lost by emigration. Yet it cannot be contended
that Germany was becoming overpopulated; "crowded" in
the economic sense. On the contrary the industrial development of the country absorbed the natural increase of population and dried up the flow of emigration by finding work
within the borders of the Empire. The means of subsistence
were increasing more rapidly than the numbers of the people,
and the standard of living rose even for the poorest classes.

The rural population remained almost stationary, which
suggests the thought that had Germany lacked the wealth
Agriculture in coal on which her industries were based, her
population might have increased but little more
than that of France. Yet agricultural progress was by no
means neglected. Nearly half the land was under crops,
and most of the rest forest land or good pasture. Germany
led the world in the production of potatoes and sugar beets
and was very nearly self-supporting with respect to all the
principal grains and vegetables of the temperate zone. The
government carefully conserved agriculture as the basis of
the national economic life so that in time of war if the
Empire became a beleaguered fortress the garrison need not
starve. Great Britain, with the strongest navy in the world,
took the risk of becoming one vast workshop and buying
grain from overseas; Germany refused to follow this example.
Bismarck protected agriculture by tariffs which increased

the price of bread to the townsman in time of peace but saved him from utter famine in time of war. Like German industry, German agriculture was highly organized. By 1914 there were some 25,000 agricultural co-operative societies of various types within the Empire.

Western Germany, like most of continental western Europe, was farmed by peasant freeholders, but east of the Elbe much of the land was divided into great estates worked by gangs of laborers. The "agrarian" or countryman's movement in German politics was often allied with extreme conservatism. Serfdom lingered in Prussia till 1810, and a hundred years later its impress was still felt on Prussian institutions, such as the laws punishing with imprisonment farm laborers and domestic servants who broke their contracts. The poverty of rural life in eastern Germany and the grinding tyranny of the landlords were, no doubt, contributory factors in the rapid growth of the cities. Many landlords were forced to give seasonal employment to Slavic laborers from Russia and Galicia (Austrian Poland) to offset the "land flight" of their German tenants and laborers. The dominant political power of the Prussian "Junkers" ("squires") sustained the policy of agricultural protection for Germany as a whole and kept on the statute books of the Kingdom of Prussia the reactionary laws of labor contract.

Prussia had given a marked impetus to German trade and manufacture even before the consolidation of the Empire by entering into trade treaties with other German states, thus forming a *Zollverein* or customs union. The Empire included and made permanent the *Zollverein* (which included Luxemburg as well) but through Bismarck's influence higher rates were imposed on foreign goods and from 1879 onwards Germany was increasingly committed to the policy of a protective tariff. His attitude on the tariff question was opportunist

Bismarck endorses protection

and realistic. "For the abstract teachings of science in this connection I care not a straw," he said. "I see that protectionist countries are prospering, that free-trade countries are retrograding." The trend in Germany after 1870 and, it must be admitted, in nearly all other countries, was toward economic nationalism and away from the liberal internationalism preached by the free trade economists from Adam Smith to Richard Cobden.[1] The ideal was no longer the individual merchant free to "buy in the cheapest market and sell in the dearest" but the self-sufficient nation with balanced industry and agriculture, adequate colonial markets, a national merchant marine and direct governmental aid to business.

German trade abroad was carried increasingly in German ships. Such important transatlantic lines as the North German Lloyd and the Hamburg-Amerika developed under the patronage of the government. German consuls in foreign countries fostered in every possible manner the efforts of German traders to open up new territory. Quite reluctantly Bismarck yielded to the spirit of the age and consented to throw the protection of the government over the German merchants who had established trading posts in Africa and the Pacific isles. Here, as in the matter of tariffs, he followed expediency rather than theory. He was no lover of overseas adventure and had not used the opportunity afforded by the Franco-Prussian War to annex any of the French colonial dependencies. On the contrary, he encouraged French colonial ambitions to distract national attention from Alsace-Lorraine and perhaps incidentally to prevent France from seeking alliance with such colonial rivals as Britain and Italy. But when the partition of Africa and the Pacific seemed imminent he concluded that Germany must have a share so that her commerce would not

— and agrees to establish a modest colonial empire

---

[1] For the revival of protectionist agitation in Britain, see Chapter IV.

suffer. He did not wish, however, to extend German dominion beyond the limit of existing German interests. The
dream of a vast overseas empire that would rival the British
and be supported by as strong a fleet Bismarck considered
as quite outside practical politics, fearing that it might lead
to conflict with Great Britain or a neglect of Germany's
European position.[1]

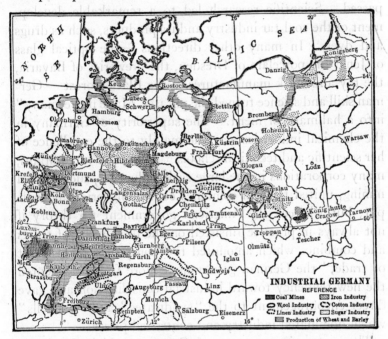

INDUSTRIAL GERMANY

REFERENCE

Coal Mines   Iron Industry
Wool Industry   Cotton Industry
Linen Industry   Sugar Industry
Production of Wheat and Barley

The greatness of Germany has been well said to rest
rather on coal and iron than on "blood and iron." The
three greatest coal-producing countries of the *German
manufac-
tures*
modern world, the United States, Great Britain
and Germany, are also the three greatest industrial countries. The full value of the iron ores of Germany
was not realized in 1871 because the rich deposits in Alsace-
Lorraine had too much phosphorus to make good steel.

[1] For the partition of Africa see Chapter V; for the wider colonial ambitions of
Germany after Bismarck's time see Chapters X, XI and XII.

During the following decade, however, two British metallurgists, Thomas and Gilchrist, had worked out a process of freeing the iron from phosphorus at the same time it was being converted into steel. German iron and steel production far outdistanced the Belgian, overtook and passed the French and seriously rivaled the British, though it was not till the new century that Great Britain was definitely surpassed. Scientific research led to a remarkable development of the coal-tar industry and its products, such as drugs and dyes. In many other directions — the optical glass of Jena, the porcelain of Dresden, the breweries of Bavaria, the toy and clock manufactures of the Black Forest — German skill and science turned the phrase "Made in Germany" into a hallmark of merit. The superiority of Germany in the chemical industries was due mainly to the excellence of her scientific and technical schools. As in the United States, many corporations in the large-scale industries, such as coal mining, united to form combines controlling price and output; but whereas the American government (in theory if not always in practice) insisted on the dissolution of trusts and combines which amounted to "conspiracy in restraint of trade," the German government more frankly accepted the new tendency toward industrial consolidation and gave direct encouragement to the "syndicates" and "Kartells" which dominated industry and controlled prices.

The economic structure of Germany which developed between the Franco-Prussian and World Wars has proved *The politi-* more enduring than the corresponding political *cal struc-* forms. Indeed the constitution of the old Em- *ture of the* pire has been twice buried by a political ava- *German Empire* lanche, by the republican revolution of 1918 and by the centralized dictatorship of 1933; little remains that a contemporary of Bismarck could recognize. In form it was a federation, including four kingdoms (Prussia, Bavaria, Saxony and Würtemberg), six grand duchies, five duchies, seven principalities, three city republics and the territory (*Reichsland*) of Alsace-Lorraine, each with its own constitution. In political motive it was an attempt to combine three principles: the predominant power of the Kingdom of Prussia, the local self-government of each individual state, and direct legislative representation of the nation as a whole.

The first aim, the predominance of Prussia, had been secured by Bismarck's insistence that the kaisership be hereditary in the House of Hohenzollern, the rul- *The Kaiser* ing family in the Kingdom of Prussia. Not only could the two offices never be divided, but the Prussian Kingship was the primary office, the Kaisership of all Germany merely derivative from it. German writers have laid stress on the fact that the Kaiser was "German Emperor" rather than "Emperor of Germany"; not a solitary sovereign but president of a federation, "first among his peers," the ruling princes of Germany. But if his legal dignity as hereditary chief of a federal state was inferior to the undivided sovereignty of a King of England or Italy, his actual power was much greater. He summoned and dissolved the Federal Council (*Bundesrat*) and, with the consent of that body, the elected legislature (*Reichstag*). He appointed imperial officials, promulgated the laws and supervised their execution. He had no direct veto on legislation, but his influence in the Bundesrat usually sufficed to block any action of which he disapproved. He was head of the navy and, subject to the special rights of a few German states in peace time, also of the army. Within Prussia his power as Kaiser was doubled by his direct authority as King. To offer him insult was a heavily punishable crime.

Most of the functions of the German Emperor were exercised through his Chancellor, who was also *The* usually (but not necessarily) Prime Minister of *Chancellor* Prussia. This office was shaped to fit the gigantic personality of Bismarck, and none of his successors proved able fully to live up to its possibilities. The Chancellor held office at the pleasure of the Emperor whether or not he had the support of the Reichstag. It is at this point that the German constitution contrasted most sharply with the constitutions of western Europe generally. A Prime Minister in Great Britain, France or any other nation with "parliamentary government" was a party politician who held office only so long as he could command a working majority in the national parliament. The German Chancellor stood above party, dependent on his sovereign alone. This certainly gave great stability to the government. From the foundation of the Empire to 1917 Germany had but five Imperial Chancel-

Germany a constitutional but not a parliamentary monarchy lors, whereas the French Republic had over fifty ministries. But this stability was won at the expense of democracy. Since the elected representatives of the German people had no power to force from office the chief responsible executive officer of the Empire it followed that whatever control the people might have over legislation they had none over the equally important field of administration. In another respect the German Chancellor differed from the Premier of a parliamentary monarchy. A Prime Minister is usually the chief of a ministry or cabinet and the views of his colleagues have much weight with him, since the cabinet must act as a unit. But the Chancellor had no colleagues; his ministers were his subordinates. The initiation of new policies rested not with a collective cabinet but with the Chancellor, the Emperor personally, or the German princes as represented in the Federal Council.

The Federal Council or Bundesrat was much more than an "upper house" of the national legislature. Theoretically *The Bundesrat* it was the heir of the old Diet of the German *Bund* which had come to an end when Bismarck established German unity; it represented the sovereignty of the German princes and the rights of the individual states over which they ruled. The delegates were appointed by the ruling sovereigns and each state delegation voted as a unit according to the instructions of its government. In contrast with the American Senate the states were unequally represented, in a rough approximation to their relative importance. Prussia cast seventeen votes out of the sixty-one. Though this was less than the share to which Prussia was entitled on the ground of population or political importance, her influence and prestige among the lesser states of northern Germany usually sufficed to rally a majority to any policy strongly desired by her government. A special constitutional provision enabled Prussia to veto military changes, and as fourteen hostile votes sufficed to defeat a constitutional amendment it is evident that the opposition of Prussia could prevent any radical reforms. As each delegation voted under the direct instructions of its home government and, as all but three German states were monarchies, this made the Bundesrat virtually a council of ruling princes. The duties of the Bundesrat were so numerous and extended that it remained in practically permanent session. It undertook the shaping of the budget and of the legislative program favored by the Chancellor, passed upon laws approved by the Reichstag, declared war, approved treaties, enjoyed general oversight of the enforcement and administration of Imperial laws, determined constitutional issues arising in the sphere of administrative law between the Empire and the states, confirmed appointments, and, with the assent of the Emperor, dissolved the Reichstag.

The Reichstag was Bismarck's sole concession to the popular demand for representative government. It was a legislative body of 397 members chosen by direct, *The Reichs-* secret and universal manhood suffrage. It was *tag* not, as its admirers sometimes claimed, "the most democratic parliament in Europe" since there was no redistribution of seats to correspond to the shifting population of the Empire and by the end of the nineteenth century a vote in a country district of stationary population had come to have several times the weight of a vote cast in an industrial suburb of Berlin.   But it was certainly the most democratic part of the machinery of the German Empire and had it enjoyed the powers of a British House of Commons or a French Chamber of Deputies, Germany might fairly have been accounted a democracy.   But as we have seen, the Reichstag possessed no power over the executive branch of the government.   Even its legislative authority was severely limited.   The most important laws were shaped by the Bundesrat before being presented to the Reichstag.   Army budgets were voted for a considerable period of years, and all Germany remembered that Bismarck had been able to collect taxes in the face of a hostile Prussian parliament and feared he might do the same in the face of a hostile Reichstag if driven to extremities.   The Reichstag was important as an index of public opinion and as a check on autocracy, but it was certainly one of the weakest parliamentary bodies in Europe.   As the political philosopher James Bryce has sapiently remarked, "An assembly elected on a comparatively narrow franchise but with wide powers does more to make a government popular than one elected on a wider franchise with narrower powers."

Though Germany never had party government under the Empire, the political parties in the Reichstag had real *Party politics in the Reichstag* importance since they represented permanent tendencies in German life and most of them reappeared under new names in the Republic. At the extreme right were the Conservative party and certain allied groups such as the "Free Conservatives," agrarians and others.   They stood for existing institutions, upheld military authority and an aggressive foreign policy, and favored the economic interests of the landlords as against the townsmen. They were the heart of every government coalition and yet sometimes "more royalist than the King" they voted against reforms desired by the Chancellor. Sometimes Bismarck therefore turned to the Liberals, representing the political traditions of the German nationalists of 1848 and the economic interests of the commercial and professional middle classes. A schism split the group into two parties, the increasingly conservative National Liberals, devoted to imperial expansion and "big business" industrialism, and the Progressives who still clung to the principle that Germany must be made a parliamentary monarchy "like England." The Social Democrats or Socialists, bitterly but unsuccessfully opposed by Bismarck, became by 1912 the strongest party in the Empire, but as the party grew in size it tempered its revolutionary program to a very mild parliamentary opposition. The Catholic Center, the product of Bismarck's struggle with the Catholic Church,[1] represented many classes and many shades of political and economic opinion, united only by a desire to safeguard the interests of the Church. Besides these major groups there were many small parties, including the national minorities of Poles, Alsace-Lorrainers, Danes and Guelphs (the last named being a group who protested against the Prussian annexation of Hanover).

In every federal government there is a conflict between the nationalist tendency to reduce the states to administrative units of the central government and the *Particularism in Germany* particularist tendency to emphasize states' rights and treat the nation as a mere alliance of sovereign states. Germany has had both her Hamiltons and her Calhouns. In some respects the German Empire was more centralized than the United States of America, in others less so. The legislative competence of the Reichstag

[1] See page 72.

and Bundesrat exceeded that of the American Congress, but much administrative power was left to the local authorities. Certain of the more powerful states enjoyed special privileges. Bavaria, next to Prussia, was the most powerful and privileged state, enjoying six seats in the Bundesrat and the permanent chairmanship of the foreign affairs committee of that body, and permitted to retain her own railway and postal system and her own organization of poor relief. Bavaria, Würtemberg and Baden had the exclusive right to levy taxes on local wines and beer. Some states enjoyed a limited control over their military establishments in time of peace, though most of them simply consolidated their armies with that of Prussia. The supreme law court of the Empire met at Leipzig in Saxony instead of at Berlin. The city-states of Hamburg and Bremen maintained "free zones" outside the tariff line in their ports.

Of course the most highly privileged of all the states was the Kingdom of Prussia. With about two thirds of the area *The Prussian constitution* and population of all Germany, the Imperial crown in her royal House, a large majority in the Reichstag and a controlling position in the Bundesrat, the Imperial Chancellor as her Premier, and a military system which was the model for the Empire as a whole, Prussia usually determined the course of German policy both at home and abroad.[1] This made her internal constitution a matter of international importance. A democratic constitution for Prussia would have meant a democratic constitution of the Empire; but the actual state government was far less democratic than that of the majority of German states or of the Empire as a whole. The King of Prussia enjoyed even wider powers as King than as Kaiser. The *Landtag* or legislature consisted of a House

[1] The predominant influence of a single state made the German federation unlike such federations as Switzerland or the United States. The position of Prussia might more aptly be compared to that of Holland among the other Dutch provinces in the days of the old Dutch Republic, or the position of Great Britain among the Dominions of the present British "Commonwealth."

of Lords, representing mainly the territorial nobility, and a House of Representatives chosen by a curious system designed to give overwhelming weight to the possession of property. Voters were divided into three classes in each electoral district according to the amount of taxes paid, and each class chose one third of the electors to which the district was entitled. These electors in turn chose the representatives. This combination of unequal representation and indirect election, aggravated by the absence of a secret ballot and the failure to redistribute seats to match the movement of population, might in some districts make the vote of an employer outweigh that of a thousand workingmen or enable a landlord to outvote all his tenants.

The most backward states in the Empire, politically speaking, were the Grand Duchies of Mecklenburg-Schwerin and Mecklenburg-Strelitz, which had no writ- *Other state* ten constitutions and no form of representation *govern-* except a medieval system of "Estates" or *ments* advisory assemblies of the landowning classes. At the other extreme were the city republics of Hamburg, Bremen and Lübeck, though even here property as well as population was considered in the electoral system. In most of the monarchical states the hereditary king, duke or prince enjoyed great power, and some degree of special representation was granted to the property owners, taxpayers, nobility or professional classes. The most considerable of these constitutional monarchies besides Prussia were Protestant, industrial Saxony and Catholic, agrarian Bavaria. As a military outpost of Empire, Alsace-Lorraine was denied the local home rule enjoyed by the states of the Em- *Alsace-* pire. The people were allowed to vote for the *Lorraine* Imperial Reichstag, but their local legislature was subordinated both to the Governor appointed by the Kaiser and to the superior legislative competence of the Imperial government. In 1911 the legislature was reorganized as a two-chambered body and given increased powers. The Governor remained, however, independent of popular control, and the three votes which Alsace-Lorraine was now permitted in the Bundesrat really strengthened the power of the King of Prussia.[1]

German political life was probably at its best just where American political life is at its worst, in municipal adminis-

Local government tration. It is true that the elective element in provincial and municipal government was always mingled with and usually subordinated to a professional bureaucracy largely independent of popular control. But these expert officials were trained for their task and there were relatively few instances of corruption or even of incompetent management. It was common for a German city to own its street railways, waterworks, gas and electric plants, markets, docks, stockyards and slaughter-houses. Cities were not permitted to grow at random but were carefully built according to plan. To the foreigner one of the most pleasing features of German life was the individuality of the German towns. In many European countries culture centered in one city and radiated thence to the provinces; France, perhaps, suffered from too much focal concentration on the unique grandeur of Paris. But this was emphatically not the case in Germany, as Berliners were often reminded! Not only such historic capitals as Dresden and Munich but even such smaller cities as Jena, Nüremberg and the like blended delightfully the traditions of the Middle Ages with the commercial energies of the modern time.

Bismarck's heart was always at the Foreign Office (except

Bismarck's domestic policy in the purely personal sense in which it was rather among the grand forests in which he loved to wander and hunt) and he turned to domestic problems reluctantly. Nevertheless, he recognized his

---

[1] But they could not be counted for Prussia on constitutional amendments or to give Prussia a majority in the Bundesrat which she would not otherwise have had.

responsibility.   As Chancellor he had to construct a program
of internal legislation as well as a network of foreign alliances.   His most important policies in the former field
might be summarized as the decision to adopt a protective
tariff, the decision to annex colonies overseas, the repression
of socialism combined with a positive program of social
reform, a somewhat maladroit attempt to curb the political
influence of the Roman Catholic Church, and the continual
strengthening of the army.   In pursuit of these objectives
he learned to play the game of party politics with no little
skill.   Himself a Conservative, he turned with impartial
readiness to an alliance with any groups which would support the official program.

The venture of Bismarck into state socialism is of particular interest, for the German social insurance laws have
proved models for similar legislation in many *Social*
other countries.   Class-conscious socialism was *insurance*
abhorrent to him and he invoked the law to repress its propaganda.   But what has been termed "monarchical socialism," the benevolent interest of a paternal government in
the welfare of its subjects, appealed to him as praiseworthy
in itself and also as a good way of promoting loyalty to the
crown.   It is significant that the Social Democrats and Progressives for the most part opposed the new laws, because
of their political hostility to the Chancellor, while the Conservatives supported them.   The law of 1884 placed the
cost of accident insurance on the employers.   Insurance
against disability due to illness, on the other hand, was divided by the law of 1883 between employers and employed;
the workers contributing two thirds of the whole.   In 1889
an old-age pension system was established.   In this instance
the state added a subsidy to the fund created by equal contributions of workers and employers.   Nothing that Bismarck ever did bore more permanent fruit.   Party Socialists
who had opposed his program later accepted it as an in-

stallment towards their own Utopia, and doctrinaire capitalists came to see in it a welcome safeguard against revolution.

On the other hand, Bismarck's struggle with the Catholic Church proved to be, if not his greatest blunder, at all *The Kul-* events his most open humiliation. This so-*turkampf* called "struggle for civilization" (*Kulturkampf*) was entirely in the political field; it had nothing to do with religion and would probably have run much the same course if Bismarck had chanced to be a Catholic instead of a Protestant. There were several reasons for Bismarck's disquiet. His chief enemies abroad had been the Austrians and the French, his most bitter opponents within Germany were the Prussian Poles; in all these cases he had found priests active in anti-Prussian propaganda. At the Vatican Pope Pius IX was actively engaged in controversy with the Italian government, which had incorporated the Papal States into its new kingdom and looked abroad for diplomatic aid to restore his "temporal power" as sovereign prince in Rome. Such a movement would disturb the peace of Europe and not serve Germany's interests. In 1864 in a *Syllabus of Errors* the Pope had condemned many heresies and errors of religious "liberalism" and also the view that the State was superior to the Church or rightly independent of its influence.[1] In 1870 a general Council promulgated the dogma that the Pope was "infallible"; that is, not subject to error when formally defining a doctrine of faith and morals. All these events reminded Bismarck unpleasantly of the long struggle in medieval Germany between the Popes and Emperors. Recalling the penance done by Henry IV before Pope Gregory VII at the Italian town of Canossa, he defiantly exclaimed, "We are not going to Canossa!" When certain German Catholics were dismissed from their church for opposing the Pope, Bismarck decided to champion their rights.

---

[1] *E.g.*, that, "It appertains to the civil power to define what are the rights and limits within which the Church may exercise authority."

But for Bismarck to defend anything meant to attack its opposite. Beginning as a champion of religious liberty, he ended as something very like a persecutor. He expelled the Jesuit order from Germany, broke off diplomatic relations with the Vatican, and patronized a series of laws in Prussia (usually called the "Falk laws") providing that persons holding ecclesiastical offices in Germany must have been educated in German schools and universities, placing church schools under public inspection and regulation, dissolving religious orders and interfering with church discipline, and making civil marriage compulsory even if a religious ceremony were added. Many laws applied only in Prussia but other German states were urged to copy her example. The chief effect of Bismarck's anti-clerical campaign was to create a new political party, the Center, which from that time forward vigilantly safeguarded the interests of the Roman Church. Very frequently Bismarck needed their votes to carry other measures in the teeth of liberal or socialistic opposition. So Bismarck dropped some of the anti-clerical laws, modified the operation of others, permitted vacant bishoprics to be filled, restored governmental subsidies and resumed negotiations with the Vatican. His "trip to Canossa" was made easier by the accession to the Papal throne in 1878 of Leo XIII, a tactful and diplomatic pontiff who was eager to accept the olive branch which Bismarck extended. Bismarck, who rarely persisted in a mistake, made no further attempt to interfere in the internal affairs of religious communions.

The postulate of Bismarck's foreign policy was a strong army. He did not need any more wars after his triumph over France, but he did desire to dominate the *Bismarck's* whole course of European diplomacy so that it *military* might never take a turn injurious to German *policy* interests. In one of his most eloquent parliamentary addresses he proclaimed, "We must make greater exertions than

other powers on account of our geographical position.   We
lie in the middle of Europe; we can be attacked on all sides....
The pike in the European fish pond prevent us from becoming carp.... By courtesy and kind methods we may easily —
perhaps too easily — be influenced, but by threats never.
We Germans fear God and nothing else in the world!''   He
was not above fomenting war scares in the press to frighten
penny-pinching delegates in the Reichstag to vote large army
appropriations.   To make the government more independent
of the parties he insisted on having his military budget voted
for seven years at a time.

Next to the making of Germany, Bismarck's greatest
achievement was the imposing structure of alliances which
The Drei-   he created to defend his work.   He did not feel
kaiserbund   so much that Germany needed allies as that
France must be prevented from having them.   The desire
to detach other powers from France was the starting point of
his policy.   His first and favorite plan was a league of the
Emperors of Germany, Austria-Hungary and Russia (*Drei-
kaiserbund*), and to this expedient he recurred time and again
whenever he could bring the jealous powers into agreement.
Great Britain was inclined to aloofness from continental alliances, was on fairly friendly terms with Germany and,
what was still more to the point, was in sharp colonial rivalry
with France.   Italy was but a minor power, and her interests
in some important respects ran counter to those of France.
Therefore if France found allies against Germany, the most
probable and most formidable would be Russia or Austria-
Hungary.   No definite alliance was made, but negotiations
in 1872 and 1873 brought the three Emperors to a formal
understanding to consult together if the peace of Europe were
threatened.   Bismarck cleverly played on the conservative
prejudices of the three autocrats, convincing them that republican and "revolutionary" France was the standing
danger to European peace.   This was Metternich's old

policy, revived in the interest of Germany instead of Austria.

But whereas Metternich would probably have attempted to restore monarchy in France, Bismarck remained ostentatiously indifferent to French politics. At heart *The war* he was glad enough to have France remain re- *scare of* publican, since she was less likely to find alliances 1875 abroad in a monarchical Europe. When Count Harry von Arnim intrigued in Paris against the republic Bismarck rebuked and disciplined him. When the monarchists triumphed in the National Assembly, and Thiers, the recent convert to republicanism, was succeeded as chief executive by Marshal MacMahon, instead of rejoicing Bismarck became alarmed. This alarm was increased by improvements in the French army, by the jingoistic vaporings of some French militarists, and by the criticism of Bismarck's *Kulturkampf* in Roman Catholic countries. Some of the German officers advocated a "preventive war" before France could recover her former strength. There is nothing to show that Bismarck shared this view, but he did believe that a good scare in the press might tame French opinion. He permitted "inspired" articles to appear in the press commenting on the imminent danger of war. Unfortunately he overdid his press campaign, alarming not only the French but the British and Russians as well. He had to explain in a somewhat embarrassed fashion that no danger of war had really existed. He was much incensed at Prince Alexander Gorchakov, the Russian Minister of Foreign Affairs, for his self-complacent declaration that, thanks to Russia, "peace was now assured." The importance of this otherwise trivial incident was the demonstration that Germany could not under all circumstances count on Russian sympathy against France.

The factor which really made the agreement of the three Emperors impossible, however, was not the temporary rift between Germany and Russia but the permanent rift between Russia and Austria-Hungary. The Congress of

Berlin in 1878 had convinced the Russian government that

Effect of the Berlin Congress the Austrians were open foes and the Germans perfidious and unreliable friends.[1] Bismarck was now faced with a momentous decision. He had, to all seeming, three possible courses of action. He could refrain from any special alliance and trust to fortune that neither of the rival Empires of eastern Europe would join hands with France. He could repudiate Austria-Hungary and link the fortunes of Germany with those of Russia. He could form an alliance with Austria-Hungary and thus balk the resentment of Russia, trusting to a better day to reconquer the lost confidence of the Tsar. He chose the last of these courses and thereby laid the cornerstone for the system of alliances which dominated European diplomacy till the end of the World War.

Bismarck would have preferred a general alliance, directed as much against France as Russia, but Count Julius An-

The Austro-German alliance of 1879 drassy, the able Magyar statesman who represented Austria-Hungary, insisted on a more limited engagement. The treaty finally negotiated provided that if either Germany or Austria-Hungary were attacked by Russia, or by another power supported by Russia, the other would come to its aid. In the event of an attack by another power (such as an Italian attack on Austria or a French attack on Germany) the other contracting power would at least remain neutral. The treaty was to run for five years and be secret, but if war threatened the Tsar was to be warned that an attack on either power would be an attack on both.

Kaiser Wilhelm, who usually accepted his Chancellor's views without question, was inclined to make difficulties over the treaty of alliance. He did not believe that the Tsar, however offended for the moment over the results of the Congress of Berlin, wanted war with Austria-Hungary, still less

[1] See above, Chapter II.

with Germany. He feared that Russia if rebuffed by Germany would turn to France. Very reluctantly he accepted Bismarck's policy, more because he feared to lose Bismarck's services than because he was convinced by his arguments. Since the World War many critics, wise after the event, have maintained that the aged German Emperor was right and his brilliant Chancellor wrong. "In his great period the Iron Chancellor went with Russia and against Austria," said Prince Lichnowsky, "in the period of his decline he went with Austria and against Russia."[1] But there were many reasons which seemed cogent at the time which impelled Bismarck to his decision. The most important was that Austria-Hungary appeared to be a conservative government desiring only peace, a "satiated state" like Germany; Russia had vast and uncertain ambitions both in the Near and the Far East which might drag Germany into unwelcome adventures. A minor point was that Russia at the moment was unfriendly, while Austria-Hungary was eager to forget and forgive the Austro-Prussian War of 1866 in return for security against the immediate peril from Russia. Moreover, the Austrian Court, at least, was German, though the people were of many races, and the alliance renewed in some degree the old German unity which had lasted till Bismarck's own victory over Austria had broken it. This argument counted for little with Bismarck personally, but he weighed its effect on German opinion. Possibly the personal factor counted for something. Bismarck disliked and distrusted Gorchakov, but he felt that Andrassy was a man with whom he could work on confidential terms. In any case, he hoped that the misunderstanding with Russia would be a brief one and that he could soon enclose his Austrian alliance within the framework of a renewed and strengthened *Dreikaiserbund*.

---

[1] Lichnowsky, *Heading for the Abyss* (1928), xxv. W. H. Dawson, one of the ablest students of German policy, wrote in 1919, "It can hardly be pretended seriously that the choice which made Austria Germany's close ally and Russia her enemy was other than a blunder." *The German Empire*, II, 268.

The immediate event seemed to justify Bismarck's hopes. Russia made no move towards France and seemed to welcome overtures for the revival of the old understanding of the autocratic Empires. The new Tsar, Alexander III (1881–1894), was more concerned to repress rebellion at home than to seek new causes of quarrel with Austria-Hungary. In 1881 a three years' agreement, renewed in 1884, pledged the three powers to "observe benevolent neutrality" and try to "localize the conflict" if at war with a fourth power. This was to apply to Turkey also, but only in case the powers concerned had reached an agreement as to the results of the war. The *status quo* in Turkey and the Balkans was to be maintained and the Straits impartially closed to the warlike operations of all nations. A special protocol recognized the right of Austria-Hungary to annex the occupied provinces of Bosnia and Herzegovina whenever she pleased, provided against a Turkish reoccupation of Eastern Rumelia, and agreed not to oppose the union of Eastern Rumelia with Bulgaria. Thus the threatened conflict between Russian and Austrian ambitions in the Balkans was postponed. Special Austrian treaties with Serbia (1881) and Rumania (1883) still further strengthened the position of the German Powers.

The Drei-kaiserbund renewed, 1881

To complete the encirclement of France, Italy must be added to the lengthening chain of alliances and understandings. Bismarck found this no great task. In fact, the overtures came from the side of Italy. The Italians were eager to play the part of a Great Power and knew well enough that only by means of foreign alliances could they do so, as their own military strength was inferior to that of Russia, Germany, France or Austria-Hungary. France might have seemed a natural ally but for two reasons. One was the French occupation of Tunis in 1881, a Turkish dependency in north Africa which the Italians had for some time considered destined to be a future colony of Italy. The

Italy joins the circle

other was the agitation of some extreme French Clericals ("Ultramontanists") for the restoration of Rome to the temporal sovereignty of the Pope.   So, irritated by French colonial success and alarmed by the possibility of losing their new capital, the Italians turned to a German alliance.   The chief obstacle was the traditional hatred of the Italians for the Austrian government, so long their oppressor.   But the price of an alliance with Germany was an accord with Austria-Hungary as well.

Thus the Dual Alliance between Germany and Austria-Hungary was supplemented by a Triple Alliance including Italy.   Germany and Austria promised to come *The Triple* to the aid of Italy if attacked by France; Italy, *Alliance of* in turn, to come to the aid of Germany in like *1882* straits.   In the case of war of a signatory power with another state her two allies would at least remain neutral, and would come to her assistance if two or more joined in the attack. The alliance was to be secret and to last for five years. Originally it was entirely defensive in character.   But, as Italy recovered from her fears of French intervention on behalf of the Pope and found new outlets for her colonial ambitions, she demanded a higher price for her adhesion to the alliance and committed her allies to recognition of her interests in the Balkans and to the support of her ambitions in the Mediterranean.

In 1887 the peace of Europe seemed seriously threatened. The aged German Emperor and his son, now an invalid, would soon leave the throne to an inexperienced *The crisis* young prince who was believed to be an ardent *of 1887* militarist.   The Triple Alliance and the League of the Three Emperors were both soon due for renewal.   In France an agitation for a more vigorous foreign policy found a leader in General Boulanger.[1]   Into this disturbed and uncertain situation Russia had thrust a flaming match by intervention

[1] For the Boulangist movement see below, page 150.

in Bulgaria. During the previous summer Prince Alexander was kidnaped by Russian agents and forced to abdicate. Britain and Austria-Hungary, traditional foes of Russian policy in the Orient, were angered almost to the point of war. France, on the other hand, saw an opportunity for a Russian alliance. Bismarck demanded from the Reichstag a new army bill; to gain his point he had to resort to the dangerous expedient of stirring up another war scare in the press, and a more genuine one than that of 1875. In April a French official, Schnaebele, was arrested on charges of espionage when he crossed the frontier. Bismarck agreed to his release when it was shown that he had entered Germany on the invitation of German officials and thus, spy or not, was under a guarantee of safe conduct. For several months Europe was closer to a general conflict than at any time since the Congress of Berlin, possibly since the Franco-Prussian War.

To Bismarck the key to the situation was to restrain Russia without alienating her from Germany. If Russia *The Medi-* were permitted to go ahead and complete the *terranean* Russification of Bulgaria, war with Austria-*agreements* Hungary might occur; on the other hand, if Germany directly appeared in the lists against Russia, war might be averted for the moment, but an alliance between Russia and France would almost certainly result. As a check on Russia, Bismarck not only renewed the Triple Alliance but encouraged the formation of a Mediterranean agreement among the British, Austrian and Italian governments. In February Italy proposed an agreement to maintain so far as possible the *status quo* on the shores of the Mediterranean, the Adriatic, the Aegean and the Black Sea and to prevent the encroachments of other powers. This was intended mainly as a check on France. The British and Austrian governments assented. In December a second agreement, on British initiative, affirmed the *status quo* in the Balkans and opposed by implication any further Russian intervention in Bulgaria (Turkey cannot "delegate her suzerain rights over Bulgaria to any other Power"). Spain agreed not to aid France in ambitious designs in northern Africa directed against Italy, Germany or Austria-Hungary. The isolation of France and Russia was complete.

Yet Bismarck could still hope to maintain friendly relations with Russia. There was no hope of resurrecting the old league of the Three Emperors; the hostility between Russia and Austria-Hungary had grown far too bitter for that. But in lieu of the old tripartite agreement he proposed a direct treaty of neutrality between Germany and Russia. As in view of his obligations to Austria-Hungary under the alliance of 1879 he could not promise not to come to the defense of his ally, Russia in turn would not promise not to come to the defense of France. Both governments agreed in June on a secret three years' pact to maintain a "benevolent neutrality" in the case of war with another country, but "this provision would not apply to a war against Austria or France if resulting from an attack by one of the contracting parties." Bismarck also recognized Russia's "preponderant and decisive influence in Bulgaria and Eastern Rumelia" and her interest in the question of the Straits.

The Reinsurance Treaty of 1887

The Reinsurance Treaty was the last of Bismarck's major diplomatic constructions. It lasted until he fell from office in 1890 and completed the most elaborate network of diplomatic agreements in modern history. During the whole of his chancellorship Bismarck had kept France without allies and therefore helpless to do more than dream of *revanche* for the Franco-Prussian War. With Austria-Hungary he held definite alliance after 1879; with Italy after 1882. Russia had been a member of the first league of the Three Emperors in 1872, and of the second from 1881 to 1887, while bound to at least a negative neutrality by the Reinsurance Treaty after 1887. Great

Summary of Bismarck's alliances

Britain, though making no formal German alliance, had been usually friendly and in 1887 associated with Austria-Hungary and Italy, Germany's allies, to preserve the Mediterranean balance of power.   Of the minor states, Spain, Serbia and Rumania had been brought into the diplomatic structure, while Turkey looked to Austria for support against Russia.   Bismarck was accused of being the victim of a "nightmare of coalitions" directed against Germany; he exorcised this nightmare by making the coalitions himself. It is due to Bismarck to say that he aimed at something more than the "iron ring" around France.   He wished also to direct the activities of all the European powers toward policies which would avoid a war with Germany or a war with each other which might embarrass Germany.[1]   The Age of Bismarck was an age of peace.

But there is another side to the picture.   Many historians have argued that the Bismarckian system was far too *Dangers of* elaborate to last.   Kaiser Wilhelm I once com- *the alliance* pared his Chancellor to a juggler who tosses five *system* balls in the air at once and catches them every time.   Some of the diplomatic understandings were hard to reconcile with each other, or with common honesty.   It is perfectly true that there was no *direct* conflict between the terms of the Austrian Alliance and the Reinsurance Treaty, since Germany was bound to support her ally only in a defensive war against Russia.   But if war had broken out between Russia and Austria-Hungary, Germany would have had to assume the very delicate task of determining who was the aggressor, a question not always easy to solve.   Still harder is it to see what position Bismarck would have taken if Russia, encouraged by the secret protocol to the Reinsur-

---

[1] "The powers were so enmeshed in an elaborate scheme of insurance treaties, reinsurance treaties, agreements and understandings that it was almost impossible for any one of them to act without bringing all the others upon the scene.   Under the circumstances there was, as Bismarck himself said, a premium upon the maintenance of peace."   W. A. Langer, *European Alliances and Alignments* (1931), p. 459.

ance Treaty, had seized Bulgaria or sent a fleet to Constantinople, while Austria-Hungary, relying on the Mediterranean agreements and the alliance with Germany, had come out as the champion of Turkish integrity and Bulgarian rights.   Again, had Italy acted up to her full rights under the revised Triple Alliance, Germany might have been involved in a needless war with France over Morocco or Tripoli. Moreover, many of the agreements were secret, though not always so by Bismarck's own wish, and several times the nations drifted towards war in ignorance of the obligations assumed by their own rulers.

A far more serious question relates not to the wisdom of the particular diplomatic combinations for which Bismarck was responsible but to the wisdom of *any* system of special alliances.   They might, and probably did, preserve the peace of Europe up to a certain point by making governments, weighted with so many responsibilities, hesitate to take risks. But they divided the powers into opposed camps, led to armament races and contests of diplomatic "prestige," and above all made it almost impossible to "localize" a war once it had broken out.   The war of 1870 had been a lonely duel. The alliance policy made it almost certain that when next France and Germany crossed swords all their "seconds" would be fighting too.   Bismarck, of course, never wished for a balance of opposed alliances; he hoped rather to dominate all Europe with a network of diplomatic agreements radiating, like the strands of a spider's web, from a German center.   But such a system could never have continued indefinitely unless Germany were to breed an unending series of Bismarcks and unless all other nations were content to acquiesce in German leadership.

The proof of this lies in the history of what happened. Bismarck passed from the scene leaving the destinies of Germany and the world to the mercy of an impulsive Kaiser, mediocre statesmen who had been dwarfed to mere bureau-

crats by Bismarck's imperious will, a cowed and bullied
The "year Reichstag, and a passive public. So long as
of Three Wilhelm I lived Bismarck's position was secure.
Emperors," He lived to the age of ninety-one, vigorous in
1888 mind almost to the last, but relying increasingly
upon his Chancellor. His immediate successor, Kaiser
Friedrich III, might have turned German history into a more
liberal channel had he lived, for he was a man of generous
enthusiasms, possessing the honesty and integrity of his
father without his stiff old-world prejudices. But he came to
the throne a dying man and illness filled the brief weeks of his
reign. Germany's third and last Kaiser, Wilhelm II, was of
a different type from his father or his grandfather. Probably
more brilliant than either, he lacked their stability of character. In some ways he was a throwback to King Friedrich
Wilhelm IV, the Hohenzollern who had reigned in the
troublesome revolutionary days of 1848: romantic, sensitive,
sentimental, erratic, with high-flown ideas of the divine right
of all hereditary princes and especially of his own royal
House. Like too many crown princes he had been snubbed
and kept in ignorance of public questions in his youth; on
coming to the throne, therefore, he desired to assert himself
vigorously and demonstrate to the world that the sovereign
of the most powerful of nations was no Chancellor's puppet.

The incidents which determined the break between the
new Kaiser and the old Chancellor were many. The Kaiser
Bismarck had a generous thought for an international
resigns, conference on labor conditions; Bismarck thought
1890 the plan impractical. Bismarck insisted on
renewing the secret Reinsurance Treaty with Russia; the
Kaiser, though not wholly opposed, had doubts on the matter
and was irritated at Bismarck's concealment of diplomatic
matters. Bismarck invited into private conference Windt-
horst, leader of the Catholic "Center" party; the Kaiser
objected. . Finally, the Kaiser demanded the right to consult

ministers directly and not through the Chancellor and, when Bismarck refused, requested his resignation. But the real underlying reason was that Germany could not have two masters. If the break had not come over the petty irritations of 1890 it would have come in any case within the next few years. Bismarck was too old to learn to serve; Wilhelm II too young to learn to wait. Bismarck lived on eight years longer in sulky retirement, venting bitter criticism on the ministers who replaced him and foreboding serious perils to the ship of state with such an inexperienced steersman at the helm.

CHAPTER IV

THE UNITED KINGDOM AND GREATER BRITAIN

CONCEDING Germany to have been after 1871 the greatest European Power, Great Britain remained the greatest World

The empire of the sea-ways Power in Europe. This distinction is no verbal quibble, it goes to the very root of the difference between two great Imperial systems. Germany was a continental state whose history had ever been an inextricable part of the general life of Europe. Her strength reposed on her army; until the eighties she had no overseas colonies, and until almost the end of the century no important navy. Great Britain was the political center of the largest and most composite empire in the world's records; an empire scattered among the seven seas and represented in every continent and in almost every important island group. These possessions were held by no uniform law but by a most bewildering variety of titles and tenure; even the term "British Empire" had rather a popular than an official sanction. The nominal bond of union was the British Crown, the most important practical tie was the British fleet, for generations the strongest in the world. Her great and growing colonial interests had caused Britain from the seventeenth century onward to assume a position of partial detachment from the diplomacy of the continent. The British often intervened in continental controversies, and sometimes most effectively, but they maintained few enduring alliances and relied in time of peace on a small and volunteer army. In the main, until the time of Wilhelm II, British and German policy revolved in separate orbits and did not conflict because they did not touch.

A visitor from Mars or Venus if shown a map of the British Empire might well be excused for overlooking one of its smallest units, the British Isles themselves. *The British* Invert a map so that the southern hemisphere is *Isles* at the top and the British Isles become "a little archipelago in the antipodes" as an Australian wag once called them. England, the most populous part of the islands, is about the size of New York State; the whole group about as large as Montana. Even on the European scale the British Isles are small. Yet on closer inspection the Martian geographer might be inclined to ascribe great possibilities to this little land. Separated by the narrow "silver streak" of the Channel from the continent, the British have been able to live their own national life more completely than any other European people. Secure behind the sea, at least till the twentieth century brought the airship and the submarine, the British early attained national unity, avoided the necessity of a large standing army, and were able to concentrate their attention on commerce and colonies instead of wasting their resources on the interminable frontier wars that make up the political history of the continent. The long winding coastline, with its numerous bays, harbors and inlets, beckons to venture on the high seas and facilitates trade with the neighboring French, Dutch and German ports. The general relief is low, save in parts of Wales and Scotland, so access is easy from one part of the country to another. The climate is surprisingly mild for islands in the latitude of Labrador. Last, but by no means least, the island of Great Britain is rich in coal and iron and thus was enabled to become the first nation to develop modern machine industry. In this respect Ireland, besides Great Britain the only large island in the group, was less fortunate and hence perforce remained a mainly agricultural country.

In political history as well as in geographical position Great Britain is unique. Whereas most nations on the

continent passed through a political evolution from feudal
The British anarchy to royal despotism, in England the
Constitu- kings became strong enough to curb the feudal
tion. lords but were forced to share their power with
the representatives of the merchants and country gentlemen
in Parliament. From "advising" and "petitioning" their
rulers these representatives developed the actual enactment
of laws, secured control of taxation, and, as a final step,
forced the rulers to accept ministers who had their confidence. No written constitution underlies the British government, though some laws and charters guaranteeing the
"liberties of the subject" have been jealously cherished.
The real British constitution is the traditional authority of
Parliament, and any law which Parliament regularly enacts
is, by that fact, constitutional.

When Queen Victoria ascended the throne in 1837 many
people predicted that there would never be another corona-
Parliamen- tion. Since then Edward VII (1901–10) and
tary govern- George V (1910–   ) have reigned, and the issue
ment and of republicanism has scarcely been raised in any
the Crown quarter, even among the Socialists. The truth
is that the powers still vested in the "Crown" are actually
held *in commission* by the King's chief ministers or cabinet.
This cabinet is in turn responsible to the House of Commons,
the elected branch of Parliament. Because the ministry is
responsible to Parliament it is the usual custom for ministers
to have seats either in the Commons or the Lords. The
Prime Minister is the responsible executive and on him falls
the threefold task of determining executive policy in cabinet
meeting, directing the course of legislation from the "front
bench" in Parliament, and controlling his own party organization on which his majority depends. If this does not exhaust his energies he may, should he wish, combine with the
premiership the actual administration of some branch of the
government, such as foreign affairs or national finance. In

one respect he is more powerful than an American President, for he personally directs the legislative program instead of merely sending messages of advice. In another aspect he is less powerful, for his tenure of office runs for no fixed term and may be ended at any time by a serious defeat in Parliament. The legislative initiative of the House of Commons and its control over the ministry and the budget should not lead to the conclusion that the monarch and the Upper House had become altogether functionless. Until 1911 the House of Lords could block legislation not to its liking, and even after that date suspend it for two years. Though the King cannot defy his ministers he can and does advise them in private, and his social position enables him to exercise a vague but powerful influence on the customs of his time. Not wholly without reason has the last two-thirds of the nineteenth century taken, in other countries as well as Britain, the label of the "Victorian Age," for Queen Victoria's court shared, symbolized and in some degree influenced the general social atmosphere of the times.

The period between the first great reform bill of 1832 and the second in 1867 was one of transition from aristocracy to democracy, marked by the great political activity *Politics in* of the commercial middle class. In 1832 there *the mid-* had been a double reform of the House of Com- *century* mons. The right to vote had been extended and made uniform throughout the nation so that the propertied classes were generally enfranchised. At the same time separate representation was taken away from small decayed villages ("rotten boroughs") and bestowed on growing towns and cities. In 1867 the franchise was broadened still farther, and many workingmen householders in the towns first obtained the vote. The British middle class was, on the whole, progressive and the period of its ascendancy was marked by many reforms: the abolition of the protective tariff, especially on grain; the extension of home rule to colonies of British blood and speech; the reorganization of local government on a basis of popular election; the legal regulation of hours of labor for women and children in mines and factories. Parliament as an institution was at its strongest; stronger perhaps even than today, because in recent years, with a widened democratic electorate, Prime Ministers and their cabinets have carried their cause directly to the voters by campaign speeches and the party press instead of making their sole appeals inside the walls of the legislature. Though the majority of voters represented commercial and industrial England, most of the members of the Commons (and, as a matter of course, the Lords) were still of the old landowning aristocracy, and there was a cozy atmosphere of personal acquaintance and family influence lingering in politics, hard to define in set terms but familiar to anyone who has read the "mid-Victorian" political novels of Disraeli and Trollope.

Until the rise of the Irish Nationalists and, later, the Labor Party, British politics had known but two major *Conserva-* parties. The Conservatives were the political *tives and* heirs of the Tories who supported the rights of *Liberals* the King in the days of Charles II. The Liberals derived their tradition from the Whigs who had championed the rights of Parliament. In theory the Conservatives were the party of resistance to change, upholding monarchy and aristocracy, supporting the established Church in Ireland and Wales as well as in England (Scotland had a separate Presbyterian establishment of her own), favoring a protective tariff, opposed to national independence for Ireland; whereas the Liberals were the party of "peace, retrenchment and reform," favoring free trade, a more democratic franchise and the rights of submerged nationalities. In practice the line between the two parties was far less clear-cut. Though the Conservatives were the party of the "landed interest" and hence of the tariff on grain, a large section of the party under the leadership of Sir Robert Peel voted to repeal these "corn laws." Though the Tories had almost to a man opposed the reform of 1832, the Conservatives of a later generation had joined with the radical Liberals ("Radicals" in common phrase) to carry another reform bill in 1867. There was little sympathy between a reactionary Whig such as Robert Lowe and such a Radical as John Bright, and as little between a Peelite free-trader and a diehard Tory. Then, as always, politics made strange bedfellows.

Perhaps the strangest commentary on the artificial and accidental character of the party system was the leadership of the two most prominent party chieftains, *Disraeli and* Benjamin Disraeli the Conservative and William *Gladstone* Ewart Gladstone the Liberal. Anyone acquainted with the men but unfamiliar with their public careers would have selected the wrong party for each to lead. Disraeli we have already met, as the leading opponent of Russia at the Berlin Congress.[1] But that was the Disraeli of later life who had won the Earldom of Beaconsfield for services in high diplomacy and for gaining the title of "Empress of India" for the Queen. When first in the public eye Disraeli was a struggling young politician of Jewish descent who wrote society novels and was handicapped as much by his reputation for undue cleverness and wit as by his "unenglish" and flamboyant manner. He had little of the conservative fear of change, and was quite willing to admit the workingman to the franchise and to protect his interests by social legislation. Gladstone started public life as a typical product of the "public school" and the university, hailed as a "rising hope of the stern and unbending Tories" by the Whig historian Macaulay. He was an unusually devout Churchman and debated against Thomas Huxley the biologist in an attempt to prove that evolution could be reconciled with the literal words of

[1] See Chapter II.

Genesis — if properly interpreted.[1] He very gradually shifted to the Liberal party, partly because he favored free trade and partly because of his sympathy with the movement for political liberty on the continent, especially in Italy. But to the end of his career he retained a stately, old-fashioned dignity of manner that contrasted oddly enough with his increasingly radical policies.

In 1870 Gladstone was in office, wrestling with the most perplexing of all British questions, that of Ireland. The *The Irish* Irish question was an unfortunate legacy of dead *question* centuries. Great Britain and Ireland had no quarrels in the nineteenth century that could not have been peacefully adjusted if they had not been poisoned by bitter memories of the past. The English conquest of Ireland had begun in the twelfth century; it was never really completed. For centuries England neglected her western estate, leaving it to the private adventure of Norman nobles, and even the firm rule of the Tudor and Stuart monarchs, and the iron dictatorship of Oliver Cromwell, established merely a superficial law and order over a people still unreconciled at heart. The old racial barrier became of less importance as knowledge of the English language spread among the native Celts, but the Protestant Reformation created a new line of division between the immigrant Protestant minority, Scottish and English, and the Catholic masses. At the opening of the nineteenth century the Irish Parliament was merged with the British into a common Parliament of the United Kingdom, but the Catholics did not obtain complete political equality with Protestants until 1829.

Now that their greatest grievance, religious discrimination, was removed the English thought that the Irish would be content. But they had still three important demands

---

[1] Disraeli, characteristically, turned the whole question off with a jest to the effect that some thought man an angel and some thought him an ape but that personally he was "on the side of the angels."

to press. Firstly, they wished to disestablish the Anglican Church in Ireland, the so-called Irish Church. *Irish reform* Secondly, they wished to break up the land monopoly; the ownership of most of the agricultural land by a few landlords who took advantage of the need of their tenants to raise rent to an oppressive figure and who had the power to turn tenants out of their holdings without warning. Thirdly, they wished to repeal the Act of Union of 1801 and restore to Ireland a separate Parliament, but on a more democratic basis than the old eighteenth-century Irish Parliament. They agitated for these reforms in many ways, by peaceful argument in Parliament and the press, by obstruction of all public business in Parliament until their grievances were attended to (the tactics worked out by the grim and taciturn Irish Nationalist leader Charles Stewart Parnell), by boycotting offending landlords and their agents, and sometimes by destruction of property or even by assassination. The English replied to this agrarian reign of terror by coercion acts, giving the judicial authorities extraordinary powers for the detection, conviction and punishment of law-breakers. Gladstone hoped to break this vicious circle of rebellion and coercion by remedying the chief grievances of which Ireland complained. In 1869 he disestablished the Irish Church, thus putting all denominations on an equal basis. In 1870 he put through a land act establishing "tenant right," granting to tenants compensation for all the improvements they had made in case they were evicted from their holdings. In 1873 he tried to establish a new university in Ireland, which was to be neutral as between Catholics and Protestants. This measure, ill-conceived in its details, seemed to displease all parties, and in the following year the Conservatives returned to power.

Gladstone's first ministry had, however, accomplished reforms unprecedented in number and importance, and not again to be equalled until the Liberal régime of 1906–14.

Most important of all was the Education Act of 1870, *Other* sponsored by W. E. Forster, establishing for the *Gladstonian* first time in English history the principle of uni-*reforms* versal education and founding free schools where the existing schools did not suffice for the instruction of all the children. The new "board schools" supported by public funds and subject to state supervision were mainly attended by the poor, the wealthier classes still preferring the old private schools.[1] In 1871 the ministry abolished the bad old custom of purchasing officers' commissions in the army. In 1872 the secret ballot was adopted for elections. In the same year the ministry forwarded the cause of peace by accepting the heavy bill of damages which arbitrators awarded to the United States for unneutral British acts during the American Civil War. In 1873 the Judicature Act reorganized the courts of appeal and much improved the judicial system of the nation. So many reform measures had "erupted" that Disraeli mockingly referred to the ministers on the front bench as a "range of exhausted volcanoes."

Disraeli's ministry was concerned mainly with foreign and imperial affairs: the settlement of the Near East, the pur-*Disraeli's* chase of shares in the Suez Canal, a border war *last minis-* in Afghanistan, an attempt to unite South *try and* *Gladstone's* Africa and the development of British India. *second* But the old statesman had not wholly forgotten his earlier interest in social reform. He improved sanitary administration, gave local authorities the power to condemn and tear down buildings unfit for habitation, and codified the labor laws, granting trades unions full exemption from criminal prosecution for "conspiracy." Gladstone, who had thought of retiring from politics, came back to denounce Disraeli as defender of the Turk against the Balkan Christians. In 1880 he returned to power and bent himself again

[1] The so-called "public schools" of England are really exclusive private schools and in no way to be confused with the new government schools.

to the endless task of finding solutions for the Irish problem. In 1881 he supported a new land act, empowering commissions to fix a "fair rent" for periods of fifteen years. He also widened the franchise in 1884 by admitting agricultural laborers to the vote, and the following year he redistributed seats, as had been done by the earlier reform bills of 1832 and 1867. On the whole, however, his second ministry was less fertile than his first had been.

For a time the Irish question dominated everything else. Gladstone's great rival died in 1881 and was succeeded in the Conservative leadership by Robert Cecil, Mar- *The Home* quess of Salisbury. A defeat in 1885 turned out *Rule move-* the second Gladstone ministry but left the Con- *ment* servatives without a secure majority of their own. The following election placed the Irish Nationalists under Parnell in a position where they held the balance of power and could turn either party out of office by siding with the opposition. Gladstone formed his third ministry with Irish support in 1886 and brought forward a plan for a separate Irish Parliament, the familiar demand once called "repeal of the Union" and now "Home Rule." But the Liberal Party split on the issue thus presented, even such Radicals as John Bright and Joseph Chamberlain deserting their leader. A combination of Conservatives and Liberal Unionists (former Liberals opposed to Home Rule) brought Lord Salisbury again into office. But Home Rule was not dead. Gladstone assumed the premiership for the fourth and last time in 1892 and brought forward a new bill the following year, differing from its predecessor in the provision that Irish representatives should attend the British Parliament whenever measures affecting Ireland were considered. As before, Ireland was to have her own Parliament for local affairs. The new measure passed the Commons only to be defeated in the Lords. Not this defeat but age and physical infirmity induced Gladstone to resign the premiership to his colleague Lord Rosebery, a very conservative "Liberal," and the Home Rule question was shelved for the next two decades.   The Conservatives after their return to office in 1895 tried to "kill Home Rule with kindness" by giving aid to Irish tenants who desired to buy up their tenancies and convert them into freeholds.

The problem of Ireland, the disorders in Egypt and the Sudan, the increasing friction with the Dutch Republics of *Burdens of*   South Africa, distracted the attention of England *empire*   from domestic reforms.   Some useful measures were indeed passed.   The scope of free education was widened.   In 1888 county councils, elected by ratepayers, relieved the justices of the peace from many administrative duties which in the course of time had been added to their proper judicial functions.   But in the main the period between Gladstone's first ministry and the great Liberal triumph of 1906 was relatively barren of fundamental domestic reforms.   The Boer War in South Africa engaged the energies and attention of Salisbury's third ministry.[1]   The spirit of imperialism was at its height.   Joseph Chamberlain divided the Conservative Party by reviving the long-dead issue of a protective tariff with a new argument.   The old justification for protection had been economic, to protect the British farmer from the competition of cheap foreign grain.   The new justification was political, to unite the British Empire into a customs union and thus strengthen its ties.   Colonial Conferences, which were held in 1887, 1894, 1897, 1902, 1907 and 1911,[2] brought together representatives of the home government and of the self-governing Dominions.   Many advocated that these conferences advance beyond consultation and achieve a real Imperial federation with a common legislature, judiciary, tariff and navy, but every proposal in this direction met with opposition to an Imperial tariff or the fear lest federation mean heavier taxation in the Dominions

---

[1] For the Boer War see below, page 110.

[2] In 1907 the title was altered to the Imperial Conference.

for Imperial defense. Fear of higher food prices to the consumer if a protective tariff were imposed on foreign wheat outweighed all Chamberlain's imperialistic oratory with the British voter.

Though the Conservatives and their Unionist allies snatched an electoral victory during the Boer War, scarcely had the war ended when signs appeared that the *The Liberal* nation was turning against them. Arthur Bal- *triumph* four, who succeeded Lord Salisbury as Premier, found it increasingly hard to hold together the free-trade and the protectionist Conservatives, and the Liberals made many gains at by-elections. At the end of 1905 he resigned, and the following election brought the Liberals into power with a majority which rendered them independent of Irish support. But it was not the old traditional "Whig" Liberalism of Russell, Palmerston, Gladstone and Rosebery, concerned mainly with political reforms and individualistic in social philosophy. The Liberal Party had to reckon with a new force in Parliament, a strong independent Labor Party, and was compelled to turn its attention to the "condition of England question" and to accept measures of a more or less socialistic character for its solution. Premier Campbell-Bannerman was followed in office by Herbert Asquith in 1908, but the real driving spirit of both ministries was an energetic young Welsh Radical, David Lloyd George, who became Chancellor of the Exchequer as soon as Mr. Asquith vacated that office. Largely under his influence and direction, the ministry entered on the most sweeping program of social reform which had ever been undertaken in British history.

The most notable of these measures was perhaps the adoption in 1908 of a system of old-age pensions pay- *Old-age* able by the nation. Labor was placated by a *pensions* *and trades-* Trades Disputes Act in 1906 which exempted *union priv-* labor unions from civil suits for damages and thus *ileges* reversed the Taff Vale judicial decision which had affirmed

their liability for property losses caused to employers by
strikes. A Workmen's Compensation Act of 1906 made
employers liable for the compensation of victims of industrial
accidents. A Labor Exchange Act tried to meet the problems of unemployment; a Trade Board Act gave local boards
the power to maintain sanitary conditions and a living wage
in certain "sweated" industries; a Town Planning Act permitted local authorities to improve tenements, and school
authorities were authorized to provide meals for school
children.

Some of these measures of social legislation received a
certain amount of support even from the Conservative
The "veto" benches, but other reforms of a more partisan
of the Lords character were rejected by the House of Lords.
Among these were a new Education Act to relieve dissenters
who did not belong to the established Church of England
from paying for religious instruction in any of the schools, a
bill abolishing plural voting (the right to vote in each constituency for which the voter held a property qualification),
and a licensing bill designed to diminish the number of places
selling intoxicants. The House of Lords in recent decades
has been continuously conservative, no matter how strong
the Liberals might be in the Commons or in the country at
large. This is not because the Lords all represented ancient
privilege or had all been attached to the Conservative Party
originally — on the contrary many had acquired their wealth
and rank recently and had received royal appointment on
the advice of Liberal ministers — but simply because they
were the *successful*, the men who had inherited or had themselves built up great fortunes, and property is always conservative because it has so much to risk in any change.
The latent conflict between the Lords and Commons came
to a crisis with the rejection of Lloyd George's budget of
1909.

In discussing old-age pensions, Mr. Balfour, the leader of

the opposition, expressed a mild wonder as to where "within the limits of free trade finance" the ministry *The budget* would find the necessary revenues. Many other *crisis* Liberal reforms were expensive, though sometimes the cost fell on local rates rather than on the national budget. The naval competition with Germany necessitated ccstly shipbuilding. Some Conservatives hoped that the Liberals would be driven by sheer necessity to adopt high tariffs, but Lloyd George had another answer ready. He would continue to rely mainly on direct taxation but would increase the rate and multiply the forms of taxation to a degree unprecedented in time of peace. Direct taxes on incomes and inheritance and revenue imposts on liquor, tobacco, licenses, motor vehicles and stamp duties would all contribute their share, and there was to be a supertax on large incomes, and a tax on the increment or increase in value of land, exclusive of improvements. In defending the budget, the Chancellor appealed to the program of social legislation which had made it necessary:

> I am told that no Chancellor of the Exchequer has ever been called on to impose such taxes in a time of peace. This is a War Budget. It is for raising money to wage implacable warfare against poverty and squalidness. I cannot help hoping and believing that before this generation has passed away, we shall have advanced a great step towards the good time when poverty and wretchedness and human degradation which always follows in its camp will be as remote to the people of this country as the wolves which once infested its forests.

By constitutional precedent rather than by positive law, the House of Lords had relinquished control over finance bills. But the majority of the peers took the view that this budget was no mere provision of revenue but an attempt to break up the large landed estates by pressure of taxation, and that so drastic a policy should not be approved "until it has been submitted to the judgment of the country."

A British ministry does not usually resign because of an

adverse vote in the House of Lords, but on this occasion the
Two elections in 1910 issue raised was of such importance that the Liberals accepted the challenge and carried the budget controversy into a general election. Lloyd George went beyond the usual courtesies of debate and denounced individual landlords by name for demanding extortionate rents from city tenants. The Conservatives defended the constitutionality of the action of the Lords in rejecting the money bill and emphasized the need for a larger navy than the Liberals had yet authorized. The poll left the Liberal and Unionist (Conservatives and Liberal Unionists) parties nearly equal in strength, but the Labor and Irish Nationalist parties who now held the balance of power hated the "veto" of the Lords even more than did the Liberals. The Labor members wanted to abolish the House of Lords outright as a mischievous anachronism; Conservatives argued that as the British constitution had no such "checks and balances" on the action of the national legislature as other democracies, there should be a conservative upper chamber to prevent rashly radical action; Liberals agreed that there should be a second chamber but held that the existing House of Lords was incompetent for the purpose and its power over legislation should be limited until it could be reformed. The death of King Edward VII in 1910 and the accession of George V brought a temporary party truce, but no solution for the constitutional problem could be reached by agreement. A new election took place with almost no alteration in the relative strength of the parties, and the ministry decided to proceed to carry out its own program without further negotiation with the Conservative opposition.

The Parliament Act of 1911 is one of the most important of constitutional statutes. It provided that financial measures should become law if passed by the House of Commons and signed by the King, even if opposed by the

House of Lords, thus settling the constitutional issue raised by the rejection of the budget. Other measures *The Parlia-* of general legislation would become law if passed *ment Act of* in unaltered form by the House of Commons over *1911* a period of at least two years; this gave the Lords a "suspensive veto" for a two-year period. The maximum duration of a Parliament, that is the period between two elections of the House of Commons, was reduced from seven to five years. The average duration of a Parliament is less than its maximum term because a Prime Minister may lose control of his majority or he may deem it wise to select a favorable moment for party advantage to dissolve Parliament rather than wait till the full term has elapsed. Another law enabled poor men to enter national politics by providing payment for members of the House of Commons, hitherto serving without salary.

Fearing that the House of Lords would never accept the drastic limitations now imposed on their legislative power, Premier Asquith took the precaution of advising the King to appoint new peers pledged in advance to vote for the contested measure. Rather than have the aristocracy diluted by the sudden addition of several hundred commoners to the peerage, the House of Lords sullenly gave way and permitted the Parliament Act to become law. The Liberals, however, never proceeded to the second part of their program, reforming the House of Lords. Though restricted in power it still remained a hereditary chamber.

The Liberal ministry did not bring forward reforms so rapidly after the elections of 1910 as in earlier years. But Lloyd George found opportunity to round out *Social* his program of social reform by introducing in- *insurance* surance against sickness and unemployment. The old-age pensions had been contributed entirely by the state, but the insurance laws made up the needed fund by contributions from employers, workmen and the state. This compulsory insurance was a wide departure from the old individualistic traditions of the country and met much criticism as an imitation of Bismarck's state socialism. Most of the attention of the ministry, however, was taken up with the re-emergence of the Irish problem. Now that the fate of the government again depended on Irish votes, the Home Rule issue could be no longer postponed.

In 1912 the Liberal ministry introduced a third Home Rule measure. Ireland was to be represented in the British Parliament on all measures but have its representation cut from 103 votes to 42. Various important matters, such as peace and war, tariffs, religious establishments, were reserved for the British Parliament. Other questions were to be transferred to an Irish Parliament chosen on a democratic basis. The measure was carried through the Commons and placed on the statute books in spite of two years' delay caused by the opposition of the Lords, but it never went into effect. The coming of the World War suspended its operation and before the war was over new measures had been brought forward to reconcile the claims of the Catholic majority with the special interests of the Protestant minority in Ulster. The district around Belfast in northeastern Ireland formed in truth a nation within a nation. Geography had bound its fate with that of the rest of the island but its national sentiment was in every respect opposite to that of the rest of the country. The people were English or Scottish in origin, zealous Protestants in religion, industrial rather than agricultural by occupation, "Unionist" rather than Nationalist in politics. They declared that "Home Rule means Rome Rule" and threatened to refuse obedience to a separate Irish Parliament. On the very eve of the World War Ulster volunteers, encouraged by the fiery speeches of Sir Edward Carson and other leaders, were drilling volunteers to resist Home Rule.

The third Home Rule bill

The economic position of Ireland had vastly improved since the middle of the nineteenth century, partly through the relief of overpopulation through heavy emigration to America, partly because of land legislation, beginning with Gladstone's attempts to fix rents and culminating in Wyndham's Act of 1903, appropriating large sums to transform tenants into peasant freeholders, and partly because of the agricultural revival brought about through the co-operative associations organized by Sir Horace Plunkett. The "misery spot" of western Europe had become a fairly prosperous agricultural nation. But the new Ireland still insisted on recognition of her separate national identity; neither kindness nor coercion had in the least diminished this demand.

Scotland and Wales as truly as Ireland had a distinct national revival, but the problems raised were far less acute. Scotland's active share in the government of *Scotland* Britain and the Empire was so large that the *and Wales* movement for a separate Scottish Parliament remained purely academic and did not get into practical politics. Scottish nationalism was in the main a revival of old historic memories and found its chief expression in literature. Welsh nationalism stressed the employment of the old native language and the demand for disestablishment of the Church of England within Wales, since the majority of the Welsh people were "dissenters." In 1912 the House of Commons voted for Welsh disestablishment, and in 1914 it became law despite the opposition of the Lords. Unlike Irish Home Rule, the new ecclesiastical system in Wales went quietly into effect at the end of the war.

THE DOMINIONS

The British Empire for all its complexity can for practical purposes be grouped into two main divisions. One includes the British Isles and the overseas Dominions; *The two* the fully self-governing portions of the Empire, *aspects of* sometimes termed a "Commonwealth of Free *Empire* Nations," because the term Empire suggests power rather

than consent. But there remains another category of possessions for which that term is strictly applicable, the Crown
colonies, the protectorates and dependencies, and the great
Indian Empire. These colonies are (with the exception of
certain small naval bases, coaling stations and the like) located within the tropics, unsuited by climate for British settlement, and important for strategic or commercial reasons
rather than as national homes. In the majority of cases
they enjoy some measure of self-government, but always
important matters are "reserved" for British officials to
handle. This chapter will treat solely of the self-governing
portions of the Empire.[1]

Before Irish Home Rule added another to the number in
1922 there were five Dominions. Three of them, Canada,
The Domin- Australia and South Africa, were federal in
ions collec- structure and arose by voluntary union of small
tively self-governing colonies. Two others had but a
single legislature, New Zealand and Newfoundland. In
strict law the Dominions, before the World War, did not occupy a position of equality with the mother country. The
British Parliament was the only Imperial Parliament and it
could, at least in theory, legislate for the affairs of the Empire
as a whole. On it, and on the ministry responsible to it,
rested the entire direction of foreign affairs and the main
burden of imperial defense. The King was represented in
the Dominions by Governors General appointed on the advice of the British ministry. Certain cases involving general
imperial interests could be carried on appeal to the judicial
committee of the Privy Council. Yet in the position of the
Dominions, as so frequently in British politics, we must look
below the surface of legal theory to find the political reality.
In practice the Dominion Parliaments had as free a hand in
their internal affairs as the British Parliament enjoyed in the
United Kingdom. The Governor General usually acted as

[1] For British possessions in India, Africa, etc., see Chapter V.

strictly by the advice of his ministers as did the King. Each
Dominion determined for itself how much aid in men,
money and ships it would give the Empire in time of war.
The British Empire was not even a customs union, each Dominion being free to protect its own industries against British
as well as foreign goods.

First among British Dominions in size, population and historic importance was the federal Dominion of Canada. It
was formed in 1867 by the union of several self- *Canada and*
governing colonies of British North America *Newfound-*
which had already won for themselves parlia- *land*
mentary and responsible government. One such colony,
Newfoundland, refused to enter the federation and formed
a separate Dominion, Britain's oldest oversea colony and
the home of a race of hardy fishermen. Modern Canada
contains nine provinces, each with its own legislature and
responsible ministry, besides territories in the far northwest
which are under direct federal authority. Three provinces
of the Atlantic shore, New Brunswick, Nova Scotia and
Prince Edward's Island, are known collectively as the "maritime provinces." Then along the St. Lawrence River lies
Quebec, more French than English in speech and still clinging
to the laws, religion and customs of the days when it was a
part of French America. North of the Great Lakes is On-
tario, the most populous colony of English origin. Then
westward lie the "prairie provinces" of Manitoba, Saskatche-
wan and Alberta, the most rapidly growing part of the Dominion as the development of transcontinental railway lines,
the poleward extension of the wheat fields and immigration
from Europe and the United States as well as from the older
provinces transformed a prairie into a granary. On the
Pacific Coast is British Columbia, continuing the Rocky
Mountain chain up from Oregon and Washington towards
Alaska.

The Canadian government followed British forms and

traditions. The executive power was in the hands of a
Canadian politics ministry responsible to an elected House of Commons. The place of a House of Lords was taken by a Senate whose members are appointed for life on the advice of the ministry. As in Great Britain there were Conservative and Liberal parties, and to an even greater extent than in the mother country the rule of stable, long-term ministries prevailed. For many years after the union of 1867 politics was dominated by the nationally minded Conservative leader, John Macdonald. The Liberal Premier, Sir Wilfrid Laurier, a French Canadian, enjoyed a similar lease of power. In 1911 he was defeated on the issue of reciprocity with the United States, and Sir Robert Borden, the Conservative leader, assumed office and held it during the World War. The chief issues of Canadian politics were the building and management of transcontinental railways to unite the distant provinces, the question of a protective tariff, especially as to how much "preference" should be granted British goods and how much "reciprocity" allowed to the United States, the question of state aid to church schools, and the extent to which Canada should interest herself in British imperial affairs and contribute to the navy. On the whole, the Conservative party emphasized the imperial connection and opposed too close commercial relations with the United States.

The Commonwealth of Australia is an island continent with only about two inhabitants to the square mile. First *The Commonwealth of Australia* used as a penal settlement by an unimaginative Britain, the discovery of gold in the middle of the nineteenth century and the development of the sheep-raising industry pointed to economic possibilities in spite of climatic handicaps. The north lay within the tropics; the vast interior was an arid desert; only the coastal fringe of the south and east was suited to close settlement. The native "blackfellows" were few in number and low in civilization; Asiatic immigration was tried, restricted and finally practically forbidden, and even European immigration not greatly encouraged. The majority of the inhabitants are therefore of pure British stock. Owing to vast distances and local jealousies the six Australian colonies did not join to form a union till 1900. On January 1, 1901, the Commonwealth of Australia came into existence. Its constitution was less centralized than that of Canada; its divisions were called states, not provinces, and they enjoyed a great measure of home rule. There was a Senate in which the states had equal representation and a House of Representatives chosen according to population. The ministries, federal and state alike, were responsible to their legislatures.

The interesting little island group of New Zealand, in area and in temperate climate, bears much resemblance to the British Isles at the farthest extremity of the *New Zea-* globe. But as the chief industry is sheep-raising, *land* perhaps the comparison is closer with the England of Elizabeth's day than of our own. The New Zealand natives, the Maori, were intelligent and energetic Polynesians, far superior to the natives of Australia, but they were too few in number, despite their warlike qualities, to offer much impediment to the English settlers. Eventually they settled down as peaceful farmers with a small share in the national legislature.

Both Australasian Dominions have been more radical in their politics than Canada. They were among the first modern communities to adopt woman's suffrage *Australasian* and the secret ballot (the so-called "Australian *State social-* ballot"). In both countries the labor unions *ism* have been powerful and active in politics, and the chief political issue has been how far the government should go in the economic field. The authority of the government has been freely used for the protection of labor by factory codes, the amelioration of poverty by old-age and invalidity pensions, for maternity grants, for opening arid lands to settlement, for the division of large estates into small holdings, and for the compulsory arbitration of industrial disputes. Yet this socialistic tendency is combined with nationalism. Instead of advocating free trade, it upheld protection; instead of treating all races equally, it insisted on the total exclusion of Asiatics and the rigid limitation of other immigration. Fear of Japan has caused even labor groups to favor military training and adequate defenses.

The Union of South Africa is the child of the Boer War, the chief colonial war of modern Britain. When as a result *The Boer* of the Napoleonic wars the British acquired the *republics* Cape of Good Hope many of the Dutch settlers were discontented. Some remained at the Cape and mingled with the British immigrants, others "trekked" inland and founded two small republics, the South African or Transvaal Republic and the Orange Free State. In 1877 the British government made an unsuccessful attempt to bring the Transvaal within the British sphere of influence. Gladstone on coming into office in 1880 reversed this imperialistic movement and in the following year agreed to restore independence to the Transvaal subject to a vague recognition of British "suzerainty." The Boers (Dutch farmers) rejoiced at the reconquest of their independence which they attributed in part to a victory of their arms at Majuba Hill. In 1884 they won the further diplomatic triumph of having the term "suzerainty" deleted, though it was replaced by a very significant provision that white men were to have equal rights to reside in any part of the Transvaal, to trade there and to enjoy equal rights of taxation with citizens of the republic. Had the Boer states remained mere ranching communities the matter might have ended there, but the rapid development of gold and diamond mining brought a huge cosmopolitan throng of engineers, capitalists, laborers, white and black, to the mushroom towns of the Witwatersrand goldfields. Such a town as Johannesburg increased in less than a decade from three thousand to a hundred thousand. The new prosperity was welcome enough, and the Transvaal authorities shifted most of the burden of taxation onto the shoulders of the immigrant industrialists, besides tapping the wealth of the mines in other ways, such as the creation of monopolies and the increase of transportation rates.

The political consequences of the Transvaal boom were less welcome. Some of the industrial leaders were men of daring ambition who would not have hesitated *Briton* to gain control of the country by weight of immi- *versus Boer* gration and then have proclaimed its union with the British Empire. Cecil Rhodes, a young Oxford graduate who had gone to South Africa to look for his health, had found opportunity to become the chief empire builder of his day. He had succeeded in pushing British Dominion far north of the Transvaal over the territory known after him as Rhodesia, and in 1890 he became Premier of Cape Colony and the leading champion of a united South Africa under the British flag. The imperialism of Rhodes found powerful backing. Sir Alfred Milner, British High Commissioner, and Joseph Chamberlain, the Colonial Secretary, were resolute to support British rights in the Transvaal. Paul Kruger, the President, saw in the encirclement of his country by British settlements and its penetration by British immigrants a direct menace to national existence. He tried to stem the tide by denying the franchise to alien residents. The "outlanders" complained of "taxation without representation" and demanded political reforms, better justice in the courts and a share in the franchise.

A premature revolt headed by Dr. L. S. Jameson discredited the cause of the reformers and embarrassed the British government, and a still more ominous event was *The Jame-* the telegram sent by the German Kaiser con- *son Raid,* gratulating the Boers on having repulsed the *1895* raiders without appealing for help to "friendly powers."

The British now felt that they had to struggle against the
Dutch republics, backed by Germany, to stay in Africa at
all; the Boers felt that the British were fomenting rebellion
to overthrow their independence. President Kruger became
more stubborn than ever, demanded the demobilization of
British forces on the frontier, and predicted that the cost of
a British victory would "stagger humanity."

At the start the Boers took the initiative, invading the
British colonies of Natal and Cape Colony and laying siege
The Boer to the cities of Mafeking, Kimberley and Lady-
War, 1899- smith. The Orange Free State, though not di-
1902 rectly involved in the controversy, sided as a
matter of course with the kindred Transvaal. All parts
of the British Empire offered help to the British South
African colonies, but continental Europe was almost unanimously pro-Boer, partly from sympathy with a gallant
struggle against odds, but mainly from distrust of British
imperialism. But no foreign power intervened and the
Boer cause was hopeless from the start, though able generals, such as Louis Botha and Christian De Wet, maintained a guerilla warfare long after the British had proclaimed the conquest of the republics. Lord Roberts and
Lord Kitchener had to wear down resistance by the slowest
methods, establishing cordons of blockhouses to intercept
raids and turning civilians out of their farms to dwell in
concentration camps so that they could give no aid to
soldiers "out on commando." The war ended with the
annexation of the South African Republic and the Orange
Free State, but the British promised the defeated Boers
eventual self-government, free use of their language and a
sum of three million pounds ($15,000,000) to restock dev-
astated farms.

In spite of the bitter memory of a recent war, the union of
Cape Colony and Natal with the conquered Transvaal and
Orange Free State was achieved with but little opposition

in 1909. The Dutch and British elements in the population were of approximately equal strength and   *The Union*
both languages were made official. The first Prime *of South*
Minister of the Union was a Boer general, Louis   *Africa*
Botha.   The union was a close one, the provinces being even
more subordinated to the general government than in
Canada.   More serious than the rivalry of Boer and Briton,
or even the economic conflicts between miner and mine
owner, was the race problem.   Native Negro races within
the territory of the Union far outnumbered the white settlers.
In Cape Colony some of them enjoyed the franchise, but for
the most part they stood outside the political life of the
country.   Could these millions of half-civilized and warlike
Africans become in time equal citizens of a Union in which
they would form a majority of the population?   Will they
accept a permanently inferior status?   Or is the solution to
be found in segregation, setting aside certain reserved districts for exclusive native occupancy?   Another racial problem was that of the Asiatic immigrant.   For a time Chinese
contract labor was used in the mines, but the Liberal victory
in Britain put a stop to it.   Hindus settled in considerable
numbers in some parts of the Union.   Asiatic labor was in
some respects more useful to the mine owner than either the
high-priced European with his trades unionism and strikes
or the easy-going native African, but many South Africans
feel that to permit Asiatic immigration would add new difficulties to a racial situation already far too complex.

CHAPTER V

THE PARTITION OF THE TROPICS

FROM the fifteenth to the twentieth centuries the energetic races of crowded Europe have utilized the new means of *The "new imperialism"* transportation and conquest which science placed at their disposal to extend their own civilization around the globe. Sometimes the European found "white man's country," lands suitable for settlement and inhabited only by scanty tribes of hunters or herdsmen. There he built a new home and planted the language, religion and laws with which he was familiar. Thus were settled the temperate zones in North and South America, Siberia and Australasia. But nearly all the land believed to be suited for European settlement had been pre-empted by 1870. The colonial movement after the Franco-Prussian War was of quite another type. The French imperialist, Jules Ferry, defined the problem with French precision in 1885:

> There is a new form of colonization: it is that which is adapted to peoples who have either a mass of disposable capital or an excess of manufactures. And that is the modern, existing form, the most widespread and the most fruitful.... Since the loss of colonies of settlement, such as Canada by the treaty of 1763 and Louisiana ceded to the United States by Bonaparte, there no longer existed such colonies on the globe, so rapid had been the English acquisitions. The only place where it remained possible to make acquisitions was in the tropics. It was no longer possible to seek outlets for a French emigration... it was a question of finding outlets for our industries, exports and capital.

There have been two main periods of colonial imperialism in modern European history. The first may be dated very *Contrast with the "old imperialism"* approximately as lying between the discovery of America and the end of the French overseas empire in 1763. In that earlier race for dominion only five nations played an important part — Portugal, Spain, the Dutch Republic, France and England.

Except where European settlement was possible, this earlier colonization consisted largely in the establishment of trading posts and monopolized trade routes with enough military force to protect them.   Where the plantation system was profitable, slavery or other kinds of forced labor prevailed. The interests of foreign traders, subject races and European settlers were all alike sacrificed to direct profits for the trading company or national government which undertook the task of colonization.   The political future was subordinated to the economic present: England and France, for example, paying more attention to a few cane sugar plantations in the West Indies than to the opportunities for expansion on the vast continent of North America.   Similarly the Dutch threw away chances of empire in South Africa and Australia in order to concentrate on the immediately profitable spice islands of the East Indies.

There followed a period of relative indifference, a trough between two waves of imperialism.   The new economic doctrine of Adam Smith and his contemporaries, *A period of* that nations profited more by freedom of trade *relative* than by attempted monopoly, made the possession *indifference* of colonies seem a matter of indifference from the standpoint of commerce; and the revolutions of the United States, French Haiti, Portuguese Brazil, and the many republics of Spanish America from Mexico to Argentina, made it seem questionable if political greatness could be securely founded on colonization.   Even Britain, which continued to expand, offsetting her loss of the thirteen colonies by the addition of Cape Colony, Australia, New Zealand and several provinces in India, showed little enthusiasm for a positive imperial policy.   Many early Victorian statesmen seemed resigned even to the prospective loss of Canada.   Disraeli in 1852 declared in a moment of petulance, "These wretched colonies will all be independent in a few years and are a millstone around our necks," while Gladstone as late as 1870 thought that at a certain stage of colonial development "separation from the mother country inevitably takes place." Tennyson reproached his fellow-countrymen for saying in effect to colonists overseas: "So loyal is too costly! Friends, your love is but a burthen: loose the bond, and go!" France, viewed by the British as their only serious colonial rival, annexed Algeria in 1830, and later made some small ventures in Indo-China and the Pacific under the restless Napoleon III, but did not rival in scale either the lost empire of the eighteenth century or the modern empire of the Third Republic.[1] Russia and the United States expanded, indeed, but overland; they had small need for tropical colonies. Holland was content to hold and develop an existing empire. The imperial exertions of Germany, Belgium, Italy and Japan lay in the future.

Though the period between the Berlin Conference of 1884–85 and the Russo-Japanese War of 1904–05 may be *Stirrings of* taken as the second age of imperialistic expan-*imperialism* sion, there was evident a changed atmosphere almost immediately after the Franco-Prussian War. In 1874 Disraeli came to the British Premiership, an avowed convert to imperialism. That same year the Fiji Islands were added to the British Empire, though requests for annexation from the islands themselves had previously been repeatedly rebuffed. In 1875, without even waiting for authorization from Parliament, Disraeli negotiated for the purchase of the shares in the Suez Canal enterprise placed on the market by the Khedive of Egypt. In 1876 he added "Empress of India" to the titles of Queen Victoria. France, with the benevolent approval of Bismarck, who desired that, in thinking of Africa, France might forget Alsace, occupied Tunis, the eastern neighbor of her old colony of Algeria. Jules Ferry,

---

[1] "Since 1877 the gain in territory has been almost sixteen times as great as in the sixty-two years before 1877." P. Moon, *Imperialism and World Politics* (1926), page 22.

who might be called the Disraeli of France except that he was probably the more active imperialist of the two, energetically supported French expansion in north Africa and southeastern Asia.   Even Bismarck, most reluctant of colonizers, tried vainly in 1880 to induce the German Reichstag to vote a subsidy for a trading company in the Samoan Islands.

There were many good reasons why the last two decades of the nineteenth century should have been a period of active colonial expansion.   The peace prevailing *Reasons for* within Europe and the solution of the great prob- *the imperi-* lems of German and Italian unity released the *alist revival* minds of the statesmen of the continent from the preoccupation with purely European affairs which had been dominant since the French Revolution.   Competition from the continental powers in turn stimulated the British, long accustomed to a virtual monopoly of overseas enterprise, once more to look to their laurels.   The intense na- *Political* tional pride and rivalry of the times found ex- *reasons* pression in building up imposing colonial domains.   Nations which had not been able to enter the first great race for empire had attained sufficient power to enter the second: Germany, Italy, the United States, Japan.   The United States, however, became a colonizer by the accident of the Spanish-American War and acquired overseas territory only in certain island groups of the Pacific and the Caribbean.

But important as were these political reasons for the new imperialist movement, there is no doubt that economic reasons were even more cogent.   The rapid in- *Economic* dustrialization of western and central Europe *reasons* created an almost insatiable demand for new markets, new sources of raw material, and new openings for capital investment.   The "backward countries" offered all these benefits, or at least held out plausible hopes for them.   In natural riches the tropics are the most favored part of the earth. Mineral wealth may chance to be found in any latitude, but only the rain and sunshine of the torrid zone bring the vegetable kingdom to its richest variety. , In the first period of tropical colonization the most valued commodities (next to gold, silver and precious stones) were the spices of the Far East and the sugar of the Caribbean. Neither trade has quite maintained its old importance, as spicery is less used by modern cooks and the sugar cane has found a new rival in the sugar beet, but other gifts of the warm latitudes have attained augmented importance. Cold storage and rapid transportation have brought the sub-tropical orange and the tropical banana to supplement the rather scanty list of northern fruits. The cocoanut is familiar and popular in both Europe and the United States, but it has a recent special importance greater than its table use. The dried cocoanut yields *copra*, one of the most valuable of vegetable fats. Our three breakfast beverages, tea from southern China, India or Ceylon, coffee from Brazil or Java, cacao (the basis of cocoa and chocolate) from equatorial Africa and America, have no equivalents in northern flora. Tropical forests, too, are rich in valuable woods, such as teak, ebony and mahogany, whose rich color and dense fiber cannot be obtained in Europe. But the most important forest product of the tropics is rubber. At first obtained "wild" from the jungles of the Amazon and the Congo it is now raised chiefly on plantations. The United States, using about seven tenths of the world's supply, grows practically none of it, depending mainly on English and Dutch plantations in the East Indies and the Malay peninsula.

Still a third group of reasons enter into the "new imperialism" the fact that scientific advance for the first time began *Technical* to make *possible* the conquest of the tropics. *reasons* The main difficulties of tropical development may be summarized as climate, sanitation, transportation, racial adjustment. Authorities are still at odds as to whether the white colonist can thrive and settle permanently within

the heat belt or whether he must forever be content to come
there temporarily as trader, planter, missionary or governing
official. Heat is not the greatest problem. Midsummer
temperatures in the Mississippi valley run as high as those of
almost any equatorial lowland at any season, and on high
tropical plateaus, such as Mexico, Peru and much of eastern
Africa, the climate is rather a perpetual spring than a perpetual summer. But tropical highlands are usually fenced
off from the sea by hot, damp jungles which can be penetrated only with great difficulty, and the intense sunlight and
absence of seasonal change in temperature are *The con-*
said to be as trying as the excess of heat. The *quest of*
steam bath of tropical sun and rain which so *disease*
stimulates organic growth multiplies many forms of animal
and vegetable life inimical to man. The smallest plagues are
the most deadly. The tigers and cobras can be easily killed,
the flies and ants less easily, while the microscopic germs of
disease for centuries baffled civilized man altogether. Malaria and yellow fever made the west coast of Africa notorious
as the "white man's graveyard" and impeded the French
construction of the Panama Canal. So long as people mistakenly believed such diseases a "corruption of the air" en-
gendered by "foul marshes" they could do nothing but keep
away from the places where they prevailed. But the discovery that malaria and yellow fever came from micro-
organisms borne by two species of mosquito opened the way
to a solution. The work of the Americans in Panama and
Cuba showed that draining or oiling stagnant water and
screening hospital windows could keep those diseases within
modest dimensions. Boiling drinking water safeguards
against many intestinal diseases prevalent in hot climates.
Perhaps the greatest remaining difficulty is the tsetse fly
which kills the beasts of burden in some parts of Africa.

    Science also is solving the problem of transport as well as
that of sanitation. The Africa of ancient and medieval times

was the southern shore of the Mediterranean, north of the

The con-
quest of
distance
Sahara Desert. Beyond that lay a Dark Continent, an unknown and impenetrable land. The first age of European exploration did little more than define the coastline. The inner basin of the Congo and the eastern highlands remained almost unknown till the last quarter of the nineteenth century. As late as 1890 the English romancer Rider Haggard found plenty of room for imaginary nations in the still unexplored parts of Africa. But the building of railroads, the opening of good roads for pack-animal transport, the invention of aircraft, the means of rapid communication afforded by telegraph, telephone, cable and wireless have opened up the interior of Africa so that European colonies could be of continental scope and not, as formerly, mere trading posts along the seaboard.

The problem of racial adjustment in the tropics is not yet solved nor in a way to solution. Save in the "monsoon

Racial
problems
area" of southeastern Asia, where seasonal rains alternate with dry weather, and in a few advantageously situated islands, the density of population averages less in the tropics than in the temperate zone. Jungle and desert are always thinly peopled, and the grasslands of Africa and South America are mostly given over to pasture or very superficial agriculture. But as sanitation progresses and tribal warfare is stayed, numbers rapidly increase. Sometimes the first contact of races causes heavy loss to the native population, but the gap is soon filled by imported labor. There are fewer Indians in the Antilles than Columbus found there, but the islands are more populous than ever with the descendants of African slaves. Hawaii has lost some of her native Polynesians but acquired a large population of Japanese. Chinese labor floods Indo-China and the Malay states. Hindus have been employed as contract laborers in Fiji, British Guiana and British Africa. In all parts of the

tropical world the standard of living is low and population continues to increase to the limit of subsistence.

Since the European cannot himself labor to advantage under a torrid sun, and the native does not see why he should exert himself for the advantage of the European,   *Forced and* the problem of labor organization becomes a   *free labor* crucial one.   The first expedient was the cruelest, slavery. The almost universal abolition of slavery in the nineteenth century made this simple solution impossible.   But forced labor in a more disguised form still exists in many parts of the world.   Sometimes labor on the plantations is exacted as a tax, or a money tax is levied which the native must labor to pay.   More common is the device of contract labor, by which the native voluntarily offers his service for a term of years in return for a fixed payment, but once employed he can be held to his contract even by force.   This system bears some resemblance to the old custom of apprenticeship in Europe and colonial America, and there is much to be said in its favor if the contract has really been voluntary, thoroughly understood by both parties, and carried out in spirit as in letter — conditions which do not always obtain!   Another method is to encourage the native to work for himself and sell his surplus to the white trader, but this is possible only where he has been educated to a higher standard of living than mere subsistence.   Under any system there are possibilities of injustice, and strong, impartial administrators, who have themselves no profits at stake, seem essential as a check on the greed of unscrupulous traders and employers.   Some of the worst conditions have existed under nominally independent "native governments" where private capitalistic enterprise had an unchecked hand.   As late as 1931 Secretary Stimson had to protest on behalf of the United States against a system of virtual slavery obtaining in the little Negro republic of Liberia.

The forms of European control varied considerably in

different parts of the tropical world.   Perhaps the British

*Administra-
tive policies
of the chief
colonizing
powers* Empire presented the widest variety of types of government.   Some "crown colonies" had representative institutions, though not amounting to complete home rule, as in the West Indies; others were governed throughout by British officials; others were treated as "protectorates" in which a native ruler is maintained on the throne on condition that he will be guided by the advice of a British resident.   As a general rule, British crown colonies were open to the equal trade of all nations and were careful to respect native tribal customs.   India was not a crown colony, but ranked as an "Empire" in its own right; it was administered by the "India Office" and an Indian civil service, not by the Colonial Office.[1]   France took the bold step of according Algeria and some of her other colonies direct representation in her national legislature as though they were parts of France; other colonies, such as Tunis, were counted as protectorates over nominally sovereign native governments.   The French tendency was to maintain discriminatory tariffs in the colonies to foster French trade. The Dutch, on the whole, inclined to govern indirectly through native chiefs.

The work of Catholic and Protestant missionaries is a tolerably familiar story, but its historic importance is *The rôle of the missionary* usually underestimated.   The missionary comes with the single purpose of preaching his faith, but unconsciously he becomes an advance agent of all Western culture.   Finding that the sick clamor for healing, he brushes up what medical knowledge may be his, makes what cures he can, and writes home to the missionary board to train the next representative in medicine *before* he is sent to a land where there are sick bodies as well as sick souls. He founds a school, and finds it frequented by young men who have no intention of changing their religion but eager

[1] For British India, see below, pages 137–141.

to learn the secrets of secular civilization. In order to make the Word of God understood he translates the Bible, and sometimes finds it necessary to invent an alphabet and thus transform a tribal dialect into a written language. The indirect effects of missionary enterprise are always important, but direct conversions vary with the type of religious tradition encountered. Nature religions, the crude myths invented by primitive men to explain the world they live in, seem to have little power of resistance. Practically the whole Pacific island area was converted from paganism to Christianity in two or three generations, and missionary success in southern Africa has been but little less remarkable. On the other hand, "prophetic" religions which rest on revelations and sacred writings win few converts from each other. In spite of much Christian teaching, the vast majority in such countries as China, India and northern Africa retain their ancient faiths, and Mohammedanism is winning converts in some parts of Africa more rapidly than Christianity. Most students of African affairs predict that within a few decades Christianity and Islam will have divided all Africa between them to the exclusion of former pagan cults.

Tropical Africa was in 1870 the greatest material prize open to diplomacy, an unconquered wilderness larger than the whole of Europe. Northern Africa was a *Africa* different world, a region of civilized though sometimes stagnant monarchies long in touch with European diplomacy, Mohammedan in religion and "white" (a deeply sunburned white!) in race. South of it lay the Sahara Desert, a far more real barrier than the Mediterranean Sea. Then the Sudan, or prairie "black man's land," merging gradually into the equatorial jungles. This jungle, broken by wide expanses of highland and grassy country, continues south till increasing aridity brings again the prairie and desert, the South Africa of gold, diamonds, cattle, sheep and ostrich feathers. In tropical Africa no strong civilization had ever

arisen to resist European encroachment. Despotic kingdoms existed in a few places, but most of the natives still
lived in small tribes or tiny village communities. Very
little of Africa was as yet under European control. In the
extreme north of the continent France held Algeria, at the
extreme south British and Boers were settled near the Cape,
in the tropical latitudes Britain, France, Spain and Portugal
held about half the coastline, but their colonies did not extend
far inland and in many cases amounted to little more than
neglected trading posts.

David Livingstone, a Scotch missionary who combined the
enthusiasm of the crusader with the zeal of a scientist, was
Livingstone   one of the first explorers of the unknown hinter-
and Stanley   land of south central Africa. He viewed with
horror the Arab slave trade which was wrecking and debasing
all that there was of native Negro civilization and tried to
awaken Europe to the need of curbing it. Once when he was
cut off from all contact with the outside world, the New York
Herald sent Henry M. Stanley as journalist-explorer to find
him. Stanley became fascinated with the possibilities of
empire and commerce in the deep rich heart of the Congo
River basin, and attracted the attention of King Leopold II
of the Belgians, a shrewd monarch who was before all else a
man of business. At King Leopold's instigation an international geographic conference took place in Brussels in
1876, and an International Association of the Congo was
organized (at first under the timid title of a "committee for
the study of the upper Congo") in 1879. Stanley would
have preferred British rule in the Congo basin, but his efforts
in effect gave a rich colony to the Belgian King.

Other nations became interested. The French explorer
The Berlin   De Brazza staked out claims to part of the region
Conference,   which became the French Congo. The British
1884-85
recognized Portuguese sovereignty over the
mouth of the Congo on the basis of some ancient explora-

tions in order to bottle up Leopold's projected dependency. An international conference held at Berlin attempted to settle the Congo problem and at the same time lay down general rules for the partition of central Africa.   The International Association of the Congo now became the Congo Free State under King Leopold's personal administration.   Provisions, later practically disregarded, assured equal trading rights and freedom of navigation to all nations.   Slavery and the slave trade were condemned, but the sale of liquor and of firearms to native races was not generally restricted till another conference, held in Brussels in 1890.   The Berlin Conference wisely provided that no colonizing power should extend its African territory without due notice to others, that disputes must be settled by peaceful arbitration and that territories annexed must be effectively occupied.

The Congo Free State was a highly enlightened experiment in the administration of a backward area; it seemed an ideal arrangement to place so rich a tropical *The Congo* treasure house under the benevolent supervision *Free State:* *a tragedy* of a monarch who had long been interested in *of good* African affairs and who ruled too small a country *intentions* to arouse the jealousy of the Great Powers.[1]   Had Britain, France or Germany taken over the Congo the colonial balance of power might have been seriously endangered.   Unfortunately for the world, and especially for the Congolese natives, Leopold II was at heart more interested in building up a private fortune than in carrying civilization into "darkest Africa."   Rubber and ivory proved profitable.   The annual rubber output of the Free State increased from some thirty thousand dollars in 1886 to eight million in 1900. Foreign competitors were hampered, huge private monopolies created, and the idle natives driven to work in the

---

[1] Unfortunately no system of international inspection or control existed to hold the trustee to his duty; that lack was supplied by the "mandate" system established after the World War; see Chapter XVIII.

name of taxation. While warring against Arab slave traders and justifying his despotism on the ground that slavery must be suppressed Leopold was turning, whether he fully realized it or not, the whole Free State into a gigantic slave plantation. When the proper quota of rubber was not turned in, half-savage native regiments were turned loose in "punitive expeditions" to burn villages and kill or mutilate their inhabitants. Isolation favored abuses. Not only Europe at large but many officials in the Congo remained ignorant of cruelties that took place in remote corners of the territory. But gradually the truth appeared from accounts of missionaries and foreign consuls stationed in the country; foreign opinion, especially British, demanded investigation, and domestic critics, such as the humanitarian Belgian Socialist Émile Vandervelde, echoed the cry. At last Leopold consented to sell his private sovereignty to the Belgian nation and in 1908 the Free State became the Belgian Congo. Conditions have greatly improved, partly from reforms introduced by the new régime but partly, it must be owned, from the fact that wild rubber is no longer so profitable as formerly. Similar atrocities took place in the rubber forests of Putomayo in South America. Wherever huge, immediate profits can be gathered by exploiting a local product for a world market by forced native labor the worst conditions are almost sure to arise.

A German empire in Africa developed at the same period as the Congo Free State. Though Bismarck had been slow German to act he proceeded with vigor when once he had Africa made up his mind. In 1883 he extended protection to one Lüderitz, a merchant from Bremen, who had settled in southwestern Africa, a rather barren stretch between British Cape Colony and Portuguese Angola. The British, who owned an outpost at Walfisch Bay, were slightly disturbed and endeavored to evade the issue presented. At last the Chancellor's brittle patience snapped and in April,

1884, he formally proclaimed a protectorate over the unclaimed part of the coast.   Dr. Gustav Nachtigal in the same year explored Togoland and Kamerun, and by treaties with the native chiefs, laid the foundation of two more colonies in equatorial Africa.   Dr. Karl Peters, in the meantime, was engaged in empire building in East Africa.   Here, again, the British and the Portuguese were Germany's rivals; the Portuguese striving to hold old claims to the coast, the British to annex land rapidly enough so that the whole region would not fall to Germany.   Negotiations were long and complicated, but eventually Great Britain obtained in Kenya and Uganda territory about equivalent in importance to German East Africa or Tanganyika.   In 1890 Germany bartered all claims to Uganda and Zanzibar in exchange for the island of Helgoland in the North Sea.   Though the arrangement was denounced as "trading a suit for a button," the insignificant European island proved an important naval defense to Germany during the World War.

On the whole the British attitude toward German colonization was not very far from that of Gladstone who declared with his accustomed orotund formality, "If Germany is to become a colonizing Power, all I can say is 'God speed her.'   She becomes our ally *Anglo-German colonial relations* and partner in the execution of the great purposes of Providence for the advantage of mankind."   There were several reasons for the British sanction of German colonization: a desire to avert hostilities with the most powerful nation of the continent, a desire for German diplomatic support of British policy in Egypt, and a feeling, at least till the end of the nineteenth century, that France was a more vexatious rival than Germany.   Yet even in Bismarck's time the total effect of many small colonial controversies vexed the otherwise friendly relations of the two governments, and after statesmen and publicists had departed from Bismarck's conservatism to talk of "a German India in Africa," "Berlin

to Bagdad" and other visions of the new imperialism, the
British transferred their rivalry from France and Russia to
Germany. Even then it proved possible, in 1898, and again
in 1913, to come to an agreement as to the shares of Portuguese Africa which each would be entitled to claim in case
those feebly held and badly managed colonies ever came on
the market, and the fact that Portugal was an ally of Britain
does not seem to have proved any impediment to such secret
bargaining.

The German colonies ventures in Africa were never a
marked success. Hardly one per cent of Germany's trade
was with her own colonies and very few Germans
settled within their limits. Except for the
southern part of German Southwest Africa, a
region mainly desert, the whole of Germany's African domain lay within the tropics. Only the highlands of
East Africa, difficult of access, were suited to white settlement. For years the cost of administration outran the direct
profits or even the indirect commercial benefits of possession.
The Germans had no such long experience in tropical administration as the British, French and Dutch, and they handled
native labor, by which alone a torrid region can be profitably
developed, with excessive harshness. An unsympathetic
native policy resulted in an uprising of the Hereros in Southwest Africa in 1904 which cost more to put down than all the
wealth which that colony had produced. Many Germans
at that time were ready to abandon colonial empire altogether rather than let it remain a continuous fiscal and moral
deficit against the nation. But the Kaiser and his ministers
insisted on continuing an imperialist policy, a better management of the colonial office began under Dr. Bernhard Dern-
burg after 1907, and the boundaries of Kamerun were increased at the expense of the French Congo as the price of
recognizing French claims in Morocco. Though Germany
had not made her African colonies pay, she had laid excellent

*Estimate of
German
colonial
activity*

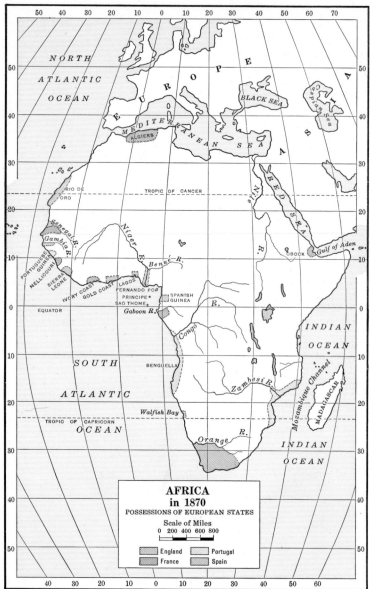

50 40 30 20 10 0 10 20 30 40 50 60 70

NORTH
ATLANTIC
OCEAN

EUROPE

BLACK SEA

Caspian Sea

ASIA

MEDITERRANEAN SEA

ALGIERS

RIO DE
ORO

TROPIC OF CANCER

Nile R.

RED SEA

Senegal R.

Gambia R.

PORTUGUESE GUINEA

MELLICOURI

SIERRA LEONE

IVORY COAST

GOLD COAST

LAGOS

FERNANDO POO

PRINCIPE

SAO THOME

Niger R.

Benué R.

SPANISH GUINEA

OBOCK

Gulf of Aden

EQUATOR

Gaboon R.

Congo

R.

INDIAN
OCEAN

SOUTH

BENGUELLA

ATLANTIC

OCEAN

Walfish Bay

TROPIC OF CAPRICORN

Zambesi R.

Mozambique Channel

MADAGASCAR

INDIAN
OCEAN

Orange R.

AFRICA
in 1870
POSSESSIONS OF EUROPEAN STATES
Scale of Miles
0 200 400 600 800

England   Portugal
France   Spain

40 30 20 10 0 10 20 30 40 50 60

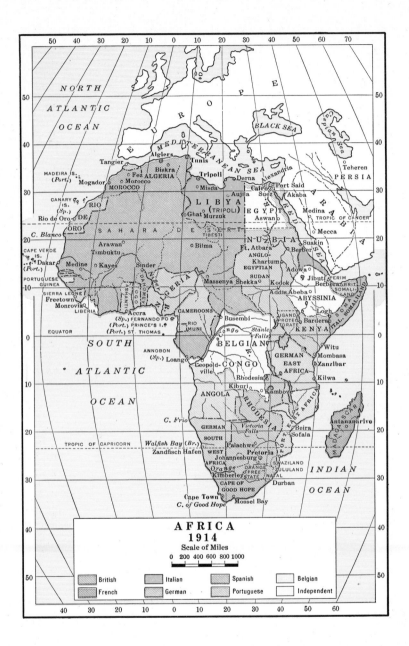

AFRICA
1914
Scale of Miles
0 200 400 600 800 1000

British   Italian   Spanish   Belgian

French   German   Portuguese   Independent

foundations for the future by scientific surveys, and expensive investments in buildings, roads and railways. Even on its weakest side, the treatment of native races, the German record though less creditable than the British or French might be favorably compared with the Belgian and Portuguese.

The rivalry of France with Britain at first presented issues far more serious than Germany's entrance into the territorial scramble. The French were the most active of *French* all colonizing powers during the last quarter of *Africa* the nineteenth century. They had the tradition of past greatness to sustain them, remembering how for over a century and a half they had striven with Britain for the mastery of India and America. They had an opportunity to find compensation overseas for the unforgettable humiliation of 1870 in Europe. They had experience and ability as colonizers, and to a greater extent than other alien rulers a knack of getting along tactfully with native races. By 1914 France held by one form of tenure or another the Mediterranean states of Algeria, Tunis, Morocco (barring a small zone of Spanish influence), the immense expanse of the western Sahara, the equatorial jungle of the French Congo, numerous outposts on the western coast, such as Senegal and Dahomey, French Somaliland and the great island of Madagascar in the east. Most of this empire formed a united and continuous domain covering the greater part of western Africa. But at one point French ambition received a decided check. British influence prevailed over French in Egypt and Egypt's southland dependency, the Sudan.

Egypt has never since Roman times been a mere European "colony," and only in consequence of the World War did she become for a brief time a British "protector- *Anglo-* ate," during the interval between her status as a *French* dependency of Turkey and her recognition as an *rivalry in* "independent" kingdom in 1922. Nevertheless, *Egypt* Egypt has been justly regarded as one of the prizes of European imperialism; diplomatic forms have gloved the iron hand of foreign rule without relaxing its grip. Though nominally subject to the Ottoman Empire, Egypt in 1870 enjoyed virtual autonomy and might have retained it with wiser government. But Ismail Pasha, the Egyptian heredi- tary governor or Khedive, was an unfortunate ruler. He combined a passion for European improvements with a reck- less disregard of their cost. He crushed the peasantry with taxation and thus undid half the benefit of his own reforms. By 1879 the government was in bankruptcy, no longer able to repay its indebtedness to European money lenders. Al- ready in 1875 Disraeli had bought up the Khedive's interest in the Suez Canal, an enterprise of French engineers opened to international traffic in 1869. Thus the first diplomatic victory went to Britain. Nevertheless Britain and France, acting in the interest of Egypt's creditors, found it possible to establish a joint financial control from 1879 to 1883 and to force the resignation of the spendthrift ruler.

But it proved easier to deal with a recalcitrant ruler than with an aroused and resentful nation. While the pliant *British* Khedive Tewfik Pasha now placed in office *military* yielded to the foreign demands for retrenchment *occupation* and reform, a discontented Egyptian officer, Ahmed Arabi (better known by his title of Arabi Pasha), raised an anti-foreign insurrection. Nationalism had reached the East; there was a popular outcry of "Egypt for the Egyptians!" Riots in Alexandria made matters urgent, but France and Turkey (the paramount power in legal theory) failed to act. Great Britain, therefore, alone assumed the responsibility for a bombardment of Alexandria in 1882 and the subsequent military occupation of the whole country. A new organic law for Egypt, drawn up by Lord Dufferin in 1883, constituted what was in form a representative consti- tutional monarchy subject to Turkish overlordship but was in actual practice a new British dependency. Major Evelyn

Baring, later Earl of Cromer, governed from 1883 to 1907 as Consul General and diplomatic agent. His commands were always tendered as "advice" but officials who failed to follow his advice were forced out of office. On the whole the Egyptians profited from British occupation. Sound financial administration not only balanced the budget but relieved the peasantry from forced labor and oppressive taxation. Cotton production was widely extended. The great Assuan dam, completed in 1903, backed up the waters of the Nile for two hundred miles to supply a reservoir in the dry seasons. Yet the many advantages brought to Egypt by the British neither reconciled the natives to foreign rule nor convinced European rivals that under cover of a "temporary" occupation the British were not really planning a permanent addition to their empire. The agreement with France in 1904, the breaking of the nominal tie with Turkey in 1914, and the grant of a partial and conditional independence to Egypt in 1922, helped simplify one of the most complex and anomalous situations in all colonial history. The acquisition of Egypt led, moreover, to another troublesome imperial entanglement in the Sudan.

Premier Gladstone who had intervened in Egypt in 1882 was none the less at heart reluctant to extend imperial commitments. He favored withdrawing British and Egyptian forces alike from the Sudan, a huge *The revolt in the Sudan* province lying south of Egypt and nominally dependent on it. Here a Mohammedan fanatic commonly termed the Mahdi had established a despotic empire. General Charles Gordon was sent to withdraw the garrison at Khartum on the upper Nile. Gordon was one of the most picturesque soldiers of adventure in modern times. His simple Puritan piety reminds the American of "Stonewall" Jackson, and no doubt he seemed to many British hero-worshipers a reincarnation of one of Cromwell's generals. By aiding the Chinese Emperor to crush a revolution he had acquired both military fame and the nickname of "Chinese" Gordon. The British would have been wiser to have selected a man who was less of a hero and more of an obedient agent. Gordon could not bear to abandon a great and fertile province to bloodshed and slavery. He delayed withdrawal until he was cut off, the relief expedition sent to rescue him arrived too late, and Khartum was sacked. The death of Gordon in 1885 was a damaging blow at British prestige and the opportunity to avenge him did not come till 1898.

This long delay gave other powers some right to say that "Egypt" (really the British authority in Egypt) had abandoned any claim to the effective occupation of *The Fashoda "incident"* the Sudan. The brave French explorer Captain Marchand started on an expedition from French Congo to the Nile; though his enterprise was ostensibly one of scientific exploration he carried with him the French flag and French hopes of empire. In July, 1898, he raised the flag at Fashoda on the Nile. In September of the same year Herbert Kitchener destroyed the Sudanese army in a great battle at Omdurman. Then hearing that the French had reached the Nile he hastened to meet Marchand. There was no conflict, both men simply referring the case to their home governments. Had France possessed a navy able to cope with the British and feared nothing from Germany war would probably have followed. But the British well knew that France could not risk a war with the strongest naval power and also that Alsace-Lorraine was closer to French interest than any post on the Nile could be. In the negotiations that followed Great Britain insisted on the main point, the complete control of the Nile valley under the joint authority of Great Britain and Egypt. France, however, obtained a free hand in the Sahara and the western Sudan and promptly proceeded to unite Algeria, French Congo, Senegal and Dahomey by military missions.[1]

[1] For French expansion in Morocco see Chapters X and XI.

Italy has been among the less fortunate of the colonizing powers. Like Germany, and for an identical reason, the long delay in attaining national unity, Italy came *Italy and* late into the race for empire; and she entered it *Abyssinia* with military and economic resources much inferior to the German. Disappointed at the French occupation of Tunis, Italy had to wait almost a generation longer before obtaining compensation in Tripoli, and Tripoli appears to be the least valuable of the north African states. In eastern Africa Italy obtained two strips of coastland, Eritrea and Italian Somaliland, the latter increased in 1924 by the cession of Jubaland from British East Africa. But the main prize on which Italy was set was Abyssinia, an independent and mountainous country inhabited by a proud, warlike people of mixed white and black race, Christian in religion. Menelik, a ruler of some military competence, succeeded in defeating an Italian army at Adowa in 1896. The imperialistic cabinet of Francesco Crispi fell and the Italian government agreed to recognize Abyssinia's complete independence.

With the exception of Abyssinia, the little Negro republic of Liberia, founded by freedmen from the United States, was the only part of Africa to retain independence *Other* from European control. Quietly and rapidly the *African* British, French and Portuguese pushed their *annexations* coastal colonies in towards the interior to keep abreast of their new German, Belgian and Italian rivals as well as of each other. Spain's small coastal and island settlements in west Africa, on the other hand, were never greatly extended. The British made much use of private enterprise; chartered companies laying the foundation for the prosperous protectorate of Nigeria in west Africa and Rhodesia in south central Africa. The almost complete European conquest of the second largest continent within less than a generation, without a single war among the partitioning powers, was one of the most amazing feats of modern times. On the other hand, experience has moderated the enthusiasm of the first explorers and empire builders. Each new colony was hailed as fabulously wealthy in mineral and agricultural resources, but only a few were ever placed on a paying basis.

Another tropical area partitioned during the same period was the island world of the Pacific. Here conditions in *The parti-* many respects paralleled those of central Africa. *tion of the* Native tribes and kingdoms too weak to resist *Pacific* European aggression or even to maintain internal order stood guard over tropical raw products desired by European markets. Conquest was the inevitable result; in fact some of the unstable native governments, as in Hawaii and Fiji, petitioned for foreign annexation some time before it was granted, and in other cases, such as Samoa, the fiction of native independence proved a convenient cover for the most ruthless exploitation by foreign consuls and traders. Nearest to Asia lie the largest islands, the East Indies, inhabited by brown-skinned Malayan peoples probably akin to the Mongolian race of eastern Asia. Most of this region is Dutch, but the British and Americans acquired some important portions. In New Guinea and in the neighboring Melanesian islands to the east as far as Fiji most of the population is black, perhaps allied to the true Negro of Africa. Farthest away from Asia are the "many islands" (Polynesia), including Hawaii, Samoa, Tahiti and many other groups, inhabited by a light brown race certainly related to the Maoris of New Zealand and possibly — though this is still an open question — to the "white" races of Europe and western Asia.

The Dutch East Indies are a relic of the older period of colonial conquest. They are the reward of The Netherlands *The Dutch* for possessing sea power and commercial enter- *East Indies* prise at an early date and with the exception of British India may be accounted the most valuable of all tropical empires.   Netherlands India, as it is sometimes called, covers about 734,000 square miles and has a population of fifty million, or about seven times that of the mother country.   Some of the larger islands, such as Sumatra, Celebes and the Dutch portions of Borneo and New Guinea, are still wild country, only partly developed.   But Java has been for centuries the best developed agricultural estate in the tropics.   At first the Dutch exploited the inhabitants as well as the resources of the island.   By the so-called "culture system" a portion of the land was set aside for producing export crops of sugar, coffee, indigo, tea, spices and tobacco. Forced labor on these plantations and the oppression exercised by native rulers or Regents, acting as agents of the Dutch administration, provoked much protest and led after 1860 to the gradual abandonment of the system.[1]   But under a régime of free labor Java has continued to be a revenue producer, and rubber, copra and mineral products rival the older wealth of sugar, coffee and spices.   Within half a century after 1880 the population of Java almost doubled.   At present Java, though mainly agricultural, has a population equal to that of England on an area no greater.   In recent years the Dutch have built schools and opened native advisory assemblies, but they have given no special encouragement to missionary work and do not desire to Europeanize the native Javanese, who are instructed in their own language and culture rather than the Dutch.

Britain-in-Asia includes several colonies outside the Indian Empire.   The island of Ceylon, immediately south of India, is governed as a separate crown colony.   It is a *The British in the East Indies* main center of the tea trade.   Near the equator the port of Singapore, the southern gateway to the Far East, dominates the Malay States under British protection.   In northern Borneo there are some peculiarly

---

[1] These evils were exposed in E. D. Dekker's novel *Max Havelaar*, which from its popularity and influence has been termed the "Dutch *Uncle Tom's Cabin.*"

interesting experiments in colonial administration.   One part
of the island is governed by a chartered company, the British
North Borneo Company; another is ruled as an hereditary
monarchy under a British dynasty, the descendants of
"Raja" Brooke who took the throne of Sarawak at the bidding of native Malay and Dyak tribesmen.   Australia gov-
erns British New Guinea, including the old colony of Papua
and the recently acquired "mandate" of German New
Guinea.

The German attempt to found a Pacific empire coincided
with the beginnings of German Africa.   In 1884 German
The Ger- traders hoisted the flag over the unoccupied coast
mans in the of northeastern New Guinea.   The Australians
Pacific of Queensland, without waiting for any sanction
from the home government, attempted to forestall the German action by a previous landing in southeastern New
Guinea.   The western half of the island was conceded to
belong to the Dutch.   Hence a single island — a large one
to be sure — was divided among three colonizing powers.
The German portion took the name of Kaiserwilhelmsland
and the offshore islands were christened the Bismarck archipelago.   Germany also secured the western Solomons and,
farther north, the Caroline, Marshall and Ladrone Islands
and, eventually, a share in Samoa.

The Samoan island group is small but it occupies a large
place in diplomatic history because of the intense rivalry of
The Samoan German, British and American merchants and
condomin- consuls and their intricate intrigues with a weak
ium native government.   The Samoans are among
the most attractive representatives of the Polynesian race;
tall, handsome, intelligent and gentle, they have captured
the admiration of many European visitors.   The famous
Scottish novelist Robert Louis Stevenson spent his last years
among them almost as a patriarchal chieftain, championing
their rights with trenchant pen.   His *A Footnote to History* is

an important though not unbiased source of information on Samoan politics. But among the many Samoan virtues political acumen and business energy were not numbered. Nominally independent, Samoa became a battleground of imperialistic and commercial rivalry; kings were deposed and exiled as one or another foreign influence prevailed, and had not a timely hurricane smashed the assembled warships of the powers in 1889 there might easily have occurred some "regrettable incident" which would have made inevitable a naval war between Germany and the Anglo-Saxon powers. Instead the three interested nations agreed to set up a joint protectorate or condominium over the islands. The experiment worked badly, however, national jealousies continued, and in 1899 Germany and the United States divided Samoa between them, Great Britain relinquishing all her claims in return for compensation elsewhere.[1] In the New Hebrides after 1906 there was a similar Anglo-French condominium, more durable but not much more satisfactory.

Britain and France divided between them most of the outlying Oceanic islands. The British annexation of Fiji in 1874 led to the absorption of neighboring groups such as the Gilbert, Ellice, Tonga and British Solomons, besides New Zealand's ac-quisition of the Cook Islands and some smaller *Other European Pacific colonies* islets. France obtained the Society Islands, with Tahiti, the Marquesas and Tuamotu groups, also New Caledonia which was for some time used as a penal colony. Brown Polynesian and black Melanesian accepted Christianity and civilization with astonishing avidity. Men still alive can remember when cannibalism was rife in these now decorous and well-ordered communities. But contact with the white man's civilization has spread disease, in some cases diminished the native population, and done little to make the easy-going islanders industrious laborers. The natives are

[1] After the World War German Samoa became a "mandate" of New Zealand.

usually regarded like the reservation Indians in the United States and protected as wards of the state against their own improvidence. The burden of agricultural development is often divided between the white plantation owner and the imported coolie laborer from Asia.

The United States, which never shared nor sought to share in the partitions of Africa and of Asia, has acquired *America in* several Pacific island colonies. Tutuila in *the Pacific* Samoa, Wake, Midway, Guam and the once independent Polynesian kingdom of Hawaii form a series of stepping stones across the Pacific to the Philippines. The Philippine Islands were a quite unexpected acquisition. With Cuba and Porto Rico in the West Indies, a few Pacific islands and a short stretch of coastline in northwestern Africa, they formed the remnant of the once great colonial empire of Spain. By location and race they belong rather to the Malayan East Indies than to the mid-Pacific island world of Polynesia, and ordinarily would have been considered quite outside the limits of the American sphere of influence. But a war with Spain in 1898 arising over Spanish misgovernment in Cuba found Commodore George Dewey in Asiatic waters, and his victory at Manila placed the islands in American hands. Germany, which had hoped herself to purchase the Spanish islands in the Pacific, was much disconcerted and only partially appeased by the opportunity to purchase the Carolines and some other small Spanish groups.[1] The war with Spain indirectly facilitated the American acquisition of Hawaii. Hawaii, like Samoa, found the pretense of independent national sovereignty a burdensome fiction, but President Cleveland opposed annexation. Under President McKinley, however, the islands were taken over and made a self-governing territory of the United States. The Philippines, on the contrary,

---

[1] Since the World War the German islands north of the equator have passed to Japan; those to the south, either to Great Britain or her dominions.

were understood to be not permanent territories but wards of the nation to be fitted for eventual — though undated — independence, and in the meantime were placed under a special colonial régime, very paternalistic at first but with an increasing degree of native home rule.   No other colonizing nation devoted so great a share of attention and effort to spreading education among the masses of the people, but one result was to create a large class of nationally conscious Filipinos eagerly demanding an early termination of foreign tutelage.

The largest and most populous of all tropical dependencies is British India and the associated native states.   Modern India begins with the transfer of authority *British* from the East India Company to the British *India* Crown in 1858.   For years the East India Company had been rather a political and administrative body than a merely commercial venture, and so wise a philosopher as John Stuart Mill regretted that it should cease to administer Indian affairs, but most Englishmen thought that such indirect control worked awkwardly and had given rise to many abuses, culminating in the terrible Sepoy rebellion, a mutiny of native soldiers in 1857.   A Viceroy was placed in immediate charge of British India with a large civil service subordinate to him, and a Secretary of State for India sat in the British cabinet.   In the lower ranks of the army and of the civil service there were many natives, but at first the higher positions were mainly reserved for the British.   The new government abandoned the policy intermittently pursued by the East India Company of annexing native kingdoms to British India; they were permitted to retain their independence on condition of accepting British "advice" as to foreign policy and necessary internal reforms.   British India continued, indeed, to expand, but on the frontier rather than in the interior.   A "scientific frontier" to the north was fixed to forefend a possible Russian invasion, Afghanistan was compelled to adopt a friendly policy as a "buffer state" between Russian and British Asia, and upper Burma was annexed to the east, partly as a counter-stroke to French aggressions in Indo-China on the other side of Siam.

India is rather a continent than a nation. British India has a population of nearly 250,000,000, and the native *Complexity* states, for whose welfare the British are almost *of Indian* equally responsible, more than 70,000,000. If *problems* the latter are included, India represents about three fourths of the population of the whole British Empire, and Christianity is the third religion in the Empire, being exceeded by both Hindus and Moslems! In India the religious division is more important than the complex divisions of race and language. Over 200,000,000 adhere to the Hindu or Brahmanic faith, and these Hindus are in turn divided into hereditary social classes sanctioned by religious custom, the "castes." Highest of all stands the priestly caste, the Brahmin, who may be defiled by the mere close presence of an inferior. Then comes the warrior, then the "middle class" merchant or peasant, then the humble laborer, and finally the "outcast" who may perform only the degraded tasks. The Mohammedans, over 60,000,000 in number, are for the most part quite hostile to the Hindus, and their importance far outruns their number, for their creed has attracted the most warlike races. In Burma and some other districts there are over 10,000,000 Buddhists, but the main conquests of the faith of the gentle prophet Gautama Buddha have been made in the Far East, outside his native India. Christian missionaries have won a few million converts, and there are also the warlike Sikhs, the Parsee traders, and the wild jungle tribes with their myriad forms of nature worship.

In ruling India, therefore, the British had such a task as the Japanese would have had if fortune had placed in their hands the whole of Europe! The vast numbers of the people, their diversity in language, race, religion and civilization, their mutual antagonisms, their wide *Aspects of* *British rule* divergence from the common ruling power as well as from each other make the comparison scarcely an exaggeration.   For the most part the British permitted the traditional village life to continue without any attempt to impose European institutions or to educate more than a selected minority.   Even Christian missions were tolerated rather than actively supported by the government.   The main task of the British was merely to preserve order, to maintain justice in the courts, to promote prosperity by building railways, highways, canals and factories, to fight famine, and cautiously to introduce some Western concepts of sanitation.   That in all these respects British rule brought great blessings to India only the uninformed can doubt. Yet there have been drawbacks to British rule.   The peasantry are almost as poor as ever and famines have by no means ceased.   Taxes are heavy, and while the revenue raised is spent in India, much of it goes to keep up a large army of occupation.   Another grievance is that skilled native industries have been crushed out of existence by the competition of the cheap manufactured goods of Great Britain.   Even law and order have been bought at the high cost of surrendering, not indeed political liberty (for India before the British came was subject to native despots or foreign conquerors from the north), but some possibility of initiative, variety and experiment.

Even had British rule been better than it was, or better than any alien rule can be, India would have become discontented in the twentieth century, as all Asia *The nation-* caught the European fever of nationalism.   The *alist move-* awakening of Turkey, the rebirth of Japan, the *ment* revolutions in China, could hardly leave the proud and ancient nations of India contented subjects of a foreign bureaucracy.   Many moderate Hindus adopted the formula of

"Dominion Home Rule," a status similar to that of Canada; others demanded complete independence and were willing to resort to revolution and assassination to secure it.   Perhaps the most interesting and typically "Oriental" phase of the nationalist movement was that of Mohandas K. Gandhi, better known by his popular religious title of Mahatma Gandhi, who had championed the rights of Hindus in British Africa before returning to India to begin a more general assault on British imperialism.   He held that the real evil was not so much the mere political rule of Britain over India but "Western industrialism and imperialism" generally; that India should return to a simple life, reject imported products, revive native handicrafts and live austerely as befitted a spiritual nation.   His program forbade the use of violence and proposed to attain independence by passive resistance and a systematic boycott of all governmental activities ("non-co-operation").   None of his followers should hold office, attend public ceremonies, bring cases into British courts, pay taxes or obey British legislation.   The personal sincerity and saintly simplicity of this Tolstoy of India won him thousands of followers, even among those who were too impatient to accept entirely his policy of non-resistance.

The British faced by a growing demand for Indian self-government, cautiously introduced reforms in political ad-

The Mor- ministration.   Lord Curzon, the Conservative
ley-Minto Viceroy from 1898 to 1905, was the last to main-
reforms tain the old system of exclusively British control.   Though his administration was competent and conscientious, some of his policies, such as the partition of Bengal province in 1905, roused nationalist resentment, and Earl Minto, his Liberal successor, began a policy of concession, supported by Lord Morley, the new Secretary for India.   The number of elected members in the provincial legislative councils was increased (1909) and native Indians ad-

mitted to the Governor General's Council and as advisers
to the Secretary for India.   Three years later the capital
was transferred from Calcutta to the ancient city of Delhi.
Hindus were admitted more readily to executive positions.
But these cautious concessions whetted the appetite for more,
and the nationalist movement was renewed after the World
War on a greater scale than before.[1]

[1] For postwar India see Chapter XXX.

CHAPTER VI

FRANCE AND THE DUAL ALLIANCE

THE French Republic was after 1871 unquestionably the
most important democracy of continental Europe. With

The ven-
turesome
Republic
the exception of Switzerland, France was the
only considerable European nation in which
democracy then took the form of republicanism,
and for a long time the dynastic question was a live issue
even in France. Not till the end of the nineteenth century
did royalist groups abandon the hope of a monarchical
restoration. So many revolutions and sudden changes of
régime had marked the period since 1789 that few observers
either in France or abroad expected the hurried and provisional constitutional arrangements set up after the Franco-
Prussian War to outlast a decade or so. How surprised they
would have been had they known that during and after the
World War France would be generally considered the sta-
blest government and her voters the most conservative
public in Europe; that the whirlwind of revolution would
sweep over Russia, Germany, Italy and Spain and leave
France almost untouched!

The omens of 1871 for civil peace were certainly not good.
Since 1789 the people of Paris had been more radical than

The Paris
Commune
those of the "provinces"; they had been at the
core of every revolution and had a tradition of
armed insurrection. The prolonged siege of the city by the
Germans had brought it to the verge of famine; gaunt, hungry men whose fathers had died on the barricades in 1830 or
1848 saw the one consolation prize for all their sufferings, the
republic about to be snatched away from them by a reactionary assembly meeting in the old royalist town of Versailles.
The radical city government, or Commune, declared oppo-

sition to monarchy and even to centralized national government under any régime, demanding the reconstitution of France as a loose federation of municipal democracies free to conduct their own economic and social experiments. Because of the similarity of name, many have confused this "Communard" movement with "Communism" in the sense of radical socialism, and the confusion is made the easier by the fact that many of the leaders of the Paris Commune *were* Communists as well.   But as the movement included all shades of radicalism from a merely political republicanism to the reddest shades of anarchism, it is important not to identify this anti-monarchist insurrection in Paris with the full economic program of the "Communists."

With France at large expressed by the National Assembly, Thiers could not if he would have given the assurances demanded by the city of Paris.   He resolved to use force to crush the rebel city.   During April and May, 1871, Paris endured a second siege, on this occasion by Frenchmen, while the German army of occupation looked on in cynical neutrality and congratulated themselves that they were "not as others — even these French!"   In their last frenzy the Communards burned a number of public buildings and killed their hostages, among them the Archbishop of Paris. This brought down on the insurgents a signal vengeance when the city was taken.   Thousands died in bitter street fighting and thousands of the survivors were exiled to penal colonies. The international prestige of France received a greater blow than from the Franco-Prussian War.

Though the Bonapartists had been too thoroughly discredited by the Franco-Prussian War to hope for a speedy restoration of the Empire, the adherents of the Bourbon monarchy had good prospects.   Many conservative peasants and business men feared that republicanism might turn "red" and mean such experiments in socialism as had marked the early career

Plans to revive the Bourbon monarchy

of the Second Republic in 1848 or a revival of the Paris Commune of 1871. The Catholic clergy were in large majority favorable to monarchy as the best prospect of protecting the interests of the Church. The remnant of Bonapartists, despairing of any immediate restoration of their own dynasty, turned to a Bourbon restoration as a better embodiment of the principle of "authority" than a republic would be. The National Assembly which was undertaking the reconstruction of France would in all probability have offered the crown to the old dynasty but for the fact that there were two Bourbon claimants and neither could command sufficient support. The Comte de Chambord, grandson of the Charles X deposed by the revolution of 1830, called himself Henri V and clung to an integral program of "divine right" monarchy, refusing even the smallest concessions to the spirit of the age. The "Orleanist" candidate was the Comte de Paris, grandson of King Louis Philippe who had reigned from 1830 to 1848. After prolonged negotiations, the two factions united on the Comte de Chambord, who was childless and would be succeeded by the Orleans dynasty. Then, when all seemed settled, "Henri V" threw away his chances by insisting on restoring the old white flag of the Bourbons in place of the national tricolor which had waved over the wars of the revolution and of both Napoleons. The Orleanists would not submit to that, and their chief spokesman, Adolphe Thiers, "head of the executive power" in the provisional government, came out for a republic as "the form of government which divides Frenchmen least."

Though the royalists were unable to fill the vacant throne at the moment, they were still far from accepting the re-*The constitutional laws of 1875* public in principle. An adverse vote forced Thiers to resign the executive authority in 1873 and the National Assembly chose one of the few military men who had emerged from the war with Prussia

with undamaged reputation, Marshal MacMahon. Many
of his own supporters regarded him as a provisional executive to keep the country quiet and orderly until a King could
be found to succeed him.[1]   The Wallon amendment, introducing the title of President of the Republic for the new
executive, carried in 1875 by majority of a single vote.   By
a curious paradox which has often been remarked, the hap-
hazard, provisional constitution adopted in 1875 to meet a
temporary emergency has outlasted all the polished and
rounded "perpetual" constitutions of the First Republic,
the First Empire, the restored Bourbon monarchy, the
Second Republic and the Second Empire!   It did not even
contain an explicit declaration of rights, as was the wont of
French constitutions, but merely organized the powers of
the government.

The French written constitution, like its unwritten British model, was based on the principle of parliamentary control over the executive through the collective *The French*
responsibility of the ministry to the popularly *executive*
elected branch of the national legislature.   The four most
powerful of modern nations during the brief lifetime of the
old German Empire (1871-1918) represented four distinct
methods of organizing the executive power: (1) a monarchical head governing through a Chancellor of his choice, the
German plan; (2) a monarchical head governing through a
cabinet responsible to the House of Commons, the British;
(3) an elective head governing through a cabinet of his choice,
the American; (4) an elective head governing through a
Council of Ministers responsible to the Chamber of Deputies, the French.   The French President was evidently the
least significant of the four chief executives, since he had

[1] Very interesting parallels to this situation have occurred since the World War,
notably in Hungary where a royalist majority were forced for diplomatic reasons to
choose a provisional "Regent" instead of a King, and in Germany, where many
royalists voted for Marshal Hindenburg as the best choice possible so long as the
republic lasted.

neither the hereditary dignity of the British King and German Kaiser nor the actual power of an American President; he neither *reigned* nor *governed*.   The President was chosen by the two legislative chambers, the Senate and the Chamber of Deputies, voting jointly as a National Assembly.   His nominal term of office was for seven years and he was made eligible to re-election, but by a series of strange accidents the presidential term of office has become very indeterminate. Adolphe Thiers (1871–73), who had the power but not the name of President, resigned because of legislative hostility; so did his successors Marshal MacMahon (1873–79) and, in his second term, Jules Grévy (1879–87).   President Sadi Carnot was assassinated in 1894; Casimir-Périer resigned in 1895; Félix Faure died in office in 1899.   In the new century things went better, Presidents Émile Loubet, Armand Fallières and Raymond Poincaré completing each his full term. But after the World War several administrations were interrupted by resignation or death.[1]

The Council of Ministers appointed by the President was collectively and individually responsible to the Chamber of Deputies.   The Premier, or President of the Council, was the real ruler of France, but his tenure was apt to be very brief, as an "interpellation" in the Chamber of Deputies, challenging the ministry on some trivial detail of policy, could at any time force a vote of want of confidence and the resignation of the ministry.   The average duration of a ministry under the Third Republic has been less than a year; from the adoption of the constitution of 1875 to the outbreak of the World War France had fully fifty ministries.[2]   But it should be remembered that a new cabinet as a rule retains part of the personnel of the old; that changes in policy as a result of a cabinet

The ministerial kaleidoscope

---

[1] For post-war France see Chapter XXVIII.

[2] A complete list of ministries from 1876 to 1920 may be found in E. M. Sait, *Government and Politics of France*, pages 447–49.

shake-up are the exception rather than the rule; that almost
never is a special election called (as is the British custom)
because of the fall of a ministry, and finally that a trained
permanent civil service gives great stability to French administration under any government.   A capable Foreign
Minister may sustain a continuous policy under half a dozen
Premiers, and a Premier forced from office may return to
it, perhaps many times.   When the "tiger" of French politics, Georges Clemenceau, was reproached with having upset so many ministries by his factious opposition, he is said
to have retorted that he had overthrown only one cabinet,
for they were all alike!   Nothing is more striking than the
contrast between the superficial instability of French politics and the stable and conservative trend of French
policy.

The legislative power was divided between a Chamber of
Deputies, chosen for a four-year term by direct and universal
manhood suffrage, and a Senate chosen by in-
direct election for nine years, one third being   *The French
legislative*
renewed each third year.   The two bodies meet
and vote together as a National Assembly to elect a President
or amend the constitution.   The Chamber of Deputies, enjoying control over national finances and the rise and fall of
ministries, was much the more powerful of the two bodies.
The Senate, selected by electoral colleges of deputies, department and district councilors, and delegates from each
commune, was designed as a check on the supposed radicalism of the Chamber.   Originally it had a group of members
holding office for life, but this provision was later abandoned.
The most discussed question under the Third Republic
was whether members of the Chamber of Deputies should be
elected for single districts (*scrutin d'arrondissement*) as is
the American House of Representatives, or by a general
ticket for the whole of a department (*scrutin de liste*), in the
manner of an American Electoral College.

France is one of the most strongly centralized of nations. There is no "state" or provincial legislature to share the law-making powers of the National Assembly, and local administration is carried on in accordance with orders received from Paris. The largest unit of local government, the department, is governed by a Prefect, appointed by the President on nomination of the Minister of the Interior. The Prefect is at once the chief executive officer of the department and the agent of the central government, and he is assisted by an elected council of very restricted powers. Each department in turn is subdivided into districts or *arrondissements*, each district into cantons, and each canton into communes. The commune is the real cell of the body politic, the basic political division which touches the immediate interests of the people. The communes, over 36,000 in number, range in size from great cities to small villages of less than fifty inhabitants. Paris, the capital and metropolis of France, is a somewhat special case, as it is a commune including several *arrondissements* and is more directly under the immediate supervision of the national government than are the smaller communes. Many Frenchmen have urged a greater degree of local home rule than now exists ("regionalism"), but it is significant that a number of the new constitutions of southern, central and eastern Europe have copied the French type of local administration.

French local government

Elections held under the new constitution returned a republican majority to the Chamber of Deputies and a large republican minority to the Senate. President MacMahon, a monarchist by conviction, could not work in harmony with a republican legislature. He demanded the right to select ministers by his own judgment irrespective of the opinion held by the Deputies. This was challenged as unconstitutional by the popular republican orator Leon Gambetta. A special

MacMahon versus Gambetta

election in 1877 tested the issue. The republicans held the Chamber of Deputies by a larger majority than before and the next year conquered the Senate. Responsible parliamentary government was thus established as a precedent, since unbroken. In 1879 President MacMahon resigned and a republican successor, Jules Grévy, was chosen. All branches of the government were now in the hands of friends of the constitution.

The Third Republic was still in peril, however, and perhaps survived as much through the dissension of its foes as by its inherent strength. There were three monarchist factions, the Legitimists, adherents of "Henri V," the Orleanists, and the Bonapartists. More important than any of these was *Anti-republican parties and movements* a conservative group who were not committed to any one royal candidate but held that the republic was still on trial and that some "strong government," whether royalist, imperialist or dictatorial mattered little, might be preferable. This group included most of the clergy, many officers in the army, peasants and shopkeepers who still shuddered at the memory of the Commune, ardent patriots who thought the republic too weak to win victory against an autocratic German Empire in the "next war." The blunders of the republicans played into their hands. After the death of Gambetta in 1882 there were few outstanding political leaders and many very mediocre professional politicians, some of whom were corrupt. President Grévy, though personally honest, was forced to resign office because of charges that his son-in-law Daniel Wilson had sold his influence to persons desirous of obtaining membership in the Legion of Honor. The incessant shifting of ministerial posts seemed to indicate instability, and this impression was enhanced by the failure of the deputies to organize strong, well-disciplined party groups. The republican majority fell apart into personal factions, scarcely deserving the name of party, and quite incapable of sustaining any ministry in office long enough to carry out an important program.

The forces of discontent found their leader at last in the person of General Boulanger, the idol of the militarists. *The Boulanger fiasco* He was a fairly competent officer, an aggressive War Minister and a picturesque "man on horseback" to capture the enthusiasm of the crowd. By cleverly promising a revision of the constitution, its nature entirely unspecified, he succeeded in attracting to his standard a motley following ranging all the way from monarchists, who hoped that a military dictatorship would be a stepping stone to a Bourbon restoration, to radical republicans, who were ready to use any broom that promised to sweep out the machine politicians and clear the path for radical reforms. The Comte de Paris, Orleanist pretender, favored his cause; so did such militarists as Henri Rochefort and Paul Déroulède, and, for a time, the radical republican Clemenceau. In 1889, after winning several electoral victories in the provincial departments, he appeared at the head of the poll in Paris. Had he shown a more decisive spirit at that crisis he might have repeated the career of Louis Napoleon or anticipated that of Mussolini or Hitler. But the government struck before he was ready, summoned him to appear before the Senate on charges of conspiracy against the Senate and condemned him when he refused to appear. Boulanger had fled to Belgium, his party collapsed and he finally committed suicide. The Third Republic was strengthened by the failure to overthrow it.

Georges Clemenceau, who did much to build up Boulanger and then to pull him down again when convinced the *Clemenceau versus Ferry* republic was in danger, is perhaps the most remarkable political figure of the entire Third Republic; in many ways a French Bismarck, resembling the Iron Chancellor in earnest patriotism, truculence of manner, incisive cynicism of utterance, self-reliance and capacity for rapid and efficient action, differing from him in little but political creed. He was rarely conservative but combined in a curious fashion radicalism, reaction and opportunism. He held a local office in Paris at the time of the Commune, though he opposed the excesses of the Communard movement. For many years he led the Extreme Left in the Chamber of Deputies, opposing the majority of ministries for the most diverse reasons — lack of zeal for republicanism, a too conciliatory attitude toward the Catholic Church, neglect of the national defenses, or preoccupation with overseas imperialism. Alone in the Chamber of Deputies he voted against the Treaty of Bardo annexing Tunis (1881). Jules Ferry, the father of modern French colonialism, was his most hated antagonist. Both men sincerely sought the greatness of France, but Ferry thought that only by building up an overseas empire could France recapture the proud place among the nations lost by the Franco-Prussian War, while Clemenceau feared (as Bismarck hoped) that Tunis and Indo-China would make France forget Alsace and Lorraine. Though only in office for brief periods Ferry initiated the protectorate over Tunis, the occupation of Madagascar, the exploration of the Congo, and an extension by conquest of French Indo-China. A minor defeat of the French troops in the Far East brought down his ministry, but he remained influential among the moderate republicans until his death in 1893. Clemenceau long survived his opponent, lost his radical reputation as a more "extreme left," arose among the Socialists, formed strong ministries in 1906 and 1917, and had the satisfaction of carrying France through the last stages of the World War and presiding over the ensuing Peace Conference.

The complete diplomatic isolation of France during Bismarck's Chancellorship was due in the main to his own shrewd diplomacy but was in part the price which France

paid for republican government and colonial empire. All
other major powers of Europe were monarchical, and viewed
Approaches   the Third Republic as a dangerously radical ex-
toward the   periment or a sign of a weak and unstable govern-
Dual Alli-   ment, by either interpretation diminishing the
ance   value of France as an ally. The race for colonial empire, as Clemenceau had foreseen, alienated Britain and Italy. By 1890 the former objection, at least, had
lost much of its force. Whatever the errors and corrup-
tions of the Third Republic, it had proved both conservative
and stable, it had already lasted longer than any other régime since 1789, and weathered every storm from the Communards to the Boulangists. Russia, no longer bound by
diplomatic understandings with Germany, might hope to
find in France a powerful counterpoise to the Triple Alliance.
As for France, she was ready to welcome any powerful ally
to break the prison of her diplomatic isolation. The double
tragedy of the Franco-Prussian War and the Communard
insurrection, the uninspiring parliamentary bickering of
domestic politics, the failure to maintain an even pace with
Germany in the increase of population and industrial wealth,
had given many Frenchmen a sense of humiliation and inferiority reflected in the generally pessimistic tone of the
national literature. Some had found partial compensation
for these humiliations in the new colonial empire, some in
the struggle for political democracy and social reform, but
nearly all rejoiced at the prospect of a powerful foreign alliance.

Yet negotiations proceeded at a very leisurely pace.
Tsar Alexander III was conservative even for a Russian
The wooing   autocrat; of all European sovereigns he was most
of Russia   hesitant to strike hands with a democratic or republican régime. Still Frenchmen subscribed heavily to
the Russian loan of 1888, and the English historian G. P.
Gooch remarks significantly, "Such sums are only lent by

one Great Power to another when an alliance is in being or in sight." Russia purchased rifles of French manufacture. The press of Paris, once so solicitous over the fate of Russian Poland, placed expediency before sentiment and became with suspicious unanimity cordially pro-Russian. In 1891 a state visit of French warships to Russia met with unexpected cordiality; the Tsar even consenting to listen to the band play the revolutionary *Marseillaise* because it was also the national hymn of France. Russia offered an *entente* based on an agreement to confer on any issue that threatened European peace and work out a common policy to meet the emergency. France, not satisfied, demanded definite military stipulations, and in 1892 obtained a general agreement, but the two governments still differed on some points of detail and the Tsar would not accept the proposed French amendments. Not till January, 1894, were negotiations finally concluded.

The Franco-Russian alliance, made definite by the secret military agreement, was defensive, as the Triple Alliance had been. Should France be attacked by Germany, or by Italy with the support of Germany, Russia would come to the aid of France. Should Russia be attacked by Germany, or by Austria-Hungary with the support of Germany, France would come *The military convention of 1893* to the aid of Russia. Mobilization by any member of the Triple Alliance would be the signal for immediate counter-mobilization by France and Russia.[1] France would contribute to a campaign against Germany at least 1,300,000 men; Russia, mobilizing more slowly, and perhaps having to face Austria-Hungary or Turkey, would contribute seven or eight hundred thousand. The general staffs of the two armies were to co-operate in time of war and exchange information in time of peace, and neither nation would make separate peace. The Dual Alliance was to terminate simul-

[1] Changed in 1906 to apply only to German mobilization.

taneously with the Triple Alliance,[1] against which it was directed, and all its clauses were to be kept most rigorously secret. But of course secrets of such magnitude cannot long be wholly kept; while the official text of the treaty was not published till Russia dropped out of the World War, the fact of the alliance was universally suspected and by 1895 openly admitted by the French government.

The Dual Alliance restored balance of power diplomacy. Instead of the Bismarckian ideal of a single power, the German Empire, dominating European diplomacy by alliances, ententes and special understandings, the older ideal of preserving peace by the distribution of political and military power among several great nations prevailed. There was not yet, however, the complete marshaling of the powers into two camps which existed in 1914; rather a balance of three quite independent forces, the Triple Alliance, the Dual Alliance and the British Empire. If anything, the British, irritated by French colonial "pinpricks" and always apprehensive of Russian ambitions in Asia, inclined more to the German side than to the French. The Dual Alliance was certainly not strong enough to embark on an aggressive policy and it was thoroughly understood by both governments that no war was to be instituted for the reconquest of Alsace-Lorraine by France or the occupation of the Straits by Russia. If these prizes should fall to them as the result of a defensive war, that would be another matter. Though the Kaiser privately raged at the Tsar's treason to the common cause of monarchy, many Germans were actually relieved because they thought that Russia would be a restraining influence on French policy. The immediate effects of the alliance were for the most part beneficial. France recovered confidence and freedom of action but became rather less chauvinistic than before; Russia

Effects of the Dual Alliance

---

[1] In 1899 this time limit was removed and the military convention was made to run as long as the diplomatic accord of 1891.

found a ready market for her financial securities; the peace of Europe seemed more firmly consolidated. If an alliance between the most democratic and the most autocratic powers in Europe seemed anomalous, it must be remembered that most alliances are "marriages of convenience" rather than "love matches."   Common fears supplied the place of common sentiment.   On the remoter effects of the alliance the verdict of history is less certain.   It is at least possible that France might better have suffered continued isolation than tie her fortunes to a government so ambitious in the Near and Far East and so unsound in its domestic institutions.   The French statesmen are not to be blamed for failing to read in the future the war of 1914 and the Bolshevist revolution of 1917, but they did know even in their own day that Austro-Russian rivalry in the Balkans was a more probable cause of European war than either Africa or Alsace.

The increased prestige which the Russian alliance brought to the Third Republic was much needed as an offset to certain domestic crises of the eighteen-nineties.   *The Drey-* Scarcely had the Boulangist movement sub- *fus case* sided when France was in an uproar over the alleged bribery of certain politicians in the interest of the private French company which was engaged in the construction of a canal at Panama.   Scarcely had this "Panama scandal" passed from the front pages of the press when it was reported that a captain of artillery had sold military secrets to Germany. Captain Alfred Dreyfus was an Alsatian Jew, personally unpopular, who appears to have been selected as a "scapegoat" to cover the delinquencies of a number of his military associates and superiors.   He was condemned for treason in 1894 and sentenced to banishment on Devil's Island, a penal colony off the coast of French Guiana.   Colonel Picquart, the novelist Émile Zola, and a number of radical republican politicians became convinced of his innocence and worked for a new trial.   The case was reopened by the agita-

tion, new evidence to prove the guilt of Dreyfus was produced, but some of the incriminating documents were shown
to be forgeries and Dreyfus, though again condemned, was
recommended for mercy and pardoned in 1899.   Final vindication came with a review of the case by the Court of
Cassation in 1906.   The Dreyfus incident, trivial enough
in itself, furnished an opportunity for bitter attacks on the
republicans as enemies of the "honor of the army," while the
radicals retorted that the whole affair was an attempt to
railroad an innocent man to jail to hush up army scandals.

Sensing a common danger, the republicans drew their
ranks together.   The party known as "Radical and Radi-
The anti-   cal-Socialist," the strongest and best disciplined
clerical   of the republican groups, was really a federation
campaign   of factions hostile to the influence of the clergy
in politics, taking as their motto Gambetta's old slogan,
"Clericalism — That's the enemy!"   The wise and politic
Pope Leo XIII had indeed reminded the French Catholics
that the Church of which he was head could be reconciled
with republican as well as with monarchical government, but
many of the priesthood and also of the laity who placed the
interest of the Catholic Church above other considerations
(the "Clericals") still remained actively hostile to the French
Republic and used the Dreyfus affair as a pretext to stir up
opposition to it.   The quarrel was an old legacy of the first
French revolution which had for a time disestablished the
Catholic Church in France, confiscated its property and
treated its orthodox adherents as enemies of the State.
From that time onward the average Clerical viewed republicanism as a menace to the Church, and the average Radical viewed the Church as a menace to human progress.

To save the Republic, the Radicals united with more conservative republican groups to the right and the Socialists
to the left in a common "bloc" or coalition which ruled
France during the comparatively long ministries of Waldeck-

Rousseau (1899–1902) and Combes (1902–05) and initiated laws restricting the monastic orders and separating Church from State. By the "associations law" of 1901 religious orders unauthorized by the government were dissolved. In 1905 the connection between the French government and the Roman Catholic Church, resting on the agreement made by Napoleon in 1801 (the Concordat), was terminated. Salaries paid to the clergy were discontinued, though pensions were granted to the older priests. The churches, while remaining national property, were to be managed by religious corporations — *associations cultuelles* — as trustees. The new and very conservative Pope Pius X objected to the separation of Church and State, and in particular to the organization of lay corporations to manage church properties. He forbade French Catholics to recognize the new law, and for several months there was a deadlock which threatened to result in the closing of churches all over France. Finally a working compromise permitted the Catholic authorities to manage Church property after their own traditions. Though the mass of French people are still Roman Catholic, their government is divorced from all religious functions. The Radicals were also insistent that the state-supported schools retain their secular character and permit no religious instruction.

The separation of Church and State

France may almost be said to have invented socialism; at all events many of the earliest nineteenth-century theorists who advocated collective ownership of property were Frenchmen. Yet the Socialist party did not become as strong in France as in Germany. This was mainly due to the fact that France underwent no such rapid and profound industrial revolution. Even in the twentieth century the peasants of the countryside outvoted the artisans of town and city, and peasants owning their own acres are very seldom socialistic in their politics. Moreover, French socialism was long divided into hostile factions, and

Socialism in France

not until 1905, with the foundation of the Unified Socialist
Party under the leadership of the great orator Jean Jaurès,
did it become a major political force.   The new party made
erstwhile Radicals, such as Clemenceau, and even former
Socialists who fell from party regularity by entering "bourgeois" ministries, such as Aristide Briand and Alexandre
Millerand, now seem conservative.   Indeed the long and able
ministries of Clemenceau (1906–09) and Briand (1909–11)
were distinguished by their resolute rigor in suppressing
strikes and labor disorders.   When Premier, Briand told
the Deputies that if he had not found a legal way to suppress
a railroad strike, namely by calling the railwaymen to military service, he would have suppressed it anyhow.   During
the World War, however, even the Unified Socialists supported the national cause and after the Russian revolution
a Communist "left wing" split from the party.   The most
distinctively national tendency in twentieth-century French
socialism was the "syndicalist" movement.   The Syndi-
Syndicalism   calists advocated the control of industrial properties by trades unions ("syndicats") rather than
by the State and advocated violent methods such as the
general strike and "sabotage" or covert damage to the employer's property.

After the triumphant struggle with the Royalists and
Clericals, the Third Republic felt a security and self-con-
The nation-   fidence never known before.   Even the new dan-
al revival,   ger of radical socialism did not cause great alarm.
1906–14   Against foreign dangers France was protected
not only by the Russian alliance but also by the *entente* with
Great Britain (1904) and a growing friendship with Italy.
All commentators on the Third Republic have stressed the
new hope and vigor in the national life in contrast with the
discouragement of earlier years.   Though the radical parties
were in the saddle, they believed as much as their reactionary critics in ample preparedness.   In 1913 the term of

military service, reduced to two years in 1905, was again increased to three.   Throughout the World War France was ruled by the most radical Chamber of Deputies that had ever been elected, yet neither in patriotic spirit nor in the assertion of authority did the Third Republic prove weaker than Napoleonic Empire or Bourbon monarchy.

CHAPTER VII

OTHER STATES OF WESTERN EUROPE

By 1870 nearly all parts of western Europe were organized on lines of national sentiment.   Even countries such as

Western Europe the home of nationalism and democracy

Switzerland and Belgium which had more than one native language showed little or no desire to change their status.   A few nationalist malad-justments remained — Alsace-Lorraine, Ireland, Norway and perhaps the Catalan provinces of Spain — but they could not be compared in number or urgency with the national problems which disrupted Turkey in 1878 and 1912, Russia in 1917 and Austria-Hungary in 1918.   Much as the numerous states to the south, west and north of Europe's central core, the German Empire, differed in size, strength, language, race and religion, they had all been affected to a greater or less degree by the democratic trend of the times.   All had constitutional governments and most of them had parliamentary responsibility as well, but usually after the French rather than the British model — ministries resting insecurely on a coalition of numerous party factions rather than on a stable and disciplined party majority.   In outward form, however, most were monarchical, and the wide choice of ministers which the instability of parties made possible gave the western continental monarchs a freer hand than the British King, though less independent power than the rulers of Russia, Austria-Hungary or Germany.

ITALY AND THE PAPACY

Next in importance to France and Britain among the states of western Europe, Italy ranked as one of the Great

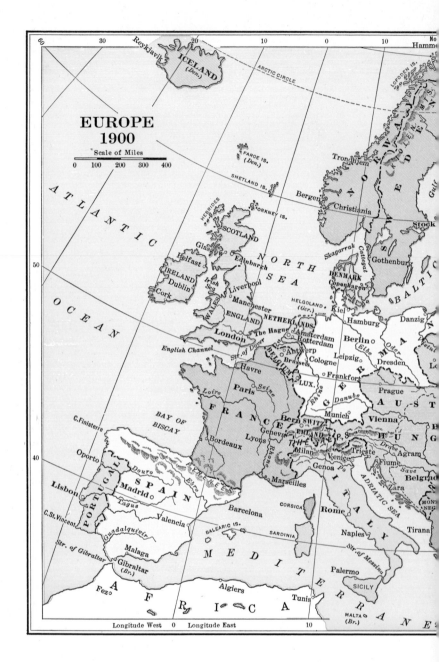

EUROPE
1900

"Scale of Miles
0   100   200   300   400

ATLANTIC

OCEAN

ICELAND
(Den.)

ARCTIC CIRCLE

Reykjavik

FAROE IS.
(Den.)

SHETLAND IS.

HEBRIDES

ORKNEY IS.

SCOTLAND

Glasgow
Belfast   Edinburgh
IRELAND
Dublin
Cork   Irish Sea
Manchester
WALES   Liverpool
ENGLAND
London   The Hague
English Channel   Str. of Dover
Havre
Paris   Seine
FRANCE
Bordeaux
Loire

BAY OF
BISCAY

C. Finisterre

Oporto
PORTUGAL   Douro
SPAIN
Lisbon   Madrid
Tagus
C. St. Vincent   Guadalquivir   Valencia
Malaga   BALEARIC IS.
Str. of Gibraltar   Gibraltar
(Br.)
Fez   Algiers

A   F   R   I   C   A

NORTH
SEA

NORWAY

SWEDEN

Trondhjem

Bergen
Christiania

Skagerrak   Cattegat   Gothenburg
Stock
BALTIC

DENMARK
Copenhagen
HELGOLAND
(Ger.)   Kiel
Hamburg   Danzig
NETHERLANDS
Amsterdam   Berlin
Rotterdam   GERMANY
Antwerp   Cologne   Leipzig   Dresden   Lo
BELGIUM   Brussels
LUX.   Frankfort
Rhine   Elbe
Danube   Prague
SWITZ.   Munich   Vienna   AUST
Bern   Geneva   Trieste   HUNG
ITALY   Milan   Venice   Agram   G
Rhone   Po   Fiume   Belgrad
Lyons   Genoa   Zara   MONT-
Marseilles   ADRIATIC SEA   NEG
CORSICA   Rome   Tirana
Barcelona
SARDINIA   Naples
MEDITERRANEAN
Str. of Messina
Palermo
SICILY
Tunis
MALTA
(Br.)

Longitude West   0   Longitude East   10

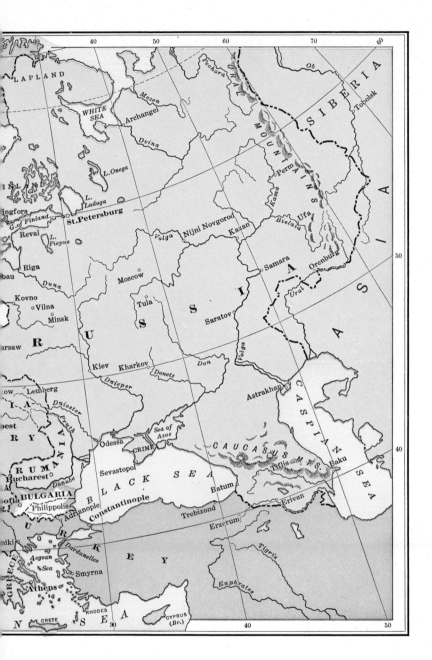

Powers. Her population, military and naval establishment, historic greatness and powerful alliances enabled Italy to play the rôle in the face of serious economic handicaps. Though dowered with every variety of natural beauty, Italy was far *Italy and her economic limitations* inferior to such countries as Britain, France, Germany and the United States in mineral wealth; inferior also to France, Austria-Hungary and Russia in extent of agricultural lowland. Italy was perhaps the only European nation after 1870 which really had a "surplus population" which could not be supported either by farming or manufacture. The natural result, since the birth rate remained high, was the annual emigration of hundreds of thousands of sturdy south Italian peasants to new homes in the United States or the temperate parts of South America.

Poverty was thus the greatest handicap of the newly united monarchy. It was aggravated by the decision of the government to build a strong army and navy, embark on a colonial policy in Africa, and conduct an extensive program of internal improvements, all of which required heavy taxation. *Progressive north and backward south* The whole peninsula was forced to live up to the pace set by the energetic Piedmontese who had secured its unity. When the Kingdom of the Two Sicilies (Sicily and the mainland around Naples) was added to Italy in 1860 the nation acquired a beautiful and historic region but also a serious problem. In southern Italy there were arrears of centuries of misgovernment to make good. The overcrowded land was held by great landlords and farmed in primitive fashion. Illiteracy was the rule and not the exception. Crimes of violence, brigandage and private revenge were not only common but in many cases sanctioned by public opinion. Misrule and oppression had taught the people to look on every outlaw as a potential Robin Hood, and many decades of better government were necessary to weaken that tradition.

The new Italian constitution was merely an extension of the old constitution of the Kingdom of Sardinia (Piedmont), *The Italian government* a parliamentary monarchy after the British fashion, though resembling France in the multiplicity of parties and the centralization of local government in the hands of the national authorities. Federal government, as in Germany, might have seemed the more natural constitution for a country so recently welded together from provinces which had for many centuries been sovereign States, but most Italians felt that just on account of these diversities a strong uniform law was necessary to maintain national unity. A Chamber of Deputies represented the people, but until 1882 there was a high property qualification for the franchise and until 1912 a literacy test. A Senate, appointed for life by the King on the advice of his ministers, acted as a slight check on the Chamber, but the latter controlled the ministry and really governed the nation. Thoroughly democratic in form, Italy encountered most of the difficulties of an inexperienced popular government and others, such as the quarrel with the Papacy, peculiar to her own circumstances.

In the language of diplomacy, the chief internal difficulty of the newly united kingdom was the hostility between the *Vatican versus Quirinal* Vatican (the Papal court) and the Quirinal (the royal court). The Pope, regarding the unification of Italy as a mere usurpation, refused to recognize the rule of the King over the former Papal States including the capital at Rome. Pius IX (1836–78), and his successors Leo XIII (1878–1903), Pius X (1903–14) and Benedict XV (1914–22) all refused to accept the offer of compensation made by the Italian government and remained voluntary "prisoners of the Vatican," confining themselves to the walls of the Papal palace. Not till 1929, when a special Concordat between Pope Pius XI and Premier Mussolini ended the seventy years' quarrel begun by the Franco-Austrian War of 1859, was the breach wholly healed. The abstention of many of the more devout Catholics from Italian political life left politics for many years to anti-clericals who were not affected by Papal remonstrances. The "Roman question" also complicated foreign policy. One of the reasons why Italy sought an alliance with Germany was the exaggerated fear that France, Austria or some other Catholic State might challenge the Italian hold on Rome.

The making of Italy was, perhaps, the most romantic chapter in modern history and called to the front some of the most remarkable personalities, men of the type of *Parlia-* Cavour, Mazzini, Garibaldi. Their work once *mentary* completed, the daily routine of parliamentary *doldrums* government presented less dramatic tasks and was carried on by comparatively mediocre men. The government was not, in the main, oppressive or violent. Cavour had left his fatherland a golden legacy in his last advice not to govern by martial law but rather slowly educate the backward provinces into freedom. Yet the average Italian seemed less awake to his responsibilities than the average Frenchman; he took little interest in politics, permitting it to develop into a professional game of party bosses who sometimes staged a sham battle in public and divided the spoils of office in private, much in the manner of the mercenary *condottieri* who fought for Italian cities in the Middle Ages. The politician who most nearly rose to eminence was Francesco Crispi, advocate of the Triple Alliance and colonial imperialism. The failure of the Italian attempt to conquer Abyssinia discredited his ministry and his policy and turned the attention of the government homeward to a rather discouraging picture of poverty, emigration, crushing taxation and revolutionary discontent. In 1900 King Humbert, successor of Victor Emmanuel II, was assassinated by an Italian anarchist.

Affairs went better in the new century. In the north an

important manufacturing district developed around Milan,
National using the "white coal" of water power to supply
recovery the lack of mines. National finances improved.
The philosophical historian Benedetto Croce goes so far as
to depict those years in radiant phrases.[1]

> Italian life after 1900 had overcome the chief obstacles in its
> course, and, confining itself within the channels imposed upon it,
> flowed on for the next ten years and more, rich both in achieve-
> ment and in hope. It was not that Italy entered upon a period
> of felicity, or "golden age," for such times are known neither to
> philosophy nor history.... But, as in the life of the individual
> there are years when a man reaps the fruits of the pains which he
> has endured and the experiences which he has gathered... so it
> is in the life of nations.

A new and somewhat perilous vigor returned to foreign policy.
In 1911 Italy went to war with Turkey over Tripoli (Libya)
and emerged the next year not only with the African colony
but with the Greek-speaking Dodecanese islands as well.
Though the Triple Alliance lasted until the World War, Italy
felt sufficiently free of her obligations to seek close friendship
also with the Triple Entente.

SPAIN AND PORTUGAL

Spain no longer ranked among the Great Powers in 1870
and did not even seek alliances with them. Yet she was the
Revolution innocent cause of the Franco-Prussian War, for
in Spain had not a revolution left vacant the Spanish
throne there could have been no Hohenzollern candidate to
fill it. After the veto of France had precipitated the war
neither Spain nor Prussia renewed the candidacy and the
revolutionary assembly or Cortes offered the throne to
Prince Amadeo of Savoy (1870–73) in the hope of stabilizing
the government and strengthening national ties with Italy.
The experiment was a failure, as Amadeo resigned when experience showed that he could not count on the support of a

[1] B. Croce, *A History of Italy, 1871–1915*, page 214.

united nation. Some wanted to restore the old ruling Bourbon line in the person of Alfonso XII, some to turn back the pages of history to a still older branch of the dynasty (the "Carlist"), some to create a centralized republic like France, some to recognize the principle of provincial home rule ("regionalism") and make a federal republic like the United States.

For almost two years the provisional republic struggled on in the face of growing anarchy and civil war, and at last, as was not uncommon in modern Spanish history, *Spanish* the army stepped in and decided the question *government* for a hesitant nation. Alfonso XII was restored *after 1875* to the throne of his ancestors in 1875 and a constitution drawn up the following year provided for a parliamentary monarchy with a popularly elected Cortes and a conservative Senate, partly appointed, partly elected and partly drawn from the nobility. The Cortes controlled the ministry, at least in form, but in practice parliamentary government became an alternation of Conservative and Liberal ministries sharing the spoils of office in rotation by private agreement. Owing to the ignorance and lack of political experience of the masses elections were "made" by local party bosses and the voters usually returned without question whatever man was nominated. In 1890 universal manhood suffrage was established. The infant King Alfonso XIII succeeded his father in 1886 but did not actually begin to reign until 1902, the Queen mother Maria Christina acting as Regent in the meantime. After Alfonso became King he usually inclined toward the liberal side, but this did not save him from several attempts against his life.

The reasons for the comparative failure of popular government in Spain were rather economic than political. The country much resembles southern Italy: a rugged, mountainous plateau, hot and arid in the interior, sustaining an impoverished and illiterate peasantry with bad political traditions.   Spain had only about half the population of

Economic and social problems of Spain

France or Italy, and even for her size was not a wealthy nation.   Spain had some mineral wealth, but not enough to develop great industries, and her rocky soil was too much monopolized by thriftless landlords.   Yet if conditions in modern Spain be compared with the depths of misery existing in the seventeenth, eighteenth[1] and early nineteenth centuries, there is much reason for encouragement.   Religious freedom was gradually extended and even the political unrest resembled rather the "growing pains" of a young nation than the decadence of an old one.   At least in Catalonia, including the eastern seaport of Barcelona, there was rapid economic progress.   Just because the Catalans were the best educated and most progressive Spaniards they were most insistent on political reforms even at the risk of revolution.   Though neutral in the World War, Spain was afterwards to experience new convulsions which led through dictatorship to another republican experiment.[2]

The close of the nineteenth century witnessed the loss of Spain's colonial empire in the Pacific and in the Caribbean.

Spain's lost colonial empire

A revolution in Cuba evoked sympathy in the United States, the active aid of insurgent volunteers and, finally, official intervention.   The result of the Spanish-American War of 1898 was the independence of Cuba and the transfer of Porto Rico and the Philippines to American rule.   What had been in the sixteenth century the greatest of world empires was finally reduced to a narrow "sphere of influence" in northern Morocco and a few small holdings on the west coast of Africa.   This loss of empire was, however, a probable blessing to Spain, as she needed all her energies and capital for internal improvements, and in later years, at all events, her colonies had been more of a burden than an asset.

[1] Save for a partial revival under the "enlightened despotism" of Charles III.
[2] See below, Chapter XXVIII.

Spain's little neighbor Portugal, a mere coastal fringe of the Hispanic peninsula, is still one of the chief colonial powers of the world, possessing large territories in both *The Portu-* east and west Africa, though they have been of *guese Re-* little profit to the mother country. An old alli- *public* ance with Britain secured Portugal's independent position in the world. In the main, however, the problems of Spain were repeated in Portugal. A population heavily handicapped by poverty, ignorance and political inexperience, was growing increasingly resentful of traditional institutions which seemed only so many barriers to national progress. But the revolutionary movement attained an earlier triumph. King Carlos (1889–1908) lacked the manliness of Alfonso XII and Alfonso XIII; he was disliked as an individual as well as a monarch. In 1908 he and the crown prince were assassinated in the open streets of the capital. His successor Manoel II was too weak to make good the lost prestige of the crown, and in 1910 was driven into inglorious exile. Since that time Portugal has been a republic, alternately democratic and dictatorial, and constantly disturbed by socialistic outbreaks to the "left" and monarchist conspiracies to the "right." The revolution is notable as the only extension of republicanism in Europe between 1875 when Spain returned to monarchy and 1917 when Russia became a republic.

SWITZERLAND

The success of democratic institutions varies directly with the educational standards, economic well-being and political experience of the people among whom they are *Europe's* established. Democracy worked least smoothly *model* under such adverse conditions as existed in *democracy* Portugal; most efficiently, perhaps, in Switzerland. Lord Bryce's opinion that "Democracy is there more truly democratic than in any other country," concisely expressed the opinion of many students of comparative government.

Modern Switzerland has been called one of those happy nations that have no history, and it is true that since 1848 there has been no major internal crisis and that the Swiss have been able to dispense with any foreign policy save a vigilant neutrality. But Swiss political institutions have been studied by foreign historians with exceptional care. The Swiss government may be classed as a parliamentary republic, but it differs in at least three important respects from France. Instead of a single executive head and a partisan ministry, there is a plural executive, a Council of seven members elected by the National Assembly, one of whom bears the title of President though he has little more power than any of his colleagues. Not all legislative power is vested in the two houses of the Assembly, for there is a provision for direct popular legislation through the initiative and referendum. Instead of a centralization of power there is a high degree of local home rule in the states or "cantons" which make up the federation.

The diversity of languages and faiths in Switzerland made the federal form of government a practical necessity. A *The cantons* majority of Swiss speak German as their native tongue, but in the western part of the country French prevails, in the extreme south Italian, and in one canton many speak an old Latin dialect, the "Romansch." The religious division does not even coincide with the linguistic, as some parts of French Switzerland are Protestant and some parts of German Switzerland are Catholic. There is a much greater diversity of local institutions among the Swiss cantons than among the American States. In most of them a legislature is chosen by direct popular vote, but usually even in these cases frequent appeal is made to the voter by the referendum. In a few of the smaller cantons direct democracy is carried to its logical conclusion and there is no legislative body at all except the mass assembly of the voters.

A landlocked country, covered with rugged highland,

without much mineral wealth and with very limited arable lands, Switzerland might have been expected to *Farming the* be an insignificant nation, a Serbia or Bolivia of *Alps, and* western Europe. But the Swiss turned their *the tourists!* very disadvantages to profit. Lacking coal, they turned their waterfalls to the work of manufacture. They placed under cultivation all the land that could be farmed, extending stock-raising to the very edge of the glaciers, and making the Alps themselves productive by systematic development of the tourist industry. Not all visitors to the "playground of Europe" were transient mountaineers; there were large foreign colonies of Germans, Frenchmen, Austrians and Englishmen who had been attracted to the country as permanent residents by the charm of the scenery, the healthful climate or the organized amusements, together with a small sprinkling of political refugees from every revolution-ridden country.

THE NETHERLANDISH NATIONS

In the little lowland corner of Europe between Germany and northern France were three constitutional monarchies of democratic flavor, the Kingdom of the Nether- *Luxemburg* lands, the Kingdom of Belgium and the Grand Duchy of Luxemburg. Luxemburg was a political accident, made into a sovereign state because diplomats could not agree to unite the tiny Duchy with any other neighboring state. After 1867 her neutrality was guaranteed by the powers. Luxemburg belonged to the German customs union (*Zollverein*) until the end of the World War. Smaller than Rhode Island and with less than half its population, Luxemburg was yet important as a strategically located state lying on the borderland of French and German speech and possessing valuable iron deposits. The personal union between Luxemburg and the Kingdom of the Netherlands terminated in 1890.

Belgium was a dynamo in the very center of industrial Europe, the most densely inhabited State of the continent.

Belgium, the "little giant" of Europe Though not a Great Power in the political or military sense, Belgium on the eve of the World War ranked immediately after Germany and France in industrial output, exceeded Italy in foreign trade, led the world in proportion of railway mileage to extent, and sustained a population of more than seven million on an area less than that of Maryland. Even in the Middle Ages the Flemish towns of northern Belgium were known throughout the civilized world for the excellence of their wares, and adequate coal deposits permitted the Belgians to make an easy transition from mastery of handicraft to mastery of machine technology. Like Switzerland, Belgium was without a national language. Northern Belgium speaks Flemish, a tongue akin to Dutch; southern (or "Walloon") Belgium, French. The linguistic frontier cuts the country almost exactly in half and runs close to the capital at Brussels. Both parts of the country are Roman Catholic, which is the chief explanation of their separation from their Protestant Dutch neighbors to the northeast. Parliamentary institutions were established in the Kingdom of Belgium in 1831, immediately after separation from the Netherlands, and the neutrality of the new nation perpetually guaranteed by the powers in 1839.

In 1865 the wise King Leopold I was succeeded by his son Leopold II (1865–1909). Leopold II had many strong *Belgian politics* qualities and even his villainies worked more harm to his own reputation than to the prosperity of his subjects. The wealth which he looted from the Congo Free State [1] he spent lavishly in Belgium; he had an intelligent interest in diplomacy, and though as reactionary as he dared to be in maintaining his royal prerogatives he was too prudent to let matters come to an open issue. His

---

[1] See above, pages 122–124.

successor King Albert (1909–34) is best known for his gallant resistance to German invasion in the World War. All three rulers permitted the peaceful development of constitutional government. After 1893 manhood suffrage existed, but additional votes were given to property owners and the highly educated. Three main political parties contested for power: the Catholic or Clerical group, conservative and attached to the principle of religious instruction in the schools, the middle-class Liberals and the Socialists. One vexing political question that never found completely satisfactory solution was the adjustment of the rival claims of the French and the Flemish languages for public use.

The Kingdom of the Netherlands,[1] the successor of the Dutch Republic which in the seventeenth century rivaled England as the foremost commercial and naval power in the world and inflicted signal defeats in turn on British, French and Spaniards, had *The Kingdom of the Netherlands* ceased long before 1870 to rank among the Great Powers. Yet it would be misleading to speak of a "decline" of the Netherlands in the sense in which we can speak of a decline of Spain in the seventeenth century or of Poland in the eighteenth. Though outstripped by larger nations in the race for political power, the Dutch retained most of their commercial wealth and still ranked high among the world's shippers. The Dutch colonial empire in the East Indies was more populous and prosperous than it had been in the days when the ships of the Republic monopolized the spice trade and roused the envy of every other European nation. Within their own country the Dutch continued their old policy of reconquering lands from the shallow seas that encroached upon them; building dykes, draining swamps,

---

[1] Often called "Holland" after the most important province, just as we frequently say "England" for brevity when "Great Britain," "The United Kingdom of Great Britain and Ireland," or even the "British Empire" would be more accurate. Convenience will always win the popular preference over accuracy.

constructing canals, establishing farms and even cities below sea-level.

Even as a Republic, the Netherlands had usually been governed by the descendants of William of Orange who first *Dutch* liberated the country from Spanish rule, and the *politics* transformation of the Republic into a Kingdom in 1814 did little more than give formal recognition to an established political tradition. But among the Dutch, as among their close kindred the English, constitutional liberty came much earlier than democracy. The aristocracy of wealthy merchants held to power as stubbornly as the English landlords, and several successive reforms, in 1848, 1887, 1896 and 1917 were required to make the franchise universal for the States General or national parliament. The individual provinces enjoyed a wide measure of home rule, perhaps not so much as a "sovereign" Swiss canton but more than a French department, as each had its local legislature. The long tradition of political liberty made parliamentary government workable in spite of the sub-division of parties into various groups, conservative (both Protestant and Catholic), liberal or socialistic. As in Belgium, the major political issues were colonial administration, the extension of the franchise, and the extent to which religious instruction should be fostered in the schools.

All three netherlandish nations found the great commercial advantage of a location between France and Germany *Military* partly offset by the military risk. In spite of *problems of* solemn pledges to the contrary, Germany in-*the nether-* vaded both Belgium and Luxemburg in 1914. *landish* The Netherlands and Belgium had to spend *monarchies* large sums in building forts and maintaining armies to protect their independence. The Dutch had been much alarmed when Queen Wilhelmina (succeeding William III in 1890) married a German prince lest dynastic forces draw them into the orbit of mighty Germany, but the World War, though it brought many embarrassing problems, did not force them to face a foreign invasion. This was partly because the Netherlands, unlike Belgium and Luxemburg, lay a little off the direct line from the German frontier to Paris,[1] and partly because the Dutch possessed in their easily flooded lowlands a natural safeguard almost as effective as the Swiss enjoyed in their Alpine highlands.

THE SCANDINAVIAN NATIONS

In Europe's far north the three Scandinavian nations formed a distinct sub-type of European civilization. Swedes, Danes and Norwegians were alike of the blond north European race, commonly called "Nordic." They spoke closely related Teutonic languages, *Scandinavian civilization* and were with but few exceptions Lutheran Protestants in religion. Although the Scandinavians retained the forms of monarchy they developed a very high degree of democracy, a democracy the more secure since it rested not alone on political forms but on universal education and a wide distribution of property as well. In one respect the Scandinavian countries carried democracy farther than even the republics of France and Switzerland. Norway before the World War, Denmark and Sweden immediately afterwards, admitted women to full parliamentary suffrage. Legislation in all three countries has been strongly "feminist," favoring the fullest civil rights for women. The Scandinavian countries no longer have the political importance which they enjoyed in earlier centuries when it was still possible for a small nation to be a "Great Power," but their standard of living is higher than in the days of their greatness.

Though Denmark profited indirectly from the World War by recovering northern Schleswig, none of the Scandinavian

---

[1] An earlier plan of the German General Staff than the one adopted in 1914 provided for an invasion of France by way of the Netherlands as well as Belgium and Luxemburg.

nations participated in the World War. The common need
Separatist for neutrality bound them together more closely
tendencies than their common civilization had bound them
in the days of peace, for the Norwegians, Swedes and Danes
have preferred national independence to the advantages of
political union. In fact, the tendency has been away from
union, as is shown by the separation of Norway from Sweden
and in the home rule movement in Denmark's dependency
of Iceland. Since the war, indeed, we can speak of five
Scandinavian countries, as Finland (mainly Swedish in culture though not in race) has become independent of Russia,
and Iceland independent in all but name of Denmark.

The Kingdom of Sweden and Norway was one of the more
durable of the anti-national political experiments of the
Congress of Vienna. The same dynasty ruled in
The King- both countries, but each country retained a
dom of Swe- separate parliament. The Norwegian parliament
den and or *Storthing* was the more democratic of the two,
Norway as Sweden had a powerful class of nobles which was practically non-existent in Norway. But the unequal progress
which democracy had made in the two parts of the realm was
not the main cause of separation. The real issue was Norwegian nationalism. Though Norway had been joined to
Denmark for centuries before being handed over to Sweden,
the people still cherished memories of Norwegian independence in the Middle Ages, and refused to consider themselves
either Danes or Swedes. During the nineteenth century
they developed a vigorous national literature which intensified their feeling of individuality, even to the point of creating
a separate national tongue (the "Landsmaal") out of a synthesis of peasant dialects, the literary language being considered "too Danish." They felt that Sweden as the preponderant partner in the union was keeping Norway in a
subordinate position, very much as the Belgians felt toward
the Dutch from 1814 to 1830, the Scotch toward the English

in the eighteenth century,[1] the Hungarians toward the Austrians after 1867. "When two ride on the same horse, one rides behind." They demanded a flag of their own and a separate consular service.

King Oscar II (1872–1907) felt that he dared not grant separate consular representation to Norway, as one nation could not carry on a double foreign policy. In 1905 the *Storthing* declared the union dissolved and a subsequent popular referendum over-whelmingly favored independence. Many of the leading *Norwegian independence* Norwegian nationalists were republicans as well, but Norway needed recognition by her monarchical neighbors and therefore agreed to accept a Danish prince who ruled under the title of King Haakon VII. In 1907 the neighboring powers signed a treaty guaranteeing Norwegian independence. Norway has been called the most democratic monarchy in the world. Under the union manhood suffrage had been established, and in the days of independence the vote was extended to women also, in 1907 to taxpayers, in 1913 to all women alike.

Sweden with a magnanimous spirit rarely shown in history acquiesced without war in Norwegian independence and the two nations agreed to leave unfortified their common frontier. In 1909 manhood suffrage *Sweden since the separation* was granted, after the war woman suffrage as well. Sweden became a political democracy, but King Gustavus V, who succeeded Oscar II in 1907, was not content to withdraw altogether from politics. Shortly before the outbreak of the World War, Sweden was swept with panic lest Russia should follow up her absorption of the Grand Duchy of Finland, a country which had once belonged to Sweden and still had many Swedish-speaking in-

---

[1] The more obvious parallel of Ireland would overstate the case; the Irish till 1922 had no national recognition and felt themselves a mere "conquered province." The same may be said of Hungary before 1867.

habitants, by a direct blow at Scandinavia. King Gustavus threw his influence to the parties which supported increased military preparedness and his view triumphed in the elections. This fear of invasion accounts in great measure for the alleged pro-German, but more accurately anti-Russian, sympathy of many Swedes during the war.

Denmark, successively shorn of Norway by the Congress of Vienna and of Schleswig-Holstein by Bismarck, was much diminished from her former political importance. *Denmark, the land of the small farmer* Unlike Norway and Sweden she had a colonial empire, but not one of much value. Iceland, Greenland and the Faroes were little more than fishing grounds to the mother country, and the Virgin Islands in the West Indies, sold to the United States in 1917, ranked among the lesser groups of the Caribbean. Denmark's task was to find in freedom and prosperity a substitute for past greatness. A majority of the Danes lived in the country and farming was the leading national industry. Most of the farms were very small, about half of them being mere market gardens of a dozen acres or less, but intensive cultivation rendered them highly profitable. Probably no country in the world had a more successful dairy industry, paid more attention to the scientific education of the farmers, or more fully took advantage of co-operative methods of marketing produce. All Scandinavian countries had a high educational standard, and Denmark was particularly famous for an excellent system of "People's High Schools" established for adult education of the peasantry.

Denmark was, however, slow in developing political institutions to match her democratic national life. Up to the *Democracy in Denmark and Iceland* middle of the nineteenth century Denmark remained an absolute monarchy, in sharp contrast with Sweden which had at all periods of her national history enjoyed some measure of representative government. After a constitution had been granted in 1849

difficulties arising over the Schleswig-Holstein question delayed the inauguration of parliamentary government for
many years. Even when Prussia removed this difficulty by
the simple expedient of conquest, King Christian IX (1863–
1906) refused to yield control over the ministry and the military budget to the popularly elected branch of parliament
(the *Folkething*), fearing that the Radical Party would diminish the army below the limit of safety and thus invite attack from Germany or Russia. With the new century
Christian IX and his successors Frederick VIII (1906–12)
and Christian X (1912–   ) gave up the struggle against the
rising tide of democracy and made no attempt to revive
personal rule. At the end of the World War Iceland, already enjoying a considerable degree of home rule, was
granted complete independence save for the fact that the
King of Denmark is also by law King of Iceland. Iceland
may be called a Danish "Dominion" in the British sense.
Though Iceland has barely a hundred thousand inhabitants,
there is no more interesting country. For over a thousand
years the Icelanders have preserved an ancient Norse speech
and a remarkable literary tradition. To a unique degree
they have combined the primitive simplicity of their Viking
ancestors with the highest culture of modern Europe.

A brief study of modern Europe must needs concentrate
on the larger and more politically active nations. Nevertheless, one charm of Europe to the visitor is the   *Small-state*
life of the lesser states. The world is the richer   *culture*
for the fact that Portugal is not quite Spain, that Norway
is both like and unlike Sweden, that the Netherlands is not
a part of Germany, that Belgium is not a mere group of
French departments. There is even a certain pleasing individuality about nations on the "comic-opera" scale, such
as Andorra, a republic poised on the Pyrenees between
France and Spain; Monaco, on the Mediterranean, a principality only too well known as the site of "Monte Carlo";

CHAPTER VIII

RIVAL EMPIRES OF EASTERN EUROPE

EASTERN EUROPE consists of three main regions, the vast Russo-Polish plain which narrows to the north German low-land in the west and rises to the Ural mountains *Lands of* on the Asiatic frontier; the plains of the Danube *the "Old* basin within the Carpathian wall; the rugged *Régime"* Balkan highland. The Balkan area, as we have seen, broke in the nineteenth century into national fragments liberated from the alien power of the Ottoman Turks. The great plains north and south of the Carpathians were divided among the Russian, Austro-Hungarian and German Empires, the three Great Powers in which monarchical authority had not yet succumbed to liberalism and parliamentary democracy. "Europe," said the French historian, Charles Seignobos, "was thus divided between two political orders, founded on two social orders — in fact, into two different worlds between which the Elbe was approximately the boundary." Germany, as befitted the central state of Europe, was neither wholly of the old nor of the new; her industry and culture were Western but she submitted in political matters to the leadership of the "East-Elbe Junkers," the landed aristocrats of eastern Prussia. Nationalism as well as democracy was less fully realized in eastern than in western Europe. Austria-Hungary and Russia contained an even greater variety of nationalities than all western Europe, but they were artificially held together by the bureaucratic machinery of the central government. Once the governments were shaken by war, the two Empires fell apart into their national units.

AUSTRIA-HUNGARY

Austria-Hungary was a relic of the old dynastic.Europe as it used to be before the French Revolution "nationalized" *The Dual* the nations. Alone among the Great Powers of *Monarchy* the world, Austria-Hungary had no one dominant nationality. Germany, Russia and Turkey had their national minorities, but they were only minorities; everyone knew that a German was not a Pole, a Russian was not a Lithuanian, a Turk was not an Armenian. But the word "Austrian" no more called to mind a single national type than the word "European." Like Switzerland, though on a larger scale, the country was a mosaic of racial and linguistic units. The ruling dynasty was German and the court at Vienna, the center of political and social life, German also. But the government, after a brief period of repression from 1849 to 1866, had abandoned any attempt to stamp a German character on the polyglot population of the Empire. Rather was it the policy of the Viennese court to preserve a balance of power among the peoples of the Empire, favoring those which seemed harmless and repressing those threatening to become dangerous.

One nationality, the Magyars of Hungary, even enjoyed a position of legal equality with the Germans of Austria. *Government* Austria and Hungary had separate constitutions *under the* and parliaments. Their relations to each other *Ausgleich* were regulated by the constitutional arrangement — the *Ausgleich* — of 1867. In addition to the unity afforded by the crown of the Emperor of Austria who was also King of Hungary, there was a common ministry for foreign affairs, the army and finance. Tariff and financial agreements were made on a ten-year basis, a most unsatisfactory arrangement since it led to prolonged negotiations and the chance of a national crisis every decade. There was no common parliament, but equal delegations chosen by the legislative bodies of Austria and of Hungary discussed and

regulated affairs of common interest. Bosnia and Herzegovina, occupied by Austro-Hungarian forces in 1878 and
formally annexed in 1908, were administered under the
joint control of Austria and Hungary.

The Austrian lands curved around the solid mass of the
Kingdom of Hungary like a hand grasping a ball. Both
countries lacked national unity; Austria lacked *The Aus-*
even geographical unity. Her seventeen prov- *trian lands*
inces, which did not at all correspond to the real national
units of the country, enjoyed a considerable measure of home
rule. The most numerous of these national units was the
German, yet of more than 28,000,000 Austrians at the opening of the World War only 9,000,000 were Germans. By
favor of the court and by their wealth, energy *Germans*
and culture, they played a part in Austrian life
greater than their numerical strength would warrant, yet so
far were they from being able to Germanize Austria — to
make no mention of Hungary — that some extreme nationalists favored severing connection with their non-Teutonic
compatriots and entering the German Empire to save what
was still German from being submerged by other nationalities.

Next in importance were the Czechs of Bohemia and Moravia, some 6,000,000 in number, a Slavic people who looked
back to an ancient independence and demanded *The Slavic*
as a minimum concession a position of home rule *nationalities*
equal to that won by the Hungarians. The Czechs, who
occupied the quadrilateral plateau of Bohemia, were particularly prosperous and, alone among the Slavic peoples,
equaled the Germans in educational standards. In the
province of Galicia beyond the Carpathian wall dwelt two
other peoples, a dominant Polish element and a much submerged Ruthenian group. The Ruthenians were a branch
of the Ukrainians or Little Russians who lived in southwestern Russia. The southern branch of the Slavs, the

so-called Yugoslavs, were represented in Austria by the three nationalities, Slovene, Croatian and Serb, and the two latter were found in Hungary and Bosnia as well. Apart *Latins and* from the Germans and the Slavs, there were *others* Italians among the mountains of southern Tirol and in the ports along the Adriatic coast, a few Rumanians in Bukovina to the east of Galicia, and a large number of the two wandering nationalities of eastern Europe, the Jews and the Gypsies.

The political life of Austria was colored throughout by the problem of nationality. Many political parties were *Austrian* organized on national lines; others represented a *politics* double sectioning of nationality and opinion, such as German Liberals, "Old" or "Young" Czechs (conservative and liberal), and the like. The national feuds stifled democracy in the cradle. The Austrian constitution was not illiberal, particularly after successive extensions of the franchise in 1873, 1896 and 1907 had made elections direct and given an equal vote to men over twenty-four. The aged Emperor Francis Joseph (1848–1916), though reactionary, especially in the early days of his reign when he stood as the main obstacle to both German and Italian national unity, came in his later years to a more conciliatory temper and preferred compromise to repression as a means of government. Parliamentary government might well have developed had it been possible for the nationalities to work together. Even the Slavs, could they have united on a common program, might have controlled the Austrian half of the Dual Monarchy. But time after time parliamentary procedure broke down in a deadlock and sometimes in actual rioting. The Austrian lower house or *Reichsrat* was probably the most disorderly legislative body in Europe; the German and Czech delegates in particular carrying their national feud to the floor of the house, and many sessions ended in storms of mutual recrimination followed by scenes of personal violence. Absolutism profited by this paralysis of constitutional government. The Emperor and his ministers allied with any racial groups which would give them a working majority for necessary legislation, and when no majority could by any means be obtained they fell back on "exceptional laws," "emergency decrees" and other extra-parliamentary devices.

Hungary was quite as much divided as Austria among contending nationalities, but enjoyed two important advantages over the senior partner in the Dual *The Hunga-* Monarchy. Geographically Hungary was fairly *rian lands* compact, lying within the Carpathian wall and occupying the central plain of the Danube; a country, at all events, if not a nation. Hungary also had a dominant nationality which maintained its ascendancy more successfully than did the Germans in Austria. The Magyars or "true Hungarians" were a people of Asiatic origin, though mainly of European physical type, remotely allied by language to the Finns and Turks but not at all to either the Germans or the Slavs. In former times they had suffered much oppression from the Austrian Habsburgs and in 1849 made a brave though unsuccessful effort to erect an independent national republic. Most of the Magyar population was *Magyars,* compactly grouped on the Danubian plain. *Slavs, Lat-* Around this Magyar core were alien nationali- *ins, etc.* ties: Slovaks, akin to the Czechs, in the north along the Carpathians; Yugoslavs, both Croatian and Serb, in the south; Ruthenians and Rumanians in the east; Germans along the Austrian frontier on the west; Italians in Fiume on the Adriatic; Jews in the towns, Gypsies in the countryside. Sometimes these nationalities were strangely mixed, as in Transylvania, where embedded in the heart of a large Rumanian population was an isolated group of Magyars (the "Szeklers") and another of Germans (called "Saxons"). In all there were on the eve of the war some ten million

Magyars, rather less than half the population of Hungary even if the Magyar-speaking Jews be counted as of Magyar nationality.

Hungarian politics, like Austrian, was a mere by-product of national rivalry, but the racial conflict was more success- *Hungarian* fully kept out of parliament. Hungary was at *politics* once more parliamentary and less democratic than Austria. More parliamentary, because the Magyars held a large majority in both chambers of their legislature and were often able to organize sufficient party support for the ministry; less democratic because this result was obtained by a narrow franchise, excluding three fourths of the male population from the vote. No effort was spared to keep the Rumanians and Slovaks out of parliament. Every known form of chicanery and intimidation was practiced in turn and so successfully that in 1910 out of 413 deputies to the lower house only eight were non-Magyars. Partial home rule was granted, it is true, to Croatia-Slavonia, a Slavic province in southern Hungary, but the paper liberties of the province were often suspended because of disputes between the native Yugoslavs and their Magyar rulers. The real political conflict in Hungary was not between the parties but between the enfranchised dominant Magyar nationality (though some of the poorer Magyars failed to attain the property qualification for the suffrage) and the practically disfranchised non-Magyars.

Even the Magyars had their differences, however. The old liberal followers of Francis Déak were content with the *Ausgleich* of 1867, though refusing to accept anything less, but there was a radical minority which held that Hungary had not obtained from Austria all that should have been demanded. In particular they objected to the use of German in the army as the "word of command" and insisted that Hungarian regiments be addressed in Magyar. Against this demand Francis Joseph cleverly countered with the threat of universal suffrage, a demand which struck terror to the Magyar oligarchs as it would mean some two hundred Slavic or Rumanian deputies in parliament and an end to all attempts to "Magyarize" the whole of Hungary. Up to the outbreak of war Hungary toyed with various plans of electoral reform but dared not open the floodgates of national rivalry by any really fundamental or democratic measure.

Owing to the explosive forces within the Dual Monarchy, Francis Joseph and his ministers were practically forced to adopt a policy at once reactionary and oppor- *Dualism* tunist; reactionary, because any change, even *versus* in the direction of progress, might upset the *federalism* delicate balance of power which preserved the monarchy; opportunist, because to carry through any policy whatever to its logical extreme might have the same effect. To Germanize Austria-Hungary, when the German element was scarcely a quarter of the whole population and less than a half even of Austria's, was out of the question; to reconstruct the whole realm on a federal basis, like that of Switzerland, theoretically the best solution, met with too much opposition from "vested interests," especially of the German magnates in Bohemia, the Magyars in Hungary and the Poles in Galicia. One plan was endlessly discussed, "trialism" or the transformation of the Dual Monarchy into a triune state in which the Slavs, or at all events the Czechs and Poles, would hold equal place with the Germans and the Magyars. But there were many practical difficulties. The joining of even two national states under separate governments and a common crown is attended with difficulties and apt to lead to agitation for complete separation,[1] to attempt it with three might lead to an administrative breakdown. Moreover the Magyars refused to consider for a moment the loss of any part of their "thousand year old realm" of Hungary. When Francis Ferdinand, heir to the throne, seemed to

[1] As witness Sweden and Norway.

favor trialism, he roused against himself the implacable hostility of the Magyars and equally the hostility of their enemies the Serbs, who feared that independent Serbia might be forced inside the projected German-Magyar-Slavic empire. The easiest plan was to postpone a final solution from generation to generation and trust everything to chance or providence.

The national question dominated the foreign as well as the internal politics of Austria-Hungary. One main weakness of the state lay in the fact that national minorities in many cases were close to the frontier of other fellow nationals. Just beyond the border of Italy lay the "unredeemed Italy" of Trieste and the Trentino (southern Tirol); close against Serbia were the Serbs of Bosnia; the Rumanians of Transylvania were doubly insurgent because oppressed at home and because they could look across a frontier to the independent Kingdom of Rumania; the Poles of Galicia were separated by an imaginary line from the Poles of Russia. The diplomacy of Austria-Hungary devoted itself to maintaining a close alliance with Germany and Italy, so that there might be no official encouragement given to propaganda for separating the Italian districts from Austria or for merging Austria in the German Empire; to weakening the power of Russia, so that Russian imperialists could not plan the annexation of the Slavic provinces of Galicia and Bohemia; and to keeping the Christian kingdoms of southeastern Europe weak and divided, so that Serbia might not hope for Bosnia nor Rumania plot to gain Transylvania. Each progressive step of the Balkan nations seemed to the Austrian government a fresh menace to its security. For this reason, Austria-Hungary favored the Turkish cause at the Congress of Berlin in 1878, viewed with disfavor the victory of the allies in Balkan Wars of 1912–13, and resolved at any cost, even that of a general European

Influence of the national question on Austro-Hungarian foreign policy

war, to crush Serbia before that kingdom waxed strong enough to sever the Yugoslav provinces (Serb, Croat and Slovene) from the Empire.

THE RUSSIAN EMPIRE

Of European countries Russia stood easily first in area, population and resources. Nearly half of the continent, and perhaps rather more than half of the arable low- *The Rus-* land, owned obedience to the Tsar, and his do- *sian colos-* main did not stop at Urals but continued across *sus* Asia to the Pacific, comprising altogether more than a seventh of the land surface of the globe and almost thrice the area of the continental United States. To be sure, much of this land was too cold or arid for settlement, but between the frozen tundras (marshes) of the Arctic plain and the Steppes (grassy prairies) of central Asia lay a broad belt of forest land and farming country capable of almost unlimited development. Russia possessed the widest grain fields in Europe, produced the greater part of the world's flax, and ranked (including Finland) first in the timber trade. Some of the world's richest petroleum deposits were found near the Caspian Sea. Mining was of some importance, and Russia enjoyed almost a monopoly in the production of platinum, a metal more costly than gold. In spite of the austere climate and an exceptionally high death rate due to popular ignorance of medicine, the Russian population increased with unrivaled rapidity. The census of 1897 placed it at 128,000,000, and by 1914 it was unofficially estimated at 170,000,000.

Russia should have been the most formidable of the Great Powers, and in the nineteenth century many thought that she was. We have seen with what anxious — *and its* trepidation so bold a statesman as Bismarck *feet of clay* labored to keep on as good terms as possible with Russia and how Russia's advance in the Balkans and in central Asia gave British statesmen most of their nightmares. The Russian army was, on paper, the largest in the world and had the greatest reserve of available man power behind it, and until the Japanese war the Russian navy was usually ranked among the three or four strongest European fleets. A fairly typical judgment was that of an American publicist, who declared "it is evident enough... that among the nations of the Eastern Continent, England and Russia only have a future... we can see everywhere, except in England, America and Russia, signs that the limits of growth are not far off." [1] Few either of the friends or the enemies of Russia realized to how great an extent the natural advantages of the country were nullified by the backwardness of the people and the manifold inefficiencies of the central government.

Many made the mistake of thinking that they saw Russia when they really saw only the shadow of Peter the Great.

Eastern and western aspects of Russian culture   That civilizing barbarian, perhaps the most remarkable sovereign ever born to a throne, had, indeed, imposed a "western" character on the Russian government and on the educated classes. He and the rulers who succeeded him established a centralized national monarchy of the type which prevailed generally in continental Europe of the seventeenth century: an absolute sovereign, surrounded by a polished and fashionable court, ruling through a bureaucratic civil service and relying on a drilled and uniformed professional army. In the eighteenth century a ruler of German birth, Catherine the Great, added an extra polish of western culture to the somewhat crude surface of Peter's modern State. In the nineteenth century Russian authors, though complaining that Russia had contributed nothing to the common stock of civilization, were even then engaged in creating one of the most remarkable of modern literatures. But the cosmopolitan culture

---

[1] W. D. Foulke, *Slav or Saxon?* (1897), page 4. In Rudyard Kipling's nineteenth-century stories and poems the "next war" is almost invariably assumed to be one between Russia and Great Britain.

RACES IN
CENTRAL AND EASTERN EUROPE
1914

TEUTONIC

Italian
Rumanian

Turks
Magyars
GREEKS
ALBANIANS

Russians
Poles
Ukrainians or Ruthenians
Czechs & Slovaks

Slovenes
Croats & Serbs
Bulgars

of a small class of educated Russians only threw into darker contrast the isolation of the Russian masses from European civilization. A majority of the people could not read or write. They farmed their lands by primitive methods disused in western Europe for centuries. Famines occurred, not merely as the result of some devastating war or extraordinary natural calamity, but recurrent whenever the land was visited by floods or drouth. The average standard of living in rural Russia was about that prevailing in the river valleys of India and China.

Russia was handicapped also, though not so greatly as Austria-Hungary, by lack of national unity. The Russians, a Slavic people, formed nearly two thirds of the population of the Empire. Three dialects of *"All the Russias"* Russian must, however, be distinguished: Great Russian, the literary language of the nation and the speech of the Muscovite "kernel" of the whole Empire, White Russian, spoken by a few million dwellers in the fenlands of western central Russia, and Little Russian (also known as Ukrainian and Ruthenian), spoken by the peasants of the south. The non-Russian peoples of the Empire may be grouped into two classes: those from whom the Russians might learn civilization, and those to whom Russia transmitted civilization. The former group included the Poles, Finns, Estonians, Letts, Lithuanians and Jews, who all compared favorably with the Muscovites from the standpoint of economic, educational and political development. On the other hand, the Tatar and Turkish tribesmen of southeastern Russia and central Asia, the isolated fragments of Mongolian and Tungusic peoples in northeastern Russia and Siberia, and many other waifs and strays of nomadic barbarism were undoubtedly raised to a higher level of civilization by being absorbed into the Empire. The Russians are among the great pioneering peoples of the earth, flinging out an advance guard of "rough rider" Cossack herdsmen, followed by priests,

officials and tough, stolid peasants born to conquer the wilderness. They fraternized readily with the natives and soon
succeeded in impressing a Russian character on all peoples
with whom they mingled except where they encountered
a civilization higher than their own.

Down to the revolution of 1905 Russia was an absolute
monarchy without a parliament and without a constitution.
The The Tsar, Autocrat of All the Russias, was the
Tsardom sole lawgiver and supreme executive of his realm.
The only limits to his power were the possible weakness of
his own will and the sullen inertia of his officials, who sometimes nullified the best intended reforms by leaving them so
far unexecuted as they dared. These officials (the *tchinov-
niks*) formed a vast administrative machine, largely as-
similated to the hereditary nobility, who governed the country in much the same way that the class of officers govern
an army, except that few armies have been so little efficient.
The personality of the Tsar was obviously of the greatest
moment to Russia, and here again, as in almost all respects,
Russia was unfortunate. The nineteenth-century rulers
were patriotic in intention but none of them measured up
to the difficulties of the time. Some were resolute reactionaries, such as Nicholas I and Alexander III, and others
vacillating and inconstant progressives, such as the first and
second Alexander.

Alexander II (1855–81) aroused brighter hopes, perhaps,
than the wisest statesman could have fully satisfied. His
Reforms of predecessor, Nicholas I, had crushed the liber-
Alexander II ties of the Kingdom of Poland with an iron
hand, discouraged Russian reformers by imprisonment and
exile, and pursued an adventurous foreign policy culminating in the disaster of the Crimean War. Almost any
successor would have been a welcome change, and the young
Alexander began his reign most auspiciously. The greatest
economic and social evil of Russia was serfdom, which lin-

gered in Russia for generations after it had been abolished in other European countries, even the most autocratic.[1] By a series of decrees he freed the serfs, first on royal and princely estates and then on the estates of the nobles. The decree of 1861 alone liberated some 23,000,000 human beings from bondage and was probably the greatest single act of emancipation in human history. In 1864 the Tsar created a system of district and provincial councils (*zemstvos*), not to share the legislative authority but to aid him in the work of local administration. He also reorganized the courts and introduced trial by jury in certain criminal cases.

The Polish rebellion of 1863 discouraged the Tsar who concluded, as so many reformers have done, that he who sows benefits reaps only ingratitude. The latter part of his reign was marked by fewer reforms and by some backward steps. He diminished the power of the *zemstvos* and initiated many arbitrary arrests and prosecutions for political offenses. Like more than one of his predecessors, Alexander had considered the establishment of a constitution and a representative body, but, again like them, he never found the propitious moment to translate his dreams into action. In 1881, after prolonged hesitation, he concluded to make a beginning of representative government, but on March 13th the last of many attempts to assassinate him succeeded and left his work of reform unfinished. As is usually the case with political assassinations, the murderers had done more harm to their own cause than to their foes'. The autocracy was in no wise shaken by the death of the autocrat, and the new Tsar Alexander III (1881–94) abandoned all idea of constitutional reform and turned with brutal energy to the work of repression.

The "Tsar Liberator" turns reactionary and is assassinated

[1] It disappeared first in England of the principal European countries, from local economic causes rather than legal enactment, in the fourteenth and fifteenth centuries; France abolished its last relics in 1789, Prussia in 1810.

The history of Russia from the accession of Tsar Nicholas
I (1825–55) to the present time must be written in terms of
Springs of   revolution. Russia was perhaps the only modern
revolution   country in which it was almost impossible to be
in Russia   a thinker — an "intellectual" as the phrase went
— and not be a revolutionist. In Germany autocratic
government has always had able apologists, the older British
universities have usually been conservative, in France, while
many authors have been radicals, others have boasted of
aloofness from politics and devotion to "art for the very
sake of art," but the Russian government was forced to
treat every university and almost every school as a potential
hotbed of revolution, and the great majority of Russian
writers, however diverse their remedies, were at one in the
belief that the existing régime was hopelessly diseased.
There were three main sources of revolutionary sentiment,
the discontented minor nationalities, the land-seeking peasants, and such "intellectuals" as were willing to face the
risks of opposing openly the powers that be. To these may
be added, but hardly before the twentieth century, a fourth
radical element, the class-conscious urban workingman who
had been reached by the propaganda of Marxian socialism.

Not every nationality constitutes a national problem and
not every national problem is equally acute. The White
Discontent   Russians of the west, for example, hardly felt
of the na-   themselves to be a separate nationality, the
tional mi-   Ukrainians or Little Russians were divided in sen-
norities   timent, but the Poles were almost unanimously
resentful towards Russian rule. The Finns and Swedes in the
Grand Duchy of Finland enjoyed a certain measure of home
rule and were long the only people in the Empire to have
parliamentary institutions; for that very reason they were
the more watchfully jealous of Russian encroachments on
their ancient freedom. There was some discontent among
the Estonians, Letts, Lithuanians, Baltic Germans, Ru-

manians of Bessarabia, Georgians and Armenians in the Caucasus, but the most serious problems were those of Poland, Finland and the Jews. The Russian Jew as a rule lived in Poland or the Ukraine, in fact he was debarred from the old territory of Great Russia and permitted only within the "Pale" of Russia's western provinces. He usually spoke a German dialect (Yiddish) and stood apart from his Slavic neighbors in religion and in social customs. As the law forbade him to take up land, rise in the army or civil service, or (except in limited numbers) enter the universities and the professions, he was usually forced to live by finance and retail trade. This made the peasantry hate him as an alien and a usurer and gave rise to frightful race riots.

A typical outbreak of mob violence took place in Kishinev, a Bessarabian city, in 1903. Goaded to fury by an anti-Semitic newspaper the townspeople raided the *The* Jewish quarter and killed or injured hundreds *Kishinev* of Jews. The police and soldiers seem to have *massacre* done nothing to stop the mob; they waited in grim neutrality for the riot to burn itself out. These massacres ("pogroms") were not wholly unwelcome to the authorities who disliked the Jews as a troublesome, alien element and were glad to find a scapegoat for the economic troubles of the time, feeling that the popular fury turned against the Jews might otherwise have been directed against themselves. The view was a short-sighted one. Russia's persecutions alienated foreign sentiment from Russia,[1] especially in Britain, France and the United States, made the Russian Jews revolutionary in sentiment, and accustomed the people

---

[1] This had a very practical side to it. The refusal of the House of Rothschild, a Jewish financial group, to handle Russia's loan of 1891, in consequence of the anti-Semitic policy of the government, almost shipwrecked the negotiations for the Dual Alliance with France; popular British prejudice delayed for years the "entente" between Britain and Russia; American hostility toward the Tsardom was a powerful factor in neutralizing anti-German sentiment during the early part of the World War. In all these cases and many others Jewish resentment abroad played an important part.

to violent mob action, a dangerous lesson for an unpopular government to teach its subjects.

So far as the Russian peasant was revolutionary, the cause was the land question. The peasantry for the most *The* part were docile, obedient, reverent towards *agrarian* "Holy Church" and "their little father, the *problem* Tsar." But land was their livelihood and land they lacked. Alexander II, who was not in close touch with the actual living conditions of the poor, made the pardonable but serious error of supposing that personal liberty was what the serf wanted most, and that the land would without question belong to the nobles as a property right. He accordingly restored to the landlords half their estates and purchased the other half from them. The land so purchased was given to the peasants, but only on condition that they paid back the money in installments to the government. Moreover, in those parts of Russia where the communistic system of managing the land prevailed, the village commune or *mir* became the indebted owner, and the peasant was held responsible not for his personal debt alone but for his share of the community debt. It would probably have been wiser to give each emancipated peasant an outright share of land, free of debt, and large enough to support his family; such a policy would have created in time a class of conservative peasant proprietors such as forms the ballast of modern French society. Alexander III had wisdom enough to see part of the problem and grant a partial cancellation of the indebtedness of the peasantry to the government, but the peasant holdings still remained too small, considering the very primitive agricultural methods prevailing, and land shortage kept a large part of the nation in hungry discontent.

The *intelligentsia* or "intellectuals" of Russia were, we have seen, discontented with existing conditions but not agreed as to the way out of the woods. Some argued that Russia was a backward country which had everything to learn from abroad; that she should go to school to France, Germany, Britain and the United States, as once *Westerners* Peter the Great had learned to build ships in *and* Dutch shipyards and how to win victories over *Slavophils* Charles XII of Sweden by carefully noting the methods by which Charles had defeated *him*. These "Westerners" wanted to break up the *mir* into individual farms or transfer all land to the state, to replace village handicrafts by machine technology, to introduce parliaments, juries and all the political forms of western lands. The "Slavophils" on the other hand held that the Russians had a special mission in history, that they should remain aloof from the sordid materialism of mercantile Europe and develop their primitive agricultural communism into an ideal social order without passing through the purgatory of capitalism. There were radicals and conservatives in both camps. Count Sergius Witte who became Minister of Finance in 1892 envisaged the future Russia as a greater Prussia, efficient, industrial and bureaucratic; Prince Peter Kropotkin, scientist and anarchist, believed that the Paris Commune of 1871 pointed the way to a future of happy industrial municipalities without religion, property or law. Among those who believed in Russia's spiritual mission there was an equal divergence, ranging from Konstantin Pobiedonostsev, the reactionary Procurator of the Holy Synod (administrator of the State Church), to Count Tolstoy, the prophet of a curious "Christian anarchism" which held that political government and private property were alien to the spirit of the Slavic peoples and equally so to that of the New Testament.

The first definite and modern revolutionary party were the "Decembrists" [1] who opposed the autocracy of Nicholas I, but having no roots in the nation at large, *Revolution-* were easily crushed. The lesson of their failure *ary parties* was taken to heart by the *Narodniki* or Populists who went as

[1] From the attempted revolution of December, 1825.

voluntary missionaries among the peasants to stir up among them a longing for better conditions so that the next reform movement would have behind it widespread popular support. The more extreme radicals who were willing to resort to violence to gain their aims were popularly called the Nihilists.[1] With the coming of the industrial revolution other important groups arose, Constitutional Democrats (popularly "Cadets") who wanted a constitution of the western type, Social Revolutionaries who preached a peasant socialism, Social Democrats, strong among the workingmen of the towns, who adhered to the "orthodox" theories of Karl Marx. In 1903 the Social Democrats split into two factions, not as to the party aims but as to the party methods. The larger faction or *Bolsheviki* (from *bolshinstvo* = majority) agreed with their leader Lenin that the party should be governed by an iron dictatorship and that there should be no co-operation with middle-class liberals and progressives; the minority or *Mensheviki* favored a more opportunist policy and a more generous co-operation with other radical parties.

The revolution was made more probable by the accession to the throne in 1894 of Nicholas II. He was the type of *Nicholas II* ruler under whom revolutions usually occur and has frequently been compared to King Louis XVI of France; the ruler who is too slow in granting reforms to conciliate his subjects and lacks the stern resolution to keep them always in awe. The early part of his reign merely continued and extended the repressive policy of Alexander III. Pobiedonostsev supplied the underlying theory of both reigns. His doctrine was that Russia must keep in quarantine from western ideas, and especially the liberalism which always led to revolution and decadence. The press was merely an enemy to sound government, parliament served only the "self-interest of its members," democracy

[1] The term was originally a literary one for impatient young radicals who desired to leaving nothing (*nihil*) standing of existing institutions.

was a "fatal error"; the true political trinity for Russia was to be Orthodoxy, that is, adherence to the Greek Orthodox Church and repression of Roman Catholics, Protestants and Jews, Nationality, that is, the compulsory Russification of the minor nationalities of the Empire, and Autocracy, the preservation undiminished of the arbitrary power of the Tsar. Plehve, Minister for the Interior, was the mailed fist of Nicholas's reactionary early reign. Behind him was a formidable organization of secret police, commonly termed the "Third Section," which had the arduous duty of counter-mining the conspiracies of the revolutionary parties. This counter-espionage led to the employment of dangerous tools, sometimes the same individual was a revolutionary "terrorist" and an agent of the secret police. He might in reality be serving either side and betraying the other, or betraying both and serving only his own profit.

Under the financial ministry of Count Witte Russia ceased to be an almost exclusively agricultural nation. Count Witte was a shrewd man with a gift for *The work* finance. Professor J. H. Robinson has termed *of Count* him "the Colbert of Russia," and the Irish jour- *Witte* nalist E. J. Dillon "Russia's unique statesman." His policy was to strengthen Russia by governmental protection of industry. He bought up private railways, nationalized the liquor traffic, established the gold standard, subsidized new industries, enacted high protective tariffs, and protected the workingman by factory codes. He was forced from the ministry in 1903 by the intrigues of reactionaries such as Plehve, but the revolution of 1905 frightened the Tsar into making him· head of Russia's first constitutional government. He performed an equally important service to Russia in the diplomatic field by negotiating the Treaty of Portsmouth with a skill which almost redeemed the manifold military blunders of the Russo-Japanese War.[1] As a con-

---

[1] For Russian foreign policy in the Far East see Chapter IX.

stitutional statesman, however, he was less successful than as administrator and diplomat. The revolutionists disliked him as a conservative, while to the reactionaries he seemed a dangerous liberal. Distrusted by both sides and treated with ungenerous suspicion by the Tsar, he was compelled to leave his constructive plans but half completed.

The turning point in the reign of Nicholas II was the Russo-Japanese War caused by Russia's aggressive imperialism in Manchuria. Many reactionary officials *The first Russian revolution, 1905* hailed it as the best means of awakening a national patriotism which would cause the people to forget their revolutionary dreams, but this calculation implied a victorious war. Even the most patient nations will seldom forgive a military defeat, still less a positive military disgrace. The military machine broke down so completely under the test of conflict that every patriot and every lover of efficient government echoed the revolutionary demand for a cleansing of the corrupt and self-seeking bureaucracy which governed the nation. The irresolute Tsar wavered from day to day between concession and resistance. He permitted the troops to fire on a crowd bearing a petition, the massacre of "Red Sunday," January 22, 1905. He appointed the reactionary General Trepoff as chief of police. He exiled to Siberia thousands of men whose only offense was advocacy of reform. But he relaxed the censorship, made vast promises of liberties to be granted all his subjects, and in October, 1905, took the decisive step of granting a national parliament, the Duma.

The manifesto of 1905 was the end of absolute monarchy in Russia, but the principle of parliamentary responsibility *Russia under the constitution* was not yet considered and the executive government remained in the hands of the Tsar and his personally chosen ministers. Associated with the Duma in the work of legislation was an Imperial Council, in part appointed by the Tsar and in part chosen from privileged orders and official bodies. None the less it was important that the Autocrat should have laid down "an immutable rule that no law can come into force without the approval of the Duma." The first Duma was too radical; the Tsar dissolved it, and many of its deputies met at Viborg in Finland protesting against the hasty dissolution and urging the people to refuse taxes. But the appeal did not meet with the expected success; the nation was not yet ready to support its representatives by a general armed insurrection.

A second Duma met in 1907. Like its predecessor it was controlled by a radical majority and dissolved after a few stormy and fruitless sessions. But the Tsar *The reaction, 1907-14* now felt strong enough to risk a reactionary *coup d'état* and he had in his service an unusually able minister, Peter Stolypin, who supplied the resolution which he himself lacked. By Imperial decree, without consent of the Duma, the Tsar altered the electoral law. The Asian provinces were largely disfranchised, Poland lost some representatives, and the voting power of the landed aristocracy was increased at the expense of the more liberal bourgeoisie and workingmen of the towns. As a result the third Duma was more conservative than its predecessors. The Socialist and other radical parties had been weakened by persecutions and disfranchisement, the Constitutional Democrats were discredited by the failure of the Viborg manifesto, the dominant political group was the "Octobrist," so called because content with the reforms granted by the Tsar in October, 1905. The fourth Duma, chosen in 1912, was of similar character. The government exiled to penal colonies in Siberia thousands of political prisoners, all legal liberties that stood in the way of police repression were canceled or disregarded, and reactionary gangs, the so-called "Black Hundreds," attacked liberals and Jews with the passive encouragement of the authorities. Stolypin's cruel repression made him the best-hated man in the Empire, the hangman's rope was popularly nicknamed "Stolypin's necktie," and he was assassinated by a radical in 1911, leaving power to ministers as conservative as himself but less resolute and less able.

Yet Stolypin was far too intelligent a man to believe that mere repression, however cruel, would avert the possibility *Stolypin's* of revolution. He had a constructive land policy *agrarian* which aimed to detach the peasant from the *policy* revolution by improving his economic condition. He believed that communal control of the land, however altruistic in theory, encouraged shiftlessness. Why should a peasant introduce improved methods if he did not himself reap the profit? So he sanctioned legislation permitting peasants to free themselves from the control of the *mir* and farm their own lands in individual allotments. In parts of southern Russia this was already the custom, now individual farming was to become the rule in Great Russia as well. At the outbreak of the World War, Russia was in a state of transition from collective to individual ownership.

One victim of the reaction was the Grand Duchy of Finland. By law and treaty the Grand Duchy was a sepa- *The repres-* rate government united with Russia by the per- *sion of* son of the Tsar and its separate rights were in *Finland* the main respected until the reign of Alexander III. Nicholas II proved even more hostile to Finnish liberty than his predecessor and made every effort to replace Finnish by Russian officials, curtail the public use of the two native languages (Finnish and Swedish), and limit the powers of the Finnish Diet to the most petty local affairs. The outbreak of the revolution enabled the Finns to restore their constitution and even reform it in a democratic direction. The new Diet was elected by universal adult suffrage on a basis of proportional representation. But with the end of the revolution the Tsar's government, while respecting the existence of the new Diet, withdrew one power after another from its competence and established Russian control in all matters of interest to the Empire as a whole. Judges who ventured to protest against these illegalities were sometimes arrested and deported from their country.

To the defeated Russian radical between 1907 and 1917, it must have seemed that nothing had been won except a paper constitution and a weak and apologetic legislature, both existing by the sufferance of the Tsar. It is true that, in spite of a few military mutinies and the picturesque episode of certain warships hoisting the revolutionary flag, the army as a whole had remained obedient and that city strikes and peasant riots stood no chance against the disciplined forces at the disposal of the government. But in 1905 for the first time the Russian workingman, not as a secret and individual conspirator but as an organized unit in an open insurrection, had measured his strength against the government. Though the government had triumphed, its weakness had been so demonstrated to the world as to weaken its prestige with its own subjects as well as with foreign nations. *Another* unsuccessful war and who could tell what might not happen?

Significance of the first Russian revolution

That other war was not far distant. The foreign policy of Russia is so intertwined with the general history of Europe that it may better be considered in connection with the problems in which Russia was interested than with the internal history of the nation.[1] But it may here be said that Russia cherished hopes which could not be realized without war, and for war Russia was singularly unprepared. The peace-loving Nicholas II, founder of the Hague Court, permitted his country to drift into war with Japan as a result of his Far Eastern policy, and into war with Austria-Hungary and

The menace of Austro-Russian rivalry

[1] See especially Chapters II, III, VI, IX, X and XI.

Germany as the result of his Near Eastern policy. The fact that the two military monarchies of eastern Europe were in opposite diplomatic camps was a first-rate danger to the peace of Europe. Russia, though the more backward of the two, was also the stronger, not only from sheer weight of numbers but because she could appeal to the millions of Slavs within Austria-Hungary who resented German or Magyar overlordship. But behind Austria stood Germany with the best army and probably the strongest industrial system in Europe. The prize for which both contended was the mastery of the Near East, not necessarily by open annexation but by establishing complete political and economic ascendancy in that part of the world. The origins, progress and results of this momentous rivalry form the main theme of European diplomatic history from the Congress of Berlin in 1878 to the disappearance of the old Russia in the revolutionary earthquake of 1917.

CHAPTER IX

EUROPE AND THE FAR EAST

SEPARATED from Europe and India by the broadest deserts and highest mountains in the world the Far Eastern nations have for centuries formed a civilization apart. *The Old Régime in the Far East* Until late in the nineteenth century they were isolated as much by their own policy as by distance and natural barriers; they at once despised the foreigner as a barbarian and feared him as a possible conqueror and exploiter. They were content with their own civilization, dignified by ancient tradition and the sanctions of religion and adjusted to their racial desires by ages of social experience. The center of this civilization was China; the "marginal" nations such as Japan, Korea, Manchuria, Mongolia, Tibet, Turkestan, and perhaps Indo-China and Siam (though here the Indian influence is also evident) owed most of their culture to contact with the Chinese. Chinese culture was self-centered, looking around the world from their "Middle Kingdom" [1] they saw nothing to compare with their own achievements. As a symbol of their conservatism stands the Chinese wall, the greatest achievement of pre-industrial engineering, a wall to keep "outer barbarians" from raiding the provinces of the Chinese plain.

The Chinese Empire with its dependencies covered an area greater than that of the United States and had about four times as many people. No complete and *Importance of China in world politics* accurate census has ever been taken, but most estimates place the population of China towards the end of the nineteenth century at about 400,000,000, or approximately one fourth of the entire human race. As a people the Chinese are industrious, thrifty and

[1] Compare "Mediterranean," the sea "in the midst of the earth."

enduring. They thrive in all climates from the rigorous winters of northern Manchuria to the perpetual summers of Java and the Philippines. They are accustomed to want and hardship, and the chief reason put forward for excluding them from Australia, Canada and the United States is that they can endure a degree of poverty which would be intolerable to races accustomed to a higher standard of living and would in consequence displace from employment the higher priced white laborer. The resources of China are adequate for almost limitless industrial development. Both oil and coal exist in considerable quantities and there are large deposits of iron ore and other valuable commercial minerals. As the best European mines are exhausted the comparatively untouched mineral resources of China will become of increasing importance. At present China is still mainly agricultural, and the margin between successful farming and famine is very narrow. When the rivers rise, tens of thousands are killed by floods; during a dry season millions die of hunger. In the almost universal absence of hygiene, pestilences spread almost unchecked. Many of the most terrible epidemics which have swept over Europe originated on the teeming plains of eastern Asia. Under such circumstances human life ceases to be greatly valued, and it is not surprising that a fatalistic indifference to death is one of the characteristic Chinese traits.

The old Chinese civilization, with all its defects, was in its own way as remarkable as the civilization of Europe. The *Chinese civilization* Chinese were acquainted with such luxuries as silk and porcelain ("China" ware) at a time when our North European ancestors were skin-clad barbarians. They knew of the printing press, gunpowder and the compass. They had a written language of their own in which each word was represented by a distinctive character. In the decorative arts the Chinese, and the Japanese as well, achieved miracles of painstaking skill which surpass in their own kind the best European work. Daily life was enriched with an elaborate ritual of politeness which would have done credit to the French Court of Louis XIV. Even those Chinese who admit the superiority of the West in science and invention do not concede to us any superiority in the "art of living."

Nor was Chinese civilization wholly a matter of externals. The whole life of the people has been shaped by the teaching of a group of philosophers who lived several cen- *Spiritual* turies before the Christian era and preached the *foundations* virtues of courtesy, benevolence, fair-dealing, *of Chinese* reverence and filial piety. Confucius (to give *life* his name its familiar Europeanized form) was the most influential of these philosophers and his works are still studied as the classics of the language. Whether or not we can speak of a Confucian "religion" is a question of definition. He taught ethics rather than theology, and it might be safer to say that his principle of reverence for ancestors, parents, wise men and rightful authority has saturated all the Chinese religions than to attempt a census enumeration of "Confucianists." The religion of China was not a variety of sharply contrasted and mutually hostile sects, as in Palestine, Turkey or India, but a synthesis or alloy of several different religious traditions. Under the old Imperial government there was a cult of public ceremonial in honor of "Heaven," many Chinese professed Buddhism or Taoism, and some were converts to Mohammedanism or, later, to Christianity, and there were innumerable popular superstitions as to "demons" and "evil influences," but Confucian ideals influenced everyone. The weakness of Chinese religious life was in the confusion between ethical and merely prudent or conventional conduct and the absence of any appeal to the imagination. It is as if we had no Bible except the Book of Proverbs.

The political principle taught by the Chinese philosophers

was "enlightened despotism." The rule of kings and princes *Chinese government* was taken for granted, but it was understood that they should be fathers of the people and ever solicitous to promote their moral and material welfare. A ruler who misgoverned his subjects beyond the point of endurance might be rightfully deposed. "He who puts an unrighteous judge to death," said Mencius, "is no regicide but a minister of justice." The republican revolution of the twentieth century was no novelty in Chinese history, except in the failure to establish a new dynasty in place of the old. In theory the Emperor was absolute monarch and the ceremonial of the court was of the most elaborate Oriental type, even European ambassadors being compelled to perform acts of submission before being admitted to the august presence of the "Son of Heaven." But despotism in China, like despotism in Russia and in all extensive empires with inferior means of communication, meant in practice bureaucracy, the rule of a trained official class. The Chinese officials were selected in part by court favor, but very largely on the basis of civil service examinations. This modern-seeming system is many centuries old. Those who passed a threefold series of rigorous competitive examinations were sure of a position in the public services. The subject matter of the examinations was entirely literary, it tested only familiarity with the classic authors and ability to write graceful essays on suggested topics, but as for centuries the higher schools in Europe taught little save the Greek and Latin classics it should not be hard for us of the West to understand the conservatism of the old Chinese system of public examinations.

The ruling dynasty in the nineteenth century was not of Chinese origin. In the seventeenth century the Manchus, *China under the Man- chus* a Mongolian people somewhat remotely akin to the Chinese but inferior to them in civilization, overran the country. But in the long run the Chinese absorbed their conquerors without being able to overthrow them, just as the English absorbed the Norman knights and barons who conquered them. The conquerors adopted the civilization of the masses around them, and the racial barrier became of little importance. Unfortunately few of the Manchu rulers were able to maintain high standards of efficiency in administration. Corruption pervaded every department of government. Officials were not expected to live on their salaries and seldom did so. Judges were often dishonest and the legal system so inefficient that foreigners would consent to trade in China only on condition that they be exempted from the jurisdiction of the native courts. The public finances were badly administered and the whole system of taxes and customs needed to be straightened out by honest and capable officials.

The merits and defects of the Chinese, their devotion to peace and their lack of public spirit, alike handicapped the Empire in dealing with such patriotic and warlike nations as Japan and the European powers. *Early contacts with* Throughout ancient and medieval times there *European nations* had always been a thin trickle of trade between Europe and eastern Asia and an occasional traveler, such as Marco Polo, would bring back tall tales of the strange Oriental civilizations. In the sixteenth century Portuguese traders began a more direct trade with China and Japan and they were soon followed by the Dutch, French and British. But there was an early reaction against the foreign traders, the ports were closed and the first Christian converts — mainly Roman Catholic — persecuted. Trade dwindled to an inconsiderable traffic, carried on under the most humiliating conditions, the Chinese Emperors blandly informing the British diplomats that their Celestial Empire had no need for the products of barbarous nations! Not till the middle of the nineteenth century were normal commercial relations established and then only by the use of force, and force exerted in a highly dubious cause.

One of the most important articles of commerce was opium, exported from British India. As opium smoking had reached the dimensions of a national vice, the Imperial government very rightly resolved to halt the infamous traffic. Unfortunately the methods used by the authorities in this, as in nearly all matters, were at once too violent and too feeble; too violent because they involved the illegal arrest of British subjects or agents and the confiscation of their property, too feeble because they did not suppress the illicit trade carried on with the connivance of their own corrupt officials. The result was a small naval war with the British ending with the Treaty of Nanking in 1842, ceding the island of Hong-Kong to the British as a permanent base for their Oriental trade and opening other ports to foreign ships. In 1858 another conflict terminated in the Treaty of Tientsin, signed by the Russians, French and Americans as well as the British, opened additional treaty ports, established toleration for Christian missionaries and began regular diplomatic relations between the foreign governments and Imperial court at Peking, though it required another campaign, the capture of the capital and the burning of the Emperor's summer palace to enforce its terms.

The "opium wars" and freedom of trade

The Tai-Ping rebellion of the eighteen-fifties was in part national and in part religious. A fanatic, influenced perhaps by Christian missionaries, proclaimed a new synthetic religion which combined Christian elements with some of the older Chinese traditions and announced that he was the new Emperor, founder of the Tai-Ping or "Great Peace" dynasty. He exploited the popular resentment against the Manchus and attained considerable success, especially as the incompetent Imperial armies were being hard enough pressed by British and French forces bent on spreading freedom of trade by military action. The final defeat of the Tai-Ping movement was due largely

The Tai-Ping rebellion

to the employment of foreign officers, most eminent among them being the British officer Charles Gordon, whose "Ever Victorious Army," organized in the European fashion, reached a standard of efficiency new to Chinese warfare, and the American soldier of fortune Ward.   Gordon left the service of the Empire in indignation when promises of mercy to the rebel chiefs were violated, and it is hard to resist the conclusion that he fought in a bad cause, as the decadent Manchu dynasty was hardly worthy to rule.   From first to last the rebellion is said to have cost China more lives than were lost by all the nations engaged in the World War.

One of the officials whose perfidy aroused the anger of the chivalrous Gordon was to become the greatest statesman of nineteenth-century China.   Li Hung-Chang was *Li Hung-* by no means a faultless patriot.   Not only was *Chang* he unscrupulous where the interest of his country was concerned, a vice too common in diplomats of all nations, but he feathered his own nest from the public funds to a degree that would be impossible to justify by any system of ethics, Christian or Confucian.   Yet he brought to the service of the Empire courage, an unwearied patience, a keen insight into the realities of each new situation and, greatest of all, the ability to risk everything by telling unpopular truths. In his memorial of 1867 he bluntly thrust in the face of the self-deceiving government such admonitions as:

> The truth is, that at present foreigners are powerful and the Chinese feeble.   And whence arises the power of the former? It certainly is not innate in them, but depends on the fact that "the requisites of government are sufficiency of food, sufficiency of military equipment, and the confidence of the people in the ruler" (Confucian Analects).   And how is the weakness of China to be accounted for?   This also is not innate, but is a result of the truth of the above axiom not being sufficiently realized.

Slandered as lacking in patriotism and being too much a friend to foreigners, he labored all his life to save China by playing for time with courteous delay in his foreign policy while administrative reform strengthened the nation till it could maintain its independence.

If the first serious foreign encroachments against China were British, the French were not long behind and proved *French ag-* even more land-hungry. Over the small native *gressions in* states between China and Siam, the Chinese *Indo-China* Empire claimed a nebulous suzerainty which, like the Turkish sovereignty over the Mohammedan states of northern Africa, or the English claim to paramount lordship over Scotland in the Middle Ages, was rarely acknowledged and often resisted. For practical purposes the Empire of Annam was independent and even able to carry on imperialistic wars against neighboring states. In the days of Napoleon III France made a beginning of a new Oriental empire by the conquest of part of Cochin-China, thus avenging the murder of some Christian missionaries. With this foothold already gained, the Third Republic soon established a French protectorate over Cambodia, on the Siamese frontier, Tonkin, adjacent to China, the Empire of Annam in between the two, and Laos to the west of Annam. The combined Indo-Chinese annexations were larger than France in area and had a population of some twenty millions. The conquest of Tonkin involved a war with China. In 1885 China renounced all claim to Tonkin and Annam, but a small military disaster suffered by the French army caused an outburst of indignation in the French Chamber of Deputies and compelled the resignation of Jules Ferry, the most aggressive champion of colonial imperialism who ever held the premiership.

Siam, though menaced by the French conquest of the Indo-Chinese kingdoms to the east, and the advance of the *Siam* British in Burma and the Malay peninsula to the west and south, has not only remained independent but become a stable kingdom under its own native government though with much employment of foreign ad-

visors in its service. The British and the French both preferred to keep a "buffer state" between their colonial domains, believing that too close neighborhood might create
troublesome problems.

A greater menace to China came from her nearer neighbors, Russia and Japan. Russia, already in possession of
the eastern half of Europe and the northern half   *Russian*
of Asia, had no particular need of new lands, but   *advances*
greatly desired warm water ports to give her more   *in Asia*
adequate access to the seaways of the world. By 1860 Russia had secured the island Sakhalin,[1] north of Japan, and the
maritime provinces north and east of Manchuria, giving Siberia a long frontage on the Pacific and permitting the
establishment of a naval base at Vladivostok. In the meantime Russia was advancing toward the frontier of India by
successive additions of territory in central Asia, in Turkestan,
Khiva, Bokhara and Merv, only the buffer state of Afghanistan saving British India from direct contact with Asiatic
Russia. Fortunately for China, the aggressions of Russia
aroused the keenest alarm in both Britain and Japan, and
Chinese statesmen such as Li Hung-Chang were able to play
off Russia and her Anglo-Japanese rivals against each other.

Japan is a land of borrowed culture as compared with
China, in the same sense that ancient Rome was a land of
borrowed culture as compared with Greece. This   *The awak-*
does not imply that the pupil was a mere imi-   *ening of*
tator. Rome was able to develop a far stronger   *Japan*
political and military system than Greece; Japan in the same
fields excelled China. China when first opened to European
influences was a huge, amorphous Empire with little patriotic spirit and a rooted contempt for the soldier's trade, socially a democracy and politically a bureaucratic despotism.
Japan at the same period was a unified national state, feudal
in organization and aristocratic in temper. Religiously

[1] The Japanese claims to the island were extinguished by treaty in 1875.

Japan shared with China the rites of Buddhism and the tradition of reverence for ancestors. But the ethical basis of Japanese life was in many respects the opposite of that of China. Instead of the practical, prosaic "business man's" code of the Chinese, the Japanese were stirred to deeds of nobility and patriotic heroism by the chivalric code of *bushido*, the personal honor of the warrior. Japan from the thirteenth to the nineteenth century resembled in a thousand ways western Europe from the ninth to the sixteenth century. But, unlike Europe, Japan was compelled by foreign pressure to pass in a single generation from the Middle Ages to our own times. The modernization or westernization of backward, tradition-bound peoples is a common story in the nineteenth and twentieth centuries, repeated with variations in Russia, Turkey, India, Persia, north Africa, China and Japan, but nowhere else was the process of adjustment so swift and successful as among the Japanese.

After a period of trade, on no very large scale, with the Portuguese and the Dutch, the Japanese closed the door to *America opens the door* foreigners. Hoping to open up Japan to commercial intercourse with the outside world, the United States sent Commodore Perry in 1853 with letters and presents to the Japanese government. This began negotiations, both American and British, which in the course of a few years opened treaty ports, established uniform customs dues and gave foreign residents the rights of "extraterritoriality" or exemption from Japanese courts. Contact with foreign nations brought about a great revolution within Japan.

Japan had been in form an absolute monarchy; the Emperor or Mikado was revered as of divine origin *Japan enters the "Era of Enlightenment"* and the royal line had been unbroken since the dawn of national history. His actual power, however, had passed to the *Shogun* very much as in early medieval France the power of the Merovingian Kings

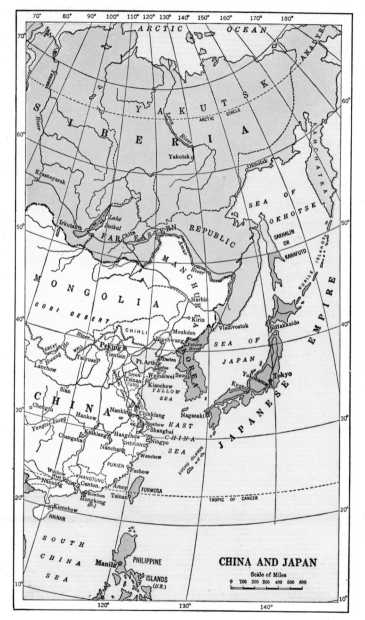

CHINA AND JAPAN

Scale of Miles
0   100   200   300   400   500   600

had passed to their "Mayors of the Palace." Below the monarch and his powerful minister were the feudal nobles, the *daimios*, and the military knighthood the *samurai*. The new Mikado, Mutsuhito (1867–1912), was resolved that both he and his nation should emerge from dignified retirement into the active life of modern times; with his reign begins the Japanese new era of enlightenment, the *Meiji*. The Shogunate was ended and the Mikado added political duties to his previous religious and ceremonial functions. Feudal rights and servile status were abolished by successive decrees, the army reorganized on European lines, the laws rewritten to correspond with modern ideas of legal right, railway and steamship lines were instituted, universities and technical schools founded, the cities were policed, lighted and made sanitary, and reforms of every sort which had been the work of some four hundred years in the most progressive European countries were transplanted in two generations to Japan. Yet these revolutionary changes were not brought about without some reactionary rebellions in the provinces, notably an uprising of the Satsuma clan in 1877. Even today party lines follow to some extent the old clan and provincial groupings and many old feudal customs and loyalties survive.[1]

Both China and Japan were undergoing modernization, but Japan much the more swiftly of the two. In 1894 the two Oriental powers broke into war over Korea, a province nominally subject to the Chinese Empire. Japan was speedily victorious. The modern armies and navies which existed largely *The Chino-Japanese War, 1894-95* on paper in China existed in physical fact in Japan. In 1895 China was forced to sign the humiliating Treaty of Shimonoseki, acknowledging the independence of Korea, surrendering the Liao-tung peninsula in southern Manchuria and the island of Formosa south of the Japanese archipelago, and

[1] Such as the customary suicide (*hara-kiri*) of any person of rank who has fallen into disgrace.

paying a substantial war indemnity. But the rapid rise of a new Great Power in the Far East alarmed the continental European statesmen. Russia, Germany and France combined to force a downward revision of the drastic terms of peace. Japan had to retrocede her Manchurian gains to China.

Russia in protesting against the Japanese seizure of the Liao-tung peninsula was putting in one word for China and *The Russians in Manchuria* two for herself. The Russians obtained a lease of twenty-five years for Port Arthur and Dalny in southern Manchuria, thus winning a new naval base in the East. But Russian ambition did not stop there. Railroads were to be built throughout Manchuria and linked with the trans-Siberian line, exclusive mining concessions negotiated with the Chinese government, and in a short time all Manchuria would fall within a Russian sphere of influence. Korea, now nominally independent but notoriously too weak a realm to stand alone, would then be added. Thus Russia would gain a great new empire, hold the best position of any European nation for commanding Chinese trade, and reduce Japan for all time to the position of a group of offshore islands with no footing on the mainland.

Germany proved as contemptuous as Russia of Chinese rights and Japanese susceptibilities. Germany's gratuitous *The Germans in Shan-tung* support of Russia's Far Eastern policy had alienated the Japanese. The murder of two German missionaries by Chinese in 1897 provoked armed intervention in the province of Shan-tung and won for Germany in 1898 the leasehold of the port of Kiao-chau for ninety-nine years. The acquisition of a German naval base at the expense of China led Russia to hasten her demand for the lease of Port Arthur and inspired the French to demand a lease at Kwang-chau and the British another at Wei-hai-wei. Between enemies demanding annexations and friends demanding "compensation" it seemed for a time that China would follow the fate of Africa and India and become subject to European partition and control.

The actual annexations amounted to merely a few sea-ports and even these were usually politely disguised as "leaseholds." [1] Even were China to lose her vast but thinly peopled outlying dependencies of Manchuria, Mongolia, Tibet and Chinese Tur- *Concessions and "spheres of interest"* kestan, as she had already lost Korea and Indo-China, the great mass of Chinese people would still live under their own government. More menacing was the growing tendency of foreign powers to mark out economic "spheres of interest" within which the fortunate possessor would have a monopoly of mining rights, railway routes, banking facilities and commercial concessions. In a weak or back-ward country commercial zones often harden into zones of political dominance and foreshadow the eventual lines of partition. Germany held such a sphere of influence in the densely settled province of Shan-tung, the home of the im-mortal Confucius. France claimed special rights in the southern provinces bordering on the French colonies of Indo-China. Great Britain had a somewhat vaguer claim to com-mercial privileges in the populous valley of the Yangtze. Japan aspired to a sphere of influence in the province of Fukien.

One alone of the powers with extensive commercial in-terests in the Pacific stood apart from the scramble for exclusive commercial concessions, acquired no leased port and hoped for no share of Chinese *The United States and the "Open Door".* territory. The United States formulated the policy of the "Open Door" which may be ex-pressed in the words of Secretary John Hay in his letter to the powers in 1899:

The recognition that no Power will in any way interfere with any treaty port or any vested interest within any leased terri-

[1] Compare the British leasehold of Cyprus from Turkey after 1878. The desire to "save face" by legal fictions is common to the Chinese, the Turk and the European diplomat!

tory or within any so-called "sphere of interest" it may have in China.

That the Chinese treaty tariff of the time being shall apply to all merchandise landed or shipped to all such ports as are within said "sphere of interest" (unless they be "free ports"), no matter to what nationality it may belong, and that duties so leviable shall be collected by the Chinese Government.

That it will levy no higher harbor dues on vessels of another nationality frequenting any port in such "sphere" than shall be levied on vessels of its own nationality, and no higher railroad charges over lines built, controlled, or operated within its "sphere" on merchandise belonging to citizens or subjects of other nationalities transported through such "sphere" than shall be levied on similar merchandise belonging to its own nationals transported over equal distances.

The main purpose of the American declaration for the Open Door was to prevent American commerce from being driven from the Chinese market, but it had the incidental effect of helping to preserve China from partition. The "Hay Doctrine" deserves to stand by the Monroe Doctrine as a preserver of the national independence of weak states.

The incessant encroachment of foreign powers on Chinese territory, arousing a sullen resentment against all foreigners *Failure of the Chinese reform movement* and their religion, was one of the chief causes of that strange outbreak of fanaticism known to history as the Boxer movement. Another cause was the failure of the reform movement of 1898 initiated by the well-meaning Emperor Kuang Hsü. His career, like that of Joseph II in eighteenth-century Austria, shows how little can be accomplished by an "enlightened despot" whose enlightenment is not shared or understood by his subjects. He tried to modernize the examination system, abolish sinecures, reorganize the army, navy and financial administration and extend the schools. At every step he made fresh enemies and a large reactionary party gathered around the Empress Dowager, Tzu Hsi, a woman of remarkable strength of character, commonly termed the

"Old Buddha" by foreign journalists. A reactionary *coup d'état* placed Tzu Hsi in power and ended the reform projects of the Emperor. The old régime was about to make its last stand against twentieth-century civilization.

The "shock troops" of the anti-foreign movement were the members of societies organized for propaganda, the most famous of which bore the name of "Fists of   *The Boxer* Righteous Harmony," later westernized as "Box-   *Rebellion* ers." At first the Manchu government stood aloof from the movement, condemning the anti-foreign riots and the murder of Christian missionaries. Yuan Shih-Kai was instructed to crush the disorders in Shan-tung and many other provincial governors followed the same policy. But as time went on the authorities at Peking began to waver. Large bodies of the regular army joined the mobs against the foreigners. In June, 1900, Baron Von Ketteler, the German Minister, was murdered and other foreign ministers besieged in their own legations. The government wavered pitiably between secret encouragement to the outbreaks and public disavowal of them. Only the elderly Li Hung-Chang had the insight and courage to tell the ruling Empress the whole truth. "Under any enlightened sovereign," he said, "these Boxers with their ridiculous claims of supernatural powers, would most assuredly have been condemned to death long since.... You should take steps immediately to appoint a high official who shall purge the land of this villainous rabble, and who shall see to it that the foreign ministers are safely escorted."

The imminent peril to thousands of foreign traders, missionaries and officials in China forced the powers to act together in spite of their mutual rivalries. The   *Repression* whole civilized world was afraid that the next   *by an allied* news from Peking might tell of the massacre of   *army* all the foreign refugees in the legations. An international relief force of Japanese, Russian, British, American, German, Italian and French troops commanded by a German general,

Count Waldersee, advanced to Peking and entered the city. The heroic garrison of the legations still held out, facing odds of hundreds to one.   The Imperial government withdrew all support from the anti-foreign movement and sought only to avert the wrath of the victorious foreigners.   There is only too much evidence that Russian, German, French and Italian troops repaid the Boxer atrocities in kind.[1]   The German government was not ashamed to share in the plunder won by its armies, and it is pleasant to note that as one result of the World War Germany had to return to China astronomical instruments stolen from Peking.   Perhaps the most shameful incident in the suppression of the Boxer movement, though the record of no army was wholly blameless, was the massacre of some five thousand Chinese civilians by Russian troops in the Siberian town of Blagovestchensk.

The terms of peace imposed on the Chinese government for permitting the massacre of foreigners were sufficiently *China pays* severe to teach a lasting lesson, though they would have been still more humiliating had it not been for the skillful negotiations conducted by Li Hung-Chang.   Personally he was acceptable to the allies, as they knew that he had sincerely striven to his utmost against the Boxer movement.   China was forced to make public apology for the murder of the German minister, punish officials involved in the Boxer riots, pay indemnities to foreign governments for individuals who suffered in the rebellion, permit the establishment of permanent guards for the Peking legations, and repress anti-foreign propaganda.   The United States voluntarily remitted about half the indemnity due American nationals, and the funds thus saved enabled China to send students to American universities.   Among the American-trained Chinese have come many leaders of the present Chinese Republic.

[1] For one testimony from many see the account of the Tientsin massacres given by Herbert Hoover, then a mining engineer in China, cited in *The Independent*, November 22, 1900.

In a well-meant effort to check the aggressions of Japan in Manchuria, Li Hung-Chang had relied perhaps too much on Russia. Now it appeared that Russia's ambition *Russia and* to absorb the province was in way of being *Japan clash* realized. It was a prize worth fighting for, if *over Manchuria* conquest is ever worth the cost of war. Manchuria was a vast and thinly settled region in the temperate zone, rich in mineral wealth and farmland. If Russia had need for more Asiatic ports, Japan had a still greater need for undeveloped lands; not for settlement — the Japanese prefer to live in their own island Empire — but for commercial exploitation. Japan, like Italy, received only a single gift from Nature, the gift of beauty. Those radiant islands are too hilly for the best agricultural development and yet at the same time inferior to the Asiatic mainland in mineral resources. The Russian government held possession of Port Arthur and evaded all Japanese representations that it should be relinquished to China. The Tsar Nicholas II loved peace but probably believed that Japan would yield without a fight. His agents in the Far East, such as Admiral Alexieff, held no such delusion. They knew that Manchuria and Korea must be won by battle but they expected a short and easy war. When had an Asiatic people, unaided, triumphed in a major war with a great Christian and European Empire? Never since the decline of Turkish power in the seventeenth century!

Far better than other European powers, Britain appreciated the renaissance of Japan. The British were among the first to pay Japan the compliment of abandon- *The Anglo-* ing "extraterritoriality" and accepting for their *Japanese* nationals the jurisdiction of the native courts. *alliance of 1902* Seeking to establish a balance of power in the Far East which would halt the Russian advance, they made an alliance with Japan in 1902 to maintain the *status quo* and the general peace in the Far East. If, in defense of this policy, either nation were assailed by two or more other powers the alliance would become a military league. Thus Great Britain was not obliged to join Japan in the war against Russia, but had some other power, such as France or Germany, joined Russia against Japan they would have had to face the British fleet. At one time the adhesion of Germany to the alliance was under consideration, but the German government did not view the idea with favor, for at the moment German diplomacy was wary of England, contemptuous of Japan, and solicitous of Russian good will.

In February, 1904, the Japanese ended their long and futile negotiations to force Russian withdrawal from Manchuria and Korea. In deciding for war Japan decided *The Russo-Japanese War, 1904-05* also from the very first to take the offensive, as the ultimate man power of Russia was so much greater than that of Japan that delay would mean certain defeat. On February 8, a Japanese fleet under Vice-Admiral Togo struck the Russian fleet at Port Arthur, and simultaneously with this naval demonstration General Kuroki landed an army in Korea and began his advance to the Yalu river, the Manchurian frontier. While one Japanese army crossed the Yalu, another closely invested Port Arthur and Dalny in the Liao-tung peninsula, and a third advanced into the heart of Manchuria. General Kuropatkin, the Russian commander, withdrew before the Japanese and held to the defensive, knowing that every mile of Japanese advance took them farther from their base of supplies. Port Arthur, besieged by land and sea and isolated from all Russian support, held out for several months. When General Stössel surrendered in January, 1905, the disappointment in Russia was great and the commander was later prosecuted for surrendering too easily, but for all that the heroic endurance of the garrison through seven months of bombardment and assault is the one episode of the war which the patriotic Russian could remember with any pride.

In the meantime several Japanese armies under the general leadership of Marshal Oyama were converging upon the Russians in central Manchuria.   General Kuro- *Japan* patkin made his stand at the fortified railway *conquers* town of Liao Yang; the Japanese successfully *Manchuria* assaulted the position and forced the Russian army back on the city of Mukden.   The fall of Port Arthur set free another Japanese army and when the battle was renewed the Japanese confronted the Russians south of the city with approximately equal forces and repeated their victory.   General Kuropatkin lost about a third of his army and was compelled to retreat still further to the north.

But the decisive action of the war was fought at sea. Russia had a great fleet in Baltic waters.   Could that be sent to the Pacific the Japanese armies in Man- *The Rus-* churia might be isolated from their homeland *sian fleet* and deprived of essential military supplies.   The *destroyed* venture was doubtful, but the need was desperate.   So in March, 1905, Admiral Rozhestvensky sailed for Asiatic waters.   In May his fleet encountered Admiral Togo's in the battle of Tsushima Straits, and nearly the whole of the Russian fleet was destroyed by the superior tactics and gunnery of the Japanese.   At one blow Russia ceased to be a naval Great Power.

Important as was the naval battle which decided the fate of the war, one trivial incident of the outward voyage came near eclipsing the whole war in importance, for it *The Dog-* almost brought on a conflict between the Russian *ger Bank* and British Empires.   The Russian fleet in *incident* passing through the North Sea came upon a number of British fishing vessels.   In a moment of inexplicable panic the Russians decided that Japanese torpedo boats were concealed among them and fired, killing several men.   The indignation of the British public, already favorable to Japan on general grounds, was very great, but none the less the government consented to refer the whole matter to a special commission. Russia made peace by the payment of an indemnity to the fishermen and their families. The Dogger Bank incident is memorable as one of the most significant victories ever won in the cause of peace and international conciliation.[1]

After the battle of Mukden and the destruction of the Russian fleet, the war had reached a deadlock. It is true *President Roosevelt ends the war by mediation* that Japan had enjoyed an almost uninterrupted succession of brilliant victories, but — and this is a fact overlooked by many civilians — wars are not won by "points" but by ultimate staying power and the ability to deliver a decisive knockout blow. This Japan could not do; in fact, had the Russian government been able to inspire among its subjects the same unquestioning patriotic enthusiasm that moved the Japanese the war might have continued for years until Russia's superior resources brought eventual victory. But the Russian government was shaken by rebellion and had to set its own house in order before it could effectively undertake the reconquest of Manchuria. Both nations wished peace; each feared that to ask it would be interpreted as a sign of weakness. President Theodore Roosevelt at Japan's request undertook mediation; he saw that now was the moment when a friendly neutral power could offer it without offense to either side. In August, 1905, peace negotiations were opened at Portsmouth, New Hampshire. Japan was represented by Baron Komura and Mr. Takahira, Russia by Count

[1] "It was in fact an arbitration *sui generis*, of a kind new and unprecedented in the history of international relations; for it was not only applied, at a time of great excitement, to a question affecting the national honor and vital interests of both parties to the dispute, but it introduced into our administration of international justice a new method of procedure in cases of alleged violation of the law of nations. It has set a precedent for the establishment of tribunals combining the functions of an International Court of Arbitration with those of a Court of Inquiry for the investigation and trial before the bar of the public opinion of the world, of those charged with international crimes and misdemeanors." (A. S. Hershey, *International Law and Diplomacy of the Russo-Japanese War*, 1906, pages 240–41.)

Witte and Baron Rosen. The Russians had the more difficult task, for they had to win back by diplomacy some part
of what had been lost in war.

The two chief points of controversy were the payment of a
war indemnity and the cession of the island of Sakhalin off
the coast of Siberia. For a time there seemed   *The peace*
danger that the conference might break up on   *of Ports-*
these issues, but President Roosevelt continued   *mouth, 1905*
to urge the need for compromise, and at last Japan agreed to
drop the demand for an indemnity and to accept the part of
the island of Sakhalin south of fifty degrees of north latitude [1]
instead of the whole. On September 5, 1905, the peace was
signed. Russia recognized Japan's "paramount political,
military and economic interests" in Korea and agreed not to
interfere with any measure of direction, protection or supervision which Japan might adopt for that country. Both
nations agreed to evacuate Manchuria and restore it to Chinese administration, but the leased territory of Port Arthur
and its environs in the Liao-tung peninsula passed from
Russia to Japan, together with certain railway concessions
and mining rights.

The so-called "Hermit Kingdom" of Korea had long
shared the contented isolation of China and Japan. The
people were unwarlike and their government so   *Japan ab-*
inefficient that after China had been forced to   *sorbs Korea*
abandon her nominal overlordship the only question was
whether the country would fall to Russia or Japan. When
at Portsmouth Russia gave Japan a "quit-claim deed,"
Korea had no more chance of preserving independence than
a mouse allowed a brief run within paw's reach of a cat. In
1905 a Japanese Resident General took charge of the foreign
affairs of Korea. The dormant patriotism of the Koreans
awoke, but too late. An insurrection merely gave the Japanese opportunity to enforce the resignation of the Emperor of

[1] Renamed Karafuto.

Korea and extend the powers of the Resident General to all departments of national administration. In 1909, Prince Ito, who had held that office, was assassinated, the Japanese decided to abandon the sorry pretense of Korean independence, and in 1910 annexed the country outright, renaming it Chosen.

In Manchuria also the Japanese improved the position won by the Treaty of Portsmouth, securing virtual control of *China's bor-* the coal mines, timber concessions and railway *derlands:* projects of southern Manchuria, while respecting *Manchuria,* Russian vested interests in northern Manchuria. *Mongolia,* Mongolia was another Chinese dependency all *Turkestan,* *Tibet* but lost to the foreigner. It is a wild, hungry land of desert, grassland and plateau from which for thousands of years Mongol and Tatar tribes have gone forth to conquest.[1] Tsarist Russia supported a movement for independence among the tribesmen of Outer (western) Mongolia. Though the Russian revolution of 1917 halted this imperialist adventure, the ties which bind Mongolia to China are of the slightest. Tibet, the rugged mountainous plateau which lies between China and India, was long unvisited by Europeans and until recently it was death for a foreigner to put foot in the sacred capital of Lhasa.[2] In 1904 Colonel Younghusband, on behalf of the government of British India, entered Lhasa and compelled the Tibetans to open trade and refrain from making agreements with Russia or other foreign powers without British sanction. In 1907, when Russia and Britain were more friendly, both agreed not to seek spe-

[1] Scientific attention has recently been attracted to Mongolia by the discovery there of dinosaur eggs and other unique fossils. Many believe that the Mongolian highland was an early home of the human race.

[2] Tibet is interesting chiefly for the dominant power of the Buddhist priests who have almost transformed the country into a vast monastery. Tibetan Buddhism is so corrupted by formalism and superstition that Gautama Buddha would hardly recognize his own religion should he revisit that most devout of countries; as one illustration, the rotation of a prayer wheel gave the same spiritual "credit" as saying a prayer!

cial concessions from Tibet and to respect the sovereign rights of China. Turkestan, a country much like Mongolia, suffered like it from Russian encroachments, and yet a large part still remained nominally subject to China.

But the real weakness of the Chinese Empire was at its center. The gain or loss of outlying dependencies mattered less than the revelation of national inefficiency *National* taught by the Chino-Japanese War and the Boxer *movement* outbreak. Even the Empress Dowager had *Manchu* become convinced that some degree of moderni- *rule* zation was essential to save what was precious in the old ré-gime, and reforms that had been rejected when proposed by the Emperor Kuang Hsü, such as the introduction of modern subjects into the civil service examinations, were now adopted. A constitution and a parliament were promised. But the Manchu dynasty had lost its hold on the obedience of the people. The old bottles could not retain the strong new wine of democracy and nationalism. The Manchus were not a numerous element in China, they had adopted many Chinese customs, they held only about a fifth of the posts in the civil service and their privileges were few and slight. Such pretensions as they had, however, were displeasing to the Chinese and especially to the ardent young republican leaders, for the most part trained in foreign schools, who captained the nationalist movement.

The most prominent leader of the republican revolution of 1911 was Sun Yat-Sen, a stormy petrel of Chinese politics, who had been actively engaged in plots against *Sun Yat-* the Manchu dynasty for over fifteen years. *Sen* Much of his life had been spent abroad because his life was not safe in China. Even in London he had been kidnaped and imprisoned in the Chinese legation, and only the intervention of the British government saved his life. A revolutionary convention named him the first President of China, and with him were associated many students from American universities and a former minister to the United States, the wise and witty Wu Ting-Fang, sometimes termed the "Franklin of the Chinese revolution." Politicians of narrower vision, and generals discontented with the Manchu service, joined the idealistic students of Young China and within a few months the new régime was solidly established throughout southern China.

In the north there was panic. The new Emperor Pu Yi who had succeeded the Dowager Empress in 1908 was a *Yuan Shih-* child and none of those who supported his cause *Kai* could cope with the rebellion. At last it was decided to recall to office the ablest of the conservatives, Yuan Shih-Kai, the man who had aided the Dowager Empress Tzu Hsi to overthrow the reformer, Emperor Kuang Hsü, and had later protected foreigners in Shan-tung during the Boxer disturbances. Once dismissed from office, on the courteous pretense of a "lame leg," he now refused to return to service, remarking that his leg was not yet well! Eventually an offer of supreme command over the Imperial armies restored his health. He had no love of republics, but realizing that it was too late to save the Manchu dynasty he entered into negotiations with the republicans of the south. President Sun Yat-Sen sacrificed his own ambition for the unity of the nation and resigned his office in favor of Yuan Shih-Kai. The baby Emperor, Pu Yi, was deposed and the whole Imperial family pensioned off and permitted gracefully to retire.[1]

Thus far everything had gone as smoothly as is ever possible in revolutions. The Manchu dynasty had vanished *The Repub-* with a minimum of resistance, and the country *lic does not* was united under the new republican flag of five *prosper* horizontal stripes[2] in place of the picturesque old banner of the Imperial Dragon. It became fashionable

[1] With Japanese aid he later became Emperor in Manchuria (Manchukuo).

[2] Symbolizing the five nations of the Republic — Chinese, Manchus, Mongols, Tibetans and the Mohammedans of Turkestan.

for Chinese men to abandon the "pigtail," now regarded as
a symbol of subjection, and for women to throw aside the
bindings which had confined their feet and made the wealthier ladies a class of cripples.   China, which in all other respects had lagged so far behind Japan in the adoption of
western institutions, had at a single step passed from being a
bureaucratic despotism like Russia to a democratic republic
like the United States, while Japan remained at a half-way
stage, a constitutional but not yet parliamentary monarchy,
like Germany.   The fundamental difficulty was the same
which has spoiled so many European democratic movements
in the past hundred years, the difficulty in bridging the gap
between a small, instructed revolutionary minority and the
traditional, conservative, politically inexperienced masses
of the people.   The masses were perhaps glad to see the
Manchus go, but they had few ideas as to what further
changes the revolution might bring.   Politics remained a
question for the students, the officials, the professional politicians and — most unfortunately — the generals of the
army.

Hardly had the new government organized, before quarrels broke out between President Yuan Shih-Kai and his
radical Parliament.   In part the differences   *Civil war*
were sectional.   Northern China was con-
servative, militarist, agrarian, traditionally loyal to a central
government and remote from foreign influences; southern
China was commercial, democratic, and more devoted to
local self-government than to the unity of the nation.   Yuan
Shih-Kai seemed to embody the spirit of the north, the traditions of the mandarins of the old Empire, while Sun Yat-
Sen voiced the enthusiastic hopes of the young rebels of
Canton.   At one time Yuan Shih-Kai made a tentative attempt to revive the monarchy but the attempt was a failure
which did much to destroy his own prestige.   Throughout
the World War and for more than a decade thereafter, the

Republic was shaken by intermittent storms of civil war which rarely involved any intensive fighting but prevented any stable central government from arising to command peace at home and respect abroad.

The overthrow of the Manchu dynasty was regarded with sympathy in liberal European and American circles. *Foreign affairs of the Chinese Republic* The financiers of six nations — Great Britain, France, Germany, Russia, Japan and the United States — joined in an offer of a great loan for internal reorganization, but the restrictions imposed on the Republic were so numerous as to cause President Wilson to withdraw the sanction of the American government lest it "might conceivably go the length in some unhappy contingency of forcible interference in the financial and even the political affairs of that great Oriental State" — in other words, lest it make China a second Egypt. More immediately perilous to national independence was the attitude of Japan. When the World War broke out Japan seized the German leased port of Kiao-chau and thus became master of "nine points of the law" in the Shan-tung peninsula. She then took advantage of her improved strategic position and the fact that all rival powers, except the United States, were then involved in the European conflict, to press on China a series of demands designed to establish definitely a Japanese sphere of influence over Manchuria, eastern Inner Mongolia, and the provinces of Shan-tung and Fukien in China proper.

These demands, and others of a more general character which were later abandoned, contradicted the principle of *Japan's "twenty-one demands," 1915* the Open Door, and menaced not only Chinese independence but European and American trade as well. China was asked to appoint Japanese advisers in political, financial and military affairs, to grant the right of land ownership to Japanese hospitals, churches and schools; to admit Japanese police into the Chinese service at certain "important places," to buy war munitions from Japan, to grant railway contracts in the Yangtze valley. Peking protested, students rioted and merchants boycotted Japanese goods, but there was no hope of effective foreign aid, and so when Japan abandoned her claim to a general control of Chinese affairs the Chinese government accepted the terms relating to specific local concessions.[1] These related to: (1) recognition by China of the rights acquired by Japan as successor to Germany in Shan-tung; (2) an extension of the Japanese lease of Port Arthur and Dalny to 1997, extension of the lease of the Manchurian railways, and general priority of rights in commercial concessions in southern Manchuria and Inner Mongolia; (3) recognition of the rights of the Hanyehping Company, financed by Japanese capital, in developing the iron and coal resources of the Yangtze valley, (4) an agreement not to grant to foreign nations concessions in the province of Fukien.

That Chinese hopes of freedom and national revival should have enhanced civil strife and foreign aggression is disappointing enough. Young Turkey had suf- *China in* fered in the same way as Young China, and both *transition* could ruefully ponder the small grain of truth in the reactionary contention that reform merely precipitates trouble. Yet there has been substantial progress through it all. Modern education in particular made important advances, and foreign educators such as Bertrand Russell and John Dewey were amazed at the rapid growth in popular enlightenment. Nor have the troubles of a time of revolution been as disastrous to the Chinese as an American or European would expect. The real life of the nation is in its self-contained villages and a blow at the center is not fatal to the daily routine of the masses in the provinces. They go on about their business as if revolution were merely an inconvenience

[1] For the later development of Chino-Japanese relations see Chapter XXX.

CHAPTER X

THE RISE OF THE TRIPLE ENTENTE

EACH new study of the background of the World War seems to lay less stress on the immediate events of 1914 and more on the diplomatic revolution at the opening of the century which isolated Germany and sur-rounded her with an "iron ring" of potential *The diplo-matic revo-lution* foes similar to that which Bismarck had once forged to encompass France. The loss of Russia from Bismarck's diplomatic combination was, perhaps, inevitable in view of the irreconcilable rivalry of Russia and Austria-Hungary in the Near East. The Triple Alliance of Germany, Austria-Hungary and Italy, together with the minor states which were more or less within their sphere of influence, such as Rumania, still formed a stronger combination than France and Russia so long as Great Britain remained aloof. But the ten years following the formation of the Dual Alliance greatly weakened Germany's position. The British abandoned all idea of a German alliance and sought a friendly understanding with France, Italy ceased to be a reliable partner, Serbia became definitely hostile, Rumania became doubtful, Japan and Portugal were almost certain to support British policy. The next ten years, from the Anglo-French *entente* of 1904 to the outbreak of the World War, developed the implications of this situation, hardened vague tendencies into definite alignments and accentuated the rivalry of the opposed diplomatic leagues.

Germany as a result of these changes lost her European hegemony and found herself for the first time since the Empire was established facing superior odds. But the picture should not be oversimplified. Two considerations

must be borne in mind. In the first place, Germany was
never isolated to so great a degree as was France from 1870

*Germany
still formi-
dable*

to 1892. To the very end Austria-Hungary remained a faithful, though often embarrassing,
ally. Again, the loss of friends and the rise of adversaries were in part balanced by Germany's own rapid
increase in population, wealth and power. If the reign of
Wilhelm II represented steady loss for Germany in the field
of diplomacy, it represented also steady gains in every other
factor that can make for success in war. Therefore when
war did come the result remained doubtful till four years of
struggle had exhausted Germany's resources and brought
into the field against her neutral nations, such as the United
States, which were not involved in the shifting of peace-time
alliances.

Might-have-beens in history are always interesting.
During those plastic years, 1894–1904, the general coalition

*British
isolation*

against Germany came very near to becoming
instead a general coalition against Great Britain,
and as late as 1905 the Kaiser made frantic though unsuccessful efforts to revive the idea of a "continental league"
against "the yellow peril" (Japan and China) and "the
Anglo-Saxons" (Britain and America). The acuteness of
the colonial rivalry between Britain and France during the
eighteen-nineties, the jealousy which all the continental
powers felt in some degree at the dominant strength of the
British navy and the vast extent of the British overseas
Empire, and the growing keenness of international commercial competition would have made a continental coalition a natural outcome of the "new imperialism." If
France had been able to forget Alsace-Lorraine, if German
diplomacy had been wise enough to conciliate other nations
instead of frightening and estranging them, if the British
had remained in the transient mood of arrogant aloofness
which is so accurately reflected in Kipling's verses of the

period,[1] the Triple Alliance and the Dual Alliance might have blended into a five-power pact directed against the British Empire, and secondarily perhaps against Japan and the United States.

The decision of Wilhelm II and his ministers that Germany must have a navy commensurate with her military and commercial greatness was probably the turning point in Anglo-German foreign relations. Bismarck had foregone a navy — for the tiny fleet of his day, not comparable to that of France, let alone of Britain, scarcely deserved the name. The British navy of the early nineties could probably have encountered, unaided, the combined forces of either the Triple Alliance or the Dual Alliance with good prospect of success.[2] When a temporary naval panic would sweep Victorian England the armaments of France were usually the cause, though even France was not a very serious rival. But the new Kaiser was more consistently bent on making Germany a great naval power than on any other policy of his entire reign. As early as 1897 he appointed Admiral von Tirpitz, a "big navy" zealot, as head of his Admiralty, and publicly announced that "I will never rest till I have raised my navy to the same standard as that of my army."

In 1898 the German government secured from a hesitating Reichstag a naval bill which for the first time made Germany one of the Great Powers at sea. The Kaiser was

Germany builds a navy

---

[1] As in his "Song of the Dominions" (1898):
"On thy house and my house lies half the world's hate.
For my house and thy house no help shall we find
Save thy house and my house — kin cleaving to kind."
Contrast his tribute to the *entente* with France written in 1913:
"the linked and steadfast guard set for peace on earth"!

[2] The official standard was that the British fleet should be at least equal to the naval strength of any two other nations. But in the twentieth century the British, in following this formula, took account of European fleets only and did not reckon that of the United States as a possible part of any hostile combination, and after 1904 they regarded the French fleet rather as a potential ally than as a probable enemy.

jubilant — and incautious. With his usual love of the striking phrase, he used to express his satisfaction dur-

*Inception of
the Anglo-
German
naval race*

ing the years when his fleet was in building by
such sayings as "the trident belongs in our
hands," "our future lies on the water," and
refer to himself as "Admiral of the Atlantic." A Navy
League was founded to carry on propaganda for a bigger
navy. Unfortunately, to justify a navy as large as was desired, the taxpayers must be convinced that there was danger from Great Britain, and the Navy League became an
agency of anti-British agitation. The preamble of the law
of 1900 hinted directly at possible conflict with Great Britain: "Germany must possess a fleet of such strength that
a war against the mightiest naval Power would endanger
the supremacy of that Power." The desire for a great
navy arose partly from the renewed interest in colonial
development that very naturally accompanied Germany's
rapid industrial and commercial expansion and partly from
personal and national pride. The Kaiser was fond of the
sea, spending much of his life aboard his yacht; he felt
humiliated that Germany should be much behind other
nations in anything, especially anything relating to military
prowess; and, most of all perhaps, he desired to make his
reign memorable by some striking personal achievement,
such as would be the building of a German navy. The new
generation in Germany shared his sentiments. There is
no reason to suppose that the German government had at
this time any definite expectation of a war with Great
Britain, still less a determination to start one, but it was
unfortunate that the beginning of the most momentous
armament race in history happened at a time when Anglo-
German relations were already strained by other causes and
that it led Germany to reject offers of friendship, alliance and
naval limitation repeatedly proferred by Great Britain.

The colonial rivalry between Great Britain and France

reached its climax in 1898 in the "Fashoda incident" and
the exclusion of France from the valley of the   *Diplomatic*
Nile.[1]   The British government at the same   *"incidents"*
period met with repeated rebuffs from both Germany and
Russia while striving to rescue the Armenians from Turkish
oppression and massacre.   When in 1896 the German
Kaiser telegraphed his congratulations to President Kruger
of the Transvaal for having repelled the Jameson Raid[2]
without invoking the aid of friendly powers, the British
press construed the act as a direct provocation.   In his
memoirs the Kaiser defended his conduct in the matter as
forced on him by his advisers against his own judgment,
but it is of very little importance whose was the original
idea of sending the telegram as by accepting advice the
Kaiser assumed full responsibility.   During the Boer War
the impression of continental hostility was deepened.   With
practical unanimity the press of France, Germany and other
continental states denounced the subjugation of the Boer
Republics.   The attitude of the Kaiser, warned perhaps by
the storm of protest which his Kruger telegram had raised,
was "correct" throughout the war, but as much could not
be said for the German nation at large.   One unpleasant
incident was an exchange of insults between Joseph Chamberlain, colonial secretary and the most prominent man in
the British cabinet at the moment, and the German Chancellor.   Irritated by allegations that the British army had
been guilty of atrocities in the South African War Chamberlain very undiplomatically retorted that Germany had
waged war far more ruthlessly in times past, notably in
1870.   Chancellor von Bülow in reply said that those who
criticized the German army were "biting granite."

Though the American press and public had in the main
joined the continental Europeans in denouncing the Boer
War, on most other issues of the time the two English-

[1] See above, page 130.   [2] See above, pages 109–110.

speaking nations were in sympathy. In 1895 there had been
The Anglo- a controversy over the boundary between Ven-
American ezuela and British Guiana. The British insisted
entente on drawing the boundary entirely in accordance with their own views, and President Cleveland,
regarding this as contrary to the principles of the Monroe
Doctrine, demanded arbitration, and permitted his Secretary of State to assert that the United States was "practically sovereign on this continent" with respect to the
"subjects to which it confines its interposition." But this
was the last war scare that ever arose between the two
countries. The British, while not accepting Secretary
Olney's interpretation of the Monroe Doctrine, did agree
to an arbitration of the question at issue. During the
Spanish-American War, the British press was pro-American,
the continental press pro-Spanish. The conduct of the
German Admiral Diedrichs at Manila Bay, ostentatiously
friendly toward the Spanish and obstructive toward Admiral Dewey's fleet, stood in marked contrast with the
attitude of British officers. The Armenian massacres
aroused as keen resentment in America as in Britain.
Finally, the Far Eastern question brought the British and
American governments into very close and friendly co-operation, and at the same time emphasized the isolation of Great
Britain in Europe.

Russia's aggressive policy in Manchuria and Korea had
the support of both Germany and France, as rival bidders
Repercus- for Russian favor. The three powers had joined
sions of in forcing Japan out of Manchuria after the
eastern Chino-Japanese War.[1] Great Britain had mark-
Asia on
European edly abstained, and in 1902 had singled out
diplomacy Japan as her ally in the Far East. The British
had given strong support to Secretary Hay's policy of the
"Open Door"; some of the continental powers, especially

[1] See above, page 214.

Russia, were more hesitant. In the Russo-Japanese War, Great Britain and even the United States qualified their official neutrality by enthusiastic popular applause for the Japanese; Germany and France sympathized with Russia. In the case of France the reason is obvious, Russia was the great ally on whom the French had built so many hopes of increased diplomatic influence, but the attitude of Germany requires some explanation. In large part it was due to the personal diplomacy of Wilhelm II. He disliked the Orientals and was a convinced believer in the "yellow peril," and he was at the same time earnestly striving to reconquer the lost friendship of Russia. In this endeavor he was able to work on the weak and unstable mind of the Tsar, who shared with him a distrust of French democratic government and English liberalism, and sway him towards Bismarck's old policy of a League of the Three Emperors. But Wilhelm was more ambitious than Bismarck. Though he disliked the French government, he cherished for a time the hope that France would not consent to isolation and would forget her old quarrel with Germany when it became evident that Russia had been lost to her. Thus a continental *bloc* of the Triple Alliance and the Dual Alliance would be created under German leadership and "Anglo-Saxon imperialism" be forever checked.

No revelation of secret diplomacy in modern times is more amazing than the correspondence between the Tsar Nicholas II and the Kaiser Wilhelm II. The letters are intimate and undignified, and the considerations of state put forward in them are naïve in the extreme. It must not be rashly assumed, however, that the Kaiser placed his full mind before his friend "Nicky"; he was using the arguments which would most influence him. In 1898 he conveyed to the Tsar Chamberlain's project for an Anglo-German alliance [1] and asked

The "Willy-Nicky" correspondence

[1] See below, pages 241–242.

"what you can offer me and what you will do for me if I refuse the British offers." The Tsar merely replied that he also had rejected flattering offers from the British. But during the Russo-Japanese War, when the Tsar was smarting under British manifestations of friendship for Japan, the Kaiser renewed his suggestions for an alliance with Russia with better prospects of success. He suggested a Russo-German alliance to which France would have to adhere and incidentally remarked that in building up her fleet Russia would do well to buy from Germany; "our private firms would be most glad to receive contracts"! The Tsar said that he, too, believed "that Germany, Russia and

The Björkö treaty, 1905 France should at once unite upon an arrangement to abolish Anglo-Japanese arrogance." In July, 1905, a secret treaty between the two monarchs was signed at Björkö on the Baltic. If either power were to be attacked by a third European power, its ally would aid it with all its forces in Europe and not make separate peace; the treaty was to go into effect as soon as peace was made between Russia and Japan, and its terms communicated to France after it had become effective.

But when the Tsar communicated his agreement with the Kaiser to his ministers they were not pleased and he

Russia rejects the Björkö treaty had to listen to an unusual amount of plain speaking. The Tsar was still an autocrat, he could have insisted on his treaty and found new ministers to carry out his wishes, but the domestic situation was threatening, the Kaiser was no longer with him to insinuate persuasive arguments, and the flat insistence of Counts Witte and Lamsdorff that France would never agree to such a compact influenced his impressionable mind. He reluctantly agreed to inform the Kaiser that the new treaty could not come into effect unless France approved it in advance. This ended the last attempt at a continental league. Why did the Kaiser fail? His projected Russian alliance was not only a good one in the interests of Germany but it appealed almost as much to the Tsar, and, while France would probably not have entered into partnership with Germany, at least the Kaiser's plan might have disrupted the Franco-Russian alliance. There seem to have been two reasons for his failure: one, that he made the attempt too late, when Russia was already closely bound to France and France to Britain; the other, that his policy was too largely a personal one and had been neither supported by public opinion nor worked out by the diplomatic "experts"; it took Count Witte in Russia completely by surprise and von Bülow, the German Chancellor, complained that the Kaiser had not communicated to him some important alterations in the substance of the German proposals. Though the full details of the Russo-German negotiations were kept secret till the World War, the British suspected that the German government was pursuing a policy friendly to Russia and hostile to themselves, and they were more than ever convinced that Germany was indeed *the* enemy.

The isolation of Germany is not, however, fully explained by the failure to isolate Great Britain. Why, for example, should there not have been an Anglo-German alliance instead of an Anglo-French *Entente*? *Background of Anglo-German relations* Abstractly, from the standpoint of nineteenth-century history, that would have seemed the more natural combination. The British and Germans were alike "Teutonic" in language, at least partly "Nordic" in race, "Protestant" in religion and, what amounted to more than all such ties, closely allied in recent political controversies. In the days of Frederick the Great and in the days of Napoleon British and Prussian regiments had fought side by side against the French. There had been no recent war between Great Britain and any German state; none at all between Great Britain and united Germany. The British royal house was mainly German in blood (though for the matter of that so were most other European dynasties, since the numerous German monarchical states provided so many eligible princesses for foreign marriages), Victoria and her husband Prince Albert had been German in sympathy and their daughter was mother of Wilhelm II. Bismarck, as we have seen, managed to maintain generally friendly relations with the British in spite of minor colonial controversies. German liberals were enthusiastic "Anglomaniacs," for they thought they saw in British parliamentary institutions a golden mean between their own autocracy and French revolutionary republicanism. On the other side of the narrow seas, British historians such as Freeman, essayists such as Carlyle, novelists such as Kingsley, statesmen such as Joseph Chamberlain, represented a large body of opinion when they eulogized their "Teutonic kinsmen." Carlyle hailed the defeat of France in 1870 as the "hopefullest public fact" of his time! Were there nothing else to draw the two powers together, their common antagonism to France and their common dread of Russia might have sufficed.

Of course, there were other facts to set against these. The building of the German fleet, the increase of German com-

Causes making for friction

mercial competition, the growth of the German colonial empire, the frequent diplomatic indiscretions of Kaiser "Wilhelm the Sudden," the rather aggressive manners of the young German Empire were bound in any case to disturb the British, while on the other hand the British Empire seemed to impatient German imperialists a huge land and sea monopoly barring their progress in every direction, and they were further irritated by the rather patronizing tone adopted toward the continental nations by some Victorian statesmen. Kaiser Wilhelm's touchy vanity was constantly being wounded by what seemed to him British slights and condescensions. The militaristic historian Treitschke had for years urged that only on the ruins of the British Empire could be built the Greater Germany of the future.   No fairer expression of this mutual misunderstanding can be found than the words of the German historian Karl Nowak: "Time was bound to soften the rather rough edges of German statesmanship. There could hardly fail to come a type of statesman who did not confuse persuasiveness with stark force, other people's hesitations and reservations with traps and trickery, projects and proposals with pressure, diplomacy with the German's all too downright plain-spokenness.   If, in the meantime, the British statesmen were to realize that it was not in the nature of things that one of two friends should for all time be strong and poor and the other strong and rich... then the way might after all be open one day to an Entente, perhaps even to more than that." [1]

Yet these asperities did not prevent suggestions from both countries for close political agreements between them. Bismarck had more or less tentatively suggested *Approaches* on several occasions that Great Britain should *toward an* form a defensive alliance with Germany, at least *alliance* as against France, and though nothing was done in the matter, owing to the traditional British dislike of broad general alliances, the British government entered into the Mediterranean agreements of 1887 with Germany's allies, Austria-Hungary and Italy, to maintain the *status quo* in the Balkans and north Africa.   The eighteen-nineties marked the height of Anglo-French colonial antagonism, and in 1898, in spite of the friction so recently aroused by the Kaiser's telegram to Kruger, the question of an alliance was again mooted. This time the approaches came from Britain and the Germans were coy.   The driving spirit behind the project was Joseph Chamberlain, who informed the German Ambassador, Count Hatzfeldt, that the time had come to abandon

[1] K. F. Nowak, *Germany's Road to Ruin* (1932), page 74.

the policy of isolation and that the British preferred a German alliance but might have to turn elsewhere if it could not be obtained.   This offer, transmitted to the Kaiser, was at once communicated by the latter to the Tsar as a proof of Germany's preference for Russia over Great Britain.   Chamberlain knew that his overtures had been coldly received but not that his confidence had been betrayed, and, as late as November, 1899, he publicly stated that "the natural alliance is between ourselves and the great German Empire." This open proffer of friendship was rather contemptuously rejected by the German ministry.   In 1901 Chamberlain once more, in spite of these repeated rebuffs, opened negotiations, but the Germans demanded that if an alliance be made it include the entire Triple Alliance and obligate Great Britain to come to the rescue of Germany, Austria-Hungary or Italy if any one of them were attacked by two powers. Lord Salisbury, the Prime Minister, who had in the main been friendly towards Germany, advised that such conditions be rejected and even questioned if a simple alliance with Germany would any longer be welcomed by public opinion.

Germany rejects British friendship   The haggling spirit in which the German government received the British offers is well illustrated by a letter of Chancellor von Bülow to the Kaiser in 1901:

> The English are gradually becoming aware that they will not be able to maintain their world dominion with their own strength against so many adversaries.   It is now a matter of neither discouraging the English nor of letting oneself be prematurely pinned down by them.   The embarrassment of the English will be enhanced in the next few months,[1] and thereby the price which we will be able to demand will increase.   We must not show the English too great readiness.... The understanding which the English threaten to make with the Dual Alliance is only a bugbear for our intimidation.

[1] This was during the Boer War, when the British were most conscious of their painful isolation.

The reasons why the German government so persistently forced the British to turn from Germany to her enemies have been endlessly discussed by historians and nowhere with more acid severity than by the Germans themselves, for in the light of 1914 it appears to be an outstanding diplomatic blunder.   There were many factors: the Kaiser's persistent delusion that he could reverse the trend of alliances and bring Russia and perhaps even France over to the side of Germany, the bitter feeling roused by the Boer War in both countries, the fear that the price of a British alliance would be a limitation of the German navy.   But unquestionably the chief factor was the inept handling of all questions relating to foreign affairs after the dismissal of Bismarck. To explain this we must turn to the internal politics of Germany under Wilhelm II.

From his dismissal of Bismarck in 1890 till the end of his reign Wilhelm II was really his own Chancellor.   None of Bismarck's successors was permitted the free *The Kaiser* hand in formulating policy which he had en- *and his* joyed.   General Leo von Caprivi (1890–94) was *Chancellors* a simple, plain-dealing man of unusual honesty but also of unusual political inexperience; he was constantly embarrassed by Bismarck's faultfinding and by the Kaiser's penchant for undiplomatic speech making, and he had not himself sufficient prestige to compete with either.   Prince Hohenlohe (1894–1900) was a far more prominent man, perhaps the most eminent of modern Bavarian statesmen. But he was greatly enfeebled by age and in the main permitted events to take their course without imposing his own personality on them.   Bernhard von Bülow (1900–09) certainly lacked neither ambition nor address, he had a positive policy of his own and for some time enjoyed the special confidence of the Kaiser who thought him a second and more agreeable Bismarck.   His polish, his social talents, and his great capacity for making whatever he advocated seem plausible made many persons, including himself, believe him a great diplomat. Yet it was exactly during his Chancellorship that Germany finally alienated Great Britain, and he had already made matters bad enough by the advice which he had given for several years as Foreign Minister under Hohenlohe. He seemed unable to act straightforwardly, everything with him was a game of intrigue, which ended by making him the object of almost universal distrust. The last Chancellor before the World War, Theobald von Bethmann-Hollweg (1909–17), was, like Caprivi, an honest, simple man without much force and totally unable to dominate German policy; he had the misfortune to be in office when the crisis of 1914 compelled him to assume the responsibility for a war which he had not desired.

Though the Kaiser was the actual as well as the nominal head of the government this does not mean that he was unswayed by advice. He had a much stronger will than his friend the Tsar, but he gave his confidence in turn to many advisers, some of them, like Bülow, holders of high public office, others, like Count Philip Eulenburg, personal friends about the court, others, like Admiral Tirpitz, specialists in the business of war. On economic matters he listened to the new captains of industry, such as Albert Ballin the director of the Hamburg-Amerika steamship line. But most persistently influential of all was a dyspeptic recluse in the foreign office, Privy Councilor Friedrich von Holstein, an expert "career man" who held over in office after Bismarck's fall because he was considered uniquely well-informed on all diplomatic affairs. He was not anti-British except in the general sense that he was suspicious of all foreign nations and held Machiavelli's opinion that mankind at large were but a set of rascals on whom good faith would be wasted, but he held firmly to a dogmatic conviction, reiterated in numberless memoranda to his of-

How Germany was governed after 1890

Holstein

ficial superiors, that an understanding between Great Britain on the one hand and France or Russia on the other was quite impossible, and that therefore the British must come to Germany on the latter's own terms. Nobody liked Holstein; the men in higher office called him "mole," "hyena" and "monster of the labyrinth," but he had the double satisfaction of persuading them to follow his guidance and revenging himself for slights by wrecking some of the most brilliant careers. His cynical and immoralist views of statesmanship were well expressed in his comment on the Hague Conference, "Arbitration is all right for small states and small questions, not for large states and large questions."

After 1901 the British made several attempts to mitigate German hostility, but they had practically abandoned hope of an alliance or even an *entente*. No longer believing in the possibility of self-sufficient isolation they turned elsewhere for friends, first to Japan in 1902, then to France in 1904, and finally to Russia in 1907. The Japanese alliance was mainly directed against Russia rather than Germany, and Germany might have had a partnership in it if she had been willing to show such open preference for British as against Russian friendship. But the understanding with France was a different matter; it so plainly arose from British distrust of the policy of the German government that it at once accentuated the growing hostility between the two countries. Like the Franco-Russian alliance a decade earlier, the Anglo-French *entente* had to be reached slowly after the overcoming of many prejudices. A friendly understanding was delayed by the Fashoda incident and by the Boer War, but it is arguable that in the long run both events helped clear the air, for the first led to a definite and final demarcation of African territories and the second brought home to the British the dangers of isolation. After the Boer War few obstacles re-

Great Britain turns toward France

mained to prevent an *entente* except the soreness from old quarrels and the still outstanding problems of Morocco and Egypt.

If France was unwilling and Great Britain unable to come to a permanent understanding with Germany, the logic of *The per-* the situation certainly pointed to an agreement *sonal fac-* with each other, and in the long run the force *tor: Edward* *VII and* of this logic would have overridden personal *Delcassé* preferences and prejudices. But the path to such an agreement was greatly facilitated by the coming into power of new men in both countries. Edward VII became King in 1901. He had no policy apart from that of his ministers, the attempt of his German critics and his less discreet English admirers to make him out "the author of the *entente*" shows merely ignorance of the working of the British government; a King cannot disregard his ministers, nor his ministers disregard parliament, press and public. But the fact that he was himself a lover of France and a warm advocate of friendly relations across the Channel made the task of his cabinet much the easier. Friendly visits paid by Edward in 1903 to France and by President Loubet to England were advance witnesses of diplomatic co-operation. In 1898 Théophile Delcassé became the French Foreign Minister and he remained in office till 1905, outlasting several cabinets. His policy was in the main that of Clemenceau, that France must never forget that Germany was her real foe and permanent peril and that peace and friendship with Great Britain was worth having even at the cost of colonial compromises.

With the single exception of the Balkans, no part of the world played so persistent a rôle in twentieth-century diplo-*The* matic controversy as Morocco. Morocco was *Morocco* the last part of Africa open to the international *situation* scramble for colonies; Algeria and Tunis were already French, Egypt although nominally Turkish was in

reality British, Tripoli though also under Turkish suzerainty
was generally understood to be Italy's allotted share whenever Italy was ready to occupy. Nor was there any real
possibility of Morocco standing alone. Like the other
Mohammedan states in Africa, Morocco was at once weak
and corrupt, entangled in debt and unable to prevent
popular tumults against foreigners which gave pretext for
European intervention. Even the efforts of the Sultan for
reform, being expensive, bogged the nation further in debt.
The three powers most interested in Moroccan conditions
were Britain, which had by far the largest trade, France,
which had interest in protecting the Algerian frontier from
bandit raids, and Spain, Morocco's nearest European neighbor. Germany's interests were less direct, and for some
time the Kaiser professed almost complete indifference to
the question, probably because his mind was full of his personal plans for an alliance with Russia and he did not wish a
quarrel with France which might complicate the situation.
But other Germans, mindful of the commercial interests
which the Fatherland had in Morocco, cherished hopes of a
"sphere of interest" in part of that country, the only north
African state not yet pre-empted.

Of the four European powers most apt to intervene in
Morocco France was keenest on the quarry. Britain, Germany and Spain would have been content to let *Log-rolling*
the question stand open for a few years more, *in north*
but France, irritated by disorders along the *Africa*
Algerian boundary, wanted what amounted to "police
power" in the whole of Morocco (except for some small zone
which might be thrown as compensation to Spain) and the
quickest way to this goal would be an agreement with the
other interested powers. Fortunately, as regards Britain,
France had compensation to offer. The British occupation
of Egypt, anomalous in so many ways,[1] was difficult to de-

[1] See above, pages 127–129.

fend from the legal standpoint, and other nations could and frequently did embarrass British policy by appealing to the "sovereign rights" of Turkey or the French rights, theoretically equal to the British, of financial administration. Why should not the British offer a free hand to France in Morocco in exchange for a similar free hand for themselves in Egypt? At once the greatest obstacles to the friendship of the two powers would be removed and the possibility of a general diplomatic accord would be strengthened. There were some minor disputes between the two countries which might be adjusted at the same time: disputes as to Newfoundland fishing rights, boundary delimitations in western tropical Africa, the status of Siam, Madagascar and the New Hebrides islands.

The *entente cordiale* between Great Britain and France was not an alliance, such as Germany's with Austria-Hungary, France's with Russia, or Britain's with Japan. An alliance is a legal document specifically stating the conditions of political or military co-operation. An *entente* is a much vaguer thing, and may perhaps be defined as the *fact* of co-operation without the *pledge*. From 1904 to 1914 Great Britain and France did, though without legal obligation, act as though they were allied. The specific and legal part of the *entente*, which was not the most important, consisted of a treaty of general arbitration signed in 1903 and a series of colonial agreements signed in 1904. By the arbitration treaty "differences of a juridical order," unless they involved the honor or "vital interests" of the powers concerned or could be solved by the ordinary processes of diplomacy, should be submitted to the Hague Court. The most important colonial agreement, embodied in the treaty of April 8, 1904, provided that the French would "not obstruct the action of Great Britain" in Egypt by asking that a time limit be fixed for the British occupation, and that the British would recognize the right

The entente cordiale

of France to preserve order in Morocco and "provide assistance for the purpose of all administrative, economic, financial, and military reforms." France pledged herself to come to an agreement with Spain about Morocco but — significant omission! — made no reference to Germany. In secret clauses appended to the treaty, provision was made for the possible case that Great Britain might exercise still closer control over Egypt or that France should proceed to a partition of Morocco between herself and Spain.

The Anglo-French *entente* was unquestionably the most important factor in the "diplomatic revolution" at the turn of the century. Perhaps second in importance *Italy swings* was the changed attitude of Italy. As the *toward* French Republic was in violent controversy *France* with the Roman Catholic Church and already contemplating its disestablishment in France, certainly there was no danger of the old bugaboo of a French army supporting Papal claims in Rome. Time had healed the quarrel over Tunis, and in 1899 Delcassé assured the Italians that France would in no case intervene in Tripoli. This opened the way to a definite agreement in 1900 that France would not interfere with Italian policy in Tripoli and that Italy would not interfere with French policy in Morocco. Chancellor Bülow with his easy surface optimism assured the Reichstag that Germany had nothing to worry about, "In a happy marriage the husband must not be angry if his wife takes an extra dance with another partner; the main thing is that she does not elope with him." But in 1902 Italy took the further step of agreeing with France to remain neutral in a war involving France, if France had been attacked or had suffered "direct provocation." This greatly weakened the Triple Alliance, for obviously it gave Italy the power to determine in all cases whether she was obliged to stand by Germany and Austria-Hungary or not, since there exists no definition of what constitutes a "direct provocation." The Anglo-French *entente* also made a great difference to Italian policy, for all Europe understood that Italy, with her long coastline, could never risk a conflict with the British fleet. In their private correspondence and memoranda both Bülow and the Kaiser confessed frankly enough that they could no longer be sure what Italy might do in the event of a European war.

The failure to bring about a general alliance between Great Britain and Germany did not preclude common action *Anglo-Ger-* on certain specific questions of overseas imperial-*man co-op-* ism. The results of these attempts at co-opera-*eration in China,* tion, however, were not reassuring to either *Venezuela,* country. In 1900 Great Britain and Germany *Africa* agreed on a common policy opposing further partition of China, but disputes later arose as to whether the agreement covered Manchuria where the German government gave tacit support to Russia's policy of aggression. Venezuela might in some ways be termed the "Morocco of America," a weak, disorderly republic always at odds with foreign powers. A Venezuelan boundary dispute had led to the last serious quarrel between Great Britain and the United States in 1895, and an Anglo-German naval expedition to enforce the collection of debts by blockade led in 1902 to strong remonstrances from President Roosevelt. The British adopted a pacific attitude a little sooner than the Germans, so Germany bore the brunt of American displeasure. The British press commented on the whole episode in unfavorable terms, and Kipling (that faithful thermometer of popular sentiment!) called the Germans "the breed that have wronged us most" and "the shameless Hun." In 1898 Great Britain promised to allow Germany a share in the colonies of Portugal if they should ever come into the market and to make concerted arrangements as to loans to Portugal. But Portugal refused to sell, made other financial arrangements, and in 1899 concluded a treaty with Great Britain renewing the old Anglo-Portuguese treaty of alliance of the seventeenth century.   Probably in all three of these cases both governments were acting in general good faith towards each other, but it is easy to see how mutual misunderstandings led to reciprocal charges of perfidy.

A much more important problem in the dynamics of imperialism was the question of the Bagdad railway.   The familiar phrase "Berlin to Bagdad" is often ap- *Berlin-* plied in two very different senses.   Sometimes it *Bagdad* is used with reference to a purely commercial enterprise, the completion of railroad connections between Mesopotamia and the Straits, which would in turn connect with other routes, completed or projected, from Constantinople to central Europe.   Sometimes it is used to imply all the imperialistic ambitions which such a route might make possible. British and French investors as well as German sought railroad concessions in Asiatic Turkey, an excellent field for foreign capital, since the Ottoman Empire lacked the capital and the technical skill to develop its own routes.   In 1903 the Bagdad Railway Company, a private corporation under German direction, finally obtained an agreement with the Ottoman government to link the railroads of Anatolia (Asia Minor) with the Persian Gulf.   Foreign capital was needed. At first Premier Balfour and Foreign Secretary Lansdowne favored the participation of British finance in the enterprise, but so great was the public hostility to any more Anglo-German joint enterprises that the government retreated and abandoned participation in the project.   Many afterwards considered this decision unwise, since French and British financiers might by working together have taken the main control of the railroad out of German hands.   But in 1903 Britain and France were not as close friends as they were eventually to become.

At one time or another, though in no case consistently, Russia, France and Britain opposed the German railroad enterprise.   This was not wholly because of the economic

interests involved, though the power to develop the resources
The Drang of Mesopotamia was a prize worth winning.[1]
nach Osten The real objections to the plan were strategic.
The railway project coincided too ominously with the attempt of the German government to win a political and
military ascendancy over the whole Ottoman Empire not to
awaken the suspicions of the Russians, still dreaming of
Constantinople, and of the British, nervous as to the safety
of Egypt and India. Dr. Paul Rohrbach was incautious
enough to point out in his book on the Bagdad project that
"We can never dream of attacking Egypt until Turkey is
mistress of a developed railway system." Ports on the Persian Gulf would also make possible, or at least conceivable,
attacks on India. Austria-Hungary also desired friendly relations with Turkey in order to hold in check the Christian
Balkan States, especially Serbia. In its widest extension,
Berlin–Bagdad implied a glorified system of alliances from
the North Sea to the Persian Gulf, a sort of Bremen–Berlin–Budapest–Belgrade–Byzantium (Constantinople)–Bagdad–Basra Bahn! If we may continue the enticing allitera-
tion, the real fear was that an imperialistic Germany might
some day add Brussels and Boulogne to one end of this line
and Bombay to the other.

This "drive to the east" did not, of course, imply a German conquest of Turkey or even the establishment of any
The Ger- formal protectorate. On the contrary, what Ger-
man-Turk- many sought was the position, so long held by
ish entente Britain, of champion and "next friend" of the
Ottoman Empire. Bismarck's ostentatious indifference to
the Near Eastern question was replaced in the time of Wilhelm II by a feverish desire to cultivate the good will of the
Turks. The Turkish army received instruction from German

---

[1] "The Bagdad line was probably the most valuable single prize still unappro-
priated... in the colonial world." F. Schevill, *History of the Balkan Peninsula* (1922),
page 448.

experts and bought German munitions. As early as 1895 Germany, in the person of the young Kaiser, rejected suggestions from Premier Salisbury that the time might soon come for reopening the question of the partition of Turkey. In Armenia and Crete he supported Turkish supremacy and he blocked British efforts to force the Sultan to grant reforms. In 1898 he made an official visit to Palestine by way of Constantinople. He enjoyed the trip tremendously, especially the triumphal entry into Jerusalem, but he did not forget his political purposes and at Damascus he announced that he would always be the friend of the Sultan and "the three hundred million Mussulmans scattered over the earth." As a very large proportion of the world's Mohammedans were subjects of Asiatic Russia, British India, Egypt or French north Africa, this appeal to Pan-Islamic sentiment was the cause of quite a flutter among the diplomatic dovecotes. With the Young Turk revolution of 1908, the Kaiser's influence, so largely based on his personal support of Sultan Abdul Hamid, seemed shaken, but it was not long before Germany again was in close understanding with the new rulers of the Ottoman State.

Another voyage of the "travel Emperor" (*der reise Kaiser*) which had important diplomatic results was to the Sultan of Morocco. Chancellor Bülow, much disturbed at the turning of both Britain and Italy toward France, decided to strike straight at the new French ascendancy over Morocco. Germany had been no party to the bargains by which Britain, Spain and Italy had been one by one induced to give France a free hand in that country; she was in no way bound to recognize France's newly assumed powers in that country. Bülow, perhaps on Holstein's advice, urged Kaiser Wilhelm to visit Tangier and announce Germany's Morocco policy on the ground itself. In accordance with this plan the Kaiser announced that he addressed the Sultan "in his capacity of in-

The Morocco question reopened, 1905

dependent sovereign" and urged an open door policy, giving equal rights to the commerce of all nations. Though the Kaiser does not seem at this time to have cared personally about Morocco, he loyally backed up the game his ministers were playing. Bülow followed up the Tangier incident by a circular to the powers requesting an international conference on the Morocco question. Foreign Minister Delcassé, apparently confident of British support, at first stubbornly refused a conference. But Premier Rouvier who wanted peace became seriously alarmed lest the refusal of a conference might lead to war. President Roosevelt promised that he would see that France had fair play at such a conference if, to avert war, she would consent that it be held. Rouvier decided to dismiss Delcassé, whose bellicose attitude stood in the way of a settlement.

Germany had gained two points, the dismissal of her chief enemy, Delcassé, and the calling of a conference of the *The Algeci-* powers to reaffirm the independence of Morocco *ras Confer-* and to regulate Moroccan affairs. But in the *ence, 1906* conference itself Germany noticed an ominous drawing together of France, Russia, Spain, Italy, Great Britain and even the United States, leaving her no consistently loyal friend save Austria-Hungary. The bullying methods to which German diplomacy had resorted before and during the conference alarmed or irritated other powers. The upshot of the conference was the Act of Algeciras, affirming Moroccan independence, guaranteeing all commercial rights of the powers under existing treaties, establishing an international bank and creating a Franco-Spanish police force under a Swiss Inspector-General. Germany could not reject an international settlement which conceded so much of what she demanded, yet in obtaining partial control over the policing of Morocco France had won a position which in the long run would bring the nation more and more within the French "sphere of influence." At the most, the vigorous intervention of Germany had delayed by several years a French protectorate over Morocco, while it had certainly brought France and Britain into closer diplomatic co-operation than either had anticipated when the *entente cordiale* was first established.

There was still a missing link in the anti-German coalition. If the Franco-Russian alliance and the Anglo-French *entente* were both to continue some way must be found *Anglo-* to reconcile Great Britain and Russia. There *Russian* was great need for this reconciliation on any ac- *relations* count if the two powers were to continue at peace. It is true that the Near Eastern policy of the British and Russian statesmen was not as sharply hostile in the eighteen-nineties as it had been from the time of the Crimean War to the Bulgarian crisis of 1887, but this was largely because the center of Russian interest had temporarily shifted to the Far East and, as we have seen, quarrels about Manchuria could be as dangerous to both countries as quarrels about Macedonia. The new century only made the tension worse. The Anglo-Japanese alliance of 1902, the Russo-Japanese War, the Dogger Bank incident, the secret but not wholly unsuspected negotiations between the Kaiser and the Tsar, repeatedly strained relations almost to the breaking point. There were a whole series of problems arising in the "Middle East" — Russian intrigues in Afghanistan, Russian influences in Tibet, Russian plots to control Persia and the Persian Gulf. The Tsar personally inclined strongly to a German alliance and some of his ministers disliked Britain as Russia's traditional and most inveterate foe. In Great Britain, where public opinion and the press influenced foreign policy more than was the case in other countries, the desire of the foreign office for closer relations with Russia was hampered and delayed by the strong dislike the "man in the street" had for the Russian government, its autocratic forms and its persecution of the Poles, Finns and Jews.

Nevertheless, the logical step was at last taken, and by a Liberal ministry.   Sir Edward Grey, who had succeeded Lord Lansdowne at the foreign office, was a warm friend of the *entente* with France, and as he was suspicious of German policy, he believed it essential to strike hands with Russia.   The method chosen was identical with that followed in the case of France, the settlement of outstanding colonial disputes. Both powers agreed to respect the territorial integrity of Tibet and to refrain from interfering in its internal affairs. Great Britain promised to respect the independence of Afghanistan, and Russia recognized British control over the foreign policy of that buffer state between their dominions. But by far the most important agreements were with respect to Persia.   Northern Persia was to be a Russian sphere of interest in which the British government would seek no political or commercial concessions; a small section of southern Persia, near Afghanistan, formed a similar British sphere, and a neutral zone was established between the two in which either country might seek concessions.   Russia and Japan also came to a friendly understanding as regards their Manchurian interests, thus terminating the possibility of a renewed Russo-Japanese War.

The Anglo-Russian entente of 1907

Persia was the sacrifice on the altar of peace.   Although the usual assurances of her independent sovereignty were given, the Russians took them no more seriously than did the French their assurances of the independence of Morocco.   Persia is an arid, rugged highland, three times as large as France but very thinly peopled.   In 1906 the Shah of Persia was forced to grant a constitution and a parliament (the majliss) and in 1909 he was deposed. A new patriotic movement swept Persia, akin to the attempts to modernize Turkey, China, Japan and other Oriental countries.   An American expert, Morgan Shuster, was appointed in 1911 as Treasurer General to straighten out the national

The fate of Persia

finances. Russia, not wanting Persia put in a position where she would be independent of Russian influence, intrigued against the reform government, supported the cause of the deposed Shah, occupied northern Persia with Cossack troops and forced Shuster's resignation. Liberal Britain looked on appalled but powerless; not daring to contest Russia's intervention too vigorously lest Russia revert to the Björkö policy of backing Germany against the British. "Persia tried my patience more than any other subject," said Sir Edward Grey, "I once told Benckendorff that if Russia made things too difficult the policy of friendly agreement might become impossible. In that case I should resign, for I could not myself pursue any other policy." Still Persia preserved at least nominal independence, and after the Russian revolution of 1917 there was less interference in the political affairs of the country, though foreign investors are much interested in the oil wells which have been discovered on Persian soil.

From 1907 to 1914 the interlocking action of the Franco-Russian Dual Alliance, the Anglo-French *entente* and the Anglo-Russian *entente* was commonly summed up as the Triple Entente and set over against the Triple Alliance of Germany, Austria-Hungary and Italy. As Japan had her own alliance with Britain, only the United States among the Great Powers of the world stood outside the two diplomatic camps. This sharp and definite alignment made every diplomatic incident seem a victory for one group and a defeat for the other, and every increase in any army or navy seem an ominous shift in the balance of power. Yet it required the rivalry of several years to harden the alliances into swords of war. The diplomatic situation in 1907 was no longer so plastic as it had been in 1900 or even in 1904, but Great Britain was not completely committed to France and Russia and the attitude of Italy was more than doubtful.

CHAPTER XI

TRIPLE ENTENTE VERSUS TRIPLE ALLIANCE

ONE ill effect of the marshaling of the European powers into separate leagues of allied and associated states was that it *Rival al-* weakened the idea of general co-operation of all *liances or* the powers. The best hope for peace that Europe *united* had during the first fourteen years of the new *Concert?* century was in strengthening the vague but important tradition of the "Concert of Europe." In dealing with Turkey and the Balkan states particularly, it had long been the custom for Germany, Austria-Hungary, Italy, Russia, France and Great Britain to take no action until they had reached an agreement as to the policy to be pursued. The practical result was too often to let matters drift while the Turk continued to misgovern and his Christian subjects to plot and carry on petty wars, but even this was better than to make the Near Eastern question the cause of a general European conflict. The partitioning of Africa was also peacefully effected by agreement among the powers, and the crushing of the Boxer movement in China brought into co-operation not only the European nations but also the United States and Japan. The Algeciras Conference had in all probability averted a Franco-German war over Morocco. The Concert had many faults. It had no structure, no legal basis, no times or places for regular meeting. It usually excluded the small countries from its debates and was often cynical and brutal in its handling of the rights of such countries. But because it stood for the common interests of all the great states it was a better basis for world peace than the balance of power maintained by the rivalry of hostile alliances.

The most ambitious attempt, previous to the creation of the League of Nations in 1919, to embody European internationalism in a definite legal form was the *The first* establishment of the Hague Court. This orig- *Hague* inated from an international conference at The *Conference,* Hague, the capital of the Netherlands, sum- *1898* moned by Tsar Nicholas II in 1898. The Russian autocrat, though too weak a man to keep his country at peace either at home or abroad, felt a vague attraction toward the ideal of universal peace. More concretely, he was alarmed at the rising cost of preparedness against Germany and Austria.[1] His invitation was accepted by other European nations, the United States and Japan, and in May of the following year the diplomats assembled. The Conference of 1899 achieved part of its task, the establishment of a permanent arbitral tribunal and a code of international customs designed to keep in bounds the horrors of warfare. But in the more important aims of making arbitration compulsory in certain cases and of diminishing the burden of armaments, the Hague Conference failed altogether. The best that could be achieved was the expression of a pious wish for the limitation of armaments which each power could agree to or reject as it chose.

The second Hague Conference which met in 1907 accomplished little more. Sir Henry Campbell-Bannerman, the British Liberal Prime Minister, tried to raise *The second* the question of limitation of naval armaments; *Hague* Germany opposed its discussion. An interna- *Conference,* tional prize court was instituted and some prin- *1907* ciples of international law further formulated. But as to disarmament, President Nelidow was forced to inform the

[1] E. J. Dillon, who was in close contact with Count Witte, traces the plan to a proposal of General Kuropatkin, War Minister, for an Austro-Russian agreement to stop expenditure on new artillery. Witte broadened this suggestion into a general proposal for a disarmament conference to which all nations would be invited. The Tsar was pleased with the idea and gave it his official sanction.

Conference, "If the question was not ripe in 1899, it is not any more so in 1907." Germany was particularly intransigeant, the Kaiser threatening withdrawal if either compulsory arbitration or limitation of armament were placed on the agenda, but it must be said that few states except Russia showed much interest in disarmament at the first Conference and few except Great Britain at the second. Between the two Conferences it was estimated that the world expenditure on armaments had increased by more than a fourth. The second Hague Conference was more inclusive than the first as it included delegates from the Latin American countries as well as from Europe, Asia and the United States.

The failure of the second Hague Conference to take any effective steps toward the safeguarding of peace was matched *The London Naval Conference, 1909* by the failure of the London Naval Conference in 1909 to codify the laws of naval war. The Declaration of London, covering such points as blockade rights, contraband, prizes, right of search and the like, was not ratified by Great Britain and several other powers, and thus never went into effect. The British were almost as reluctant to limit their naval rights as belligerents as were the Germans to limit the size of their navy. Armaments by land and sea continued to grow unchecked and with ominously accelerating speed.

The constant hailstorm of disturbing diplomatic "incidents," the growing unfriendliness of the German press, and *The naval race in the North Sea* the "speeding up" in Tirpitz's program of naval building made the British public more seriously concerned for their national safety than they had been since Nelson's victory at Trafalgar. The French, especially after a naval agreement with the British in 1912, gave up their attempt to rival Germany in the North Sea and concentrated their fleet in the Mediterranean, where they had no effective rival except Italy. Until the German navy became a menace, it had been the British custom to scatter ships all over the world in order to defend every distant colony and maintain British prestige wherever traders went. This easy-going policing of the seas was ended under the vigorous administration of Admiral Fisher, one of the most picturesque old sea-dogs who ever directed a navy. He ruthlessly scrapped obsolete ships, introduced modern equipment, withdrew warships from distant outposts and concentrated the bulk of the navy in the North Sea, ready for an instant blow at Germany, even hinting that it might be a good idea to "Copenhagen" the German fleet before it got any bigger.[1] With Germany and Great Britain filling their home waters with ever larger fleets it was no longer of much use to pretend that they were built for the world at large and without special reference to an Anglo-German war. As one British publicist ironically put it, "Our power is concentrated, watching our dearest friends, those Germans who have no intention whatever of coming near England!"

In 1906 the British launched the Dreadnought, the first large warship fitted with turbine engines and ten twelve-inch guns. Never was vessel more ironically named, for the launching of this warship precipitated the greatest of naval panics. It so greatly outclassed all previous types of battleship as to render almost obsolete the existing British capital ships. The Germans saw their chance and accelerated their building program. They had the great advantage over the British in building their navy "right" on modern lines from the very start; they were not encumbered by having a large amount of capital sunk in old-fashioned boats. In 1908 Germany was building ships of the new type so fast as to bring their navy closer to British strength than ever before; the British took alarm and the newspapers clamored for eight new Dreadnoughts ("We want eight and we won't wait!" was the popular slogan). From 1909 onwards the British

[1] Referring to the seizure of the Danish fleet by Great Britain in the struggle with Napoleon.

government began again to outbuild the German fleet, resolved to pay any cost rather than the cost of unpreparedness
at sea.

This naval race was most distasteful to the British taxpayer, and the Liberal government repeatedly besought
Germany to agree to a naval holiday, either in
the form of a total cessation of new construction
for a period of years or an agreement based on a
fixed ratio of capital ships (battleships and battle
cruisers) between the two powers. In 1907 and 1908 the
British government, through many channels and in many
forms, repeatedly proposed a mutual limitation of naval
armament. The Kaiser, offended at the bare suggestion,
wrote on the margin of an ambassadorial despatch, "good
relations with England at the price of the building of the
German navy are *not* desired by me," and when Sir Charles
Hardinge insisted too bluntly that Germany "must" build
more slowly the Kaiser retorted, "Then we shall fight, for it
is a question of national honor and dignity." Renewed proposals were answered contemptuously by Chancellor Bethmann-Hollweg in 1911 that the question of disarmament was
"insoluble so long as men are men and States are States."
Other overtures were no more successful.

Germany rejects the "naval holi-day"

As Great Britain was an island power dependent on imported foodstuffs for daily bread, and, moreover, the center
of an empire scattered in every part of the earth,
it was obviously out of the question that the
British should permit another European navy
seriously to rival theirs. Even the Germans
acknowledged so much, though they roused apprehensions
by refusing to accept fixed formulas of relative strength.
The British had "gone the second mile" repeatedly by offering every possible concession that did not sacrifice their
naval margin of safety. They very naturally, though no
doubt mistakenly, concluded that the German government

Anglo-Ger-man rela-tions at their worst

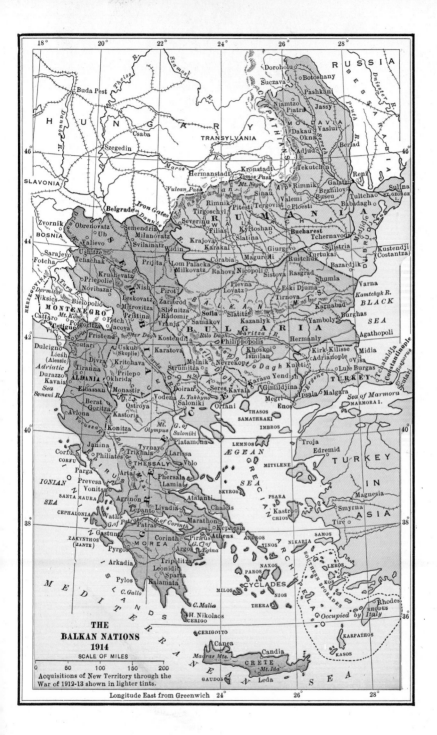

THE
BALKAN NATIONS
1914

SCALE OF MILES

Acquisitions of New Territory through the
War of 1912-13 shown in lighter tints.

Longitude East from Greenwich

was bent on an early naval attack on the British isles. The press was in a panic. To allay British fears the Kaiser made public what was meant to be a reassuring interview in the *Daily Telegraph* in October, 1908. He said that the English were mad to regard him as unfriendly, that he had stood their friend during the Boer War and even suggested the plan by which the war was eventually won, and that he had personally withstood the bitter anti-British feeling of the German masses. As might have been expected, this interview raised a storm in both countries. Chancellor Bülow apologized for his Imperial master before the Reichstag in terms so deprecatory that the Kaiser never forgave him. The British were more impressed by the Kaiser's admission that the German people were hostile than by his assertion that personally he was friendly.

The British government refused to consider the plea of Lord Roberts that they should follow the example of Germany, France and all the other continental Great *Military* Powers and introduce conscription; they went no *"conver-* *sations"* further than to permit Lord Haldane as War *within the* Minister to organize a reserve "territorial" force *entente* of volunteers. They rejected also suggestions from France for a definite military agreement parallel to that existing between France and Russia. But from the time of the first Morocco crisis to the World War there were frequent and detailed consultations between military and naval specialists of the two countries extending even to plans for landing British forces on the continent. The placing of the fleets practically imposed a moral obligation on Great Britain to stand by France in the event of war, unless France were indefensibly in the wrong, because the French had left the protection of their northern coasts to the British. The military conversations were less binding, as the French experts had alternative plans for land warfare if the British expeditionary force failed to reach the continent. As early as 1906 the French and British military authorities discussed what aid might be sent Belgium in the very probable event that Germany, operating according to the plan of the German General Staff, invaded France by way of neutral Belgium. France and Russia, frankly allied, were in even more constant touch as to their military plans.

Throughout the reign of Nicholas II Russian diplomacy hovered uncertainly between expansion in the Near East *Trends of* and expansion in the Far East. The former *Russian* policy involved hostile relations with Austria-*diplomacy* Hungary and probably with Germany, but it could, under the changed conditions of the twentieth century, be reconciled with friendship towards Britain. The latter policy involved hostility towards Britain and made possible friendly relations with the Triple Alliance. Till the close of the Russo-Japanese War, the Tsar and his ministers seemed on the whole to prefer Far Eastern imperialism, but Russia's sharp check at the hands of Japan caused many Russians to say: "If we cannot realize our new dream of warm water ports in Manchuria and Korea, should we not revert to our old dream of Constantinople and the Straits?" This consideration, much more than any pressure from France, seems to have shifted Russia from antagonism towards Great Britain to co-operation with her. Alexander Izvolski, Russian Foreign Minister from 1906 to 1910, and afterwards Ambassador to France, was an ardent partisan of the Triple Entente and of concentration on the question of the Straits. His successor at the Foreign Office was Sergius Sazonov, a more conservative diplomat, lacking Izvolski's "bounce," but in the main interested in the same problems.

Izvolski so badly bungled the crisis created by Austria-Hungary's annexation of Bosnia and Herzegovina in 1908,[1] that he failed to obtain the expected compensation for Russia, the opening of the Straits to Russian warships. But

---

[1] See above, Chapter II, for the Bosnian crisis.

in the following year he arranged an accord with Italy at Racconigi, the main terms of which were that *The Bos-* both countries were to support the principle of *nian crisis and the* nationality in the Balkan States, which seemed *Racconigi* to point to a partition of European Turkey, *Accord* that new agreements made with regard to the Balkan region should have the consent of both nations, and that Russia would support Italy's interests in Tripoli if Italy would support Russia's interests in the Straits question. The agreement was kept secret even from Italy's allies, and marked a still further relaxation of the ties which bound Italy to the Triple Alliance. But Russia, while gaining one of her objectives, the sowing of dissension between Italy and her allies, had failed in the more important one of opening the Straits.[1] When the issue was again tentatively raised in 1911 by the Russian Ambassador at Constantinople it was so coldly received by both France and Britain that the Russian government disavowed its representative.

Then Russia turned to Germany with the aim of securing a freer hand in the Near East. Germany promised not to seek concessions within the Russian sphere of *The* influence in northern Persia; Russia promised *Potsdam Accord,* in turn not to interfere with the completion of *1910* the Bagdad railway and, by oral assurance, not to be a party to any attack on Germany. So far as the terms of the agreement went, it resembled the Anglo-French *entente cordiale* of 1904 which "swapped" an Egyptian policy for a Moroccan one in much the same way that this Potsdam Accord swapped Persian concessions for interests in Mesopotamia. As S. B. Fay aptly says, "The Potsdam conversations and agreements of 1910–11 are another indication of the fact that questions of economic imperialism are far easier for governments to handle successfully than questions affecting prestige, alliances or armaments; in fact the former may some-

[1] See pages 52–53.

times serve as a convenient bridge to the latter." Yet the
Potsdam Accord did not lead to a permanent *entente* between
Germany and Russia, as it still left unappeased all the
quarrels between Russia and Austria-Hungary.

As between France and Germany, Morocco continued to
be the chief stumbling-block.   The first crisis had been
Morocco   ended by the Algeciras Conference, but the in-
again   herent contradiction between Moroccan "independence" and French "police power" was certain to lead to
further complications.   In 1908 the French authorities
captured some army deserters who had sought refuge in the
German consulate at Casablanca.   The Hague Tribunal
found a pacific settlement for this incident, but it demonstrated the danger of France's anomalous position in the
country.   In 1909 Germany, preoccupied with the Near
Eastern situation, promised to recognize the political ascendancy of France in Morocco, provided that Germany retain
her economic equality in the Moroccan market.   But the
German government had no intention of letting French predominance become an actual French protectorate — the
probable ultimate result — unless Germany were "compensated" elsewhere for her complaisance.   When civil war in
Morocco induced the French to send a military expedition
to the city of Fez, Kiderlen-Wächter, the German Foreign
Minister, decided that the time had come to act.   The new
policy was much more his than either Kaiser Wilhelm's or
Chancellor Bethmann-Hollweg's, but he secured the assent
of his superiors to force a crisis, and in 1911 a German warship, the *Panther*, was sent to Agadir to "protect the important German interests in the territory in question."

France, unsupported, would probably have been forced to
retreat from her plan of bringing Morocco into her north
The Agadir   African empire or else to pay whatever price
crisis, 1911   Germany demanded.   But the British were as
reluctant as the French to see German power established in

Morocco near Gibraltar and the entrance to the Mediterranean. Besides, they believed that Germany's action at Agadir was more than a blow at France's colonial policy, that it was an attempt to separate France and Britain and prove that the *entente cordiale* could be shaken by a German threat. In order to make plain the British position in the matter, Lloyd-George, the Chancellor of the Exchequer, warned Germany in a public address that:

> If a situation were to be forced upon us in which peace could only be preserved... by allowing Britain to be treated, where her interests were vitally affected, as if she were of no account in the cabinet of nations, then I say emphatically that peace at that price would be a humiliation intolerable for a great country like ours to endure.

These words were the more impressive from the fact that Lloyd-George was one of the most pronounced anti-militarists in the cabinet and the advocate of a good understanding with Germany.

Germany's position was now most difficult. Kiderlen-Wächter seems to have desired nothing more than the cession of the whole of French Congo to Germany as *The final* compensation for giving France free rein in *Moroccan* Morocco. But a section of the German press *settlement* had begun to clamor for a German colony in western Morocco. The French press was so angry that it was difficult for the government to offer any concessions. The British government had made the most direct public threat of war since Anglo-German rivalry began. There was something of a banker's panic, which may have contributed to preserving the peace. Within the French cabinet there was a division of opinion as to what should be conceded. On November 4, 1911, Jules Cambon and Kiderlen-Wächter finally reached a settlement after four months of discussion. France for the first time obtained permission from Germany to follow her own policy in Morocco to its logical conclusion of a protectorate, and in return for this permission ceded about a hundred thousand square miles of the French Congo. The French lost no time in improving their opportunity. In 1912 Spain was allotted a special zone of influence in northern Morocco, Tangier was internationalized, the rest of Morocco became a French zone; in the same year the Sultan of Morocco reluctantly agreed to the French protectorate. General Lyautey, a most skillful and diplomatic officer, put down every nationalist uprising and yet so conciliated national sentiment that on the whole this newly won dependency was a source of strength rather than weakness to France during the World War. The Spaniards had far more trouble in their tiny sphere, about a twelfth of the whole country, than the French in all the rest of it.

The French absorption of Morocco determined for the Italians the moment of their intervention in Tripoli. The *The Tripoli-* Italians had been strangely slow to act on their *tan War* diplomatic "rights" in the Turkish dependen-*1911* cies of Tripolitania and Cyrenaica (collectively, Tripoli or Libya) between French Tunis and Egypt. As early as 1887 Italy had secured the passive approval of Germany, Austria-Hungary and Great Britain to maintain Italian as against French interests in Tripoli; [1] in 1900 she had bargained with France and offered support of French policy in Morocco; in 1909 Russia's assent had been won by the secret agreement of Racconigi. The terms of the Triple Alliance, in its later renewals, directly supported Italian colonial interests. Yet not till 1911 did Italy act and even then without being able to find much excuse for intervention, as the disorders in Tripoli were not very serious, certainly not at all comparable with those which had provoked French intervention in Morocco. Nearly all the other powers disapproved of Italy's action, Germany especially, as it endangered good relations between the Triple Alliance

---

[1] These assurances were made still more definite in 1902.

and the Ottoman Empire, but no power was in a position to object to Italy's using the permission and following the example of her neighbors by sharing the spoils of north Africa. In the course of the war Italy seized also the Greek-speaking Dodecanese islands in the Ægean and held them as security for Turkey's coming to terms.

The chief importance of the Tripolitan War was the encouragement it gave to the Balkan kingdoms to proceed with the partition of European Turkey. They *The Balkan* had long contemplated — one might even say *war cloud* always contemplated — such a partition, but it required prolonged and difficult negotiations to bring them into agreement. The Balkan States mirrored in miniature all the suspicions, jealousies and antagonisms of the Great Powers. It was as hard to get the Greeks and Bulgarians into friendship as it had been to reconcile Great Britain and Russia. But the shrewder Balkan diplomats, such as Tsar Ferdinand of Bulgaria, his minister Gueshov and Premier Venizelos of Greece, with the aid of Russia's active friendship, succeeded at last in bringing Greece, Bulgaria, Serbia and Montenegro into a league. Probably the governments would have preferred to wait longer before turning their secret alliance into an open crusade for the partition of Turkey, but public opinion, stirred by the tyranny of the Young Turks in Macedonia and encouraged by the Turco-Italian War and the uprising of the tribesmen of Albania, would not permit delay. The Great Powers bent on averting war warned the Balkan league that:

> If despite this note, war does break out between the Balkan States and the Ottoman Empire, we shall not admit, at the end of the conflict, any modification of the territorial status quo in European Turkey.

This warning the Balkan allies naturally ignored. They knew by long experience that the Concert of the Powers always adjusts its program to an accomplished fact.

On October 8, 1912, Montenegro, the smallest of the Balkan kingdoms, declared war on the Ottoman Empire.

The first Balkan War, 1912 Almost immediately Bulgaria, Serbia and Greece joined in an ultimatum to Turkey, knowing in advance that it would be rejected. The reforms demanded in Macedonia Turkey might have conceded, but the right of the Balkan states to oversee the administration of those reforms would virtually have surrendered her sovereignty in that region. So the Turkish government hastily patched up peace with Italy and bent all energies to the war in the Balkans. Most students of European diplomacy and military science predicted a Turkish victory, and the Turks certainly shared that opinion. The Ottoman army had a glorious tradition, resting on the valor and endurance of the tough, stocky peasant soldiers from Asia Minor, and to the natural fighting qualities of the Turk had now been added the science of the West: instruction by German officers, equipment with German cannon.

The Balkan nations were not so rash as they appeared to be. In discipline, leadership, equipment and patriotic en-

Why the allies won thusiasm they were equal to the Turks, and their strategic situation was much superior. European Turkey had so long and winding a frontier that no army which the Empire could put into the field could protect every part of it. The Greek navy dominated the Ægean, thus not only permitting Greece to annex at will the islands, but also preventing Turkey from sending reinforcements to Macedonia from her Asiatic provinces, save across the narrow Straits. This difficulty of bringing Asiatic troops to European battlefields in time for decisive action practically nullified Turkey's advantage in man power. Many of the levies from Asia Minor did not understand the new ways of fighting. They objected to the presence of Christians in the ranks of "the army of the Prophet," and many conscripted Christians objected to serving against their fellow Christians of the Balkan states. The "new model" army which the Young Turks had organized proved less efficient than the old Turkish army simply because the soldiers had not yet time to become accustomed to European methods of organization and discipline. In the World War, after the army reforms had become more familiar, Turkey recovered most of the military prestige lost in the Balkan War.

Forces from Serbia and Montenegro at once occupied the Sanjak of Novi-Bazar, thus uniting the two Serb kingdoms to the utter disgust of Austria-Hungary, whose *The war in* diplomacy had long been directed to keeping them *the west* apart. Macedonia, caught between Serbian armies from the north and Greek armies advancing from the south, was overrun in a few weeks. The Serbians won a victory at Kumanovo, captured the important city of Monastir, and marched into Albania to seize the port of Durazzo. The Greeks advanced to Saloniki, the chief Macedonian seaport, laid siege to Janina (in the Greco-Albanian borderland of Epirus), and added Crete and other islands to their realm by naval capture. The northern Albanian fortress of Scutari, besieged by Montenegro, held out for several months, as did Janina, attacked by the Greeks. But the western campaigns provided few real tests of military prowess as the bulk of Turkey's forces were concentrated in Thrace.

The Bulgarian armies, supplemented later by a Serbian contingent, hammered the main Turkish front in the neighborhood of Adrianople. At Kirk Kilisse and *The campaign in* Lule Burgas the Bulgarians triumphed and *paign in* drove back the Turkish army behind the forti- *Thrace* fications which protected Constantinople (the Tchataldja lines). But the Bulgarians, who had already sacrificed more lives than any other of the Balkan allies, were still held at bay before Adrianople and before the Tchataldja entrenchments. The Thracian campaign resulted in a temporary deadlock, though the honors of war were certainly with Bulgaria. In December, 1912, Turkey and Bulgaria agreed to an armistice, which was accepted by the other belligerents with the exception of Greece.

Delegates of the belligerent nations met in London to discuss terms of peace where they could keep in touch with *The first* each other and with the Great Powers. Though *London* the Great Powers abandoned their original posi- *peace* tion that there should be no change in the terri- *conference* torial status of Macedonia and European Turkey generally, they still insisted on a veto power over the details of the peace settlement. In particular they insisted that Albania should be erected into an independent principality under the collective guarantee of the powers and not simply partitioned among Serbia, Montenegro and Greece. This demand was certainly justified on grounds of nationality, for the Albanians were neither Greeks nor Slavs, but the real reason for uging it was that Austria-Hungary did not wish Serbia to have ports on the Adriatic. Other difficulties arose with regard to Thrace. The mere rumor that Adrianople would be surrendered brought back into office the Young Turks (Committee of Union and Progress), resolved to see the war through to the end. Negotiations were interrupted and hostilities resumed.

Throughout February and March, 1913, the Turks attempted to regain their lost ground in Thrace, but by the *The second* end of March Adrianople was forced to surrender. *London* The Greeks were already in Janina, and in April *conference* Montenegro achieved the conquest of Scutari. The Great Powers, however, forced Montenegro to surrender her prize to the infant state of Albania. As Turkey had lost everything in Europe except Constantinople and the Straits, even the Young Turks were now convinced of the necessity of suing for peace. On May 30, 1913, the Treaty of London was concluded, ending the first Balkan War. European Turkey was limited to a zone of the Straits, lying east of a

line drawn from Enos on the Ægean to Midia on the Black
Sea. The island of Crete went to Greece, but the status of
other Ægean islands and the frontier of Albania were left to
the Great Powers to determine. Unfortunately no decision
had been reached as to the partition of Macedonia. Bulgaria claimed Thrace as far as the Enos–Midia line by right
of conquest and nationality, and the claim was allowed by
her allies; but she also claimed the greater part of Macedonia
on the ground of nationality and treaty rights and this claim
was contested. Greeks and Serbs alike held that Macedonia
was theirs by nationality, and that the secret pre-war agreements as to the division of Macedonia must be set aside since
the creation of Albania disappointed Serbia's hope for an
Adriatic port. Rumania, which had taken no part whatso-
ever in the war, put forward a claim for "compensation"
to restore the Balkan "balance of power." Bulgaria, in the
elation of her greatest victory, was expected to yield western
Macedonia to Serbia, southern Macedonia to Greece, and a
strip of land south of the Dobrudja to Rumania, while
Turkey eagerly awaited a chance to reconquer Adrianople.
Beset on four sides, Bulgaria should in prudence have yielded
somewhere, but pride counseled defiance.

Two ominous events hastened a second Balkan War. A
Greek fanatic assassinated King George, and his successor
Constantine was expected to follow a more ag- *The second*
gressive policy. In Bulgaria the conservative *Balkan*
Premier Gueshov was compelled to resign office *War,* 1913
to the more chauvinistic Danev. Militarist sentiment rode
high in both countries. Greece and Serbia formed a secret
alliance to protect their holdings in Macedonia from a Bulgarian attack. In a last effort to avert war, the Tsar of Russia demanded the submission of the whole Macedonia question to him as arbiter. Greek and Serbian armies already
occupied the greater part of Macedonia and thus held "nine
points of the law" against Bulgaria. The temptation for a

sudden attack was too great for the Bulgarians to resist. Up to this point Bulgaria could rightly count on much foreign sympathy. She had borne the greatest burden of the war, her national claims in Macedonia were at least as good as those of Serbia or Greece, and her diplomatic attitude, though stubborn and ungenerous to her allies, at least conformed to the letter of her rights. But now Bulgaria put herself entirely in the wrong. Without declaration of war, her armies at the end of June attacked the forces of Greece and Serbia. Montenegro and Rumania joined against Bulgaria, the Turks recaptured Adrianople, and within a month Bulgaria was suing for peace. This second Balkan War, arising as it did from the bitter rancor of nations recently in alliance, was marked by exceptional ferocity. So many charges and counter-charges of cruelty were made that an investigating committee was later sent to find out the truth, and it came to the depressing conclusion that all the belligerents had been guilty of indefensible violations of international law. As one diplomat phrased it, the war of liberation had degenerated into a war of partition, and that in turn into a war of extermination.

Peace was made at Bucharest, August 10, 1913, between Greece, Serbia, Rumania and Montenegro on the one hand and Bulgaria on the other. Rumania obtained

The treaties of Bucharest and Constantinople the entire southern Dobrudja from Silistria to the Black Sea; Serbia annexed western Macedonia as far as the new Greek frontier, including the city of Monastir and the upper Vardar valley; Greece obtained a great extension of territory in southern Macedonia, including the whole Ægean coast from Saloniki to beyond Kavalla. Turkey imposed a new treaty on Bulgaria at Constantinople in September. The frontier was still to run, as agreed in London, between Enos and Midia, but was to be bent inland between those points in such a way as to give Adrianople and most of eastern Thrace back to the Ottoman Empire.

The most important and permanent result of the Balkan Wars was the end of Turkey as a European state. Although the Turks still held Constantinople, Adrianople and the Straits region, this was a mere outpost of Asiatic Turkey, and the "center of gravity" of the Ottoman Empire henceforth lay in Asia

A balance sheet of the Balkan Wars

Minor. Turkey had lost two thirds of her European population and five sixths of her European area. Of the Balkan allies Greece gained most. The area of the kingdom was practically doubled and its population increased from about 2,750,000 to 4,750,000. Greece now included all Thessaly and southern Epirus, southern Macedonia, Crete and all the Ægean islands except those held by Italy since the Tripolitan War and a few retained by Turkey to protect the entrance to the Dardanelles. Serbia had likewise almost doubled in area, adding to her former territories western Macedonia (including the district known as "Old Serbia") and the part of Novi-Bazar not given to Montenegro. She was still denied access to the sea but now had common frontiers with two friendly seaboard countries, Greece and Montenegro. Both Serbia and Montenegro increased their population by about one half, giving Serbia a population of nearly 4,500,000, and Montenegro almost half a million. Bulgaria both gained and lost, as against her acquisitions in eastern Macedonia and western Thrace must be set the southern Dobrudja, transferred to Rumania. Her net gain in area was less than one fifth and in population probably not more than a twentieth. The possession of a coastline on the Ægean was not of as much value as one might think, as Greece held the best Macedonian ports.

The new country called into existence by the Balkan Wars had about the same area as what was left of European Turkey. Its population was less than a million.

Albania

Of all the Balkan kingdoms Albania was the wildest and most backward, containing not a single mile of railway, divided into clans rather than into political units. The Concert, however, treated Albania like other Balkan states and, following its usual practice, found a German prince to rule it. In 1914 Prince Wilhelm of Wied took the title of Mpret of Albania and endeavored to Europeanize his little realm. But he had been on the throne only a few months when the World War swept his sovereignty aside, and Albania, nominally neutral, became a battleground of Austrians, Italians and Serbs. Under various native dictators and provisional governments, the warlike highland clans managed to maintain their independence against the encroachments of both Serbs to the north and Greeks to the south.

Since the desolation and atrocity of the World War and the anarchic instability which followed it have reproduced *The Euro-* on a grander scale the evils of the Near East, *peanization* much has been said by publicists of "the Balkani-*of the Bal-* zation of Europe." There is force in the phrase, *kans* but it is allowable to dwell for a moment on the more cheerful topic of the Europeanization of the Balkans. One hundred years before the Balkan Wars, Greece, Serbia, Montenegro, Bulgaria, Rumania and Albania were enslaved provinces of an alien despotism; Turkey was at the lowest point of a long cycle of degeneration. In 1913 the Balkan kingdoms were free and proud peasant democracies and even Turkey had awakened from her Byzantine sloth. Though the force of nationalism brought war rather than peace to the Near East, it brought some measure of political freedom, and with it the fruits of freedom such as industrial activity, popular education and social experiment. The faults of the Balkan states in the twentieth century were frontiersmen's faults, the crudity of young communities, and with them went a hopeful energy which is the virtue of youth. There is every reason to expect that southeastern Europe will in the future play a much greater part in the positive progress of civilization, even though it will doubtless continue to furnish some of the most vexing problems of diplomacy.

Of all the European Concert, Austria-Hungary was most closely affected by the Balkan Wars. The basis of Austro-German policy in the Near East in recent years had been the military and political strength of the Ottoman Empire. Now the Turkish power had been almost swept from Europe and at a *Austria-Hungary and the Balkan Wars* time, too, when the Turkish government had placed reliance on German artillery and German training. Nor was that the worst. Victor in both wars was Serbia, dangerously elated by victory and more than ever hostile to Austria-Hungary because Austrian diplomacy had once more barred her from the sea. Austria-Hungary had disapproved the formation of the Balkan league in the first place, had refused to join Russia in attempting to prevent war among the allies, and had encouraged (though not caused) Bulgaria to break up the alliance. Had Bulgaria won the second war Austria-Hungary would have had a diplomatic victory to compensate for the weakening of Turkey. At one time Count Berchtold, Austro-Hungarian Foreign Minister, approached Germany and Italy with proposals for an attack on Serbia even at the risk of a European war. This was early in July, 1913, almost exactly a year before the assassination of the heir to the Austrian throne gave Austria-Hungary the pretext for hostilities; in 1913 the only pretext advanced was the one which can always be found, "the balance of power." Germany and Italy emphatically disapproved. Chancellor von Bethmann-Hollweg replied that "the hostilities which have now broken out between Bulgaria and Serbia-Greece in no wise as yet disturb the rule of policy hitherto traced by Austria-Hungary" and pointed out that, even if Serbia won, Bulgaria would not forgive her, and this hostility would weaken Serbia more than small territorial gains in Macedonia would strengthen her.

Though Austria's allies held back Berchtold from hurling Europe into a general war to humiliate Serbia in 1913, the *Tightening the alliances* long series of crises in the Balkans starting in 1908 had greatly contributed to the growing tension between Russia and Austria-Hungary, just as the various Moroccan crises from 1904 to 1911 had increased the hostility between Germany and France. Each year the diplomatic rapids ran more swiftly toward the cataract of 1914. In 1912 the British cabinet, after having failed to reach a reassuring understanding with Germany through the peace mission of Lord Haldane, took a long step toward converting the *entente cordiale* into an alliance by approving an exchange of notes between Sir Edward Grey, the Foreign Secretary, and Paul Cambon, the French Ambassador at London, to the effect that "if either government had grave reason to expect an unprovoked attack by a third power... it should immediately discuss with the other whether both governments should act together to prevent aggression and to preserve peace, and, if so, what measures they would prepare to take in common" (November, 1912). This agreement, to be sure, merely bound France and Britain to take counsel together when trouble threatened, which they would no doubt have done without any written agreement, but it at last placed on diplomatic paper the understanding which hitherto the British had preferred to leave entirely unwritten. In December, the Triple Alliance was renewed, although not due for renewal until 1914. Renewed military and naval understandings and renewed assurances of diplomatic support, especially in the Near East, bound together more closely the powers in both diplomatic groups.

Nevertheless, at the very time when the British were binding themselves more closely to France and Russia, they were also working to avert war with Germany. On the whole, Anglo-German relations were much friendlier during the period from 1910 to the actual outbreak of the war in 1914 than they had been during the period 1904–09. The storm center of Europe was now the Near East rather than the North Sea. *Attempts at an Anglo-German understanding* To avert war the British government was prepared to grant a cessation of naval building by both countries, a settlement on mutually satisfactory terms of the Bagdad Railway question and an enlargement of Germany's share of the Portuguese colonies in Africa if Portugal should ever alienate them, and a pledge not to join in any aggression against Germany. To make this offer Lord Haldane the Minister of War went in February, 1912, on a special mission to Berlin. He was not only a statesman of ripe experience but an ardent admirer of German national life and culture who had once called Germany his "spiritual home." On the other side, Chancellor Bethmann-Hollweg was desirous of ending Anglo-German hostility, though his influence was practically nullified by the great power at court of Admiral Tirpitz.

On the first two points of agreement not much could be achieved. Germany insisted on the new naval law and refused a "naval holiday" though agreeing to retard for a time the rate of shipbuilding. The German Chancellor demanded an ironclad guarantee of British neutrality "if war is forced on Germany"; *Results of the Haldane mission* Great Britain would not promise more than to abstain from "aggression." In other words, Great Britain would leave France and Russia in the lurch if they attacked Germany, but would not pledge herself to remain neutral if Germany attacked them; it is difficult to see what more Germany could have expected, and her insistence on an absolute formula of neutrality only convinced the British cabinet that Germany's plans envisaged at least the possibility of undertaking an offensive war. Colonial negotiations were carried on with greater success, thanks very largely to the tact and friendliness of Prince Lichnowsky, German Ambassador to Great Britain. The old agreement of 1898 for a partition of the Portuguese African colonies, contingent on Portugal's willingness to sell out,[1] was revised to give Germany a much larger share, a great part of Angola, northern Mozambique, and the islands of San Thomé and Principe. The Bagdad railway question[2] which had caused more bad feeling between the two countries than anything else save naval competition, was also settled to the satisfaction of both parties. Germany was allowed to extend the Bagdad Railway as far as Basra and granted important commercial concessions which almost transformed Mesopotamia into a German sphere of interest. The British retained their influence on the shore of the Persian Gulf, thus preventing Germany from threatening India. Both the African and the Turkish agreements were, of course, soon invalidated by the World War.

Coincident with the rivalry of alliances and coalitions which absorbed the attention of the Foreign Offices was an *The arma-* equally keen competition among the War Offices. *ment race* Nearly every European nation (among the larger states Great Britain was the only exception) had adopted in some form the Prussian principle of universal military training in time of peace. During 1912 and 1913 important increases were made in the military establishments of Russia, Austria-Hungary, France and Germany. The German Army Bill of 1913 added to the number of men summoned annually for training; the French simultaneously prolonged the period of required military service from two to three years. This made the French and German armies approximately equal in size, though Germany was somewhat superior in equipment and greatly so in reserve man power. The Russian army was almost as large as the French and German combined — on paper — but was rendered partly ineffective by inadequate rail routes.

[1] See above, page 250.   [2] See above, pages 251–252.

In the few months between the close of the Balkan Wars and the opening of the World War the Near Eastern question remained the center of diplomatic concern. *The Straits* Though such matters as the tracing of the bound- *question* aries of the new Albania caused small irritations, *again* the most dangerous problems concerned the Straits. In 1913 an able German officer, General Liman von Sanders, was appointed General Inspector of the Turkish army and the reorganization of the Turkish army was in general entrusted to German experts, just as British naval officers gave advice with regard to the Turkish fleet. So far there could be little objection from Russia. But when it was learned that General Liman von Sanders was also to be in direct command of the Turkish army corps at Constantinople the Russian government feared that a permanent German control of the Straits might result. Much irritated and alarmed Foreign Minister Sazonov tried to swing the Triple Entente into united action to force Turkey either to cancel the appointment or grant liberal "compensation" for it. In January 1914, however, a peaceful compromise was arranged by which Liman von Sanders remained Inspector General but ceased to exercise direct military command at the Straits. In February, a conference of Russian civil and military heads discussed the prospects of a sudden seizure of the Straits which would present Europe with an accomplished fact. But the conclusion reached was that since such an action would in any case bring about a general European war, it might well wait the result of such a war, and the whole question was shelved until some new turn in the diplomatic situation would give an opportunity to revive it.[1]

The Russian statesmen, as nearly as can be determined,

[1] Of course it does not follow, as some hasty writers have inferred, that this meant that Russia planned to start a general war. Certainly they thought one probable, and in the near future, but they may have expected to fight on the defensive in some quarrel instigated by Austria or Germany.

seemed to expect an early dissolution of the Ottoman Empire
Russia on which would raise in its acutest form the old
the eve of question, parent of so many wars, as to who
the war would be the heirs of the Turk. They were resolved that at all costs, including that of war, Constantinople
and the Straits must not pass to any other Great Power than
Russia, though if Turkey could maintain her hold, without
becoming a mere dependency of Germany (as Egypt was of
Britain), Russia would not force a change. They were
pleased at the new French three-year service law and at the
vigorous tone given to French diplomacy by the new President Poincaré, who kept in close touch with his Russian
allies by official visits and conversations. Russia was able
also to embark on naval conversations with Great Britain.
On the whole, however, Great Britain and Russia still stood
much farther apart than Russia and France, and it was only
through France that Russia could influence British policy.
The attitude of Sir Edward Grey in supporting the Austrian
demand for an independent Albania, and later in helping Germany find an acceptable compromise in the Liman von
Sanders affair, showed that in Near Eastern matters the
British still held an independent line. Thus matters stood,
when the explosion between Austria-Hungary and Serbia
forced a decision on hesitating Russia.

CHAPTER XII

CLOUDS OVER EUROPE

EVERY historian has one great and unfair advantage over every statesman: he can look backward and be wise after the event. But this advantage carries with it a *Was the* serious risk, the danger of writing history as *World War* though it were a well constructed tragic drama *inevitable?* in which every act and every speech is calculated to lead to a predetermined catastrophe. Was the World War of 1914 inevitable? Perhaps so. Perhaps everything is inevitable — John Calvin was of that opinion! But such an opinion is an act of faith, it carries us beyond the bounds of positive knowledge. If we keep within the limits of what we *know*, all we can safely say is that European tensions had increased with dangerous rapidity from the eighteen nineties to 1914. The crowded years from 1911 to 1914 were particularly full of menace; they contained three small wars, Italy's seizure of Tripoli from Turkey, and the two wars among the Balkan states, they witnessed a narrowly averted struggle over Morocco between France and Germany, they were marked by rapid accumulation of armaments and by an alarmingly fatalistic tone in the press which had fallen into the habit of speaking of the "coming war" as a mere matter of course. We can at least say that if war had been averted in July 1914 it would have been an unusual triumph of pacific statesmanship over most formidable difficulties. Nor, in view of the electric atmosphere of the period, can we feel confident that a collision between the alliances, if averted at that time, would not have come within two or three years thereafter.

Before we take up the diplomatic crisis of 1914 let us look

at the Europe, so near to us in time, so far away in its institutions and outlook, in which the crisis arose.
The dip-
lomatic   Europe was divided into many national states,
"map" of   each in legal theory an absolute "sovereign
1914
power" accountable for its acts to no one. Six
of these states possessed sufficient military, naval or economic strength to be counted "Great Powers," and their
joint activity was the "Concert of Europe." Three of these
powers, Germany, Austria-Hungary and Italy, had a long-
standing alliance, first completed in 1882 but renewed from
time to time, the Triple Alliance. Two other powers, Russia and France, allied since 1893, formed a Dual Alliance.
Great Britain, though not bound by alliance to either camp,
had come in point of fact after 1904 to co-operate with the
Dual Alliance, and thus all three powers were often collectively called the Triple Entente. Outside Europe two powers were acknowledged to be "great," Japan and the United
States of America. Japan after 1902 was bound by alliance
to Great Britain; the United States alone had no diplomatic
ties.

The smaller states of Europe did not keep to independent
orbits but circled around the Great Powers like planets
Position of   around a central sun. Portugal was allied with
the lesser   Great Britain. Belgium, fearing a German in-
powers   vasion, had defensive military understandings
with France and Britain. Turkey was practically committed
to Germany, fearing a Russian descent on Constantinople
and the adjoining Straits. Rumania was formally attached
to the Triple Alliance, but in actual fact hesitating between
both diplomatic camps. Greece and Bulgaria were also
neutral, in the sense of being divided in opinion, but Bulgaria had suffered a recent defeat from Serbia and would be
apt to oppose her in any future war. Serbia and Montenegro were definitely pro-Russian and anti-Austrian. Only
Spain, Switzerland, Holland and the Scandinavian countries

had a hopeful prospect of remaining neutral in any general war; even that would depend on the chance that no strategic advantage lay in the invasion of some one of them.

One of the greatest dangers to the peace of Europe lay in the existence of nations which had no place on the map but which cherished hopes of future independence. *The suppressed nationalities* These cases were particularly numerous in eastern Europe. Poland, once one of the European Great Powers, was divided among Russia, Austria-Hungary and Germany. The Poles, more patriotic in the days of their subjection than they had been when independent, formed a vast conspiracy against the three Empires which ruled them. Russia had a whole series of national problems along her western border — Poles, Finns, Estonians, Letts, Lithuanians, Baltic Germans, Jews of the "Pale," Ukrainians, Rumanians of Bessarabia. Within Austria-Hungary two unlike peoples, the Germans and the Magyars (Hungarians), maintained an uncertain ascendancy over Italians, Rumanians and many branches of the Slavs. The Czechs of Bohemia and the Yugoslavs (Slovenes, Croats and Serbs) of the southern provinces were openly disaffected and ripe for rebellion. These were not internal questions merely; they were international as well. The repression of a small group of Danes in northern Schleswig kept Denmark in constant alarm about Germany; the Russian violations of the chartered liberties of Finland not only offended but terrified the Swedes; the ties of alliance between Austria-Hungary, Italy and Rumania were weakened almost to worthlessness by popular resentment in Italy and Rumania at the treatment of their fellow-nationals in the Dual Monarchy. Ireland's dislike of British rule did more than anything else to weaken the natural ties of friendship between the United States and the British Empire, since millions of American voters were of Irish descent and sentiments.

A single illustration may serve to show the dynamite that lay in these unsolved problems of nationality. Alsace-

The Zabern incident Lorraine is a borderland of French and German speech. In Alsace more persons spoke German than French. Yet when Germany conquered the territory in 1871 the elected representatives unanimously protested and they continued their attitude of protest down to the World War, especially since Germany, resenting this attitude, garrisoned the provinces as though they were peopled by enemies. To the French the loss of their border provinces was an open wound, an unforgivable affront; no French statesman thereafter could propose an alliance or even an open friendly understanding with Germany and continue to hold office. In 1913 two German officers, Colonel Reutter and Lieutenant Forstner, established a reign of terror in the Alsatian town of Zabern. Insults hurled by both sides, arbitrary arrests, the imprisonment of civil judges for protesting against military violence, the sabering of a lame cobbler, a formal vote of censure of the military authorities in the German Reichstag, defiance of that censure by the German government, and congratulations to the authors of the outrages by the German Crown Prince, marked the course of events. If France had been still in the chauvinistic mood of three or four decades earlier war might have followed.

But there were problems of class as well as of nationality, and in 1914 Europe seemed as near to general revolution as

Social discontent to general war. Socialism had long ceased to be a novelty in Europe, but in the years immediately preceding the war a radical "left wing" group of Socialists, impatient at the slow progress made by the increasingly conservative official parties and their parliamentary representatives, called for "direct action." Socialism was to be brought about not by voting but by general strikes, sabotage or destruction of property, and the forcible seizure of mines and factories by workingmen's syndicates — hence the term, "syndicalism." The elections on the eve of the war showed in most countries the greatest strength the radical parties had ever polled. This was notably true in Germany, where the Social Democratic party in the election of 1912 became the largest in the Reichstag. In Britain the Labor party increased its strength at practically every election. In France the royalist groups dwindled to insignificance and the Socialists increased in strength, though not to the same extent as in Germany. Violent and destructive strikes became increasingly common throughout Europe, and America as well. Russia on the eve of the war was threatened with a general strike; the revolutionary forces which had been trampled underfoot in 1906 and 1907 were again awake. If the World War was latent in the national situation, the Bolshevist revolution of 1917 was equally foreshadowed by class antagonisms.

Even in stable Britain, the least excitable country in Europe, there were some curious minor evidences of unrest immediately before the war. The Protestant *Ulster and* minority in Ireland, mainly concentrated in the *the suffra-* industrial region of Ulster, were threatening *gettes* armed resistance of the Irish Home Rule bill which had passed the House of Commons and was about to be passed over the "veto" of the House of Lords. Officers of the British army threatened to resign if they were asked to coerce the Ulstermen, with whose resistance to the creation of an Irish Parliament they had full sympathy. The woman suffrage cause, which had long been the most orderly and peaceful of all political agitations, took a curious turn towards violence in the so-called "suffragette" movement. Heckling cabinet ministers, interrupting meetings and the like were soon supplemented by more strenuous methods, smashing shop windows, pouring destructive chemicals in mail boxes, cutting to pieces a picture in a national gallery, even isolated instances of arson. Across the Channel, the wife of a famous French radical politician, Joseph Caillaux, murdered Gaston Calmette, a journalist who had threatened to expose certain discreditable pages in Caillaux's career. Hardly a country in Europe but showed similar instances of growing disregard for law. "There is a risk," wrote H. G. Wells, "that the catastrophic events of 1914 may blind the historian to the significance of the spinning straws of 1913. But throughout Europe the sands were trickling before the avalanche fell. The arson of the suffragettes, the bellicose antics of the Unionist leaders in Ulster... were all parts of the same relaxation of bonds that launched the grey-clad hosts of Germany into Belgium." [1] And, in like mind, Professor J. W. Swain, "The first six months of 1914 were a period of excitement and tension in Europe, with a state of mind prevailing that was almost hysterical... It is sometimes said that the war brought a diminished respect for law; it is more correct to say that a rapidly declining respect for law heralded the war." [2]

Disorder and lawlessness were particularly prevalent in the Near East. Not only were Turkey and the Christian *The diplo-* Balkan states long accustomed to every sort of *matic en-* violence but they had not yet settled down from *tanglement* the immediate effect of the Balkan Wars of 1912–13. The tensions were most dangerous here because at this point the imperialistic ambitions of Germany and Austria-Hungary crossed the similar ambitions of Russia and both were in turn complicated by the national ambitions of each Balkan state. Southeastern Europe in 1914 was like an intricate tangle of live electric wires, spluttering sparks in every direction, while ranged around were the powder barrels of the historic jealousies and rivalries of the other nations of Europe. What did it matter to France or Britain whether Serbia gained a seaport on the Adriatic or

[1] H. G. Wells, *Joan and Peter* (1918), page 401.
[2] J. W. Swain, *Beginning the Twentieth Century* (1933), pages 346–47.

Bulgaria one on the Ægean? Nothing, directly. But France was allied to Russia and Britain a close friend of France, and these relations were certain to endure so long as France still resented German control of Alsace-Lorraine and Great Britain feared the growing German navy. If Balkan questions involved a collision between Russia and Austria-Hungary there could be no hope of "localizing the war" and keeping it from spreading to western Europe. It is commonly said that the system of alliances which was relied on to keep Europe at peace did more than anything else to bring about the World War. This is true, but not the whole truth. For Italy and Rumania were allied to Austria-Hungary, Great Britain was not allied to France, yet every diplomat in Europe knew that the force of circumstances bound Britain and France far more closely together than formal treaties did Italy and Rumania to their allies. The alliance system *plus* the conflicts of interest and prestige which brought the alliances into recurrent crises and tests of strength — *there* lay the danger!

Let us turn for the moment from the close atmosphere of the European foreign offices to the larger though vaguer forces in the background that determined peace or war. The commonest error in discussing diplomacy is to assume that the diplomat is a *Factors that "made" diplomacy* free agent who can make or break alliances at will. This may have been approximately true in the eighteenth century, though even then public opinion had to be taken into account in some countries, such as Holland and England.[1] In an age of national patriotism, economic imperialism and a widely read newspaper press the diplomat must work within narrow limits. Even in autocratic countries rulers and their ministers have their hands tied by the fear of stirring up too much opposition. The Russian Tsar

---

[1] As when Prime Minister Walpole was forced against his will by popular clamor to make war against Spain to avenge the mistreatment of English seamen.

Nicholas II would personally have preferred an alliance with Germany to an *entente* with Great Britain, for he was much under the influence of the German Kaiser and greatly resented British rivalry in the Far East, but the widespread hostility in Russia to Germany and Austria-Hungary compelled Russian diplomacy to a different course. This does not mean that modern diplomacy is democratic; nothing is less so. The average voter has his patriotism, his prejudices against particular nations or races, his moments of excitement or enthusiasm when some crisis breaks into the press, but his interest in foreign affairs is intermittent and his knowledge of them very slight. Much more important is the steadier pressure of certain powerful groups: business interests, party organizations, newspapers, propagandist associations, the army and navy, the land owning aristocracy and "society," occasionally the churches.

One of these conditioning factors has usually had ample recognition, indeed it has often been overemphasized, the *Commercial* commercial rivalry of the European nations. *rivalry* This has not often been directly or simply the cause of war, since modern capitalism is both individualistic and cosmopolitan, the rivalry of merchant against merchant rather than of nation against nation, and it makes little difference to a firm whether it loses money to a native or a foreign competitor. When the World War broke out the Germans unearthed an isolated editorial in the jingoistic *Saturday Review*, to the effect that every Briton would be richer if Germany were destroyed, and hailed it as testimony that commercial greed had brought the British into the league against Germany. The answer to this is that most merchants and even many politicians were aware that a keen competitor might also be a good customer, and while the British had lost some good foreign markets, especially in Latin America, to German competition, they had been more than compensated by the improvement of the

German market itself. American commercial competition was almost as keen as German in the period of the "diplomatic revolution" and yet Anglo-American relations were improving every year.

Not the direct but the indirect effects of commercial competition endangered peace. Infant industries demanded tariff protection; tariff barriers raised by one *Colonial* nation caused a clamor for equal "economic de- *imperialism* fenses" by its neighbors. The general tendency of tariffs has been upward from the eighteen-sixties to the present time; Great Britain alone held out until the World War as an important champion of free trade. Though tariff wars sometimes promoted ill-feeling it was generally agreed that tariff making was within the sovereign rights of each civilized power.[1] But when tariff protection and, still more important, exclusive or monopolistic "concessions" of mining, railroad, plantation or factory rights, were granted to the subjects of one nation only in a colony, protectorate or "sphere of influence," *then* the commercial conflict became also a political one. At least one large element in the race for colonial empire was the desire to keep an "open door" to national trade forcibly open (as in British India) or to close it to the foreigner (as in Manchuria and parts of French Africa).

Political rather than strictly economic motives underlay, however, a great deal of the colonial scramble. The nations of Europe are, with the exception of Russia, *Natural re-* very small on a world map and contain only a *sources and* small proportion of what their inhabitants might *national* need in case of war. Regions rich in coal (as *security* China) or oil (as Mexico, Persia, Mesopotamia), have been centers of foreign intrigue. Lands producing copper,

[1] The freedom of tariff making by "backward states" such as China was often seriously limited by treaties with foreign powers, with force to back them, but tariff treaties among more powerful nations were often "denounced" with no worse consequence than retaliatory tariffs by the other party.

cotton, rubber, nitrates (for explosives) and other products useful in war time have been exploited with special zeal. Then each power trading overseas desired naval bases, coaling stations and ports so that its ships might never be far from a friendly harbor. The desire of Russia to find ice free ports in eastern Asia, and the bitterness which the Germans felt at the British possession of Walfisch Bay, the best port in the neighborhood of their colony of Southwest Africa, are cases in point. Landlocked nations such as Serbia desired seaports so that their commerce might be more under their own control. Russia felt continual irritation at the power of Turkey to turn the key on the Russian Black Sea fleet by closing the Straits.

Finance, like trade, is cosmopolitan and to that extent pacifist. Many students of affairs believe that several *Influence* serious European crises, notably the Morocco *of interna-* crisis of 1911, might have ended in war but for *tional fi-* the timidity of the banks and stock exchanges. *nance* Japan would probably have continued her successful war against Russia had she been able to raise sufficient funds. French loans to Russia helped consolidate the Dual Alliance. But capital seeks investment in colonial enterprises and may in that way indirectly contribute to imperialistic interventions. Loans to such countries as Egypt, Morocco, Turkey, Persia and China have often been accompanied by such guarantees and conditions as have undermined national independence. Napoleon III once tried to found an empire in Mexico, using as a pretext the collection of a bad debt, and the Anglo-German intervention of 1902 in Venezuela had a similar occasion. Perhaps the fairest way of putting it is to say that capital generally desires peace because war means taxes, confiscations, loss of markets and financial panics, but that it will risk war rather than lose its total investment without a struggle.

The press and the party politicians had usually a greater

share than the business men in putting pressure on the diplomats, but their influence differed greatly in   *The press*
different countries. Bismarck was never wiser
than when he said that in the long run every government
must pay for the windows broken by its newspapers; none
the less so, because he had himself at times encouraged the
German press to fling stones with the rest! Among the
greater European powers, press and party were perhaps
strongest in Great Britain. Newspapers such as the London
Times, usually conservative, and the Manchester *Guardian*,
consistently liberal, were read by politically influential
persons in every corner of Europe. They were known to
have excellent foreign correspondence and to be in the main
quite independent of government influence. France had as
free a press as Britain, but conditions there were quite peculiar; most of the very numerous journals read throughout
France were concentrated in the city of Paris and represented the personal views of individual politicians (as Clemenceau's *L'homme libre*) or were controlled by subsidies
representing special interests.[1] Hence very few French
papers were trusted to give an uncolored account of anything; they were read for their style or their opinions. In
most continental countries the press was of less importance
because the severity of government censorship (as in Russia)
or the direct influence of government instructions (as with
Bismarck's "reptile press" in Germany) made so many newspapers little more than a sounding board for official opinion.
Some small nations, such as Switzerland, had newspapers
of wide circulation and influence outside their own borders.
In general, European newspapers gave relatively much more
space to foreign affairs than American papers were wont to
do before the World War. Weekly and monthly magazines
did much to mould the opinions of the upper and middle
classes.

[1] Russian concerns advertised heavily to promote Dual Alliance sentiment.

The attitude of the press to foreign affairs varied largely with party affiliations. Though the case of each nation *Party poli-* presented some unique features, in general the *tics and* more conservative parties and papers were the *diplomacy* more militaristic while the liberal, radical and socialistic groups were willing to make greater concessions to secure peace. In seeking alliances the parties preferred governments whose constitution they approved. All this was well expressed in one of the Kaiser's letters to the Tsar, written of course from his own point of view, "As for France, the radical party... inclines toward England but is opposed to war, because a victorious general would mean certain destruction to this republic of miserable civilians. The nationalist or clerical party dislikes England and has sympathies for Russia." But the real danger to peace lay not in the particular sentiments and prejudices of press and party so much as in the fact that everywhere, and for all factions, the easiest way to attack any government was on the ground of lack of patriotism. The fear of this forced all governments to pose as vigilant champions of the "honor and vital interests" of their respective countries and to conceal behind a screen of secret diplomacy the necessary concessions made in bargaining with foreigners. The "valor of ignorance" in the intensely nationalistic crowds who hooted every treaty as a surrender to the other party and cheered every "firm stand" and spirited defiance had more to do with bringing on the World War, and the lesser modern wars as well, than all the sins of the diplomats combined.

We may perhaps distinguish four types of agitation which trended toward war: the militarism which positively glorified *Propaganda* war or ridiculed the ideals of peace, the prepared-*making* ness agitation which deprecated war but urged *towards war* the need of preparing for self-defense, the cult of nationalism or patriotism which became dangerous when the national claims of two peoples overlapped, and the im-

perialism which sought prosperity or national greatness
through forcible expansion. Of the four, the first was incomparably of least importance. When the famous German general Helmuth von Moltke said that peace was a
dream and not even a beautiful one, and the Englishman
J. A. Cramb said that peace was less a dream than a nightmare, neither spoke for his countrymen. Here and there a
German officer, pining in the ennui of the long peace of 1871–
1914, might express a half-serious wish for a "fresh, pious
and joyous war," or a philosophic recluse like Friedrich
Nietzsche declare that "a good war justifies any cause," but
it would be a mistake to assume that these isolated voices
were really characteristic of any country or expressed the
mind of any government. There is every evidence that the
majority in each belligerent nation viewed the shadow of
impending war with horror and dread.

But it was easier to feel confident of one's own pacific intentions than of those of a rival. The literature on the
World War *before it happened* includes many *Prepared-*
hundreds of books and many thousands of arti- *ness agita-*
cles. The curious reader will find very interest- *tion*
ing predictions of such developments as trench warfare and
military aviation in *The Last Shot* by Frederick Palmer, and
Anticipations and *The War in the Air* by H. G. Wells. Early
in 1914 Sir Arthur Conan Doyle in an article thinly disguised
as fiction, *Danger!* warned his fellow countrymen that submarine attacks on merchant vessels might end British supremacy at sea. A series of imaginary invasions of England
by Germany began in 1871 with *The Battle of Dorking*,
and a popular drama on this theme, *An Englishman's Home*,
played a part in the naval panic of 1909. The French and
German predictions of war were even more numerous than
the British. The number of technical books on military affairs bought by the civilian public on the continent was extraordinary. Men who had served their term in the army

felt a personal interest in the dry details of strategy, especially when they expected to play a personal part in the drama of the next war. In 1906, eight years before the war, an article in the British *Fortnightly Review* spoke as a matter of course of "the probability, verging on absolute certainty, that... the next Franco-German struggle will commence with an act of violation at the expense of Belgian neutrality."

Nationalism or patriotism has been perhaps too indiscriminately condemned as the villain of the piece. That *National-* curious attachment of a man to one particular *ism and* group of his fellows who bear with him the label *progress* of "Germans," "Poles" or "Frenchmen" has sometimes been the main energy behind progress and has led to great cultural triumphs as well as to great wars. It united Germany and Italy in the nineteenth century, liberated the Balkan states from Turkish tyranny, contributed to the national revival of Japan and China. Very much of the best literature in Europe would have remained unwritten but for the inspiration of patriotic feeling. Nationalism underlay the modern Irish drama of Yeats and Synge, the Polish novels of Sienkiewicz, the writings of the Bohemian historians such as Palacky, the revival of classical interests in Greece and Italy, the stories and poems of the Norwegian Björnson. Music and all the arts have celebrated national triumphs or bewailed the misfortunes of the fatherland. Even gymnastic societies, such as the German *Turnverein* and the Slavic *Sokol*, began as parts of nationalist movements, and many schools and universities were founded in every part of Europe to cultivate native languages.

But it is quite tenable that Europe in the twentieth century suffered from too much nationalism. The popular enthusiasm for nationality blended dangerously *National-* with the legal doctrine that a sovereign state was *ism becomes* subject to no law, Machiavelli's principle that *militant* moral rules apply only to private and not to public affairs, and biologic teaching that only the fittest survive in the "struggle for existence." These doctrines received their most systematic exposition in Germany, partly because Germany was no longer a "satiated state" but felt cramped for colonies and partly because the Germans had a genius — or a weakness — for systematizing everything. But the same doctrines, perhaps more sketchily expressed, can also be found in the literature of every other country. In some cases the sciences of language (philology) and race (ethnology) were pressed into service and all the Teutonic or Slavic peoples were urged to unite under the banner of Pangermanism or Panslavism. But these particular professorial hobbies had little weight in practical politics; Germans and English remained mutually suspicious in spite of all the ink that was spilled to prove their Teutonic brotherhood, and Poland and Russia were deeply hostile in spite of their Slavic kinship. Wherever the spirit of nationalism took a chauvinistic turn it tended towards anti-Semitism, or persecution of the Jews, because they seemed a "peculiar people" who were not wholly merged in the populations among whom they lived.

Of the greater powers of Europe Germany was the least content with her position in the world. Her great and growing population, wealth, trade and military and naval strength contrasted too markedly with the narrow confines of Germany-in-Europe and the German colonies. *German imperialism* Grandiose ambitions were much encouraged by the propaganda of the Pan-German League (*Alldeutscher Verband*), the Defense Association (*Wehrverein*) and numerous other patriotic societies. One school of expansionists desired above all overseas colonies; "a German India in Africa" expressed their ideal, and Dr. Solf, the Colonial Minister, and Professor Delbrück of Berlin were prominent among their leaders. A more belligerent group, inspired by Admiral Tirpitz and including Count Reventlow, insisted that while colonies might be desirable, no colonial empire could be secure while Britain held the seas. Their program involved as a first step destruction of the British fleet and annexation of the Channel ports of France, Holland and Belgium. Quite different was the point of view of those who, like Friedrich Neumann, favored a union of central Europe (*Mitteleuropa*) which would start with Germany and Austria-Hungary and might in time comprise also Switzerland, Holland, Scandinavia and the Balkans. Most Germans, however, who wanted landward expansion looked beyond the Danube to the Euphrates and favored the Berlin–Bagdad ideal of a German sphere of influence over the Ottoman Empire. Dr. Paul Rohrbach was one of the chief advocates of this plan. Lastly a "lunatic fringe," who certainly were not representative of either the government or the nation at large, would be satisfied with nothing short of world dominion.[1]

Next to Germany, Russia was most desirous of expansion; but as overseas colonies were out of the question and *Other ex-* Japan had checked the dream of a Russian Man-
pansionist churia and Korea, practically all Russian im-
dreams perialistic ambitions centered in the Near East.
Great Britain and France had already undertaken nearly all the colonial responsibilities that even the most imperialistic desired them to assume — the British conquest of the Boer states in South Africa and the French absorption of Morocco were their last important colonial ventures before the war — but many Frenchmen would have risked a war to regain Alsace-Lorraine. The Italian annexation of Tripoli pointed to a revival of colonial ambitions, long subdued by a defeat in Abyssinia, and some Italians wished for national reasons to annex the "unredeemed Italy" in Tirol

[1] As in Tannenberg's *Gross deutschland* (1911) advocating annexation of central Europe, the Near East, much of Africa, China and South America! General Bernhardi's *Germany and the Next War* (1911) is a well-known but not very important specimen of this species.

and, across the Adriatic, the Italian speaking provinces of Austria-Hungary. Austria-Hungary was the least expansionist of the Great Powers because of the difficulty she had in holding together even the provinces already gathered within her "ramshackle empire," but to prevent the loss of her southern Slavic provinces many Austrian militarists favored the conquest of Serbia. The motive was defensive but the policy aggressive, and it is one of the ironies of history that in 1914 the least ambitious of the powers, Austria-Hungary, dragged into war the most ambitious, Germany, by the iron chain of an alliance.

The lesser powers had their ambitions as well, especially within the Balkan area. Bulgaria wished a "Bulgaria of the four seas" reaching the Adriatic, the Ægean, the sea of Marmora and the Black Sea; Serbia wished a "Greater Serbia" including Montenegro, northern Albania, Bosnia and Herzegovina as a minimum, and some Serbs went further and dreamed of a Yugoslav Empire comprising also the Croat and Slovene provinces of Austria-Hungary; Greece contemplated a new Byzantine Empire, centering around the Ægean and including Constantinople, Smyrna, Cyprus, Rhodes, western Thrace and southern Albania in addition to her gains in the Balkan Wars; Rumania would have liked to annex Transylvania from Hungary and Bessarabia from Russia. In many countries the political philosophy prevailed that a nation which had ceased to grow had already begun to decline; in the expressive German phrase, a race was either hammer or anvil.

One general cause of war which has been frequently and rightly stressed was the growing burden of armament in time of peace. It is not that guns go off by *The burden* themselves or that limitation of armament in- *of armament* sures peace; the whole bloody history of ancient and medieval times is a sufficient refutation of the doctrine that our modern elaborate and expensive armament is necessary to bring on war. The evil done by armament races, like the evil done by commercial competition, was chiefly indirect. If armaments could have been stabilized at any figure, no matter how crushingly huge, the danger would have been lessened. The constant introduction of new inventions, the building of larger ships and huger cannon, and the calling of more men to the colors in time of peace for required military training roused apprehensions of direct attack in neighboring powers, who, in their turn, saw no security save in enlarging their own defenses. Anglo-German relations were at their worst when naval competition was keenest, about 1908; and the large increase of the French and German armies in 1913 was almost the opening signal for the World War, at least it was a sign that the governments had practically given up hope of preserving peace by diplomacy. Other indirect effects of the armament races were the powerful political influence exerted by the army and navy officers and the manufacturers of munitions, the mischievous interference of strategic considerations in diplomacy, and the constant temptation to justify a costly military establishment by basing on it an aggressive and threatening foreign policy.

To every action there is an opposite reaction. If the twentieth century was the age of most extensive and systematic militarism, it was also an active period *Pacifism* in the history of the peace movement. Some pacifists, such as the Quakers and the followers of Tolstoi, denounced on religious and moral grounds all wars, whether offensive or defensive. A second group of pacifists rested their case on economic arguments. Norman Angell (Ralph Lane) argued ably in his famous *The Great Illusion* (1910) that the prime motive of imperialism, the increase of national wealth by the annexation of new territory, was a fallacy, since nations grew rich by trade and not by dominion and small states were often more prosperous than the heavily armed and tax-burdened Great Powers. A third type of pacifism centered its attention on political methods and advocated use of the Hague Court and other methods of arbitration to avert war. Finally, the international Socialist movement represented a brand of pacifism peculiar to itself, the substitution of the class struggle for national rivalry and the proclamation of the brotherhood of workingmen of all nations.

The peace movement was widely organized. In every important nation there were peace societies and periodicals devoted to the cause of international friendship. *Agencies at work to avert war* Some men of wealth contributed lavishly to pacifist propaganda among them Alfred Nobel, the Swedish inventor of dynamite, who provided prizes in his will for eminent achievements in science, idealistic literature, and the promotion of world peace, and Andrew Carnegie, the Scotch-American steel king who built the Peace Palace at The Hague and established the Endowment for International Peace. The universities of America and of Europe exchanged professors and students with each other and thus contributed largely to international understanding. The Rhodes scholarships by which German and American students studied at Oxford were but the most conspicuous instance of educational internationalism. At each new international crisis protests against war arose alike from bankers and merchants who dreaded loss of trade, from the labor unions and Socialists, and from the liberal wing of the press. The fact that Roman Catholics, Jews, and many of the Protestant denominations were scattered among rival nations often made religious sympathy a counterweight to excessive nationalism; though in other cases, as in India and Turkey, religious hostility tended to promote war. The age was, on the whole, humanitarian; it winced at the cruelties of war and identified religion with pacifism in a manner that may conform to the teachings of the New Testament but would have surprised a medieval Crusader or one of Cromwell's Puritan officers.

The peace movement had not been altogether barren of results. It had contributed to the marvelous and unprec-

"Peace hath her victories no less re- nowned than War" edented good fortune which kept war away from all parts of Europe, except the Balkan peninsula, from 1871 to 1914. The precedents for judicial or arbitral settlement of issues quite important enough to lead to war were many, from the set-tlement of the *Alabama* claims in 1872 [1] to the Dogger Bank inquiry of 1905. [2] The numerous crises and "incidents" which marked the partition of Africa had not resulted in a single European war. Arbitration treaties, varying in scope, had been negotiated among the western nations, in Latin America as well as in Europe and the United States. Though the Hague Court had no power to compel obedience to its decrees, many governments voluntarily sought its services and abided by its decisions. Matters not of a judicial nature lacked a tribunal, such as the League of Nations was later to furnish, but were often successfully negotiated in specially summoned international conferences and congresses.

Yet though ninety-nine Europeans out of a hundred dreaded war, they did not dread it enough to make the neces-

The last stand of peace sary concessions of national prestige which could have averted it in the crisis of 1914. Too many pictured the impending war as a brief, brisk campaign after the manner of nearly all recent wars — Bis-marck's victories over Denmark, Austria and France, Japan's one-sided victory over Russia, the easy American triumph over Spain, and the two Balkan campaigns of 1912–13. As Sir Edward Grey, the British Foreign Minister, truly said, "On the continent all the Great Powers were

---

[1] When Britain as defendant paid damages for permitting Confederate raiders to sail from British ports in the American Civil War.

[2] When Britain as plaintiff was granted damages for the destruction of fishing boats in the North Sea by the Russian fleet the previous year.

thinking of war in terms of previous experience and of the latter half of the nineteenth century... When once we were in the diplomatic crisis we were so occupied in searching for practical expedients for solution that there was no time for abstract argument about the catastrophe of modern war." [1]
It is said that in time of peace preparations must be made for war, but in time of peace preparations must also be made for peace, for when war is really imminent it is usually too late either to improvise an army or to improvise a foreign policy which will make it unnecessary to use it.

[1] Viscount Grey, *Twenty-Five Years*, II, page 32.

CHAPTER XIII

THE STORM BREAKS

THE Archduke Francis Ferdinand, nephew of Emperor Francis Joseph and heir to the thrones of Austria and Hun-

The assassination of Francis Ferdinand, June 28, 1914
gary, visited Sarajevo, the chief city of Bosnia, on June 28, 1914. His visit showed more courage than prudence, for the city population was Serb, the date chosen was a Serbian anniversary, and there had been warning that in view of the popular excitement prevailing he would be wiser to stay away. Yet very inadequate police precautions were taken, and his high spirit rose to the challenge of danger. In the morning a bomb was hurled at his car but he proceeded uninjured to the town hall. On his return a Bosnian youth, Gavrilo Prinzip, fired into the car, killing him and his wife.

Such an event in any part of Europe would have provoked a first class international crisis, but in view of the tension

Serbia as a bad neighbor to Austria
then existing between Austria-Hungary and Serbia it was an open invitation to war. Though Prinzip was not a Serbian he was a Serb, akin by race and sympathy to the men on the independent side of the ill-omened frontier which diplomacy had drawn between Serbia and Bosnia. Moreover, his act was but one phase of a widespread conspiracy involving many Serbians. For years an influential propagandist society, the *Narodna Odbrana* or National Defense, had carried on an agitation for uniting all the Serbs, and if possible all the southern Slavs, even at the cost of war and revolution. But there was a smaller and more secret organization, the "Union or Death" (sometimes nicknamed the "Black Hand") which specialized in murder plots and some members of which had been implicated in the assassination of King

Alexander in 1903, a deed which had discredited Serbia for years in the eyes of monarchical Europe. This body would not stop at propaganda or even incitement to war, it desired direct vengeance on all whom it might consider enemies of the nation. To be sure, the Serbian government was on bad terms with the "Union or Death"; Premier Pashitch dreaded that it might bring war with Austria-Hungary or cause another revolution in Serbia, and in 1917 Colonel Dimitrijevitch of the Serbian general staff, active in the organization, was executed for a plot against Crown Prince Alexander. There is also evidence that the Serbian minister at Vienna warned the Austrian authorities, through the minister of finance who administered Bosnian affairs, that Francis Ferdinand would go in peril of his life to Sarajevo. This warning would hardly have been given, even in the vaguest terms, if the Serbian government had *desired* the assassination since it might have altered the archduke's plans. But the negative responsibility of the Serbian government was great. It had, in total disregard of its pledges in 1909, permitted and encouraged anti-Austrian propaganda, it had some knowledge (we do not even yet know how much) of the assassination plot, but exerted only half-hearted and ineffective efforts either to stop the conspirators or arrest and punish them afterwards, and some of its subordinate officials connived at smuggling men and arms across the border.

What is too frequently forgotten, however, is that a small nation may be "endangered" as well as a great one, and that if Serbia threatened Austria-Hungary with revolution and disruption and individual Serbs were involved in murder plots, there had been as much aggression on the other side. Austria-Hungary had dominated Serbia by bribery and intrigue in the days of King Alexander and by bullying in the days of King Peter. She was guilty not only of the passive injury

Austria as a bad neighbor to Serbia

of holding Slavic provinces which Serbia wanted but of the active injury of blocking every effort Serbia made in the Balkans to secure seaports or advantageous trade routes. In 1913 Foreign Minister Berchtold had urged on Germany and Italy the advisability of war with Serbia, though no assassination had yet taken place. In Bosnia and Herzegovina civil government constantly lapsed into military dictatorship and the same was true in the Hungarian provinces of Croatia-Slavonia. Francis Ferdinand was popularly credited, perhaps unjustly, with desiring to annex Serbia as part of his projected third or Slavic division of Austria-Hungary ("trialism"). This seems to have been a vague dream rather than an actual plan, but so much was said about it that the Serbians can hardly be blamed for believing that their national independence was threatened. And while Francis Ferdinand, who was always something of a man of mystery, seems not himself to have wished war, he was mainly responsible for the appointment of Conrad von Hötzendorf as Chief of Staff, the hottest militarist in the whole Dual Monarchy.

The murder of the Austrian archduke was received very differently in different European capitals. The Serbians *Europe and* at Belgrade felt no sorrow; some rejoiced openly *the assassi-* that an "enemy of the Serbs" had fallen, others *nation* trembled in terror at the vengeance that Austria might demand. The Hungarians at Budapest also felt little regret, because they had viewed with much alarm the succession to the throne of a ruler believed to be anti-Magyar in his sentiments and feared that Croatia-Slavonia might be taken from Hungary and added to a Slavic division of the country. St. Petersburg, Rome, Paris and London expressed official regret but they were chiefly interested in what Austria would do. Only at Vienna and Berlin was the assassination followed by a genuine outburst of popular and official indignation. The aged Francis Joseph had not always been on good terms with his heir, but he had suffered so many domestic calamities that this one struck him with cumulative force. Military circles in Austria were wild for war. Foreign Minister Berchtold, the real head of the civilian government, as the Emperor was too enfeebled by age and prostrated by grief to take the helm, resolved that *this* time nothing should stand between him and war against Serbia. Kaiser Wilhelm II was moved chiefly by monarchical feeling; he felt that the assassination was a blow at all kings and kingship and could not believe that the Tsar of Russia would lend Serbia any countenance even if Austria-Hungary resorted to war. When he learned that the German ambassador at Vienna had warned Austria-Hungary against rash action he exploded into indignant exclamation points along the margin of the dispatch: "Is none of his business since it is solely Austria's affair what she intends to do in consequence. Then it will be said if things go wrong, Germany was not willing! Tschirschky will kindly stop this nonsense! The Serbs must be cleaned up and that *quickly*."

But Austria did not heed the Kaiser's wish. Instead of striking while the iron of public indignation was hot the Austro-Hungarian government delayed nearly a month before presenting demands to Serbia. *The long delay, June 28-July 23* The Kaiser was displeased and the diplomatic circles of Europe made uneasy by the silence of Vienna, but the general public seemed reassured. Another "incident" had passed without war! The reasons for delay were fourfold. Some time was necessary to collect evidence which would serve to justify a drastic ultimatum to Serbia; assurances must be obtained from Germany of military support in the event of a war with Russia; the Hungarian government must be won over to the support of the Austrian policy; a moment must be selected when France and Russia would not be too closely in consultation. The report of

Dr. Wiesner, the Austrian investigator, implicated a few minor Serbian officials but concluded that "there is nothing to prove, or even to cause suspicion of the Serbian Government's cognizance of the steps leading to the crime, or of its preparing it, or of its supplying the weapons." However, he and other Austrian authorities suspected, and in part correctly, that the plot had wider ramifications than had yet been revealed by the preliminary inquiry. Assurances of German support were easily obtained on July 5 without declaring to Kaiser or Chancellor the substance of the Austrian demands.[1] It was much harder to convince Count Stephan Tisza, the Hungarian Premier. He hated the Slavs more than did Berchtold himself and had been guilty of gross oppression towards them in Hungary, but he was against a war policy partly because he rightly believed that a general European war would be ruinous to Austria-Hungary and partly because he did not want an annexation of Serbian territory which would increase the number of Slavs in the Empire.

Legends of a definite Austro-German "conspiracy" to bring on a general European war at a private meeting at

Germany gives a "blank check"

Konopischt between Wilhelm II and Francis Ferdinand, a few days before the assassination of the latter, or later at a Potsdam Crown Council on July 5, 1914, attended by all the diplomatic, military and financial authorities of Germany, have been blown away by later research. The Konopischt meeting did indeed involve a discussion of Balkan affairs, but concerned chiefly the attitude of Rumania, whose dubious allegiance to the Triple Alliance gave Austria-Hungary at that time even more concern than the open hostility of Serbia. The Potsdam Crown Council, in the formal sense, never took place; but it was an exaggeration of what none the less was a crucially important incident, the personal

---

[1] The terms of the note had not yet been finally determined.

pledge of Kaiser Wilhelm that he would back Austria-Hungary in any demands which might be made on Serbia. From that day the power of Germany to work openly for peace was shackled by a rash pledge which made war absolutely inevitable unless Russia could be persuaded, or threatened, into wholly standing aside, or Berchtold's determination to make war on Serbia waver before the Russian menace. The Kaiser consulted his Chancellor, Bethmann-Hollweg, Zimmermann the acting Foreign Secretary, Falkenhayn, the Prussian Minister of War, and a few other officials; these conversations undoubtedly started the rumor of a formal Crown Council.

Germany had promised to aid Austria-Hungary even if the Austro-Serbian crisis resulted in a European war; does that mean that the German government *The German point of view* expected such a war? Apparently not. The Kaiser, after giving his rash pledge, immediately set sail for Norwegian waters in his yacht, and some of his ministers likewise remained on their summer vacations. No important military or naval preparations seem to have been made. Perhaps the inmost mind of the German civilian authorities was best expressed in Foreign Secretary Jagow's confidential note to Ambassador Lichnowsky, who was alarmed lest Germany's fatal loyalty to Austria-Hungary might jeopardize good relations with Great Britain. Jagow admitted that Austria-Hungary was a weak ally, in fact "can hardly be counted any longer as a fullfledged Great Power" but, as Germany lacked other allies and could not improvise them in a crisis, Austria must at all costs, even at the risk of war, be sustained. But the risk was not a great one. "The more determined Austria shows herself, the more energetically we support her, the more likely it is that Russia will keep quiet. Some blustering at Petersburg will not be wanting, no doubt, but Russia is not really prepared now." In this gambler's spirit the great re-

sponsibility was taken. Austria-Hungary treated her allies
with something like contempt. Italy was almost completely
disregarded, Berchtold fearing that she would demand
"compensation" in the Balkans for supporting the Austrian
policy; the text of the ultimatum to Serbia was shown to
the German Foreign Office only on the very eve of its
presentation and long after Germany had promised unconditional support.

By July 14, Tisza's most reluctant consent had been
won to Berchtold's policy, but still the ultimatum was not
Poincaré's   sent. A new obstacle had arisen. President
visit to   Poincaré visited Russia from July 20 to July
Russia   23; Berchtold did not wish to send Austria's
demands on Serbia to Belgrade while Russian diplomats
were toasting a French President, lest the "champagne
mood" as it was wittily called, might cause the representatives of the Dual Alliance publicly to commit themselves
to the armed defense of Serbia. He preferred to wait till
Poincaré was on his way home and thus delay direct consultations between France and Russia on the crisis which
he knew must result. The public addresses on either side
during Poincaré's visit were general enough but they emphasized the sincere adhesion of both France and Russia
to the Dual Alliance and very likely were supplemented by
private assurances even more specific. Hints were dropped
to the Austrian Ambassador at St. Petersburg that a
moderate note to Serbia would best assure the peace of
Europe,[1] but the main burden of conversation seems to
have been the attitude of Great Britain and in particular
the need of conciliating British opinion with regard to
Persia, where Russian aggression had been the cause of
much irritation.

Finally, on July 23, the demands of Austria-Hungary

---

[1] "Serbia has very warm friends in the Russian people," Poincaré told him, "And
Russia has an ally, France."

were presented to Serbia with a limit of forty-eight hours for complete compliance. The Serbian govern- *The ultima-* ment was asked to print an official apology for *tum at last* anti-Austrian propaganda and pledge to repress it in the future, and in particular to (1) suppress publications hostile to Austria-Hungary, (2) dissolve the Narodna Odbrana and other nationalist societies, (3) remove from the schools anti-Austrian teachers and textbooks, (4) remove from the civil and military services all officials objectionable to Austria-Hungary, "whose names and deeds the Austro-Hungarian Government reserve to themselves the right of communicating"; (5) admit Austro-Hungarian officials into Serbia for collaboration in "the suppression of the subversive movement directed against the territorial integrity of the monarchy"; (6) admit Austro-Hungarian officials also into the judicial inquiries regarding the murder plot; (7) arrest certain designated Serbians compromised by inquiries already made; (8) prevent illicit arms traffic across the frontier and dismiss and punish officials guilty of participation in it; (9) apologize for the unfriendly remarks of "high Serbian officials." The drastic character of these demands, much sharper than had been expected, and the short grace of forty-eight hours allowed for submission, caused general alarm in Europe. Sir Edward Grey declared with truth that he "had never before seen one State address to another independent State a document of so formidable a character." Yet all expressed hope that Serbia would send a conciliatory reply and war might be averted.

Just before the expiration of the time limit Serbia sent a very submissive reply, accepting most of the demands but not the participation of Austro-Hungarian officials in investigations on Serbian soil. Even *Austria-* the doubtful points the Serbian government of- *Hungary* fered to refer to the Hague Court or to the *begins the* mediation of the Great Powers. Everywhere *war* except in

Austria this reply was considered to open a way to peaceful settlement. The German Kaiser himself, who had expressed himself perhaps more violently than any other public man in Europe against the Serbs,[1] declared that "every cause for war disappears" and that on the strength of it "*I* would never have ordered mobilization." These were the wisest words of his entire reign and could he have remained in that mind and imposed his view on Austria-Hungary there would have been no World War, at all events in 1914. No doubt there would have been prolonged negotiations and exasperating delays in carrying the Austrian ultimatum fully into effect, for certain phrases in Serbia's reply pointed to possibilities of evasion of some of the more inacceptable demands, but to treat such a document as a blank refusal is proof positive that the Austrian government was bent on a punitive war and would not be content with a mere diplomatic victory, however sweeping. On July 25 Austria-Hungary broke off diplomatic relations with Serbia and commenced mobilization; on July 28 she declared war. Just what plan the Austrian government had in mind is hard to tell; it rejected on military grounds the German plan of remaining content with the occupation of Belgrade as a pledge of the enforcement of its demands, but it may have been sincere in professing that no "territorial aggrandizement" was desired, and perhaps the clue is to be found in Emperor Francis Joseph's letter of July 5 to the German Kaiser that he desired "the isolation and diminution of Serbia," the strengthening of Bulgaria, a new Balkan union "under the patronage of the Triple Alliance" and the elimination of Serbia "as a political factor in the Balkans."

Both Germany and Austria-Hungary hoped that the war,

---

[1] For instance "Grey commits the mistake of putting Serbia on a level with Austria and other great powers! This is unheard of! Serbia is a pack of robbers and has to be held accountable for its crimes!"

no longer to be averted, could be "localized" and remain a Balkan conflict merely. Though sympathy *The Rus-* with Austria, after the Sarajevo assassination, *sian view-* had been largely changed to sympathy with *point* Serbia by reason of the Austrian ultimatum and insistence on war, it was not likely that Britain, France or Italy would intervene in a military sense unless Russia chose to do so. Russia was the only Slavic and the only Greek Orthodox Great Power in Europe, the only one bound by ties of kinship and faith with Serbia. Russia was also the only Great Power with direct and immediate interests in the Near East which would be injured by the crushing of Serbia and the establishment of Austro-German ascendancy in the Balkans, though France and Britain might feel on general grounds apprehensive at this degree of realization of "Berlin to Bagdad." The key to the general European situation was obviously Russia. In the very region now at war Russia had suffered a diplomatic defeat at the hands of Germany and Austria-Hungary in 1908 and 1909, when Austria-Hungary annexed Bosnia and Herzegovina from Turkey and compelled Serbia to accept the settlement as final. Would Russia on a second and more serious occasion again submit to the humiliation of Serbia, her Balkan protegée? If so, what would become of Russian influence with the Balkan States? Would they not all turn to Germany and Austria-Hungary as the only powers able either to injure or defend them? If Russia herself, after a victorious war with Turkey, had been compelled to lay all her claims before an international European conference at Berlin in 1878, could Austria-Hungary claim the right to carry on a Balkan war in complete disregard of the point of view of all other nations? Such considerations made Russian intervention practically inevitable, though not necessarily justifiable, and one is amazed at the folly of the Austro-Hungarian government in rushing into an avoidable Balkan war with-

out first making certain of Russia's attitude. In Sir Arthur
Nicolson's phrase, to most of Europe "localizing the war
merely means that all the powers are to hold the ring while
Austria quietly strangles Serbia." That was not likely to
content the Russians!

From July 24, when the terms of Austria-Hungary s
ultimatum became generally known to the European Foreign Offices, to August 4, when Great Britain
Twelve days, July 24 to August 4, 1914 announced her intention to support Belgium by
force of arms, Europe passed through the most
intense diplomatic crisis ever known. The full
story of those days can never be told, not because we lack
evidence,[1] but because events crowded so fast on each
other's heels that the diplomats themselves could not keep
up with them and often confused different peace proposals
with each other. Negotiations, which in a more leisurely
day would have occupied many months and perhaps have
made peace possible after all, were cut short by the sinister
speed of modern military action and panic fear of immediate
attack. However we distribute blame among nations,
governments and individuals, we can all agree that the
chief villain of the piece was the "military time table," the
fixed and rigid plans which the several general staffs of the
European powers had drawn up in time of peace. Military
considerations, overriding diplomatic and statesmanlike
projects for maintaining peace, determined Austria's hasty
blow at Serbia, Russia's premature mobilization against
Austria-Hungary and Germany, Germany's premature
declarations of war against Russia and France, and the

---

[1] So abundant have been the wartime and post-war official publications on the
crisis of 1914 and so fully has the subject been treated in the memoirs of its chief sur-
viving participants, that Prof. W. E. Lingelbach justly observed in 1930 that "Already there is more direct evidence on the subject from the secret foreign office
archives than exists on any other war in history"! Revolutions in Russia, Austria-
Hungary and Germany not only opened archives usually kept secret for generations
after a war, but placed their publication in the hands of radical socialists who had no
motive to spare their former rulers. Few important secrets committed to paper can
have thus escaped publicity.

German invasion of Belgium and Luxemburg which decided the time, if not the fact, of Britain's entrance into the war.

In this confusion of detail, it will be necessary to limit our present consideration to a few outstanding facts: the mobilization of the Russian army, the principal *Russia* diplomatic projects for a pacific solution of the *mobilizes* crisis, the German declarations of war on Russia and on France, the invasion of Belgium and the consequent entrance of Great Britain into the war. Russia, as we have seen, was resolved to go to war unless Austria-Hungary would recognize that the Serbian crisis should be regarded (as Near Eastern conflicts almost invariably had been regarded) as a matter of general European interest. As a threat to compel Austria-Hungary to recognize this, Russia would mobilize her army; that is, put it in a state of readiness for instant war. Though modern means of transportation have made mobilization many times as rapid as it used to be, Russia was of all European nations the most at a disadvantage in this matter. Her vast population was thinly extended over an immense area, poorly served by railroads. The importance of this factor is graphically shown by the single fact that, although Russia had about four times the population of France (not including overseas colonies) and an army about twice as great, Germany based her whole campaign on a strong, immediate offensive against France while leaving only a relatively small defensive force to defend the Fatherland from Russia until, after a lapse of several weeks, France had been defeated and the main German army could be shifted to the east. This slowness of Russian mobilization was of vital significance in the diplomatic situation, it explains why Russia felt it necessary to start preparations so soon and also why Germany thought essential not to prolong negotiations until Russia could complete them.

On July 24 the Russian government began to consider

general measures "preparatory to war," not mobilization
Divided in the strict sense of the word but administrative
counsels steps which would facilitate it if occasion made
in Russia it necessary.   On the following day the decision
was taken and a plan of partial mobilization, against
Austria-Hungary only, was also considered.   But the military authorities disliked Sazonov's plan of partial mobilization, not only because Germany was certain to support
Austria-Hungary in the event of war but because it was
technically difficult to move troops in the south if they
could not be moved elsewhere in Russia as well.   They
urged a general mobilization, along the German as well as
the Austro-Hungarian frontier.   The Tsar hesitated between two opinions with characteristic and pitiable inde-
cision.   The Austrian declaration of war on Serbia on July
28 caused Sazonov to believe that the time had come to
order at least the partial mobilization, and it was so ordered
on July 29.   On that same day the Tsar had already
signed orders for general mobilization to be used if necessary, but had canceled them again.   But late on July 30,
the combined pressure of the military experts and of Sazonov
induced the Tsar to consent, reluctantly it appears, to
mobilize along the whole western frontier of Russia.   Fearing another change of opinion by the Tsar, his officials at
once rushed the order over the wires and "the iron dice
were set rolling."

The Tsar almost certainly desired peace, though he
lacked the strength of character to control even the policy
Russian of his own ministers and generals.   Foreign
peace ef- Minister Sazonov, much more influential in the
forts crisis, is more of an enigma and students of the
crisis are divided to this day as to how much he hoped or
desired to avert war.   Certainly he tendered numerous
overtures of conciliation, some of them very generous in
their terms, to Germany and Austria-Hungary.   He pro-

posed at various times mediation by neutral powers, direct representations to Austria, collective guarantees for the future good behavior of Serbia, a modification of the terms of the Austrian ultimatum, an extension of the time limit granted to Serbia and sundry other suggestions, provoking Sir Arthur Nicolson to say on July 27 "In three consecutive days M. Sazonov has made one suggestion and two proposals all differing from each other... One really does not know where one is." As late as July 30 he offered:

> If Austria, recognizing that the Austro-Serbian question has assumed the character of a question of European interest, declares herself ready to eliminate from her ultimatum points which violate the sovereign rights of Serbia, Russia engages to stop her military preparations.

But his suggestions were proferred without much hope. He had become personally convinced that Germany was the instigator of Austria's policy and this impression was confirmed when he asked the German Ambassador what Berlin was doing to check the precipitate action of Austria and the Ambassador could give him in return no positive assurances. Behind the scenes, to be sure, Berlin was already urging caution on Vienna, but Sazonov did not know this. In finally consenting to mobilize against Germany he was virtually consenting to war, for Russian mobilization on the German frontier would as a matter of course lead to counter-mobilization, and the German plans for mobilization against Russia implied the actual sending of troops across the frontier. The military men, such as Generals Sukhomlinov and Yanushkevitch, had no such hesitations as affected Nicholas II and Sazonov; they expected war and urged immediate action. Izvolski, Russian Ambassador at Paris, was of the same mind; he is even said to have boasted, "This is *my* little war!" — a boast which some historians have perhaps taken too seriously, as this jingo braggart was already a little out of favor at St. Petersburg.

"Mobilization is war" was a phrase used by military experts at the time of the negotiation of the Franco-Russian

The signif-
icance of
Russian
mobilization

Dual Alliance in 1892, and apparently this formula was accepted by most military men in 1914. This does not mean, of course, that every mobilization is necessarily followed by hostilities; on the contrary there have been many examples in history of mobilization followed by a peaceful settlement, such as the partial mobilization of Austria-Hungary against Serbia in 1908–09. But the fact that the German plan of mobilization implied immediate military action made it highly dangerous to provoke it by bringing Russian forces towards the German frontier even if they had been instructed not to cross it. Grey, certainly, and Sazonov, apparently, believed it possible to avert war even after general mobilization had been ordered in Russia, for they continued to offer peace proposals which, if accepted by Germany and Austria-Hungary, would have ended the crisis and with it all need for military preparation by either side. The possibility of mobilization without war has been endorsed by some able and impartial historians since the war.[1] But it implies a willingness on the part of military men in both Russia and Germany to alter old established plans of campaign at the eleventh hour; here again the "military time table" prevailed over diplomatic considerations.

Sir Edward Grey was the spokesman for Great Britain and, except so far as the attitude of others limited his free-

British
peace
efforts

dom of negotiation, conducted the whole course of British diplomacy during the crisis. There has been endless controversy as to the wisdom or folly of his foreign policy in 1914 as well as in the years immediately preceding the crisis, though even his enemies

[1] E.g. G. P. Gooch, *History of Modern Europe* (1922), page 547. "Had the German Government been as anxious for peace as the British cabinet, it might... have answered the Russian mobilization by counter-mobilization."

admitted his good faith and zeal for peace.[1] It has often
been asserted, for example, that he could have kept Europe
from war by taking a clearer stand from the start and either
have warned Germany and Austria-Hungary that a war
with Russia and France would mean a war with Britain too,
or else have warned Russia and France that they could not
in any event count on British assistance; then one side or the
other would have given way and peace prevailed. This may
or may not be true, but it is irrelevant; Grey could have
given no such assurances without the risk of perjuring himself and the government which he represented. Until
France was attacked and neutral Belgium invaded public
opinion in Great Britain was too strongly against war for
Grey to be sure that he could carry even the cabinet, let
alone the parliament and the nation, with him in a war
policy, while an unconditional promise of neutrality would
probably have broken down as the German hosts swept
through Belgium toward Paris. A far stronger case against
Grey's diplomacy is that he spoke and acted throughout the
crisis as though Great Britain were free of diplomatic entanglements, whereas the close association and especially
the secret military and naval "conversations" between the
British and the French in recent years had in fact morally
bound the British government to support France in any
defensive war, and that such obligations should never have
been incurred without franker explanations to public and to
Parliament.[2]

[1] Note the German Foreign Secretary Jagow's statement *during* the World War
"I believe in Sir Edward Grey's love of peace and in his earnest wish to arrive at an
understanding with us. But he had allowed himself to become entangled in the net
of Franco-Russian policy."

[2] An excellent commentary on the impossibility of a British government making
binding promises of intervention or neutrality may be found in a memorandum by
Lord Salisbury in 1901, "Several times during the last sixteen years Count Hatzfeldt has tried to elicit from me, in conversation, some opinion as to the probable
conduct of England, if Germany or Italy were involved in war with France. I have
always replied that no English minister could venture on such a forecast. The
course of the English Government in such a crisis must depend on the view taken by
public opinion in this country, and public opinion would be largely, if not exclusively, governed by the nature of the *casus belli*."

Sir Edward Grey, not feeling free to restrain the Triple
Alliance by threats of war or the Dual Alliance by threats
of desertion, bent all his efforts to give the Balkan crisis a
peaceful setting. If his peace proposals were fewer than
those of Sazonov they were better sustained. Before the
text of the Austro-Hungarian ultimatum was published he
urged direct conversations between Vienna and St. Petersburg to moderate its tone; France preferred Russian and
French protests to Vienna. After the ultimatum he suggested a conference of the four powers "who had not direct
interests in Serbia," that is to say Great Britain, Germany,
France and Italy, to "act together for the sake of peace,
simultaneously in Vienna and St. Petersburg." This broke
down because Germany did not want intervention between
Austria-Hungary *and Serbia*, though willing to have it between Austria-Hungary *and Russia*; France and Russia,
on the other hand, insisted that the Serbian question must
come directly into the foreground. On July 26 Grey made
a formal offer of a conference of ambassadors of the powers not directly involved on the whole situation. Germany rejected this suggestion as humiliating to her ally
and because she feared that Britain, France and Italy
would all be hostile to Austria's claims. This rejection disappointed the British Foreign Minister, but he rejoiced to
hear that direct conversations between Russia and Austria-
Hungary had been renewed with German approval.
Throughout the crisis he insisted on no one program but
offered to accept any solution that would keep the peace.
He informed Lichnowsky, the German Ambassador, that
"if Germany could get any reasonable proposal put forward
which made it clear that Germany and Austria were striving
to preserve European peace, and that Russia and France
would be unreasonable if they rejected it, I would support
it at St. Petersburg and Paris and go the length of saying
that, if Russia and France would not accept it, the govern-

ment would have nothing more to do with the consequences."
In spite of much pressure from France and Russia he constantly refused to pledge British intervention under any
circumstances, but he warned Germany through her Ambassador as early as July 29 that if France became involved
"I did not wish him to be misled by the friendly tone of our
conversation into thinking that we should stand aside."

The constant appeals for peace from St. Petersburg and
London did not leave the German government unmoved,
though it did not respond until it was almost too *German*
late. Until about July 28 Germany still ad- *peace*
hered to the position that what Austria-Hungary *efforts*
chose to do with Serbia was no concern of any other power
and that mediation, if admitted at all, should be merely an
attempt to "localize" the conflict and keep it from spreading
beyond the Balkans. But the imminence of Russian mobilization, the total opposition of Italy to Austria's whole program of war, the conciliatory reply of Serbia which had impressed even the Kaiser, and, above all, the grave warnings
from England transmitted by Lichnowsky [1] finally convinced
Bethmann-Hollweg that it was time to warn the Austrian
government that it was running past the danger signals into
a needless general European war.[2] Kaiser Wilhelm thought
a basis of compromise might be the Austrian occupation of
Belgrade, the Serbian capital which was near the frontier,
as a guarantee that the measures in the ultimatum would be
in fact carried out. Bethmann-Hollweg and Jagow seem
to have taken the same view. They sent frequent and urgent
warnings to Austria through Tschirschky, the German Ambassador at Vienna to find some basis of compromise which

[1] As P. Renouvin put it, "As far as Germany was concerned, the fear of England
was the beginning of wisdom."

[2] As late as July 27, the Austrian Ambassador in Berlin informed his government that Foreign Secretary Jagow, in transmitting British proposals for mediation,
wished Austria to understand that he by no means endorsed them but, on the contrary, favored their rejection. The telegram is very confused, and experts are still
debating as to exactly which British proposals were in mind.

would avert war with Russia, and Bethmann-Hollweg even
went so far as to say that "We must refuse to be drawn into
a world conflagration through Austria not respecting our
advice." The excellent effect of these calming suggestions
was, however, much diluted by the unauthorized inter-
ferences of some German military men, such as Moltke, the
chief of staff, who urged Austria to stand firm and mobilize
against Russia at once, to reject the British peace overtures,
and to offer Italy "compensation" sufficient to hold her to
the alliance.

The other three Great Powers did relatively little in positive support of peace. France, to be sure, supported the
French principal Russian and British peace proposals
peace and cautioned Russia not to take steps that ap-
efforts peared aggressive; but she had accorded Russia
pledges of unhesitating support if attacked. France has been
blamed for not pressing Russia to refrain from mobilization
as vigorously as Germany pressed Austria to find some peace
formula with Russia, and in this negative sense France must
share some of the responsibility for the war. Three points
may, however, be made in her favor. The Austrian ultimatum caught her by surprise while President Poincaré
and some of his most important advisors were returning from
St. Petersburg to Paris, so the French Foreign Office could
only "mark time" in the first phase of the crisis; France
thoroughly agreed with Russia that the Serbian question
was a European matter and believed that if Austria-Hungary refused to treat it as such Russia was within her rights
in mobilizing; and the attitude of the French government
and public was singularly calm (in marked contrast to the
old legend of "French excitability") and did nothing to
raise the psychological temperature of the crisis, perhaps a
more important fact than any interchange of diplomatic
notes.

Italy took from the start an attitude of neutrality; considering that Austria's policy was offensive, she would not regard it as binding her to come to the aid of her allies under the terms of the Triple Alliance. *Italian and Austrian peace efforts* She made one sensible peace proposal, that all the powers join together to induce Serbia to accept the Austrian ultimatum without any reservations, if Austria-Hungary would declare herself content and discontinue military measures. Very little attention was paid to this suggestion. Austria did more for war and less for peace than any other European belligerent, but even she did not desire a general war and was willing to promise not to annex Serbian territory [1] and to continue diplomatic conversations with Russia. This apparent yielding to the British and German mediation for peace was largely nullified by the two implicit conditions which were attached to it, that Russia must cease to mobilize and that Austria-Hungary must have a free hand to continue military operations in Serbia. Serbia's own excellent peace suggestion, to refer all disputed points to the Hague Tribunal, was once echoed by the Russian Tsar, who felt a fatherly interest in the institution which he had helped to create, but otherwise was lost to sight.

It will thus be seen that in different measure and at different times Serbia, Austria-Hungary, Russia, Germany, Italy, France and Great Britain each made or supported peace proposals which if universally accepted would have averted the World War. *The war that no one wanted* The proposals of the Triple Entente would have averted even a Balkan war. This is proof sufficient that no civilian government in 1914 wanted a general war, and dissipates the "war mythology" of long planned "conspiracies," either by a Germany consumed with lust for world dominion or by an "iron ring" of jealous foes bent on the downfall of the

---

[1] Not, however, to respect Serbian "sovereignty." Austria's concession was quite compatible with reducing Serbia to a vassal state or giving her territory to Bulgaria, Albania or any country *except* herself.

Fatherland. Unfortunately, the moment was at hand when decision would be snatched from the hesitating and bewildered civilian diplomats and determined by considerations of purely military expediency.

Russia's mobilization determined the German declaration of war, for on July 31 Germany issued an ultimatum demanding the cessation by Russia within twelve hours of all measures of general mobilization. For some time the Kaiser had become increasingly alarmed at the prospect that Germany would be caught unprepared between France and a fully armed Russia, and his irritation showed itself in sneers at the "*civilian* Chancellor" and at his advice to remain calm — "To remain calm is a citizen's first duty! Just keep calm, always calm!! A calm mobilization is something new, indeed!" When a direct appeal to the Tsar failed he gave up hope of peace. A proclamation of "threatening danger of war" was made on July 31 and followed on August first by mobilization and declaration of war. Some of the military chiefs in Germany opposed the German declaration of war but not on the ground that it was premature, merely that on a basis of expediency it was better to let war begin with some act of hostility on the border than by a formal declaration which made Germany seem the aggressor.

Germany declares war on Russia, August 1, 1914

The attitude of France put Germany in a quandary. France was more feared than Russia, and the whole German plan of campaign was based on attacking France first; military opinion held that it would be unsafe to let France remain neutral at first and then enter the war at a time when Germany's full force was engaged in the east. Moreover, the Germans were rightly convinced that France, bound by treaty obligations to support Russia, would never agree to genuine neutrality. So France was not only asked to remain neutral, but the German government planned, in case such a promise was

Germany declares war on France, August 3, 1914

made, to follow it by a demand for the fortresses of Toul and
Verdun as guarantees of neutrality! This arrogant demand
was never actually presented, however, as France replied
simply that she would consult her own interests. That
would have justified a declaration of war, since it amounted
to support of Russia, but Germany in a maladroit attempt
to make a stronger case for declaring war really weakened it.
Though France had withdrawn her army to a line averaging
ten kilometers back of the frontier [1] and had taken care to
avoid any collision of forces, the German government
snatched at some hasty newspaper rumors, such as the
bombing of Nuremberg by French airplanes (later denied
by the Mayor of Nuremberg), and declared that France had
already begun the war. The effect of Germany's brusque
attack was to destroy in France all remnant of party division. The socialists supported the national cause practically without exception in spite of their natural resentment
at the murder of their leader Jaurès by a fanatical chauvinist.
At the other extreme, royalists who had spent their lives in
futile dreams of overthrowing the Republic proudly accepted service in its ranks. A similar "rally round the flag"
had taken place already in Serbia, Austria-Hungary, Russia
and Germany. Pacifism seemed to have vanished overnight, as the common people in every nation believed that
they were fighting on the defensive.

The invasion of the neutral states of Luxemburg and Belgium had been for more than a decade an integral part of
the plans of the German army in the event of *The inva-*
war with France (the Schlieffen plan). Of *sion of Lux-*
course this intention was not openly avowed by *emburg and*
Germany, which was bound by treaties of 1839 *Belgium*
and 1867 to respect and maintain the neutrality and integ-

---

[1] The fundamental reason for this was to impress British opinion by assuming a
clearly defensive attitude. None the less the precaution was wise on other grounds,
for many an otherwise avoidable war has been started by some trivial conflict of
patrols along a national frontier.

rity of Belgium and of Luxemburg respectively. But the construction of German strategic railways to the Belgian frontier, the secret conversations of Belgian officers in 1906 with British military experts for defense against Germany, and the frequent discussions in the periodical press of Germany's military plans, showed that the invasion was no last minute resolution. The frontier between France and Germany was short, it was guarded by a chain of the strongest fortresses in the world, and behind it lay a rough, hilly country through which Germany could not lead armies vast enough to overwhelm the French defense. Worst of all, from the standpoint of the invader, the sharpest, steepest slopes of these hills face the Rhine. The plains of Belgium, on the contrary, are almost as level as one of her own Brussels carpets and form an ideal terrain for maneuvering millions of soldiers. This is what the German Chancellor meant when he justified the invasion on the ground that "we are now in a state of necessity and necessity knows no law"; it was another way of saying that the military advantage of a belligerent power overrides every right of a neutral state, even a state whose neutrality is guarded by special treaty.

In spite of the ten years of continuous co-operation which Great Britain had accorded France under the *entente*, in *A divided mind in Britain* spite of the popular hostility which had grown up between the British and Germans for an even longer period, in spite of the naval arrangements which had been made between the British and the French, the British government refused throughout July to give any categorical assurances of support to France. The truth is that dislike of participation in any continental war had become very strong in British circles. Until the danger of a German invasion of Belgium became imminent, half the cabinet opposed intervention even to save France, and when the decision for war was made at last two powerful ministers, John Morley and John Burns, resigned. Ramsay MacDonald, Keir Hardie and some other Labor leaders continued to oppose war even after Great Britain had entered. Sir Edward Grey himself, though he had worked more consistently for peace than any other European diplomat during the crisis, was accounted too belligerent by some of his colleagues. On the other hand, his Foreign Office advisers, such as Sir Eyre Crowe and Sir Arthur Nicolson, and the leaders of the Unionist or Conservative party, then in opposition, thought that he was overcautious. One precaution was taken; the fleet, assembled for review, was not dismissed but remained concentrated.

Though Germany had no hope of keeping France from joining Russia, the case seemed to be different with Great Britain. If the British, whose repugnance to entering the war was so evident, could be induced to stand aside, the prospects of victory would be much brighter. Continental opinion *Germany bids for British neutrality* held rather in contempt the small British army, but in immense respect the powerful British navy. On July 29 Chancellor Bethmann-Hollweg promised that, if war arose and Great Britain stood neutral, Germany would promise not to annex any French territory. But he refused to give any promise as to the French colonies and could not say that German armies would keep out of Belgium. As might have been expected this maladroit proposal had only the effect of convincing the British government that Germany was bent on war and determined on conquest, though as a matter of fact Bethmann-Hollweg was still working for peace. Other hypothetical questions were later asked. Would the British be satisfied by a promise not to make a *naval* attack on the French coast? Would the British abandon France if Belgium were not invaded? Sir Edward Grey uniformly answered that "our attitude would be determined by public opinion" and that "the neutrality of

Belgium would appeal strongly to public opinion." Not until August 2 did the cabinet give the French any definite assurances of support, and this was limited to naval matters. On August 3 Sir Edward Grey presented the whole diplomatic situation to the House of Commons, and on August 4 the government demanded that the Germans withdraw their ultimatum to Belgium. Chancellor Bethmann-Hollweg, overburdened with responsibility and hysterical with fatigue, broke into bitter reproaches that "Just for a word — 'neutrality,' a word which in war time had been so often disregarded — just for a scrap of paper Great Britain was going to make war on a kindred nation."

Perhaps the Chancellor did not realize all that was in that "scrap of paper." It contained not only England's *Why Great* moral and legal obligation to maintain the in*Britain* tegrity and neutrality of Belgium, but England's *went to war* security as well. That no great and aggressive continental power should conquer or occupy the netherlandish countries had been for centuries the very axiom of British foreign policy. Largely on that ground, England had fought Spain in the days of Philip II and France in the time of Louis XIV and Napoleon. A glance at the map will show that the question was vital to national security.[1] Moreover, the British public is by far the most sentimental and romantic in Europe, and the spectacle of "brave little Belgium" honoring its legal obligations in the face of certain invasion and probable conquest stirred the nation as had nothing else in the whole crisis. Of course it is probable, we may almost say certain, that Great Britain would sooner

[1] Bismarck was wise enough not only to respect Belgian neutrality in the Franco-Prussian War of 1870 but to take care to turn British sympathy against France by giving publicity to Napoleon III's intrigues to secure Belgium. If Americans will imagine some great European power seizing and fortifying Cuba and filling its harbors with submarines they can form some faint idea of the strategic interest of Britain in the safety of Belgium from foreign occupation, but to make the parallel exact one must fancy Cuba placed within a few hours' sail of New York harbor, as Belgium is placed with respect to London and the Thames valley.

or later have entered the war to save France, but the intervention might have been delayed long enough to change
the whole course of the war had not Belgium been available
as a battle cry.

Montenegro entered the war on August 7 from sympathy with Serbia, a natural step as the two peoples were of
the same race and speech. Japan and Portugal *Other na-*
became involved as allies of Britain; Japan *tions enter*
policing the Pacific and seizing the German *the war* .
leasehold of Kiao-chau on the Shan-tung peninsula of China,
Portugal formally coming into the war in 1916. Turkey
joined the German cause in November, 1914, the immediate
occasion being the refuge given to German cruisers which had
attacked Russian ports, but the fundamental cause was the
fear of Russia which had long since brought her into an
entente with Russia's enemies. Bulgaria entered the war in
October, 1915, in order to reverse the verdict of the second
Balkan War and secure Macedonia from Serbia.

After August 4, 1914, only one of the Great Powers of
Europe remained neutral. Italy from the first had refused
to support her allies, Germany and Austria- *Italy de-*
Hungary, in what she regarded as an offensive *cides, 1915*
war against Serbia, Russia and France. But there was a
long step from neutrality to active participation in the war
on the side of the Triple Entente. Germany hoped to keep
Italy neutral by small compensations [1] — the southernmost
part of Tirol (the Trentino), a slight rectification of her
northeastern frontier, a sphere of influence in Albania and
an Italian university at Trieste. These were fairly generous
terms but the Entente Allies could outbid them. On April
26, 1915, Italy made a secret treaty at London with representatives of Great Britain, France and Russia. Italy
agreed to declare war on Austria-Hungary and in return re-

---

[1] Italy could claim "compensation" for Austro-Hungarian gains in the Balkans
under Article VII of the Triple Alliance (1912 version).

ceive, in the event of a common victory: (1) the Trentino and southern Tirol as far north as the Brenner Pass, (2) a region east of the Adriatic including Gorizia, Gradisca, Istria and the islands of the Gulf of Quarnero, (3) northern Dalmatia and islands off the Dalmatian coast, (4) the port of Valona in Albania and its hinterland, (5) confirmation of her title to the Dodecanese islands in the Ægean, seized during the war with Turkey, (6) a sphere of interest in Asia Minor, (7) a right to increased empire in Africa if France and Britain annexed the German colonies, (8) a claim to share in war indemnities and facilities for a war loan, (9) an agreement not to permit the Papacy to intervene in negotiations contrary to the wishes of the Italian government. On May 23, 1915, Italy declared war on Austria-Hungary but not until August, 1916, on Germany. The Italian people in the mass sympathized with France and Britain, but their immediate national quarrel was with Austria-Hungary rather than with Germany.

In 1916 the Entente Allies won another recruit. Rumania, like Italy, had an "Irredenta." Eastern Hungary *Rumania enters, 1916* had a population largely Rumanian, though mixed with considerable minorities of Magyars, Germans, Jews and Serbs, and the Austrian province of Bukovina had a mixed population of Slavs and Rumanians. In Russia Bessarabia was a mixture of many nationalities including a million Rumanians. Between these two opportunities Rumania long hesitated, not foreseeing that fortune was to prove kinder to her than either group of belligerents and that the eventual collapse of *both* Russia and Austria-Hungary would bring her Bessarabia and the Rumanian parts of Austria-Hungary. On August 27, 1916, Rumania declared war on Austria-Hungary. As in the case of Italy, national sentiment coincided with the balance of national advantage, for ever since the second Balkan war Rumania had been more favorable to Serbia than to Bulgaria, and the Rumanians had besides a special score to pay off against the Hungarians who had mistreated their Rumanian fellow subjects.

The reasons which led the United States to enter the World War belong to another chapter. But even while the United States, China, Greece and Latin America *The Entente Allies* still remained neutral, the coalition of the Entente Allies included five Great Powers — Russia, France, Great Britain, Italy, Japan — and five of the smaller nations of Europe — Serbia, Montenegro, Portugal, Belgium, Rumania. On September 5, 1914, the British, French and Russian governments had transformed the old Entente into a wartime alliance by exchanging pledges not to make a separate peace, and to this pact Italy adhered in 1915. In all human history no such coalition had ever been formed. It included approximately half the population of the world and more than half of the armies and navies. The British command of the sea opened up to the Entente Allies trade with Asia, Africa and the Americas and closed it to their foes. Until the collapse of Russia in 1917 the general mood of the Entente was optimistic. Germany, it was conceded, might win victories owing to her high degree of initial preparedness, but each month would exhaust her wealth and reduce her man power while Russia and Britain were gradually augmenting their resources. "Time fights on our side" was the complacent saying.

The intervention of Italy on the side of the Entente put an end to the old Triple Alliance. A better term for the wartime coalition of Germany, Austria-Hungary, *The Central Powers* Bulgaria, Turkey, is the common phrase "the Central Powers"; central indeed, for by land or sea they were beleaguered at every point. In spite of this blockade and a great inferiority of man power and ultimate natural wealth, the Central Powers had on their side certain important advantages. They formed a continuous block of territory. They held by early conquest important acquisitions — Serbia, Montenegro, Russian Poland, Belgium, Luxemburg, northeastern France. Troops and munitions could readily be shifted to any front where they were needed. With geographical unity went the corresponding advantage of unity of command. The very weakness of Germany's allies made them dependent on her for diplomatic and military leadership. The warfare on every front from Flanders to Mesopotamia was conducted as part of a single campaign, the defense of particular turrets of a common fortress, whereas the Entente Allies fought the war as a series of isolated campaigns and did not achieve unity of command till 1918. Russia was almost blockaded by the German control of the entrances to the Baltic and the Turkish control of the entrance to the Black Sea; Great Britain had to ship troops overseas to any battle front, and a large part of her empire was too far from the war zone to take an immediate part in the struggle; Japan confined her activities to eastern Asia and the Pacific. On the actual battlefields of Europe the odds for either side were not very great.

The problem of war guilt, or better of war responsibility (for history deals rather with causes than with motives), has *Responsi-* already filled thousands of volumes and several *bilities* current periodicals are wholly or mainly devoted to its further discussion, but it probably never will be solved to the satisfaction of all students of the question. This should occasion no surprise. There is quite as wide a diversity of opinion over the merits of the wars of Napoleon, or, for the matter of that, of Rome and Carthage, as over the merits of the World War. Nor does this fact imply that investigation and discussion of the subject have had no practical value. Two important points have been gained. Thanks to the opening of the archives of Russia, Germany, Austria-Hungary and Great Britain and the partial opening of those in other countries, we are already in possession of most of the written records which can contribute to a verdict, and present day differences of opinion are rather as to the significance of certain events than as to the events themselves. Again, certain extreme opinions widely held during the war have been discredited, and replaced by more moderate views.

No one whose opinion is worth attention any longer believes that any civilian government wished a European war or that any except the Austrian wished even a *At least one* Balkan war. No "conspiracy" of Pan-Germans, *moral, any-* the Triple Entente, or the "capitalists" created *how* it; in the excellent phrase of Professor L. B. Namier, it was a "war of tension not of intention." For a long time to come, however, writers will differently estimate the diplomatic blunders which prevented a peaceful settlement of the crisis of 1914. Some will lay the chief stress on the Austrian attack on Serbia which broke the peace; others on the Russian mobilization which transformed a Balkan crisis into a European one, others, again, on Germany's support of Austria's aggression and her declarations of war on Russia and France which cut short negotiations. According to this emphasis, the chief immediate responsibility will be placed on the shoulders of the Austrian, Russian or German governments. But all will agree that the fundamental error was the inelastic mind which placed petty points of national prestige or the gaining of an initial military advantage above the preservation of the general peace. This is illustrated by Foreign Minister Jagow's defense of Germany's refusal of an international conference in 1914, "A fresh diminution of our prestige was not endurable for our position in Europe and in the world. The prosperity of states, their political and economic successes, are based upon the prestige that they enjoy in the world." These words might serve as an epitaph of the "old diplomacy," for the thought which they express underlay every "crisis," "incident" and "diplomatic triumph" which led the nations along a path of rivalry, sure, if followed long enough, to terminate in war.

CHAPTER XIV

THE WORLD WAR

DURING the great peace of 1871–1914 science and invention had vastly altered most human institutions and activities,
A war without precedent including the art of war. The military academies still studied the eternal principles of strategy in the campaigns of Napoleon, but on such topics as mobilization, the use of railroads, the power of artillery, the use of aviation, Napoleon's wars were as out of date as those of Julius Caesar. Even the Franco-Prussian War seemed to belong to another age, and the minor wars of the succeeding forty-three years gave hardly a hint as to what a general European conflict under modern conditions would be like. The Boer War was a cavalry campaign in a distant grassland country; the Russo-Japanese War a colonial struggle between an Asiatic nation and the most backward of the European powers; the Turco-Italian conflict a mere armed "pacification" of barbarous Tripoli; the two Balkan Wars did not involve a single Great Power.

Perhaps the greatest innovation of the new type of war was the virtual abolition of the old distinction between the
The armed nation army and the nation. Down to the French Revolution armies had been a feudal class militia or a handful of trained mercenaries, professional soldiers recruited from stolid peasants, restless adventurers or the unemployed in the city slums. The Napoleonic wars intensified the patriotic impulse by making war an affair of nations as well as kings; soldiers were now usually recruited from the nation in which they served and in some countries, such as Prussia, military duty might be asked of anyone. But there still remained a broad distinction between soldier and civilian. Even patriotic and well-intentioned

civilians in Great Britain and France thought it no sin to smuggle goods across the Channel while their countries were at war. The army represented the nation as a football team represents a college. The civilian public cheered its "team" to victory, mourned its defeat, paid its expenses. But beyond that there seemed no way to serve. The World War proved much more exacting. The obligation of service escaped practically no one. Were you a chemist? Go to the nearest factory. A photographer? Learn to be an aerial scout. A baker? Run a field oven for the soldiers. A dentist? Repair jawbones shattered by shrapnel. A landscape painter? Just the man to devise "camouflage" (protective disguise) for cruisers and motor trucks. A linguist? Please censor these letters in Russian or Portuguese. Women were no longer confined to the old tasks of farm work, hospital service and the knitting of socks. They were employed also to make shells, to run automobiles and street cars, to replace men in civilian office work, to fill every sort of post of usefulness from elevator "boy" to government clerk. It is probable that every belligerent nation at least doubled its military efficiency by using women in the fields, the factories and other services behind the lines. Even little children were invited to contribute their mite to victory by farm work, messenger service and petty economies.

Civilian life as such practically disappeared. There were the strictly military activities such as fighting and nursing the wounded; there were also necessary *War socialism* sustaining services, such as agriculture, manufacture, transportation and commerce; but all were directed by order of the government to definite ends. You could be fined or imprisoned for selling grain above a certain price, or failing to give priority on a railroad to war munitions, or corresponding with an enemy subject, or trading abroad without a license, or traveling without a passport, or printing uncensored news in a paper. Every government used the freest hand in fixing prices and wages, regulating trade, confiscating private property, taxing incomes and profits, forbidding debt collections (moratorium), and interfering without limit in the once sacred sphere of private property. This universal mobilization and socialization of industry deserves special emphasis for it underlies most of the peculiarities of the World War. It explains why belligerent nations were able to continue the fight to the point of economic exhaustion instead of surrendering as soon as the government ran short of funds. It explains why victory depended as much on civilian as on military endurance. It explains in great degree the cruelty and ruthlessness which gave the World War a sad pre-eminence among modern wars. In recent generations civilians had been granted special immunities as "private citizens." Unless they forfeited their status by spying or engaging in irregular warfare they could not lawfully be mistreated or killed or despoiled of property. But in the World War this distinction largely disappeared. Bombardments were as often directed against railroad stations, munition factories, and government offices as against fortresses. Invading armies confiscated or burned private property without compensation. Merchant ships, since they contributed indirectly to the economic efficiency of the enemy, were sunk as readily as if they had been hostile cruisers. This disregard of private rights outlasted the war and made possible the wholesale reforms and ruthless repressions which marked the succeeding "age of the dictators." It is unlikely that the drastic social reconstructions in postwar Russia, Italy and Germany would have been possible if the people had not already been accustomed to an arbitrary and absolute wartime power.

Another distinctive characteristic of the war was the development of military transportation. The automobile supplemented the railway and transformed the ordinary roads to routes of rapid transport. The most picturesque

development in this field was military aviation. Both airship and airplane were still in the experimental
stage in 1914. The Germans placed great hopes *Aviation*
on Count Zeppelin's invention of an elongated dirigible bal-
loon with a rigid metal framework. These battleships of
the air carried large crews for hundreds of miles and made
spectacular raids on London and other large cities, but their
usefulness was limited by the fact that they were also good
targets for airplane attacks and anti-aircraft batteries. On
the whole the airplane proved more valuable. It had not
the lifting power of the airship, it could not rise so rapidly
nor carry so large a crew. But it had compensating advantages. It was so cheap that it could be manufactured
in almost any quantity, it could fly at enormous speeds, and
could be specially adapted for combat with enemy planes,
for bombing forts and factories below, or for scouting and
artillery observation. The aviators were the eyes of the
army. They could map out a whole system of hostile entrenchments and direct the batteries below to concentrate
their fire where it would do the greatest damage. They
could note and photograph any very considerable massing
of forces behind the lines (small movements could be
camouflaged) and thus prevent a surprise attack. An army
without aircraft under modern conditions would be a blind
man in combat with Argus.

The development in artillery was on more familiar lines
and yet this department of military science produced some
of the most surprising novelties of the war.
The British and French were fairly well equipped *Artillery*
with light artillery, but the Germans astonished the world
by moving heavy artillery of unprecedented dimensions.
In their first campaign on the western front they attacked
French and Belgian fortresses with siege howitzers varying
from 28 to 42 centimeters caliber (11.2 to 16.8 inches) and
in their last campaign, in 1918, they shelled the city of

Paris from a distance of more than seventy miles! The Germans also (in disregard of a Hague agreement) introduced poisonous gases, such as chlorine, into trench warfare. The English, taking a suggestion from the American tractor, introduced the "tank" or armored automobile for preparing an attack. Like no previous war in history, the World War was a conflict of machines, of ingenious mechanisms on land, on sea and above the clouds. Yet nothing is stranger than the survival of the old in the midst of the new. Old fashioned devices, such as the steel helmet and the hand grenade, long obsolete in war, came again into practical use. Earthwork entrenchments with barbed wire entanglements proved more useful than the elaborate Brialmont fortresses of concrete and steel which lined the French frontier. Cavalry did not disappear, the infantryman became more important than ever and man power remained one of the cardinal factors in victory.

The demands of the new warfare on the man behind the gun were greater than at any time in the past. Owing in *Battles merge with campaigns* part to the vast size of the armies engaged and the speed with which railroad and automobile could spread them over a whole countryside, and in part to the deadlock of trench warfare which soon replaced open battles in the field, the armies of the Entente Allies and of the Central Powers were in constant touch with each other from the first to the last day of the war. In former wars battles were isolated incidents in a long campaign. Two armies would go out to meet each other, spend months in slow strategic concentrations and at last lock forces on a small plot of open country, "the battlefield." Within a few hours a defeated army would be flying in wild rout from the pursuing victors. But the World War was one unbroken battle. For the sake of convenience it may be divided into campaigns and operations but even on the quietest sectors of the line, where the daily dispatches chronicled "nothing to report," there was always more or less fighting and a slowly growing casualty list. In an active sector the strain of battle might continue weeks without intermission. "Waterloo?" said one British soldier, "*We are fighting five Waterloos a week!*" Since human nature cannot endure unrelieved tension, it soon became the custom to shift troops frequently from front to front and give them periods of comparative rest behind the lines, but even with these respites the soldier's physical endurance and sustained moral courage were tested as never before.

In one respect, at least, science wrought an important alleviation of the soldier's lot. In the wars of the nineteenth century, even down to the American *Medical* campaign in Cuba, disease usually claimed many *progress* victims for every death on the battlefield. In the twentieth century wars, such as the Russo-Japanese and the World War, hygienic precautions kept the sick list down to manageable proportions. Except for a typhus outbreak in Serbia and the great influenza pandemic of 1918, which affected civilians quite as much as soldiers, the war did not directly involve any widespread epidemic. Such familiar campaign scourges as typhoid, cholera, tetanus and gangrene almost disappeared. Of those who lived to reach the base hospitals at all the great majority recovered health sufficiently to enter active service again or be useful behind the lines. German physicians claimed that about nine tenths of their hospital cases were discharged cured and less than two per cent died.

Not all the possibilities of twentieth century warfare were at once apparent. The Germans had cut short negotiations in order to overwhelm France before Russia *The first* could fully mobilize. The improved means of *phase: the* transportation which had so greatly increased *war of* *movement* the celerity of military movements seemed to point to a brief war. When Lord Kitchener, the British

Minister of War, warned England to expect a three years' struggle he was commonly considered a pessimist; the newspapers were urging civilians to carry on "business as usual," and skilled factory workers, who later had to be recalled to make munitions, were allowed to enlist and go to the trenches.   The first phase of the war, the rush of the German army from the Belgian frontier to the outskirts of Paris, was indeed as rapid a campaign as Europe had ever known.   It held a false promise of open battles and an early decision.   Who in September, 1914, could have foretold the four years' deadlock before the victorious advance of the Entente Allies?

The German army extended from Switzerland to the Dutch frontier.   In eastern France it made little progress *The Belgian* because of the hilly country and the great line *campaign* of major fortresses guarding the French frontier — Verdun, Toul, Epinal, Belfort.   The French, misled by sentiment, sent too large a force into Alsace where they made little progress.   The acquisition of a very small part of Alsace was a small counterweight to the peril of weakening France in the north where the main German armies were advancing.   The plan used by Germany was, in its essentials, that worked out by Count Alfred von Schlieffen, chief of the German General Staff, in 1905.   This implied a mere covering force against Russia and on the southern part of the French frontier while the main German army would be sent through Belgium and Luxemburg [1] so that France might be attacked on a wider front, a flatter terrain and a more weakly defended frontier.   Count Helmuth von Moltke, nephew of the famous strategist of the Franco-Prussian War, inherited this plan but he was alarmed at its audacity and ventured to modify it by strengthening the German line in the south.   Some experts have said that this

---

[1] In its original form the plan included a march through Dutch territory also, this was abandoned to avert war with the Netherlands.

was a fatal timidity, that Germany might have won the war by staking everything on a single, concentrated, irresistible blow against northern France through the level Flemish plains. Liége, the Belgian fortress-city near the German frontier held out for several days but the German advance swept past it and the new steel and concrete turrets were smashed by heavy siege guns like eggshells under a hammer. By the end of August the greater part of Belgium was under German occupation and the combined French, Belgian, British army was in retreat along the line from Mons to Verdun.

The French fortresses of the northeast proved as unable to check the German advance as the Belgian for- *The march* tresses. The British expeditionary army landed *toward* on the continent only to engage at once in a whole- *Paris* sale retreat and almost daily battle against superior odds. Their morale remained unbroken under the severest tests an army can face, but they seemed to be thrown away in a sacrifice as vain as it was noble. The French partial offensives in the south had been costly failures; Marshal Joffre was resolved not to undertake a general offensive until it became necessary either to save Paris or to prevent the outflanking of the main army. The French government transferred some of its administrative offices to the distant city of Bordeaux as a precaution in the possible event that Paris were captured. Such a capture would not, however, be permitted in advance of a general battle, since Paris was not only the political center of France but the commercial metropolis and the chief railway center — New York, Chicago and Washington in one! The German plan was to outflank and crush the left wing of the French army in the north, roll up the French line ("Cannae" strategy the Germans called it, with a memory of Hannibal's greatest victory over the Romans), and then occupy Paris at leisure.

On September 5 began the battle of the Marne. General von Kluck swept southeast to strike at the Allied *The battle* army; General Gallieni counter-attacked from *of the* Paris (some of the reinforcements were sent out *Marne* in taxicabs!). To strengthen the flank of the German army the center was weakened; General Foch drove hard at the weak spot in the German line facing him. The British also counter-attacked and drove a wedge between two German armies. On September 10 the German forces withdrew to the Aisne. Their retreat was only in part due to the vigorous stand of the Western Allies; other factors were the disorganization into which the German plans had fallen and the consequent loss of touch between the General Staff and the armies in the field, the exhaustion of the soldiers who had been marching and fighting for over a month, the dangerous extension of the German lines of communication and supply, and, most of all perhaps, the Russian advance to East Prussia. All these considerations induced the German military authorities to abandon their western offensive and fall back on entrenched positions to the rear. The battle of the Marne was not a conclusive or decisive battle of the Waterloo type; it began a great war instead of ending one. But it saved Paris, it saved the forts of eastern France, it permitted the Allies to assume the offensive, and it shattered to pieces the war plan and "time table" of the German General Staff. An evidence of German disappointment was the replacement of Moltke by Falkenhayn as head of the General Staff; the nephew had failed where in 1870 the uncle had succeeded.

The main German army now fell back on prepared entrenchments along the river Aisne. But to the north and *The race to* west there was a great extension and consolida- *the sea* tion of the German line. The fate of Antwerp and the Flemish coast towns still hung in the balance; the Allied armies tried to hold central Belgium to save the sea-

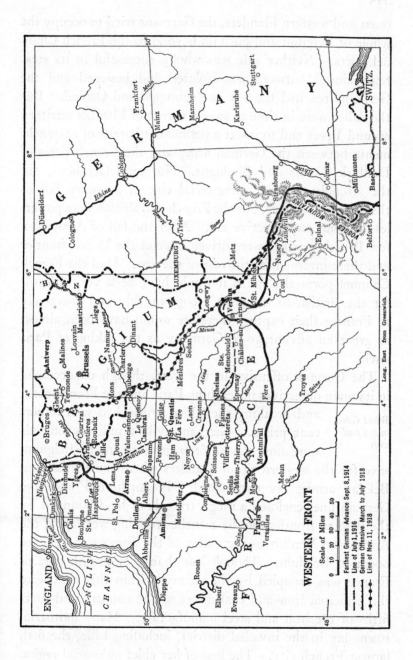

WESTERN FRONT

Scale of Miles
0 10 20 30 40 50

— — — Farthest German Advance Sept. 8, 1914
|||||||| Line of July 1, 1916
●—●—● German Offensive March to July 1918
●●●●● Line of Nov. 11, 1918

coast and western Flanders, the Germans tried to occupy the
whole of Belgium and push on beyond to the French Channel ports.   Neither side was wholly successful in its strategic aim.   Antwerp was isolated and besieged and the
Germans reached the sea at Zeebrugge and Ostend.   But
the Allies were in time to save a corner of Flemish territory
around Ypres and to insert a permanent barrier of entrenchments between the German army and the French ports of
Dunkirk, Calais and Boulogne.   Not until October 9 did
the strongly fortified commercial city of Antwerp fall to
the German artillery, but the French and British were powerless to send any effective aid.   After the fall of Antwerp a
few British marines were driven beyond the Dutch frontier
and there interned for the rest of the war.   Had the French
Channel ports also fallen it would have been very difficult
for the British to transport troops quickly and effectively
to France; their capture therefore would have been almost
as great an advantage to Germany as the taking of Paris
itself.

The German offensive in the west, though unsuccessful
in its main objectives of reaching Paris and the French coast
What Ger- and breaking the Allied army, had won impor-
many had tant prizes.   German civil or military officials
won were now the *de facto* government of Belgium,
save for the western tip of Flanders where the British and
Belgian armies lay entrenched.   In northern France the
German lines enclosed a rough triangle of land bounded by
the Belgian frontier and by trenches running west along the
Aisne from Verdun to the valley of the Somme and thence
north to Belgium.   Though less than a twentieth part of
France was occupied by the enemy, within this area were
the principal iron and coal mines of the country and four-
fifths of the iron and steel manufacture.   Many industrial
towns lay in the invaded district, including Lille, the fifth
largest French city.   The loss of her chief industrial region

greatly crippled France and forced her to rely in part on munitions supplied by Great Britain or bought in the neutral market of the United States. The coal and iron mines of Belgium, Luxemburg and northeastern France supplemented the resources of Germany and the factories were either turned into German munitions works or stripped of their machinery for the benefit of German factories. Even the crops and cattle were requisitioned for German use while their owners were forced to depend on foreign charity.

The policy of the German government in Belgium was to secure its safety against rebellion, espionage and passive resistance to German orders by crushing the *German* spirit of resistance with an iron hand. It had *rule in Belgium* long been an accepted military principle that a civilian fighting as a *franc tireur*, that is unattached to any regular army, was liable to military execution. But the Germans extended this principle from individuals to whole communities. They made a practice of holding as hostages the chief men in each town, such as the mayor or the village priest, and executing them in case any townsman attacked German soldiers. This practice of hostage taking had been widely employed in ancient and medieval warfare but was termed "obsolete" by nineteenth century writers on the laws and customs of war. Sometimes a town or a section of a city was laid in ruins as a warning. The most famous instance of this was the burning of a part of Louvain, from which the fire spread to the library and the university, on August 26, 1914. Another harsh practice was the levying of extortionate fines on conquered cities under threat of immediate destruction. There was also much criticism of the summary solution of the unemployment problem in Belgium and the occupied departments of France by compelling civilians without their consent to emigrate to Germany and labor in German factories.

Yet the spirit of Belgium was not crushed. Cardinal

Mercier, one of the chief Roman Catholic dignitaries of the kingdom, protested boldly against each new infraction of national liberty. Under the bewildered eye of German censorship a group of Belgian patriots secretly printed and distributed a national newspaper *La libre Belgique.* One of the German policies in Belgium might have had important results if the general reign of terror had not so completely alienated the sympathies of all classes of the population. This was to weaken Belgium by separating the Flemings from the French-speaking Walloons and thus split the country into two nations. But though the Flemings by race and language were closer kin to the Dutch and the North Germans than to their Walloon neighbors and there had been political feuds between the two, both alike were first of all Belgians, and the German yoke pressed as heavily on Flanders as on southern Belgium. American and British aid, distributed through a relief commission headed by the American engineer Herbert Hoover, kept Belgium from such a fate of wholesale starvation as befell Poland and Armenia.

After the Germans had fallen back to the Aisne and had pushed through Flanders to the sea, the war of movement ended in the west to be succeeded by a prolonged *The dead-lock on the western front* siege operation, the war of the trenches. At first merely emergency shelters from gunfire, the trenches were deepened and widened into complete encampments with bomb-proof shelters, underground passages and looped parapets for rifle fire. Heavy artillery, underground mines and aerial bombing might destroy a section of entrenchment and its garrison with it, but ordinary rifle or machine gun fire had little effect, especially after the soldiers were equipped with steel helmets and with periscopes for directing fire from shelter. Behind the front trenches were other lines of defense, so that the capture of a trench did not mean a break through the line. Under such conditions an advance of a few score yards or

the capture of a hill fifty feet above the surrounding plain
was heralded as a great victory worth the cost of several
thousand lives. As one commentator put it, "Though the
Powers still bore upon their banners the old insignia of lions
and eagles, the war was fought in the manner of the skunk,
the cuttlefish and the mole!"

The entrenched front protecting Paris and central France
ran through a hilly country of limestone rock. The freshly
turned earth was white with chalk, making the outlines of
the trenches as distinct as if traced on a blackboard by some
giant hand. Further to the north the trenches ran through
the flat claylands of Flanders. Here the soldiers encountered the worst hardships of the war.[1] Heavy rains in the
chalklands were absorbed by the soil; in the Flemish clay,
rain and melting snow filled the trenches and turned the
"no man's land" between the opposing lines into a sea of
mud. Often the trenches had to be built up from the ground
by sandbag parapets because to dig below the surface would
create a ditch of standing water which could not easily be
drained.

In the spring of 1915 both the British and the Germans
tried to break the deadlock on the rain-sodden plains of
Flanders. Both failed. The British were in- *The 1915*
adequately supplied with high-explosive shells *campaign in*
and relied too much on light artillery. The *Flanders*
Germans in their attempt to take the British positions near
Ypres introduced a novel weapon. In April they flooded
the British trenches with clouds of chlorine gas which
strangled and poisoned their unprepared opponents. The
Canadian regiments suffered especially. Had the Germans

---

[1] "The author has visited the fighting fronts from the sand-dunes of the Belgian
coast to the entrenched camp of Saloniki and observed during the conflict the conditions under which men fought from the polders below sea-level to the glacier-clad
heights of the Alps. He has no hesitation in saying that, of all the combatants,
those who fought on the plain of Flanders endured the most terrible physical conditions." Major Douglas W. Johnson, *Battlefields of the World War*, page 25.

been prepared to drive home a vigorous assault immediately after the gas attack they might have broken the British line and altered the fate of the war. But the use of poison gas was a novelty, and before the Germans realized its full effectiveness the British had devised protective masks. Later in the war various types of poison gas were employed by both sides, and, instead of being merely turned loose from cylinders to await the chances of the wind, were dispersed from exploding shells in the midst of the enemy trenches.

Falkenhayn, the new German Chief of Staff, staked and lost position and reputation on the siege of Verdun. Ver-

The Verdun campaign, 1916 dun was one of the great French fortresses of the eastern frontier, a pivotal point where the battle line running north from the Swiss frontier swerved sharply to the west. If Verdun were lost, the whole French line would have to be reconstructed on some less advantageous front than the heights guarding the Meuse valley. The Germans relied on the siege guns which had done such effective service in reducing the forts of Antwerp and Liége. In February, 1916, the German army reached the outlying fort of Douaumont before its advance was checked. Thereafter the assault smoldered down to stubborn, intensive siege warfare. Many hilltops and villages changed hands a dozen times in attack and counterattack until the whole crescent shaped battleground north and east of Verdun was blasted to desert and naked rock. In all ages the French soldier has been famous for his reckless gallantry in attacking the foe, but here was a new type of French soldier who could endure as well as dare, fight as bravely on the defensive as in the enthusiasm of a charge, a soldier who expressed his inmost soul not in any Napoleonic phrase about "glory" but in the quiet resolution, "They shall not pass!" In July the intensive attack on Verdun was practically abandoned. The small strip of territory which had fallen to the Germans was of little importance, but at least the campaign had served the purpose of postponing any general offensive by the Entente Allies.

In July, 1916, the British and French at last started a counter-offensive along the Somme river, partly to relieve the German pressure on Verdun, partly to co- *The Somme* operate with the war effort of Russia and Italy *campaign* in what was hoped to be the decisive struggle. The French selected as their objective the town of Péronne, the British forces to the north the town of Bapaume. As with the German attacks on Verdun, the relatively large gains of the first surprise attack were not maintained in the later phases of the battle. The Germans were well entrenched, and while the Allied troops forced back the German line six or seven miles along a wide front they had not attained either Péronne or Bapaume. In September the British first made use of the "tank," — an armored automobile which gripped the ground with "caterpillar" endless belts instead of wheels, and thus ran little risk of being bogged in the mud or upset by rough ground.[1] The great merit of the tank lay in the fact that it provided a solution for the deadlock of trench warfare. Hitherto an offensive operation had been impossible without sufficient artillery preparation to demolish barbed wire entanglements and front line trenches and thus permit the infantry to advance. Heavy artillery fire, however, gave warning to the enemy that an attack was in prospect and thus eliminated the important factor of surprise. But the weight and power of the tank enabled it to crush wire fences, earthwork parapets and even stone walls without previous artillery preparation. Like poison gas, the tank was a by-product of trench warfare which might never have been employed if the armies had kept to the open field.

In striking contrast to the stalemate on the western front was the rapid series of German victories in the East. Rus-

---

[1] To conceal the experiment until actually tested in the field, the word went out from the factories that the British War Office was making "tanks," hence the inappropriate name.

sia, to be sure, made a very promising beginning to the cam-

The eastern war of movement, 1914

paign of 1914. In August Russian armies invaded East Prussia and the Austrian province
of Galicia (Austrian Poland). But the invasion
was over hasty and met with terrible retribution.
During the last week of August a large portion of the Russian army in the north was entrapped and outflanked in the
marshy region of the Mazurian lakes, very near the site
of Poland's greatest victory over the Germans five centuries
earlier (1410). This victory of Tannenberg saved Germany
from the Russian peril, and General Paul von Hindenburg
whose intimate knowledge of the region had been largely
responsible for success became forthwith the most popular
national hero; a popularity that was one day to carry him
to the presidency of the German republic, while generals of
the ultimately victorious Allies were almost universally
unable to win political preferment. But things were still
going awry for the Austrians. They had concentrated too
large a proportion of their forces against Serbia and had
insufficient strength to meet the Russian advance. Galicia,
lying beyond the Carpathian mountain wall, was easier to
attack from the northeast than to defend from the southwest. In September the Russians seized Lemberg, the
capital of Galicia, and occupied also the province of Buko-
wina. They shut up a large Austrian garrison at Przemysl
and advanced almost to Cracow; only the coming of winter
and the Carpathian barrier saved Hungary from invasion,
though timely German aid had done much to relieve the
hard-pressed Austrians.

In the following spring the Russians renewed their offensive, capturing Przemysl on March 22, 1915, and pushing

Attack and counter-at- tack in 1915

on to the Carpathian passes. In April the prestige of Russia was at its highest point and on-
lookers confidently prophesied that the Russian
"steam roller" by sheer mass of man power would crush the

German eastern front.   The Allies looked forward eagerly
to the fall of Cracow, the invasion of Hungary and the march
on Vienna and Berlin.   But the Russian position was not
so strong as it seemed.   Russia was backward in all the industries that underlie modern war and her allies were too
distant to make good her shortage of equipment.   Hostile
Turkey closed the Black Sea to Russian trade, hostile Germany closed the Baltic, and the thin trickle of imports from
Arctic Archangel and from Vladivostok on the far Pacific
were wholly inadequate to make good the Russian losses.
Tactless attempts to "Russify" the Poles and Ukrainians
of Galicia had destroyed whatever Panslavic sentiment had
originally existed in that province.   The friction of incompetence which pervaded every branch of the Russian bureaucracy, civil or military, had already begun to slow down
the progress of the "steam roller."   A combined Austro-
German force under General Mackensen prepared for an
offensive which would not only drive back the Russian army
but break it into fragments.   On May first, 1915, von Mackensen began the attack along the Dunajec river just east of
Cracow.   The Russians were forced to a speedy retreat to
save their army from complete destruction.   By July the
Teutonic armies held all Galicia except its extreme eastern
tip.   Worse was to follow.   Having lost Galicia and East
Prussia, the Russians had to abandon Russian Poland as
well lest they be caught between the jaws of a gigantic nut-
cracker, the German army to the north operating from East
Prussia and the Austro-German forces in the south.

   Though Hindenburg had failed in his main purpose of
enveloping the entire Russian army in Poland, he had struck
Russia a blow from which she never fully re-   *The eastern*
covered and brought about the conquest of an   *deadlock,*
eastern borderland (Russian Poland, Lithuania,   *1915-17*
Courland) half as large and one-third as populous as the
German Empire.   For a time the war in the east lapsed into

a siege of the trenches. The battle front from Courland to
Bukovina was actually shorter and straighter than the
sinuous line following the boundary of Russian Poland,
hence Germany had the unusual advantage of being able to
hold an advanced position with fewer men than would have
been required to hold the original frontier. In June, 1916,
General Brussilov attempted yet another offensive, won
several brilliant successes and reconquered Bukovina and a
large part of eastern Galicia, but he failed to reach his main
objectives, Brest-Litovsk, Lemberg and Halicz, and the
summer's hopes turned gray as the reorganized Russian
army was forced once again to entrench. Russia was almost
spent. There was still man power, but equipment and
enthusiasm were alike exhausted. At all events, Russia
had already contributed her full part to the victory that she
never shared, for if Germany had not been compelled in the
critical September days of 1914 to hasten troops to the eastern front the battle of the Marne might have been a German
victory and Paris in German hands.

Unhappy Poland with no government of her own to direct
a war or defend neutrality furnished a battleground for
the rival armies. When the Russians "invaded
Austria" the burden fell not on the Teutonic
Austrians but on the Poles of Galicia; when in
turn Germany "invaded Russia" the fields and
towns that were devastated were not really Russian but, for
the most part, Polish. That the Poles were drafted into the
contending armies against their will was but the common
fate of the subject races of eastern Europe, their peculiar
hardship was that Polish subjects of Germany and Austria
were forced to fight against their own kinsmen of Russian
Poland. The sympathies of the nation were as divided as
its allegiance. In the first year of the war the Russian Grand
Duke Nicholas promised to reunite the fragments of Poland
"under the scepter of the Russian Tsar" as a nation "free

Poland, the Belgium of eastern Europe

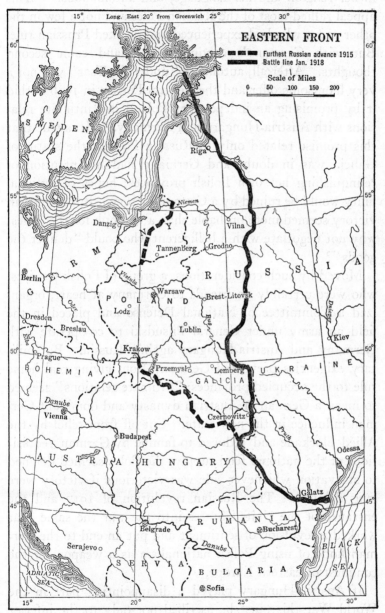

EASTERN FRONT

▄▄ ▬ ▬ Furthest Russian advance 1915
▬▬▬▬ Battle line Jan. 1918

Scale of Miles
0   50   100 150 200

in her religion and her language, and autonomous." This appeal rallied most of the Russian Poles and not a few in the other camp who had experienced and disliked Prussian rule. But with Germany's conquest of Poland came second thoughts. After all, autonomy "under the Tsar" was not a very handsome offer and the Central Powers in 1916 outbid it by promising an independent Poland in "intimate relations with Austria-Hungary and Germany." It is true that this promise related only to Russian Poland, the status of Galicia was in doubt and Germany had no intention of relinquishing her own Polish provinces; hopes of national unity would be ruined by a German victory. But a German victory seemed more probable than a triumph for the Allies; why not negotiate with a belligerent who could "deliver the goods"?

Moved by such considerations, a group of Polish patriots, who were certainly no friends to Germany at heart, organized a Committee of National Defense and placed in the field an army under General Pilsudski to co-operate with Germany and Austria-Hungary against Russia. But military exigencies prevented Germany from giving real home rule to the occupied provinces; "intimate relations" seemed to mean a German or Austrian dynasty and dominant German influence in the new state. Cut off from relief by the Allied blockade and reduced to famine by German requisitions of the national food supply, the Poles seemed doomed to starvation whichever side was victorious if victory were long delayed. The Russian revolution of 1917 and the entrance of the United States into the war the same year worked a revulsion of sentiment and put an end to the German hope of using Polish nationalism as a weapon for the conquest of eastern Europe.

If Austria-Hungary played a disappointing part in the World War this must be ascribed not only to the inferior industrial wealth, military organization and national unity of Germany's ally, but quite as much to the fact that the Dual Monarchy had to maintain forces *The Italian* against Serbia, against Russia, after May, 1915, *front* against Italy, and after August, 1916, against Rumania.[1] The Italian armies operated along the mountainous frontier of western Austria. Here the natural conditions were as different as possible from those which characterized the level plains of Flanders and Poland. In the north (Trentino and the Tirolese Alps) a bewildering maze of foothills, intersected by mountain valleys and passes, led step by step to the highest crests of the eastern Alps. In place of trenches the rocks formed natural defenses and the struggle became a series of machine gun duels above the clouds for the possession of strategic hilltops. This combat in three dimensions amid the eternal snows was unquestionably the most picturesque land warfare of the World War, but it made almost impossible rapid advance by either belligerent. Large armies could not be fully deployed amid the precipices. Austria, content to hold her own, had every advantage as against Italy, bent on conquering "unredeemed" provinces beyond the frontier.

To the east lay a somewhat more promising field of action. Along the Adriatic coast the mountains were lower, and the Italians directed their main effort *The Isonzo* towards Gorizia and Trieste. After heavy *campaign* losses, the Italians crossed the Isonzo river, occupied Gorizia, and began the slow conquest of the hills which lay on the road to Trieste. But the natural defenses of the Isonzo front, though not so striking at first glance, were almost as strong as the Alpine ramparts of the north. Near the Adriatic lay the Carso plateau, a tableland of barren limestone honeycombed with tunnels, entrenchments and machine gun nests. Through this difficult region the Italian army never succeeded in penetrating until the final

[1] For the causes which led Italy and Rumania to intervene see Chapter XIII.

collapse of Austria-Hungary near the end of the war. In
May, 1916, an Austrian counter-attack in Tirol freed most
of that mountainous province from Italian occupation and
might have entered the Venetian plains if the Russian pressure in Galicia had not compelled the abandonment of the
drive. Austria-Hungary was again placed on the defensive
until, more than a year later, Germany was able to spare aid
for a more vigorous attack.

Austria-Hungary, preoccupied with the far more significant conflicts with Russia and Italy, postponed the decisive
reckoning with Serbia until the aid of a German
*Bulgarian
interven-* force under Field Marshal von Mackensen and
tion dooms the intervention of Bulgaria on the side of the
Serbia Central Powers in the autumn of 1915 enabled
her to strike a crushing blow. Up to that time Serbia had
rather more than held her own, repelling attacks along the
Danube and its branches the Save and Drina and even spar-
ing forces for raids into Austrian territory. The diplomats
of the Entente had been "caught napping" by the politic
Tsar Ferdinand of Bulgaria. In vain they tried to persuade
Serbia and Greece to yield back part of their Macedonian
conquests of the second Balkan War; they would not concede as much as the Central Powers could offer. Greece
remained in hesitant neutrality; Premier Venizelos ardently
favoring intervention on the side of the Entente Allies, but
King Constantine, a brother-in-law of the German Kaiser,
insistent on neutrality. Though Greece had a defensive
treaty of alliance with Serbia, the only gain which the
Allies had from it was the reluctant permission to use the
Greek port of Saloniki as a basis for Allied forces operating
in the aid of Serbia. Bulgaria countered this by forcibly
occupying a part of Greek Macedonia.

The Bulgarian intervention, German aid, Greek neutrality and the inadequate force which the western Allies could
spare for the Macedonian front made the case of Serbia

hopeless. The Serbs were good fighters, trained in the Balkan Wars of 1912–13, but they had already *The Balkan* suffered heavy losses in the early months of the *campaign* war and were now confronted by much superior forces to the north and east. The little Serbian army was overwhelmed and forced to retreat to the coast through the Albanian mountains. Montenegro yielded so easily that King Nicholas was suspected of a secret understanding with the Austrians. The relief expedition sent by the Allies retreated into Greek territory and remained strongly entrenched but practically ineffective at Saloniki. Serbia, Montenegro and parts of neutral Albania and Greece came under the administration of German, Austro-Hungarian and Bulgarian officers and so remained for the greater part of the war. The Italian foothold on the Albanian coast, the Anglo-French army at Saloniki, and the uncertain attitude of Greece and Rumania alone prevented the German conquest of the Balkan peninsula from being complete.

The Entente had built high hopes on Rumanian intervention and bid high for it, offering all the extensive Rumanian-speaking parts of Austria-Hungary. The *The Ruma-* Central Powers were correspondingly alarmed; *nian cam-* Germany dismissed Falkenhayn as Chief of Staff, *paign* sending him to the Balkan front, and appointed in his place Marshal von Hindenburg, the leader who had so brilliantly conducted the campaign in Poland. Mackensen attacked Rumania from the south, advancing through the Dobrudja, the district between the Danube and the Black Sea, while Falkenhayn directed a counter-offensive in Transylvania. During September and October, 1916, he forced the Rumanians from Hungarian soil and prepared for a descent on the Wallachian plains of southern Rumania. With one army pressing north from Bulgaria and another pouring southward through the passes of the Transylvanian Alps, the whole Rumanian army was caught as in the jaws of a trap. The military supplies promised by Russia did not arrive, due to a characteristically old Russian blend of bad faith and sheer incompetence. To save their army from being wholly cut off, the Rumanians abandoned Wallachia and even the capital at Bucharest, retiring into the hilly and wooded province of Moldavia in the north. Turkey and Bulgaria were freed from a serious military peril, Austria-Hungary was safeguarded on her southeastern frontier, Rumania was practically eliminated as an active factor in the war and the military prestige of the Entente weakened throughout the Near East. Even more important were the economic effects of the victory; food for hungry civilians in Vienna, fuel for motor trucks on the roads behind the trenches and for submarines at sea — these were the chief fruits of the conquest of this land of "corn and oil."

The adherence of the Ottoman Empire to the cause of the Central Powers was a fact of the highest military sig-

Turkey in the World War   nificance. To be sure, Turkey was not one of the Great Powers and had to be supplied from Germany and Austria-Hungary with all her modern military equipment. But Turkey's ability to control and close the Straits meant the power to turn the key on all effective aid from the Western Powers to Russia; no longer was it possible to exchange surplus Russian grain for western war munitions. The Asiatic provinces of Turkey provided a good vantage ground for attacks on British Egypt and threats toward British India. Even more important was the moral strategy of the Sultan's position in the Moslem world. Turkey was the only fully independent and relatively powerful Mohammedan nation; other Moslem realms being directly under foreign rule or indirectly subject to foreign influence, and the Turkish Sultan claimed primacy among all Mohammedans as the "Caliph" or successor of the Prophet. At Germany's bidding the Ottoman government proclaimed a *jihad* or religious war against the

Entente, with the hope of stirring up rebellions in Egypt,
French north Africa and the Mohammedan provinces of
India. But no important outbreak occurred, and the
Arabs within the Ottoman Empire itself tended to side with
the British as against the Turkish Sultan. Perhaps the
religious summons would have been more effective if the war
had really been between Christendom and Islam instead of
being so obviously between rival groups of Christian powers.

The obvious course for the Entente Allies was to seize
Constantinople and the Straits, thus opening up a sea-route
to the Black Sea ports of Russia. A victory *The*
here, the most strategic point in the whole East, *Gallipoli*
would have brought Russia into the general plan *campaign*
of Allied operations and have settled for the remainder of the
war the mastery of the Ottoman Empire. But the campaign
against Constantinople, excellently conceived, was faultily
executed. Russia, hard pressed in Poland, could lend little
aid; France felt she could spare few troops from her invaded
homeland. The British had no way of estimating the strength
of the Turkish shore defenses protecting the Dardanelles pas-
sage-way, the narrow, winding strait through which all ships
must pass from the Ægean Sea to the little inner sea at Marmora. In February, 1915, a combined Franco-British naval
expedition tried to force the Straits, suffered heavy losses
from shore batteries and mines, and abandoned the attempt. Postwar opinion inclines to the view that greater
risks taken at this time might have had great results, as the
Turkish forts were already low in ammunition when the
naval attack was abandoned. But at the time the British
thought it advisable not to risk "the Nelson touch" but
patiently reduce the land batteries by military operations
before again sending in a fleet. During the last part of April
a mixed force of British, French colonial and Australasian [1]

---

[1] Nicknamed the "Anzacs" because of the common abbreviation for the Australia
and New Zealand Army Corps.

soldiers under Sir Ian Hamilton seized the southern tip and western shoreline of the Gallipoli peninsula. But the long trench warfare which followed was quite indecisive and the entrance of Bulgaria into the war made the venture almost hopeless. In December, 1915, the British began the evacuation of the peninsula, leaving behind them only an epic of wasted valor.

A similar disappointment awaited the British in Mesopotamia. The Persian Gulf and the river valleys of the Tigris and Euphrates held out a delusive promise

The first Mesopotamian campaign

of an easy advance into the Ottoman Empire based on the resources of British India. General Townshend advanced toward the city of Bagdad in 1915 with a combined force of British regulars and Indian colonial troops. Under the direction of the German General von der Goltz part of the British army was halted and surrounded at Kut-el-Amara and besieged from December, 1915, to the following April. The Turks took prisoner some three thousand British troops and about twice as many Indians. Though the material loss was small, the injury to Allied prestige in the East was very great.

Russia was equally unsuccessful in her advance into Armenia. In 1916 Russian forces penetrated far into Asiatic

The Armenian campaign

Turkey and took the fortified city of Erzerum. But lack of support and supplies halted their advance and eventually the Turks reconquered all they had lost and pushed their arms into Transcaucasian Russia. Like the Belgians and the Poles, the Armenians suffered for their geographical position. Although the Armenians were widely distributed throughout the Ottoman Empire, there being a large colony in Constantinople itself, the national homeland lay in eastern Asia Minor on the Russian frontier. The chiefs of the Turkish administration, Talaat Pasha, Grand Vizier of the Ottoman Empire, and Enver Pasha, Minister of War, came to the conclusion that

Armenian aid to Russia could be prevented only by the complete destruction of the Armenian nation. This decision was disguised as "deportation." The Armenians were driven wholesale into the desert, some were permitted to settle in distant parts of the Empire (for no massacre is ever quite complete), but the majority died of famine or were butchered on the road. No census has been taken of the number done to death, but a German authority, Dr. Lepsius, who afterwards investigated the massacre, estimated that a million Armenians, half of them women and children, were killed by the Turks. If this estimate is even approximately correct, the Armenian massacre of 1915 was probably the most extensive slaughter of non-combatants ever known in this world since the days of Timur and his Tatars. The Armenians did not suffer alone, as lesser massacres took place of Greeks, Syrians, Jews and even Mohammedan Arabs.

The British command of the sea meant that Germany's overseas colonies would inevitably, even if only temporarily, be lost. The Pacific colonies were easily taken. *The colonial* The fortress of Kiao-Chau surrendered to Japan *campaigns* after a few weeks' siege in 1914 and the Japanese also took over many German islands north of the equator. Australian forces occupied German New Guinea (Kaiserwilhelmsland), and the New Zealanders seized German Samoa. In western Africa the French and British encountered little difficulty in occupying Togoland and Kamerun, but German East Africa put up a most obstinate resistance which did not end till the war itself was over. General von Lettow-Vorbeck, with 4000 white troops and some 25,000 natives, eluded the Allied forces in the vast territory of jungle, rugged highland and roadless wilderness which was his to defend until the armistice. German Southwest Africa was taken by forces from the Union of South Africa. A few Dutch Boers, still unreconciled to British rule, seized the opportunity to rebel, and Generals Botha and Smuts had the uncongenial task of having to repress the rebellion of their former comrade in arms of the Boer War, General De Wet.

By the winter of 1916 both the Entente Allies and the Central Powers had become completely disillusioned as to any *As 1916* hope of a short, decisive war, and the exhaustion *ended* of a protracted struggle was telling seriously on the morale of both belligerent groups. The war in the west had apparently reached an unbreakable deadlock; the German assault on Verdun being already an admitted failure, and the Franco-British offensive on the Somme but a very partial success. Italy had neither conquered Austria nor been conquered by her. In Poland, the Balkans and Turkey the Central Powers had indeed won striking victories, but the British fleet still held the sea and the German colonies had become prizes of war. In 1917 the intervention of the United States and the Russian Revolution inaugurated a new phase of the war. To these new factors we must turn before resuming the military chronicle.

CHAPTER XV

AMERICA INTERVENES

UNTIL 1917 the New World had not been directly engaged in the World War, if we except Canada, Newfoundland and other European colonies. Twenty-one republics *Neutral* still stood neutral, the United States and the *America* nations of Latin America. Of all neutrals the United States was incomparably the most important. Others might be important because of their geographical situation, such as Switzerland or the Netherlands, or because they were convenient sources of raw materials needed by the belligerents. But the United States alone could fling into the balance the decisive weight of unparalleled industrial productivity, particularly a supply of the goods required for successful prosecution of the war; not "munitions" only or chiefly, but foodstuffs, cotton, copper, oil and chemicals. The Entente Allies, having command of the seas, here enjoyed every advantage. They could trade freely with the United States, and indeed all neutral countries, while the Central Powers could carry on only such overseas trade as their adversaries would permit. But the favor of the United States was desired for other than commercial reasons. Even if the nation did not intervene in the military struggle, her influence might be important in the making of peace and would certainly be so in the balance of power when the war was over. Hence spokesmen for every warring nation deluged the country with arguments for their cause, and the lesser nations and subject peoples in particular urged their claims through every channel of publicity.

The first reaction of the United States to the war was one of sheer humanitarian horror. The American public followed the windings of diplomacy less consistently than the Euro-

pean public and had a less fatalistic attitude towards war.
Few realized how tense the European situation had become
in the decade preceding the war; still fewer believed in the
possibility that the spreading conflict might involve the
New World with the Old. One of the oldest American traditions had been not to intervene in any European conflict, no
matter how greatly the public might sympathize with one
side or the other. President Wilson's declaration of neutrality in 1914 appeared to most Americans not only as proper
but as inevitable. As time went on, however, it became
daily clearer that the United States could not hope to escape
the indirect consequences of so vast a conflict. The sudden
interruption of trade with Germany caused an acute shortage
of certain drugs and dyestuffs ordinarily imported from that
country, and the cotton market of the southern states felt
the loss of foreign orders. On the other hand, Britain and
France provided increasing markets for munitions. American charity was called upon to save Belgium and Poland
from famine. Every American felt vicarious pride in the
effective organization of relief work by Herbert Hoover in
Belgium. A flood of books and magazine articles, some
scientific, some propagandist, but mainly journalistic in
type, aroused public interest in the issues and events of the
hour.

The particular question in which the United States as a
neutral was most immediately interested was the right to
Freedom of trade and travel on the high seas. One of the
the seas diplomatic traditions of the United States was
the "freedom of the seas." This freedom had been invaded
on both sides in the epic struggle of Napoleon against Great
Britain, and the attempt to defend it against the British
brought on the war of 1812. Once more the World War revived those burning issues of a hundred years before. Neither the Entente Allies nor the Central Powers were in a
position to enforce a "blockade" in the strict legal meaning

of the word. The Germans could trade not only with land-ward neutral states such as the Netherlands but even across the Baltic with Sweden. For this reason the British Orders in Council avoided so far as possible the use of the concept "blockade" and relied in part on the general sea law concerning the taking of prizes and contraband and in part on the principle of "reprisal" against alleged illegal acts by Germany. As for Germany, she could maintain no blockade at all; from the standpoint of international law a blockade must be close, continuous, impartial and complete, it is not constituted by the taking of isolated prizes or the sinking of an occasional ship. Quite aside from the technical privileges of the blockader, maritime law recognized also a limited right to intercept certain classes of goods directly used for military purposes as "contraband of war," but this term proved as elastic as the desires of the belligerents who used it. Cotton and wheat became suspect, for who could guarantee that once landed at a belligerent port they might not be diverted to military uses? Other questions arose as to the "continuous voyage" of goods shipped from one neutral port to another — New York to Amsterdam for instance — but ultimately destined for Germany or Austria.

Owing to the superiority of the British fleet the Germans did not risk a decisive battle for control of the sea. There were a few attempts to break through the block- *Running the* ade. Cruisers dashed across the North Sea *blockade* early in the war to bombard English coast towns and then scurried back for safety; the cruisers *Breslau* and *Goeben* took refuge in Turkey and thus helped bring that country into the war; a fleet of German cruisers under Admiral von Spee won a minor victory over a British force under Admiral Cradock off the coast of Chile in November, 1914, and succumbed to a larger force under Admiral Sturdee near the Falkland Islands in the South Atlantic. The individual feats of some of the German commerce raiders deserve to be remembered, notably the *Emden* of Captain von Müller and the *Moewe* of Count Zu Dohna, cruisers which kept the sea for weeks and took numerous prizes. The *Deutschland*, the world's first submarine merchantman, actually reached the United States from Germany with a cargo of dyestuffs. But broadly speaking it remained true throughout the war that all the seas of the world, with the partial exception of the Baltic, were closed to Germany and that the German navy was powerless to break the British blockade. One weapon alone remained available — the submarine.

The submarine was largely an American invention. The Germans had not specialized in this type of ship but built
The sub- submarines as auxiliary to the main fleet, as did
marine peril the British, French and Americans. Like all torpedo boats the submarine is frail and light enough to be vulnerable to a single well directed shell from battleship or cruiser; it moves rather slowly, and when once detected is easy to evade. In the one element of surprise lies all its special value. By submerging it can pass through the closest blockade and reappear where least expected. But even as a commerce destroyer the submarine was under a severe handicap, as it could not without detection take its prizes into port; in fact, to rise to the surface and challenge the merchant ship at all involved great risk, if the merchantman carried arms or was attended by a cruiser convoy. Germany was faced therefore with the hard alternative of practically laying aside her only effective weapon of naval combat or else adopting a policy of relentless submarine warfare, striking secretly and without warning at merchant vessels of the enemy or neutral traders in enemy waters.

One of the few points of sea law on which all authorities
The sub- were in accord was that no merchant ship, even
marine ver- if carrying contraband, may be sunk without spe-
sus the law cific warning and opportunity offered to secure the safety of all on board. Of course, if a merchant ship

offers armed resistance this immunity disappears. By declaring a zone of unrestricted submarine warfare along the shores of the Entente powers in February, 1915, Germany challenged principles of international law which had been generally recognized and respected for hundreds of years. The German plea that the novelty of the submarine as a weapon made obsolete all precedents, carried no conviction in neutral countries because the employment of a new weapon, however legitimate in itself, brings with it no new right to slay non-combatants and neutrals. As if to make her position still less tenable, Germany executed a British merchant captain (Captain Fryatt) for attacking and ramming a submarine, thus denying to traders the rights of belligerents as well as the immunities of non-combatants.

As the chief of the neutral nations, the United States had the responsibility of registering a protest against each new invasion of the "freedom of the seas." The American government protested against the extension of the contraband list, the interruption of mails, the boycotting of "blacklisted" neutral *America champions neutral rights* firms which had financial connections with enemy states, the misuse of neutral flags, and other acts of the British and other Allied governments which infringed neutral property rights. But the German war zone declaration, containing as it did a latent threat against neutral lives, involved far graver problems. On February 10, 1915, the American government warned that it would "hold the Imperial German Government to a strict accountability for such acts of their naval authorities and to take any steps it might be necessary to safeguard American lives and property and to secure to American citizens the full enjoyment of their acknowledged rights on the high seas." Germany offered to restrict the employment of submarines on condition that the principles of the Declaration of London with regard to contraband be accepted by the Entente Allies, thus enabling

Germany to import foodstuffs and raw materials for manufacture. This proposal was inacceptable to Great Britain,
and the German government therefore adhered to its policy
of warfare against merchant shipping. Attacks on the
American vessels *Cushing* and *Gulflight* and the drowning
of an American citizen on the British passenger liner *Falaba*
directly challenged the position taken by the Washington
authorities. But they were almost forgotten when another
disaster, similar in kind but vastly greater in degree, first
made the horrified world acquainted with the possibilities of
unrestricted submarine warfare.

On May 7, 1915, the British passenger liner *Lusitania* was
torpedoed off the Irish coast. Before the ship sailed passen-
The fate gers had been warned by German agents not to
of the board her, and her destruction was hailed as a
Lusitania great naval victory. Of the 1906 passengers and
crew on board, over 1100 drowned, among them 114 American
citizens. On that date for the first time a considerable body
of American opinion contemplated the possibility of war.
But the government at Washington, though sorely pressed,
remained true to its declared policy of neutrality and contented itself with the reiterated warning that "The Imperial
German Government will not expect the Government of the
United States to omit any word or act necessary to the per-
formance of its sacred duty of maintaining the rights of the
United States and its citizens."

A long diplomatic correspondence ensued. The German
contention was that such events as the sinking of the *Lusi-
Continued* *tania*, though perhaps contrary to international
U-boat raids law as previously interpreted, were justified not
only by the novelty of the submarine as a weapon but also
as a reprisal against the British blockade policy and by the
fact that British merchant ships were "auxiliary cruisers"
carrying munitions of war and sometimes armed for defense.
But the *Lusitania* appears to have been unarmed, and the

fact that she carried munitions did not alter her legal status as a merchant ship. Renewed loss of American lives on the *Arabic* and the *Ancona* (the latter destroyed by an Austrian submarine) darkened the prospect of peace. Finally, the destruction of the *Sussex* in March, 1916, brought matters to a crisis. President Wilson's much-enduring patience, which had subjected him to some ridicule at home as well as abroad, finally snapped and he declared that any further such acts of violence against neutral lives at sea would force the United States to sever diplomatic relations. Germany agreed not to torpedo merchant ships without affording every provision for the safety of the passengers and crew. This promise was, however, made conditional on a modification of the British blockade and did not prevent a renewal of unrestricted submarine warfare the following year.

The determination of the German government to rely on the submarine rather than risk in battle the capital ships of the navy was strengthened by the one major *The battle* naval combat of the war, the battle of Jutland. *of Jutland,* On May 31, 1916, a number of British ships in *1916* the North Sea under command of Vice-Admiral Beatty came into touch with the German High Seas Fleet under Admiral von Scheer and suffered heavy losses until the arrival of the main British force under Admiral Jellicoe reversed the odds. Admiral Jellicoe maneuvered to intercept the German fleet and compel it to decisive conflict, but night was already descending and the mists of the northern seas added to the obscurity. The German fleet withdrew safely to its base. Next only to the battle of the Marne in 1914, the naval conflict off Jutland has been the most discussed battle of the war, but the issues open to question are not the same. No one doubts that the Marne was a great and fruitful victory for France; the outstanding problems relate to the exact factors which made the French victory possible. But in the case of Jutland there is the preliminary question — who won? The Germans claimed victory on the ground that with a smaller fleet they inflicted greater damage than they suffered; the British lost three large battle cruisers and several minor vessels, the Germans lost one battleship, one battle cruiser and some light cruisers and destroyers. The British point to the fact that they held the battleground (if one may so speak of the sea) and continued their blockade of the German ports. Perhaps the fairest conclusion is that the honors of the day went to Germany, the permanent results remained with the British.

Over the protest of the neutral nations the Entente Allies had shut off the Central Powers from all access to the world's *Tightening the block-ade* markets. From the first day of the war the risk of being captured and taken to a prize court had kept even the most venturesome traders from going directly to the German ports, but until the Allies undertook the regulation of neutral trade Germany had been able to import by way of the Netherlands and Scandinavia. Already in the industrial cities of Austria and Germany thousands of people were underfed, and the governments had to ration civilian food. In June, 1916, representatives of the Entente Allies met at Paris to work out a program of continued economic co-operation extending, if need be, even beyond the war. Germany was now confronted not only with an immediate blockade but by the still more alarming prospect of an economic boycott which would prevent the revival of German commerce if peace were restored. Even a peace of victory and conquest would be a disaster to Germany if the Entente Allies could maintain a policy of granting commercial preference to each other as against goods "made in Germany." The neutrals, too, were somewhat disquieted at the prospect of a permanent economic league in which they could not become members.

The growing possibility of American intervention in the World War redoubled the intensity of propaganda on both sides. "Propaganda" came to have a very evil connotation during the war, so much so that it has taken *The war of* on a meaning almost equivalent to subsidized *propaganda* mendacity; but the word is used here in its broadest sense, as any attempt, whether by fair means or foul, to "advertise" a cause. After all, many propagandists on both sides were honest, and even the most unscrupulous usually preferred facts to falsehoods when they could find facts that "would do." Sometimes the facts were not striking enough and then fabrication crept in; as in the famous instance when the German phrase for "carcass" was deliberately mistranslated "corpse" and the reader was led to believe that the German factories which transformed the dead bodies of horses into useful articles were busied on the bodies of men! Many alleged war atrocities were of this order; many more were the honest but inaccurate product of hysteria, refugees repeating the gossip which they heard amid the confusion of invasion. Photographs were sometimes faked, as for example by painting a red cross hospital sign on a building *after* it had been bombed. War correspondents were strictly censored; the old, happy-go-lucky days of the Spanish-American War, when a few journalists half created a war and then half ran it afterwards, had passed forever; dry, curt official communications from the front, carefully devised to minimize setbacks or exaggerate the effect of victories, took their place. In general, propaganda had three purposes: to maintain the fighting spirit at home; to undermine the confidence of enemy nationals, and to capture the sympathy of neutrals, suppressed nationalities or other groups open to persuasion by either party.

In this war of propaganda the British and French were on the whole more successful than the Germans. This in part was due to the fact that the most important neutral nation, the United States, spoke the English language, in part to the control of overseas mail routes and submarine cables

by the British (but wireless telegraphy from Berlin was
Forces possible), in part to the more subtle methods
making for and superior tact of the Entente spokesmen, but
intervention in greatest part to diplomatic and military acts
of the Central Powers which provided almost unlimited ammunition to their critics. Whatever may be said of the moral
aspects of the Austrian ultimatum to Serbia, the German
declaration of war on France, the invasion of Belgium, the
sinking of the *Lusitania*, the shooting of Edith Cavell,[1] the
promotion of strikes and "accidents" in American munition
plants by embassy officials,[2] they had ten times more influence on public opinion than all the "propaganda" that
either side could devise. American financial interests were,
in the main, pro-Entente because of the growing war profits
realized through trade with France and Britain (the Central
Powers, and Russia for that matter, were almost inaccessible)
and the large credits granted to those countries. Ex-President Theodore Roosevelt, after a brief period of hesitation,
had come out flatly for the Entente cause and denounced the
Wilson administration for timidity. Walter Hines Page,
Wilson's own ambassador to Great Britain, was emphatically
of the same opinion though he had to express his views more
privately. Though few politicians dared hint at anything
except neutrality, men in unofficial position were less discreet and large sections of the press and public were outspoken in their views.

But Germany was not without friends in the United States.
The two most influential immigrant groups who made up
the American population, aside from the old British stock,
were the Germans and the Irish. Though many Germans

---

[1] Edith Cavell, an English nurse, was shot in Belgium for aiding British captives
to escape. Though women spies were shot by both sides without much public sympathy, the high character and disinterested motives of this victim of military law
made her execution a disastrous blunder.

[2] In 1915 Constantin Dumba, the Austro-Hungarian ambassador, and Captains
Boy-Ed and von Papen of the Germany embassy, were dismissed from office for illegal activities on American soil.

had left their country to find greater political liberty than existed at home, they still had a reminiscent fond- *Forces* ness for the land of their fathers. The main Irish *against* emigration had taken place during a period of *intervention* acute tension with England which left a lasting bitterness. The Russian Jewish element was naturally hostile to Tsarist Russia. Even among the Americans of British stock, memories of the American revolution and the War of 1812 were still potent, and British interference with the "freedom of the seas" awoke the echo of those old quarrels. Many who were not in any positive sense either pro-German or anti-Entente were so averse to war that they favored an embargo on the transport of all munitions, a measure which would have advantaged only the Central Powers. William Jennings Bryan, the Secretary of State, was so strongly pacifist that he resigned office rather than stand sponsor for diplomatic remonstrances on the submarine question which might lead to war with Germany. Germany was fortunate in her ambassador, Count von Bernstorff, who had much to do with persuading his government to suspend for a time the ruthless submarine attacks on merchant ships which were driving American opinion daily nearer to war. Had his advice been followed to the end, there is every probability that the United States would have remained neutral throughout the war, but the promises of a speedy starving out of the British Isles, advanced by such national heroes as Ludendorff and Tirpitz, had greater weight in Germany than the warnings of a mere civilian ambassador.

About half way between the two camps of declared interventionists and unbending pacifists stood President Woodrow Wilson and his most trusted adviser, Col. E. M. *Wilson and* House. Both unquestionably desired at first to *House* keep America out of the war. President Wilson had endured much criticism for refusing to send an army into revolutionary Mexico, to protect American interests there; he was

willing to endure more to keep from having to send a bigger
army to Europe. Indeed an obstinate adherence to his own
view of the right was Wilson's outstanding personal trait, at
once his greatest merit and his most dangerous weakness.
The fact that having once taken a stand he met opposition
would tend only the more to confirm him in his opinion.
The wishes of the financiers had little weight with him; he
was accounted generally their political enemy. In 1916 he
was chosen president for a second term, largely on the cry
that "he kept us out of war," although his Republican opponent, Associate Justice Charles Hughes of the Supreme
Court, was equally careful not to commit himself to any
promise of intervention in Europe. On the other hand, Wilson was no advocate of peace-at-any-price. He pushed
through Congress bills strengthening the army and navy.
He had given Germany warnings which if disregarded must
eventually lead to war. In February, 1916, Colonel House,
on a confidential diplomatic mission to the European capitals, let the British government know that "President Wilson
was ready, on hearing from France and England that the
moment was opportune, to propose that a Conference
should be summoned to put an end to the war. Should the
Allies accept this proposal, and should Germany refuse it,
the United States would probably enter the war against
Germany." He hinted that a fair basis of agreement would
be the restoration of Belgium and Serbia, the liberation of
Alsace-Lorraine, an outlet to the Mediterranean for Russia,
and colonial compensation to Germany for the loss of Alsace
in Europe. Nothing came of the suggestion; the Entente
Allies were not ready to go to conference and they doubted
the value of so vague a promise as the "probable" aid of
the United States.

President Wilsons's re-election encouraged him to offer
the mediation of the United States to the belligerent nations.
At the same time, but quite independently, the German

government was ready with an offer to initiate peace negotiations. In a joint note of December 12, 1916, *Wilson's*
Germany, Austria-Hungary, Bulgaria and Tur- *offer of*
key proposed immediate negotiations. On De- *mediation*
cember 18, President Wilson asked both warring groups for
"such an avowal of their respective views as to the terms
upon which the war might be concluded and the arrangements which would be deemed satisfactory as a guaranty
against its renewal or the kindling of any similar conflict in
the future as would make it possible frankly to compare
them." He stated that the United States had no desire to
intrude its mediation if the belligerents did not so desire; he
wished merely that "soundings be taken" in order to find
out how far apart in actuality were the war aims, and pointed
out with truth that the general objects proclaimed as war
aims "seem the same on both sides" but "the world has
been left to conjecture what definitive results, what actual
exchange of guarantees, what political or territorial changes
or readjustments, what stage of military success even would
bring the war to an end."

Germany and her allies replied by proposing an immediate
peace conference to be held on neutral ground but made at
that time no statement of terms. The Entente
The En-
Allies rejected the proposal for a conference, but *tente Allies*
stated publicly their conditions of peace. Hith- *declare their*
program
erto their war aims had been phrased only in
such broad terms as Premier Asquith's phrase "restitution,
reparation and guarantees." Now they specified:

> In the first instance, the restoration of Belgium, of Serbia,
> and of Montenegro, and the indemnities which are due them,
> the evacuation of the invaded territories of France, of Russia,
> and of Rumania, with just reparation; the reorganization of
> Europe, guaranteed by a stable settlement, based alike upon the
> principle of nationalities, on the right which all peoples, whether
> small or great, have to the enjoyment of full security and free
> economic development, and also upon territorial agreements and
> international arrangements so framed as to guarantee land and

sea frontiers against unjustified attacks, the restitution of provinces or territories wrested in the past from the Allies by force
or against the will of their populations; the liberation of Italians,
of Slavs, of Rumanians, and of Czecho-Slovaks from foreign
domination; the enfranchisement of populations subject to the
bloody tyranny of the Turks; the expulsion from Europe of the
Ottoman Empire, decidedly alien to Western civilization.   The
intentions of His Majesty, the Emperor of Russia, regarding
Poland have been clearly indicated in the proclamation which
he has just addressed to his armies.

A later statement from Foreign Minister Balfour, who had
succeeded Sir Edward Grey as spokesman of the British
foreign office, laid special stress on the absolute necessity of
expelling the Turkish government from Europe and liberat-
ing all the subject nationalities suffering from its misrule.

As the note of the Entente Allies on January 10, 1917,
foreshadowed in the main the actual peace settlement,[1] it

*What lay
behind the
Entente
terms*

deserves close examination.   Not all of its significance appears on the surface.   The restoration
of invaded territories and the demand for indemnities for injuries suffered in the invasion
might, indeed, be taken for granted, but the proposed rearrangement of boundaries must be interpreted in the light of
secret understandings made in the interest of France, Italy
and Russia, and of the new conviction that Austria-Hungary
was not a mere second to Germany but the core of the whole
problem.   By the Treaty of London, April 26, 1915, Italy
had been promised Tirol to the Brenner Pass, Trieste and
Istria, a share of Dalmatia, several islands in the Adriatic
and a share in Asiatic Turkey.[2]   In 1916, Rumania had been
promised the Rumanian-speaking parts of Hungary.   France,
of course, expected Alsace-Lorraine ("the restitution of
provinces or territories wrested in the past from the Allies

[1] The chief exceptions were due to the collapse of Russia in the interim.   This
made Poland wholly independent instead of autonomous under the Tsar and left to
Turkey Constantinople and Armenia which would probably otherwise have gone to
Russia.

[2] For Italy's entrance into the war, see above, pages 329–330.

by force") and had under consideration plans for annexing
also the Saar valley and erecting an independent "buffer
state" from the German provinces west of the Rhine. The
British ministry later declared that it had never expressed
approval of this particular plan. Russia had publicly promised the union of Russian, Austrian and Prussian Poland
into a united and autonomous state joined to Russia by
personal union under the Tsar. Russia had been promised
Constantinople and the Straits and extension of her frontier
in Armenia. The delimitation of boundaries between the
proposed French sphere of influence in Syria and the British
claims in Mesopotamia reached a provisional settlement in
the Sykes-Picot agreement of 1916. Japan claimed the German island colonies north of the equator and also the leasehold of Kiao-chau on the Shan-tung peninsula, leaving to
Great Britain and to the Dominions of Australia and New
Zealand the German Pacific colonies south of the equator.

One phrase in the note of the Entente Allies is particularly
interesting: "the liberation of Italians, of Slavs, of Rumanians, and of Czecho-Slovaks." As the Czechs
and Slovaks are Slavs, the phrase was as illogical *The new
weapon of*
as "British and Welsh" or "Germans and Ba- *national
liberation*
varians." But there was reason for thus singling
out for special mention one branch of the Slavic peoples; it
was an announcement to the world that the Allies would
not be satisfied merely with annexing frontier provinces of
Austria-Hungary to their own territories: "unredeemed
Italy," Rumanian Hungary, Austrian Poland and Bosnia-
Herzegovina for the respective benefit of Italy, Rumania,
Russia and Serbia. They would strike at the heart of the
Dual Monarchy, liberate a nation which though pro-Entente
in sentiment could not be claimed as subject to any one of
the Allies, and demand either the total dismemberment or
the federal reconstruction of the entire Habsburg inheritance
("liberation" could be interpreted either way). This new

policy was due in part to the influence of a brilliant group
of British and French students of eastern European affairs,
such as André Chéradame, H. Wickham Steed, and R. W.
Seton-Watson, and in part to the able propaganda of Professor Thomas G. Masaryk, the exiled champion of the Czech
national cause and soon to be the first president of his
liberated nation. Periodicals such as *The New Europe*
warned the British and French nations that they were near-
sighted, and that a victory which liberated only Belgium
and Alsace-Lorraine would be a defeat if Germany could still
dominate central and eastern Europe. This new weapon of
nationalism had two edges, however, and Germany found
the propaganda of national revolt effective also among the
Finns, Poles and Ukrainians in Russia.

The war aims of the Central Powers were less definitely
formulated than those of the Entente Allies, which is perhaps
German the reason why they preferred to unveil them in
war aims secret conference. At one extreme the Socialists
and a few pacifists in other parties would have been satisfied
with a *status quo* peace "without annexations or indemnities"; at the other extreme a group of influential industrial
and agrarian associations demanded control over Belgium "in
monetary, financial and postal matters," the annexation of
the French iron mines near the old frontier and the fortresses
of Longwy and Verdun, and the acquisition by Germany of
large parts of Russian Poland and the Russian Baltic Provinces. That the government took an intermediate stand is
indicated by the confidential terms transmitted by Ambassador Bernstorff to President Wilson on January 29, 1917.
They comprised a restoration of Belgian independence, subject to certain "guarantees" against injury to German interests, slight frontier adjustments in the west, a strategic
frontier against Russia, a restoration of colonies or territorial
compensation for their loss, the renunciation of the projected
economic boycott of Germany by the Allies, and payment

for injury to German undertakings and persons who had suffered damage by the war.

On January 22, 1917, President Wilson announced to the
Senate the result of his tender of good offices and outlined
his own views of a just and suitable peace. He *Wilson's*
urged a "peace without victory" based on the *second*
consent of all nations, great or small, and terri- *appeal*
torial rearrangements according to the lines of nationality.
As an example of this he instanced Poland — "a united,
independent and autonomous Poland." Every nation should
have commercial if not political access to the highways of the
sea, and there should be freedom of the seas "alike in law
and in fact." Armaments should be reduced and an association of nations replace the insecure principle of the balance
of power.

Thus far overtures for peace had progressed when the
German government suddenly announced a policy which
made peace impossible. Convinced that the de- *Germany*
mands of the Entente Allies made it useless to *renews sub-*
continue negotiations, the statesmen of Germany *marine war*
concluded that Ambassador Bernstorff's policy of using
America to aid in securing a satisfactory peace had failed,
and that it was time to revert to the Ludendorff and Tirpitz
policy of submarine warfare devoid of all restrictions and
reckless of all consequences. Early in January Germany
reached her fateful decision, but it was not officially announced till the end of the month. All the waters around
the French and British coasts were to constitute a war zone
barred to all ships, neutral as well as belligerent, armed or
unarmed, carrying munitions or not. The only exception
permitted was the right to dispatch one passenger ship a
week along a narrow sea-lane, a ship carrying no contraband
and decorated with broad stripes of alternate white and red.
Other sea-lanes permitted ships to approach the neutral
shores of Holland, Greece and the Scandinavian countries.

The new war zone decree went into effect on February 1,
1917. Perhaps we may say that by that act and on that

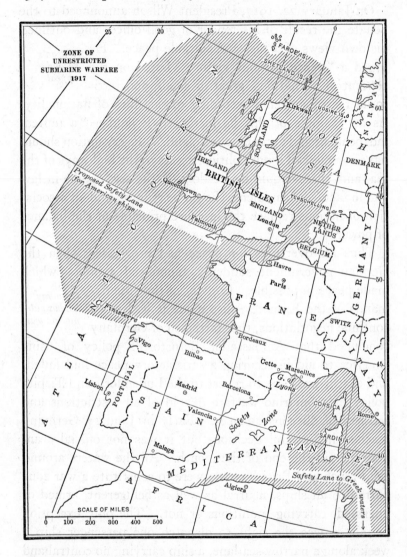

day Germany lost the war. But the gamble, though a
desperate and losing one, came perilously near success. No
possible victory on land, not even a simultaneous occupation

of Paris, Petrograd and Rome, could have so hastened the end of the war in Germany's interest as a really successful submarine blockade of Great Britain. A few months' complete interruption of overseas trade and the British Isles would be in the most literal sense starved into surrender. By April, 1917, the submarines were sinking ships several times as rapidly as they could be put out by all the shipyards of the world, and when Admiral Sims visited London, shortly after America's entrance into the war, he was told bluntly that unless the submarines could be halted the war was lost. In a single fortnight one ship out of every four that left a British port was torpedoed.

The German declaration of unrestricted submarine warfare ended at once diplomatic relations between Germany and the United States. Ambassador von Bernstorff *"Armed* and Ambassador Gerard left their respective *neutrality"* posts. President Wilson still clung to the hope that war might even yet be averted and he advocated a policy of armed neutrality, the defensive armament of American merchant ships. A majority of Congress supported his plan, but the end of the session was near and "a little group of willful men," as the President called them, talked it to death in the Senate, but this did not prevent his arming them anyway on executive authority. Again the German government was guilty of an almost incredible diplomatic blunder. Alfred Zimmermann, German Foreign Minister, notified the German Minister to Mexico that it was the intention of his government to force an early peace by "ruthless submarine warfare" and to keep the United States neutral. Should this be impossible, Mexico was invited to attack the United States and reap as reward "the lost territory of New Mexico, Texas and Arizona," and Japan was to be invited to break away from the Entente Allies and join in the war with America. The discovery and publication of this particularly crude plot nearly extinguished what was left of anti-interventionist sentiment. Several neutralist organizations merged into an Emergency Peace Federation and strove to avert war but with a growing sense of hopelessness. When the Congress met in April it was not to discuss the arming of merchant ships but to vote on a declaration of war.

On April 2, 1917, President Wilson brought to the bar of Congress the case of the American people versus the German *War at last* government. In asking for a declaration of war he surveyed the wrongs the nation had suffered in lawless outrages on the high seas and intrigues and plots within the country. He distinguished the German government from the German people and placed the whole burden of responsibility for the war on "a narrow and privileged class." He welcomed the newly established Russian Republic as "a fit partner for a League of Honor" in the crusade against autocracy. He disclaimed on behalf of the nation all conquests, annexations, indemnities or material compensation of every sort. He phrased the war aims of the American government as a "fight for the ultimate peace of the world and for the liberation of its peoples, the German peoples included; for the rights of nations, great and small, and the privilege of men everywhere to choose their way of life and of obedience. The world must be made safe for democracy. Its peace must be planted upon the tested foundations of political liberty." Congress was not unanimous, and the debate on the war, though brief, was bitter. Party lines vanished. In the House of Representatives fifty votes were cast in opposition; in the Senate six. In accordance with the vote of Congress, the president proclaimed a state of war in existence on April 6.

The war to which the nation was now pledged was to be no mere naval combat nor even an expedition of volunteers, as *Building* to Cuba in 1898, but the mobilization of every *an army* needed man and dollar and the unification of American war efforts with those of the Entente Allies. It was the first participation of armed forces of the United States in a European struggle, for the War of 1812, though coinciding in time with the last phases of the Napoleonic wars, involved no direct aid to France. Taught by the experience of Great Britain, which began the World War by relying on voluntary service and only reluctantly shifted to compulsion in 1916, the United States almost at once made service obligatory and devised a draft system to raise the necessary army. In order that the mobilization of the army might be uniform and function as a single machine, President Wilson disregarded the gallant proposal of ex-President Roosevelt, who offered to accompany a special division of volunteers to enter at once into the conflict. Volunteering, it was feared, would take the wrong men, those needed in the factories or on the farms or to act as organizers and drill masters of the inexperienced civilians in the military camps at home. No one was permitted, as during the American Civil War, to purchase exemption from service; indeed the poor man stood perhaps a better chance of exemption than the rich as he would be more apt to have a job in a munitions factory.

The first year of war was a period of mobilization and preparation. When it began there were barely 200,000 soldiers ready for action in the regular army and the mobilized National Guard; before it ended the United States had placed in service twenty times that number. Of 200,000 officers fewer than 9000 had been in service before the war; many others had experienced in the ranks as soldiers or had attended officers' training camps as civilians, but the majority had no military training whatever, and even those who had a routine officers' education needed to take a "postgraduate course" under French or British experts who had seen service under the peculiar conditions of the World War. Even by February, 1918, American soldiers were reaching France at a rate of less than 50,000 a month. Five months later they were arriving at the rate of ten thousand a day. In all more than two million, or approximately half the army, reached France before the end of the war. But the battles in which the American army proved a powerful and independent factor formed a single campaign of the summer and autumn of 1918.

The chief task of the fleet was to safeguard shipping from submarine attack, as the Germans had practically abandoned *The rout of* other forms of naval warfare. Forty-nine per *the subma-* cent of the American army traveled in British *rine* ships; forty-five per cent in American ships, including the German lines confiscated in American ports. To protect cargo and troop transport the convoy system proved essential, each group of merchant ships going to sea with a guard of cruisers. For further protection, the ships were painted with weird camouflage, not to conceal their presence but to delude the submarine commander as to their speed and direction. Routes were frequently shifted. Direct war, against the submarine was waged with depth bomb, mine barrage, scouting airplanes, swift destroyers, and the armed decoy ship made up to appear as a harmless merchantman. More than two hundred German submarines were destroyed in one fashion or another during the war, but as new ones were constantly being built the rapid decrease in shipping losses after April, 1917, must be attributed largely to skillful evasion of submarine attack. In 1918 the output of new shipping exceeded the diminishing loss from undersea attack. With the entrance of the United States and several other neutral nations into the war, the blockade of the Central Powers was made tighter than ever before; the United States, as a belligerent, carrying out the very same rigorous rationing of neutrals adjacent to Germany, which had formerly evoked vigorous American protests.

The American government had not only to build a new army and carry it overseas; it had at the same time to make

a gigantic economic effort to maintain this army and to aid
the Entente Allies to maintain theirs. From the *Behind the*
first a large part of the expenses were raised by *lines*
taxation but borrowing on a great scale also played a part.
In a series of "liberty loan drives," in which all the arts of
propaganda and advertisement were carried to the pitch of
perfection the government "sold the war to the people" and
raised over $21,000,000,000, making the American people
for the first time a nation of bondholders like the French.
President Wilson did not follow the example of most European belligerents and reorganize his cabinet on a non-partisan
basis. But many new offices were created outside the cabinet
for wartime purposes and these were usually put under successful business men with no political record. An Emergency
Fleet Corporation for the construction of new ships and a
Shipping Board to direct their operation assayed the task of
offsetting the losses in merchant shipping. Herbert Hoover,
whose efficient administration of relief in Belgium made him
an inevitable choice, became head of the Food Administration; though his task was not the same as that of similar officials in Europe, as since the United States suffered no food
shortage, rationing was voluntary, and the aim of the administration was to create a surplus which might be shipped
overseas to hungry Europe. As fuel must be conserved as
well as food, the President appointed a Fuel Administrator,
President Garfield of Williams College. Secretary of the
Treasury McAdoo and Walker D. Hines merged the operation
of all important railroad lines into a single system. Government boards determined priority in manufacture and shipment of all kinds of goods, so that war needs would be given
uniform precedence over peacetime luxuries.

The adhesion of the United States to the cause of the Entente Allies had a diplomatic importance beyond its military
and economic contributions. It was probably the chief
factor in determining the action of several Latin American

neutrals. Cuba and Panama declared war on Germany *Latin America and the war* almost simultaneously with their powerful neighbor. Of more significance was the addition of Brazil, a country too distant and populous to be considered as a mere echo of Washington diplomacy; a country, moreover, with a large German immigrant population. Costa Rica, Guatemala, Haiti, Honduras and Nicaragua followed the same policy, and a number of other Latin American republics went half way, breaking off diplomatic relations with Germany but not declaring war (Bolivia, Ecuador, Peru, Santo Domingo, Uruguay). None of these nations took any important share in the military operations of the war, but their action diminished German influence in a wide quarter of the neutral world and tested the success of Wilson's attempt to win good will by forbearance with troublesome Mexico.[1]

Other neutrals entered the war as belligerents in 1917; China and Siam in Asia, Liberia in Africa, Greece in Europe. *More than ever a World War* The Greek intervention was not wholly voluntary, the country had long been divided between interventionist partisans who followed Premier Venizelos and neutralists who looked to King Constantine. A condition almost of civil war arose between these parties, while in complete disregard of Greek neutrality an Anglo-French force encamped at Saloniki and Bulgarians occupied

---

[1] Mexico had been engaged in an almost continuous series of civil wars from the end of President Porfirio Diaz's administration in 1911. When General Huerta erected a military despotism on the corpse of President Madero, the liberal and relatively "legal" presidential successor of Diaz, President Wilson refused him recognition and countenanced the anti-Huertist "constitutionalist" revolution of Carranza. Though he landed troops at Vera Cruz in 1914, he accepted the "mediation" of Argentina, Brazil and Chile and refused to intervene on a large scale and enforce respect for foreign lives and property in spite of much criticism from a portion of the American press. When Villa raided the American border in 1916, however, he took advantage of the opportunity to mobilize along the frontier and give training to the National Guard militia as well as to the regular army. Throughout the war Mexico was neutral, though inclined to sympathize with Germany, from fear of her northern neighbor the United States. Elsewhere in Latin America, however, Wilson's forbearing conduct won friends for his European policy.

part of Macedonia. In June, 1917, the Entente Allies blockaded Greece, forced the abdication of King Constantine, and established an interventionist government under King Alexander and Premier Venizelos. In July Greece joined the Allies. The neutral world shrunk to small proportions: Spain, Switzerland, Holland and Scandinavia in Europe,[1] Abyssinia and the Spanish colonies in Africa, Persia and a few central Asiatic states of little importance, and about half of Latin America. The war was almost planet-wide; the Earth had become Mars.

[1] Albania and Luxemburg, though nominally neutral, were occupied by belligerent armies.

CHAPTER XVI

THE COLLAPSE OF RUSSIA

SINCE the great French Revolution of 1789–99 there have been scores of revolutions great and small, but most of them *An inevitable comparison* have dealt only with that superficial layer of human life called "politics," the overthrow of an alien government or the substitution of a parliamentary democracy for an autocratic monarchy. The Russian revolution of 1917 was of a more fundamental type. Like France's basic revolution it aimed at nothing less than the creation of a new social order. The points of comparison between these movements are temptingly numerous — a weak monarch, married to a reactionary German wife, a land-hungry peasantry, an unpopular clergy and aristocracy, a brief "honeymoon" of liberalism followed by a plunge into a reign of terror dominated by radical doctrinaires. But we must not be too much led by analogies. There were differences as well, and these differences were mainly to the disadvantage of Russia. France was a unified and highly patriotic nation; Russia a sprawling empire composed of diverse and mutually hostile nationalities. France began her revolution in peace though ending it in war; Russia came to the trial already exhausted by years of unsuccessful struggle with the Central Powers. France rested even her most radical experiments on the institution of private property; Russia essayed the enormous task of putting all industry on a socialistic basis. Small wonder that the Russian revolution involved an even greater amount of death and suffering than the French. Perhaps we are still too close to estimate its ultimate effect; the French Revolution *seemed* for a long time to have ended in the dictatorship of Napoleon, the Russian still seems to have ended in the dictatorship of the Communist party managers. But what the present calls an "end" is always to the future a mere "transition."

For a few months after the World War began patriotic fervor and wartime discipline seemed to have driven underground the rebellious spirit which had broken *Effect of* out in 1905 and was threatening another out- *the war on* break in 1914. Even veteran revolutionists in *Russia* many cases hoped that good might come to Russia from an alliance with liberal France and Britain against autocratic Austria and Germany. A competent Tsar and an honest court could have seized the opportunity to revive popular loyalty. But the old story of the Russo-Japanese War was repeated. Funds raised for military purposes were wasted. Supplies were kept useless in distant ports while soldiers stood under German fire waiting till their comrades were shot down so that they might have rifles. The absence of adequate munitions plants in Russia and the vast distance from sources of supply in other countries partly excuse the breakdown of the Russian military effort but cannot excuse the way in which such resources as did exist were mishandled. Ugly whispers of treason in high places circulated among the troops. Russia suffered heavier losses in killed, wounded and captured from 1914 to the revolution than did any other nation during the entire course of the war. No doubt the exertions of Russia had been of indispensable value to the western Allies by forcing the Central Powers to divide their armies between east and west, but the Russian peasant could not reckon in terms of such distant and indirect advantages. All that he could see of the war was defeat and disaster along the entire eastern front.

The Russian machinery of government broke down not at any one point but all along the line. To begin at the top, Tsar Nicholas II, Autocrat of all the Russias, was as little capable of ruling men as any sovereign who has ever reigned.

It is due to this unhappy ruler to concede that he did not personally desire the war, that he threw himself *The Tsar* into it when it began with patriotic though unintelligent devotion, and that he does not seem to have taken a personal share in the treasonable intrigues which surrounded him. But for all his excellent intentions he was clay in the hands of his advisers. Chief of these was the Tsarina, a German princess, also a Russian patriot but quite out of sympathy with the aspirations of the Russian people. She was forever goading the Tsar to punish liberals and defy the elected Duma, and exerted her powerful influence, like another Marie Antoinette, to protect reactionary officials who happened to be personal friends. Particularly notorious was the case of Rasputin, whose whole career seems like a page from a crude melodrama rather than a chapter of actual history.

Both the Tsar and his wife were religious mystics and very indiscriminate in selecting their spiritual advisers. They *Rasputin* long retained as their most trusted counselor *at court* Gregory Rasputin, an eccentric monk of coarse manners and evil reputation. He claimed the powers of a prophet and healer and was particularly valued by the royal family as affording supernatural care to the little crown prince (*tsarevitch*) whose health had given much concern. Rasputin's voice was powerful in the selection and dismissal of officials and though he seems to have known or cared little himself for either foreign or domestic policy his greed and vanity made him the easy tool of intriguers. When a group of exasperated nobles murdered Rasputin public opinion rejoiced as over a victory on the battlefield.[1] But Rasputin was not the disease, he was only a symptom, and after his death the Tsar found new advisers equally perilous to his throne.

[1] The details of this assassination were rehashed in a motion picture libel suit in 1934.

The official advisers of the Tsar were selected from the higher ranks of the bureaucracy. Many of them were Baltic Germans and had little sympathy with the war. *The* During the most critical moments of the cam- *ministry* paign of 1916 the Tsar's chief minister, Boris Stürmer, so greatly hampered the operations of the army that he was accused of treason by liberals in the Duma. Miliukov, leader of the Constitutional Democrats, declared:

> The abyss between our authorities and ourselves has widened and become impassable. We could appeal before, assuredly not to the sense and capacity of the rulers, but at least to their patriotism and good will. Could we do so now?

Stürmer's successors did nothing to improve matters. The fanatical reactionary Minister of the Interior, Protopopov, devoted all his zeal to harrying and persecuting the liberals, even discouraging the efforts of the provincial *zemstvos* (local councils) to send supplies to the army on the ground that *any* form of voluntary co-operation in Russia tended toward revolution.

The Duma was relatively honest. It is true that the franchise had been so manipulated that the influence of the landed gentry outweighed that of the peasants *The Duma* and workmen to a farcical degree. But at all events the Duma afforded a safety valve for criticism of the bureaucracy and the majority of its members, even the conservatives, were in earnest about winning the war and rooting out inefficiency and disloyalty in high places. The bureaucracy hated the free criticisms of the Duma and resolved to crush it. The bread riots of 1917, after a terrible winter of starvation in the Russian cities, afforded an opportunity. Taking the Petrograd [1] riots as an excuse, Prince Golitzin ordered the Duma to adjourn on March 11, hoping at one blow to crush the constitutional liberties of the Duma and the revolutionary spirit of the mob.

---

[1] The new, de-Germanized, name for St. Petersburg. It was to be rebaptized Leningrad after the revolution.

One vital point Protopopov and the other enemies of the Duma had overlooked. They could not rely on the army, *The March* and in an hour of crisis the test of a real govern-*revolution* ment is "whom will the army obey?" The soldiers would not fire on the crowd. They remembered their own grievances against a government which had conscripted them to fight in a vaguely conceived quarrel and had then frittered away the chances of victory by scandalous mismanagement. In some cases the soldiers shot their own officers or fought the police. A desultory battle raged in the streets of the capital, but owing to the reluctance of the soldiers to fire on the crowds the loss of life was not very great. Part of the army declared for the Duma. The order to adjourn was disobeyed and all the liberal delegates joined in proclaiming to Russia that the Duma had "found itself compelled to take into its own hands the re-establishment of the authority of the State and public order."

The unwitting Tsar, always the last to be correctly informed as to conditions in his own realm, was caught un-*Nicholas II* aware. On March 14 he was told that insur-*passes from* rection had broken out in the capital and that *history* the people demanded his abdication. On the following day a delegation from the Duma met him at Pskov and proposed that he resign the throne to the young Tsarevitch Alexis with Grand Duke Michael as Regent. The Tsar, his spirit broken, made no protest against his fate and requested only two favors: that the crown should go directly to his brother Michael so that he would not be separated from his little son, and that he be permitted to retire to his estates at Livadia "because I am so fond of flowers." His first request was granted, but vainly, as Grand Duke Michael cannily refused to take the throne until a constituent assembly had approved it. His other request, quietly to retire to the life of a country gentleman, was never accorded. He was kept in close seclusion, and

while at first treated as a simple prisoner of war, guarded
but not punished, under the later reign of terror in 1918 his
lot became as hard as that of any political prisoner whom
he had in past days sent into exile. He and his family
were subjected to every insult and abuse, ending with their
secret execution by decree of a local soviet at Ekaterinburg
in July, 1918. Thus the last of the Tsars was denied even
the dignity of public trial and execution granted to Charles I
and Louis XVI.

The authority of the revolution was now vested in the
hands of a provisional government chosen from the party
leaders of the old Duma. It was headed by *Russia's*
Prince Lvov, former President of the Union of *first repub-*
Zemstvos, who held the important position of *lican gov-*
ernment
Minister of the Interior. Guchkov, a leader of
the conservative Octobrist party, was Minister of War;
Miliukov, chief of the more liberal Constitutional Democrats, Minister of Foreign Affairs; Alexander Kerensky, the
only Socialist in the government, Minister of Justice. No
abler or more enlightened body of men have ever held power
in Russia, before or since, but they were doomed from the
start by the burden of carrying on an unsuccessful war and
by the gulf of misunderstanding which separated them from
the peasants, workingmen and common soldiers. The
provisional government desired to establish a régime that
would be stable as well as liberal, in which personal liberty
would be secure but property rights guarded with equal
care. The radicals "out of doors" demanded an immediate
and general peace, the division of the great estates (without
compensation to the owners) among the peasantry, and the
nationalization of all important industries. Only striking
military victories, holding out the hope of an early peace,
could have given the government sufficient prestige to
survive.

For the moment, however, the new provisional govern-

ment was enthusiastically welcomed.   It proclaimed a gen-
The era of eral pardon for political crimes and some eighty
good feeling thousand exiles returned from Siberia.   Complete freedom of speech and of the press was granted.   Capital punishment was abolished, arbitrary arrests made illegal, and a speedy trial for all accused persons guaranteed.
All legal discriminations against the Jews were abolished.
They were henceforth free to live where they chose, own
property of any kind, engage in any occupation, enter any
school or college, and hold any civil or military post.   The
special privileges of the Greek Orthodox Church were swept
away and complete religious freedom established.   Poland,
now wholly occupied by the Central Powers, was definitely
promised independence instead of mere "autonomy."   The
legal rights of Finland were restored.   The attempt to impose the Russian language by force on non-Russian peoples
ceased.   Optimistic people, in Russia as well as in western
Europe and America, too easily assumed that a backward,
illiterate despotism could and would transform itself overnight into a model democracy and at the same time bring
new energy to the tasks of war.   It was like the false dawn
of 1789 in France, 1848 in Germany and 1908 in Turkey;
the belief of a few generous idealists whom a revolution had
thrown into power that they could direct the further course
of the revolution into safe and sane channels.

The mob in town and country was vaguely pleased but
somewhat bewildered by these rapid changes.   In the cities
The peril good-natured crowds stood about all day listen-
of anarchy ing to orators or parading behind red banners,
enjoying the first prolonged holiday in their hard-driven
lives.   In the villages peasants were seizing the estates of
their landlords without waiting for the slow process of law.
In place of the old administrative officials who, however
incompetent and corrupt, at least had learned by dint of
long experience the routine of office, came idealistic young

social reformers who knew a great deal about revolutionary philosophy but had never before handled the machinery of government. The infection of disorder passed to the army. Soldiers turned the trenches into picnic grounds, chatted across "no man's land" with their German foes and chose committees to keep watch on their own officers. The navy practically disappeared as an instrument of war, as the sailors were more interested in fighting for the revolution than in fighting against a foreign enemy.

Because the Russian poor and their radical leaders did not fully trust the "bourgeois" provisional government, they supplemented the regular, legal authorities *The rise of* by a system of revolutionary councils chosen in *the soviets* the towns by factory workers, in the country by peasant communes, in the army by military units. These councils bore the name of "soviets" and had been organized as centers of agitation, though on a lesser scale, in the abortive revolution of 1905. Soon the agents of the government found that they could get no order obeyed unless it were also approved by the local soviet. Thus a double system of government grew up, the lawful, though provisional, national government, and the vigilant revolutionary committees directed by radical agitators who thought that the revolution was as yet but half completed. The reactionary parties and the adherents of the Tsardom had been practically eclipsed from the first moment of the revolution. This eliminated any immediate danger of a counter-revolution, but it left the stage clear for a conflict between those parties, such as the Octobrists and the Constitutional Democrats, who accepted the March revolution as a final settlement, and the various socialist factions who regarded it as but a first step to further reforms. The Social Revolutionaries, strong among the peasantry, and the Social Democrats, representing mainly the town proletariat, were the chief radical groups, and the latter was divided into two bitterly hostile divisions, the *Bolsheviki* or majority, and the *Mensheviki* or minority.   The Bolsheviki were the only large party in Russia which openly opposed and rejected the provisional government and therefore absorbed nearly every element of extreme discontent.

Having no responsibility for administration and being quite unrepresented in the government, the Bolsheviki were *The Bolshevist program* in a position to outbid other parties in promises to the people and to glean new support from every blunder of the government and every defeat on the battlefield.   Their program implied a "dictatorship of the proletariat," that is, the principle that the propertied classes should have no political rights or power, and "all power to the soviets," that is the substitution of the revolutionary councils of workingmen, soldiers and peasants for all other government agencies.   They demanded the immediate confiscation of the land without compensation to landlords, the nationalization of all productive property, and a revision of war aims looking toward an immediate peace.   Because they were "defeatist" in not looking for a victorious issue to the war, they received aid from the Central Powers and their leader Lenin returned from exile in Switzerland across Germany with the permission of the German government.   But this does not mean that the Bolsheviki were in any positive sense pro-German.   To them all "capitalistic" (i.e. non-socialist) governments were equally detestable and they would have welcomed a revolution in Germany or Austria as readily as in Russia or Italy. They desired merely to end the "imperialist war" in order to clear the ground for a general European class revolution. On their part the Germans also had no illusions.   They aided the Bolsheviki for the same reason that they had welcomed the reactionary Stürmer ministry under the Tsar and the nationalist movements in Poland, Finland, Lithuania and the Ukraine, caring little for the merits of each case but glad to help any movement that might weaken Russia or induce her to make a separate peace.

A successful revolution usually requires an outstanding leader, and the Bolsheviki had a man to play that rôle in the person of Vladimir Ulianov, better known as *Lenin* Nikolai Lenin.[1]   He was a Russian of the lesser nobility whose brother had been hanged many years before for a conspiracy against Tsar Alexander III and who had himself suffered exile for his convictions.   From the day of his return to Russia he was the sharpest thorn in the side of the provisional government, working untiringly for its overthrow.   In many ways his character suggests that of Robespierre.   Like that famous revolutionist, Lenin could sway a mob without the qualities of the demagogue.   He was dry, pedantic and dogmatic in manner, iterating and reiterating his Marxian formulas with little attempt at an appeal to the emotions.   He was imperious, dictatorial, jealous of power and ready to use any weapon of fraud or force that might hasten the proletarian revolution, but, for all that, fundamentally courageous, sincere and devoted to his cause. Unlike Robespierre, he was a very "practical politician" in the sense that, while always keeping his ultimate goal in mind, he could bide his time and shift his course when necessary to meet a particular exigency.

Paul Miliukov, Foreign Minister of the provisional government, was a liberal imperialist who wished Russia to continue in the war until a final victory brought *The second* to her Constantinople and the Straits.   But *provisional* the war-weary masses would have none of an *government* "imperialist peace" and demanded an immediate peace "without annexations or indemnities and based on the right of nations to decide their own affairs."   Public clamor and the organized agitation in the soviets induced the government to "move to the left," adopting the radical peace for-

[1] Nearly all the radical leaders were known by aliases.

mula as its own and placing more socialists in the cabinet. Terestchenko replaced Miliukov; Kerensky, the former Minister of Justice, became Minister of War. The new government was a coalition, about equally divided between socialist and "bourgeois" parties, which probably reflected fairly enough the division of opinion in the country at large at the moment. But it had lost the confidence of many conservative men who had supported the first provisional government and had not yet conciliated the Bolsheviki who demanded an all-socialist ministry from which the bourgeois parties would be rigorously excluded.

In spite of their desire to make an early peace without conquests and the unwillingness of Britain, France and *Attempt to restore the eastern front* Italy to consent to a drastic downward revision of their war aims, the new government still aimed to remain loyal to the Entente Alliance. Kerensky did all that oratory can do to revive enthusiasm at the front, but the effect of his appeals was temporary while the forces of disintegration were permanent. Not until July did the Russian army feel strong enough to resume the offensive, and this attempt served only to reveal how unreliable the Russian soldier had become. Soldiers' committees sent delegates to the soviets, supervised the officers and even issued military orders. The government had no authority and could rely only on patriotic speeches. A few Cossack regiments set a good example and a "women's battalion of death" was organized to shame the men into renewed efforts but in vain. In July a vigorous offensive into Galicia reached the city of Halicz, passing beyond the high-water mark of the 1916 campaign, but before a fortnight had passed the attack utterly broke down. Several cases have been reported of soldiers, having advanced a certain position, deliberately stopping to debate whether they should halt there or advance still further. The military result of a combat between a disciplined German army and a soldiers' debating society may be imagined! After suffering frightful losses, the Russian army abandoned Galicia and Bukovina, thus entirely freeing Austrian soil from the invader. Isolated Rumania was left to her fate.

Coincident with these disasters at the front, fresh riots broke out in Petrograd. Armed men in motors cars passed through the streets terrorizing the populace and *The third* the authorities. This July insurrection was put *provisional* down after a few days of anarchy in the capital. *government* But the rising tide of radical and pacifist sentiment forced out of office Prince Lvov, head of the first and second coalition ministries, and Kerensky became the chief of state. The new government was mainly socialist in color though it contained none of the Bolsheviki. Another change was made in the military command. In August General Kornilov succeeded Brussilov as head of the army.

Alexander Kerensky was the last hope of those who wished at once to preserve the fruits of the revolution and keep Russia in the war. His personal prestige was *Kerensky* great, for he had been one of the most popular and fearless radical leaders before the revolution and had been active in each provisional ministry. As Minister of Justice he had kept the popular vengeance within bounds and repeatedly saved Russia from the disgrace of lynch law. As Minister of War he had done more than any other man to infuse patriotism in the demoralized army. But when he became Prime Minister his personal power and his popularity alike declined. Always physically weak, his heroic exertions told heavily on his judgment, temper and power to work, and the rout of the army clouded his early optimism. A note of despair crept into his later speeches. "My strength is failing," he once said, "because I no longer have my old confidence that we have before us not revolting slaves but conscious citizens creating a new state with an enthusiasm worthy of the Russian nation. Alas that I did not die two months ago, for then I should have died in the splendid dream that once and for all a new life had dawned for Russia!"

An inevitable result of the political conflicts of the revolution was a falling-off in the productive power of the nation.

The industrial collapse Factory workers took the power from their employers just as the soldiers had done from their officers. The working day was cut from twelve to eight or six hours, wages were doubled and trebled, bosses were forbidden to discharge workmen. Strikes and street demonstrations interrupted factory routine. The always inadequate transportation system of Russia fell into complete chaos; to take a train was an adventure, the outcome of which depended on the whim of the train crew. When we add that Russia was in no case an important manufacturing nation, that many of the most important industrial centers were in Russian Poland and other provinces occupied by the enemy, that Russia could not import on a large scale from any other country, it is evident that even if there had been no defeatism at the front the Russian soldiers before long would have had to face the enemy with empty hands unless in some way the Russian mines, factories and railways could be restored to relative efficiency.

The failure of the Russian campaign in Galicia encouraged the German army to break the Russian lines farther north.

The military collapse So a vigorous offensive was started in the Baltic provinces, where part of the population was German in speech and sympathy and the Lithuanian, Lett and Estonian majority were at least divided in sentiment. In September, 1917, the Germans captured Riga, the chief city of Livonia, and next to Petrograd itself the most important Russian Baltic port. With little difficulty they seized also some island outposts and prepared for a descent on Estonia. Petrograd was in danger, and popular confidence in the Kerensky government shaken. For practical purposes Russia was almost out of the war and Kerensky informed Russia's allies that he could do little more. But neither he nor they realized how widespread had become the demand for peace at any price.

In a desperate attempt to gain moral authority for the government and restore discipline in the army, a general conference was summoned in August, made up *The* of representatives from city councils, rural *Moscow* zemstvos, co-operative societies, trades unions, *conference* commercial organizations and other public agencies. It was not a legislative body like the old Duma or the proposed Constituent Assembly but merely an advisory council for the emergency. On the whole the Moscow Conference was conservative in tenor. Premier Kerensky had to listen to many reproofs for not taking sufficiently drastic measures to repress mutiny at the front. Distinguished officers, such as Generals Kornilov and Kaledin, demanded the death penalty for deserters. Kornilov, the romantic war hero who had escaped from an Austrian prison and risen to command of the army, was the hero of the occasion and began to cherish the delusion that Russia would accept him as dictator and "savior of society" if the provisional government failed in its task.

General Kornilov, convinced by the fall of Riga that drastic measures were necessary, proposed a reconstruction of the provisional government with himself as *Kornilov* commander-in-chief holding supreme civil and *bids for* military control. This proposal alarmed Keren- *power* sky who as a socialist and veteran of the revolution feared that a military dictatorship might jeopardize all the gains of the revolution and perhaps restore the Tsardom. On September 9 he announced that Kornilov had been removed from his command. Instead of submitting, the general replied with a proclamation of defiance and marched on Petrograd with an army consisting largely of troops from

the Caucasus, the so-called "Savage Division." But the
army as a whole rallied to the government and even the
Bolsheviki gave it a transitory support as the lesser of two
evils. Kornilov's army melted like snow and his entire enterprise collapsed. The effect of the incident was most unfortunate. It deprived the army of the services of an able
general and discredited all who worked with him for a restoration of military discipline. At the same time it alienated the conservatives from the government and made
Kerensky entirely dependent on radical support. The
provisional government formally proclaimed the republic,
so as to set at rest any rumor that the Constituent Assembly
might provide for a monarchical constitution. Another
national conference met, but this time it took the name of the
Democratic Conference and was more radical in composition
than the Moscow Conference had been. It favored the calling of a provisional Parliament until a Constituent Assembly
could be elected. The Bolsheviki demanded an immediate
election.

During the early months of the revolution the All-Russian
Congress of Soviets and the Central Executive Committee
The Bolshe- which represented it between meetings were
viki capture socialist but not Bolshevist. The complex
the soviets hierarchy of soviets were radical enough to give
the provisional government a great deal of trouble but
had not yet aspired to exclusive authority or broken definitely with the national authorities. But the Bolsheviki
captured many local soviets in the summer and autumn of
1917. In Petrograd a prominent Bolshevist Leon Trotsky
(Bronstein) replaced the Menshevist Tcheidze as head of
the local soviet. This facilitated the Bolshevist plans for a
coup d'état in the capital. Though, chiefly to embarrass the
government, they had agitated for an immediate election
of the Constituent Assembly, their enthusiasm for it faded
when their capture of the soviets placed a new weapon in

their hand. Why bother with uncertain future elections when a single blow might make the Bolshevized Congress of Soviets the master of Russia? By the end of October all plans were complete for a new and more radical revolution which would wipe out all remnants of bourgeois capitalism and liberalism from the world's first socialistic commonwealth.

On November 6, the Red Guards (revolutionary regiments acting under Bolshevist orders) seized the public buildings in Petrograd. On the following day *The* they placed under arrest the ministers of the *November* provisional government, though Kerensky him- *revolution* self managed to escape. The All-Russian Congress of Soviets approved the new revolution and accepted the authority of the new government. Unlike the earlier ministries, the Council of Peoples' Commissars, which was the executive branch of the government, was drawn entirely from a single political party. It did not even represent the whole of Russian socialism, merely the Bolshevist faction. As little consideration was shown to the Social Revolutionaries and the Menshevik Social Democrats as to the bourgeois parties. Lenin, the party leader, assumed charge of the Council of Peoples' Commissars. Trotsky, the leader of the Petrograd Soviet, became Commissar for Foreign Affairs.

Foreign observers looked on the revolution in Petrograd as merely an interesting episode in the growing chaos of Russian politics. Petrograd was a disaffected *The destruc-* city with radical traditions, its garrison was not *tion of the* the whole army. But Moscow also deserted *Constituent* Kerensky. The army failed to answer his ap- *Assembly* peal. The one remaining hope of the opponents of the new dictatorship was the coming Constituent Assembly, elected on a basis of universal adult suffrage. This was the most democratic body Russia has ever known. It did not overweight the propertied classes like the old Duma, nor totally exclude them like the Congress of Soviets. Elections took place on November 25. The result showed that Russian sentiment had moved far on the radical road. The Constitutional Democrats and other middle class groups almost disappeared and even the Menshevik Social Democrats made little showing. But the Bolsheviki were disappointed in their hope of a complete triumph at the polls. Though they carried Moscow, Petrograd and other large cities, the Social Revolutionaries, strong among the peasantry and in distant provinces, had a majority. On January 18, 1918, the Constituent Assembly met in Petrograd under the armed menace of Red Guards and sailors from the Baltic fleet. The few conservative members dared not appear. By a vote of 244 to 153 the Social Revolutionaries chose their leader Tchernov against the Bolshevist nominee, Maria Spiridonova, for president of the Assembly. They refused also to accept a declaration transferring all governmental power to the soviets. The Bolsheviki thereupon left the Assembly, and on the next day forcibly dispersed it in Tsarist fashion. The dream of a democratic Russia was at an end.

The disasters of the war had brought the Bolsheviki into power; only an immediate peace could keep them there. *Russia asks peace* On coming into power the new government proposed a general armistice. The western Allies, still refusing to recognize the Bolshevist revolution as anything but a tragic interlude, paid no attention to the proposal. The Germans, on the contrary, encouraged the Russian negotiations, not indeed hoping such a general peace to ensue as Russia desired, but seeing an opportunity to make a separate peace with Russia and thus break up the coalition which hemmed them in. On December 15, 1917, a definite armistice signed at Brest-Litovsk by representatives of Soviet Russia and of the Central Powers put a term to Russia's participation in the war.

In capturing the public buildings of Petrograd the Bol-

sheviki obtained possession of the secret documents of the
old Russian government. Trotsky, as Commis-   *Publication*
sar for Foreign Affairs, ordered their immediate   *of the secret*
publication. At the same time he warned the   *treaties*
Central Powers that they had as many skeletons in their
own closets:

> When the German proletariat, by revolutionary means, gets
> access to the secrets of its government chancelleries, it will pro-
> duce documents from them of just the same nature as those
> which we are now publishing.

A prophecy fulfilled to the letter in the following November!
The Soviet government followed its repudiation of Russia's
diplomatic obligations by repudiating all foreign financial
obligations as well, and the national loans advanced mainly
by France were wiped off the slate.

On December 22, 1917, formal negotiations opened. The
German government sent Foreign Secretary Richard von
Kühlmann, Austria-Hungary sent Count Czer-   *The Brest-*
nin. These civilian emissaries would have made *Litovsk ne-*
a conciliatory peace to hasten the withdrawal *gotiations*
of Russia from the war, but they were overruled by the military authorities who realized the utter prostration of Russia
and were not afraid of abusing their victory. General Hoffmann, one of the German military delegates, frequently interrupted proceedings with threats which seemed to embarrass his civilian colleagues as greatly as they embarrassed
the Russian envoys. Impatiently he blurted out the hard
truth:

> I must protest against the tone of these proposals. The
> Russian delegation talks to us as if it stood victorious in our
> countries and could dictate conditions to us. I would like to
> point out that the facts are just the reverse and that the vic-
> torious German army stands in your territory.

Kühlmann apologized on one occasion for this truculent attitude. "If General Hoffmann," he said, "expresses these
terms more strongly, it is because a soldier always uses

stronger language than diplomats." The Russian delegates, acting under the instructions of Trotsky as Commissar for Foreign Affairs, had a most difficult task. They realized that Russia had no heart and no arms for a renewal of the war and that resistance would mean destruction. On the other hand, to yield too much and too easily would seem to justify the taunt of their political opponents that they were "German agents." They followed, therefore, an intermediate course, not openly rejecting the demands of the Central Powers but playing for time and secretly endeavoring to foment revolutionary movements among the German soldiers. This had little influence at the time, while the Germans were still confident of an early peace with victory, but later, when the tide of war began to turn against them, the seeds planted by Trotsky's agents began to sprout.

The main point at issue in the prolonged debates of Brest-Litovsk was the fate of the nationalities torn from the Russian Empire by war or revolution; especially

Self-deter-mination and the nationalities Poland, Lithuania, Courland, Livonia, Estonia, Finland and the Ukraine. The Russian delegates made no claims to these countries, but insisted that the German and Austro-Hungarian armies evacuate all former Russian territories and leave them to the "self-determination" of their inhabitants. The Central Powers conceded the "principle" of self-determination but refused the military evacuation which alone could have given it reality. They knew well enough that the masses of the Polish, Lithuanian and Ukrainian peasantry were not friendly, but they hoped by political and military pressure to coerce their provisional governments into accepting treaties and constitutions "made in Germany." Various Teutonic princes were tentatively proposed for Poland and the other Baltic countries but nothing was definitely settled. In each case it was hoped that, whatever constitutional arrangements might ultimately be made, commercial treaties and military alliances would bind the new nations of eastern Europe into such dependence on the Central Powers that even without annexations the war might be counted a victory. This, of course, was exactly what France and Britain feared.

Of all the losses threatening Russia the sorest was the Ukraine or "Little Russia." Such lands as Poland and Finland had never been thoroughly Russified *The* and their loss would strike no blow at Russian *Ukrainian* unity though it might reduce Russian resources. *republic* But in the vast plains of southwestern Russia lived a people akin to other Russians by language and culture. These Ukrainians ("borderlanders") numbered some 30,000,000 in Russia and counted as kinfolk more than 4,000,000 Ruthenians in Austria-Hungary. With the Russian revolution of 1917 the Ukrainians put forward demands for autonomy and took advantage of the Bolshevist upheaval to enlarge autonomy into complete independence. The Central Powers insisted on separate negotiations with the Ukraine and aimed to split it from Russia proper. Further to conciliate the Ukraine, they "rectified" the frontier a little at the expense of Poland and thereby alienated the Poles, who were already debating the value of an "independence" in such close subordination to Austria and Germany.

Finland never had anything in common with Russia except a common — and involuntary — subjection to the Tsar. Alien in race, language, faith, history, *The* tradition, culture and national sentiment, the *Finnish* Finns desired only to find the first opportunity *republic* to break the connection. The Russian republic had offered Finland autonomy, but the revolution made this hard to define. Under the Tsars, autonomy had meant a personal union between the Empire of Russia and the Grand Duchy of Finland with the Tsardom as the common link; but there

was now no ruling family to command the allegiance of any
Finn, and to become a part of Russia by any new or closer
tie ran counter to every national instinct.   With the Bolshevist revolution Finland flung off even the name of allegiance, and in December, 1917, became an independent state.

Unfortunately the Finnish republic came into existence
at a time of economic crisis and acute class hostility.   A
The class new diet had been elected and the Socialists lost
war in their former majority.   A radical wing of the
Finland party, sympathizing with the Russian Bolsheviki
and desirous to establish a dictatorship of the proletariat
in Finland on the Russian model, started an insurrection.
In the chaotic civil war which followed, the rivalry of the
Finnish-speaking peasants with their Swedish compatriots,
the rancor of the tenant against his landlord, the fear that
the conservative parties were selling the national independence to Germany, the counter-fear that the radicals would
bring about reunion with Soviet Russia, and the desperation
born of a terrible famine which was slaying the poor by
thousands, all played a part in confusing the issues and en-
hancing the bitterness of the struggle.   The Finnish Bolshe-
vists and their Russian allies ravaged southern Finland,
butchering without mercy all the "bourgeoisie" who opposed them.   A volunteer militia of "White Guards" in
northern and western Finland opposed the advance of the
"Reds" and appealed for foreign aid.   Sweden was afraid
to act, lest she be drawn into the vortex of a war with Russia,
the western powers were too busy to help, but Germany
spared some regiments, sent aid to the Whites and crushed
the Bolshevist rebellion.   In their gratitude for German aid,
the Finns came greatly under German influence.   In March,
1918, a peace treaty between Germany and Finland provided for friendly neutrality on the part of the latter and
close diplomatic and commercial ties with Germany.   Even
a German prince was suggested, the reaction against red

radicalism having converted many Finnish republicans to monarchy.

In February, 1918, the peace negotiations with Russia broke down. The Ukrainian Rada (parliament) made a separate peace, much to the disappointment of *Russia* the western Allies who had hoped that since the *makes* Ukraine was non-Bolshevist it might continue in *peace with-* *out a treaty* the war even if Soviet Russia withdrew. The peace with the Ukraine on February 9 was followed on February 10 by the withdrawal of Soviet Russia from the war. On Trotsky's advice the Russian delegation refused to sign any peace treaty but declared war at an end. No doubt Trotsky hoped that this unusual step would appeal to the German Socialists and bring about a general strike if not an actual rebellion in case the German militarists tried further to prosecute the war against an unresisting socialist republic. Vain delusion! The German armies advanced into Russia encountering no real resistance, and the German Socialists contented themselves with mild parliamentary remonstrances. Some of the more fiery spirits among the Bolsheviki counseled armed resistance to the new German invasion, since it was not directed against a Tsarist or "bourgeois" Russia but against the proletarian revolution. But Lenin advised submission, pointing out the impossibility of effective resistance and the certainty that a German triumph would overthrow the Bolshevist régime.

On March 3, 1918, the treaty of Brest-Litovsk was signed. Those who signed it must have felt that they were signing the death warrant of Russia as she had *The Treaty* been. All the borderlands of Russian Poland, *of Brest-* Lithuania and the Baltic Provinces passed from *Litovsk* Russian rule and their future fate was left to German determination. Turkey reoccupied Erivan, Kars and Batum in Russian Armenia. Russia had to acknowledge the separation of Finland and the Ukraine. By a later agreement

Russia had to pay a war indemnity of 6,000,000,000 marks ($1,500,000,000) for war losses to German subjects and for the care of Russian prisoners of war. The Entente Allies refused to recognize the treaty or the government which had made it, but the President of the United States sent a message of sympathy "to assure the people of Russia" that the American government "will avail itself of every opportunity to secure for Russia once more complete sovereignty and independence."

Rumania, left without support from Russia or the Ukraine, had no choice but to make peace on whatever terms the *The Treaty of Bucharest* Central Powers would grant. The southern Dobrudja, won from Bulgaria by Rumania in the second Balkan War, was returned to Bulgaria. The northern Dobrudja, Rumanian since 1878, passed under the joint control of the Central Powers, as the Turks raised some objection to giving the Bulgarians the whole district. Along the Austro-Hungarian frontier a narrow ribbon of territory was torn away to give the mountain passes of the Carpathians to the Dual Monarchy, but as compensation for these losses Rumania was allowed to occupy part of Bessarabia at the cost of Russia. Economic provisions of the peace gave the Central Powers leasehold control over the petroleum fields of Rumania, modified the Rumanian tariff and regulated the administration of the Danube river. Rumania agreed to make peace in March, 1918, and the details were finally agreed to in May. The rich grain harvests of Rumania and the Ukraine relieved the threatened pressure of famine in Germany and Austria.[1]

Acting under German pressure the Russians tried to disarm the Austro-Hungarian prisoners, mainly of Czecho-Slovak nationality, who had been captured by Russia dur-

[1] The treaty with the Ukraine was nicknamed "the bread peace," because of the food supplies imported by Germany and Austria-Hungary after Brest-Litovsk. Count Czernin comments: "The millions whose lives were saved by those 42,000 wagon-loads of food may repeat the words 'bread peace' without a sneer."

ing the early phases of the war. They were ardently pro-
Entente in sympathy and had in many cases *The anaba-*
surrendered voluntarily in order to escape the *sis of the*
hated Austrian service. Refusing to disarm, *Czecho-Slo-*
they seized rolling stock on the Trans-Siberian *vaks*
railway and fought their way across Siberia to the far eastern
port of Vladivostok, opposing German and Austrian armies
in the Ukraine, Bolshevist Red Guards sent to disarm them,
and German prisoners of war. This successful retreat was
one of the most dramatic chapters in the war and did much
to win the good will of the Entente towards the demand for
Czecho-Slovak independence, but it sharpened the antagonism between the Entente and Soviet Russia.

The eastern battlefront had disappeared and the resources
of the Central Powers could now be concentrated against
the western Allies. Poland, Lithuania, Cour- *Russia in*
land, Livonia, Estonia, Finland, even Rumania, *1918*
had become dependencies, client states, of the Central
Powers. The nationalities of the Caucasus were in rebellion. Only in Russia proper could the Bolsheviki establish
a consolidated rule and even there they were everywhere
threatened by foreign intervention or domestic counter-
revolution. Japanese and Czecho-Slovaks guarded Vladivostok. American and British soldiers occupied the Arctic
seaboard of European Russia, at Archangel and along the
Murman coast. In Siberia a forlorn band of exiles from
the former Constituent Assembly tried to maintain the
nucleus of a liberal republican government at Omsk, but in
November, 1918, the scattered anti-Bolshevist factions in
Siberia were forcibly welded into a whole by the dictatorship
of Admiral Alexander Kolchak. The revolution that was
to bring to Russia "peace, bread and freedom" had substituted a dozen civil wars for one foreign war, had permitted
famine to spread throughout the land, and had given the
people no freedom but the choice of submitting to the iron

dictatorship of the Bolsheviki or to the scarcely less drastic rule of the scattered counter-revolutionary armies. The Bolsheviki presented a compact front and a more than military discipline to their disunited and irresolute adversaries and eventually established over a somewhat diminished Russia a firmer rule than Tsardom ever knew.

CHAPTER XVII

THE COLLAPSE OF THE CENTRAL POWERS

NINETEEN hundred and seventeen was an eventful year in the World War but not a decisive one. The effect of Germany's submarine campaign was counterbal- *Defeatism* anced by the entrance of the United States into *in 1917* the war. The growing weakness of Russia was offset by unmistakable signs of economic exhaustion in Austria-Hungary and to a lesser degree in Germany. The considerable gains made by the British and French on the western front, which would have been very welcome in 1915 or 1916, fell so far short of popular hopes of victory as to provoke a reaction of profound discouragement. It was a war-weary year marked by many peace proposals and movements of popular discontent. Only in Russia did this go the extreme of revolution and surrender, but in every belligerent nation — with the exception of the United States which was still in the stage of preparation for effort — symptoms of collapse could be discerned.

From October, 1914, to March, 1917, the western battlefront had remained almost stationary, the greatest changes being the German advance on the outer forts of *The German retreat* Verdun and the Anglo-French drive north and *man retreat* south of the Somme. Tactical gains had been *in France* made from time to time but no general strategic movement seemed possible for either side. The German command decided, however, that the time had now come for a considerable withdrawal to stronger prepared positions in the rear (the "Hindenburg line"), obtaining a more defensible battlefront at the cost of about a thousand square miles of

French territory. Before the retirement was effected, the Germans systematically laid waste the entire abandoned area, burning towns and villages, cutting down fruit trees, throwing rubbish in the wells, destroying the roads, so that the advancing armies would face a man-made desert. In the hope of broadening this retreat a British army near Arras and a French army near Soissons struck at the pivots, north and south, of the new Hindenburg entrenchments. In both cases the initial success was encouraging. The British captured Vimy Ridge and the French occupied the famous Chemin des Dames, a road cresting the heights north of the Aisne. Later in the year the French recaptured nearly all that they had lost before Verdun and the British literally blasted their way forward through the mud of Flanders by heavy artillery fire and underground mine explosions. But there was still no decisive break through the line, nor prospect of any.

Very ominous was the fact, carefully concealed at the time by censorship, that in one of General Nivelle's offensives several French regiments had flinched *Clemenceau, the last resort of France* from the attack as a useless bloody sacrifice. The superb morale of the French soldier had been the very cornerstone of the Entente strategy from the beginning of the war. The civil government also showed weakness. Until Georges Clemenceau took the premiership in November, 1917, the ministers had not dared risk a conclusive struggle with the forces of "defeatism." Radical pacifist papers, such as the *Bonnet Rouge*, carried on open propaganda against the prolongation of the war while professional politicians, their most prominent exponent being the veteran parliamentary leader Joseph Caillaux, more cautiously hinted that too high a price might be paid for victory. The government turned to Clemenceau reluctantly, as he had the reputation of being an uncomfortable, obdurate, intractable sort of man whose sharp journalistic criticisms of statesmen and generals had given the censor much trouble. He had those prickly qualities without question, but all his faults were balanced by his white hot patriotism and his indomitable resolution. From the day of his premiership to the end of the war there was no longer any question of a weakening of the French will to victory. He replied to all question of policy that his program was only "I make war," and he had such doubters as Caillaux arrested for disloyalty. In Marshal Ferdinand Foch, who had been before and was again to be a political enemy of Clemenceau, France found a similar tenacious will to place in supreme military command of the Allied armies.

Great Britain was less exhausted than France but at the same time less engrossed in the immediate combat and able to view the war in a more impersonal spirit. A *British war* pacifist minority represented by the Union of *politics* Democratic Control and some of the leaders of the Independent Labor Party had opposed the war from the beginning. Now even conservatives began to wonder if the game were worth the candle. Lord Lansdowne, an eminent leader of the Conservative Party, declared in November, 1917, "if the war is to be brought to a close in time to avert a world-wide catastrophe, it will be brought to a close because on both sides the peoples of the countries involved realize that it has already lasted too long." In 1916 David Lloyd George, a man with much of Clemenceau's combativeness, had replaced the former Prime Minister, Herbert Asquith, whose calm and deliberate mind was better suited to working out the problems of peace time than to meeting the urgent emergencies of war. A small "war cabinet" which included only a few of the ministers of state made decisions for the whole government. Conscription was introduced for Great Britain, but not in Ireland where a serious rebellion in Easter week of 1916 showed an untamed spirit of national resistance which the British government preferred not to rouse.[1]

Italian defeatism was far more widespread than French or British. Italian opinion had been divided as to the ad-

Italian defeatism vantages of entering the war; Germany was not considered "the" enemy so much as Austria. Moreover, the military situation was most discouraging. The Italian offensive toward Trieste had ended in a prolonged deadlock, an endless, wearisome struggle in which the capture of a barren ridge of limestone was a "great victory" for which thousands of lives must be spent. Bread riots in the factory towns, indiscipline in the trenches, whispers of the new doctrine of Bolshevism among the more radical, alarming rumors of civilian famine circulated by German agents among the war-weary soldiers, dulled the fighting edge of some divisions on the Isonzo. Here, therefore, the Germans planned an attack, not only in the hope of taking advantage of defeatism in Italy but in the desperate need of forestalling the equally serious defeatist movement in Austria-Hungary.

Thrice already Germany had been called on to lend a "stiffening" of leadership to an Austrian offensive: against

The Caporetto disaster the Russians in Galicia, against the Serbians, and against the Rumanians. Once again, this time against Italy, German divisions formed the spearhead of an Austrian attack. During the last days of October, 1917, a violent assault, aided by all the terrors of modern artillery and poison gas, overwhelmed the Italian forces on the upper Isonzo, just across the Austrian frontier. At Caporetto the Italian line broke and permitted an Austro-German army of invasion to penetrate past the frontier hills to the Venetian plains. The whole Italian army was thus forced to retreat, as otherwise there might be danger that unbroken regiments still holding to their original positions

[1] For the revolutionary movement in Ireland see below, Chapter XXIX.

might be surrounded. After the first rout, the Italians managed the retreat with skill and made full use of the rivers of
the Venetian plain to delay the enemy. Along the Piave the
Italian line held. Venice was saved and the patriotic energy
of the nation restored. But Austria had also been freed from
pressure and saved to the Central Powers for another year.

As some slight offset to the crushing defeat of Russia and
Rumania and the collapse of the Italian invasion of Austria,
the Entente recovered its lost prestige in the *A silver*
Ottoman Empire. In March, 1917, a British *lining in the Orient*
army entered Bagdad, thus avenging the former
Turkish victories in Mesopotamia. In December another
force under General Allenby entered Jerusalem. In both
campaigns the British were greatly aided by the Arabs,
subjects of the Ottoman Empire and zealous Mohammedans
by faith but convinced by the propaganda of Colonel
Lawrence and other British agents that the interests of the
creed of Islam were not bound up with the political fortunes
of the Turkish Sultan. One Arabian state, the Kingdom of
the Hedjaz, proclaimed open independence of Turkey, while
the Arabs of Syria, Mesopotamia and Palestine, hostile at
first, shifted to a watchful neutrality and finally a sympathetic co-operation as the British armies advanced.

The resumption of unrestricted submarine warfare had
closed the door to peace opened by President Wilson's mediation, and the gestures toward peace from Russia *Peace*
were treated with indifference by the Entente *overtures in 1917*
Powers and led the Central Powers only to take
advantage of Russia's extremity in the negotiations at Brest-
Litovsk. Nevertheless war aims and peace proposals were
more frequently discussed than before. On July 19, 1917,
the German Reichstag passed a resolution in favor of a peace
of "mutual understanding" with the comment that "forced
acquisitions of territory and political, economic, and financial
oppressions are incompatible with such a peace." This

formula was vague enough, but it seemed to point toward a restoration of the frontiers of 1914, Germany agreeing to abandon all conquests if the Entente Allies would do the same and further discard all plans for a commercial boycott such as were projected at the Paris conference in 1916. The peace resolution was carried by a coalition of the Socialists and the Center (Roman Catholic) parties against the opposition of the Conservatives and National Liberals who more nearly represented the views of the government. Chancellor Michaelis, the authorized spokesman of the Kaiser, was evasive, declaring that he accepted the Reichstag resolution "as I understand it."

In August Pope Benedict XV ventured the task of neutral mediation in which President Wilson had failed. He urged the belligerent nations to subordinate territorial questions to the important issues of disarmament and arbitration and to renounce indemnities and claims for reparation. All the leading nations expressed courteous approval of the Papal peace initiative, but all refused to restate their terms of peace in more acceptable fashion. In fact Chancellor Michaelis bluntly told the German Reichstag that he "must at present decline to specify war aims" and President Wilson declared that "We cannot take the word of the present rulers of Germany as a guarantee of anything that is to endure, unless explicitly supported by such conclusive evidence of the will and purpose of the German people themselves as the other peoples of the world would be justified in accepting."

The Pope offers an olive branch

Austria-Hungary, next only to Russia, was the power most weary of the war, not alone because of military and economic pressure but because a war to the bitter end might mean complete disruption, the loss of all Slavic and Latin provinces. From the German point of view Austria was no longer "pulling her own weight in the boat"; however useful as a source of commodities and

Austrian efforts for peace

recruits, she had become incapable of initiating any successful campaign except under German leadership. From the
Austrian angle, Germany was a bullying partner, ever pro-
longing the war for the sake of imperialistic gains which were
in her interest alone. In November, 1916, the aged Francis
Joseph died and an untried ruler came to the helm. The new
Emperor Charles (Karl) was restive under German domination and desired an early peace even at the cost of some
sacrifices on the part of both realms. He tried to get into
touch with Britain, France and Italy by means of various
channels in neutral Switzerland. In a noteworthy letter sent
through Prince Sixtus of Bourbon to the French government
he even secretly promised to support the "just claims of
France to Alsace-Lorraine." Czernin, his foreign minister,
sounded out German opinion but with no success; to all proposals for concessions and compromises on the Alsace-Lorraine question Germany turned a deaf ear.[1]

The question then remained, could or would Austria-
Hungary have made a separate peace and left Germany in
the lurch? The Entente Allies thought not. On several
fronts Austrian armies were really under German command,
German and Austro-Hungarian troops were freely mingled,
and any open attempt to break with Germany might have
led to a German *coup d'état* at Vienna and the replacement
of Charles by a more docile ruler. The Entente statesmen
turned away from the tempting Austrian proposals, the most
generous offered by any of the Central Powers during the
entire course of the war, as the bait in a trap, a mere attempt
to sow dissension among the Allies. Another reason for rejection of the Austrian peace proposals lay in the fact that
Italy was not satisfied with what was promised her and
thought to obtain better terms by continuing the war — this
was before the Caporetto disaster!

[1] Von Kühlmann, the German foreign minister, declared in 1917 that "the
question for which Europe is being turned into a rubbish heap is Alsace-Lorraine."

Where princes of church and state had failed could labor succeed? In general the trades unionists and socialists of *Labor ef-* Europe were closer together in their minimum *forts for* peace terms than were the aristocracies, the busi- *peace* ness men or the professional diplomats and parliamentarians, and the Russian revolution created new hopes that peace might be brought about either through Russian and American mediation or by a general European revolution. The British Labor Party put forth a detailed peace program, stressing the establishment of a League of Nations and "self-determination" as the basis for fixing the new frontiers. An attempt to hold a labor conference in neutral Stockholm in 1917 failed as several of the Entente nations refused to participate. The German Socialists were sharply divided, the majority group, headed by Ebert, Scheidemann and other influential politicians, voted for war credits and favored a peace which would have left frontiers much as they were in 1914; a minority of Independent Socialists attacked the war as imperialistic and demanded the application of self-determination to the national minorities in central Europe as well as in enemy countries.

Premier Lloyd George redefined the British position on January 5, 1918. For the Entente the winter of 1917–18 *British war* was the dark hour before the dawn; Russia had *aims re-* been eliminated, Italy thrown back on the de- *stated* fensive, and Germany was preparing the heaviest attack of the war on the western front. Under the circumstances the British statement was very moderate and even in some respects represented a retreat from positions previously taken. Assurances were offered that "a break-up of Austria-Hungary is no part of our war aims" provided that "genuine self-government" were granted to the minor nationalities of the Dual Monarchy. While Arabia, Armenia, Mesopotamia, Syria and Palestine were to be freed from Turkish rule and the Straits internationalized, "we do not challenge the maintenance of the Turkish Empire in the homelands of the Turkish race with its capital at Constantinople." With these concessions, the terms stated followed the lines marked out by the Entente reply to President Wilson a year earlier. All occupied territory must be evacuated and restored to complete independence. Reparation must be made for injuries inflicted by invasion. France must gain Alsace-Lorraine and Italy her unredeemed provinces.

On January 8, 1918, President Wilson laid before Congress a statement of his views of the eventual peace settlement. Because it was far more definite than any other *Wilson's* public peace program issued during the war and *fourteen* because it formed, in part, the basis on which *points* peace was later actually negotiated, the address of President Wilson has a unique significance. In summary:

I. Open covenants of peace, openly arrived at.

II. Absolute freedom of navigation upon the seas... except as the seas may be closed... by international action.

III. The removal, so far as possible, of all economic barriers and the establishment of an equality of trade conditions among all the nations consenting to the peace.

IV. Adequate guarantees given and taken that national armaments will be reduced to the lowest point consistent with domestic safety.

V. A free, open-minded, and absolutely impartial adjustment of all colonial claims.

VI. The evacuation of all Russian territory.

VII. Belgium... must be evacuated and restored, without any attempt to limit the sovereignty which she enjoys.

VIII. All French territory should be freed and the invaded portions restored, and the wrong done to France by Prussia in 1871 in the matter of Alsace-Lorraine... should be righted.

IX. A readjustment of the frontiers of Italy... along clearly recognizable lines of nationality.

X. The peoples of Austria-Hungary... should be accorded the freest opportunity of autonomous development.

XI. Rumania, Serbia and Montenegro should be evacuated, occupied territories restored, Serbia accorded free and secure access to the sea.

XII. The Turkish portions of the present Ottoman Empire should be assured a secure sovereignty, but the other nationalities which are now under Turkish rule should be assured an undoubted security of life and an absolutely unmolested opportunity of autonomous development, and the Dardanelles should be permanently opened.

XIII. An independent Polish state should be erected which should include the territories inhabited by indisputably Polish populations, which should be assured a free and secure access to the sea.

XIV. A general association of nations must be formed under specific covenants for the purpose of affording mutual guarantees of political independence and territorial integrity.

In numerous subsequent statements President Wilson increasingly stressed the last point, the League of Nations, as "the most essential part of the peace settlement."

While these diplomatic interchanges were proceeding both sides looked forward to a final struggle in the spring of 1918.

*Prepara-
tions for
the 1918
offensive*
Russia had collapsed in 1917, it was practically certain that Austria-Hungary would follow that example in 1918 unless a military decision were reached. The German High Command realized that it *must* be the last campaign for never again could conditions for victory be so favorable. Russia had reached the lowest point of dissolution in the anarchic interval between the old régime and the new. Italy still reeled from the blow of Caporetto. The other Entente Allies, save only France and Britain, were too distant or weak to play a decisive part in the struggle. The British and French must then be defeated, and at once, because the failure of the submarine campaign left an open road across the Atlantic for the new American armies. A few months' delay and Germany would be faced with greater odds than ever before. Too frequently had the Entente Allies consoled themselves with the half truth that "time fights on our side," for while the prolongation of the war had permitted the full mobilization of the British Empire it had also permitted Russia to break under

the strain of repeated disappointment. But now there seemed some truth in the saying, for America had taken nearly a year to organize her military resources and stood ready to fling them into the balance against Germany.

While the Russian situation was still doubtful Germany played a waiting game, economizing man power by remaining on the defensive and by ingeniously adapting the *The German plans* conditions of trench warfare so that smaller forces could hold the front. The new entrenchments covered a wider zone and hinged on small concrete-domed machine gun nests (the "pillboxes") which could give the enemy endless trouble to eliminate by artillery fire before any safe advance was possible. The German offensive tactics also aimed at an economy of men. Instead of flinging their hosts forward in living waves, as formerly against Verdun, the new method relied on the skill of a few chosen veterans, "storm troops," who seized strategic points in the hostile line and thus permitted the "infiltration" of the army through the breaches so created. These improved tactics were due largely to the twin dictators of Germany and indeed of all the Central Powers, Generals Paul von Hindenburg and Erich von Ludendorff, whose victories against Russia had placed them in supreme direction of the whole war.

Of course the necessity of a German offensive was as apparent to the French and British as to the Germans themselves. But the preparations were masked with *March 21,* sufficient care so that it remained uncertain ex- *1918* actly where the blow would be delivered. Along the western front Germany had 192 divisions against 169 for the Entente Allies; the transfer of German troops from the Russian front had given Germany a slight but sufficient numerical superiority for an offensive. From their superior forces the Germans selected the best storm troops and attacked along a fifty-mile front from east of Arras south to La Fère. The British were pushed back almost to Amiens, losing within a few days ground which had taken them three years to occupy together with nearly 90,000 prisoners of war. They suffered, though fighting on the defensive, losses as great as the Germans spent to win the battle. But there was no such "break through" as the Germans had made against the Russians in Galicia or the Italians at Caporetto. The British saved the integrity of the battle front and with it the war.

The results of the first attack had been so encouraging as to spur the German High Command to fresh efforts. They *Thor's hammer strikes again* struck again at the British, this time south of Ypres in the hope of capturing Channel ports which might be transformed from British transport landings to German submarine bases. Farther south German cannon bombarded Paris from a distance of seventy-five miles. A third German offensive, directed against the French lines between Rheims and Soissons, reached by the end of May, 1918, the old battle line of the Marne river. Soissons was taken and German trenches advanced to within forty-four miles of Paris. By July this effort reached an end. Every attack had won important territorial gains, but neither Paris nor the Channel ports were yet in German hands, and the hungry civilians and weary privates had expected at least one of these fruits of victory. The farthest extension of the German advance, and for that reason its weakest point, was the sharp salient whose base extended from Soissons to Rheims and whose apex reached Château Thierry. In June the American Second Division halted the German offensive by vigorous counter-attacks at Belleau Wood, the first important victory ever won by an American army on a European battlefield. But in July Ludendorff launched a fourth and final attack, striving to widen the Marne salient. Rheims still held out but on the west, near Soissons, the Germans advanced their trenches some six miles. Here the offensive halted.

One of the first effects of the March disaster was to teach

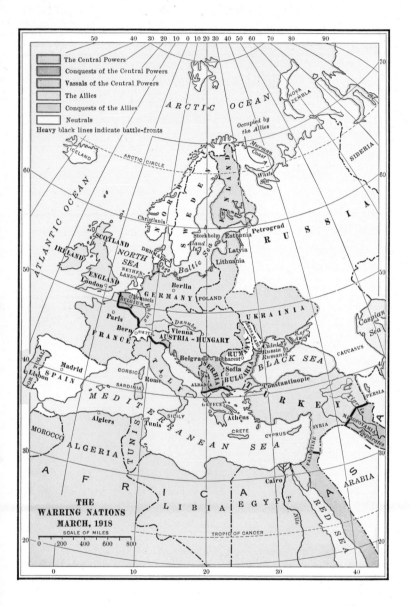

THE
WARRING NATIONS
MARCH, 1918

SCALE OF MILES

0   200   400   600   800

the Entente a lesson which should have been learned three and a half years earlier and could have been *The rally of* studied from all Germany's military successes — *the Entente* the need of unified command. The Central Powers, dominated by the German General Staff had fought the war as a unit; the Entente Allies as separate nations. Now in the ultimate emergency a supreme commander in chief was placed over the entire western war zone, Marshal Ferdinand Foch. The British brought every available man across the Channel and American soldiers were packed like sardines in transports for rapid shipment across the Atlantic. By midsummer Germany had lost her superiority of numbers and no way of restoring it was possible. Even as things were, the last recruits from Germany were inferior in fighting quality to the veterans and could not be relied on as storm troops. Desertions became frequent in the army; sailors in port were almost openly mutinous. Foch launched a counter-attack. On July 18, French and American troops struck at the western flank of the German salient from Soissons to Château Thierry. The Germans, unable to resist the pressure, withdrew from the Marne to the Aisne. South of Amiens the British advanced on August 8. For the first time in the war the German soldiers failed to rally to an attack.[1] The Canadians under General Currie were particularly successful in driving back the German lines in Picardy, capturing entrenchments long supposed impregnable. To the south the French gave effective support to the British drive.

There could be little doubt now of the outcome; the Central Powers had no further reserves to use while the Entente had all the men, munitions, money and enthu- *The last* siasm of America to draw on. An American *struggle* army, independently organized, crushed the salient at Saint-

---

[1] Ludendorff's own comment is interesting: "August 8th was the black day of the German army...I was told of deeds of glorious valor, but also of behavior which I should not have thought possible... whole bodies of our men had surrendered to single troopers or isolated squadrons."

Mihiel where for four years the Germans had held an isolated outpost in the Meuse valley south of Verdun. Without respite the battle merged into the general October campaign of the Meuse–Argonne in which twenty-nine American combat divisions took part, a force twelve times as great as General Grant led through the Wilderness in the bloodiest days of the Civil War. In January, 1918, the Americans held but one per cent of the front line trenches, and even in May only four to seven per cent, but in this last campaign American forces occupied more than a fifth of the entire battle line. While the American army pushed on towards Metz and Sedan the British seized railroad centers in French Flanders and Picardy and the Belgians reoccupied the Flemish ports. Already in April and May by daring raids on Zeebrugge and Ostend the British had practically put an end to the German use of these ports as submarine bases. In October Italy completely routed the Austrian forces. By November the whole German army was in full retreat to the frontier, the navy had become completely unreliable, the munitions workers were threatening a general strike and the nation marching with rapid strides toward revolution.

In the meantime Germany's allies, even more demoralized, one by one made separate peace. The first to do so was Bul-
Bulgaria surrenders garia. The Bulgarians, naturally a warlike people, had made their full contribution to the war in their campaigns against Serbia and Rumania in which they eagerly avenged the losses of the second Balkan War. But their army was the smallest of the armies of the Central Powers, and there lay behind it no store of national wealth or industrial productivity. The Entente had for a long time made no move in the Balkans, but a large army of Greeks, Serbs, French, British and Italians lay encamped from Saloniki to the Adriatic and in September it advanced in Macedonia. At the end of the month Bulgaria signed an armistice and on October 4 King Ferdinand abdicated in favor of Prince Boris.

The capitulation of Bulgaria involved that of Turkey, as no further aid could now be sent from Germany.   The British followed up their successes of 1917 at Bagdad *The Otto-* and Jerusalem by the conquest of Syria, the oc- *man Empire* cupation of Damascus, the seizure of railway *makes peace* centers along the Berlin–Bagdad route, and an advance on Mosul in northern Mesopotamia.   Enver, Talaat and other leaders of Turkish imperialism resigned office to men more acceptable to the Entente.   The new Sultan, Mohammed VI, begged for an armistice.   On October 30, 1918, the Ottoman Empire agreed to open the Straits to warships of the Entente Allies, to place Turkish territory at the disposal of the victors, to return prisoners of war and to demobilize the Turkish army.

Of all the Great Powers on either side, Austria-Hungary had staked the most on the war.   Defeat for Germany, France, Russia, Italy or Great Britain might *Austria-* mean national humiliation, loss of territory, *Hungary* heavy indemnities, perhaps a setback of a gen- *ceases to* eration or more in national prosperity.   But in *exist* each case there would remain a core of nationality, an irreducible homeland, within whose contracted frontiers political unity would continue to exist.   Austria-Hungary had no "core"; defeat for her meant dissolution.   For a few months there had been a flash of warlike enthusiasm among some, at least, of the Danubian nationalities.   But the weary campaigns against Russia, Rumania, Italy and Serbia soon wore away the first outburst of patriotic devotion.   In the next stage, loyalty to a particular national ideal replaced the common loyalty to Emperor and Realm. The Tirolese peasant and Viennese burgher fought no longer for the artificial structure of Austria-Hungary, but they still fought for the cause of Teutonism, the common bond among the German peoples, whether Austrian, Prussian, Saxon or Bavarian.   The Magyar was increasingly willing to sever the bond which united Hungary with Austria but he still fought on in fear lest defeat might involve a partition of the Kingdom of Hungary. Even the Croat, who would not fight against his Serbian kinsman, could be used on the Italian front, and not a few Galician Poles at first subordinated their quarrels with the Austrian government to their greater hatred of Russia. Only the Czecho-Slovaks had all to gain and nothing to lose from a victory of the Entente.

Various events in the course of the war alienated the subject nationalities of Austria-Hungary from their govern-

The uprising of the nationalities ment. The intervention of Rumania made a potential rebel of every Rumanian in Transylvania. The Russian revolution freed the Poles from their fear of Tsarism. The reply of the Entente Allies to President Wilson's request for a statement of peace terms encouraged the Czechs and Slovaks to hope more definitely for independence. The accession of the Emperor Charles brought to the throne an inexperienced ruler who, with many excellent intentions, could not command the sentimental loyalty which had been accorded the aged Francis Joseph. The Corfu agreement of July 20, 1917 brought the Serbs, Croats and Slovenes together in planning for a common Yugoslav fatherland which could come into existence only by the complete breakdown of the Dual Monarchy. The Declaration of Corfu provided for the creation of a constitutional, democratic and parliamentary monarchy under the reigning Serbian dynasty with equal rights for the three languages (Serb, Croat, Slovene) and the three most common faiths (Greek Orthodox, Roman Catholic and Mohammedan) of the Yugoslavs. At first Italy opposed this movement, for while she had no particular quarrel with Serbia she hoped to gain lands beyond the Adriatic in which the Croatians were also interested, but at a Congress of nationalities held in Rome in 1918 the Italian representatives endorsed the plan for a united Yugoslavia. As early as 1917 Polish and Czecho-Slovak legions had been organized on foreign soil in Russia, France and the United States, and in 1918 the Entente Powers recognized Polish and Czecho-Slovak National Councils in Paris as the authorized spokesmen for the would-be independent republics.

Austria would have been glad by 1918 to have made peace on promise of autonomy to the subject nationalities of the Empire, but the moment had passed when such *The birth of* terms were acceptable. Austrian Poland was *Czechoslo-* now at one with Russian and German Poland in *vakia* the demand for complete national independence; the Yugoslavs had ready their Corfu program; and on October 18, 1918, the "provisional government" of Czechoslovakia issued its declaration of independence, notable for its radically democratic and progressive character.

> The Czechoslovak State shall be a republic. In constant endeavor for progress it will guarantee complete freedom of conscience, religion and science, literature and art, speech, the press, and the right of assembly and petition. The Church shall be separated from the State. Our democracy shall rest on universal suffrage; women shall be placed on an equal footing with men, politically, socially and culturally. The rights of the minority shall be safeguarded by proportional representation; national minorities shall enjoy equal rights. The government shall be parliamentary in form and shall recognize the principles of initiative and referendum... the large estates will be redeemed for home colonization; patents of nobility will be abolished.

When the Austro-Hungarian government approached President Wilson for an armistice in October, the President replied that the national claims of the Czecho-Slovaks and Yugoslavs must be accepted as part of the peace. As these claims now went beyond "autonomy" to full independence, this meant the complete dissolution of the ancient Empire.

On November 3, 1918, Austria-Hungary accepted an armistice presented at the point of the victorious Italian bayonets. That was almost the last act of Austria-Hungary

as a state, for its provinces and nationalities were already
Chaos in in full process of organizing governments of
central their own.   Seven independent governments
Europe were heirs to the old Empire — Italy, Rumania,
Poland, Yugoslavia, Czechoslovakia, Austria and Hungary.
All frontiers were provisional; until the peace conference
met, hardly a man could be sure of what nation he was

THE PARTITION OF AUSTRIA-HUNGARY

a lawful subject.   Trade almost ceased in the Danube
valley, as each new government impounded all the rolling
stock and shipping on which it could lay hands.   The
Emperor Charles, repudiated by all the new succession
states, went into exile.   Strange local movements appeared
for an even more complete fragmentation of the Empire,
for a Ukrainian East Galicia, a German Kingdom of Northern Bohemia, a Republic of Cis-Carpathian Ruthenia, an
independent Transylvania, an independent City of Fiume.

Self-determination seemed working towards absurdity as every islet of population proclaimed its sovereignty with flag and postage stamp. Where hunger ruled most harshly the embittered poor went beyond nationalist democracy and demanded socialism. Factories lay idle and farmers refused to exchange good beef and butter for worthless paper money. Not the Empire only but society itself seemed on the verge of utter dissolution.

Germany without allies and facing increasing odds had no heart to struggle on alone. The legend industriously promulgated by German reactionaries of a later *Germany* day that defeat was due to treason at home (the *during the* so-called "stab in the back") is a mere myth *war* and an unmerited insult to a valiant nation. Not until victory was impossible from the military standpoint did the German people abandon their docile obedience to the military and civil authorities; but it is also true that one reason why the military situation *had* become hopeless was the economic exhaustion of the nation. Germany had, indeed, escaped any important invasion [1] and had suffered no such direct devastation as her armies inflicted on Russia, France, Belgium, Serbia and Rumania; her food supplies also were so well husbanded [2] and her conquests of other peoples' territory so pitilessly exploited that literal famine, such as swept Armenia and Poland, was avoided. But years of underfeeding took their toll. A memorial of the German Public Health Board at the end of 1918 contained the following grimly significant statement:

The year 1914 showed no perceptible increase of mortality... During the years 1915 and 1916, the increase of civilian mortality was not yet very heavy, amounting to 9.5 per cent in the former year and somewhat over 14 per cent in the latter in excess of the

[1] The brief Russian incursion into East Prussia and the occupation of a tiny tip of Alsace by France are the only exceptions.

[2] Walter Rathenau organized a Department of Raw Materials which not only economized supplies but, assisted by German chemistry, found substitutes for many commodities cut off by the blockade.

1913 rate. The last two years of the war, however, reveal very profound effects of the blockade. In 1917 the death-rate increased to 32 per cent, and in 1918 even to 37 per cent above that of 1913. The great increase began in December, 1916, in the months known in Germany as the "turnip winter."

Underfeeding was but one phase of the creeping paralysis of poverty which benumbed the entire economic life of the nation as the blockade shut off all access to the highways of the world.

Politically Germany passed under the joint dictatorship of Hindenburg as Field Marshal and Ludendorff as Quarter-master General from August, 1916, to the end of the war. The Kaiser himself lost his control of national policy, for at every attempt to assert his will the two generals threatened resignation and he no more dared dismiss them than his grandfather had dared accept the frequently proffered resignation of Bismarck. Chancellors were appointed and dismissed at the will of the military High Command. Bethmann-Hollweg, who had spent his administration weakly consenting to policies which he disapproved, resigned in July, 1917, to be succeeded by the even more colorless Dr. Georg Michaelis, who gave way in turn the next November to Count Georg von Hertling. The military High Command extended its control even to lesser civic officials, securing the dismissal of Foreign Secretary von Kühlmann for a speech on foreign affairs which lacked the note of confidence in final victory. The High Command, and especially Ludendorff, meddled also in diplomatic and constitutional matters, dictating the terms of the treaties of Brest-Litovsk and Bucharest, drawing the boundaries of Poland, insisting on the resumption of submarine warfare which brought the United States into the war, delaying a reform of the Prussian franchise, or opposing the introduction of ministerial responsibility to the Reichstag. The real meaning of "German militarism," a phrase often misunderstood, lies here. It is not that Ger-

The military dictatorship

many had a great army (the Russian was larger) or was especially fond of war (Germany had been at peace from 1871 to 1914), but that the military authorities were, even in peace, quite independent of civilian control unless some strong-willed Bismarck were Chancellor, and in case of war controlled the civilian government. Militarism in that sense France had never known since Napoleon, nor England since Cromwell; if Wilson, Lloyd George and Clemenceau were "dictators," as they were sometimes called, at least they were civilian dictators, Pershing did not govern the United States, Haig the British Empire or Foch the French Republic.

The lack of success of the military dictatorship undermined its prestige. By the end of September Ludendorff seemed to have lost hope and he suggested a *Stirrings of* more popular ministry and an offer of armistice *democracy* negotiations. In accordance with these suggestions Prince Max of Baden was appointed Chancellor and instructed to ask for peace. Associated with him as Secretary for Foreign Affairs was Dr. Solf, an able colonial minister. Both men were liberals. The accession to power of each new war Chancellor — Michaelis, Hertling, and Prince Max — was hailed as a victory for public opinion and parliamentary control (though the military High Command had behind the scenes forced each change), but nothing was done to write the principle of ministerial responsibility into the constitution until the final armistice negotiations. Probably the most significant political advance made by Germany during the war was not any ministerial change or constitutional reform, but the discovery of a common purpose by the Center (Catholic), Progressive and Socialist parties, hitherto widely sundered. These three parties advocated constitutional reform and an early peace on the lines of the Reichstag resolution of 1917. Powerless to control either foreign or internal policy during the war, they acted as a slight check on the influence of the imperialistic parties and the military advisers of the Crown and when peace came they provided a ready-made working majority for the republican régime.

President Wilson was resolved to use the military break-down of Germany to democratize the nation. When *The armistice negotiations* Chancellor Max proposed a general armistice, he replied with the query whether Germany meant to accept the terms "laid down by the President in his address to the Congress of the United States on the eighth of January" (i.e. the "fourteen points") and "whether the Imperial Chancellor is speaking merely for the constituted authorities of the Empire who have so far conducted the war." In answer the German note accepted the fourteen points as the basis of peace negotiation, agreed to evacuate occupied territory and assured President Wilson that "the great majority of the Reichstag" supported the ministry. President Wilson pressed still further for ex-plicit assurances that submarine attacks on merchant ships would cease, that no further destruction of property would be perpetrated by the retreating armies, and that the trans-fer of executive power from the Kaiser to ministers responsi-ble to the Reichstag should be real and permanent. Not until reassured on all these points did the President agree to take up peace negotiations with the European Allies with whom thus far Germany had no direct dealings.

On the whole, Britain, France and Italy found in the fourteen points a convenient outline of the terms of peace. *Two amendments to the "four-teen"* They insisted, however, on two amendments or restatements. First, that with respect to the "freedom of the seas... they must reserve to themselves complete freedom on this subject when they enter the Peace Conference." Second, that the President's reference to restoration of the invaded terri-tories must be construed to cover reparations "for all dam-age done to the civilian population of the Allies and their property by the aggression of Germany by land, by sea and from the air." Perhaps President Wilson's earlier notification to the Austro-Hungarian government that "autonomy" for the subject races of the Empire must now be considered as equivalent to independence may be counted a third amendment to the peace terms. It was, then, not on the basis of the original declaration of President Wilson, but upon that declaration *as amended* in these particulars that Germany surrendered. Marshal Foch and most other military heads considered that if Germany would accept an armistice whose terms would make impossible a renewal of the war it would be needless to prolong the conflict merely for a completer military triumph.

On November 11, 1918, the armistice came into effect and for the first time since August, 1914, the guns were silent. The terms were imposed unconditionally. *November* Germany must cease all military operations, *11, 1918* evacuate Belgium, France, Luxemburg and even Alsace-Lorraine, surrender prisoners of war, hostages and refugees, surrender a specified amount of artillery and war material, retire behind the Rhine and permit an occupation of the Rhineland by Allied troops, cease fighting in East Africa where a small German colonial force still held out, abandon all rights claimed under the treaties of Brest-Litovsk and Bucharest. The armistice negotiations which were begun with the German monarchy were concluded with the German Republic, for in the meantime the smoldering revolution had burst into flame.

The "revolution from below" as distinguished from belated official reforms began with a naval mutiny. Not content with refusing active service, the sailors *The* at Kiel established revolutionary councils on the *German* Russian model and seized political power in *revolution* several northern ports. The Socialists had prepared the trades unions to expect an outbreak if peace were not at once concluded, so the example of the sailors was followed by uprisings throughout the country. On November 7, Bavaria passed under the rule of a workers' council led by Kurt Eisner, a Jewish pacifist of high ideals. Two days later the Berlin workingmen went on strike and demanded a republic. Acting on the advice of military men solicitous for his safety the Kaiser and his eldest son fled to the neutral Netherlands. Chancellor Max surrendered the executive power to Friedrich Ebert, the leader of the majority or conservative wing of the Socialist party. All over Germany dynasties tumbled and ruling princes fled to neutral ground. Few revolutions have been made so easily, but it was less a revolution than an abdication; the sovereigns, great and small, made no attempt to defend their rights, the aristocracy and bourgeoisie stood neutral and inactive, the real conflict was between the more and the less radical socialistic factions.

The first task of the government was to curb its own "lunatic fringe." On the issue of supporting the war the *Socialism or Bolshevism?* Social Democratic party had split into two factions, but some of the pacifist Independents, such as Karl Kautsky and Eduard Bernstein, while criticizing the majority Socialists for supporting the war now thought of reuniting the party. But others felt that the majority Socialists had committed an unpardonable sin to the proletarian cause which must be effaced in blood. Nothing but a clean sweep of the Russian type could really save Germany. This group, corresponding to the Bolsheviki or Communists of Russia, took the name of Spartacus, leader of a slave rebellion in ancient Rome.[1] In December the Spartacist group attempted to seize power by insurrection, but Noske, acting as Socialist Minister of War, did not hesitate to turn machine guns against the rebels. The revolt

---

[1] "Every schoolboy" will recall the address of Spartacus to the gladiators, which he used to recite on Friday afternoons along with Catiline's defiance and Rienzi's appeal to the Romans.

was crushed in blood and its leaders, Karl Liebknecht and
Rosa Luxemburg, were assassinated by an angry mob after
arrest. In March, 1919, new riots in Berlin were again
crushed by Noske. In Bavaria the Spartacists had a moment of success. The assassination of Kurt Eisner by a
reactionary aristocrat led to an uprising in Munich which
brought into power a Communist dictatorship and a brief
reign of terror. But the pious Catholic peasantry of Bavaria
had no sympathy with the Munich insurrection and the
only lasting effect of the episode was a strong reaction
against all radicalism which made Bavaria the most mon-
archically inclined state in the republic.

Kaiser Wilhelm II did not abdicate at once; perhaps he
thought the revolution a mere flash in the pan. But on
November 28, after more than a fortnight of *The Weimar*
exile, he issued a proclamation releasing his sub- *Assembly*
jects from their oaths of allegiance and asking them to support any lawful government against "anarchy, famine and
foreign domination." The election of January, 1919, on a
basis of adult suffrage was a victory for democratic liberalism. The three parties supporting the provisional government (the majority Socialists, the Catholic "Christian
People's" party which succeeded the old "Center," and the
"Democrats" as the Progressives were now called) controlled
about four-fifths of the membership. The Nationalists.
("National People's"), successor to the old Conservatives;
the People's Party, formerly the National Liberals, and the
Independent Socialists were the chief groups in opposition.
Many Spartacists refused to take part in the election. The
Socialists retained the provisional presidency, held by
Ebert, and the premiership, taken by Scheidemann, but
they were forced to admit some Catholics and Democrats
into the ministry. The meeting of the Assembly at Weimar,
the city of Goethe and Schiller and the focus of the liberal
movement of the early nineteenth century, was a symbol

of the liberal triumph, a gesture to the world that neither the old Prussian autocracy nor the Communist mob was in the saddle. "Even so," wrote George Young, "might a demoralised and democratised England placate a victorious and Victorian America by transferring Parliament to the Shakespeare Theatre at Stratford-on-Avon!"

The celebrations of the armistice were not the mere usual jubilations over victory which have closed wars in the past, *Europe wel-* but a joyous outburst of relief from a huge im-*comes peace* personal calamity which had come to seem as much beyond human control as an earthquake. The war had continued so long by its own deadly momentum that in every country fear of an enemy victory had become merged with a vaguer but vaster fear of a complete breakdown of all civilization, the sliding of Europe into a bottomless abyss of famine and anarchy. There was hope that the armistice day would usher in a peace which would *not* be merely an armistice between two wars but of eternal duration. It is significant that from this war arose a custom of international scope, that of honoring the tomb of an unknown soldier, the universal sacrifice of the human race, instead of raising monuments to generals and warrior kings.

With what injuries to civilization must we debit the war? For centuries it will be too soon to reckon them. Germany *The balance* is still paying in impaired political traditions and *sheet of the* racial qualities for the Thirty Years' War of the *World War* seventeenth century and Britain has not yet wholly outlived the financial burdens of the Napoleonic Wars. Of course the real injuries of war must be distinguished from mere "book losses." For example, a war loan is often incorrectly regarded as a way of deferring the payment for a war to future generations, but really it is a mere adjustment of credits; the actual wealth in the terms of production is taken and spent at the moment, once and for all, whether raised by tax or loan, though the taxpaying portion of the public is later required to reimburse the bondbuyers and a lasting burden of debt created. Let it be admitted also that much of the economic wastage of wartime is counterbalanced by the temporary stimulus to production caused by "war orders" and the introduction, under the spur of necessity, of more efficient methods. Other assets of an economic character are the erection for military purposes of roads, wharves and other public works which are useful in time of peace; the stimulus to invention in certain fields, notably aviation and medicine; the physical and technical training which some men are able to gain from a brief experience of army life. War also, like other great calamities, brings some imponderable benefits, especially the testing and breaking down of unsound institutions and inefficient governments which might have long endured the easier tests of peace.

The negative side of the balance is the more evident. The war took from civilian life some 65,000,000 physically fit men, killed eight or nine million, maimed for life *The cost in* about an equal number and inflicted wounds *life* more or less serious on at least 21,000,000. The number of men mobilized during the war almost equaled the entire population of the German Empire; the number killed exceeded the population of Belgium. France alone spent almost as many lives in the war which restored to her Alsace-Lorraine as the whole population of those provinces. An influenza epidemic in 1918, not of war origin but spread in part by troop movements, took in half a year more lives than four years of battle.[1] Civil wars and famines which indirectly resulted from the World War, especially in Russia, took the lives of other millions, but for this we have not even approximate estimates. The war and the influenza epidemic alike selected their victims in greatest number from healthy young men between adolescence and middle age, just the

[1] About six million in India alone.

group most productive in physical labor and in fatherhood. The heaviest mortality rate of all was among the junior officers in the trenches, men with the training and quality of leadership, and among the courageous, quick-thinking aviators. If heredity be a fact, the generation following the World War and perhaps many generations to come will be of inferior racial quality to that which endured the war.

The economic cost of war must ever be of secondary importance to its cost in life, in disability and in racial quality. *The cost in* But since civilization is built from accumulated *wealth* wealth, economics, too, has its human values. The direct and immediate cost of the war, based on official statements and with all due allowance for duplication, is placed by several careful authorities in the neighborhood of $186,000,000,000, a greater sum than the capitalized wealth of any one belligerent nation with the exception of the United States. If we add to this the calculable value of the indirect costs of war, such as destruction of property, the loss of production, the cost of war relief, the injury to neutral markets, and the productive value of soldier and civilian lives we have a grand total of at least $338,000,000,000.[1] This last figure does not include some real but quite incalculable economic injuries, such as postwar depressions, permanently disorganized trade routes, and the impetus given to anarchy and civil war.

Other injuries inflicted by the war pass the power of statistics to reckon. Every big war in modern history has been *The moral* followed by a "reconstruction period" character- *cost* ized by profiteering, reckless expenditure, lax moral standards, lawlessness and intolerance. The aftermath of the World War showed all these symptoms in greater or less degree in every nation. As a general principle is best

---

[1] See for example E. Bogart, *Direct and Indirect Costs of the Great War* (1919). The rapid fluctuation of nearly all currency systems since Bogart wrote has deprived these statistics of much significance. In any case they are minimum rather than maximum figures; some other estimates run as high as $500,000,000,000.

shown in a concrete example, consider the single crime of political assassination. The war began with the murder of an Austrian Archduke, a crime shocking because of its then exceptional character. In the years which have passed since then there have been several hundred important political murders, including in their number Jaurès, leader of French Socialism; Count Stürgkh, Austrian Premier; Count Tisza, ex-Premier of Hungary; Tsar Nicholas II of Russia; Kurt Eisner, head of the revolutionary government in Bavaria; Mathias Erzberger and Walter Rathenau, two of the most prominent of the early republican leaders in Germany, and ex-Chancellor Kurt von Schleicher; President Narutowicz of Poland; Premier Collins and Vice-President O'Higgins of the Irish Free State; Stambulisky, the peasant dictator of Bulgaria; Premier Duca of Rumania; President Doumer and Foreign Minister Barthou of France; Premier Inukai of Japan; Chancellor Dollfuss of Austria; King Alexander of Yugoslavia, and scores of men of but slightly less distinction. To political enthusiasts of every type from the Russian Communist to the German reactionary the individual had ceased to have value. The war which demonetized the ruble and the mark demonetized also human life.

CHAPTER XVIII

THE PEACE OF PARIS

THE Peace Conference charged with the settlement of the questions arising from the World War met at Paris in com-

All roads lead to Paris

pliment to France as the nation which had made the greatest contribution to victory by land. Although the treaties with the Central Powers are known by the name of the suburbs where they were signed (Germany at Versailles, Austria at Saint-Germain, Bulgaria at Neuilly, Hungary at the Trianon, the first Turkish treaty at Sèvres), the preliminary negotiations among the Allied and Associated Powers were conducted in the city of Paris. Here assembled the accredited delegates with their retinue of military attendants, special advisers, diplomatic agents, clerks and typists. For a few months Paris was a world capital, as there met the responsible civilian leaders of all the Great Powers and most of the small, authorized to conclude far-reaching agreements as to European frontiers, colonial possessions, commercial treaties, armament limitations, the recognition of new governments, the adjustment of loans and indemnities, and the "sanctions" which would make peace secure. No previous peace congresses, not even those of Westphalia in 1648, Utrecht in 1713, Vienna in 1814–15 or Berlin in 1878, dealt with half so wide a range of problems. The problem of the rights of labor, hardly mentioned in any previous peace treaty, occupies a whole section of the Treaty of Versailles. The constitution of the League of Nations also presented completely new problems. Frontiers had to be redefined for almost the whole of central and eastern Europe, for Asiatic Turkey and for all the former German colonies. Solutions adopted for the problems of reparations, war debts and commercial agreements would affect the whole world balance of trade for at least half a century.

The greatest difficulty of the Peace Conference lay not in the making of treaties but in combining that task with the immediate government of a continent boiling *The im-* with revolutionary discontent and faced with *mediate* the thousand problems of demobilization and *crisis* reconstruction. It was mainly this duality of function which made the process of peace making seem so slow. While the world outside the closed doors at Paris supposed the diplomats to be asking themselves, "Where shall the Polish frontier be drawn?", or "How much indemnity can Germany pay?", they were more commonly discussing such questions as "How can we get the Poles and Ukrainians to stop fighting in eastern Galicia?", "How can we get the German army out of the Baltic Provinces without letting in the Russian Bolsheviki?", "Should we sanction the landing of Greek troops at Smyrna?", or "How can we persuade the Rumanians to evacuate Hungary?" The Peace Conference, to borrow the language of political science, was a legislative and executive as well as a constituent assembly. Had it been possible to delegate either the daily problems of government or the making of the treaties to anyone other than the responsible prime ministers the work could have been more smoothly and quickly done; but it was not possible, the decisions taken in both fields were too vital not to have the full authority of each government behind them.

After the armistice two months were lost before the Peace Conference formally opened its sessions. As the problems of the peace had such outstanding importance, *Other* the Conference could not get under way until *causes of* the responsible heads of the chief Allied and As- *delay* sociated Powers were present.[1] Premier Clemenceau of

---

[1] The United States, having concluded no formal treaty of alliance, was one of the " associated " states.

France had to devote immediate attention to the rehabilitation of the devastated departments just abandoned by the German army. Premier Lloyd George, conscious that Parliament had outlived its normal term, thought that the coalition government of which he was head should test its strength at the polls before venturing to make peace in the name of the British Empire. President Wilson had business in Washington that no one else could constitutionally perform; in fact he was compelled to return to America during the Conference because of the winter session of Congress. Other delegates came from distant nations and required weeks to reach Paris. The attempt of a communist fanatic to kill Premier Clemenceau, the presiding officer of the Conference, again delayed affairs a few days soon after the sessions had opened. There was much less social activity and merrymaking than at Vienna a century before, but a great deal of the time of the delegates was wasted in receiving formal "deputations" representing an endless variety of national, partisan or factional interests affected by one phase or another of the peace.

Nor were the delegates to the Conference ready with their terms of peace. On the contrary they so greatly feared dissension with each other that they resolved not to permit the enemy representatives to enter the Conference until they had reached an agreement among themselves. Perhaps they had in mind the skill with which Talleyrand, representing defeated France at Vienna, had taken advantage of the dissensions among the powers which had vanquished Napoleon and resolved that in that particular at least history should not repeat itself. It is true that the diplomats could not consider all possible alternatives for each problem that arose or choose exactly what solution they might individually prefer. The general outlines of the peace were fixed before ever the Conference met in at least three ways. Firstly, Germany had surrendered not uncondition-

The unready peace

ally but on terms, the "fourteen points" as amended in the
armistice negotiations.   Secondly, several of the Allies had
entered into secret compacts with each other, especially with
regard to the frontiers of Italy and the partition of Turkey.
Thirdly, and this was by far the most important limiting
condition, the actual political situation in Europe must be
taken into account.   For example, even if Britain, France
and Italy had desired to reconstruct the Austro-Hungarian
Empire they could hardly have done so; revolution had already partitioned it and the only task remaining in that
matter was to determine the exact detail of the boundaries.
Equally impossible would it have been to reconstruct the old
Russian Empire and force the provinces which had seceded
from it back into their old union.   If the break-up of these
empires into national fragments was a great act of liberation,
as some say, or a disastrous blow to European unity and
stability, as others say, in neither case does the Peace Conference deserve either blame or praise.   It merely recorded
an existing fact.

But many portions of the Versailles Treaty and the other
Paris agreements were not covered by the secret treaties or
the fourteen points or prejudged by popular revolution.
The fourteen points were far from clear in certain details.
Exactly how far did "indisputable" Polish or Italian territories extend?   To what concrete decisions would a fair-
minded rearrangement of the Balkans or colonial Africa lead?
In what degree was Germany liable for reparations?   Neither
President Wilson nor anyone else had made these things
clear.   The secret treaties were also an inadequate basis for
the peace settlement as a whole.   The United States was
not bound by them; in fact Wilson always insisted that
he had no official knowledge of them, though he must have
known of their existence since they were given wide circulation in the American press after the Bolsheviki had
opened the Russian archives.   Russia no longer claimed

anything under the terms of these agreements; and, if she had, she would have forfeited all such rights by making a separate peace at Brest-Litovsk.   Other parts of the treaties were no longer appropriate to the changed situation; they "dated."   For instance, Italy's best claim to a part of the Dalmatian coast was strategic and lay in the fact that in 1915 the Italians felt that they needed good harbors east of the Adriatic to protect themselves from a vengeful Austria-Hungary after the war.   But the complete dissolution of that Empire had left Austria with no seaports at all and far too weak to menace Italy in any way.   The issue now lay between Italy and Yugoslavia, that is to say between two allies.

One of the most serious difficulties confronting the Conference was the degree to which publicity should be given to *The prob-* the negotiations.   All diplomatic precedents were *lem of pub-* on the side of secrecy.   But President Wilson *licity* had declared for "open covenants openly arrived at," and no declaration of his had wider popular appeal. Moreover, the press is in modern times a vast political power, and the anger of the newspaper world at being completely shut off from news of the most important events in modern times would lead to attacks on all the decisions of the Conference.   A compromise was reached by which the press might be present at full sessions of the Conference, but the meetings of special councils or committees where the real work was done would be secret and their conclusions published only through brief official statements.   On the whole the Conference chose the risks of secrecy rather than the risks of publicity, though on one occasion President Wilson almost broke up the Conference by appealing over the head of the Italian government to the Italian people on the Adriatic question.   That incident shows that the risk involved in public discussion was a real one.   Without numerous compromises no treaty could possibly have been made, and diplomats feared to risk their popularity with their fellow countrymen by seeming to concede too much. Secrecy, however, had its own disadvantages. It surrounded the Conference with an atmosphere of intrigue in which any sensational rumor was widely credited. The rigid press censorship in Paris, where long white columns of blank paper frequently replaced the first-page news, and the refusal to publish in full the text of the preliminary terms of peace presented to Germany,[1] caused acute exasperation.

On the picturesque but infrequent occasions when the whole body of peace delegates met, every speech made in English was immediately translated into French, *Plenary sessions of the Conference* and every speech made in French translated into English; thus preserving, as also in the text of the Treaty of Versailles, the absolute equality of the two languages. Each Great Power — Britain, France, Italy, Japan and the United States of America — sent five representatives, and some of the British Dominions had delegates of their own. The lesser nations had from one to three delegates apiece. The Conference lacked, no doubt, some of the color of diplomatic gatherings in the old days when peace treaties were made by kings and princes. Save for Prince Feisal of the Arab Kingdom of the Hedjaz, who wore with dignity his white Syrian robes, and the Maharajah of Bikaner, in the uniform of an Indian warrior prince, the delegates wore the conventional clothes of the gentleman of western Europe — and often rather sloppily! Yet personalities stood out from the mass all the more clearly because they had been forced by a democratic age to make their own way instead of being born to the life of ruler, courtier or diplomat. To consider for the moment only the lesser countries, no one

---

[1] This was largely at the insistence of Premier Lloyd George who feared that chauvinistic opinion would make impossible any concessions to Germany if each such concession could be openly branded a "retreat." Of course, the Germans were given the full text, and it is an amusing fact that the public of the Entente nations first read their own treaty in a translation from the enemy press!

could overlook the tawny lion's mane of Paderewski, once the world's most popular pianist and now the premier of the young Polish Republic; or the keen face of Venizelos, the Ulysses of modern Greece, probably the shrewdest diplomat at the Conference; or the practical, businesslike Benès, President Masaryk's able representative from Czechoslovakia; or the two former Boer generals, Botha and Smuts, now representing His Britannic Majesty from South Africa; or the scholarly Vandervelde, veteran leader of Belgian Socialism. Men of such caliber had almost as much influence on the decisions of the Conference as if they represented powerful nations, but their real influence was exerted in private consultation with the British, French and American delegates rather than in the formal assemblies of the Conference.

The real decisions of the Conference were taken not in plenary session but in the meetings of the prime ministers *The Supreme Council* and foreign secretaries [1] of the five Great Powers, commonly called the Supreme Council or the Council of Ten. Toward the middle of March it became evident that the "Ten" would not have the treaty ready soon enough to meet popular expectation. Therefore President Wilson and Premiers Lloyd George, Clemenceau and Orlando agreed to meet for private and, at first, unrecorded conversations until agreement was reached on such outstanding questions as the Adriatic and the left bank of the Rhine. Japan, not interested in these purely European matters, did not join these meetings and for some weeks Italy was unrepresented while Orlando was in Italy. Thus many important clauses of the German treaty were first determined by the decision of three men only, Wilson, Lloyd George and Clemenceau. Of course these decisions had formally to be ratified by the whole Conference, but in no case were they in fact overruled.

[1] In the case of the United States, the President and the Secretary of State.

In 1814, when the Congress of Vienna met to settle the
destinies of Europe, the dominant figure was Prince Metternich, the embodiment of Austrian aristocracy. *The "Big*
The Russian Tsar and the King of Prussia were *Three"*
present in person. Prince Talleyrand represented France;
Lord Castlereagh and the Duke of Wellington, Great Britain.
In 1919, with the power of decision equally concentrated in
the hands of a few, a different type of man had risen to leadership. Woodrow Wilson, son of a Presbyterian minister, had
entered politics from the somewhat unusual angle of a teacher
of history; David Lloyd George, a self-made Welsh lawyer,
had forced his own way into the charmed circle of the British
"ruling class"; Georges Clemenceau, radical journalist, was
regarded in his early career rather as a revolutionary critic
of all governments than a man to be entrusted with the administration of any. The "big Three" of the Conference
were alike in their "bourgeois" origin and their liberal political background. In personality, however, they contrasted
sharply. Clemenceau, elderly, cynical, dogmatic and yet
quite capable of compromise, concentrated his attention on
one object, the security of France. He accepted the League
of Nations but tried to turn it into a military alliance; he
strove to strengthen and enlarge the friendly states of eastern
Europe, such as Poland; he tried to wrest the Rhine provinces
from Germany, but abandoned the project to the dismay of
his own supporters because he did not wish to risk alienating
Britain and America. Lloyd George, pugnacious and brilliant, always ready to alter his plans in detail, not well informed as to continental European problems but marvelously
quick to comprehend the shifts of public opinion, desired
mainly a settlement which would give lasting peace to Europe
and permit the revival of British trade. He had posed before the electorate on the eve of the Conference as a jingo
eager to "hang the Kaiser" and make Germany pay the full
costs of the war, but at the Conference he quickly revised

his views and became a powerful advocate of leniency to the defeated. Wilson, interested mainly in upbuilding the League of Nations but desirous also to maintain the spirit of his other thirteen points, found himself usually in agreement with the British policy. He brought to the Conference a somewhat old-fashioned dignity, a broad international outlook, a rigid and resolute idealism and great personal prestige. Unfortunately, his authority was not as great as it seemed in either continent. The United States, divided politically, had already elected an unfriendly Senate, and the cheering crowds who greeted him in Europe were ready to turn against him as soon as he opposed any of the many conflicting national aspirations which sought his support.

Foreign Ministers Balfour of Great Britain and Pichon of France, as well as Lansing, the American Secretary of State, *Other Great* felt themselves badly snubbed as the "Three" *Power rep-* displaced the "Ten." In all three delegations *resentatives* amateur "new diplomacy" in a hurry rather tactlessly ignored professional "old diplomacy" with its deliberate methods. When Wilson wanted advice he rarely turned to Lansing but to his intimate adviser Colonel House; similarly Clemenceau relied more on his personal friend André Tardieu than on any other member of his delegation. Clemenceau and Tardieu both had the advantage of speaking English and of personal acquaintance with the British and American people. Premier Orlando of Italy lacked this advantage, and further lost much diplomatic ground by showing an untimely stubbornness on minor points while letting greater issues go by default. Sonnino, his able and aggressive Foreign Minister also was uncompromising. Other delegates of the Great Powers were occupied mainly with questions of detail. Besides Lansing and House, Wilson had brought with him General Bliss, a statesmanlike officer who had served on the Supreme War Council, and Henry White, ex-ambassador to France, the only Republican in the delegation. Besides Balfour, Lloyd George was aided by Lord Milner representing Imperial interests, Bonar Law, a Conservative party leader, G. N. Barnes, representing British labor, and the delegates from the Dominions. Besides Pichon and Tardieu, Clemenceau had for colleagues, Jules Cambon and L. Klotz. Marquis Saionji and Baron Makino, the chief Japanese representatives in the main were concerned only with questions of eastern Asia and the Pacific.

While the Supreme Council reserved to itself the power of decision, it entrusted the task of detailed shaping of the treaty clauses to special commissions and com- *Special* mittees. The labor clauses of the Versailles *commissions* Treaty (part XIII) and the economic clauses (part X) were approved with very little alteration in the form in which they left the commissions which drafted them. The Covenant of the League of Nations was also the work of a commission, though since President Wilson and other plenipotentiaries appeared on this particular body it had unusual diplomatic authority. On most of the commissions experts and specialists, some taken from the technical staffs of foreign ministries and others drafted for the occasion from the universities, substituted for the accredited delegates.

The treaty with Germany was handled first of all as the most urgent and because certain important questions, such as the League of Nations, could be worked out *The prob-* in the German treaty and then embodied with *lem of Ger-* little or no alteration in later agreements with *many* Austria, Hungary, Bulgaria, and Turkey. With respect to Germany the major problems may be summed as: (1) German unity; (2) the western frontier; (3) the eastern frontier; (4) colonies; (5) reparations and commercial rights; (6) disarmament; (7) the punishment of war criminals. The first question was easily disposed of; some Frenchmen had toyed with such suggestions as separate treaties with individual German states, an independent republic west of the Rhine, the isolation or partition of Prussia, but the Conference dismissed all such solutions without long consideration.[1] Austria was, however, forbidden to join Germany without the consent of the Great Powers as represented in the Council of the League of Nations, a consent which France, at least, would not be apt to give.

Alsace-Lorraine, with the boundaries of 1871, went back to France unconditionally, without plebiscite, and the ces-
The west- sion, unlike all other territorial changes, was
ern frontier dated back to the armistice. Belgium obtained a very slight frontier rectification, including Eupen, Malmédy and Moresnet. The Grand Duchy of Luxemburg was withdrawn from the German customs union. Northern Schleswig was permitted to vote on the question of union with Denmark. The island fortress of Helgoland was dismantled. These decisions were easily taken and involved little controversy. But two difficult problems arose with respect to the west: the Rhine military frontier and the Saar valley. Marshal Foch contended earnestly for a permanent military occupation of the Rhine frontier. The Saar valley with its important coal mines had been in large part French territory till 1815 and had been a subject of secret treaty negotiation with Russia during the war. The French advanced another claim to it as compensation for the deliberate wrecking of French coal mines during the German retreat. The British and American delegates feared that a permanent garrison on German soil or a permanent separation of the mainly German-speaking population of the Saar from the Reich would "create a new Alsace-Lorraine problem" and prevent any permanent reconciliation of the nations.

The final upshot was a compromise. Germany was pledged for all time to maintain no armies or forts west of the Rhine or within fifty kilometers east of it. An Allied

[1] For a good discussion of this topic, see A. Tardieu, *The Truth about the Treaty* (1921).

army of occupation would be maintained west of the Rhine for fifteen years after the coming into force of *The Rhine* the treaty. The Saar valley was placed under *and Saar* the protection of the League of Nations for a *compromise* period of fifteen years, at the end of which time the permanent

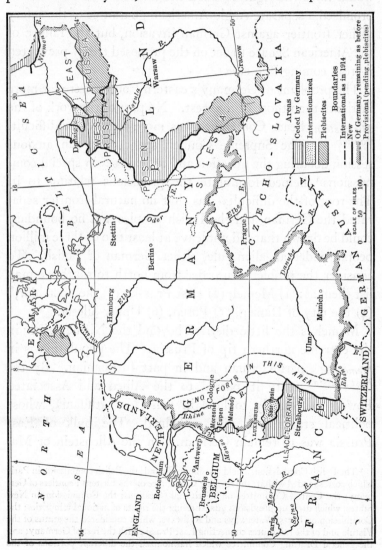

GERMANY AFTER THE TREATY OF VERSAILLES

residents (so that France could not "colonize" the district
with immigrants) would vote as to whether the region should
remain an independent state under the League, be joined to
France, or return to Germany. In the meantime France
would have the right to work the mines. France was also
promised a separate Anglo-American guarantee of the safety
of her frontier against German invasion, but the failure of
the American Senate to act on the proposed treaty prevented
it from coming into effect.

The problems of Germany's eastern frontier were far more
intricate than those of the west. No part of the work of the
The eastern Peace Conference was more complex or difficult.
frontier   The Supreme Council spent many an anxious
session debating the question and at least seven special commissions [1] helped formulate the provisions relating to it.
The root of the difficulty was that no natural frontier separated the German and the Polish peoples and no boundary
could be drawn that did not leave at least two or three million
people under an alien rule, either German or Polish. To
consider the problems in order from north to south we may
list them as: (1) Memel, (2) East Prussia, (3) the "corridor,"
(4) the city of Danzig, (5) Posen, (6) Upper Silesia.

Memel is the little district beyond the Niemen river in
the extreme northern tip of Prussia. The population is in
Memel and part German and in part Lithuanian. By the
East Prussia treaty it passed to the Allied and Associated
Powers collectively to hold in trust for Lithuania, whose
political status was still undefined. The bulk of East
Prussia was to remain German. In the Allenstein or Ma-

---

[1] The Polish Commission, a field mission in Poland; the Polish commission in Paris
which corresponded with it; the revising Committee on the Eastern Frontiers of Germany; the Central Committee on Territorial Questions; the Commission on New
States, which drew up provisions guaranteeing the rights of national minorities; the
Commission on Ports, Waterways and Railways, which considered the status of the
Vistula and of the rail routes connecting East Prussia with the rest of Germany; and
the general Drafting Committee which harmonized the different portions of the
treaty and put them in legal form.

zurian region of southern East Prussia a plebiscite was ordered, and a similar plebiscite provided for the Marien-werder district of West Prussia. Both plebiscites eventually went in favor of Germany.

West Prussia is more Polish in character than East Prussia, because of the historical accident that placed East Prussia first under the rule of the Teutonic *The Polish* Knights, an order of medieval crusaders, and *Corridor* later under that of the Hohenzollerns, long before *and Danzig* Frederick the Great added West Prussia to his dominions. Danzig is the seaport of the Vistula river, around which is grouped the entire Polish nation. Not to give Poland West Prussia and Danzig would place a large Polish population under German rule, and cut off from all direct access to the sea one of the principal nations of Europe. On the other hand, to award them to Poland would be to isolate East Prussia geographically from the rest of Germany and put the German town of Danzig under alien control. It was one of those exasperating circumstances when any solution whatever would do great wrong and injury to someone. The compromise reached by the Conference gave to the Poles their West Prussian "corridor" to the Baltic but placed Danzig under a special régime as an independent city under the protection of the League of Nations. For commercial purposes Danzig was included within the Polish customs zone but its municipal government is German in character. The arrangement much resembled that provided for the Saar, with the important difference that no provision was made for terminating it by plebiscite.

Posen is a broad agricultural region in the eastern part of Prussia. Though its population is mixed the majority is Polish, and the task of the Conference was merely *Posen and* to trace a new frontier as closely as possible to *Upper Sile-* the boundary of nationality. The case of Upper *sia* Silesia was far more difficult. Silesia, the Austrian province annexed by Frederick the Great for Prussia, is mainly German, but in the hilly southern extremity, known as Upper Silesia, there is also a large Polish element. In just this region there are mines which before the war produced almost a fourth of Germany's supply of coal and an even greater proportion of Germany's lead and zinc. Some of the Poles are peasants whose ancestors have lived there since the Middle Ages, and others are miners and factory hands tempted across the border of Russian Poland by the prospect of better wages. At the urgent and special insistence of Lloyd George, who feared that to take the coal mines of Silesia away from Germany would wreck German prosperity and with it any prospect of obtaining reparations, Wilson and Clemenceau reluctantly consented that Upper Silesia should determine its destinies by plebiscite. In the first draft of the treaty it had been awarded outright to Poland on the basis of census statistics showing a Polish majority.

The entire colonial empire of Germany, in Africa and the Pacific, passed into the hands of the victors. No considerable German population thereby came under foreign rule, as most of the German colonies were unfit for European settlement. The British, as had usually been the case in general peace negotiations, took particular interest in territorial changes outside Europe and won a "lion's share" of the colonial prizes. German East Africa passed under British administration,[1] and parts of Togoland and Kamerun, though the greater share of these latter colonies went to France. German Southwest Africa was joined to the Union of South Africa. German New Guinea and the neighboring islands passed to Australia; German Samoa to New Zealand. Thus three of the British Dominions obtained colonial empire in their turn. Japan was awarded the German islands north of the equator. The distribution of colonial conquests formed no part of the Treaty of Versailles, as it sufficed for

Colonies

---

[1] A small part was added to the Belgian Congo.

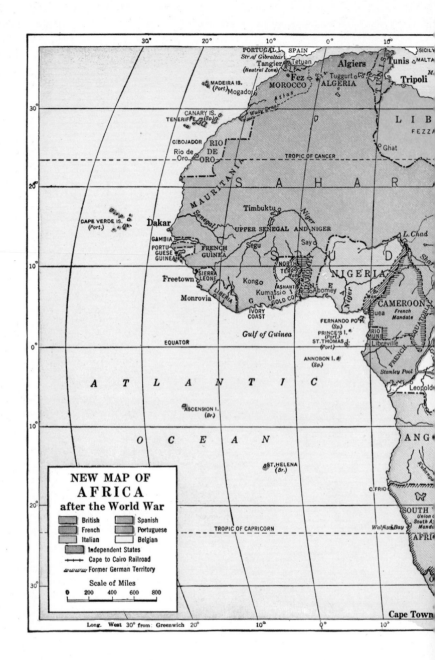

NEW MAP OF
AFRICA
after the World War

British   Spanish
French   Portuguese
Italian   Belgian
Independent States
++++ Cape to Cairo Railroad
www Former German Territory

Scale of Miles
0   200   400   600   800

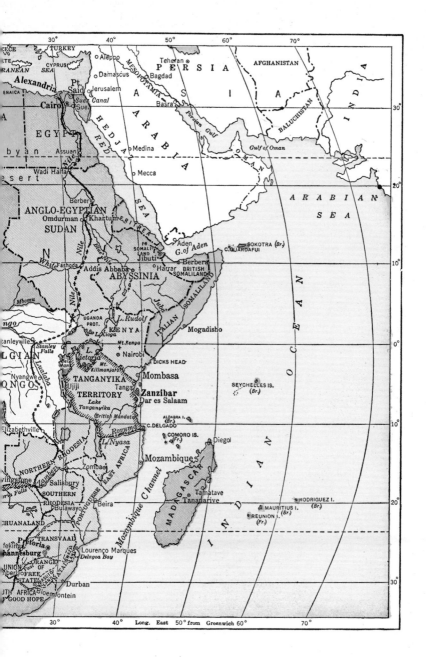

Germany to waive title on behalf of the Allied and Associated Powers collectively.

The Treaty did provide, however, a general system by which the transferred colonies should be administered. Instead of obtaining title "in fee simple" the oc- *The man-* cupying power was given merely a "mandate" *date system* or trusteeship and must render annual reports to the League of Nations as to its administration. Something remotely analogous to the mandate system can be found in earlier treaties, as when King Leopold II of Belgium was given control of the Congo Free State and again when the Congress of Berlin awarded to Austria-Hungary the right to administer Bosnia-Herzegovina and to police the Sanjak of Novi-Bazar. But never before had there been a permanent international body like the League of Nations to oversee the working of such a trusteeship. Three classes of mandates were recognized: (A) territories formerly Turkish, such as Syria, Mesopotamia and Palestine, which were expected soon to be established as independent nations but required foreign aid during a transitional period; (B) the former German colonies in tropical Africa where "equal opportunities for trade and commerce" must be granted to all members of the League; (C) "territories such as South-West Africa and certain of the South Pacific Islands," also formerly German, which "can be best administered under the laws of the Mandatory as integral portions of its territory" subject only to certain laws to protect native interests.

One of the most discussed provisions of the Versailles Treaty relates to the Chinese province of Shan-tung. Here Germany held a lease of the naval base of Kiao- *The* Chau and some commercial concessions, railway *Shan-tung* franchises and mining rights. By the treaty these *question* rights were transferred from Germany to Japan. President Wilson and other American delegates desired that Germany's holdings in China be returned to the Chinese government instead of being reassigned to Japan; but since Japan held actual possession, with wartime treaties to back it, there was no dislodging her. The best concession that President Wilson could obtain was the verbal promise, not written into the treaty, that Japan would later negotiate with China as to the terms on which Kiao-Chau would be restored.

Besides losing her colonies, Germany forfeited other benefits which she had enjoyed as a world power. In China,

Germany loses commercial privileges Siam, Morocco, Liberia and Egypt the special treaty privileges of the German Empire were terminated. The waterways across Germany — the Rhine, Elbe, Oder, Niemen and Danube — were placed under international administrative commissions so that France, Czechoslovakia, Poland, Lithuania and the Danubian States might not be impeded by hostile German legislation in the use of these rivers, and the Vistula came almost wholly under Polish control. The Versailles Treaty specified which general, commercial and other treaties made before the war between Germany and any of the Allied and Associated Powers should be revived; all others being terminated by war. For a brief period of transition to normal times Germany was forbidden to discriminate against the commerce of any of her wartime foes, but most of these restrictive provisions ran for not more than five years. Other terms of the treaty related to patent rights, shipping, private business contracts and other commercial interests.

The portion of the Treaty of Versailles which has been most discussed is that section which deals with reparations.

The problem of reparations There are three types of war indemnity: a punitive indemnity imposed as a fine or levy over and above the costs of war; an indemnity which aims to balance those costs; and an indemnity which merely covers reparation for certain categories of damage. The first two kinds of indemnity, though advocated in theory by some of the delegates, such as Premier Hughes of Australia, were

ruled out for two reasons. Firstly, that all the wealth of
Germany could not have paid the full costs of the war and
it would be useless to demand the impossible. Secondly,
that Germany had surrendered on conditions; one of them
being that she was liable to compensate the victors "for all
damage done to the *civilian* population of the Allies and their
property by land, by sea and from the air." The phrase was
vague enough, but it could hardly be stretched to include
purely military expenditures such as the manufacture and
purchase of munitions. As Mr. Dulles forcibly put the point
of view of the American delegates:

> We are not here to consider as a novel proposal what repara-
> tion the enemy should in justice pay; we have not before us a
> blank page upon which we are free to write what we will. We
> have before us a page, it is true; but one which is already filled
> with writing, and at the bottom are the signatures of Mr. Wil-
> son, of Mr. Orlando, of Mr. Clemenceau, and of Mr. Lloyd
> George. You are all aware, I am sure, of the writing to which
> I refer: it is the agreed basis of peace with Germany.

The American point of view prevailed. The reparations demanded from Germany and her allies included neither punitive fines nor complete war costs, but were based on restitution for damage done.

The real bone of contention was to fix the classes or categories of damage for which Germany was liable. France
desired to make them very comprehensive, so that Germany
would bear as large a share as possible of postwar reconstruction. The British also were "loose constructionists"
as they feared that a strict definition of damage would confine it to the direct destruction wrought by invasion and ignore the heavy indirect losses of the British public. The
American delegation stood almost alone in striving to give
"civilian damage" a literal construction. Finally a compromise was reached, largely on the advice of General Smuts
of South Africa, who urged that "while direct war expenditures... could perhaps not be recovered from the Germans,

yet disablement pensions to discharged soldiers, or pensions to widows and orphans, or separation allowances paid to their wives and children during the period of their military service are all items representing compensation to members of the civilian population for damage sustained by them." The treaty as finally shaped made Germany and her allies liable for: (1) injury to civilians caused by acts of war; (2) injury to civilians from mistreatment of any sort; (3) mistreatment of prisoners of war; (4) military pensions, separation allowances, and assistance to prisoners of war and their families; (5) reparation for forced labor and levies and fines in occupied territories; (6) injury to all property with the exception of military works or materials belonging to the Allied or Associated States or any of their citizens; (7) in the special case of Belgium, because of the violation of international law involved in the invasion of that country, Germany to assume the nation's war debt. The treaty stipulated also the restoration of live stock taken from occupied territory during the war, of works of art and historic souvenirs, and of other purloined property.[1] Elaborate provisions were laid down for the payment of the first installments of the indemnity in the form of specified amounts of shipping, coal, drugs, dyes, cable lines, and other immediately available assets. As it was impossible to tell in 1919 what sum Germany could pay or to how much the classes of damage for which Germany was held responsible might amount, a special Reparations Commission, representing the chief creditor nations, was established to fix the total by May 1, 1921.

Napoleon Bonaparte had once imposed disarmament on Prussia by treaty stipulations limiting the size of the Prussian

Disarmament   army. The result had been to transform the Prussian military machine from a professional standing army of the eighteenth century type into a military

---

[1] Including *inter alia* the Koran of the Caliph Othman and the skull of the Sultan Mkwawa of German East Africa!

training school which fitted the whole male population for battle. Warned by Napoleon's error, the statesmen of 1919 reversed the process. They fixed the German army at a maximum of 100,000 men, but they coupled this limitation with provisions which restored the old-fashioned professional army. Compulsory military service was forbidden; all enlistment must be for a long term and voluntary. The General Staff was dissolved. Thus ended the "Prussian system" of universal service, annual classes called to the colors, and organized reserves which had won victory in the wars of 1814, 1864, 1866 and 1870. Other provisions fixed the size of the German navy, forbade the use of submarines and poison gases, ordered the surrender of specified stocks of munitions, required the demolition of certain fortresses, and established Commissions of Control to see that the treaty provisions were executed. Beyond a vague declaration of future intention, nothing was done to limit armament among the victor powers.

The Versailles Treaty arraigned "William II of Hohenzollern, formerly German Emperor, for a supreme offense against international morality and the sanctity of treaties," and provided for the surrender and trial of "all persons having committed an act in *Punishment of war criminals* violation of the laws and customs of war" who might be accused by any of the Allied or Associated Powers. No other part of the treaty has broken down so completely. The refusal of the Dutch government to permit his extradition ended all talk of punishing the Kaiser, somewhat to the relief of the statesmen who made the demand in deference to the supposed opinion of their public. As for the Germans guilty of wartime cruelties and illegalities, but few of them were ever brought to trial and they received light sentences from the German courts which were permitted to handle the cases.[1] Perhaps it was as well, for the decisions of a foreign

[1] See C. Mullins, *The Leipsig Trials*, 1921.

tribunal would have been discounted from the start as mere
hostility to the German army, and the Kaiser would have
been more dangerous as a "martyr" — in the style of Napoleon at St. Helena — than as a voluntary runaway in a
neutral state.

Some few concessions were made to Germany in response
to the objections raised by the German delegation. Ger-
The treaty many obtained a plebiscite in Upper Silesia,
signed at which later enabled her to regain part of that
Versailles territory; assurances were given that the right
of the Saar valley to vote freely on the question of return to
Germany after fifteen years would not be affected by any remaining reparations indebtedness; the Polish corridor was
narrowed a little; a longer period was allowed for the decrease
of the German army, and a period of four months granted to
consider counter-proposals with respect to reparations. As
amended, the treaty was returned to the Germans with a
demand for unconditional acceptance. Count Brockdorff-
Rantzau, who had conducted the peace negotiations on behalf of Germany, resigned rather than sign the treaty; the
German sailors sank many of their warships rather than surrender them, and some French battle flags of 1870 were
burned to prevent their return to France. The decision
to accept the peace was carried through the National Assembly with difficulty and after stormy debates. But there
was nothing for a defeated and disarmed Germany to do except submit. At the old royal palace of Versailles on June
28, 1919, in the same hall where the German Empire had
been proclaimed in 1871, the treaty was signed. The Chinese
delegates alone withheld their signature, as a protest against
the Shan-tung award. As soon as peace was concluded the
fountains of Versailles burst into shower, the guns rang out
in salute, and the French people renewed the joyous celebrations which had marked armistice day. But for the peace
commissioners there was no holiday. They had to turn their

attention to the problems of Austria, Hungary, the Balkan States, Turkey and Russia, questions no less difficult than those concerning Germany.

By the Treaty of Versailles Germany lost over 27,000 square miles, an area greater than that of the Netherlands and Belgium combined. Her population was *Germany* reduced to a little over 60,000,000 (as compared *after the* with some 67,000,000 in 1914). Germany lost *treaty* the rich iron mines of Lorraine; rather more than a fourth of her coal, especially the Saar and Upper Silesia; from twelve to fifteen per cent of her cereal and vegetable crops; all her colonies, with their tropical products; the greater part of her merchant marine. She had signed a "blank check" for a reparations bill which was later fixed in 1921 at 132,000,000,-000 gold marks.[1] Her army was left smaller even than the Polish, and insignificant as compared with the French. Her navy, recently second only to the British, virtually ceased to exist. Foreign armies were encamped on German soil, to be maintained at German cost for fifteen years. These were severe terms and gave the Treaty of Versailles the nickname of the "Carthaginian peace." But the phrase is inapt. Carthage was destroyed; Germany remained a powerful factor in world trade and world politics. After all, the lost territories were for the most part inhabited by majorities of alien nationality, whereas Napoleon in his day had not hesitated to annex purely German territories. Germany suffered no such thoroughgoing partition as she had herself inflicted on Russia at Brest-Litovsk a few months earlier. The indemnities demanded created an indebtedness hardly greater than the war debts, foreign and domestic, which weighed down victorious France. Germany, no doubt, lost the war; it would be hard to say that anyone had won it!

Many parts of the peace settlement, such as the clauses dealing with the League of Nations, were worked out once

[1] See Chapter XXV.

for all in the Versailles Treaty and incorporated into later

The Austrian settlement treaties without alteration. Other parts of the settlement, such as reparations, economic restrictions and disarmament, had been worked out in principle with respect to Germany and could be applied to her allies with such alterations only as were necessary to adapt them to the circumstances of each country; for example, the Austrian army was limited to 30,000 men in place of Germany's 100,000. The new problems involved in the later treaties were mainly territorial. Austria-Hungary had already been partitioned by revolution; only detailed frontier adjustments remained to be worked out. But these were difficult enough, as at every step the rights of national self-determination conflicted with the interests of geographical unity, administrative convenience, or commercial advantage. Completely consistent application of the national principle would have replaced the old Empire with an economically impossible patchwork of tiny political units at least a score in number; on the other hand, disregard of the principle would repeat the errors made by the Congresses of Vienna in 1814–15 and Berlin in 1878 and, like those former settlements, pave the way for future wars and revolutions.

The province of Galicia, or Austrian Poland, went to the resurrected Polish Republic. The chief problem related to the eastern part of the province; western Galicia

Galicia is strictly Polish in character but in the east the majority of the population is of Ukrainian or Ruthenian nationality, akin to the natives of "Little Russia." On strictly democratic principles it should have been united with the Ukraine. But there were difficulties. The Polish element in eastern Galicia, like the German in Upper Silesia, is a dominant minority, accustomed to rule and possessed of wealth. The chief city Lemberg (or Lvov) is Polish. The historic traditions of the region associate it with the west,

with Austria and Poland, not with Russia. The prevalent
religion is not the Russian Orthodox, but the Uniate Church,
which combines somewhat of the ritual and customs of the
Orthodox Church with allegiance to the Roman Catholic
communion. There is a large Jewish population, neither
Polish nor Ukrainian but at times persecuted by both. Finally, the Ukraine itself was at the time in a state of complete chaos and civil war; no one knew whether it would
turn out to be an independent nation or a part of Soviet Russia. So the whole of Galicia went to Poland with
provision for "home rule" in the eastern part of the province;
a condition not very faithfully kept. The whole case is
worth studying as a good illustration of the difficulty, or
rather impossibility, of finding any completely satisfactory
solution of the national problems of eastern Europe.

Another perplexing tangle arose with regard to the coal-
mining area of Teschen on the borderline between Poland
and Czechoslovakia. When Premier Lloyd *Teschen*
George, in illustrating the complex problems of
peace making, confessed that he had never before heard of
Teschen, he was in no worse case than most of those who
laughed at his ignorance. Yet this small district almost
brought the two friendly and allied nations of Poland and
Czechoslovakia to war. It is a most unfortunate fact that
districts rich in coal, such as Teschen, the Saar and Upper
Silesia, are so often in Europe to be found on or near an international boundary and thus serve to instigate quarrels
between neighboring nations. In the end a Council of ambassadors of the Allied Powers divided Teschen, and two less
important disputed districts, Spits and Orawa, by a compromise line which satisfied neither country but at least averted
war. The Russian boundary of Poland was not settled by
the Peace Conference; a provisional boundary was indeed
indicated (the so-called Curzon line) but this included only
the unquestionably Polish districts in the east and left the

disputed areas to be settled by war between Poland and Soviet Russia.[1] The frontier between Poland and Lithuania took an even longer time to establish.

Czechoslovakia is a composite state made up by adding the Austrian provinces of Bohemia, Moravia and Austrian *Czecho-* Silesia [2] to a strip of northern Hungary just *Slovak fron-* south of the Carpathians. More fortunate than *tiers* Poland in one respect, Czechoslovakia has some good natural frontiers, the quadrilateral plateau of Bohemia, ringed with mountains, being one of the most definite geographical regions in Europe, and the Carpathians making an acceptable frontier with Poland. Only on the side facing the Hungarian plain was there no natural boundary fence. But to follow the mountain frontiers the new state had to violate the national principle and include over 3,000,000 Germans; to give it access to the Danube river the southern boundary was advanced far enough to include 750,000 Magyars. A small district of Ruthenian population, about 400,000 in number, was joined to eastern Czechoslovakia to make contact with Rumania; the Ruthenians, however, were at least closer kin to their fellow Slavs in Bohemia and Slovakia than to their former rulers, the Magyar Hungarians. Czechoslovakia is an inland country; no one but Shakespeare has been able to devise a "seacoast of Bohemia." [3] Its inland situation, its preposterous frontier line, its mixed population of several nationalities, made many critics of the peace predict short life for the new republic,

---

[1] For Polish relations with Russia and Lithuania see Chapters XXI and XXII.

[2] Also a tiny fragment of Prussian Silesia cut off from Germany by the new German-Polish frontier.

[3] One project put forward at the Peace Conference was to connect Czechoslovakia and Yugoslavia by a "corridor" between Austria and Hungary, but this plan was rightly rejected as involving too great a violation of the national principle, since most of the inhabitants of the corridor would be Germans or Magyars. Another plan, more seriously considered, was to lop off and give to Germany whatever German-speaking districts could be detached from the Bohemian plateau. But this plan was rejected on economic grounds, and in any case would have made little difference in the size of the German minority in Bohemia as a whole.

but thus far the patriotic spirit of the dominant Czech and Slovak element and the wisdom and moderation of their chosen rulers have not only overcome the natural difficulties of the situation but maintained what has been, ever since the war, the most democratic and prosperous of all the "succession states" which shared in the partition of the Dual Monarchy. The boldest experiment of the map makers has proved to be the most successful.

What was left of Austria was a little Alpine republic, almost wholly German in population, cut off from the sea and from the richest of the former provinces of the *The* old Dual Monarchy. The Peace Conference as- *Austrian* signed to Austria a little strip of western Hungary, *remnant* inhabited by Germans, and authorized a plebiscite in the Klagenfurt district on the frontier of Yugoslavia. Austria won the plebiscite and retained the territory. But these slight concessions hardly weighed against so many losses. An Empire of fifty millions was reduced to a tiny state of some 6,500,000 which had to support a capital city, Vienna, with nearly two million. The task would have been impossible but for foreign charity.

The most serious diplomatic difficulty which arose in establishing new frontiers in former Austro-Hungarian territory was with regard to the eastern boundary of *Italy and* Italy. In the north Italy was given the natural *the Adriatic* frontier of the Brenner Pass in accordance with *problem* the promises of the wartime Treaty of London (1915). The whole southern Tirol thus went to Italy with a mixed population of about 400,000 Italians and 230,000 Germans. The problem of the eastern frontier was more difficult as it involved a larger population and placed in opposition the claims of two Allied nations. The Serb-Croat-Slovene Kingdom, more generally called Yugoslavia, was represented at the Peace Conference among the victor nations because Serbia had succeeded in uniting under banner all the southern Slavs along the Adriatic coast; but the Italians were angrily conscious that, at least during the first two years of the war, the Croats and Slovenes had been loyal soldiers of Austria, and

THE ADRIATIC QUESTION

that while they could not be safely used against Russia or Serbia they showed little reluctance to fight against the Italians. The national feud was older than the war, for the Austrian government had long played up the reciprocal jealousies of Slav and Latin in order to maintain rule over both. From the Italian point of view, therefore, the new Yugoslav Kingdom had simply taken the place of the old Austria-Hungary as Italy's rival on the Adriatic. By virtue of the Treaty of London, Italy claimed the whole Istrian peninsula, with its valuable ports at Trieste and Pola, and a large share of the Dalmatian coast with the islands which fringe it. By virtue of the right of "self-determination" they claimed also the city of Fiume.

Fiume is an Italian-speaking town of about 50,000 which before the war was the main seaport of Hungary, although the countryside which surrounds it is neither Italian nor Hungarian but Slav. To award it to *Fiume* Italy would deprive Yugoslavia of her best port. Good harbors there are in plenty along the eastern Adriatic, but the value of most of them is lessened by the broad barrier of inhospitable highland which shuts off the sea from the inland river valleys. Only in the north, and especially at Fiume and Trieste, can the trade of the Danube valley be advantageously connected with the shipping routes of the Adriatic. The question of Fiume became a storm center at the Peace Conference. The Italians did not press very earnestly for their claims in Dalmatia,[1] though promised them by treaty, but they were very insistent on Fiume, which was not. President Wilson proposed a compromise line recommended by the geographers on his staff. This granted to Italy Trieste, Pola and most of the Italian communities in the disputed region; but since for economic reasons it allotted Fiume to Yugoslavia, Premier Orlando and Foreign Minister Sonnino refused to consider it. Finally, President Wilson made a direct appeal to the Italian people over the heads of their representatives, to put the general peace above a small immediate territorial gain. Fiume had, however, become a matter of national sentiment to the Italians, a cause and symbol not to be surrendered. The disposition of a seaport no bigger than Atlantic City seemed about to disrupt the whole peace settlement. The Italian delegates returned to Rome, found that they had parliamentary support for their

[1] Within the Treaty of London line in Dalmatia were 600,000 Slavs and only 18,000 Italians. One Italian propagandist admitted the fact, but declared it of no importance as the Slavs "were recent intruders, having come in the sixth century"!

demands, and then hastened back to Versailles to be in time
for the final steps of the German treaty. The matter at issue, not being directly involved in the Treaty of Versailles,
was left for later negotiation.

Gabriele d'Annunzio, poet, patriot, aviator and roman-
ticist in politics, resolved to cut the Gordian knot himself.
The Treaty With a small force of adventurous volunteers he
of Rapallo seized Fiume and established a dictatorship over
the surrounding region in the name of the Regency of the
Quarnero, with the intention of adding it later to Italy. The
Italian government seemed as embarrassed as the other
powers at this rough-rider diplomacy. At last in 1920 Italy
and Yugoslavia composed their quarrel by the Treaty of
Rapallo. Italy obtained the entire Istrian peninsula at the
head of the Adriatic with a far advanced eastern frontier
that reached to Fiume and at some points went beyond the
Italian claims under the Treaty of London. Fiume itself,
however, was to be an independent free port open to the
trade of both kingdoms. Dalmatia went to Yugoslavia,
but the city of Zara and some of the Adriatic islands along
the Dalmatian coast went to Italy. In 1924 a supplementary agreement transferred Fiume to Italy, though
Yugoslavia has commercial access to the Adriatic at the
neighboring suburb of Susak. The total Italian gains in
Europe as a result of the war amounted to a little less than
9000 square miles with a population of 1,600,000. Italy
obtained also the right to fortify Valona (Avlona) in Albania
and some extension of her colonial possessions in Africa.

Austria signed the Treaty of St. Germain in September,
1919, three months later than the German peace at Ver-
Hungary sailles. Hungary signed the Treaty of the Trianon
and Ru- in June, 1920, twelve months later. The reason
mania for the exceptional delay was the communist revolution in Hungary, the Rumanian invasion that followed it,
and the prolonged state of civil war and political disturbance

that resulted from this double disaster. In angry reaction against the projected partition of their "thousand year old realm" the proud Magyars placarded the streets with the legend "No, no! Never!" The moderate liberal government of Karolyi resigned, and power was seized by a group of communists, allied to the Russian Bolsheviki. Many Magyars who were not themselves communists tolerated the movement in the hope that revolution would sweep away the territorial claims of the Rumanians, Czecho-Slovaks and Yugoslavs. They were soon undeceived. In August, 1919, the Rumanians occupied Budapest. They hated Bolshevism, which to them meant the Russian danger, and they hated Hungary for the long oppression of the Rumanians in Transylvania and the recent plundering they had suffered from German and Magyar troops during the war. With zeal they performed their task of spoiling the spoilers. They seized grain and livestock, moved railroad cars onto their own lines, even stripped the linen from the hospitals. At last the Peace Conference, though pleased to see an end to the red dictatorship in Hungary, became alarmed. Sharp notes of reprimand were dispatched to Rumania, ending in a threat to consider Rumania no longer one of the Allies unless Budapest were evacuated. And now a third obstacle arose; with communism and foreign occupation out of the way, the Hungarians reacted towards monarchy. But the neighboring states that had profited at Hungary's expense, Czechoslovakia, Rumania and Yugoslavia, objected to a restoration of the Habsburgs as portending an "irredentist" campaign to reconquer Hungary's lost territories, and the Allied and Associated Powers announced that they could not "admit that the restoration of the Habsburg dynasty can be considered merely as a matter interesting the Hungarian nation, and hereby declare that such a restoration would be at variance with the whole basis of the peace settlement, and would neither be recognized nor tolerated by them."

Hungary was reduced to a landlocked state of 35,000 square miles and a little over 8,000,000 population; about a *The Trianon Treaty* third the size and population of the old Kingdom. Yugoslavia took over Hungary's former dependency of Croatia-Slavonia and part of the southern Hungarian district called the Banat of Temesvar. Rumania annexed the rest of the Banat, the whole of Transylvania and a few districts of Rumanian speech immediately to the west of Transylvania. From Austria Rumania had taken the greater part of Bukovina, which brought Rumania into contact with Poland. Czechoslovakia annexed the region of Slovak and Ruthenian speech south of the Carpathians. The remnant of Hungary had at least one advantage over the remnant of Austria; at least there was food. What was left of Hungary consisted mainly of the Alföld, the rich agricultural plain centering around the Danube river and the city of Budapest.

Because of the important national minorities included within their new frontiers, the Allied and Associated Powers *Minority rights* negotiated special treaties with Poland, Rumania, Czechoslovakia and Yugoslavia, by which the latter nations assumed the obligation of granting equal rights to other races and peoples within their borders. These treaties differ slightly in detail, but in general they grant to all inhabitants full civil and religious liberty, the right of citizenship to native-born inhabitants of any race, the free use of any and all languages in private business and private schools, with instruction "through the medium of their own language" in public schools where a particular national element is very numerous, and some particular privileges such as the right of the Jews to enjoy their Sabbath holiday. The protection of minority rights was entrusted to the League of Nations. Unfortunately, minority rights are more easily guaranteed on paper than in actual administration. Endless complaints of discrimination have been heard since the war from every one of the newly established or newly enlarged states of eastern and central Europe. Many of these complaints are of course exaggerated or unfounded,— mere "irredentist" propaganda for stirring up world opinion in favor of a revision of the peace treaties; but, true or false, they are symptoms of continuing discontent and national friction.

In November, 1919, several months before peace had been concluded with Hungary, Bulgaria accepted the Treaty of Neuilly. A narrow strip of mountainous fron- *Bulgaria* tier in the west went to Yugoslavia for the better protection of the Macedonian provinces. Western Thrace, the Bulgarian coastline on the Ægean, went to Greece. The American delegates proposed international control of this region, which had a largely Greek population but gave Bulgaria her only access to the Ægean Sea; but the European Allies thought the simplest solution would be to transfer the district to Greece. Bulgaria's claims, on national grounds, for Macedonia from Yugoslavia and the Dobrudja from Rumania were ignored. In 1914 the most powerful of the Balkan nations, Bulgaria was in 1920, with the exception of Albania, the least in area, in population and in military power.

At the end of the World War Greece seemed about to begin a career of brilliant national expansion. Venizelos, the shrewdest of Balkan diplomats, sketched out *Greater* a plan for a Grecian Empire surrounding the *Greece* Ægean; cogently arguing that it was irrational to treat Greece as a compact expanse of agricultural territory, like Rumania or Bulgaria, and on that basis to fix her boundaries; Greece was a maritime state, built on the seaways and should include all the coasts of the Ægean which had a majority of Greek population. Both eastern and western Thrace should be Greek (except that Constantinople might be an independent port) and on the coast of Asia Minor

Smyrna and its neighborhood should come under Greek protection. He hoped that in the course of time Great Britain would voluntarily cede Cyprus and Italy Rhodes, to add to the island possessions of Greece. At first the Allies viewed the Greek plan with some favor, though acute friction arose with Italy when in order to protect the citizens from the Turks; Greek troops were landed at Smyrna, near to the provinces of southern Asia Minor where Italy also claimed an interest. But the fall of Venizelos from power and the return of King Constantine to the throne forfeited for Greece the good will of the western Allies, especially France, with the result that Greece was left alone to impose her program — if she could — on the Turk. The victory of Turkish arms put an end for the time to the dream of a Pan-Ægean Empire; Greece abandoned Smyrna and retired from eastern Thrace, having won from the war practically nothing except Bulgaria's former coastland of western Thrace.

During the war Albania, though technically neutral, was used as battleground for both sides. Tentative plans had *Albania* been considered for the partition of the country, giving Serbia Scutari in the north, Greece the southern districts of mixed Hellenic and Albanian population, and Italy the purely Albanian center. But the Peace Conference finally decided to leave Albania independent within her old boundaries, though Italy retained the right to make use of the port of Avlona on the Adriatic.

The Ottoman Empire also had been scheduled for partition in the event of a victory for the Entente Allies. Russia *The Turkish* was to have Armenia and Constantinople; *settlement* France, Syria; Britain, Mesopotamia and, on *(1) What* behalf of the Jewish colonists, Palestine; Italy, *was planned* a commercial zone in the region of Adalia; Greece, the Smyrna region. Arabia would be independent under her own kings, though in alliance with Great Britain. The

Straits would be open to commerce alike in peace and war. Turkey would still retain in full sovereignty only the inner highlands of Anatolia around the ancient city of Angora and would sink to be a minor Moslem state like Afghanistan. The collapse of Russia and the military recovery of Turkey after the armistice swept aside much of this program and necessitated a complete recasting of that part of the peace settlement.

The first attempt at a definite settlement of the Turkish question was embodied in the Treaty of Sèvres (1920). As previously arranged, Syria passed to France and Mesopotamia to Britain, Palestine became a Jewish homeland under British mandate, Cyprus and Egypt were freed from dependence on Turkey, and the Arab Kingdom of the Hedjaz became independent. To this extent the wartime aspirations of the Entente Allies were fulfilled. But Russia no longer laid claim to Armenia or Constantinople. Nobody wanted a mandate for inaccessible, mountainous Armenia, but President Wilson was asked to establish the new Armenian frontier. Greece obtained the Smyrna district and eastern Thrace, but Constantinople remained the Turkish capital and the Allies abandoned their boast of expelling the Turk from Europe. The Straits were neutralized, however, and their fortifications dismantled. *(2) What was enacted, The Treaty of Sèvres*

No sooner had the Allied Powers imposed their peace on the Turkish government at Constantinople than they found that the real strength of the Turkish nation was no longer there. A vigorous Nationalist party, paralleling in its zeal for reform and its patriotic ardor the Young Turks of 1908, arose in Asia Minor. Allied warships that could overawe Constantinople had little effect on the provisional government set up at Angora. An experienced Turkish officer, Mustapha Kemal, assumed the powers of a dictator and disregarded completely *(3) What was accomplished, The Treaty of Lausanne*

the commands of the nominal Sultan. The moment was favorable. The United States and Russia had practically withdrawn from direct interest in the affairs of Turkey; France and Italy both had serious grievances against Greece, the one nation still actively in arms against the Turks; a new crusade would add to the staggering burden of war debts which weighed down Britain, France and Italy, and perhaps cause discontent among the millions of Mohammedan subjects of those three powers in Morocco, Algeria, Tunis, Tripoli, Egypt and India. The French voluntarily abandoned Cilicia and limited their interests to Syria. Smyrna was reconquered and Armenia overrun. Only the British forces at the Straits prevented an armed invasion of European Greece and a renewal of the Balkan Wars.

Naturally under such circumstances Turkey could ask — or almost dictate — favorable terms. By the Treaty of Lausanne (1923) the Treaty of Sèvres was drastically revised. The old European boundaries of 1914, including all eastern Thrace from Constantinople to Adrianople, were restored to Turkey with little change, though the Thracian frontier, like the Straits, was to remain unfortified. Greece lost the Smyrna region. The demand for an independent Armenia was tacitly dropped; indeed the Russo-Turkish frontier of 1923 lay further east than the frontier of 1914. Turkey promised equal rights to her Christian subjects, but the scattered Armenians who had escaped massacre had either to accept Turkish rule or cross the border into Russian Armenia. The "capitulations" (special privileges of foreigners resident in Turkey) were abandoned. Except for the regions south of the Anatolian highland — Syria, Mesopotamia, Palestine and Arabia — the Ottoman Empire had held its boundaries as they were left by the Balkan Wars of 1912–13.

One task the Paris Peace Conference found insoluble. After settling the frontiers, indemnities and commercial rights of enemy states, the Peace Commissioners hoped to reach an agreement as to what policy they should pursue towards Russia. But what *was* Russia? In 1919 a Bolshevist government held sway in Moscow and Petrograd but it was still contesting for its existence with counter-revolutionary armies in Siberia, along the Arctic, and along the Black Sea. Finland, Poland, and the Baltic republics of Estonia, Latvia and Lithuania were adjusting their frontiers with Russia and with each other by force of arms. The Ukraine maintained a precarious independence while torn by civil war. Under the circumstances the best proposal the Peace Conference could agree on was to

Russia and the Prinkipo Conference

> invite every organized group that is now exercising or attempting to exercise political authority or military control anywhere in Siberia or within the boundaries of European Russia as they stood before the war just concluded (except in Finland) [1] to send representatives... to the Princes Island, Sea of Marmora, where they will be met by representatives of the Associated Powers, provided in the meantime there is a truce of arms among the parties invited.

The armistice asked for did not take place, the various partisan groups continued their struggle, and the Prinkipo (Princes Island) Conference was abandoned. The French felt so sorely Russia's desertion of the Allied cause that they permitted no Russian unit to march in the triumphal procession of the Allied and Associated armies on July 14, 1919, although Russia had made the heaviest sacrifices of the war.

The Paris Peace Conference began amid an atmosphere of exaggerated hopes and ended in universal disappointment. So much was inevitable and might have been prophesied by anyone acquainted with the great wars of the past. Idealisms born of keen national danger do not much outlast the passing of the danger which

Failures of the Peace of Paris

---

[1] The independence of Finland was taken for granted; this was not so of the Baltic and Caucasian States, nor of the Ukraine.

begat them; jealousies revive among the victorious powers, and the inevitable compromises which follow if peace is to be made at all prove disappointing to everyone. When Clemenceau took his treaty to the French Chambers he was bitterly attacked for having cravenly yielded French interests to the "Anglo-Saxon bloc" of Britain and America. All his services in the war failed to win him the presidency of France even after he had consented to become a candidate, and he died an embittered and disappointed man. President Wilson went home to find the American Senate in open revolt against the Covenant of the League of Nations, the part of the peace settlement dearest to his heart. Italian discontent at inadequate gains paved the way for the ultra-nationalist dictatorship of Mussolini. Premier Lloyd George was more fortunate than his colleagues, but he did not escape bitter criticism in the press, from Tory organs like the *National Review*, which accused him of sacrificing stern justice to the sentimental bleatings of American pacifism, to the radical *Nation*, which blamed him for imposing a ruinous peace on Germany to satisfy the chauvinistic French. The small states were equally dissatisfied. Venizelos was repudiated by Greece as definitely as Wilson by the American public or Clemenceau by the French. The failures of the peace were indeed obvious enough. The Russian question had not been settled at all; the Turkish and Balkan questions were adjusted mainly on the good old plan "that he should take who has the power and he should keep who can"; the Austro-Hungarian settlement was a series of illogical compromises between national and economic claims that never quite satisfied either; the German treaty bristled with dangers for future peace. When General Smuts declared that he signed the peace not because he approved of it but merely to end the state of war, he probably spoke the mind of half the Peace Commissioners who signed with him.

Yet it would be unfair and unhistorical not to credit the
Peace Conference with important positive achievements.
In many directions it advanced far beyond former
diplomatic precedents.   It remapped Europe
more nearly in accordance with the principle of
national self-determination than ever before in
the whole course of history.   There were violations of the
principle of nationality at Paris in several instances for reasons of special strategic or economic interest; for example,
the refusal to permit Austria to unite with Germany.   But
the emancipation of Poland, the resurrection of Czechoslovakia, the union of the Rumanians, the union of the Yugoslavs, the recognition of the independent status of the former
Russian borderlands of Finland, Lithuania, Latvia and Estonia, carried to a triumphant climax the work of creative
nationalism which began before the war with the union of
Germany and Italy, the independence of Belgium and Norway and the emancipation of the peoples subject to the Turk.
Another tribute to the ideal of self-determination was the
frequent use of the plebiscite, or direct consultation of the
people, in the fixing of frontiers.   This device was used in
Allenstein,[1] Marienwerder,[1] Klagenfurt,[2] northern and central Schleswig[3] and Upper Silesia[1] (and eventually for the
Saar in 1935); and that most of the plebiscites were honestly
conducted is shown by the fact that in all cases except the
northern Schleswig zone they went in favor of the defeated
enemy states.   (Napoleon III would have known how to
make them yield another result!)   Treaties protecting minorities, though hard to enforce in practise, were another
recognition of liberal and humane ideals; and so was the
establishment of the "mandate" principle for the surrendered
German colonies and the protectorates taken from Asiatic

*Achieve-
ments of
the Peace
Conference*

---

[1] On the German-Polish border.

[2] On the Austro-Yugoslav border.

[3] On the German-Danish border.

Turkey. Very great care was taken to afford victor and vanquished nations better facilities for international trade, the use of rivers and straits and overland access to seaports; to facilitate naturalization; to provide rules for commercial aviation; to hasten the exchange of prisoners and refugees, and in every way restore the normal life of peace.

The boldest and most promising experiment of all was the creation of a League of Nations, a dream as old as civiliza*The League of Nations* tion, but never seriously attempted in "practical politics" till 1919. The League was an intrinsic part of the peace settlement and a necessary method of enforcing many of its provisions, but as it involves problems of its own, it will be more fully discussed in another chapter.

CHAPTER XIX

THE LEAGUE OF NATIONS

THE Covenant of the League of Nations has too often been considered a mere irrelevant addition to the Treaty of Versailles. As a matter of fact it was an inevitable part of the peace. Not President Wilson only, but most of the responsible statesmen of the Allied and Associated Powers had pledged themselves to its establishment, and to have repudiated or postponed their promise would have invited revolution in many nations of Europe. The war had cost far too much for the suffering millions to tolerate a settlement which contained no attempt whatever to prevent its recurrence. Another reason for the early consideration of the problem of establishing a League of Nations was the need of creating some political machinery to carry on the new tasks of international administration created by the treaties themselves. Had there been no League, other international agencies would have had to be devised to administer Danzig and the Saar, to oversee the mandate system, to examine complaints of violated minority rights in the new states of eastern Europe, and to perform a thousand and one other tasks imposed by the treaties. The decisions which were really open to the peacemakers related to points of detail: how should the League be organized, what nations should it include, what powers should it be assigned? At one extreme conservative lawyers like Secretary Lansing hoped it would be no more than a revamped and improved Hague Conference and Court; at the other extreme some Frenchmen wanted it to be a coercive military league with a permanent general staff. Utopians hoped for a "parliament of man, a federation of the world," but none of them were in

The Covenant an inevitable part of the settlement

the Peace Conference or, if there, long withstood its atmosphere of bargain and compromise.

In creating the League of Nations the Peace Conference was working out one of the oldest ideas in the world. The *The League idea in the past* writings of Hebrew, Greek, Hindu and Chinese philosophers are full of the idea of a world peace based on the common brotherhood of humanity. Christianity and Islam tried to make this peace actual on the basis of a common creed. From the Roman Empire, which included the whole civilized world as known to Europeans, the Middle Ages inherited the concept of a universal Empire led and directed by Council, Pope or Emperor. The tendency in modern times has been directly away from this ideal; to assert the separate sovereignty of each national state. But, thanks to Grotius and other writers on international law, the idea gained currency that even sovereign kingdoms were governed by the customs and conventions of civilized humanity. The wars of religion brought forth "the Grand Design of Henry IV" (really the work of his minister Sully) for a European federation; the European Parliament proposed by William Penn; and the League of sovereign princes advocated by the French philosopher Saint-Pierre. Immanuel Kant, the Prussian philosopher, influenced by the democratic ideals of the enlightenment, struck a new note in his essay on *Eternal Peace* by advocating instead of a single powerful monarch or league of monarchs, a federation of free nations with popular governments.

After the overthrow of Napoleon an alliance of the victor powers was formed which in some respects foreshadows the making of the League after the defeat of Germany a century later. But the analogy should not be pressed too far. The Quadruple Alliance of Russia, Austria, Prussia and Britain (later France) with its annual congresses resembled the League only in that both professed to maintain the peace of Europe. It was a league of sovereigns rather than of nations, it ignored the minor European states, it provided no permanent agencies or political machinery but was merely an alliance similar to the temporary alliances of wartime. As directed by Metternich, its method of international conference was used chiefly for the repression of liberal movements; a kind of anti-revolutionary police. As for the Holy Alliance of the Tsar Alexander I which came into being at the same period, it was really no alliance at all but merely a manifesto that the signatory nations would henceforth be guided by Christian principles in their dealings with each other and with their subjects. The Quadruple Alliance left one useful legacy of its rather discredited existence, the custom of calling general diplomatic conferences of the powers, the "Concert of Europe," to settle such tangled problems as the Near Eastern Question. The development of an interlacing system of treaties of arbitration and the establishment of an arbitral tribunal at The Hague supplied to a limited extent the need for an international guarantee of peace. But any further step was considered quite impracticable until the outbreak of the World War.

The war itself was the greatest stimulus to plans for securing lasting peace. Official statements from all the principal belligerent nations forecast, rather *The League* vaguely, an association of nations to prevent war, *idea in war-* and many private organizations, such as the *time* British Labor Party and the American League to Enforce Peace which included such prominent leaders as ex-President Taft, worked out more definite suggestions. The mere fact that the Allied and Associated Powers comprised more than half the world and that the exigencies of war compelled them to pool their shipping, credits, munitions and raw materials was a powerful lesson in the need and possibility of international co-operation.

No nation brought to Paris a complete, ready-made plan for the League. But the American and British delegates had

in hand several tentative drafts.[1]   At Paris the Americans
and British found that they had been working
Anglo-
American   along quite similar lines, and so in a series of
influences   informal conferences which preceded the actual
meeting of the League of Nations Commission the various
drafts were blended.   This plan, put into form by Mr.
David Hunter Miller on behalf of the United States and
by Mr. C. J. B. Hurst representing Great Britain, was in
substance accepted by President Wilson and by him laid
before the Commission as a basis for discussion.   Premier
Lloyd George showed less direct interest in the League than
President Wilson.   While heartily applauding the principle
he left the adjustment of details to Lord Robert Cecil, General Smuts and other British representatives and experts.

The French contributed singularly little to the making of
the Covenant.   It would be wrong to say that Clemenceau
Continental   was opposed to the idea of the League; he valued
influences   it as one among many guarantees for the safety
of France.   But he saw in the League little more than such
a guarantee, and when he found that it could not be transformed into a definite military alliance he turned his main
attention to other matters.   M. Léon Bourgeois, the chief
spokesman for France on the Commission which drafted the
Covenant, was more idealistic.   Italy and Japan played
little part.   The smaller Allies were represented on the
Commission by delegates from Belgium, Brazil, China,
Portugal, Serbia, Greece, Poland, Rumania and Czechoslovakia.   When the first draft was completed neutral states
also offered comments and suggestions, and Germany made
very elaborate counter-proposals when the terms of peace
were presented.   Essentially, however, the Covenant was
of blended British and American authorship.

Considering the importance of the proposals before the

---

[1] For the detailed comparison of early drafts and plans see D. H. Miller, *The
Drafting of the Covenant* (2 vols., 1928).

Commission there was surprisingly little controversy. The French attempt to place military forces at the disposal of the League was the most important amendment considered and rejected. President *Work of the Commission on the League* Wilson's proposal for religious freedom and equality among all Member States of the League was dropped, partly because Japan sought to broaden it into a declaration against racial discrimination. As this would have been widely interpreted in America and Australia as permitting Asiatic immigration, it was outside practical politics. The establishment of the mandate system for former German colonies and Ottoman provinces (article 22 of the Covenant) was the subject of prolonged discussion, but rather in the Supreme Council than in the Commission. The warmest debate during the drafting of the Covenant related to the rather trivial matter of what city would house the League headquarters. M. Hymans, head of the Belgian delegation, urged — with the support of France — the claims of Brussels, as the best way of rewarding Belgium for her services in the war. Sentiment, however, was not permitted to prevail. Britain, Italy, the United States and most of the other delegations supported Geneva in Switzerland, partly because of its beautiful and convenient location, but partly also because it was on neutral soil and would demonstrate to the world that the League of Nations was no mere continuation of the wartime alliance.

Article Ten of the Covenant, later called by President Wilson "the heart of the Covenant," provoked much less discussion in Paris than it later did in Washing- *Article Ten* ton. As adopted by the Conference it read:

> The members of the League undertake to respect and pre-serve as against external aggression the territorial integrity and existing political independence of all Members of the League. In case of any such aggression or in case of any threat or danger of such aggression the Council shall advise upon the means by which this obligation shall be fulfilled.

It is interesting to note that in an earlier draft by President Wilson specific provision was made for peaceful alteration of national boundaries by action of the League:

> The Contracting Powers unite in guaranteeing to each other political independence and territorial integrity; but it is understood between them that such territorial readjustments, if any, as may in the future become necessary by reason of changes in present racial conditions and aspirations or present social and political relationships, pursuant to the principle of self-determination, and also such territorial readjustments as may in the judgment of three-fourths of the Delegates be demanded by the welfare and manifest interest of the peoples concerned, may be effected, if agreeable to those peoples; and that territorial changes may in equity involve material compensation.

The proposal was dropped as most of the peace commissioners and some of Wilson's own advisers thought it unwise to permit the League to alter national boundaries by a three-fourths vote. Of course the right of nations, acting on their own initiative, to alter frontiers by purchase, treaty agreement, or any other method except international war, is not in any way affected by Article X, which debars only military violence.

The first draft of the Covenant was subjected to much discussion and some revisions were made. After President *The Monroe* Wilson's return to Europe the League of Nations *Doctrine* Commission reassembled and several changes were made in response to these criticisms. Perhaps the most interesting amendment was Article XXI explicitly recognizing the Monroe Doctrine, or similar "regional understandings," the first time in history that European powers gave formal and official sanction to that assertion of American policy. Question has been raised whether Article XXI was necessary in view of the fact that Article X, forbidding wars of aggression against Member States, seemed to cover the main object of the Monroe Doctrine, the protection of Latin America from European colonization and conquest. But since in the event that some Latin American nation remained outside the League Article X would not have assured its safety, there may have been some value in the explicit statement.

The Covenant invited to immediate membership in the League twenty-seven Allied and Associated Powers,[1] the entire "victor group" in the World War, and *Who were* thirteen neutral nations. Enemy states and a *members?* few neutrals, such as Mexico and Russia, where no recognized government existed at the moment, were not invited to be among the "charter members," though in the future any independent nation might join the League with the approval of two-thirds of the Assembly. Any Member State might withdraw after two years' notice of its intention and the fulfillment of existing obligations. Separate representation was accorded to the self-governing British Dominions of Canada, Australia, South Africa and New Zealand, and to the Empire of India. This did not increase the voting power of the British home government, as the provision was inserted to satisfy the Dominions themselves, who desired an opportunity to express their views directly in the League Assembly instead of leaving everything to the British Foreign Office. On several occasions Dominion delegates have voted in opposition to those of the mother country.

The League of Nations is not a World State, a true Federation of Nations, or a Super-State in any sense. It is created by the Member States, it has no policies ex- *The struc-* cept the policies of the Member Governments, and *ture of the* it has no treasures or armed forces except as these *League* may be voluntarily furnished by the Member States. On the other hand, the League is more than a mere alliance or conference, as it has a structure of its own and, as a corporate body, can and does carry on diplomatic correspondence, ad-

[1] Thirty-two if the British Dominions and India be separately reckoned.

minister important territories and perform other political functions.   Perhaps the League may best be defined for practical purposes as an international *agency* to which the Member States which compose it have transferred certain duties and through which they have agreed to exercise certain of their sovereign powers.   The primary organs of the League are (1) the Council, (2) the Assembly, and (3) the Secretariat, the last being a clearing-house of information and diplomatic correspondence required to keep the various Member States in touch with the work of the League.   In addition, there are closely associated organizations such as the Court of International Justice, the International Labor Office, technical organizations dealing with economic and financial affairs, public health, transportation and the like, advisory commissions on such matters as armaments, mandates, the repression of the opium and "white slave" traffic, and administrative commissions for such areas as Danzig and the Saar. The budget was apportioned among the Member States "in accordance with the apportionment of the expenses of the International Bureau of the Universal Postal Union." [1]   The annual expense was insignificant, amounting to a total *yearly* cost for all the work of the League less than the *hourly* cost of the last months of the World War!

In making the League Covenant, as in making the American constitution, one problem was to balance the interests *The Council* of the greater and lesser states.   In the Covenant *and Assem-* this was solved by creating an Assembly in which *bly* each Member State, from Great Britain to Haiti, from France to Albania, had three representatives, and a Council in which the Great Powers had permanent seats and the other places were distributed among such lesser nations as the Assembly might select by vote.   On the first Council Britain, France, Italy, Japan and the United States of America were offered the permanent places and Belgium,

---

[1] Another method of apportionment was later adopted.

Brazil, Spain and Greece the temporary posts. The American chair has always been vacant, but Germany and Russia, after admission to the League, obtained permanent seats, and the number of non-permanent places for the minor states was later increased from four to six (1922), nine (1926), ten (1933). The Council and the Assembly both have power to mediate in international disputes, but as the Council is the smaller body and in more frequent session it has been the real executive arm of the League. The Assembly had, however, two important powers, besides its general deliberative functions; it selected the non-permanent members of the Council and voted on new admissions to the League membership. Amendments to the Covenant required the assent of all the governments represented on the Council and of a majority of those represented in the Assembly.

The main purpose of the League of Nations was to prevent a recurrence of international war. By Article VIII of the Covenant the Council was required to formulate *Procedure* plans for the reduction of armaments. By *to prevent* Article XI, really a more sweeping assertion of *war* jurisdiction than the much discussed Article X, "the League shall take any action that may be deemed wise and effectual to safeguard the peace of nations" and any Member State may bring to the attention of either Council or Assembly "any circumstance whatever affecting international relations which threatens to disturb international peace." By Article XII the Member States pledge themselves to submit disputes either to arbitration or to the mediation of the Council and "agree in no case to resort to war until three months after the award by the arbitrators or the report by the Council." Articles XIII and XIV authorize arbitral tribunals and a Permanent Court of International Justice. Article XV provides that disputes which cannot be settled by court or arbiter be submitted to the Council. If the Council makes a unanimous report (excluding, of course, the parties to the controversy), it is held to be conclusive and no nation in the League may go to war against the nation accepting the decision. If the Council disagrees, the Member States are free to act as they think best. The Council may authorize the Assembly to handle the dispute, in which case a majority of all the Member States and the representatives of all the states represented in the Council must concur in the decision. By the wise provisions of Article XVIII secret diplomacy was forbidden, since no treaty or other international engagement of any Member State was to be binding unless publicly registered with the League. By Articles XIX and XX treaties dangerous to world peace might be reviewed by the League and abrogated if inconsistent with the provisions of the Covenant.

By Article XVI a nation which resorts to war in violation of the Covenant is regarded as in a state of hostility to all *Penalties for law-breakers* the other Member States of the League, who are expected to "subject it to the severance of all trade or financial relations," the economic weapon of the blockade and boycott. The Council may also in extreme cases recommend to the nations upholding the Covenant the use of military, naval and air forces. Of course these recommendations to become effective would need also action by the home governments of the nations concerned. The Council has no armies of its own, and the obligation to resort to war against an offending state is at most a "moral obligation" not legally enforceable. The Covenant does, however, impose the legal obligation not to aid the government adjudged to be in the wrong or to interfere with the actions taken by the League for its coercion. The League may also defend one of its Member States against attack from a nation outside the League (Article XVII).

Against rebellion and civil war, however, the League is powerless to act. If the Council upon investigation discovers that a dispute arises from "a matter which by international law is solely within the domestic jurisdiction of that party," the Council must refuse to take ac- *No "right* tion. This means that the League of Nations en- *of interven-* joys no such power as was claimed and exercised *tion"* by the Quadruple Alliance under Metternich's direction to in, tervene in the internal politics of any nation. To take con, crete cases, if Ireland or India should rise in rebellion against the British Empire, the League could not act to aid the British in suppressing the rebellion. Or if France and Poland thought it expedient to overthrow Bolshevism in Russia they could not act through the League or with its authorization unless Russia began the war. The League acts only to prevent *international* war. The point is worth stressing as it has been widely misunderstood. It is often said, for instance, that since the League was established there has been "more fighting in the world than ever," but most of these conflicts were purely internal and thus outside the jurisdiction of the League, as in China, Mexico, Russia, Ireland and many other countries.

The Permanent Court of International Justice is foreshadowed in Article XIV of the Covenant, which provides that the Council shall make plans for its establish- *The Court* ment, that the Court shall be competent to ad- *of Inter-* judge any international dispute submitted to it, *national* and that the Court may advise the Council and *Justice* the Assembly whenever requested to do so. In a sense, then, the Court is one of the League agencies. But though authorized by the Covenant it was not actually founded until 1921 and did not hold session until 1922. In its own sphere of action the Court is independent of both Council and Assembly. It deals with cases in which definite legal interests are involved, such as the interpretation of a treaty or the application of principles of international law. Thus, for example, a boundary dispute arising from the confusing language or inaccurate geography of old charters can be brought into the Court and there decided. But if two colonizing nations are fixing the extent of a "sphere of interest" no court can decide the question as there exists no legal basis for the decision. It is a question of the balance of power, not the determination of legal right. Until the League of Nations was established disputes of this latter type could be settled only by diplomatic bargain or by war.

The Hague Tribunal established in 1899 by the first Hague Conference was in some degree a precedent for the Permanent *The Hague* Court of International Justice.[1]   Both were es-*Tribunal* sentially judicial rather than diplomatic or po-*and the International* litical bodies; they could deal only with cases of *Court* legal right submitted to them by the interested parties and they had no means of enforcing their decisions. The essential difference between the two organizations was in their constitution. The Court of Arbitration at The Hague was not a permanent organic institution but merely a panel or list of judges from which arbitrators might be selected for the particular dispute of the moment. The Court of International Justice maintains a permanent "full time" bench of fifteen judges who are already impaneled to hear any case that may be brought before them. The selection is made by the Assembly and the Council of the League and only those candidates with an absolute majority in both are elected. In this ingenious manner a Court is created which is small enough for efficiency and yet no mere tool of a few large nations. The honor and dignity of the office, the long term of service [2] and the adequate remuneration granted have made the Court attractive to the highest authorities on international law.

The Paris Peace Conference regarded as one of its fundamental tasks the preparation of a charter for the protection of the international interests of labor. Precedent existed for this

[1] Sometimes popularly called the World Court.
[2] Nine years, with privilege of re-election.

in previous international treaties and conventions respecting
the rights of immigrant laborers, the prohibition *The protec-*
of the use of poisonous white phosphorus in *tion of labor*
matches, and the prohibition of night work for women. A special commission under the chairmanship of Samuel Gompers,
the veteran head of the American Federation of Labor,
worked out a plan for an International Labor Office, annual
Labor Conferences, and a code of principles to govern working conditions before the League of Nations Covenant was
completed. The most important part of the plan was the
establishment of an International Labor Office for the "collection and distribution of information in all subjects relating
to the international adjustment of conditions of industrial
life and labor, and particularly the examination of subjects
which it is proposed to bring before the Conference with a
view to the conclusion of international conventions." Albert
Thomas, the able French labor leader, was the first Director
of the Office. He was assisted by a Governing Body representing governments, employers and labor unions and by a
staff of several hundred experts and clerical workers. Annual Labor Conferences were assigned the duty of preparing
recommendations for the protection of labor, which may
take one of two forms, a general "recommendation" for
legislative and administrative action, or a definite "draft
convention" drawn up in form suitable for immediate embodiment into law. No government, of course, is bound to
accept against its will the proposals of any Conference; but
if a law, once adopted, is afterwards disregarded, the International Labor Office may order an inquiry and publish the
truth about the matter. In the Conferences each Member
State has four representatives, two representing "government," one "capital" and one "labor." The United States
accepted membership in 1934.

The Treaty of Versailles, in addition to establishing the
International Labor Office and making provision for annual

Conferences, laid down a series of nine principles which
The labor   should govern the spirit of labor legislation: (1) la-
"bill of   bor "should not be regarded merely as a com-
rights"   modity or article of commerce"; (2) right of free
association "for all lawful purposes"; (3) a living wage; (4)
the eight-hour day; (5) a weekly day of rest; (6) abolition of
child labor; (7) equal pay for women "for work of equal
value"; (8) equitable treatment for all workers in each country; (9) a system of inspection for the enforcement of laws
protecting labor.   Though not all these provisions have yet
been embodied in concrete form in the statutes of the nations,
under the auspices of the Labor Conferences draft conventions have been prepared for the eight-hour day and forty-
eight hour maximum week in industry,[1] for limiting the labor
of women and young persons at night and in dangerous
trades, for prohibition of child labor in various trades, for
protection against lead poisoning, for public employment exchanges.   Some of these conventions have been widely ratified, and others have at least stimulated national legislatures
to take action on their own account in the interests of labor.

Although the League of Nations was organized primarily
to prevent war, it has hitherto found most of its tasks to lie
Humanita-   in the field of "public welfare work."   Under the
rian activi- able administration of Dr. Fridtjof Nansen, the
ties of the Norwegian scientist and explorer, over 400,000
League   prisoners of war, belonging to twenty-six nationalities, were safely returned to their homes.   The League
also aided in caring for several hundred thousand Greek and
Armenian refugees expelled from Turkey, and organized the
medical services of Europe to keep typhus from spreading
from Russia into western Europe.   It has held conferences
to check the international traffic in opium, the sale of ob-
scene literature, professional prostitution, and the sale of
arms to native tribes.   By establishing a committee on in-

---

[1] A movement for the forty-hour week has more recently been started.

tellectual co-operation it brought together scientists and scholars from recently hostile nations for the purpose of facilitating the exchange of scientific, artistic and literary information and the movement of students and teachers from one country to another. In several instances, most notably in the case of Austria, it has brought about the financial rehabilitation of a distressed nation.

The war had consumed the wealth of Austria, the revolution which followed and the loss of the non-German provinces prevented any speedy reconstruction on the basis *The League* of the old prewar economy, and the decision of *saves Austria* the Peace Conference prevented the union of the *tria* Austrians with their fellow Germans in the Reich. American charity tided over the first few months of peace but could not undo the effects of the triple wound inflicted by the war, the revolution and the peace settlement. In 1922 the League of Nations was charged with the duty of finding a solution of Austria's difficulties. For a time the government, on its financial side, practically went into a receivership. The ordinary civil government continued to perform its duties, but in all matters connected with financial reform it was subordinate to Dr. Alfred Zimmermann, the Dutch financier who represented the League of Nations. An international loan of some $130,000,000 (650,000,000 gold crowns) was floated and provided a substantial basis for a reformed currency. To forestall the need of any new inflation the budget was balanced by drastic economies. A new national bank, independent of the local government, carried out the reform policy in detail. Many changes were ordered in tariffs and taxes. As a result of these heroic measures Austrian industry and finance were stabilized until the great depression swept over the world a decade later. In 1924 a similar program was applied to the finances of Hungary. In this instance an American financier, Jeremiah Smith, represented the League of Nations.

No one has denied the League great credit for its many humanitarian achievements. But many have anxiously asked the question: "Will the League of Nations save the world from war or be merely another such organization as the Red Cross to bind up the wounds which war inflicts on humanity? In the event of another such major crisis as that of 1914 would the Council act, or would it be paralyzed by factions so that it could arrive at no agreed verdict? Suppose the Council to make its unanimous recommendation, would the Member States obey? Would the sanctions invoked be of a military or an economic sort? Would they suffice to restrain the aggressor?" The League has acted in several minor crises, sometimes with complete success; as often succeeding merely in postponing the issue and evading an actual outbreak of war. Frequently the powers have preferred to handle a crisis through other agencies than the League. In questions outside Europe, as in Manchuria, the Member States were sometimes reluctant to use the machinery which the League provided.[1]

Has the League curbed war?

In several instances of threatened war the League of Nations found a peaceful solution, though not always one acceptable to both parties in the dispute. One of the earliest cases of mediation by the League was the dispute between Finland and Sweden over the Aaland Islands, an archipelago lying in the Baltic midway between the two countries. The case for Sweden was that the islanders were Swedish in language and desired annexation. The case for Finland was that the islands had long been a part of the Finnish state, under the Russian Grand Duchy as well as under the present independent republic. Cogent geographic and strategic arguments were advanced by both sides. After several months of investigation the Council confirmed the report of

Where the League has mediated

The Aaland islands

[1] For the Manchurian crisis see Chapter XXX.

the special commission which had the matter in hand, award-
ing the islands to Finland on legal grounds, but providing
that they should remain unfortified and that the interests
and language rights of the Swedish-speaking islanders should
have special legal protection.

Other frontier disputes dragged on for a longer time. In
the case of Vilna, a Polish city surrounded by Lithuanian
countryside, war was with some difficulty averted
between Poland and Lithuania after an irregular *Vilna*
Polish force had seized it. In 1923 the Council of Allied
Ambassadors (a successor, with diminished power, of the
Supreme Council of the Paris Peace Conference) awarded
Vilna to Poland, although Lithuania protested against the
decision. The League of Nations did not arrive at the final
settlement, but its intervention postponed the crisis till national passions had somewhat allayed. In 1924 a neutral
commission created by the Council of the League arranged
the terms on which the district of Memel was transferred to
Lithuania. In the Balkans the League put a stop *Memel, Al-*
to hostilities that were threatening to flare up *bania and*
along the frontier between Albania and Yugo- *Mosul*
slavia. In a protracted controversy from 1924 to 1926 between Turkey and Great Britain, as mandatory power over
Iraq (Mesopotamia), the League adjusted the international
boundary in the neighborhood of the rich oil field of Mosul.

More threatening to the general peace were three other
frontier questions: the Polish-German boundary in Upper
Silesia, the crisis arising between Greece and *The Silesian*
Italy over the Greco-Albanian frontier, and the *plebiscite*
war actually begun between Greece and Bulgaria in 1925.
The plebiscite on Upper Silesia was taken March 20, 1921.
Over 700,000 votes were cast for Germany; not quite 500,000
for Poland. Germany claimed that the whole district should
be returned to her, the more so since its wealth of coal and
metal was needed to make good the loss of Alsace-Lorraine

and permit her to attain prosperity. A line of division
separating the Polish from the German districts was not
contrary to the Treaty of Versailles which stated that "The
result of the vote will be determined by communes according
to the majority of votes in each commune" and that the
commission in charge of the plebiscite should make "a recommendation as to the line which ought to be adopted as
the frontier of Germany in Upper Silesia." But the result
was almost impossible to interpret in detail; German districts
were surrounded by Polish, and Polish by German; any new
frontier which could be devised would separate mines from
factories, cut workingmen's dwellings from their place of
labor, intersect railway lines, and disturb economic adjustments which had lasted for generations. The Treaty also
stated that "regard will be paid... to the geographical and
economic conditions of the locality." How could that be
reconciled with a frontier following the intricate interwind-
ings of the German and Polish national settlements?

Agricultural Upper Silesia was, without much question,
handed back to Germany as a result of the plebiscite. For
The Silesian the industrial south four proposals were consid-
award ered: (1) the German plan of leaving the whole
district to Germany, supported by some Englishmen on
economic grounds; (2) the official British plan of giving the
mining districts of Pless and Rybnik to Poland but leaving
the industrial center to Germany; (3) the French — and
Polish — proposal to grant most of the industrial area with
its mixed population to Poland; (4) the compromise line
suggested by Italy, midway between the French maximum
and the British minimum concessions to Poland. No agreement was reached, the war sentiment in Germany and Poland
rose dangerously, and in despair rather than hope the whole
question was turned over to the League of Nations for solution in August, 1921. Two months later the Council reported a settlement, based on the report of experts from neu-

tral countries who had examined the question as impartially as possible. A compromise line was adopted, following in a general way the result of the voting, but, in order to lessen the economic injury inevitably caused by the partition of a unified industrial area, reciprocal rights of trade and freedom of movement were granted for a term of fifteen years, in order to give time for the industrial life of Upper Silesia to adapt itself to the new frontiers. The Silesian award was a notable victory for the League because of the importance of the interests concerned and because other channels of diplomacy had been tried to no avail until the League was granted jurisdiction.

The most dramatic crisis which confronted the League in its early youth was the seizure of the Greek island of Corfu by the Italian fleet. There had for some time *The Corfu* been bad blood between Italy and Greece, mainly *incident* because of overlapping interests in Asia Minor, and this reached its climax in 1923 after the murder of several Italian boundary commissioners, presumably by Greek bandits, along the Greco-Albanian frontier. Premier Mussolini demanded an official apology and heavy indemnities, and to enforce compliance with his demands bombarded and then occupied the island of Corfu. Greece appealed to the League of Nations, urging that since both Italy and Greece were Member States of the League and danger of war was imminent the case for intervention by the League was as clear as ever could be. Premier Mussolini, and Salandra, the Italian representative on the Council of the League, replied that the matter concerned only Italy, that there was no danger of war, and that any intervention by the League would be an infringement of Italy's national dignity and sovereign rights. But the Italian contention that the Corfu affair was outside the competence of the League was not generally accepted by the other Member States. Lord Robert Cecil on behalf of Britain, Hjalmar Branting on behalf of Sweden, and

several other officials of the League urged that if so evident a
crisis were passed over the public would lose all confidence
in the ability of the League to prevent international wars.
Eventually the Council found a compromise solution which
both Italy and Greece accepted. As a concession to Italy,
the terms of settlement were drawn up, not by the Council of
the League, but by the Council of the Allied Ambassadors.
Greece paid the required indemnity for the murder of the
Italian commissioners. Italy withdrew from Corfu on
September 27, 1923. This prompt withdrawal greatly relieved the Greeks who feared that Mussolini designed to
make Corfu an Italian naval base commanding the Adriatic.
Whether the incident may be counted a victory for the League
is open to legitimate debate. On the one hand, it is contended that only the intervention of the League and its mobilization of public opinion made possible a peaceful solution.
On the other hand, it is true that final jurisdiction was
handed over from the League to that wartime survival, the
Council of Ambassadors. At all events, a very probable war
was averted, and averted by the method of international conference which, rather than any article of the Covenant, is
the real "heart of the League."

A more obviously successful test of the machinery of the
League of Nations was furnished in 1925 when a command
The Greco- from the League halted a conflict actually begun
Bulgarian on the Greco-Bulgarian frontier. Outposts on
crisis of either side had exchanged shots over the bound-
1925 ary, and the Greeks, inflamed by exaggerated
reports of the incident, believed that the Bulgarians had begun an invasion. They therefore advanced an army on Bulgarian soil, but before any serious battle had taken place
the troops were withdrawn because of the remonstrances of
the League and the threat of a punitive blockade of the
Greek coast if hostilities were continued. The contrast
with the second Balkan War of 1913, when a similar local

conflict between Greek and Bulgarian forces developed into a serious war before the old-fashioned "Concert of Europe" could agree on any course of action, added greatly to the prestige of the League. Unfortunately in dealing with conflicts outside Europe, as in Manchuria between China and Japan, and in the Chaco region between Bolivia and Paraguay, the intervention of the League was less successful.[1]

The membership in the League increased from its thirty-two "charter members" to a maximum of sixty by the addition of neutral and former enemy states and lost *Expansion* altogether its appearance of being a mere con- *of the* tinuation of the wartime "Allied and Associated *League* Powers." All the neutrals first invited to join sent acceptances. In the case of Switzerland the question was put before the voters and carried by referendum, a few of the German-speaking cantons voting in the negative. Switzerland also obtained assurances that her traditional neutrality in war would not be infringed by joining the League. Other neutral states, not included in the original invitation, were afterwards admitted; for example, the Baltic republics of Finland, Estonia, Latvia and Lithuania. A new Dominion, the Irish Free State, was added within the British Empire. All the Central Powers, Germany, Austria, Hungary, Bulgaria and Turkey, eventually joined, as did Soviet Russia. The United States alone among the Great Powers of the world was never a member, but on many occasions co-operated with the various agencies of the League. On the other hand, there were some losses. Brazil and Costa Rica withdrew; and in 1933, the blackest year for world peace since the armistice, Germany and Japan gave notice of an intention to withdraw which, if unaltered, would become effective in two years. Many pessimists predicted that the League would be reduced to a mere alliance of Britain,

[1] See Chapter XXX. For the intervention of the League in the Hungarian and Saar disputes of 1934–5 see Chapters XX and XXVII.

CHAPTER XX
THE SEARCH FOR SECURITY

THOUGH the League of Nations increased in membership and, on the whole, in prestige, though it found solutions for many obscure but none the less important prob- *A new* lems, it failed to give Europe that definite sense *diplomacy?* of security for which the authors of the Covenant had hoped. The accent shifted steadily from a League to Enforce Peace, the original ideal, to a League for Conciliation and Co-operation, perhaps as useful in its own way, but exercising no force except publicity and appeal to the moral sentiment of the world. Alongside League diplomacy there still remained Great Power diplomacy, depending on alliances, ententes and subtle shiftings in the balance of power almost as though the World War had taught no lessons to Europe. Almost — but not quite. Great Power diplomacy used the machinery for peace provided by the League of Nations on many occasions and, even when rejecting League agencies, often used the League method of open "round table" conference. Many writers spoke of a "new diplomacy," marked by open covenants (though not always "openly arrived at"), formally published and registered treaties, and direct negotiation between responsible Premiers in place of the traditional "secret diplomacy" of the foreign offices. This is not to say that the new diplomacy was in all respects superior to the old. Some critics insisted that postwar diplomacy was crude, amateurish, "shirt-sleeve" statesmanship, overinfluenced by public clamor and the press, and that it lost more than it gained by abandoning the formalities and suavities of an elder day. Critics of a more radical school brought the opposite complaint, that diplomacy had changed too little rather than too much, that whether in shirt sleeves or in silken coat it remained selfishly national.

Some writers have called the decade immediately following the war a period of French predominance, even of French hegemony. There is much truth in such a view. *The diplomatic map after Versailles* France had by far the strongest of European armies, while Germany had been as completely disarmed as treaty provisions ever *can* disarm a great nation. Belgium, Poland, Czechoslovakia, Rumania and Yugoslavia were quite definitely in the French camp, and most of the other minor powers were either neutral or friendly. But, for all that, France felt no security. In some respects her diplomatic position was weaker than on the eve of the World War, when Russia was a close ally, Britain an open friend and Italy a secret one. The very completeness of the victory over Germany had made Britain and Italy feel that the close alliance of wartime was no longer necessary. Aside from her obligations to the League of Nations, Great Britain tended to revert to a policy of old-fashioned "splendid isolation" and, desirous of rebuilding German trade, frowned on the French policy of coercing the defeated.[1] Italy sought rather to rival France than to sustain her. Soviet Russia was distinctly hostile, and the motley group of little client-states gathered around France was but an indifferent substitute for the old alliance with Tsarist Russia. France herself, exhausted by her losses in war and burdened with debts both domestic and foreign, was content with what Versailles had brought her and sought no new gains; fear rather than ambition was her prevailing mood.

Postwar Europe was thus not dominated by the strength of a single power, as in Bismarck's time, nor yet divided sharply into two rival camps, as in the critical decade from 1904 to 1914. Rather, each Great Power stood iso-

---

[1] See Chapter XXV for the economic background of Anglo-French estrangement.

lated from the rest, save as they might be united by membership in the League of Nations, and each tried *Franco-* to bring within its orbit as many of the lesser *Italian* states as possible. The isolation of Germany and *rivalry* of Soviet Russia was fairly complete, though Russia had some influence in China, Persia and Turkey, and Germany some well-wishers among her former allies, Austria, Hungary and Bulgaria. The British had friends scattered around the world from Portugal to Japan, but as they avoided too intimate obligations to the lesser continental European nations, most of these sought closer shelter either with France or with Italy. Which they chose depended less upon the skill of French or Italian diplomacy than upon their relations with each other. The very fact that France was friend and patron of the Yugoslavs, for example, made Hungary, Bulgaria and Albania, all more or less hostile to Yugoslavia, enter into friendly relations with Italy. These alignments were shifting and unstable; thus Austria, which in the early 'twenties had been strongly pro-German and hostile to Italy, was by 1933 seeking the protection of Italy to avert annexation by Germany.[1]

Perhaps the most significant and stable diplomatic group after the World War was the so-called "Little Entente" of Czechoslovakia, Rumania and Yugoslavia. It *The Little* was first formed by agreements in 1920 and 1921 *Entente* to prevent a Habsburg restoration in Hungary. "It is not sentimental reasons," said Foreign Minister Benès of Czechoslovakia, "which dictate our standpoint of uncompromising opposition to a return of the Habsburgs. It is our conviction that a Habsburg restoration would signify a permanent, never-ceasing struggle for the heritage of the former Empire." The combined population of the participating powers almost equaled that of prewar Austria-Hungary; when acting as a unit, therefore, the Little Entente might be counted

[1] See Chapter XXIII for Austrian affairs.

as equal to a single Great Power. Its position was strengthened by the general diplomatic support accorded it by France and Poland, and by friendly negotiations with Russia in 1934.

Besides special alliances and diplomatic understandings, such as those which bound Albania to Italy, Belgium to *Pacts of* France and the nations of the Little Entente to *non-aggres-* each other, security was sought by means of *sion* "peace pacts" or agreements of non-aggression. Some of these were of general character, such as the abortive Geneva Protocol, the most important attempt yet made to "put teeth in the League of Nations," approved by the League Assembly in 1924, and the Paris Peace Pact of 1928. Others were more limited in scope, such as the Locarno Peace Pact of 1925, guaranteeing the security of western Europe, and the "Four Power Pact" of 1933 intended to assure peace among the governments of Britain, France, Germany and Italy. This significant trend in postwar diplomacy deserves some consideration.

The Geneva Protocol provided that the nations adhering to it agree: (1) not to resort to war against other nations *The Geneva* observing the Protocol, whether members of the *Protocol* League or not; (2) to recognize as compulsory the jurisdiction of the Court of International Justice in certain specified matters of a "justiciable" character; (3) to refer political quarrels to the League or to arbitral bodies; (4) not to mobilize armed forces during the course of arbitration of a dispute; (5) to consider as an aggressor any power resorting to war in defiance of the agreement; (6) to consent that aggressor states pay the costs of war to the limit of their ability, but that war indemnities should not include cessions of territory; (7) to participate in an international conference on the reduction of armaments, as a preliminary to the coming into effect of the Protocol. Had the Geneva Protocol been ratified it might well have been as great a forward step as the making of the League itself, but it was too advanced for its time. Great Britain, moved in part by protests from the distant Dominions which did not want to be involved in purely continental European disputes, did not ratify. The failure to attain any considerable measure of disarmament by agreement would in any case probably have invalidated the Protocol.

The effort was not wasted, however. Though no general "security pact" was ever established, the powers turned to consider the possibility of a local guarantee for the peace of western Europe. Fortunately for the world, the German government at the moment was internationally minded and the French conciliatory; one might almost say it was the only moment in the entire period from 1870 to the present when France and Germany were *simultaneously* ready for a binding and enduring peace! Britain, Italy and even Belgium had long sought friendlier relations with Germany, and all the nations, in particular France and Czechoslovakia, were eager to salvage something from the wreck of the Geneva Protocol. The first and most important of the Locarno agreements was the Security Pact for Western Europe, a treaty of mutual guarantee signed by Gustav Stresemann for Germany, Aristide Briand for France, Austen Chamberlain for Great Britain and Benito Mussolini for Italy. It provided for: (1) the maintenance of the western frontier of Germany and of the demilitarized zone within Germany as fixed by the Treaty of Versailles; (2) an agreement never to resort to war along the Franco-German or Franco-Belgian frontier except in immediate self-defense or to support action by the League of Nations; (3) an agreement that the Council of the League might call on the powers signatory to the Pact to aid in enforcing its provisions; (4) an agreement to submit justiciable questions to the World Court, and political questions to a conciliation commission, with right of appeal to the League, if

The Locarno Peace Pact, 1925

the ordinary processes of diplomacy should not avail. It was understood that as a part of the settlement Germany should be admitted to the League of Nations on a footing of entire equality with other Great Powers.

Germany signed treaties of arbitration with Poland and Czechoslovakia as well as with France, Britain, Italy and Belgium. The treaties with Poland and Czecho-slovakia, however, contained no territorial guarantees and thus implicitly permitted Germany to seek a revision of her eastern frontiers provided that she did so exclusively by political and diplomatic methods without resort to armed force. France gave Poland and Czechoslovakia additional security by entering with them into an open defensive alliance. All these treaties were registered with the League of Nations and formally signed in London after the German government had secured approval from the Reichstag.

Locarno and central Europe

Germany's application for admission to the League created difficulties which for a time threatened to wreck the whole Locarno settlement. Poland, Spain and Brazil, claiming to rank as "Great Powers," requested permanent membership in the Council on equal terms with Germany, France, Italy, Japan and Great Britain. Germany refused to have the question of her own admission made conditional on the claims of any other nation. Mr. Unden, the Swedish delegate on the Council supported Germany's stand and offered Sweden's temporary seat to Poland as a solution of the difficulty, but Brazil remained unreconciled and threatened to leave the League. The Council adjourned in March, 1926, with the question still unsettled and Germany very naturally angered at the unexpected rebuff. In September, however, Germany was admitted, and the would-be "Great Powers" were conciliated by an amendment to the Covenant which granted nine seats to the non-permanent members of the League Council and

Germany and the League

provided that their terms should run for three years. The adhesion of Germany seemed the final witness to the success of the League and also to the reconquest by Germany of Europe's confidence and good will; it was the high-water mark of postwar pacifism. But the victory of the reactionary and chauvinistic National Socialists under Chancellor Hitler a few years later undid all the work of reconciliation begun so auspiciously by Briand and Stresemann. In 1933 Germany, discontented at the failure of a disarmament conference to grant full and immediate equality to her national armaments, withdrew from the League of Nations and from the conference as well.[1]

Aristide Briand, the liberal and pacific French statesman who did so much to advance the interests of international concord in the decade following the war, had pro- *The Paris* longed conversations in 1927 with Frank Kellogg, *Peace Pact,* the American Secretary of State, seeking a gen- *1928* eral peace pact between the two countries. It was finally decided to make the agreement an international one, open to the signature of any government. In 1928 an agreement was concluded in Paris by the representatives of fifteen nations to the effect that:

> The High Contracting Parties solemnly declare, in the names of their respective peoples, that they condemn recourse to war for the solution of international controversies, and renounce it as an instrument of national policy in their relations with one another.
>
> The High Contracting Parties agree that the settlement or solution of all disputes or conflicts, of whatever nature or of whatever origin they may be, which may arise among them, shall never be sought except by pacific means.

This agreement was signed by nearly every government, including even those outside the League of Nations, like Soviet Russia and the United States of America. Literally lived up to, it would have banished international war forever from

[1] For German policy after the World War, see Chapter XXVII.

the earth; for although some nations made reservations respecting wars of self-defense or wars to enforce the pacific decisions of the League of Nations, only a previous act of aggression would make those reservations applicable.   But the Pact is not "implemented" by any machinery at all; it depends wholly on the sincerity and good will of the signatory powers, and experience has shown that excuses can always be found for its violation.   When Japan sent armies against China in 1932 they trampled alike on the Covenant of the League, the Paris Peace Pact, and the Nine Power Treaty elaborated at Washington for the security of the Pacific area.[1]   The problem of peace is not to get governments to renounce war on paper but to induce them in a particular emergency to remember their promise.

The swift rise to power of the militant reactionaries in Germany after the economic depression of 1929 had a pro-
Diplomatic   found effect on European international politics.
shifts of the   By reawakening dormant fears of an armed and
'thirties   menacing Germany it brought Great Britain,
Italy and Russia into closer sympathy with France.   Austria definitely welcomed Italian protection.   Germany's diplomatic position grew weaker in proportion as her armament grew stronger.   On the other hand, Poland tended to break away from French leading strings and assume an independent position.   This was partly because the conclusion of a commercial treaty and a ten year peace pact with Germany allayed Polish fears that the triumph of Hitler's National Socialist party in 1933 would mean an immediate attack on the Polish Corridor; Poland now had some hope that even if a diplomatic storm were about to break the lightning would strike elsewhere.   Another reason for Poland's coolness to France lay in the fact that France felt bound to offer at least formal opposition when in 1934 Poland "denounced" the minority rights treaty which she had signed on becoming an

[1] For the Manchurian crisis, see Chapter XXX.

independent state and asserted that, while she would pursue a tolerant policy toward her own national, racial and religious minorities, no intervention by the League of Nations or any of its members in her national affairs would be tolerated.

In an effort to offset the blow to European peace caused by Germany's threatened withdrawal from the League of Nations, as well as from the disarmament con- *The Four* ference then in session, Italy proposed a new *Power Pact,* regional peace pact, based on an agreement of *1933* Germany, France, Britain and Italy, to endure ten years with prospect of renewal. These powers were to accept "the principle of revision of the peace treaties," with a saving clause that this work must proceed "within the framework of the League of Nations"; that Germany should enjoy "equality of rights" in armament, to be reached "by stages," and that in all questions, "European or extra-European" the signatories should adopt "a common line of conduct." France thought the concessions made to Germany were too far-reaching, the smaller states in the League of Nations feared that the League itself would be virtually superseded by an alliance of the Great Powers, and to meet these objections the Four Power Pact was watered down very considerably. In its final form, the signatory governments were required to consult together and pursue "a policy of effective co-operation"; to "examine" proposals "relating to methods and procedure calculated to give due effect to these articles"; to "re-examine" questions left unsolved by the disarmament conference, and "to consult together as regards all economic questions which have a common interest for Europe." In this form the treaty was certainly innocuous enough to suit everyone, and perhaps vague enough to solve nothing, but the very fact of the existence of such a peace agreement is evidence that the principal European powers dreaded war and felt the need of new guarantees of peace in addition to

the already numerous pacts and agreements which had filled
the uneasy years since the armistice.

In view of the altered diplomatic situation France endeavored to take advantage of the friendlier attitude of

France Russia and Italy while still retaining her influence
"mends her over Poland and the Little Entente. The task
fences" was not an easy one. Every step towards Italy
awoke suspicion among the Yugoslavs; every step towards
Russia tended to alienate Poland. Foreign Minister Louis
Barthou went on a mission of reassurance to the states of
southeastern Europe and King Alexander of Yugoslavia
visited France as a guest of the Republic. The visit ended
in tragedy at Marseilles. In October, 1934, an assassin
broke through the guard of honor which escorted King
Alexander and Foreign Minister Barthou and shot them
both. Though France could hardly be blamed for a deed
that seems to have been caused by the rivalry of nationalities within Yugoslavia,[1] the event was seriously disquieting
in view of the acute hostility existing between Yugoslavia on
the one hand and Italy and Hungary on the other, and the
uncertainty as to what foreign policy might be followed by
the Regents who assumed the control of Yugoslav affairs.

In particular, the Yugoslavs blamed Hungary for giving
aid and comfort to Croatian malcontents whose plots had

The Yugo- caused the assassination. They feared that this
slav-Hunga- was part of an irredentist campaign to disrupt
rian crisis Yugoslavia and bring about a revision of boundaries favorable to Hungary. Twenty years earlier Austria-
Hungary had brought almost identical complaints against
the Yugoslavs in Serbia and Bosnia. The danger of war
seemed real enough. Italy and Austria expressed sympathy
for Hungary; France, Czechoslovakia and Rumania for
Yugoslavia. Yugoslavia expelled a large number of Hungarian residents from her territories. There were rumors of

[1] See Chapter XXIII.

shooting along the frontier. Fortunately, however, there was now a Geneva to mediate between Belgrade and Budapest. Both parties submitted their cause to the League of Nations which arranged a compromise settlement pledging Hungary to take "appropriate punitive action" against officials whose culpability might be established but leaving the carrying out of details to the Hungarian government. Once again peace had her victory, "no less renowned than war."

Perhaps the most remarkable diplomatic shift of the new time was Russia's admission to the League of Nations. After Germany had joined, Russia and the United *Russia joins* States were the only Great Powers which had not *the League* been admitted. Lenin, and the Bolsheviki generally, denounced the whole organization as a sham structure of bourgeois pacifism to conceal a capitalistic alliance against the Soviet Union. The hostility was felt on both sides. In those earlier days even if Russia had applied for admission it is doubtful if her application would have been welcomed, and France, angered at Russia's repudiation of her foreign debts, might well have led the opposition. Indeed, if anything, Russia felt more sympathy for her recent enemy Germany than for France. By the Treaty of Rapallo (1922), an outgrowth of the economic conference held at Genoa earlier in the year, Germany gave formal recognition to the Soviet government, renounced claims for debts and damages, and established normal commercial relations. Some small states near the Russian border had given Soviet Russia recognition as a necessary preliminary to the determination of frontiers, and some larger powers had entered into *de facto* relations with her, but Germany had been the first major power to admit Soviet Russia to full diplomatic equality. Only fear of Russian communism kept Germany from seeking even closer relations with a power which shared with her a common grievance against France, against Poland and against the whole "Versailles system." When Germany concluded the Locarno Peace Pact and entered the League, Russia regarded it as a diplomatic set-back, though she found partial compensation in concluding a pact of neutrality and non-aggression with Germany in 1926.

But new conditions brought a serious change. Russia, increasingly intent on plans of international reconstruction *Russia ap-* and seriously alarmed by Japan's activity in the *proaches* Far East, became less scornful of efforts for inter-*the West* national peace, even if initiated by "bourgeois" governments. Though the Soviet authorities had treated the Geneva Protocol and the Locarno Peace Pacts as mere diplomatic traps, they agreed to sign the Paris Peace Pact for the renunciation of war. On their own account they offered pacts of conciliation and non-aggression to all their neighbors and they proposed (not, perhaps, without some inward chuckles at the embarrassment they were causing to the more conservative diplomats of the West) universal and complete disarmament at successive conferences on arma- ment limitation. Other foreign powers followed Germany's example and granted full recognition to Soviet Russia. Britain, France and Italy had accorded it in 1924; the United States, most wary of all, in 1933. The outlawing and perse- cution of the Communists in Germany in 1933 definitely terminated any prospect of a Russo-German *entente* against the Western powers. Fear of Germany in Europe and of Japan in Asia at last induced Soviet Russia to hold out a friendly hand to France and to the League of Nations.

France, Britain, Italy and most of the lesser European states, including the Little Entente and even Poland, favored *The final* the admission of Russia. It did not pass without *step* some opposition, however. In committee Portu- gal, Switzerland and the Netherlands voted in opposition and several small states, mainly in Latin America, abstained from voting. Dr. Giuseppe Motta, representing Switzerland, made a notable speech, scoring the Russian government for its despotic and intolerant internal policy, and even Eamon de Valera, who, as Ireland's representative, voted for admission, said that he would feel happier about it if Russia would guarantee religious freedom.   Russia's entrance to the League in 1934 revived discussion of a possible "eastern Locarno" or security pact for eastern Europe on lines similar to the security pact for western Europe which had been negotiated in 1925, but the doubtful attitude of Germany and of Poland delayed the conclusion of such an instrument.

Closely related to the problem of security was that of disarmament.   The World War had failed to relieve Europe or the rest of the world from the cost of military *Security* preparedness.   Though treaties had limited the *and disarmament* armed forces of the defeated nations, other powers maintained military establishments on a larger and more costly scale than in 1913.   Had there been no other cause, the multiplication of new states and new frontiers in eastern and central Europe would have increased the military burden of Europe.   Prevailing costs were generally higher owing to the well-nigh universal inflation of European currencies; man for man and gun for gun, even an unchanged military system would have cost more in 1920 than seven years before, and of course every military establishment had to be reorganized in the light of the lessons taught by the war.   Tanks, aircraft and huge siege cannon had come to stay.   But the economic burden of the rival national armaments was the least of the evil; the real peril was that the rivalry itself might arouse antagonism and Europe be once again divided into hostile armed camps.   Yet the world seemed caught in a vicious circle; if armament races were among the forces making for war, the dread of war forbade any nation to disarm.   Many well meaning people in safer parts of the world, such as Britain and the United States, wasted ink scolding countries like France and Poland for maintaining large armies with the money that might have been spent in paying their international debts; but they had no answer when asked: "And if we do disarm, and war does come, what then? Will *you* guarantee our safety?" Yet the vanquished, too, had a case; the Germans could — and did — retort, "You disarmed us, and in your very Treaty of Versailles you stated that our disarmament was intended 'to render possible the initiation of a general limitation of the armaments of all nations.' [1] Did you mean what you said? Or is security something that is good only for France and Poland and not for Germany?"

The first and, to the present time, the most successful victory for armament limitation was the conference called at

The Washington Conference, 1921-22 Washington to consider the Pacific question. The alliance between Great Britain and Japan was about to terminate and there was little chance that it would be revived in its old form. Much of its usefulness had passed, as neither Russia nor Germany now endangered British interests in the Far East (except as Russia might spread the propaganda of international communism). Yet simply to terminate the alliance and provide no substitute might run the risk of a three-cornered naval race among the chief naval powers interested in the Pacific area — the British Empire, the Japanese Empire and the United States of America. The evil memory of the Anglo-German naval race which menaced the peace for fifteen years before the outbreak of the World War pointed clearly enough to what might result.

In addition to the three powers whose fleets dominated the island world of the Pacific, France, Italy, China, the *Curbing the battleship* Netherlands, Belgium and Portugal were represented. The United States put forward a drastic program of limitation and reduction of capital ships which, with a few amendments, was adopted. For a ten-year period

[1] Treaty of Versailles, Part V preamble.

the building of new battleships and battle cruisers was inter-
dicted and many older warships were scrapped and the construction of several in process of building abandoned. The
total tonnage of the chief naval powers in capital ships was
fixed at the ratio of 5 to 5 to 3 for the British Empire, the
United States and Japan; France and Italy were equalized
at about 1.67 in the same proportion. No sixth navy on
earth was large enough to awaken concern. With regard to
minor craft, the Washington Conference was less successful.
France refused to give up the submarine, which the British
wanted wholly abolished, and no formula of limitation for
light cruisers and minor craft could be found; though the
Conference agreed to condemn the use of submarines against
merchant and passenger ships, besides reaffirming the old
Hague Conference declaration against the use of poison gases
in warfare.[1]

The supplementary conference at Geneva in 1927 to limit
the minor craft of the great naval powers was a failure.
The United States insisted on a rigorous application of the principle of equality of armament with *The Geneva
naval con-
ference of
1927*
Great Britain. The British, admitting that the
principle was valid with respect to battleships
and battle cruisers, held that an exception should be made
in their favor with respect to small cruisers, since the coastline of the British Empire presented a far longer naval frontier to defend than that of any other power on earth. There
was an unfortunate revival of secret diplomacy which shook
popular confidence, when it was discovered that the French
and British diplomats had made a pre-conference agreement
to stand together on questions relating to naval limitation.
Certain munitions industries engaged in another and even
more sinister sort of "secret diplomacy" by hiring ostensibly
disinterested press agents and publicists to attack the work
of the conference.

[1] For other actions of the Washington Conference, see Chapter XXX.

A more successful conference took place at London in 1930. France and Italy were here represented, as well as Britain, Japan and the United States. On this occasion the chief difficulty arose between France and Italy. Italy demanded equality with France in all classes of war vessels as well as in capital ships; France insisted on maintaining her existing margin of superiority. The differences between France and Italy proved too great for adjustment and were left to direct negotiation between the parties concerned, but Britain and the United States at last groped their way to a compromise formula which granted to the British a superior total tonnage and a greater number of small cruisers, but permitted the United States to have a slight surplus in large cruisers.

The London naval conference of 1930

Naval disarmament had at least a promising beginning, but the persistent attempt under the auspices of the League of Nations to bring about limitation of land armament proved less successful. Why should there be this difference? In the first place, only a few navies in the world really "mattered." The first rank was occupied by Britain and the United States, the second by Japan, the third by France and Italy; no other nation was a naval menace to any of those leading five, and naval disarmament was, under the circumstances, merely a matter of adjustment among five fleets. But on land, if only by reason of geographical position, many armies are significant. Poland cannot be ignored, nor Czechoslovakia, nor Belgium. In the second place, an "army" is hard to define in set terms. It means nothing to say that a nation has an army of "one hundred thousand men" unless it be known also whether they are professional veterans, a conscript levy, a half-trained militia, or an armed police force; whether they are armed with modern tanks and heavy artillery; whether they have good roads and railroads for transportation; whether the factories of the nation suffice for making

Attempts at disarmament by land

munitions or whether the tools of war must be purchased abroad. Russia had the largest army in the world, alike in 1914 and 1920, but Germany, for all that, had a more formidable army in the former year and France in the latter. Again, how equalize the position of a nation which is defended by mountains, like Switzerland, or can be in large part flooded, like Holland, with the flat Polish plain? What is the military value of the English Channel? Of the Atlantic Ocean? How many soldiers offset one railroad? How many are equal to one Alp? Unless all these difficulties be borne in mind it is easy to condemn the diplomats of postwar Europe even more than is just. The long labors of the "preparatory commission" of the League of Nations and of the Disarmament Conference which opened at Geneva in 1932 failed to reach any important conclusion, and in 1933 the withdrawal of Germany practically suspended negotiations.

Each nation approached the problem, sincerely desirous of reduced armaments if only because of the economic burden which they imposed, but concerned first of all *Rival plans* about its direct national security. Germany, *of disarma-* with increasing insistence, demanded equality of *ment* armament or disarmament; either France must cut her army to the German level or Germany be permitted to build hers up to the French. France objected that with Germany's superior population and industrial wealth and equivocal armed "police" forces Germany would really be stronger than France. The French favored a plan to transform the League of Nations into a military alliance bound by pacts of mutual assistance; if that were done, certain "heavy weapons," essential to modern offensive warfare, might be transferred to the League as trustee. Great Britain and Italy tried to mediate between the French and the German positions. Maxim Litvinov, on behalf of Soviet Russia, proposed a complete abolition of all military forces, and President Hoover of the United States suggested a reduction of one-third of existing military establishments and the abolition of siege guns, gas warfare and bombing planes. Aircraft and chemical warfare presented two of the knottiest problems. Airplanes can be quickly and rapidly built, or made over from commercial planes; they do not require the long preliminary preparation of a battleship or cruiser. Chemical warfare, such as the use of poison gas, though banned by international agreements is still widely discussed; experts themselves were widely divided as to whether it would always remain a minor menace or was destined to become *the* warfare of the future, displacing artillery as guns displaced bows and arrows. In general the British and Americans, partly protected by the sea, laid the greater emphasis on direct limitation of armaments; the continental powers, France at their head, on "security pacts" and leagues as the necessary basis for subsequent disarmament.

As the year 1934 closed, the prospect of an immediate radical reduction of armies, navies and air fleets was not brilliant; *Whither Europe?* Japan pressed a demand for complete equality with the British and American navies and, when the demand was not granted, denounced the naval provisions of the Washington treaty; Great Britain and the United States increased their fleets toward the maximum allowed by the treaties of Washington and London "to provide work for the unemployed"; Germany openly announced that the armament restrictions in the Treaty of Versailles were no longer binding on her since the Entente Powers had failed to disarm; France, though she had reduced the term of required military service, clung to conscription and invested enormous sums in a new system of frontier fortification. Even the addition of a "Four Power Pact" to a "Paris Peace Pact"; the search for an "Eastern Locarno" to supplement the Western; the feverish activity of diplomats within and without the League of Nations to "explore avenues" and "seek formulas" testified as much to dread of war as to love of peace. Twenty years after Sarajevo "security" was still a will-o'-the-wisp. There was, however, a much greater popular will to peace; a sufficient proof of this is that scarcely a year had passed since the armistice without seeing the peaceful settlement of some crisis quite serious enough to have plunged the continent into war. There was also, in the League of Nations and in the "new diplomacy," quicker means of obtaining concerted action to fend off conflict than the traditional method of foreign office correspondence which failed to apply the brakes in 1914.

CHAPTER XXI

SOVIET RUSSIA

IN 1919 the hope of a general European revolution was the main concern of Bolshevist policy. Russia to the in-

The European background of the Russian revolution ternationally minded Communists was but an entrenchment of capitalism seized by the proletariat, to be held at all costs, but not for its own sake; rather to aid the battle along the whole line. Indeed, many revolutionary leaders hoped for more promising results in central and western Europe than in Russia. The origins of modern socialism were largely German or French, Karl Marx was its prophet and the Paris Commune of 1871 its most cherished tradition. The class to which all forms of socialism made the most appeal was the industrial proletariat; the men of the factories, mines and railways. In no other great European nation was this class relatively so small as in Russia, the land of the peasant. Again, every new religion, whether theological or political, spreads most rapidly where the written word can supplement the voice of the orator. Obviously the doctrines of Marx and Lenin could be taught more quickly to the literate German than to the illiterate Russian. Of course prosperity and social security are barriers to revolution, but the end of the war found Austria starving, Poland disorganized, Germany bitter in defeat, France impoverished, Italy almost bankrupt, even Great Britain facing unemployment and industrial depression. Communist insurrections did in fact break out in several parts of Europe, notably Hungary and Bavaria. For almost a year after the war the commonest of questions was, "Will all Europe go Bolshevist?"

The gradual cooling off of the European situation was not for a long time recognized by the Russian government, as it

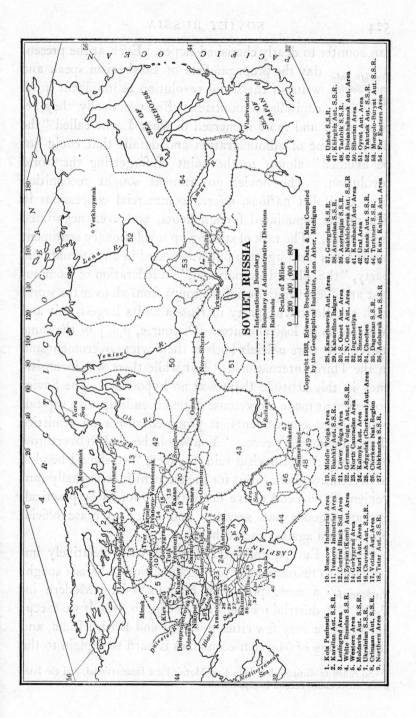

ran counter to dearly cherished hopes. Even at the present
Foreign pol- day the propagandists of Bolshevism speak and
icy of Soviet write of the social revolution as imminent in all
Russia   capitalistic countries. But practically they became more and more immersed in what Lenin called "the
daily routine of administration and details that could not
be avoided" almost to the point of forgetting the world
revolution. The Soviet government sought recognition
from capitalist nations, offered commercial concessions in
lieu of the repudiated foreign debts, and even negotiated
fresh loans. The task of stirring up revolutionary sentiment
abroad was not forgotten but was vested in an international
party, "the Third International," [1] a federation of Communist and "left wing" Socialist groups from all over the world
with the Bolshevist party of Russia as its largest unit and
Moscow as its logical center. Of course, many of the same
individuals were officials both in the Soviet government and
in the Third International. But while there was inconsistency in this attitude there was no hypocrisy. The Soviet
government made no pretense of real friendship with capitalistic foreign governments; it proposed rather an armistice
than an enduring peace. "You would be glad to overthrow
our system," Bolshevism said in effect; "we should be glad
to overthrow yours. But for the moment it is mutually convenient to suspend active hostilities, so let us be practical,
exchange goods and services, and agree to cease official
propaganda against each other."

Finding Europe and, still more, America relatively im-
pervious to revolutionary propaganda, Soviet Russia sought
Propaganda a more promising field in Asia. Modern in-
in Asia   dustrial methods are foreign to Asia, if we except
Japan and a very few cities in China and British India, and
the meaning of Marxian economics is hard to explain to the

---

[1] So called to distinguish it from Karl Marx's First International, and the later
moderate Socialist Second International.

wild horsemen of the central Asian steppe or the drudging Chinese peasant in his rice field. But Turkey, Persia, India and China were at least linked together in a hearty dislike of the pushing imperialism of the western capitalist nations. So the Bolsheviki who had preached internationalism in Europe preached national liberty to Asia, partly no doubt from a genuine dislike of colonial imperialism, but partly also as the readiest way to embarrass the British and French governments. As Russia of the Tsars had been among the most aggressive of colonizing powers, the necessary first step in winning the confidence of Asiatic peoples was the complete repudiation of former Russian territorial ambitions. Russia renounced all claim to Constantinople, the Straits, or any part of Asia Minor from the Ottoman Empire, and surrendered to Persia, Afghanistan and China the treaty rights and claims secured by the old imperialistic diplomacy. Even the Asiatic peoples formerly included within the Russian Empire, such as the Armenians, Georgians, and Tatars of the Caucasus and the myriad tribes of central Asia, were offered the new status of allies in a federal union of "soviet republics." Even when Russian armies subdued a national revolt, as they did in Georgia, it was in the name of the "proletariat" rather than that of Russia or her rulers.

For the first three or four years of its existence the Soviet government had to fight for life against many other rival governments on Russian soil as well as against *Russian* unreconciled border peoples. The counter-revo- *civil war* lutionary forces included every sort of political and economic creed: reactionary nobles, disestablished clergy, moderate constitutional monarchists, democratic republicans, particularist champions of local national minorities, adventurers, disaffected politicians, and even radicals who found the existing rule too tame for their taste.[1] The anti-Bolshevist

---

[1] Just as Robespierre suppressed the ultra-radicals under Hébert, so the Bolsheviki adopted some of their severest measures against the anarchists and against Social Revolutionary terrorists.

forces relied on the support of foreign armies and on the conservative instincts of the peasantry, just as did the counter-revolutionary armies of La Vendée, Brittany and the Gironde in the great French revolution; and equally in vain. For the foreign intervention was half-hearted and served only to rouse patriotic resentment by identifying the counter-revolutionists with treason and foreign invasion, while the peasants feared that any reversal of the revolution might endanger their hold on confiscated land.

The strongest and most promising counter-revolutionary movement had Siberia for its base. Siberia lay far from the *The Sibe-* central power of Moscow and the pioneer peasan- *rian war* try were perhaps more politically alert than those of Great Russia. The seizure of Siberian railroads by the Czecho-Slovak armies during the last months of the World War facilitated local organization against the Bolshevist power. In 1918 a merger of anti-Bolshevist groups established a provisional government at Omsk, under the leadership of exiled members of the Constituent Assembly. But the provisional government was rent by faction, it was too liberal in flavor to suit the more reactionary elements in the counter-revolution, and it was soon overturned by a coup d'état and Admiral Kolchak made dictator. This alienated many previous supporters of the Omsk government and deprived it of all title to be considered the true democratic embodiment of the Russian popular will. What was, perhaps, more to the point, it failed to bring about the expected efficient direction. During the summer of 1919 the tide turned against Kolchak and in the following February he was shot by mutineers in his army. Japan temporarily occupied Vladivostok, and for a short time an independent buffer state, the Far Eastern Republic, existed east of Lake Baikal. Eventually Soviet Russia absorbed all the Asiatic domains which had belonged to the old Russian Empire.

For a time a provisional government under the liberal

socialist Tchaikowsky maintained itself at Archangel under the protection of a British expeditionary force, but the expected rally of northern Russia against Bolshevism did not take place and in September, 1919, the British, American and other *Civil war in the European provinces* foreign forces were withdrawn, leaving northern Russia to Bolshevist occupation. There seemed better prospect of resistance in the south, where the Ukraine, the Cossacks of the Black Sea region, the states of the Caucasus, and the Moslem tribes around the Caspian were alike distrustful of the centralized dictatorship of Moscow and Petrograd. In this disaffected region loyal fragments of the old Russian imperial armies, with a small amount of aid from the British and French, attempted to reconquer Russia from the Black Sea. But General Denikin and his successor General Wrangel found it impossible to consolidate the Ukrainian peasantry against the Soviet government, and so long as they remained distrustful or suspicious the advance of the anti-Bolshevist army was through hostile territory. True, the Ukraine did not love the new-fashioned Muscovite Bolshevism; but still less did it love the old-fashioned Muscovite imperialism which threatened to succeed it. The remnants of Wrangel's defeated army, with thousands of civilian refugees including many of the old Russian aristocracy, were transported from the Crimea to Constantinople, where they lived on alien charity in the bitterness of indefinite exile. An attempt by General Yudenich, using Estonia as a base, to strike a blow directly at Petrograd equally came to nothing. By the end of 1920 Soviet Russia had vindicated her existence so far as arms could do it.

In a sense, Soviet Russia may boast of having been "at war" on various occasions with Germany, Austria-Hungary, Turkey, Great Britain, France, Japan and the United States of America, to make no mention of the Czecho-Slovak legionaries in Siberia and the border states of the Baltic,

Black Sea and Caucasus. Apologists of Bolshevism have
The Russo- indeed often insisted that, with whatever failures
Polish War it may be charged, it had withstood the hostility
of 1920 of "the whole capitalist world." But a distinction must be made. The "war" between Soviet Russia and
the Great Powers scarcely deserves the name as no one of
them put forth a tithe of its strength or regarded itself as
doing more than aiding the more conservative Russian
parties to reconquer their own land from the Bolsheviki.
The conflict with Poland, on the other hand, was international war in the strict sense of the word, a national struggle
over disputed territory, straining the resources of both belligerents and terminating in a formal treaty of peace.

The Paris Peace Conference which had so meticulously
marked out Poland's western frontiers had left her eastern
Poland's borders unsettled. The so-called Curzon line
unmarked indicated only the unquestionably Polish dis-
eastern tricts. To the east of it lay a broad belt of terri-
frontier tory inhabited mainly by Lithuanians, White
Russians and Little Russians (Ukrainians), but with a considerable and influential minority of Poles and usually a
trading class of Jews. Historically this region had once
been Polish. Marshal Pilsudski hoped to reconquer it from
Russia, trusting that the Lithuanians and Ukrainians would
prefer federal union with Poland to Russian Bolshevism.
This confidence was justified only in part. Lithuania failed
to respond and remained neutral even when Bolshevist forces
marched across her territory; the Ukraine was hopelessly divided among Russian "reds" who looked to Soviet Russia,
Russian "whites" who looked to the counter-revolutionary
armies of the south, Ukrainian nationalists who wanted independence, Polish landlords who wanted union with Poland, and simple peasants who wanted nothing but peace
and the land.

In spite of having to carry on war in the south against

Wrangel and tread out the last sparks of rebellion in Siberia, Soviet Russia had armies to spare for the war *The Russian* against Poland. Many Russians who had no *high tide* sympathy with Bolshevism, even royalist generals of the old régime, offered their services to the Red Army organized by Trotsky from motives of loyalty to Russia or hatred of Poland, Russia's ancient rival. Indeed, to continue civil war against the Soviet government when a foreign army was entering Russia seemed dangerously akin to treason. During the summer of 1920 Russia reconquered almost the whole Ukraine, invaded Lithuania and Galicia and even threatened Warsaw itself. In the north the Russian cannon could be heard from the frontier of East Prussia. Would Germany be tempted to seize this opportunity to league with Russia against their common enemy, Poland? So France feared, but Germany remained quiescent, dreading a class war more than a triumph of Polish arms.

Soviet Russia now felt able to dictate terms. True to her policy, she laid little stress on national questions, offering Poland a frontier slightly better than that of the *The tide* Curzon minimum though far short of what Pil- *ebbs* sudski had hoped to gain; insisting, rather, on the disarmament of Poland, attempting to set up soviet institutions in the disputed borderlands, and urging Polish workingmen and peasants to begin a class war against the landlords and bourgeoisie. But Poland, where national pride was strong in all classes, rallied under the shadow of disaster. President Pilsudski directed the military efforts of his countrymen with the advice of the French general Weygand. Some French munitions were rushed to Poland in spite of obstacles encountered at the port of Danzig where the local German population was hostile to the Poles. The Russians in their advance had been guilty of the same error that the Poles had made in their first flush of victory, — they had advanced too rapidly with inadequate support behind the front line.

Taking advantage of this error, the Poles struck at the extremities of the Russian line and forced a general retreat. On October 12, 1920, Soviet Russia accepted an armistice which was followed on March 18, 1921 by the Treaty of Riga.

The new frontier of Poland, running north and south in an approximately straight line from the eastern extremity of *Russian* Galicia to the Dvina river, included most of the *boundaries* debatable borderlands of mixed Polish and non-*established* Polish population. Treaties concluded in 1920 with Finland, Estonia, Latvia and Lithuania established Russia's northwestern boundaries. Finland made the gain of Pechenga, a port on the Arctic Ocean, in addition to the territory of the old Grand Duchy; but the district of Karelia, Finnish by race though historically a part of Russia, remained under Russian rule. Estonia and Latvia obtained frontiers corresponding to their ethnic limits. Lithuania was cut off from Russia by a narrow strip of Polish territory. Rumania held the disputed province of Bessarabia in defiance of Russia's refusal to recognize its cession. The Ukraine, no longer supported by foreign or counter-revolutionary Russian armies, was overrun by the Bolsheviki and reunited with Russia as a federal member of the Union of Soviet Republics. A similar fate befell White Russia and the nations of the Caucasus.

Republican France, assailed in 1792 by the "confederate kings" had made "terror the order of the day" so that *The Reign* France, willing or unwilling, would be united *of Terror* against the common peril. Soviet Russia under analogous circumstances resorted to the same cruel defense. In both cases the official terror was, strictly speaking, merely a peculiarly drastic kind of martial law which treated all political opposition as treason punishable by death. But even without foreign intervention there would have been violent deeds in the course of the revolution, and popular usage lumps all these together under the name of Reign of

Terror. Used in this broader sense we may distinguish three aspects of the Terror: the atrocities of the civil war, the "mass terrorism" of the mobs, and the legal and official prosecution of dissenters from the government policy.

Of the civil and border wars of Russia we have already spoken. Civil war, especially when it is also a class war, is usually the cruelest of all wars; it has no code or *Atrocities* tradition, such as slightly humanizes, or at least *of the civil* regularizes, the "great game" of international *war* war; it brings the conflict into each neighborhood instead of cooping it up in a limited "war zone," and it causes every belligerent to be regarded as a traitor and every neutral as a spy. The Bolshevist leaders were fighting with ropes around their necks, they knew that a victorious royalist general would simply have hanged them all as traitors to Russia. Expecting no mercy, they showed none. Both the "red" revolutionists and the "white" counter-revolutionists made a regular practice of shooting the officers whom they captured and offering to the privates a choice between enlistment in the victorious ranks or immediate execution. Partisan bands of "reds," "whites" or "greens" (peasant groups), under no real discipline, committed the worst atrocities. In the Ukraine lawless armed bands butchered at least 120,000 Jews, mostly unarmed civilians.[1]

On several occasions and for several reasons the mob rose to punish some hated class or party. During the first phase of the revolution, in 1917, two types of mob ac- *Mass* tion were common, the pillage of landlords' *terrorism* estates and the lynching of unpopular army or navy officers. Naturally, the seizure of the land by the peasants did not proceed peaceably; there was no time to arrange for a formal and legal transfer of titles and many peasants, unwilling to await such action, simply burned down the landlord's château

---

[1] For the detailed evidence, see Elias Heifetz, *The Slaughter of the Jews in the Ukraine in 1919* (1921).

and chased him off the estate. Mutinous sailors of the Baltic fleet drowned their commanders under the ice, soldiers in the trenches shot their officers in the back, Bolshevist Red Guards massacred young cadets in the officers' training schools. At a later stage in the revolution peasants who refused to surrender grain and meat for the worthless paper money which was all that the cities could offer them were raided and terrorized by armed mobs, and wealthy peasants (the "kulaks" or "tight-fists") were attacked by the landless poor. This form of class war was often deliberately encouraged by the Bolshevist authorities. Again, after a group of Social Revolutionaries (the largest party in Russia, as the elections for the Constituent Assembly in 1917 had demonstrated), attempted to bring down the Bolshevist régime by a campaign of assassination,[1] thousands of adherents of the party, the innocent with the guilty, were shot by firing squads or butchered by the mob.

The legal agency of the Terror bore the formidable name of the All-Russian Extraordinary Commission for Combating *The legal* Counter-Revolution, Profiteering and Sabotage; *persecution* more briefly the Chresvaicheka or simply Cheka. This revolutionary tribunal enjoyed the powers and employed the methods of the old secret police ("Third Section") of the Tsars. It employed many spies, including some who had learned their art under the old régime but had changed sides to save themselves. Any person of the propertied classes or known to belong to any political party save the one in power might be arrested on suspicion, detained for months in prison without trial, and then suddenly dismissed to freedom or placed before a firing squad without explanation. The most indefensible method employed by the government was the custom of seizing relatives of a suspected person as hostages for his good behavior. Many were shot

---

[1] The German Ambassadors to Soviet Russia and the Ukraine were killed as a protest against the peace of Brest-Litovsk and an unsuccessful attempt made to assassinate Lenin as a protest against the dictatorship.

whose only offense was relationship to an officer in counter-revolutionary armies. During 1918 and 1919 the Cheka formally executed at least ten thousand persons; how many unrecorded deaths there may have been it is bootless even to guess, though we may be certain that the newspaper rumors of a million or more deaths were either exaggerated or included the casualties of the civil war. After 1920 the tale of annual executions dropped to a few hundred, and in 1922 its powers and duties were transferred to the General Political Union or OGPU.[1] The latter body is believed to have carried out one or two thousand formal executions, though exact information is lacking. The Reign of Terror has not been directed exclusively against the former upper and middle classes and the conservative parties; radicals also have suffered either for acts of official dishonesty (which were counted as "sabotaging the revolution") or for opposing the ruling clique. Among the most recent victims of the law have been engineers, both Russian and foreign, who failed to carry out the plans of industrialization which the government had projected, and adherents of the exiled Bolshevist leader Trotsky. Besides the death penalty, milder sentences of imprisonment, exile to prison camps, banishment from Russia, confiscation of property and debarment from the Communist party membership have been freely imposed on political dissenters. There exists no legal protection against arbitrary arrest and punishment for anyone who stands in the way of the dictatorship or impedes its policies.

The Bolshevist régime had in fact much in common with other dictatorships, such as those later established in Italy, Germany and Austria. Its strongest side was that it really governed; certainly the Tsar had never been obeyed with more fear and trembling even in the days of Ivan the Ter-

---

[1] The powers of the OGPU were eventually transferred to the Commissariat of Internal Affairs and to the ordinary criminal courts, but political prosecutions, though less numerous, did not cease. As recently as 1934 scores of suspects were shot to avenge the assassination of a Soviet official.

rible. Visitors to Soviet Russia, even while civil war was
Dictatorship still raging, remarked the orderliness of the
and disci- streets and the efficient repression of private
pline crimes. Carlyle and other admirers of "strong
government" would have found much to commend in Lenin's
Russia as well as in Mussolini's Italy. Such British observers
as Bertrand Russell, H. N. Brailsford and H. G. Wells have
spoken of the "Puritan" coloring of Soviet Russia, for all its
official atheism, stressing the simple life of the rulers, their
insistence on hard work, their fanatical devotion to a creed
(the Gospel according to Karl Marx), and their indifference
to such peace-time luxuries as individual freedom, comfort
or happiness. To this we owe the curious paradox that some
American and British business men who had no sympathy
with socialism have spoken with respect of the iron discipline
of Soviet Russia and even intimated that it might be the
very thing needed by the shiftless Russian peasantry,[1]
whereas liberal Socialists such as Karl Kautsky in Germany,
Ramsay MacDonald in Britain and John Spargo in America
could hardly find terms strong enough to condemn its un-
democratic character. Anarchists, such as Emma Gold-
man, have attacked the Soviet government as the very negation of personal liberty.

The Bolshevist, or "majority" faction of the Russian
Social Democratic Party, the only party whose existence has
The Com- been tolerated in Russia since 1917 is, in its inter-
munist party national aspects, termed Communist. Its economic aims, however, are those of orthodox Marxian Socialism, the collective ownership of the principal means of production and distribution, and should not be confused with
the Utopian "communism" of Fourier or Saint-Simon or

---

[1] H. N. Brailsford, a radical British publicist, had some sympathy with this viewpoint. "The negative, wrecking peasant tendency was repressed and the more
positive creative instincts of the civilized urban artisan gained the upper hand.
They could triumph only by a firm dictatorship, and it is essentially a dictatorship of
the urban proletariat over the backward countryside" (*The Russian Workers' Republic*, 1921, page 250).

with the rebellion of the Paris "Commune" in 1871. It is a pity that the same word has been used in three different senses in the history of radical thought! Communism in the modern sense is simply radical Socialism proceeding abruptly to its goal by means of a party dictatorship instead of waiting for success by parliamentary methods. The party is more important in the government of Russia than any political machinery devised in the Soviet constitution; indeed that constitution had no other aim than to keep the party in power till its work was complete and Russia transformed into a completely socialistic state. The Central Committee and the executive Political Bureau of the party are the source of national policy; and the recognized party leader, no matter what strictly governmental position he may hold, or even should he hold none at all, is the dictator of Russia. The "politics" of Russia consist of the factional struggles within the party. Since the last embers of civil war were trodden out in 1920 no one has disputed the dominance of the Bolsheviki; they are the only political party which has governed any important nation continuously since the World War. Even the death of the revered Lenin did not shake the Communist dictatorship, it merely precipitated a struggle over its leadership.

The number of active members of the Communist party is variable, as every now and again the responsible chiefs hold a "purification" and weed out doubtful, hereti- *Gideon's* cal, laggard or merely opportunist members.[1] *band* About 1,500,000, approximately one per cent of the population, is a fair average of the membership in recent years. This should not be taken to imply that "only one Russian in a hundred favors the present government." To be an active Communist it does not suffice to support the party at

[1] Men whom Lenin is said to have termed "radishes," — red outside but white at heart! The jealousy with which the ranks of the Italian Fascisti, the German Nazis and dominant or privileged parties in other countries are guarded from "dilution" is a fair parallel to the case of Russia.

the polls. The Communist party is a selected group of veteran revolutionists and their trained disciples; membership is a privilege won with difficulty and lost with ease. Men have been dismissed for attending church services of any denomination, for loose conduct in private life or graft in public office, for slackness in propagandist zeal, for inefficiency, for too persistent criticism of the party policy, for having "bourgeois" friends or relatives. Membership carries with it little privilege save a share in political power and it imposes heavy obligations. Communists are called the "shock troops" of the revolution and must be ready at any moment to put aside their private affairs for any assignment of duty. Most of the leaders were themselves of bourgeois origin, because it was rare in Tsarist Russia for a workingman or peasant to have sufficient education to make him a leader of any movement; but the rank and file of the party are drawn from the factory workers in the towns, and future disciples are trained in such organizations as the Young Pioneers and Communist Youth.

A party which never meets defeat at the polls has usually loaded the dice in its own favor by political or constitutional *How the* arrangements, and Russia is no exception. The *party keeps* Communist monopoly of political power was *its power* safeguarded in five ways: (1) the disfranchisement of the propertied classes and of other social groups likely to be hostile, (2) the greater proportionate representation of the cities, centers of Communist sentiment, as compared with the rural districts, (3) the employment of an exceedingly elaborate system of indirect election, easily open to political manipulation at every stage, (4) the occasional quashing of local elections which returned active opponents of the government, (5) the complete denial of the means of political propaganda — party organization, the press, radio, the motion pictures and public meetings — to all hostile political groups. With every avenue of peaceful persuasion cut off, the opposition parties have either abandoned the struggle or contented themselves with returning a small minority of "no party" delegates to some of the Soviets. The constitution in its actual operation is the very antithesis of democracy; it is not even the "dictatorship of the proletariat" which it formally professes to be. Lenin defined it more accurately when he said, "We understand by the words 'Dictatorship of the Proletariat' what is actually the dictatorship of its determined and conscious minority."

The structure of government is extremely complex, partly because of the indirect system of elections and partly because of the local autonomy granted to the minor na- *The hier-* tionalities of the Soviet Union. The unit or *archy of* "cell" is the local council or Soviet. In the *Soviets* country the matter is relatively simple; as nearly every one is a peasant the old village commune or *mir* becomes the electoral unit of the local Soviet. In the towns there has been some attempt to represent the working classes by units of occupation in place of merely geographical units of residence, and the workshops and factories send a number of the delegates. The country village Soviets sent delegates to a District (*Volost*) Congress, which in turn sent delegates to a County (*Uyezd*) Congress, and this in turn to a Regional (*Oblast*) Congress. The District Congress, in addition to sending members to the County Congress, chose also members of the Provincial (*Gubernia*) Congress.[1] The District and County Congresses represented only the peasant villages and country towns, but the Urban Soviets sent delegates directly to the Regional and Provincial Congresses. Thus both the Regional Congress and the Provincial Congress contained both urban and rural delegates, but the towns were represented in proportion to the number of *voters*, while the countryside was represented in proportion to five times that number of *inhabitants*.

[1] To some extent these old political divisions have been replaced by new units. See W. R. Batsell, *Soviet Rule in Russia* (1929).

The central organization of the Russian Socialist Federated Soviet Republic, often called the R.S.F.S.R. for the sake of much needed brevity, is the All-Russian Congress of Soviets containing one delegate to each 25,000 voters chosen by the Urban Soviets and one delegate to each 125,000 inhabitants from the Provincial Soviets, representing both town and country. The authority of the All-Russian Congress is practically unlimited. The whole field of civil and criminal legislation is open to it and all executive branches of the government are responsible to it. But the Congress is so large and unwieldy that its chief actual function is to select an All-Russian Central Executive Committee, which is the effective agent of the Congress and the most important legislative body in Russia. We are not yet at the top of the hierarchy. The All-Russian Executive Committee entrusts the details of administration to a Council of People's Commissars and has a standing committee, or Presidium, to watch over the work of the Commissars between sessions.

The All-Russian Congress of Soviets

The constitution of the R.S.F.S.R. was complex enough in all conscience, but new machinery has been added to insure the proper representation of the minor nationalities. Theoretically Russia is but one of seven federated republics forming together the Union of Socialist Soviet Republics or U.S.S.R. There is a Union Congress of Soviets which chooses a Central Executive Committee which is divided into two bodies, a Council of the Union and a Council of Nationalities, the latter intended to give representation to numerous small ethnic units as well as to the seven constituent republics. The Union Council of People's Commissars and the Union Presidium parallel those of the R.S.F.S.R. and the other six states of the Soviet Union. Next to the R.S.F.S.R. the most important state in the Union is the Ukrainian Socialist Soviet Republic with nearly thirty million inhabitants. The White Russian So-

The new federal structure

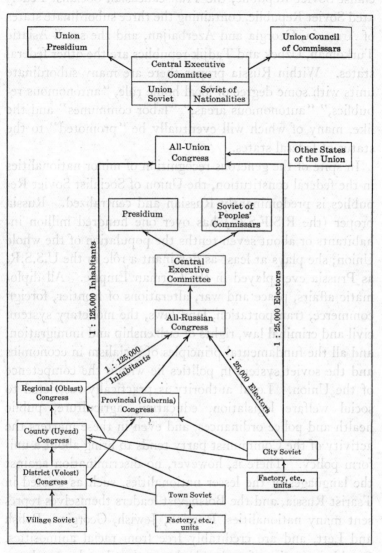

THE SOVIET HIERARCHY

In reading this chart it should be borne in mind that it is somewhat simplified, that local political units are in a state of transition, and that actual practice does not always conform to theory; the Province and the Region, for example, are sometimes used alternatively as electoral units for the Russian and all-Union Congresses of Soviets.

cialist Soviet Republic, the Transcaucasian Socialist Federated Soviet Republic, containing the three subordinate states of Armenia, Georgia and Azerbaijan, and the small Asiatic Turkoman, Uzbek and Tadjik republics are the other federal states. Within Russia proper there are many subordinate units with some degree of local home rule, "autonomous republics," "autonomous areas," "labor communes" and the like, many of which will eventually be "promoted" to the status of federal states.

In spite of the generous recognition of minor nationalities in the federal constitution, the Union of Socialist Soviet Republics is predominantly Russian and centralized. Russia proper (the R.S.F.S.R.) has over one hundred million inhabitants or about seven-tenths the population of the whole Union; she plays at least as dominant a rôle in the U.S.S.R. as Prussia ever played in the German Empire. All diplomatic affairs, peace and war, alterations of frontier, foreign commerce, transportation, land laws, the monetary system, civil and criminal law, rights of citizenship and immigration, and all the fundamental principles of socialism in economics and the soviet system in politics lie within the competence of the Union. Local authority is practically restricted to social welfare legislation, education, agriculture, public health and police ordinances, and even in these matters the activity of the Communist party tends to bring about a uniform policy. There is, however, no discrimination against the languages of the lesser nationalities, such as existed in Tsarist Russia, and the Bolshevist leaders themselves represent many nationalities, Russian, Jewish, Georgian, Polish and Lett, and are creditably free from racial animosities. On this one point of *national* tolerance, and perhaps only on that point, the Russian government is more liberal than other European dictatorships.

The elaborate governmental structure of Soviet Russia, though in effect merely the machinery which the party

dictatorship operates, has several points of interest. The
system of disfranchising the propertied classes [1]
is a novelty; history has known many instances
of a "property qualification for the franchise"
but not hitherto of property as a *dis*qualification! The system of indirect elections contrasts markedly
with the American constitution, which elects Congress directly and the President at one remove (the electoral college)
and that a merely nominal one. But indirect voting has been
used in many countries and is perhaps adapted to very backward or illiterate populations who cannot comprehend national issues but know which of their immediate neighbors
they can trust to represent them. The more direct representation and the greater proportionate voting power of the
townsman, as compared with the peasant, reverses the favor-
itism shown to the country districts in England till 1832, in
Prussia till 1919 and in some New England legislatures today.
The most discussed innovation in Russia is occupational representation, voting by industries and workshops instead of
by wards and election districts. But the principle is neither
peculiar to Russia nor carried out logically within the Soviet
system. The higher Congresses of Soviets and especially
the All-Russian and Union Congresses are as purely territorial in their basis as any American Congress or European
Parliament. Special class representation has existed in
many European constitutions, especially for "upper houses,"
and the "Fascist" constitutions in Italy and Austria ignored
geography almost entirely and based representation on occupational corporations created by the state. This was, in
fact, the original medieval idea, the representation of economic classes — "Estates" — rather than of localities; ex-

*Soviet gov-
ernment in
comparative
politics*

---

[1] Specifically excluded from the franchise are (1) persons employing labor to increase their profits, (2) persons living on unearned incomes, (3) persons engaged in
private trade, (4) the clergy of all denominations, (5) members of the old royal family or the Tsarist police, (6) criminals and the insane, (7) persons not engaged in
socially useful labor (with an exception for those too old to work).

clusively territorial representation came in with modern democracy which ignores classes.[1] The future of the Soviet system is wholly a matter of speculation, though it may evolve towards democracy if the peasants acquire political ambition with their growing education.

The civil law of Soviet Russia is not vastly different from other codes of continental Europe and most of its provisions are to be found in "capitalist" legislation, but the rights of private property are more restricted. Absolute title to real estate is not recognized, as the land is in theory a public monopoly. Inheritance rights are limited to a small sum. Marriage is a purely civil procedure, and divorce may be granted at the application of either party. The criminal law is indulgent to ordinary crime, aiming at the reformation of the criminal, but severe towards political offenses. For the administration of justice there is a hierarchy of Peoples' Courts. Public prosecutors and defenders are provided, juries are employed in important cases. Judges, jurors and lawyers must all be citizens and judges must either have legal experience or, as a substitute, experience in trades union or labor organization.

Russian law

The world has been more interested in the economic than in the political experiments of Soviet Russia. Dictatorships were established after the war in many countries, but the denial of private property remained peculiar to Russia. The rulers of Soviet Russia would, however, be the first to admit that theirs is not yet "the Socialist State" of their aims; many concessions have had perforce to be made to "capitalism" and the resulting system is illogical and incomplete, a mixture of socialism, "state capitalism" and private ownership. The land is publicly owned but in great part still privately

Stages of economic development

[1] "Proportional representation," which finds place in many postwar constitutions of a democratic sort, is a third type of representation, a grouping by political opinion rather than by either residence or occupation.

managed. The greater industries, such as mines and railroads, are public monopolies; the larger factories are state
directed, and foreign trade is rather completely in the hands
of the government. But much private retail trading has
been tolerated and valuable oil districts have been turned over
to the management of foreign investors to attract capital into
the country. The economic history of Soviet Russia can be divided into three chapters: the revolutionary period, from 1917
to 1921; the period of the "new economic policy," 1921–28;
the period of the first and second "five-year plans," since 1928.

The early phase of the Bolshevist revolution was not only
the period of greatest political violence but also of the greatest economic misery. In part this was an in- *Disruption*
heritance from the war times. As early as 1916 *and famine*
the transportation system of the nation, always miserably
inadequate, had bogged down and the great cities were faced
with a shortage of everything. In 1917 bread riots had
precipitated the revolution. The ensuing civil wars, the
violent seizure of estates and factories, the first crude experiments in workers' management of trade and industry, the
flotation of unlimited quantities of worthless paper money
and the general anarchy of the countryside made confusion
worse confounded. The country would no longer sell to the
town, as the town had little of value, either in money or
goods, to give in return. Forced requisitions and confiscations of the crops had only the effect of decreasing agricultural production; the peasants raised only enough to keep
themselves alive. In the Volga region in 1921 a serious
drouth, supervening upon the artificial crop shortage,
brought about perhaps the most serious European famine in
modern times. Several million peasants died of starvation
in spite of all the relief which the government could give
them, and several millions more would have perished except
for the activity of American relief officials.

Then, and ever since, the greatest unsolved problem of

Soviet Russia has been the position of the peasantry. The

The land problem peasant does not neatly fit into the categories of Marxian economics which divide humanity into "bourgeoisie" and "proletariat," for he is at once a manual laborer and a capitalist controlling his own "tools of production." The expropriation of estates belonging to Church, State and private landlords during the revolution added some 121,500,000 acres to peasant holdings.[1] For this confiscated land no compensation was ever paid. But the peasants were not permitted to "own" the land they acquired, they were merely tenants at will of the nation, the supreme landlord, and at first disastrous attempts were made to nationalize the entire surplus of grain production. Later a share of the crop was taken in taxes and the peasant was free to sell the rest as he pleased. Tactless handling of the peasant problem by the urban dictators of Russia has repeatedly brought on local famine conditions only less in scale than the great Volga famine. The attempt to foment class war against the Kulaks or wealthier peasants has had as its chief effect the discouragement of individual initiative for agricultural improvement. Alexei Rykov, one of the Bolshevist leaders protested against the exaggerations of this tendency:

We can't fight for culture in the village if we reckon as kulaks peasants who are using metal spoons instead of wooden ones... If the peasant works the land well they burden him with the individual tax. Then who will undertake to work the land well? I don't think there will be any such idiots who will do this when they know that for this they will be subject to the individual tax, their children will be driven out of school, and they themselves will be deprived of electoral rights.[2]

The "grain strike" of the peasants and the consequent

---

[1] Professor Vinogradoff's estimate.

[2] Cited from *Pravda* for December 4, 1928 by William Henry Chamberlain, *Soviet Russia* (1931), page 201. In spite of all the efforts of the government to make farming a collectivized industry, there were still over 25,000,000 separate farm homesteads in Russia a dozen years after the Bolshevist victory.

danger of national famine combined with the startling decrease in industrial output convinced Lenin and *The NEP*
the other practical minded Bolshevist leaders
that the socialization of Russia had been hurried too much
and that a temporary compromise with capitalism was essential to prevent an absolute collapse of Russian economic
life. Of what use would be a successful operation for the
removal of capitalism from Russia if the patient died in the
process? So he advocated a "new economic policy" which,
while retaining the ultimate socialistic objectives of the government, bent immediate attention to the restoration of
normal production. The main features of the new policy
were: (1) assurances to the peasants that they would not be
disturbed in the occupation and control of their lands; (2) a
fixed tax on produce instead of the general nationalization of
surplus foodstuffs; (3) permission to individuals to engage,
within limits defined by law, in retail trade and manufacture; (4) the leasing of industrial enterprises, especially in
mining and the oil fields, to foreign investors with a division
of profits between the capitalist and the Soviet government;
(5) the restoration of discipline in the factories, with wider
powers for factory managers, higher pay for better work, and
"efficiency systems" such as the Taylor method of motion-
saving. Lenin cherished a favorite dream that electric power
could be developed in sufficient quantity to run Russian
industry and so increase the national wealth that the foreign
investor would no longer be an essential factor in Russian
economy. In some such way the industrial mechanism
might be recaptured on behalf of pure socialism. In the
meantime Utopia must wait.

The new economic policy saved Russia at the moment of
crisis. Never again did industrial production fall so low as
in 1920, when the iron and textile industries almost ceased
operation. By 1923 production had won back about half
the ground lost since the revolution began and, except in

agriculture, it made still further gains in the years following.

Partial re-vival of production   Yet the new policy was not universally popular. Quite apart from the theoretical objection that it was a retreat from socialism to partial capitalism, many resented the rise of a new class of profiteers (nicknamed the NEPmen) made possible by the toleration of private trade. The price of manufactured goods continued to rise and that of agricultural commodities to fall, thus making it harder than ever for the peasant to get the agricultural machinery which he needed. The rising curve of industrial prices crossing the falling curve of agricultural prices was termed the "scissors," whose blades must be closed to bring together town and country.

In 1922 Lenin's health began to fail, and in January, 1924, he died. No one else in the Soviet government enjoyed a *The rise of Stalin* tithe of his prestige when he was alive, and after his death he was almost canonized and his tomb became a shrine for thousands of pilgrims. For a few years after Lenin's death political power was shared by a group of party leaders — Kamenev, Zinoviev, Rykov, Bukharin, Kalinin, Trotsky, Stalin and a few others. Though Kalinin, as Russian president of the Union Central Executive Committee (the nearest equivalent to a "President of the Union" which the Russian system affords), held the highest nominal office he had less power or prestige than the brilliant Leon Trotsky, organizer of the Red Army, or the hard-tempered party manager Stalin, and the struggle for party control increasingly narrowed down to those two leaders. Ultimately Stalin was victorious, in spite of the fact that Trotsky quoted the venerated Lenin to the effect that Stalin was too "crude and narrow minded" for party leadership. Trotsky's adherents were forced from office, compelled to recant or be read out of the party, and in extreme cases driven into exile. Such was the fate of Trotsky himself, who carried with him into foreign lands the conviction that Stalin had betrayed the Communist cause by concentrating attention on Russia and ignoring the general European revolution. Kamenev and Zinoviev, who had joined Stalin for a time against Trotsky, were in turn flung from power as radical "deviationists," while Rykov and Bukharin were reduced in authority as too conservative. The men who occupied high posts in the government after 1930 were mainly obedient disciples of Stalin and few of them bore names hitherto famous in party history. Stalin became almost as powerful as Lenin had been, and the dictatorship of a party machine was again the dictatorship of an individual.

Stalin was a Georgian from the Caucasus whose real name was Joseph Djugashvili, but like most of the revolutionary leaders he was commonly known by his alias. *Russia's* Stalin, "the man of steel," was certainly a fitting *new ruler* designation for the ruthless, energetic, ambitious man who stepped into the shoes of Lenin. He had suffered much for the faith, spending many years in prison or exile and enduring the cruelest treatment from the Tsar's police with stoical patience. He had fought bravely and effectively during the revolution against the conservative "white" armies; even those Communists, and they were many, who opposed him as an Asiatic foreigner or as a crude and violent partisan without the education that a statesman should have, admitted his courage, devotion and constant party loyalty. Without Lenin's intellectual originality, he had something of his shrewdness, tact, resolute purpose and executive energy. The man of action swept out of his way the men of ideas or broke them to his service. He was aided by an iron physique and could carry a load of work and responsibility which would have crushed many of his rivals and associates.

The greatest achievement of the Stalin administration to the present has been the "five-year plan" for the industrialization of Russia. This plan had a double objective: to complete the socialization of industry and agriculture and

to introduce modern machinery and efficiency methods;
The Five- in short, a wedding of the economics of Karl
Year Plan, Marx with the technology of Henry Ford. This
1928-1932 was certainly very different from the dreams of
the earlier Utopian socialists and communists who, as late as
William Morris, thought that industrialism was a twin disease with capitalism and both would perish together, leaving
economic life simpler as well as more democratic.[1] In a
sense, Stalin was continuing the work begun by Peter the
Great at the end of the seventeenth century, the "westernization" of the slack, dreamy, rather impractical, half-
Orientalized Russian people. The modernistic outlook, the
impatient temper and the ruthless methods of the two reformer despots have curiously much in common. Just as
Peter built an army and a navy, established a Germanized
bureaucracy, subordinated the priesthood to the State, and
thrust his courtiers into western clothes, so Stalin envisaged
Russia's future in the terms of tractors, collective farms,
electric power plants and spreading railway systems. But
the industrialization of Russia was undertaken not primarily
for its own sake or to increase national prosperity; it had also
a two-fold connection with Communism, by increasing the
efficiency of state-directed enterprise the weeds of individualism and capitalism which had sprouted in the relatively tolerant epoch of the NEP could again be "plowed
under" without disaster, and by balancing agriculture and
industry Russia could be made a self-contained economic
unit, no longer dependent on manufactures imported from
hostile capitalistic nations.

The schemes for the industrialization of Russia were carefully studied before they were launched. Preparatory work
occupied the committees and bureaus of the Communist
party and the various economic, industrial and scientific
organizations of the bureaucracy for some three years before

[1] This also was the tradition of the Tolstoyan anarchists.

a general plan was laid before the fifth All-Union Congress of Soviets.[1]   A State Planning Commission (Gosplan) assumed general direction of details.   Though the plan was not finally approved till 1929, the year 1927–28 was taken as the "basic year" for purposes of comparison, and it was hoped that by 1933 oil and coal production would be doubled, iron output trebled, electric power increased fourfold, general agricultural output increased by more than half, general industrial output more than doubled, a fifth of all individual farms put on a collective basis, agricultural machinery made everywhere available, schools provided for all children, unemployment totally abolished.

The Soviet government launched its scheme of industrial reconstruction with a fervor that can be compared only with the mobilization for a patriotic war or a religious *The plan in* crusade: The vocabulary of war was freely em- *action* ployed in this "great offensive" against poverty. So simple a matter as establishing village schools became a "war on the illiteracy front," the buying of a tractor "a new gain in the agricultural sector," the establishment of a collective farm "a drive against the Kulaks."   Many workingmen voluntarily gave up their holidays to hasten the completion of a particular piece of work.   Factories which surpassed their quotas were accorded honors; factories which lagged were subjected to government investigation and sometimes the managers were punished.   The importation and production of luxuries were discouraged.   All Russians should live like Spartans until the *piatiletka* (five-year plan) was completed.   The workers were consoled for their present privations, like soldiers in wartime, by the enthusiasm of working for a common victory and the hope of a better day when victory was attained.   It must be conceded to Russia, and to some other European dictatorships as well, that if they brought to the tasks of peace all the intolerance of war, they were able to mobilize as

[1] G. T. Grinko, *The Five-Year Plan of the Soviet Union*, page 29.

well its enthusiasm and devotion, and thus attain in some
sort the "moral equivalent of war" of which William James
had written. "If the Soviets were to fall today," wrote one
of the most careful students of Russia's industrial reconstruction, "the one idea that would be sure to survive them
is that of national planning. It is not an original idea with
them... but they have given the idea color and drama... Not
an economist or industrialist of note but has pondered over
its meaning and possibilities. Not a diplomat or statesman
but has taken it to heart."[1] "National planning" indeed
became something of a catchword not only in Fascist Italy
and Nazi Germany, but even in the individualistic United
States during the economic depression of the early 'thirties.

In many respects the five-year plan exceeded the expectations of its sponsors. Such giant enterprises as the Magni-

*The second
five-year
plan, 1933-
1937*

togorsk steel works and the Dnieprostroy power
plant rank among the world's greatest industrial
achievements. Though the key industries of
coal, iron and steel fell considerably short of their
quotas, the production of oil and machinery exceeded theirs.
On the whole, the first five-year plan may be accounted a
quantitative success. Even while it was still in operation a
second five-year plan was projected, envisaging a more than
doubled output of coal, iron and oil, a more than trebled output of automobiles and agricultural machinery, more than
twice as great an aggregate national income, and the "final
liquidation" of all "capitalist elements in society."

In the main we must look in another direction than quantitative industrial production for the failures, and they were

*Failures of
Soviet plan-
ning*

many, of the magnificent Russian effort. One
fault was an excessive emphasis on speed of production resulting in the output of a large amount
of "shoddy" and inferior commodities, the frequent inability
of the railroads to find freight cars to transport accumulated

[1] Maurice Hindus, *The Great Offensive* (1933), pages 55–56.

stocks of goods, and the waste of valuable machinery by placing it in the hands of workers and peasants untrained to use it. For these failures the government rather ungenerously sought a scapegoat by placing the blame on "engineers of bourgeois mentality" who had been "sabotaging the revolution." Many engineers and technical experts, Russian and foreign, were tried and condemned to imprisonment or execution, though for diplomatic reasons the sentences against foreigners were usually commuted to banishment. Another fault was the tactless and intolerant handling of the peasantry in the effort to force them into collective farms.

The temporary truce with the peasant proprietors under the "new economic policy," often interrupted even in those days by sporadic attacks on the wealthier individuals, came to an end with the inauguration of the five-year plan. The word went around that the whole "kulak" class was to be "liquidated" which meant that those of its members who would not willingly join the new collective farms would be stripped of their property as the old landlord class had been in the first stage of the revolution. The poorer and "middle peasantry" were stirred up to class hate against the kulaks and at the same time persuaded to join the co-operative farms by skillful propaganda, such as motion pictures graphically contrasting the miseries of the isolated farm with the advantages of the collectivist system. Heavy special taxes and levies forced most of the kulaks into ruin; they slaughtered their cattle and reduced themselves to voluntary poverty, or gave up the struggle and entered the co-operatives, or, if too defiant of the authorities, were driven into banishment in penal labor colonies in the far north. In one way these tactics were very effective; by 1932 the collective farms, counting together the co-operatives and the state farms,[1] embraced

Liquidating the "kulaks"

---

[1] The farms run directly by the government were mainly for experimental or propagandist purposes; they played a smaller rôle in general agricultural economy than the local "collectives."

eighty per cent of the planted fields in the country. But agricultural production, in spite of all the wealth of agricultural machinery now for the first time available to Russian farmers, made very little gain and in some cases actually decreased. In 1929 and 1930 about one-third of all the livestock in the country was killed off, partly to meet a food shortage and partly as a protest against the exactions of the authorities. A moderation of the "drive" against the independent farmers brought about a partial restoration of Russian agriculture, but it is evident that one of the most urgent tasks before the Soviet government is to heal the wounds that its own policy has caused.

Before the revolution Russia was the most illiterate of the larger nations of Europe, and what schools and universities *Education* did exist were badly crippled financially by war *in Soviet* and revolution and educationally by the bitter-*Russia* ness of the class struggle which resulted in the death or exile of many of Russia's best teachers. Under such handicaps it is remarkable that the Soviet government has been able to make such progress in spreading elementary education. Schools of every sort and grade have been established and the number of pupils in the schools more than doubled. Absolute illiteracy is becoming rare except in very distant and backward peasant communities. Schools for children orphaned by famine or civil war or cast adrift by their parents because of poverty have reclaimed thousands of useful citizens who without them would have become professional beggars or criminals. Nor has the Soviet government given any narrow interpretation to "education" as meaning merely elementary schooling. There is a sort of "university extension" in the form of classes in various industrial techniques for adults. Communist principles are taught in every imaginable way, by newspapers (practically all government owned), by public pageants, cartoons, moving pictures and decorated "propaganda trains" filled with speakers. The Soviets encourage and to some extent endow dancing, music and the theater for workers' recreation. Earnest, though only partly successful, efforts are made to develop a new "proletarian culture" in architecture, sculpture, the drama, verse and fiction.

Yet in this very field of educational and cultural activity where so much has been achieved one encounters some of the greatest drawbacks of the new régime. In- *Persecution* tolerance, rising to positive fanaticism, has *of the intel-* crippled the search for truth and beauty in *ligentsia* Russia to an appalling degree. No church schools or other private schools are permitted; in some cases they have existed, but in disregard of law. The universities are distorted into propagandist agencies or curtailed into mere technical schools. No professor or teacher who is not in hearty agreement with the Communist policy may teach the social sciences and he is rarely fortunate if permitted to teach anything. Many professors are refugees in more liberal countries, notably in Czechoslovakia where an entire Russian faculty has been organized. Philosophy is, in general, banned as smacking of "bourgeois ideology," and the libraries are swept clean of "counter-revolutionary books" including some of the great classics of the past. Preference is given to "proletarian" children in the schools and universities; the children of the "bourgeoisie" and the "intelligentsia" must wait their turn till the laborers' children, however ill-prepared, have been given class room. Only in natural science and technical studies is education free from censorship, and even here the hunger and discouragement of the teachers and their inability to obtain adequate funds to carry on their work have been benumbing to effort. Art has been made the bondservant of party propaganda; there is no career for poet, dramatist, painter, sculptor, novelist or essayist who is not completely orthodox in his socialism and willing to devote a large part of his attention to embodying the class struggle or the five-year plan in artistic form. The artistic achievements of post-revolutionary Russia, rated at their highest, cannot be compared with those of Tolstoy, Turgenev, Dostoievski, Gogol, Pushkin, Tschaikowsky, Rimski-Korsakov and a score of other geniuses who made nineteenth century Russia great in spite of its misgovernment and obscurantism. A revolutionary Inquisition can sometimes be as deadly to the free activities of the human spirit as a reactionary one.

Most of all this is true in the sphere of religion. The old Orthodox Church was intolerant enough, as witness its bitter *Religion in* persecution of the Jews, and as a close ally of an *Soviet Rus-* oppressive government it was hated by all pro-*sia* gressive Russians. The Bolshevist régime is in one sense tolerant. It permits public worship by any sect, and all over Russia churches still stand open. But this is bare toleration; it does not amount to religious freedom. No priest of any creed may vote or hold office; no church may establish a school or teach religion save in its regular services; no church, by recent legislation, may even undertake charitable or philanthropic work. To be ardently religious, whether as Orthodox, Catholic, Protestant, Mohammedan or Jew is immaterial, is to become a political suspect, to be debarred admission to the Communist party and therefore from all political life. The government conducts an avowed atheistic propaganda in all the public schools, which the children are compelled to attend, and encourages "Leagues of the Godless" and other anti-religious movements. That church treasures have been seized and many poorly attended churches closed seems to have been due more to economic reasons than to anti-religious policy, but the attitude of the government is fairly well expressed in its contemptuous placard "Religion is the opium of the people!" One branch of the Orthodox Church broke off from the conservative authority of Patriarch Tikhon and tried to make a compromise with the revolution under the name of the "Living Church," and the Roman Catholics and some Protestant sects, notably the Baptists, have won converts, but each movement in turn when it reached a certain degree of popularity began to meet with obstacles and discouragements from a hostile government.

Yet it is an open question whether Soviet Russia can be said to be without a religion; obviously it is a question of definition.   At least the government recognizes *The ortho-* the need for certain enthusiasms and idealiza- *doxy of* tions.   Church festivals have been replaced by *revolution* revolutionary holidays; church pageants by Communist demonstrations; ikons by red flags; reverence for the saints by reverence for the heroes of Socialism.   Unfortunately in gaining a religion Russia gained with it a "theology" and a rather arid and scholastic one at that.   The literature of Bolshevism is turgid with pedantic phrases about "counter-revolutionary mentality," "petty bourgeois ideology," "proletarian culture" and the like.   Fine distinctions are drawn between "right wing defections" and "left wing deviations"; between an "upper peasantry" to be persecuted and a "middle peasantry" to be cultivated.   The writings of Karl Marx, and latterly of Lenin and Stalin, are treated as almost verbally inspired, and every questioning of party dogma is viewed with genuine horror.   At times one seems to be back among the Greek monks of the fourth century or among the Scottish sectaries of the seventeenth.   In such an atmosphere of narrow concentration on "the one thing needful" all human values which cannot be related to the social tasks which the government has stamped with its approval are apt to be disregarded or even condemned.   In a vegetable garden flowers are considered weeds!

CHAPTER XXII

NATIONS OF THE BALTIC

THE two largest ethnic units in Europe are the Russian at the eastern extremity of the continent and the German at the center; between them is a broad zone of minor

The liber-
ated nations nationalities. Until recently these lesser peoples
of eastern were divided among four large military empires
Europe
— German, Austrian, Russian and Ottoman Turk. The Balkan struggles of the nineteenth and early twentieth centuries, the collapse of Russia in 1917 and the defeat of Germany and Austria-Hungary in 1918 replaced the bureaucratic uniformity of the four empires by the independent national states lying west of Soviet Russia and east or southeast of Germany: Finland, Estonia, Latvia, Lithuania, Poland, Czechoslovakia, Austria, Hungary, Rumania, Yugoslavia, Bulgaria, Albania and Greece. The first six of these states owe their independence to the World War and the subsequent peace settlements; Rumania was doubled and Serbia expanded into Yugoslavia, absorbing Montenegro; Greece and Albania only slightly altered; Austria, Hungary and Bulgaria diminished.

The five Baltic republics form a natural geographic group. Only Poland ranks high among European states in popula-

The Baltic tion or military power, but her northern neigh-
republics bors, Lithuania, Latvia, Estonia and Finland,
occupy important portions of the Baltic shore and, granted that they are only the "pawns of diplomacy," they are pawns very strategically placed on the European chessboard. Imperialistic ambitions in either Germany or Russia would endanger their independence; their precarious situation naturally dominates and colors their internal as well as their foreign politics.

Finland, a nation of the far north, has an area a little greater than Norway or about twice that of New England and a population of over 3,500,000. The Fin- *Finland* landers are a mixed people; not every Finlander is a "Finn," for along the coast there is a Swedish speaking element amounting to more than a tenth of the whole population and exercising a cultural and economic influence far beyond its numbers. The true Finns speak a language of north Asiatic type,[1] but physically they are as apt to resemble the tall, blond Swedes as the short, dark Lapps; many of them blend the two, having the round Asiatic head combined with the fair Scandinavian coloring. The Finns are famous the world over for physical strength and endurance, and their champions have taken many of the athletic records in international contests, particularly for long-distance running. In general culture, apart from race and language, the Finns can be classed as Scandinavian: they are Lutheran Protestant in faith, universally educated, with qualities of industry, good citizenship and respect for womanhood which have attracted the admiration of foreigners. Hardy foresters and seamen, or peasants wringing a scant living from a stubborn soil, the Finns cherish a strong affection for their country and are resolved to maintain the independence which they won with the break-up of the Russian Empire in 1917.

The tradition of national self-government is old in Finland. For centuries the country was a Swedish province with representative institutions of her own, and *Finnish in-* even under Russian rule Finland was given a *stitutions* special status as a Grand Duchy with a Diet or parliament. It is true that the last two Russian Tsars, Alexander III and Nicholas II, frequently violated the constitutional rights of Finland and subjected the country to direct autocratic rule, but such usurpations always met the most obstinate popular

---

[1] A non-Aryan tongue, akin to Lapp, Estonian, etc.; more remotely akin to Magyar.

resistance. After the separation from Russia, Finland hung perilously poised between the danger of a Bolshevist dictatorship and the danger of becoming a dependency of Germany.[1] Escaping both perils, Finland decided to become a democratic and parliamentary republic. The President was to be elected for a six-year term by a specially chosen electoral college and enjoy considerable power. The Diet, consisting of only one chamber, contained two hundred members chosen in the most democratic fashion by direct, proportional, secret and universal adult suffrage. Woman suffrage in Finland, in fact, goes back to the days of the Grand Duchy.

The echoes of the stormy period of civil war which ushered in national independence have not yet ceased. The Communist party is under the ban of the law and not permitted to organize; it recalls too many memories of massacres by the "Reds" and suggests too great a danger of Russian intrigues against national independence. Even the Social Democratic party, representing official and orthodox socialism, has been viewed somewhat askance by the "bourgeois" groups. It is, however, the largest single party in the Diet. In the center sit the liberal and democratic Progressives and the rural Agrarian party, each of which has given one president to the republic. After the fall of General Mannerheim's provisional government which carried the nation safely through the civil war, Karl Stahlberg — a professor of law and a Progressive leader — was chosen the first constitutional president (1919–25). He was succeeded by President Lauri Relander (1925–31), an Agrarian leader. On the right sit the Swedish People's party, representing chiefly the nationalistic interests of the Swedish minority in the country, the conservative National Coalition party, and a small but arrogant Fascist group, the National Patriotic party, formerly called the Lapua group, who de-

Finnish politics

[1] For the revolution and civil war in Finland in 1917–18, see Chapter XVI.

mand "strong government" and the ruthless repression of all socialists. In 1930 some irresponsible hot-heads of the Lapua movement kidnaped ex-president Stahlberg, intending to deport him across the Russian border, and in 1932 a Lapuan group attempted a rebellion against the government. Both attempts were severely punished. The general reaction towards a moderate conservatism placed in the presidency in 1931 Pehr Svinhufvud, a distinguished jurist who had been imprisoned under the Tsar for upholding Finnish legal rights and who had later been associated with General Mannerheim in the provisional "White Guard" government which had accepted the aid of German troops to crush the Bolsheviki of Finland.

Next to safeguarding the constitution against Communist or Fascist conspiracies, the most urgent domestic problems have been the land question and prohibition. *National* In a peasant nation whose chief wealth lies in its *problems* forests, the problems of land ownership and management are vital. Prohibition lasted from 1919 to 1932, a period curiously coincident with the similar experiment in the United States. Foreign policy has been concerned mainly with Sweden and Soviet Russia. The League of Nations awarded to Finland the Swedish-speaking Aaland islands in the Baltic,[1] but refused to take cognizance of the Finnish protests against Russian misgovernment in Eastern Karelia (an adjoining Russian district containing a large Finnish population) on the ground that Russia was not a member of the League and could not be "brought to court" for her treatment of national minorities. By the Treaty of Dorpat (1920) Russia awarded to Finland the Arctic port of Pechenga. Like most of the smaller European nations, Finland is pacifist and internationalist and a strong supporter of the League of Nations.

The Estonians are akin by race and language to the Finns

[1] See Chapter XIX.

and but for the intervening Gulf of Finland the two states
might have merged.   Estonia further resembles
Estonia   Finland in having been greatly affected by a long
period of Swedish rule; like Finland it is Lutheran in faith.
But Estonia had less self-government under Russia than did
Finland.   Instead of being a Grand Duchy with large powers
of local home rule, Estonia was but an undistinguished part
of the Russian "Baltic Provinces" ruled by the Tsar's officials and dominated economically by a small group of German landlords, the so-called "Baltic barons."   Estonia has
about a third as many inhabitants as Finland (1,100,000)
on an area approximately equal to that of the twin New
England states of Vermont and New Hampshire.   Most of
the people are farmers, and the chief problem of domestic
policy has been the partition of the former great estates
among the peasantry.

The birth of the young Estonian republic was a difficult
one.   The collapse of Russia meant for a time the attempt of
Estonian   Germany to establish another foreign domination
problems   based on the power of the resident German landlords and an army of occupation.   Soviet Russia attempted
to spread Bolshevism in the little country; the reactionary
"White" Russian forces desired to reannex it as part of the
old Empire.   At last by the Treaty of Dorpat in 1920 Soviet
Russia agreed to recognize the complete independence of
Estonia in return for commercial access to the nation's Baltic
ports.   The constitution adopted was a purely democratic
one, providing, like the Finnish, for a single-chambered parliament chosen by universal, direct, proportional adult suffrage,
but the President was given less power.   In fact, there was
strictly speaking no President at all, as the acting prime
minister was also *ex officio* President or "State Head."   In
1934 the constitution was revised, however, to provide for
an elected President, and tendencies toward an executive
dictatorship became evident.   Parliamentary government

was temporarily suspended and the cabinet legislated in its place.

Latvia is a little larger than Estonia (about 25,000 square miles in area) with a population of not quite two millions. The people are in no way kin to the Finns or Estonians; they speak an Aryan tongue very similar to Lithuanian. But like their neighbors to the north they are mainly Lutheran and bear many cultural impresses of their old connection with Sweden. Again like Estonia, Latvia suffered greatly from the double tyranny of the Russian bureaucracy and the German squirearchy, who between them completely dominated the life of the Baltic provinces until the Russian revolution of 1917. Latvia also passed through a confused period of civil war in 1918 and 1919 with German "Balts," Russian Bolsheviks and native Letts struggling for ascendancy. After much difficulty they extorted recognition from Russia, adjusted their frontiers, founded a purely democratic republic, and settled down to their main task of expropriating the German landlords. The constitution greatly resembled that of Estonia, but the offices of president and premier were made separate, although the former was elected by the parliament. In 1934 Premier Karlis Ulmanis proclaimed a temporary dictatorship and representative government was suspended.

Lithuania lies to the south of Latvia and the two peoples are closely allied in race and language. The Lithuanians are predominantly Roman Catholic, however, as their historical affiliations have been rather with Catholic Poland than with Protestant Sweden. In the Middle Ages Lithuania was a great nation covering about ten times the contracted area of the present republic. For a long time the Grand Duchy of Lithuania was united to Poland on a basis of strict legal equality. Nevertheless union came in time to mean practical subordination. When Poland was dismembered in the eighteenth century the Lithuanian por-

tion fell to Russia. Like the other Baltic states, Lithuania
suffered from the ravages of the contending armies during
the World War, suffered German occupation and Bolshevist
uprisings after the Russian revolution, and emerged as independent republic crippled by poverty and with uncertain
frontiers. The constitution followed the same lines as those
of the other Baltic states, — parliamentary government
through a single-chamber legislature elected by universal
suffrage, with proportional representation of parties.

The course of democracy has not run smoothly in Lithuania. The chief difficulty lay in the sphere of foreign affairs.
Vilna and Lithuania had regarded the city of Vilna and the
Memel region around it as constituting part of the republic, but an irregular Polish force under General Lucien
Zeligowski seized the disputed district. Poland disavowed
his act but was willing to profit by its fruits, Lithuania
lacked the force to evict him, and the League of Nations tried
in vain to arrange a plebiscite. Following the recommendation of a local assembly chosen at Vilna — elected, to be sure,
under Polish auspices — the League of Nations Council
decided in 1923 that Poland have the disputed region, and
the Council of Ambassadors confirmed this decision. Lithuania refused to acquiesce and still maintains a formal protest.
Partial compensation was found at Memel. The town and
district of Memel had been taken from Germany at Versailles
by the Allied and Associated Powers with the evident intention of ultimately ceding it to Lithuania; but the Germans
objected and so did the Poles, so the actual transfer was delayed. It must be remembered that for two or three years
after the war most observers expected Lithuania to be
federated with either Russia or Poland. Impatient at this
delay Lithuania resolved on direct action; taking a leaf from
Poland's book the Lithuanians in 1923 suddenly occupied the
Memel district. The Allied powers were taken aback at this
shirt-sleeve diplomacy, but referred the matter to Europe's

maid-of-all-work the League of Nations, which in 1924 recognized Lithuanian sovereignty over Memel subject to local autonomy for the district and certain regulations for the port. Including Memel but not including Vilna, Lithuania has approximately the area and population of Latvia (21,000 square miles; 2,300,000 inhabitants).

Largely as a result of dissatisfaction with Lithuania's position in foreign affairs, which was attributed to the natural weakness of parliamentary democracy, some ad- *Dictator-* herents of the conservative Nationalist Union *ship in* party resolved on a *coup d'état.* In 1926 a mili- *Lithuania* tary group overawed a too liberal parliament and imposed the continuance in office of President Antanas Smetona and Premier Augustine Valdemaras, who ruled with dictatorial power for several years. A new constitution in 1928 transferred the election of the president from the parliament to the people. In 1929 J. Tubelis succeeded Valdemaras as Premier, and in 1931 Smetona was for a third time elected President. Full restoration of parliamentary government still remained in abeyance.

The most southerly of the Baltic republics, Poland is the only member of the group able to play a prominent part in the great game of international politics. Poland *Poland* is about the size of Finland, but owing to a milder climate and richer farmlands supports nine times as great a population. There are about 32,000,000 inhabitants, a population exceeding that of Spain and Portugal combined and not far short of that of England. Poland is centrally situated and nearly every mile of her frontiers has been the subject of bitter controversy. Like many nations in eastern Europe, Poland is cursed with too brilliant a past. Although the native Polish element is hardly more than two-thirds of the population of the republic, there are ambitious imperialists who long for the restoration of the "historic frontiers" of the nation in the days before the country was partitioned by the robber-kings of Russia, Prussia and Austria. Such a consummation, even if it could be achieved, would be a doubtful blessing, as it would place the Polish element in a minority and burden the resurrected nation with the ancient feuds which formerly helped bring about its downfall. Poland under modern circumstances will do well if she can even hold her present frontiers against such powerful neighbors as Russia and Germany.

The Poland of medieval and early modern times included not only modern Poland but Lithuania and much of the Ukraine in addition. Next to Russia, Poland was the largest territorial unit in the old Europe, and as a military power waged war on equal terms with the Turkish Empire at its strongest and on more than equal terms with half-barbarous Russia. The central authority was deplorably weak, but even in this respect Poland compared favorably with Germany, which had only such unity as the personal prestige of the Holy Roman Emperor might give it, or Italy, which had no central government even in name. During the era of the Reformation, Poland decided to remain Roman Catholic, but there was comparatively little persecution of the Protestant minority. Not until the seventeenth century did Poland show fatal symptoms of political weakness. The feudal age lasted too long, and the powers of the nobility and gentry (the *szlachta*) tended to increase at the expense of both Crown and Commons. The executive power was vested in a King elected by the nobles for life, and usually chosen from some foreign dynasty which had no real influence or interest in the country. The jealous nobles, fearful of despotism, so limited his power that he was helpless for good as well as for evil. This would not have mattered in itself, since the experience of eighteenth-century England shows that an aristocracy of landlords can govern with tolerable efficiency under the fiction of a "rubber stamp" monarchy. But the Diet instead of being well organized

The Polish national tradition

like the English Parliament had the absurd rule that its most ordinary decisions had to be reached, like those of a jury, by unanimous agreement. A single deputy, exercising his "liberum veto" could block any law or even adjourn the Diet altogether. The system was hailed as "golden liberty" but in fact it amounted to anarchy, or rather the despotism of the strong, unscrupulous and violent among the nobility. The peasants were propertyless serfs without rights or citizenship. The commercial middle class was largely alien, chiefly German or Jewish. During the early eighteenth century Poland was hardly more than an ill-governed appanage of the Crown of Saxony.

Such a social, economic and political organization, suitable enough perhaps for eleventh-century Europe, was an anomaly in the eighteenth century. Poland's nearest *The national* neighbors, Russia, Prussia, Austria, Sweden, *revival* Turkey, were strong national monarchies and all save Sweden were absolute despotisms. In 1772, 1793 and 1795, three successive partitions divided Poland among the neighboring realms of Russia, Austria and Prussia. A belated attempt to reform the constitution only hastened the catastrophe, but at least it showed that there were patriots in Poland still. Under foreign oppression, the Poles recovered their national morale. All the activities of the Polish spirit, from Chopin's music to Sienkiewicz's historical novels, were pressed into the service of patriotic propaganda. Gymnastic and scientific societies, savings banks and farmers' co-operative associations, alike took on a nationalistic coloring. When the collapse of the three partitioning powers in 1918 made Polish independence possible, there was a Polish nation as well as merely a Polish State.[1]

The World War and the Russo-Polish War of 1920 which almost immediately followed it, if indeed it is not to be re-

[1] For the establishment of Polish independence and the fixing of her national frontiers, see especially Chapters XVIII, XIX, XXI.

garded as a mere continuation of it in a local area, left Poland

Troubles of a young republic independent and victorious but reduced to utter poverty. The tasks before the young republic seemed almost beyond human power. Three administrative systems, German, Austrian and Russian, had to be welded into one. A sound currency must be established in place of paper and promises. Large minorities of disaffected Ukrainians, Jews and Germans must be placated or coerced into submission. Frontiers had to be adjusted with Soviet Russia, Czechoslovakia, Germany and Lithuania. Thousands of farmsteads had to be rebuilt and hundreds of thousands of orphans and war refugees fed. Textile mills must be reopened and new railways built to bind the nation into an economic unit. Russian Bolshevism must be held at bay. A permanent constitution must be enacted. And, as means to accomplish all this, Poland had a patriotic but volatile democracy without much political experience and divided into a score of shifting parties and factions.

Once in a while something appropriate happens in history; something that a romantic dramatist or novelist would have

Pilsudski and Paderewski invented. Such was the leadership of the Polish republic in its earliest days by an army officer and a musician, jointly symbolizing the militant patriotism and the love of art which have always characterized the Poles. Joseph Pilsudski, a general of ability who had served Germany against Russia and then suffered imprisonment for refusing further service after the Russians had been driven from Poland, became acting president. Ignace Paderewski, the most famous pianist of his day, became premier. Although Pilsudski had been accounted pro-German in foreign affairs and mildly Socialist in domestic matters, while Paderewski was pro-Entente and conservative, in reality both men were simply Polish nationalists and little else. Their differences related only to means, not to aims. Paderewski represented Polish interests so ably in

Paris that he won most of what he asked and more than he could reasonably be expected to obtain. A diplomat of marked ability, an orator of singular force and charm, and a patriotic leader whose personal ascendancy had no rival except Pilsudski, Paderewski lacked a fourth asset of states-manship, administrative technique. His greatest services to Poland were rendered at Paris rather than at Warsaw. Soon he tired of office and parliamentary bickerings and left the premiership. Pilsudski also stepped into the background and concerned himself with the details of military adminis-tration; but his personal prestige, the memory of his victories over the Russians and his own impatient temper made him formidable to the politicians.

The Polish constitution, like all the new Baltic instruments of government, was purely democratic. None of the abuses of the old Polish Commonwealth before the par- *The Polish* titions reappeared in the new republic. All *constitution* classes were equal before the law, parliamentary decisions were by majority instead of unanimity, the whole framework of government was rather a copy of the contemporary French constitution than of any historic Polish model. Legislative authority was vested in a representative assembly chosen for five years (the *Sejm*) and a Senate. The suffrage was uni-versal, secret, direct and proportional. The *Sejm* had con-trol over finance and over ministerial policy. The Senate, only a fourth as large as the *Sejm*, was included as a conserva-tive second chamber to act as a check on hasty legislation, but it had less power than the lower house; Poland was the only one of the new Baltic republics to have a revising second chamber at all. The President was to be elected in the French fashion for seven years by joint vote of both houses. Poland, again like France, was not a federal but a unitary government, though Eastern Galicia, with a large Ukrainian element in the population, enjoyed a certain local autonomy.

This constitution is now largely of historic interest, for in

1926 the republic, like so many of the new European de-
Polish poli- mocracies, fell under a dictatorship. All the
tics Baltic states have shown, and to a rather extreme
degree, the continental European tendency towards a multiplication of small parties and factional groups. This rendered ministries shifting and unstable, apt to evade problems
and dodge responsibilities since they could not rely on a
solid, dependable majority to carry out any policy whatso-
ever. At the right sat the National party, a conservative
and somewhat imperialistic group, at the left the Socialists
and Communists, in the center a wide and varied range of
peasants' parties of different degrees of radicalism. The national minorities, Ukrainian, Jewish and German, had parties
of their own formed on "racial" lines. How high party feeling rose is indicated by the assassination of President Gabriel
Narutowicz, the first constitutional chief magistrate of Poland, immediately after taking office in December, 1922.
Pilsudski, the provisional President, had refused to be a
candidate on the ground that the office was not attractive to
him since it gave the occupant too little power. Narutowicz
was the candidate of the radicals, liberals and racial minorities; his election gave great offense to the conservative Nationalists, and a fanatic attached to that party seized an opportunity two days after his inauguration to shoot him.
Stanislas Wojciechowski was then elected, a former minister
of the interior in Paderewski's administration.

Marshal Pilsudski had been on good terms with both his
successors in the presidential chair, but he intensely disliked
Pilsudski's the futility of parliament and the policy of many
coup d'état, of the fluctuating ministries. When his personal
1926 enemy Vincent Witos, leader of the most conservative of the many peasant parties, became for the third
time premier, his brittle patience snapped. He accused the
government of corruption as well as of inefficiency and demanded that Witos be dismissed at once. The President

them entirely or substituting appointment altogether for election. His chief aim was to strengthen the executive power, and his latest project was a plan by which the President would be elected directly by the people but the choice lie between two candidates only, one nominated by the retiring President and one by an electoral college drawn mainly from the National Assembly. The President, so chosen, would have great executive power and the ministry would be responsible to him instead of to the *Sejm*. The elective *Sejm* would continue to exist, shorn of much of its former power, but the Senate would be partly appointed by the President and partly chosen by veterans of the army.

One of the greatest problems of Poland is the lack of national unity. Though the Polish element has a decisive majority, there are large Ukrainian, White Russian, German, Jewish and Lithuanian minorities. Poland and the Russian Ukraine (which once was Polish) taken together include nearly half the Jewish population of the world. The Polish Jew is distinct from his Gentile neighbor not only in creed, but usually also in speech, customs, traditions, opinions and occupation. He is a townsman, keen in business but often poor from lack of opportunity for betterment, orthodox, faithful to his Sabbath and the ritual of the Mosaic law, speaking many tongues but most at home in his dialect of German (Yiddish). Poland has not seen such massacres of the Jews as the Russian Ukraine, or legal restrictions so extensive as in Nazi Germany or pre-war Rumania, but there have been many isolated acts of violence and the economic struggle is often bitter, taking the form of a boycott of Jewish shops by nationalistic Poles. Minority rights treaties guaranteed on paper the equal civic status of Jews with Christians in the states freed by the Entente victory in the World War, but such guarantees are hard to enforce in practice. In 1925 the Polish government came to an agreement with the chief Jew-

The minor nationalities in Poland

ish party groups who agreed to cease anti-national agitation in return for better protection of their civil rights and economic interests. The Ukrainians of eastern Galicia have complained that the self-government granted them was inadequate, and the Polish authorities suppressed insurrections of the peasantry, sometimes with cruel severity. Germany has complained of the confiscation of German estates in the "corridor," discrimination against German residents in the Polish part of Upper Silesia, and disregard of the rights of the neutralized city of Danzig. Several times these complaints have been brought to the attention of the Court of International Justice and of the Council of the League of Nations. In 1934 Poland repudiated the treaty guaranteeing minority rights which she had been compelled to accept when the powers first recognized her independence.

Poland is an agricultural plain with relatively slight industrial or mineral resources, though the partition of Silesia brought to the nation the coal it required and some important metal mines. For an agricultural country, Poland is rather densely peopled *Economic life of Poland* and the standard of living is not high. The new immigration restrictions of the United States have closed the principal outlet for surplus population. But recovery from the World War and the Russian War has been surprisingly rapid. With the counsel of Professor E. W. Kemmerer of Princeton University the currency was stabilized and the budget balanced, the gold zloty replacing the depreciated Polish mark. The new frontiers are economically more rational than the sinuous boundaries of Russian, Austrian and Prussian Poland during the period of partition; the Vistula valley should prosper more under a united government than when it was arbitrarily divided among three alien rulers. On the whole, if peace prevails we may confidently risk the prophecy that Poland will rise to the economic and cultural level of the most advanced states of Europe, for no one who is acquainted

CHAPTER XXIII

NATIONS OF THE DANUBE

THE Danube, even more than the Rhine, is a river of many nations. Rising in Germany, it flows through Austria, touches Czechoslovakia, penetrates the heart of *"Danubia"* Hungary, cuts a corner of Yugoslavia, forms a frontier between Bulgaria and Rumania and empties into the Black Sea where old Rumania meets her new province of Bessarabia, taken from Russia. In a world constructed on economic principles rather than on political prejudices these states might well be united into a "Danubia," ampler even than the old Austro-Hungarian Empire; but as things are, such an empire would be a hotbed of nationalistic rivalry and probably end, as did the Dual Monarchy, in revolution and secession. Occasional treaties of commercial reciprocity, inadequate as they are, give some hope that the political divisions which are likely to persist may not necessarily preclude a considerable degree of economic union.

Austria holds a unique position among the Danubian states in being a national fragment rather than a complete nation. The Austrians are Germans with but few excep- *Austria's* tions; and if swayed by commercial interest *German orientation* towards Hungary and other Danubian states, they are moved even more strongly by national sentiment towards union with the German Reich. Yet neither "Danubia" nor "Pan-Germany" proved politically possible in the years immediately following the World War. France ardently opposed Austro-German union, the so-called *Anschluss* movement, on the ground that it would mean the end of Czechoslovakia, which would then be enclosed on three sides by German territory; and also because the enlarged Germany would have an even greater population than the Ger-

many of 1914, the gain of Austria more than compensating
for the loss of Alsace-Lorraine and Prussian Poland.   Italy
was less concerned, but preferred, on the whole, that a weak
buffer state like Austria should lie between her frontiers and
those of Germany.   The British cared little which way the
matter was decided, but earnestly desired that no question
be raised which would precipitate a continental crisis.   The
lesser Danubian states feared any expansion of Germany to
the south or east.   So every proposal for closer union between Germany and Austria met with a veto from foreign
powers.   In 1931 the two countries agreed on a reciprocity
treaty which would have removed tariff barriers entirely
within a few years and created an Austro-German customs
union (*Zollverein*).   Fearing that economic union might
foreshadow political union, France and other powers raised
strenuous objection.   The Court of International Justice by
an eight to seven vote proclaimed the proposed customs union
illegal on the ground that it ran counter to a pledge given by
Austria in 1922, when an international loan was floated for
Austria's benefit with the proviso that Austria would abstain
from any financial or economic engagement calculated to
compromise her independence.

During the first dozen years of her existence as an independent Republic, Austria's difficulties were rather economic
Austria as   than political.   She faced literal famine at the
a democracy end of the war, and bankruptcy was averted only
by the aid of foreign powers tendered through the agency of
the League of Nations.[1]   But Austria escaped at first the
violent swings of the political pendulum from Communism
to royalism which agitated the neighboring republic of
Hungary.   A purely democratic constitution of the parliamentary type was established, resembling the institutions of
Switzerland much more than those of pre-war Austria.   The
franchise was universal, equal, secret, direct and propor-

[1] See Chapter XIX.

tional. The Federal Assembly had two houses, a National Council and a senatorial Federal Council, the latter chosen by the legislatures of the several provinces, in which no province might have less than three or more than twelve representatives. The combined Federal Assembly elected a President for four years, who shared the executive power with a Chancellor and a ministry appointed by him but responsible to the National Assembly.[1] The greatest difference between the Austrian constitution and the generally similar new constitutions of Poland, Czechoslovakia and the Baltic states was that Austria was federal instead of centralized; each province (*Land*) having its own legislature with powers about as extensive as those of an American state. The chief reason for the adoption of a federal form of government in so small a nation was the mutual distrust of Vienna and rural Austria. The capital was strongly socialist, cosmopolitan, radical and religiously sceptical; rural Austria was conservative, piously Roman Catholic and nationally altogether German. Neither city nor countryside could be permitted to dominate; hence local home rule was the only solution.

Only two large political parties developed in postwar Austria, the Christian Socialists and the Social Democrats. The former, in spite of their name, were really conservative Clericals who represented the great bulk of "bourgeois" and peasant Austria; the latter were orthodox Marxian Socialists, strong *Austrian politics under the democracy* among the workingmen, especially in Vienna. As neither party seemed willing to press the question of union with Germany against the opposition of foreign powers, smaller groups such as the Pan-Germans, the Heimatschutz and the National Socialists (corresponding to Hitler's party in Germany) took up this issue for active agitation. In its first phase the Austrian government was socialistic in color, Karl

[1] The ministers, however, were not to be members of the Assembly themselves.

Renner of the Social Democratic party heading the provisional government. The elections of 1920, however, strengthened the Christian Socialists, who secured the election of Michael Hainisch as President in 1920 and again in 1924. He was succeeded by Wilhelm Miklas of the same party in 1928, re-elected in 1931.[1] The Christian Socialists usually also controlled the ministry. Chancellor Ignaz Seipel of that party guided Austria through the difficult days of post-war financial reconstruction, when the country was virtually in a state of "receivership" administered by foreign financial experts, and Chancellor Engelbert Dollfuss held office during the second economic collapse, coincident with the world depression, and transformed the republic from a democracy to a dictatorship.

While the Christian Socialists were directing federal affairs into conservative channels, the Social Democrats at *Vienna, a socialist metropolis* least had the city of Vienna as a laboratory test-tube in which they could conduct experiments. They municipalized nearly all the public utilities of the city and insisted that rents should be paid on the basis of the old depreciated currency (worth about one-fourteen thousandth of face value) so that landlord interests were practically "liquidated" for the benefit of tenants. As private enterprise would not build under such conditions, the city erected apartment houses for the workers on an enormous scale. The *Karl Marx Hof* was the largest apartment house in Europe. Conservatives outside the capital as well as within it viewed these tendencies with alarm. In 1929 Chancellor Johann Schober forced a series of constitutional compromises, increasing the powers of the president and substituting popular for parliamentary election for that office, transferring part of the revenues of the city of Vienna to the province of Lower Austria, and increasing national

---

[1] By a constitutional amendment of 1929 the election should have been directly by the people; it was agreed to save cost, however, by having election by the National Assembly as formerly.

control of the Viennese police. As the economic crisis deepened, however, the tension between metropolis and countryside increased.

The world wide economic depression affected Austria with
peculiar severity. In 1931 the chief bank, the *Kreditanstalt*,
failed; and in 1932 the little nation, already *Austria*
staggering under an enormous debt, had to seek *faces*
further foreign loans. The growing shadow of *revolution*
poverty, the disappointment over the foreign veto on a
customs union with Germany, and the rapid growth of the
National Socialist movement in Germany, all tended to revive the dormant agitation for the *Anschluss*. Adolf Hitler
himself was Austrian by birth, and union with Austria was a
central plank in his political platform for Germany.[1] The
National Socialists had practically absorbed the older Pan-
German party, and in addition to their own organization
had begun to "bore from within" the *Heimwehr*, a sort of
middle-class militia which had hostility towards socialism as
its chief principle. On the other hand the Viennese Social
Democrats were aroused to vigilance by the triumph of reaction in Germany, and they had an armed militia of their
own, the *Schutzbund*. Nations with private armies are rarely
far from civil war, and in 1932 it seemed that constitutional
government in Austria might be ended by a sudden seizure
of power by the Nazi "brown shirts," by the Viennese Socialists or by the conservative *Heimwehr*.

Chancellor Dollfuss, a smiling little man whose diminutive
stature and conservative policy gave him the nickname of
"Millimetternich," believed that liberal and *The Doll-*
democratic institutions were too weak to survive *fuss dic-*
this triple peril to the state and to his party, the *tatorship*
Christian Socialist. He did not wish to yield either to the
Nazis or to the Socialists; he opposed the *Anschluss* chiefly on
religious grounds, fearing lest the interests of the Roman

[1] For the Nazi movement, see Chapter XXVII.

Catholic Church might be endangered if Catholic Austria were merged in a mainly Protestant Germany, and he had a pronounced aversion to the radical program of the Social Democrats. With the *Heimwehr* he might make an alliance; the other two private armies were to be crushed. In 1933 he assumed virtually dictatorial powers. He outlawed the Nazis and the Communists and then proceeded against the Socialists. Fearing the loss of their liberties, the Viennese Socialists clung to their arms in defiance of government orders and civil war followed.

The struggle was brief and one-sided, but hotly contested so long as resistance was possible. In February, 1934, the *The siege of* Social Democrats declared a general strike, and *Vienna* the government responded by outlawing the party and seizing its offices in the capital. There was much shooting in the streets, and in some cases artillery fire was directed against the new model tenements which the municipal government had erected and which their tenants refused to leave when ordered to do so. Mayor Karl Seitz and other Socialist leaders were imprisoned. Thousands of workingmen filled the concentration camps. The government had carried out part of its task, — it had crushed the Socialists and had made alliance with the *Heimwehr*. But the price was heavy. The embittered workingmen of Vienna could no longer, as formerly, be used as allies against the Nazis; to them the difference between Dollfuss and Hitler was henceforth merely a choice between the devil and the deep sea. Liberals at home and abroad who had previously applauded "brave little Austria and her brave little Chancellor" for standing up against German bullying were almost equally alienated. The *Heimwehr*, reactionary and militaristic, was in a position to dictate to the government the terms of its support. Parliamentary liberalism was dead.

Dollfuss determined to see matters through to the end. The old Federal Assembly was summoned to vote its own extinction. Practically none save members of the Chancellor's own party, the Christian Socialist, attended; *Austria goes the Social Democrats had been outlawed, and Fascist* many of their leaders were still prisoners. Before this "rump parliament" a new constitution was presented which was largely imitated from Fascist Italy, though with touches of Austrian clericalism in its religious phraseology. The word "republic" was dropped, and Austria declared to be a "Christian German Federal State on a corporative basis." The laws were not declared to be based on popular sovereignty but on the will of God "from whom all laws emanate." Direct popular election wholly disappeared, but an exceedingly elaborate and cumbersome legislative system, resembling in many respects the French constitution under Napoleon, was established. There were to be four advisory Councils: a Council of State, appointed by the President for ten-year terms; a Federal Economic Council, chosen by corporate bodies representing the industrial units into which capital and labor were henceforth to be blended; a Federal Cultural Council, representing legally recognized religious and educational bodies; and a Federal Provincial Council, representing the governor (in the case of Vienna the mayor) and a financial representative of each province. United as a Federal Assembly, the four Councils met to nominate a President, who was then to be elected by the Mayors of Austria for a period of seven years. A Federal Chamber, consisting of twenty delegates each from the Council of State and the Federal Economic Council, ten from the Federal Cultural Council, five from the Provincial Council, would accept or reject without debate laws and decrees laid before it by the government. Behind this elaborate camouflage all real power was concentrated in the hands of President Wilhelm Miklas, Chancellor Dollfuss and his ministry, and Prince Ernst von Stahremberg, the leading spirit in the *Heimwehr.*

With the Socialists crushed, the chief remaining peril to the Dollfuss government was the possibility of a Nazi move-

The Nazi rebellion ment within Austria, aided from over the border by Germany. Against this peril foreign aid was essential. In February, 1934 France, Britain and Italy in a joint note reiterated their old stand "as to the necessity of maintaining Austria's independence and integrity in accordance with the relevant treaties." Chancellor Dollfuss entered into friendly negotiations with Italy and with Hungary, creating an informal entente which would be a diplomatic counterweight to Germany and yet not commit Austria to dependence on France. These dealings with Italy, however, seemed like double treason to the Austrian Nazis: was it not bad enough to reject union with Germany; must Austria seek support from her hereditary foe Italy as well? Filled with indignation they plotted a sudden *coup d'état*. The Chancellor and other members of the government were to be seized in the Chancellery at Vienna and held hostages while a pro-Nazi government would be proclaimed to the crowd and supported by uprisings in the provinces. In the atmosphere of gangster rule which had come over central Europe even so wild and melodramatic a plot was not impossible; in fact, it very nearly succeeded.

Disguised as members of the *Heimwehr*, a force of National Socialists entered the Chancellery, seized Dollfuss, Major

The murder of Dollfuss, July, 1934 Emil Fey and other dignitaries of the state, and broadcasted over the radio that Dollfuss had resigned and that Anton Rintelen, the Ambassador to Italy, supposed to be friendly to the Nazis, had become Chancellor. But the army and the genuine *Heimwehr* militia quickly surrounded the building. A safe retreat was offered to the conspirators if they would surrender their hostages. Unfortunately this was no longer possible, for an excited young fanatic had shot Dollfuss and his comrades had let the Chancellor bleed to death without permitting a surgeon or a priest to be summoned. After such a deed no mercy could be expected. Dr. Kurt Rieth, the German Ambassador, was removed from office for acting as an intermediary between the conspirators and the Austrian authorities; his intentions may have been merely to prevent bloodshed but his official position gave too much currency to rumors that Germany sympathized with the audacious attempt. The German government had many other embarrassments to meet: "unauthorized" outbursts in the press, quickly suppressed, untimely rejoicings among Nazi exiles just over the border in Bavaria, the fact that the rebels in Austria belonged to the same party as that which ruled in Germany and that Germany's dictator was himself an Austrian Nazi.

With less provocation than Austria had received from Germany in 1934, Austria had gone to war with Serbia in 1914. But Austria could not punish Germany *The Sarajevo of 1934* as she had Serbia, for in this instance the offender was a Great Power and the injured nation a small and weak state which would be fortunate if it could even protect itself against fresh outrages. So if war came in 1934, as it had twenty years earlier from like cause, it would not on this occasion begin by an Austrian declaration of hostilities. The danger lay in Italy and in Germany. Might not the German Nazis force Hitler, even if himself reluctant, into some unwise action while civil war raged in Austria? And if that should happen would not Mussolini send his troops, already massed on the frontier to wait events, into Austria to safeguard the independence of that convenient "buffer state"?

Fortunately, nearly everyone kept his head. Prince Ernst von Stahremberg restored law and order at the cost of several hundred lives, where Nazi uprisings were quelled in the provinces, but he did not at once *The cloud lifts — at* proceed to make himself an avowed dictator. *least for the moment* He stepped aside and permitted President Miklas to appoint as the martyred Dollfuss's successor the energetic civilian Minister of Education, Kurt Schuschnigg. As Chancellor Schuschnigg was said to be monarchist in sympathy, adherents of the exiled Archduke Otto, son of the last Emperor Karl, began to hope for an eventual Habsburg restoration. France, Italy and the Little Entente abstained from hasty action. Hitler, risking his popularity with the more revolutionary Nazis, repressed all attempts in Germany to express sympathy with the Austrian rebellion and offered to send the moderate and conservative Franz von Papen as German Ambassador to Vienna in place of the incautious Rieth. The peace of Europe, shaken as it had not been since the armistice, was saved, but Austria still remained a danger zone.

Austria reacted into a conservative dictatorship from the mere dread of communism; Hungary which actually passed *Socialism and communism in Hungary* through a period of communist rule reacted in the same way more than a decade earlier. The military collapse of Austria-Hungary overthrew the proud oligarchy of Magyar nobles and country gentlemen who had guided the fortunes of the nation ever since Hungary won home rule from Austria in 1867. The suppressed national minorities were now independent states, and some of them had Magyar minorities of their own.[1] Count Michael Karolyi, a nobleman of ancient blood but liberal and pacifist opinions, assumed the ungrateful task of reconstructing the war-shattered state. Like Kerensky in Russia he tried to steer a middle course between communism and capitalism, and like Kerensky he failed. In despair he abandoned the task and permitted without resistance the seizure of power by Bela Kun and his Communist associates. Soviet Russia had provided a model; the Hungarian Communists did little more than imitate it. They formed soviets on the Russian pattern, excluded the bourgeoisie from political life, seized the factories, proclaimed the nationalization

[1] For the effect of the peace settlement on Hungary, see above Chapter XVIII.

of the land, reorganized the army as a class-conscious Red Guard, suppressed the non-communist press, turned unoccupied houses and rooms over to workingmen, in a word tried overnight to realize the whole communistic program.

But where liberal socialism had failed, radical communism did not succeed. Dictator Bela Kun, who held the post of Commissar of Foreign Affairs, found it impossible *The collapse* to prevent the partition of Hungary on which the *of Red* Entente Allies had agreed or the armed invasion *Hungary* of Hungary by Rumania. Nor were his enemies entirely from without. The revolution, after all, was a Budapest rather than a general Hungarian movement; the devout, conservative, tradition-loving peasantry viewed it with horror and were not reconciled even by the prospect of dividing the landlords' estates among themselves. The nobility and the bourgeoisie rallied around the counter-revolutionary standard of Admiral Nicholas Horthy. In vain the government spread "red terror" and multiplied executions among suspected bourgeois or peasant counter-revolutionists. Before the advance of the Rumanian army of occupation Soviet Hungary collapsed and Bela Kun fled the country. From March to the beginning of August, 1919, Hungary had been under the red dictatorship, a brief experience but long enough to provoke a reaction that was to endure for many years. The moderate socialistic government of Julius Peidl that followed the fall of Bela Kun had scarcely been established before it was in turn swept away. A period of confusion followed. With the Rumanian army occupying the capital, the counter-revolutionists tried in vain to restore the monarchy with Archduke Joseph as Regent and Stephen Friedrich as Premier; the Entente powers vetoing any plan of Habsburg restoration.

The elections of 1920 returned a large monarchist majority. The two strongest parties were the Christian National, conservative and clerical, and the agrarian Small

Landowners' party.   Seeing that the mass of the Hungarians
The Hun- desired a restoration of the monarchy, King
garian reac- Charles (Karl IV) made two attempts in 1921
tion to reascend the throne from which the revolution
of 1918 had driven him.   It is significant that he had better
hopes of success in Hungary than in the native Austria of his
Habsburg forefathers; the monarchist reaction was far stronger
in Hungary than in any other of the succession states.   Nevertheless he failed.   The Little Entente imposed an absolute
veto, threatening war if Hungary restored any Habsburg to
the vacant throne.   Charles died in exile the following year.
But Hungary did not become a true republic merely because
foreign diplomats had forbidden the restoration of the monarchy.   Supreme power remained in the hands of Admiral
Horthy as Regent (*Reichsverweser*), the very title implying
that Hungary's dictator was but a place holder for an absent
king.   Closely associated with Regent Horthy was Count
Stephen Bethlen, who headed the ministry for ten years
(1921–31).   Many of the institutions of the old, pre-revolutionary Hungary were restored.   The franchise was slightly
restricted and the secret ballot abandoned.   A conservative
upper chamber was established, consisting of representatives
of the nobility, of county and municipal councils, of the
churches and universities, and of commercial and industrial
bodies.

The government of Horthy and Bethlen organized most
of the conservative parties into a National Union group hold-
Hungarian ing a large and permanent majority in parliament.
problems   Liberal and Socialist republicans, heavily outvoted, formed a small critical minority to the "left"; legiti-
mist royalists, who resented the shelving of the monarchical
question and demanded the immediate coronation of Archduke Otto, the successor to King Charles's claims, formed
a similar opposition to the "right."   Some of these latter
found the Horthy-Bethlen dictatorship not nearly dictatorial

enough and clamored for more stringent punishment of radicals and more rigorous restriction of the Jews, the only important national minority left within the confines of postwar Hungary. Such reactionary associations as the "Awakening Magyars" avenged the red terror of the days of Bela Kun with a "white terror" of violent and lawless deeds against suspected radicals. Under pressure from such ultra-nationalist groups all sorts of petty legal restrictions against the Jews, such as the limitation of their number in the universities, found favor. The chaotic finances of Hungary were reconstituted on a sound basis by loans negotiated through the League of Nations and an international supervision of Hungarian finance. Jeremiah Smith, an American expert, accepted the duty of administering the plan. The chief economic problem of Hungary is the negotiation of commercial treaties with neighboring states to overcome her present disadvantage as an inland country. In foreign affairs the Hungarians have recently shown a tendency towards close and friendly association with Italy, and in lesser degree with Austria and Germany, to withstand the pressure of the neighboring Slavs. They have not abandoned hope of reconquering their lost provinces and restoring their ancient throne, but Premier Bethlen and his successors, Julius Karolyi and Julius Gömbös, were forced to postpone those ultimate goals to the immediate problems of national reconstruction.

Czechoslovakia remained loyal to republican, democratic and liberal institutions long after they had been abandoned by most nations of eastern, southern and central Europe. This was due to several favoring factors. Instead of the humiliation of defeat, the *The Czecho-slovak democracy* nation felt the elation of triumph and newly achieved independence. Though lacking seaports and ringed with foreign and often unfriendly states, Czechoslovakia had a better balance of agriculture and industry than the other succession

THE REPUBLIC OF
CZECHOSLOVAKIA
Scale of Miles
0   50   100

states. The people, especially in Bohemia, were well educated and their national traditions were favorable to democratic self-rule. Finally, and not least in importance, the
young republic was fortunate in its chosen leaders. Thomas
G. Masaryk, thrice elected President of Czechoslovakia, and
Edward Benes, the skillful director of the foreign policy of
the republic, were drawn into politics from university life.
If there be a certain symbolic fitness in the fact that Poland
chose a romantic soldier and a romantic musician respectively
as her first President and her spokesman at the Paris Peace
Conference, it was perhaps equally significant that for those
two vital posts Czechoslovakia selected two scholars.

The Czechs of Bohemia and Moravia and their kinsfolk
the Slovaks numbered together about nine millions. The
important differences between these two nationalities were
merely such as arose from the historical accident that the

Czechs had long been associated with the German Austrians whereas the Slovaks had been subject to the Mag- *National* yar Hungarians. Both peoples were Slavic by *traditions* speech, broad-headed Alpines by racial type, Roman Catholic in religion, in all three respects resembling their neighbors the Poles. But for all that Poland and Czechoslovakia seem little alike in national characteristics. The Czechs have less romanticism; they are typically hard-headed and practical. "Bohemian ways" are the habits of the wandering gypsies in Bohemia, not those of the industrious Slavic peasants and townsmen of that prosperous province. Although most Czechs and Slovaks are Catholic, their national tradition is curiously allied to Protestantism, because the reconversion of Bohemia to the Catholic Church coincided with the loss of national independence in the Thirty Years' War; hence even the Catholic Czechs and Slovaks seem to have little of the intense devotion to the Church which characterizes the Poles. Medieval Bohemia (with the associated provinces of Moravia and Silesia) was a self-governing kingdom of mixed German and Czech population within the frontiers of the Holy Roman Empire. Under the leadership of John Huss and his successors Bohemia had defied both Church and Empire, but in 1526 the Austrian Habsburgs were accepted as rulers, and in 1620 the defeat of the Protestant party meant the loss of autonomy and three hundred years of subjection to the Austrian Germans. In 1848 Bohemia made a fierce effort to reconquer her independence, but without success.

A main interest of Czechoslovakia is education. Prague is one of the oldest of European universities and education is more nearly universal in Bohemia than in any *Czecho-Slo-* other Slavic country. Slovakia was education- *vak culture* ally more retarded because of the long feud between Slavic and Magyar languages in Hungary. The Czech literature is less famous than the Russian or Polish, Karel Capek the dramatist being one of the few Czech writers known to the

West,[1] but in music the Czechs and Slovaks yield to none. Dvorak and Smetana are known to every music lover. The Czecho-Slovaks delight in pageantry, vast open air choruses of singers and exhibitions of gymnasts (the *Sokols* or falcons, equivalent to the German *Turnverein*), and in many of the arts, from civic architecture to glassware, they have shown undoubted love of beauty, but most of their achievements are of a workaday sort such as business efficiency and political good sense.

But the Czechs and Slovaks are by no means the only peoples in Czechoslovakia. In making the republic little *Problems of* attention was paid to exact correspondence of *the national* political and ethnic frontiers,[2] in fact no bound-*minorities* aries geographically possible would have so corresponded. Within the mountain walls that fringe the new nation live over three million Germans, three-quarters of a million Magyars, nearly half a million Ruthenians, and numerous Poles, Jews and others, totaling in all more than a third of the whole population. Even the Slovaks, though so closely akin to the Czechs, often resent the "big brother" airs of their more successful kinsmen and complain that the Czechs obtain an undue share of political power and appointments. Fortunately Masaryk and Benes have endeavored to pursue a just and enlightened policy toward the minor nationalities and have tried to secure a faithful observance of the minority rights treaties which Czechoslovakia, in common with the other new states of central and southeastern Europe, was required to sign. In many cases minor officials have undoubtedly been guilty of irritating discriminations. As in Poland, the national minorities have formed political groups to protect their interests.

---

[1] His drama, *R.U.R.*, added the term "robot" to our language.

[2] For the Czecho-Slovak problem at the Paris Peace Conference, see above Chapter XVIII. I. Bowman estimates that only ten per cent of the international boundaries of Czechoslovakia correspond with the racial frontier (*The New World*, 1928, page 332).

The main features of the Czecho-Slovak constitution resembled those of Poland and, like the Polish, were largely
imitated from French institutions. The Na- *The Czecho-*
tional Assembly, consisting of a Chamber of *Slovak con-*
Deputies and a Senate, was the supreme reposi- *stitution*
tory of legislative power. Both bodies were elected by universal, secret, direct and proportional suffrage, but the age
limit, both for voters and members, was higher for the
Senate; the Deputies held office for six years and the Senators
for eight. The Senate was the less powerful body and did
not, like the Chamber of Deputies, control the rise and fall
of ministries. The President was elected by the two houses,
voting jointly. His veto might be overridden by an absolute
majority of both houses or a three-fifths vote in the Chamber
of Deputies. The Deputies, by a sufficient majority, might
repass a measure against the opposition of the Senate, and
in some cases the government might refer a bill to popular
referendum. The executive power was divided between the
President and his ministers who, following parliamentary
tradition, crystallized in this instance into definite constitutional law, were responsible to the lower house.

The new constitution worked more smoothly than the
Polish, the Austrian or the German in spite of the fact that
the Czecho-Slovak republic was cursed with a *Czecho-Slo-*
bewildering multiplicity of parties. Some of *vak politics*
these parties represent national minorities, some class interests, some religious concern, some theoretical shades of
radicalism or conservatism. Yet the government of the
day has usually been able to find a working majority amid
the maze of "National Socialists," "Peoples' Catholics,"
"German Agrarians," "Tradesmen's Party" and a dozen
other shifting groups. Both the Socialist and Communist
parties were large, but they did not co-operate with each
other. President Masaryk was elected by comfortable majorities in 1920, 1927 and 1934 in continuation of his term as
provisional president from 1918 to 1920.

The chief issues of internal politics, aside from the permanent question of the national minorities, have been the break-
Internal ing up of landlords' estates into small peasant
problems farms and the adjustment of relations between
church and state. From 1920 onward the government pursued a policy of purchasing at a rate fixed by law the excess acreage of the wealthy German, Magyar or (more rarely) Slavic nobles and gentry. The land thus expropriated by the state was sold at very easy rates to working farmers; adding in half a dozen years more than half a million to the number of peasant proprietors. The Roman Catholic Church was recognized by law and, in 1928, diplomatic relations with the Vatican established. There has, however, been a schism; nearly a million Catholics formed a separate Czecho-Slovak National Church, using the Czech language and permitting priests to marry. There are also not a few Protestants and many, especially among the urban workingmen, who profess no particular creed.

Of all the belligerent nations in the World War none made more satisfactory territorial gains than Rumania. The col-
Greater lapse of Russia enabled her to seize the province
Rumania of Bessarabia; the collapse of Austria-Hungary
enabled her to take over all the Rumanian speaking districts of the Dual Monarchy. Addition of new territory after the war more than doubled the area and population of the country and at the same time filled out its boundaries from an irregular crescent to an approximate circle, so that the new frontier line to be defended was no longer than the old.[1] With some 18,000,000 inhabitants, Rumania since the war has been the most populous country of southeastern Europe. The wide expanses of fertile soil along the lower Danube, the great forests of the hills, the mineral wealth, especially in oil, afford a sufficiently broad economic base to sustain this population.

[1] Rumania of 1914 can be pictured as the moon in its first quarter; Rumania after the war as the moon at full.

The expansion of Rumania, however, has increased her national problems. The most serious is that of Transylvania, once the eastern frontier of Hungary and now the *Nationality* heart of greater Rumania. Rather more than *problems* half of the Transylvanians are Rumanian by speech and sentiment but there are large and important minorities, especially the Szeklers, a branch of the Magyar or Hungarian people, and a stray colony of German Saxons. Both Germans and Magyars considered themselves superior in education, political capacity and economic efficiency to the Rumanians, and they do not take kindly to the reversal of their fortunes. Religion, too, was a factor, for the Rumanians are of the Orthodox faith, while the Szeklers and Saxons are either Roman Catholics or Protestants. In the province of Bukovina, formerly Austrian, the Rumanian element is mixed with Ruthenians (Ukrainians) and Germans. The Banat of Temesvar, divided between Rumania and Yugoslavia, contains many Magyars and Germans. In Bessarabia, though the Rumanians are perhaps the dominant element, there are almost as many Ukrainians, not to mention many Jews and scattered minorities of Russians, Bulgarians, Germans and Turks! One of the older Rumanian districts, the Dobrudja, lying between the Danube and the Black Sea, has a hopelessly mixed population of Bulgarians, Tatars and other elements. Rumania obtained most of it in 1878 as compensation for the loss of Bessarabia to Russia and gained the rest from Bulgaria after the second Balkan War in 1913; by the Treaty of Bucharest (1918) the Central Powers took the whole district with the probable intention of giving it to Bulgaria, but the subsequent victory of the Entente Allies restored it all to Rumania. Rumania lies in the belt of east European Jewish population which covers Poland, the Ukraine and many parts of the old Austria-Hungary as well. There are some 800,000 Jews in the country and their position has been one of extreme difficulty. Before the World

War the Rumanian Jew was, as a rule, denied citizenship
and forced to be a "man without a country"; since then his
position has been regularized in law, but there is much popular prejudice and, as in Poland, Hungary and Germany, a
tendency to combat the economic efficiency of the Jewish
trader by use of the boycott. Though there are probably
less than four million non-Rumanians in the whole country,
a smaller proportion than the national minorities in Czechoslovakia, the dominant majority has been less considerate of
minority rights and the problems of nationality even more
acute.

A personal struggle over the succession to the throne has
given an operatic picturesqueness to Rumanian politics
The dynas- which otherwise might be lacking, for the war
tic question was not followed by any such revolutionary overturn as took place in most parts of eastern and central
Europe. In the general "cascade of thrones" which the
eminent Rumanian statesman Take Ionescu correctly prophesied in 1914 would result from the war,[1] King Ferdinand
and his government were spared, probably because his country emerged on the victorious side. But Ferdinand died in
1927 and his son Carol had already been excluded from the
succession for his desertion of his wife, Princess Helen of
Greece, in favor of his mistress Madame Lupescu. So his
claims were passed over, and Ferdinand's grandson, the five-
year old Crown Prince Michael, was recognized as King.
Actual power was in the hands of Queen Marie, Ferdinand's
widow, and the ministry, both very hostile to the exiled
monarch. Rumania seemed stable enough, in spite of this
alteration of the succession. The forms of parliamentary
government had been retained, and in 1923 a constitutional
reform established universal suffrage in place of the old restricted franchise. But political life continued to be dominated by the Liberal party of Jon Bratianu under his sons

[1] See C. D. Hazen, *Europe since 1815* (1923), preface.

Jon and Vintila, the so-called "Bratianu dynasty." The old Conservative party, crushed by the accusation of pro-Germanism during the war, had virtually retired from the scene. The Liberal party itself, in spite of favoring the extension of the suffrage and the expropriation of large landowners, had become the real conservative group, nationalistic, centralizing and opposed to the claims of national minorities; "making" elections in traditional fashion by government arrangements at the polls.

A new, more radical liberalism arose under the name of the National Peasant party, a federation of several groups under the able leadership of Dr. Julius Maniu, *The return* demanding elections free from governmental *of King* interference, local home rule for the various *Carol* provinces, and a friendlier attitude toward foreign investors. In 1928 the new party was victorious at the polls. The defeat of the National Liberals removed the chief obstacle to Carol's return, for his personal enemies were now out of office. Seizing his chance, he returned from France by airplane in 1930 amid the cheers of the army and the somewhat fickle populace. King Michael returned to his toys and Regent Queen Marie to writing memoirs while Parliament recognized the returned prodigal as King Carol II. The National Peasant and National Liberal parties alternated tenure of office under the new rule. There were also many small parties, some representing the Hungarian, German and other national fractions, others various degrees of radicalism or reaction. In 1933 the Liberal Premier Ion Duca was assassinated by an ultranationalist Fascist group, the "Iron Guards," who correspond in a general way to the German Nazis and the Hungarian "Awakening Magyars" and profess bitter hostility to the Jews and all who tolerate them.

Rumania is a peasant country, four-fifths of whose people live by agriculture. Even before the war much had been done to break up the great estates, and since then the process has been much accelerated. Constant complaint has been *The land* made that in the newer provinces, such as Tran-*question.* sylvania, Magyars and other non-Rumanian land-lords have lost their property without adequate compensation. Hungary alleged that this violated treaty rights of former Hungarian residents of Transylvania who had kept their estates when they "opted" Hungarian instead of Rumanian nationality. It required nearly a decade of negotiation to adjust this difficulty which caused constant friction between Hungary and Rumania, menacing to the peace of Europe. But at all events the evil of landlordism was almost eliminated and nearly all the land passed into the hands of peasant cultivators. Perhaps for this reason, socialist and communist movements have made little headway in Rumania.

Prior to the World War the southern Slavs (Yugoslavs) were intricately divided, by natural barriers, political bound-*Yugoslavia* aries, religious confessions, differences of dialect *and her* and custom, in such a way as to obscure their es-*peoples* sential unity of race and language[1]. One branch of the southern Slavs, indeed, developed a separate national consciousness and has never participated in the movement for Yugoslavic unity: the Bulgarians. The Serbs, Croats and Slovenes, inspired by the enthusiasm of war, came to an agreement for national unification by the Pact of Corfu (1917), which promised a constitutional, democratic and parliamentary monarchy, with equal rights for the three dialects, the two alphabets (Latin and Cyrillic) and the three predominant creeds (Orthodox, Roman Catholic and Mohammedan) of the nation. The Serbian dynasty (Karageorgevitch) was to become the dynasty of the nation, just as the Sardinian dynasty (House of Savoy) had become the ruling line of united Italy. Except for filling the throne, the Serbs

---

[1] R. J. Kerner has pointed out that before the war the Yugoslavs were "divided into thirteen separate administrative units depending upon fifteen legislative bodies."

were to enjoy no pre-eminence over the Croats or Slovenes; Serbia was not to be a "Prussia." Such concessions were necessary, as the Croats and Slovenes regarded themselves superior in culture to the rather primitive Serbian peasant democracy and would not accept even "liberation" and "racial unity" if it meant subordination within the new kingdom. One group of Croatian particularists under the leadership of Stephen Raditch took the name of the Croat Peasant Party and demanded an independent Croatian republic; later the group changed its tactics and became a parliamentary opposition party, limiting its demands to local home rule.

Over four-fifths of the fourteen million people of Yugoslavia belong to one of these three closely kindred groups, and the chief political task of Yugoslavia has been the attempt, often far from successful, of securing their harmonious action. But there are other national minorities which, although small, are also very troublesome — Bulgars in Macedonia; Hungarians, Rumanians and Germans in the Danube valley; Albanians in the south; a few Italians on the Dalmatian coast. Perhaps to these may be added the Mohammedan Serbs of Bosnia and Herzegovina and the minority of Montenegrins who resented the loss of national independence and joined the deposed and exiled King Nicholas in his protest. By the loss of Fiume in 1924 [1] Yugoslavia was deprived of a good port but at the same time was freed of the greatest point of friction with Italy, and the failure to win the plebiscite at Klagenfurt reduced the size of the German element.

After considerable delay a constituent assembly at last broadened out the old Serbian constitution to fit the new Yugoslavia. King Alexander, who succeeded his *The new* father Peter in 1921, was the ruler and Belgrade *constitution* continued to be the capital. His powers were limited by the constitution and his ministers were responsible to the *Skupshtina* or Parliament, a single chamber chosen by uni-

[1] A free and independent city from 1920 to 1924.

versal manhood suffrage each four years on a basis of proportional representation. The Croats and Slovenes complained, however, that the new government was too greatly
centralized and that too little autonomy was granted the
provinces. Out of this quarrel arose a storm which was to
wreck the constitution. Premier Nicola Pashitch, leader of
the dominant Radical party, viewed the affairs of the kingdom too much from an exclusively Serbian point of view;
Raditch cared little for Yugoslavia except as it promoted the
local interests of the Croatians. The two leaders cordially
hated each other. Pashitch died in 1926 and Raditch was
assassinated in the parliamentary chamber in 1928, but the
quarrel continued.

Fearing civil war, King Alexander proclaimed a virtual
dictatorship in 1929. This did not mean an establishment
A "royal dictator-ship" of absolute monarchy, for the king promised to
restore popular government as soon as he had
imposed peace and unity on the kingdom; ~~he was acting Cromwell rather than Charles I~~! He urged his subjects to forget all local or particularist loyalties and trans-
formed the official name of his realm from the Kingdom of
the Serbs, Croats and Slovenes to the simpler form of Kingdom of Yugoslavia. Parliament was dismissed, the constitution suspended, the press curbed, the old units of local
government wiped out and replaced by new. In 1931 he
decreed a new constitution. The old *Skupshtina* continued
to exist as a Chamber of Deputies [1] but over it was placed a
Senate, half elected for six years and half appointed by the
King. The nine "banats" into which the country was divided were given local diets. Equal rights were accorded to
the Serb, Croat and Slovene tongues in official use. In a
measure constitutional democracy was restored, but some
features of the dictatorship still lingered under the new régime. The old political parties were dissolved by law and

[1] The electoral franchise was broadened to include women.

no new parties might be established if based on regional or class distinctions. A party obtaining a plurality of the votes would be given two-thirds of the deputies, a device borrowed from Italy. Under the new system a single ticket, representing a coalition of several parties under the name of the Yugoslav National party, swept the field and filled all the seats in both chambers.

On the surface all was loyalty; beneath it lurked much discontent and even conspiracy. Macedonian Bulgars and Croatian separatists were particularly bitter. *The murder of King Alexander* When in 1934 King Alexander paid a visit of state to France, assassins were on his trail and one fanatic shot him as he rode through the cheering streets of Marseilles, killing also Foreign Minister Barthou of France. The tragedy was not merely a personal one, but a danger to the peace of Europe as it came only a few weeks after wholesale political murders in Germany and Austria and only a few days after Premier Mussolini had threatened Yugoslavia with his wrath because of the violently anti-Italian tone of the Yugoslav press. Had the incident taken place on Italian, Austrian or Hungarian soil there is no telling what outburst of Yugoslav indignation might have followed. Fortunately no foreign government could be directly blamed (though French police protection had certainly been inadequate and Italy and Hungary had given asylum to some Croatian agitators) and after the pacifying intervention of the League of Nations the crisis passed without war. The danger of revolution was more pressing, and to avert it the government hurried from his English school the youthful crown prince and placed him on the throne as King Peter II of Yugoslavia; the real power being in the hands of a Regency headed by Prince Paul.

In spite of war, boundary troubles, political strife, dictatorship and regicide, the economic progress of the nation has not halted. The scars of the war have for the most part been

healed, though perhaps Yugoslavia will never be wealthy,
Economic   as much of the country is rugged highland
problems   and the excellent ports are separated from the
plains of the interior by barrier ridges of arid hill country.
Agriculture is the occupation of the majority of the people;
Serbia was a country of small farms but many great estates
existed in the former Austro-Hungarian provinces, which
are now being divided among the peasants. Though illiteracy is still common, schools are multiplying and, with
some foreign aid, excellent technical and medical training
can now be provided. On the whole the Serbs have gained
by exchanging their Balkan isolation for participation in the
main stream of central European life. Whether their new
fellow countrymen, the Croats and Slovenes, have gained or
lost is perhaps a more open question, the answer to which will
depend on the degree of liberalism and tolerance which the
dominant Serbs are able to weave into the fabric of their
new commonwealth.

CHAPTER XXIV

THE NEW NEAR EAST

BULGARIA, like Yugoslavia, is a country which touches at once the Danube valley and the Balkan highland, but, whereas the vast northwestward extension of the new Yugoslavia has shifted her "center of gravity" towards central Europe, Bulgaria, confined within narrower frontiers than before the war, remains primarily *Bulgaria after the war* interested in the affairs of southeastern Europe. Bulgaria faced the losses and sacrifices imposed by the second Balkan War and the World War with commendable courage, not perhaps wholly unaware that the maladroit diplomacy of her own rulers was in part to blame for her being twice on the losing side. Bulgaria under the Treaty of Neuilly (1919) was reduced to an area of 40,000 square miles, about that of Kentucky. Her only ocean frontage faces the Black Sea. Her population of about six million is less than that of any other nation of southeastern Europe with the exception of Albania. With none of her immediate neighbors was Bulgaria very friendly, for Turkey holds Adrianople, Greece western Thrace, Rumania the Dobrudja, and Yugoslavia Macedonia; to all of which Bulgaria would like to make claim. Germany and Hungary perhaps sympathized with Bulgaria but could do nothing to aid her, Italy to some extent viewed her as a useful check on Yugoslavia, but no real alliances or definite ententes could be said to exist. In 1925 a frontier "incident" nearly led to war between Bulgaria and Greece; in fact hostilities were averted only by peremptory action of the League of Nations.[1]

In her isolation and defeat Bulgaria turned against her misguiders. King Ferdinand had to abdicate and let the throne pass to his son Boris III. In 1919 Alexander Stambulisky, leader of the radical peasants, became premier.

[1] See above, Chapter XIX.

He had opposed Bulgaria's entrance into the war on the side
The peasant of the Central Powers and on elevation to power
dictatorship he caused the arrest and punishment, by imprisonment and fine, of the ministers who had been responsible. The
forms of the constitution were little changed but Stambulisky ruled as a virtual dictator. He regarded himself as responsible neither to king nor to parliament, but to the class
which he represented. Though there were few great estates
or large cities in the country many of the poorer peasants
vaguely felt that they had been cheated by urban politicians,
middlemen and officials. Stambulisky advocated a foreign
policy of peace, conciliation with other Balkan states, fulfillment of the distasteful clauses of the peace treaty. He enacted legislation limiting profits and confiscating unused
land. His most interesting experiment was the compulsory
labor law, which he designed to replace the compulsory military service which had been abolished by the peace treaty.
Men, women and children were ordered to set aside certain
days for unpaid public labor. The Stambulisky dictatorship
was commonly called "socialistic" or even "communist" but
it had little in common with Russian Bolshevism. Essentially it was peasant or agrarian rule, taking private property
in land for granted; in the phrase of the day it was "green socialism" in contrast to the "red" variety of the Marxians.

Stambulisky's foreign policy seemed humiliating to military men and fanatical nationalists, as it appeared to mean
The bour- permanent acquiescence in Bulgaria's inferior
geois dic- position in European affairs. His radical eco-
tatorship nomic legislation created a panic among the
traders. Professional men resented his censorship of the
press and closing of universities. Opposition political parties
objected to the monopoly of office holding by the Agrarians.
All these discontents promoted a counterrevolutionary conspiracy, and on June 9, 1923, a successful *coup d'état* overthrew
the government and placed in power a coalition of the con-

servative parties under Professor Alexander Tsankov. Stambulisky was killed a few days later and his partisans were
jailed. The radical groups, Socialist, Communist and Agrarian, driven from office, struck back by deeds of violence, rising to a horrible culmination in the explosion of a communist
bomb in the cathedral of Sofia in April, 1925. More than a
hundred worshipers were blown to pieces and the entire
cabinet narrowly escaped. The government, though carefully preserving parliamentary forms, retaliated by stringent
measures of police repression, throwing thousands of radicals
into prison and driving other thousands into exile.

The conservative coalition, called "Democratic Entente,"
remained in office under Premiers Alexander Tsankov and
Andrei Liapchev until 1931, when a more radical *The mili-*
parliamentary group called the National Bloc *tary dic-*
came into office under Alexander Malinov and *tatorship*
Nicholas Mushanov, who succeeded each other in the premiership. But the rapids had not been passed. In 1934 a group
of discontented army officers seized the government and
established a government more violently at variance with
the constitution than either Stambulisky's peasant dictatorship or the rule of the civilian conservatives which succeeded
it. A pretext for the outbreak was the dread of the Communists, a dread which had led the previous year to their expulsion from Parliament, but a deeper reason was the resentment of the military men against Bulgaria's weakness in
international politics.

Particularly acute was the national feeling with regard to
the portion of Macedonia seized by Serbia in the second
Balkan war and retained (with some additions) *Macedonia*
after the World War. Though Macedonia is an
everyman's land of numerous and intricately mixed nationalities, the Bulgarian element seems on the whole to pre-
dominate; Bulgaria has therefore watched with sympathy
the activities of "Macedonian nationalists" to resist the

Yugoslav government and with indignation the measures of repression which the Yugoslavs have taken. Bitterness has been increased by the constant influx of homeless refugees from Serbian Macedonia, and Greek Macedonia as well, across the Bulgarian frontier. The irritating question has prevented friendly relations from growing up between Bulgaria and Yugoslavia and it has added to the confusion of Bulgarian politics by creating a vociferous group of refugee politicians who are always berating the government for not taking a stronger stand against Yugoslavia, even to the point of war.

When Greece took Bulgaria's Ægean coastline after the World War it was promised that Bulgaria should have free *Western Thrace* economic access to the port of Dedeagach. Bulgaria, however, insisted that the intervening strip of territory must be made neutral and that Bulgaria have complete control of the port; Greece refused to abandon any of her territorial or political sovereignty over western Thrace and would make concessions only in the economic sphere. At Saloniki the Greeks conceded a small free zone under the jurisdiction of Yugoslav customs officers and offered a similar free zone to Bulgaria; both to remain, however, under Greek sovereignty in all matters save port administration. In 1923 Greece and Yugoslavia signed a convention, though the adjustment of details was a wearisome and vexatious business which required until 1929 to complete. The Bulgarian claims still remained only partly satisfied.

Greece, had she played her military cards as well as Venizelos played diplomacy, should have emerged from the *Postwar Greece* World War a winner. Premier Venizelos had come back from Paris with promises for an "Ægean Empire" which would include western Thrace, eastern Thrace except the immediate environs of Constantinople, and a wide sphere of influence around Smyrna in Asia Minor. But to consolidate those gains Greece had to hold her own against the Turks and retain the good will of the Entente Allies. In both respects she failed and gained nothing from the war except Bulgaria's Ægean frontage.[1] Venizelos was the only Greek leader in whom the Entente Allies had any confidence, and when he fell from power in 1920 Greece was left to struggle on against Turkey alone. Italy had already been offended at the landing of Greek troops in Smyrna, and France was furious when, on the death of King Alexander in 1920,[2] the deposed and exiled King Constantine was recalled to the throne. Constantine's victory meant defeat for Venizelos and his partisans and the triumph of those who had been hostile to the Entente Allies during the World War. The continuation of that war in Asia Minor was an undesired legacy of which the new régime wished to be rid. But the Turks would consent to no peace which involved the loss of territory to Greece. Willy-nilly the Constantinists continued the war which the Venizelists had begun, but without the support from friendly foreign powers on which their predecessors relied. They met utter disaster. Smyrna was burned, the victorious Turkish armies approached the Straits and would have pushed the war into Europe with incalculable consequences if the British had not at last bade them halt.

In 1922 the fickle and angry populace, aware of inefficiency and suspicious of treason in high places, turned against King Constantine and drove him for a second time into exile. His ministers and generals did not escape so easily; some of them were shot as traitors. King George II, son of the deposed monarch, followed in the path of exile the following year. Venizelos and his party rode triumphantly back into power, but the question still remained, should Greece make one more attempt at monarchy or become a republic? Pending a decision, Admiral Paul Konduriotis was made Regent. In 1924 the dynasty was

Constantine the twice-deposed

---

[1] For Greek claims at the Peace Conference and their fate, see Chapter XVIII.

[2] From the bite of a pet monkey which resulted in blood poisoning. But for that peevish pet Greece might now be ruler of Smyrna and Adrianople!

declared at an end and a popular plebiscite approved the establishment of a republic. Venizelos personally went into temporary retirement, but his name was still the principal line of division in Greek politics.

The exile of a king is no guarantee against the appearance of a dictator. Hardly had the new republic been established *The Pan-* when it was overturned by an ambitious army *galos dic-* officer, General Theodorus Pangalos, who be-*tatorship* *and its suc-* lieved himself to be an Hellenic Mussolini de-*cessors* voted to the task of building a strong and militant nation on the ruins of a feeble parliamentarianism. His career was, however, even briefer than that of most dictators. He seized power in 1925 and was formally elected president in 1926, but forced from office the same year. Admiral Konduriotis again set up the republic and was its provisional president until elections could be held, when he was chosen the first constitutional president. He resigned in 1929 and was succeeded by Alexander Zaimis. In the meantime Venizelos had returned to politics, strengthened and placed in power his Liberal party, organized a parliamentary upper chamber, reformed the national finances, negotiated treaties of friendship with neighboring nations and tried in every way to stabilize the republic. The economic depression, however, revived political discontent, the elections of 1932 and 1933 went against Venizelos, and in the latter year Panagiotis Tsaldaris, leader of the royalist Popular party, became premier. Tsaldaris, however, accepted the republic and King George remained an exile.

One consequence of the Turkish victory was to flood the land with Christian refugees, mainly Greeks from Asia Minor and eastern Thrace, but among them many Armenians and *Swapping* other non-Moslems. A counterstream of Turks *national* returned from Macedonia and western Thrace *minorities* to their Ottoman fatherland. In part this shift-ing of populations was deliberate, as Greece and Turkey had agreed at Lausanne in 1923 on "a compulsory exchange of Turkish nationals of the Greek Orthodox religion established in Turkish territory, and of Greek nationals of the Moslem religion established in Greek territory," subject to certain designated exceptions.[1] In all about 1,400,000 Greek refugees entered the country and some 350,000 Turks and Bulgars emigrated from it.[2] This enormous transfer of human beings to fit the arbitrary lines on the map has something about it that suggests the habit of Procrustes in chopping down the legs of his guests to fit his beds, and has indeed been attended with like suffering! Many of the refugees arrived destitute and had to be cared for by foreign charity, such as the Near East Relief, or at the expense of the impoverished Greek government with aid from the League of Nations.

But there have been public advantages as well as private tragedy in this "blood transfusion." Greece is now one of the most homogeneous nations in Europe, with less than one-twentieth of her population of alien nationality. Greek traders and mariners exiled from Turkey are already repaying Greece for her hospitality by their energy and skill. The decreased friction in regions of formerly mixed population has diminished international hostility, particularly along the Bulgarian and Turkish frontiers. In 1930 Venizelos was actually able to negotiate a treaty of friendship with Turkey, a landmark in the relations of the two most persistently hostile nations in Europe.

During the period of Venizelos's return to influence Greece improved her foreign relations in many other directions besides the peace pact with Turkey. *Greek foreign relations* Though Greece had been almost at war with Italy in 1923 when Mussolini's government seized Corfu to enforce the payment of an indemnity, and in 1925 the Greeks had actually sent troops across the Bulgarian

---

[1] Chiefly in long-established foreign colonies in Constantinople and western Thrace.

[2] See estimate by Hamilton Fish Armstrong, *Foreign Affairs*, October, 1929, p. 121.

frontier,[1] Venizelos succeeded in restoring "correct," if not absolutely friendly, relations with both Italy and Bulgaria. To achieve this end he had to declare that "there was no Dodecanese question"; in other words that Greece would not officially contest the Italian possession of the Greek-speaking islands which Italy had seized from Turkey at the time of the Tripolitan War and which Greece had long hoped would be voluntarily transferred to her by the Italians. More adequate port facilities were accorded Yugoslavia at Saloniki. Even with turbulent Albania many disputes were liquidated. The treaty of friendship with Turkey in 1930 was supplemented by a ten-year pact of non-aggression in 1933.

Albania, a country of about 10,000 square miles and a population of a million, was the smallest and youngest of

Albania

the Balkan nations, obtaining her independence in 1913 on the eve of the World War and keeping an uneasy neutrality throughout its course. Wilhelm of Wied, the King or "Mpret" of Albania, placed there by the powers before the war, relinquished the throne shortly after it began. In his absence the country staggered on from one provisional government to another. The two most prominent leaders were Bishop Fan S. Noli, a former Harvard student, and Ahmed Zogu, a Mohammedan prince. The rivalries of Catholic, Orthodox and Moslem of the tribes and clans in north and south,[2] complicated the incessant frontier disputes with Greece and Yugoslavia. In 1925 Zogu was formally elected president by a two-chambered parliament after having overthrown the regency of Bishop Noli the previous December. Italian influence predominated in the little state, and in 1926 both countries agreed on the Treaty of Tirana, which gave Italy the right to intervene to maintain Albanian independence or restore order within her boundaries should the Albanian government so request. In 1927

---

[1] For these disputes, see above Chapter XIX.

[2] The Ghegs of the north and the Tosks of the south.

this was supplemented by a twenty-year military alliance President Zogu in 1928 felt strong enough to take the throne as King Zog I and transform his virtual dictatorship into formal royalty. In fifteen years since the World War this was the sole instance in Europe of the reversion of a republic to a monarchy.[1]

The prolonged decline of the Ottoman Empire from the sixteenth to the twentieth century was frequently interrupted by more or less successful national revivals. *The rejuvenation of Turkey* Such a revival had taken place in 1908 when the enthusiastic young students and officers of the Committee of Union and Progress ("Young Turks") had taken over the destinies of the Empire and attempted to transform a backward Oriental despotism organized on a basis of religious creed into an efficient modern constitutional state organized on a basis of national language and sentiment. The experiment was only a partial success. It increased the national wealth, improved administrative efficiency and greatly strengthened the army, but it failed in the field of international relations. At the very start the new régime lost the nominal overlordship of Bulgaria and Bosnia-Herzegovina which the decadent despotism of Abdul Hamid II had been permitted to retain. A more real loss was that of Tripoli to the Italians and of Albania, Macedonia, Crete and western Thrace to the Christian Balkan States in the three years preceding the World War. In that war the Young Turks precipitately plunged to continue their old feud with Russia, and as a result shared in the defeat of the Central Powers. Their claim to be considered progressive reformers had also been stained by the massacre of nearly a million Armenians and many thousands of other national minorities. The program of modernization was still the accepted policy of the nation, but a fresh start had to be made and new leaders discovered.

[1] Hungary voted to restore monarchy, but found it impossible for diplomatic reasons to carry the restoration into effect. In all other cases where a parliamentary republic broke down it was replaced by a non-hereditary dictatorship.

Chief among the new Nationalist leaders was Mustapha
Kemal. Like many of the "Young Turks" he came from
Mustapha Macedonia in the days when it was still under
Kemal Turkish rule, having been born at what is now the
Greek port of Saloniki. He took part in the revolutionary
movement which first limited and later overthrew the power
of Sultan Abdul Hamid; but he was essentially a military man
rather than a civilian politician, and served in the Tripolitan,
Balkan and World Wars with high distinction. He took
little share in any save professional military questions until
after the surrender in 1918. Dismayed at the peace terms
which the Entente Allies seemed disposed to exact and in-
furiated at the landing of Greek troops at Smyrna, he resolved
to build a Nationalist party and a national army in the highlands of Asia Minor, whither no Greek or British battleships
could reach, in complete disregard of the feeble government
of Sultan Mohammed VI (1918–22) at Constantinople. In
1920 he established a provisional government at Angora.
In a brilliant series of campaigns he crushed the Greek forces,
reconquered Smyrna, spread the power of his government
from the frontiers of Russia to the Ægean Sea, and even
threatened Thrace. At the Lausanne Conference of 1920
the peace treaty of Sèvres was drastically revised in favor of
Turkey.[1] Independent Armenia and Asiatic Greece disappeared from the map and Turkey again held possession of
Constantinople and eastern Thrace as far as the Maritsa
river.[2] Most satisfying of all was the abolition of the
"capitulations" or special privileges which foreign powers
had previously enjoyed on Turkish soil.

Such a successful general was bound to be a popular national hero. As a matter of fact, his prestige was so great
that in a few years' time, almost without protest, he was able
to abolish the Sultanate, divorce the Ottoman State from di-

---

[1] For the Lausanne Treaty, see Chapter XVIII.

[2] Together with the town of Karagach, a railway center, on the west bank.

rect connection with the Mohammedan religion, transform
cherished traditions and customs that had behind them the weight of many centuries, implant
western institutions by wholesale in a sweeping
program of personal reform that has scarcely a
parallel in history unless it be the Europeanization of Russia
by Peter the Great.[1]   The National Assembly deposed the
last Sultan, Mohammed VI, in 1922, and in 1923 declared a
republic under Mustapha Kemal's presidency.   In 1924 the
Assembly decreed the abolition of the caliphate, or successor-
ship to Mohammed, which had hitherto been associated with
the Turkish Sultans and had given them a leadership over all
orthodox (Sunnite) Mohammedans.[2]   Not until 1928, however, were all ties dissolved between the government and the
faith of Islam, and of course the majority of Turks are still
Mohammedans in personal creed, although that fact no
longer entitles them to a superior political position.

*From theo-
cratic Sultan
to secular
dictator*

The use of the term "Turkish Republic" should not disguise the arbitrary character of Mustapha Kemal's dictatorship.   No Sultan had ever ruled more absolutely.   For years
his Nationalist party was the only one permitted to exist;
and the fact that a small and very tame opposition
group appeared in 1930 was really an added witness to his power, for the official opposition came into being
by express permission of Mustapha Kemal, who desired to
establish one as an appropriate part of parliamentary procedure!   The National Assembly unanimously re-elected
the president in 1927 and 1931.   The capital remained at
Angora, renamed Ankara, even after Turkey's enemies

*Political
changes*

[1] Of course there have been a few other cases of the rapid alteration of national
institutions, as in nineteenth-century Japan or contemporary Soviet Russia, but in
these cases the modernizing reforms were usually the work of a considerable number
of persons rather than the personal program of a single leader; and it is not unfair to
say that most European dictatorships have been directed rather to strengthening
than to modernizing or liberalizing the State,— indeed, they have usually taken
a counter revolutionary direction.

[2] The Shiite Persians had refused to recognize this primacy.

evacuated Constantinople (or "Istanbul"), and the former inland village of 5000 became a modern city of 80,000. The entire legal code was remodeled on western European patterns;[1] the Arabic alphabet, in spite of all its religious associations, was replaced by the Latin and the people were commanded to use the new script exclusively; western measurements of time in calendar and clock and the metric system of weights and measures were introduced. One curse of the old Ottoman Empire had been illiteracy; now the number of schools was approximately doubled in the postwar period and illiteracy, though still very prevalent, reduced by half.

But Mustapha Kemal was not content with altering the laws; the very daily life of the people must be westernized as *Social changes* well. With a sweeping simplicity he abolished the fez, as worn by the men, and the veil which had covered the faces of the women. He forbade polygamy and made the position of women more nearly equal to that of men. He permitted statues to be erected — to himself and others — in direct defiance of Mohammed's ban on graven images. He imposed severe restrictions on religious teaching in the schools, which greatly hampered the work of Christian missionaries but at the same time drove a wider wedge between Turkish nationalism and devout Mohammedanism. To each of these initiatives, the National Assembly responded with complete docility, though in holes and corners of the republic old-fashioned Moslems grumbled under their breath at such radical reforms. They dared not grumble too openly, for under the Turkish dictatorship outspoken critics were usually prosecuted, and even the wearing of a forbidden pattern of hat or the printing of a newspaper in the old Arabic type was an offense against the law.

The reformation of Turkish institutions improved her international status. France and Italy were well disposed

---

[1] The civil code based on the Swiss, the criminal code on the Italian and the commercial on the German.

as early as 1920 because of their quarrels with Greece, but
the long-contested frontier adjustment between   *Turkey*
Turkey and the British mandate of Iraq (Meso-   *among the*
potamia), settled with the aid of the League of   *nations*
Nations in 1926, delayed a good understanding with Great
Britain.   Soviet Russia, eager to present her government in
a favorable light to Oriental peoples, negotiated several treaties of friendship with the new Turkey.   In 1930 and 1933 outstanding differences with Greece were terminated, and in 1932
Turkey was received as a member of the League of Nations.

Though Turkey had held her own or recovered lost ground
in her European and Anatolian lands, she was unable to resume her sovereignty over the Arab-speaking   *The man-*
countries of Mesopotamia, Syria, Palestine and   *dated terri-*
independent Arabia.   All these regions were by   *tories*
majority Mohammedan in faith, though intermixed with
Christian and Jewish minorities especially in Syria and
Palestine, but the Arabs had never cherished affection for
the Turks.   The two peoples were utterly dissimilar in race
and speech,[1] indeed in everything except religion; and Mustapha Kemal's transformation of Turkey from a religious to
a secular basis made many pious Arabs thank Allah that they
did not have to submit to his decrees.   The British held a
trusteeship from the League of Nations for Mesopotamia and
Palestine, the French for Syria,[2] and even Mustapha Kemal's
excellent army was not equal to meeting the opposition of
such Great Powers.   Certain frontier adjustments were
made.   By the Angora agreement of 1920 France abandoned
Cilicia to the north of Syria.   A prolonged dispute over the
Mosul region, famous for its oil resources, resulted in a decision in favor of the British by the League of Nations in 1925,
reluctantly accepted by Turkey the following year, and in
1927 the frontier was actually demarcated.   The Turks were,

[1] The Turks were of Mongolian origin (though mixed with other races) and Tura-
nian (central Asiatic) speech; the Arabs, like the Jews, were Semitic.

[2] See Chapter XVIII.

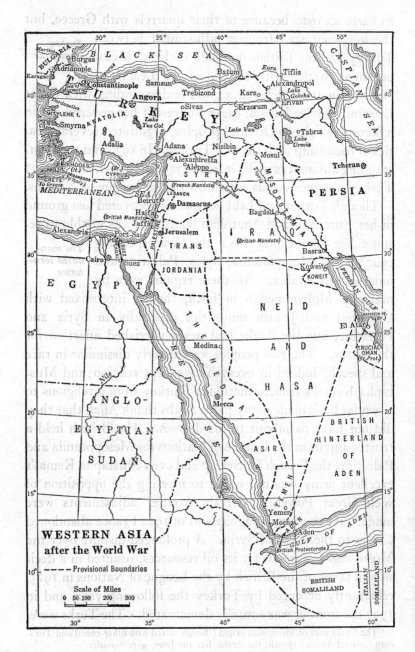

WESTERN ASIA
after the World War

– – – Provisional Boundaries

Scale of Miles
0 50 100 200   300

THE NEW NEAR EAST 613

however, given an indemnity equivalent to a ten per cent share in the oil royalties for twenty-five years. The secret Sykes-Picot agreement of 1916 between Great Britain and France for the division of spheres of influence between Syria and Mesopotamia had to be readjusted in detail; eventually Great Britain kept the Mosul oil region but shared oil rights with the French.

Iraq, the ancient Mesopotamia, traditional site of the Garden of Eden and historical site of the civilizations of Babylon and Bagdad, had before the war been considered one of the prizes of diplomacy, as *Iraq* witness the contest over railway control between Germany and Great Britain. It was commonly believed that the barren and impoverished look of the country had been due solely to Turkish misrule and that under British guidance the mandate would prove a most remunerative one. These expectations have not been wholly realized. The British discovered that the burden of looking after the affairs of a restless and somewhat fanatical Mohammedan people involved administrative costs that offset the commercial profits which might be realized. Gradually they weakened their control and eventually placed the country in a position somewhat similar to that of postwar Egypt; a country nominally independent but tied by a close alliance to the British Empire in such a way as to be kept within the British "sphere of influence" to the exclusion of all other foreign influences. To conciliate the Arabs, disappointed at not obtaining a universal Pan-Arabian Empire over Syria, Palestine and Iraq as well as over the independent Arabian states such as the Hedjaz, Great Britain made one son of King Hussein of the Hedjaz ruler over Iraq and another ruler over the Trans-Jordan district connecting Iraq with Palestine. In 1922 a treaty of "alliance" (actually of protectorate) was negotiated between Great Britain and Iraq. In 1932 Iraq was admitted to the League of Nations as an Independent Member State, for-

mally terminating the "mandate" though still bound to
recognize certain treaty rights of Great Britain. In 1933
King Ghazi I succeeded King Feisal, son of Hussein of the
Hedjaz and former Arab representative at the Paris Peace
Conference. The British army of occupation was progres-
sively diminished as Iraq was accorded a greater measure of
home rule. Iraq has a population of three millions on an
area a little greater than California.

Still more perplexing was the problem of administering the
mandate for Palestine. This country was to be a "home-
Palestine land" for Jewish immigrants but it had a considerable majority of Mohammedan Arabs already
rooted in the country, conservative, fanatical, disposed to
look askance on alien immigration. Jerusalem was a sacred
city to three religions, the Mohammedan, the Jewish and the
Christian. To hold a firm course through what at any moment might become a tempest of religious fanaticism was no
easy matter. The greatest problem was the regulation of
Jewish immigration. To permit it to proceed rapidly would
not only irritate the Arabs to the point of rebellion but swamp
the resources of what is, after all, a tiny country in spite of its
mighty history. On an area about that of Vermont, Palestine already supports over a million inhabitants of whom
nearly three-fourths are Mohammedans. The number of
Jews increased through immigration from some 80,000 to
upwards of 200,000. In 1930, following a series of riots, the
British government temporarily suspended immigration.
As there are probably over 15,000,000 Jews in the world, it
is obvious that the "Zionist homeland" can at best house
only an insignificant fraction of the number. Yet the Zionist movement, while it has made little difference to the fortunes of the Jewish people as a whole, has had an enormous
effect on the fortunes of Palestine. It has increased religious
friction, but at the same time brought a great deal of capital
into the country, stimulated industry and scientific agri-

culture and erected well-endowed institutions of philanthropy
and education.

France's one mandate in the Near East was allotted to her
not only in virtue of secret treaties concluded during the war
or in recognition of her position as a world power
at the end of it, but because for many years *Syria*
France had been cultivating close relations, commercial and
cultural, with Syria and especially with the small Christian
community of the Lebanon district. Yet the American
commission of Henry C. King and Charles R. Crane which
visited the Near East during the Peace Conference advised
against a French mandate for Syria on the ground of "the
strength, universality and persistency of anti-French feeling
among practically all Moslems" in the country, and subsequent events seemed to justify these forebodings. This is
the more surprising, since the French in north Africa have
been more successful than any other Christian nation in
conciliating Moslem sentiment. Perhaps part of the trouble
was the selection of a faulty personnel to manage the mandate. General Serrail, the French High Commissioner, by
his high-handed and arbitrary government provoked an
insurrection which was not put down until the ancient city
of Damascus had been twice bombarded from the air and
more than a thousand natives killed. The rebellion of
1925–26 resulted in a report by the League of Nations Mandates Commission which severely censured the French officials for unnecessary village burning and aerial bombardments. The French then turned to more conciliatory
methods and in 1930 set up a "Syrian Republic" subject to
special treaty relations with France, a relationship somewhat
analogous to that which the British established with Iraq
and Egypt. The Lebanon district is administratively separate, with a president and assembly of its own. Syria is
about the size of Illinois, with a population of not quite
three million. There is little mineral wealth, but well
developed agriculture, and especially a valuable silk culture.

CHAPTER XXV

RECONSTRUCTION AND DEPRESSION
IN WESTERN EUROPE

WESTERN EUROPE, as compared with eastern Europe, underwent only slight modifications of frontier as a result of
The eco- the World War, the Paris Peace Conference and
nomic after- the wave of national revolution; even Alsace-
math of war Lorraine bulks larger historically than geographically. But there are changes which the map does not
reveal, which are not even a part of political history in the
narrower sense, which may have profound political consequences. Such were the dislocations of trade, the fluctua-
tions of the currency, the indebtedness of governments to
other governments or to their own citizens, the spread of
unemployment, the enrichment or impoverishment of the
various social classes in consequence of industrial changes
or governmental policies, which in greater or less degree
affected the whole world, even the nations which were
neutral during the war. But, in general, the highly industrialized nations of the West such as Britain, France, Germany and the United States of America, were most affected
by these economic forces, since industrial communities live
by exchange and are greatly dependent on the balance of
international credits and the buying power of foreign markets.

Great wars in the old pre-industrial days were economically important chiefly because of the direct destruction
caused thereby. Certain towns would be looted or burned,
certain farmsteads robbed of their flocks and herds. Then
when it was over the plundered peasantry would slowly
and painfully rebuild all that war had shattered. Such was
indeed the aftermath of the World War in those parts of

Europe still largely dependent on subsistence farming. The effect on industrial and commercial communities was more complex. Neither Germany nor Great Britain suffered greatly during the war from direct devastation, yet they were faced with economic problems as serious as those of invaded France. Germany was unable for several years to balance the national budget and resorted to currency inflation with the result of ruining millions of formerly thrifty and prosperous citizens. Britain escaped any such financial earthquake, but found the ability of continental Europe to import British goods so seriously diminished that millions of workingmen were thrown out of employment and had to be maintained in idleness at the expense of the burdened taxpayer; her "devastated regions" were the milltowns of Lancashire and the shipyards on the Clyde. The American wheat farmer (who is not a "peasant" farming for subsistence, but a "food manufacturer" using machinery to create a large surplus for distant markets) found that he had overplanted his fields when Europe returned from the almost limitless demands of wartime to the very limited demand of an impoverished peace. He was in essentially the same position as the shipbuilder whose new craft built to meet the needs of war rotted idle at the wharf for lack of cargo. In many such ways the remote and indirect consequences of the war remained to plague the world long after the armistice.

The credit relations affected by the war were so intricate as to be easily confused. A journalist writing that a certain country was "heavily in debt" might mean, ac- *Debit and* cording to his context, that (1) reparations or *credit* indemnities were due under treaty to enemy states; (2) debts were due to allied states for war loans; (3) debts were due to foreign states for "reconstruction" or other peace time loans; (4) government bonds were held by individual foreign creditors; (5) the government had a large internal debt held by its own citizens; (6) foreigners held extensive credits against the private business enterprises of the country, quite independently of governmental action. Failure to pay, in whole or in part, might occur in any one of these six categories, but the interests affected would not be the same: where one government owed another government the loss would be borne by the general body of taxpayers of the creditor nation; where the government owed individuals the loss would fall exclusively, and sometimes ruinously, on the bondholders; where private concerns owed money the investor would stand the loss. A "moratorium" or delay in payment, a downward revision of interest, or any other adjustment short of repudiation might similarly refer to any of these types of indebtedness. Many nations were at once debtor and creditor; for instance, Great Britain and France were creditors to Germany with respect to reparations and debtors to the United States for war loans, while France was also debtor to Great Britain, and all four governments were heavily indebted to private bondholders.

The payment of reparations owed by the Central Powers fell chiefly upon Germany, as her wartime allies were in no *The repara-* condition to make very substantial payments. *tions ques-* The Reparation Commission fixed the total *tion* liability of the vanquished group at 132,000,000,-000 gold marks (or approximately $31,400,000,000), and in April, 1921, Germany was notified that she and her allies would be held to the payment of this sum. By the Spa agreement of the previous year German payments were to be distributed according to a fixed ratio among the creditor nations: 52% to France, 22% to Great Britain, 10% to Italy; 8% to Belgium; 8% to other Allied States. The relatively small sums expected from Austria, Hungary and Bulgaria were distributed in a different ratio, the shares of Greece, Rumania and Yugoslavia being very much larger; these obligations were adjusted and largely "liquidated" in the course of the next few years by mutual cancellation of claims on various accounts between the debtor states and their creditors.[1] Germany's burden, however, remained as one of the major problems affecting European peace. The total sum demanded was over thirty times as large as the war indemnity which had been imposed on France in 1871 in the expectation of "bleeding her white"; there was no possibility of paying it in gold; German paper currency was not wanted since it could not be certain to remain on a gold basis; payment in labor met with determined opposition from French trades unionists, who wanted to reconstruct the devastated departments themselves; payment in goods, or from a favorable balance of trade, would involve an immense output of German made goods and a corresponding curtailment of German imports — neither of them welcome to manufacturers in creditor countries! Even payment in raw materials had its difficulties; Great Britain, for example, was not apt to view with enthusiasm reparations payments in German coal to France and Italy large enough to spoil her own export trade. The primary question, "How can Germany afford to pay?" was complicated by the apparently paradoxical consideration, "How can Germany's creditors afford to take?"

To all the other obstacles in the way of reparations payments must be added the psychological. War indemnities to a foreign foe are paid less willingly, perhaps, than any other governmental exaction whatever. German citizens hoarded their wealth, preferably in foreign banks and deposit boxes, where the tax gatherer could not reach it. The French grumbled that the German government was in collusion with the tax dodgers and demanded "productive guarantees," that is the physical possession of German properties capable of yielding revenue as security for payments. The German objection to the principle of repara-

---

[1] For the east European financial settlements, see Royall Tyler, *The Eastern Reparations Settlement, Foreign Affairs* (October, 1930), pages 106–17.

tions was based partly on the ground that pensions and separation allowances, comprised among the categories of "civilian damage" in the Treaty of Versailles,[1] were really military expenses which should never have been included; partly on the claim that the total bill should have been diminished by the value of the lost colonies and public property in other ceded territory, and partly on the general ground that Germany was not responsible for the war.

Nothing in the Treaty of Versailles roused more resentment in Germany than the apparent implication that on *The "war* her rested the responsibility for the World War. *guilt" ques-* This implication was found in three parts of *tion* the treaty. In the preamble it was stated that the war "originated in the declaration of war by Austria-Hungary on July 28, 1914 against Serbia, the declaration of war by Germany against Russia on August 1, 1914, and against France on August 3, 1914, and in the invasion of Belgium." Article 227 arraigns "William II of Hohenzollern, formerly German Emperor, for a supreme offence against international morality and the sanctity of treaties." In article 231 "Germany accepts the responsibility of Germany and her allies for causing all the loss and damage to which the Allied and Associated Governments and their nationals have been subjected as a consequence of the war imposed upon them by the aggression of Germany and her allies." All three clauses may, it is true, be given an interpretation quite aside from the question of ultimate moral responsibility for the World War,[2] but in Germany nearly

[1] See Chapter XVIII.

[2] Of course there is no doubt that the diplomats of the victor group at Paris did believe in Germany's guilt and did assert it (for instance, in the "covering letter" that accompanied the submission of the Treaty of Versailles to Germany for final signature), but it does not follow that the Germans were, by signing the Treaty, compelled to subscribe to the same view. The preamble merely recites the dates and manner of the beginning of hostilities; the "supreme offence" of Kaiser Wilhelm II seems to refer to the invasion of Belgium rather than to the war as a whole; and even article 231 seems to have been intended by its authors merely as a legal formula for the "assumption of liability" for damage done by the act of invasion and its conse-

all parties denounced it as "the war guilt lie" and "signing away the national honor." Some of the more extreme publicists held that all liability to pay reparations would disappear if article 231 were disproved by historical research — or even repudiated with sufficient frequency and vigor! This consideration infused new life into the very dry bones of the controversy on the origin of the war; entire periodicals were devoted to the subject, and opposition parties could embarrass any German government by demanding action to erase the offending paragraphs from the Treaty.

French suspicion of Germany's good faith increased with each delay in payments and reached a climax in 1922 when Germany requested a total suspension of all *The occupation of the Ruhr* payments until her budget could be balanced and her credit restored. There was very good ground for this demand, since inflation had driven the mark down to a small fraction of its face value. But the French had been forced in the meantime to reconstruct their devastated departments largely at their own expense. Most of Germany's early payments had been offset by the costs of the Allied army of occupation on the Rhine or by payments to Belgium which had been given priority.[1] The Reparations Commission found Germany delinquent in making certain promised deliveries of wood and coal. Very significantly, the British representative on the Commission declared the default a trivial one and opposed any measures of punishment or coercion such as the French demanded. His government supported this view and no British soldiers were sent across the Rhine when in January, 1923, French and Belgian forces occupied the Ruhr district with its

quences. Certainly no theory of sole responsibility was necessary as a legal basis for reparations; no one questioned that France and Belgium were invaded and damaged, no matter what may have been the ultimate causes of the war.

[1] By article 232 of the Treaty of Versailles Germany was required "to make reimbursement of all sums which Belgium has borrowed from the Allied and Associated Governments" prior to the armistice.

wealth of mines and factories. The small district to the east of the lower Rhine was the most important industrial district in all Germany, producing, it was estimated, four-fifths of all the coal and iron remaining to Germany after the Treaty of Versailles.

Not since the two countries first joined hands in the *Entente Cordiale* of 1904 had France and Britain stood so

British in-terests con-flict with French

sharply opposed to each other as during the time of the Ruhr occupation. The British had stood for moderation towards Germany at the Peace Conference, but they were still sufficiently under the emotions of wartime to have some sympathy for the French viewpoint. By 1922 most British commentators on international affairs denounced the French policy as harsh and oppressive. The British economist, J. M. Keynes, rejoiced at the breakdown of the reparations clauses of the Treaty of Versailles and declared, "The actions of those in power have been wiser than their words. It is only a slight exaggeration to say that no parts of the Peace Treaties have been carried out, except those relating to frontiers and to disarmament." [1] Though statesmen were more cautious in their comments than publicists, the refusal of the British government to take any share in the occupation of the Ruhr bespoke a parting of the ways. With the German fleet scuttled and the German colonies lost, Germany no longer presented any immediate danger to the British Empire, while the falling off of German trade struck a crushing blow to British prosperity. British interests pointed toward the reconstruction of their former foe. On the other hand, the French claimed that they had already spent about $7,500,-000,000 on reconstruction and war pensions, almost entirely at their own cost, and they believed that Germany was still a military menace to countries which had a common land-ward frontier with her. André Tardieu, one of the most

[1] J. M. Keynes, *A Revision of the Treaty* (1922), page 180.

influential of French statesmen, complained that Lloyd George "in 1920... adopted the very policy which he had repudiated in 1919, the policy of Mr. Keynes. Commercial interests have everywhere been put first... Too many Englishmen have forgotten that — however great and decisive the part played by England in the war — her territory was neither invaded nor devastated. Too many Englishmen have failed to recognize that France, bleeding and plundered, is entitled to something better than daily advice to renounce her rights."[1]

Germany, unable to meet the French occupation by any adequate military force, resolved to see what passive resistance might achieve. The German government suspended all payments to France and Belgium for reparations, stopped taxes in the occupied zone, closed down all manufacture, halted trade and tried by every means to "freeze out" the invaders. *Germany enters bankruptcy* The French retaliated by establishing martial law, imposing heavy fines on those who disobeyed their decrees and rigorously censoring the press. To sustain resistance in the Ruhr, Chancellor Cuno unwisely accelerated the inflation of the currency until the process passed completely beyond control. As confidence in the paper mark was lost, greater and greater quantities had to be printed to meet the daily costs of government. The face value of the mark was about a quarter of a dollar. By November, 1922, it was currently quoted at 7000 to the dollar, during July, 1923, it sank to less than 1,000,000 to the dollar, and it reached final bottom in November at 4,000,000,000,000 to the dollar, "astronomical figures" indeed! Shopkeepers altered their prices hour by hour as the exchange rates shifted. Wages, altered almost daily, still lagged behind prices, and salaried men, whose incomes could not be so speedily adjusted, fell into utter destitution. But the blow fell most severely on those who lived

[1] A. Tardieu, *The Truth about the Treaty* (1921), page 447.

from fixed credits — the holders of bonds, mortgages, annuities and pensions. Many of the thriftiest Germans found the savings of a lifetime unable to buy a postage stamp. No one dared save, for money was like some fairy gold which would change to dross in one's possession; every bit of paper money — and nothing but paper was in circulation — was spent or invested in tangible goods (land, buildings, commodities) as soon as possible. This "flight from the mark into goods" as it was termed, feverishly stimulated building and some forms of industrial enterprise, it encouraged rapid spending and thus gave a false appearance of prosperity to the visitor who looked only at the surface of things and saw (outside the Ruhr) factories busy turning out goods and new houses rising like mushrooms.

Underneath the busy surface Germany was sinking into chaos and despair. In September, 1923, the government *The "Dawes* abandoned resistance in the Ruhr, and Gustav *plan," 1924* Stresemann, the new Chancellor, undertook a "policy of fulfilment,"— the endeavor to carry out the provisions of the Treaty of Versailles until they could be modified with the consent of all concerned. The French, openly triumphant at the "victory" of their Ruhr policy against the opposition of Germany and without the aid of Britain, were secretly pleased to liquidate their whole venture in the Ruhr, for the costs of occupation amounted to more than all the revenues that could be raised by the seizure of industrial properties. In November, 1923, the Reparations Commission authorized the establishment of two committees of investigation: one, under the chairmanship of Reginald McKenna of Great Britain, to discover in what manner and what quantity German capital had been sent out of the country; the other, under General Charles Dawes of the United States, to advise as to method of stabilizing the German currency and balancing the national budget so that orderly payment of reparations might again be possible. Neither committee was authorized to alter the amount of reparations, as fixed in 1921, but the recommendations of the "Dawes committee" assumed a very wide scope and covered the question of the installments which Germany was to pay and the manner of guaranteeing payment. The Reparations Commission accepted the Dawes Report in 1924, and on September first the new plan went into effect.

The Dawes Plan provided that all Germany be treated as an economic unit, implying the evacuation of the Ruhr; that annuities begin at 1,000,000,000 gold marks *A "receiver-* (about $238,000,000) and rise by stages to a *ship for* normal figure of 2,500,000,000 gold marks *Germany"* ($595,000,000) by 1928; that they might be raised or lowered thereafter according to an "index of prosperity" based on statistics of German trade and national income; that a foreign loan of 800,000,000 gold marks ($190,000,000) be extended to Germany in order to place her on a gold basis; that a "blanket mortgage" be placed on German railways and on certain industrial properties as security for payment,[1] and that a central bank under international control supervise the working of the plan. An American, S. P. Gilbert, became Agent General of Reparations. He advocated an early fixing of Germany's total debt. In the meantime Germany put her own house in order. Under the direction of Dr. Luther as Minister of Finance and Dr. Schacht as head of the Reichsbank, the further issuance of the old currency was stopped and the value of the paper mark fixed at the fantastic ratio of 1,000,000,000,000 to one, amounting in effect to cancellation; a new currency, the "rentenmark," secured on the real estate of the country, took the place of the old. Eventually the gold standard was restored.

In 1928 the interested governments agreed to assign to a new committee the task of working out "a complete and final

---

[1] Inflation had practically wiped out any previous bonded indebtedness on these properties, so these new charges could be easily handled.

settlement of the obligations resulting from the existing trea-
The Young ties" and in 1929 the committee set to work
Plan, 1929 under the chairmanship of an American financier,
Owen D. Young.   The Young committee had the power
which the Dawes committee lacked to suggest an alteration
in Germany's total indebtedness as well as merely to regulate
methods of payment.   Dr. Hjalmar Schacht obstinately
held out for reducing Germany's payments to a sum that
would but little more than pay the Allied debts to the
United States and he somewhat tactlessly hinted that if
Germany's creditors wanted more they should restore some
of Germany's lost territorial assets, the overseas colonies, the
Saar valley, the Polish Corridor and Polish Upper Silesia.
Finally a compromise was reached midway between the sums
suggested by the German and the Allied experts.   About
$165,000,000 a year was to be levied unconditionally, a rail-
way tax being the guarantee, for a period of thirty-seven
years; the rest of the amount would be made up from the national budget, but be subject to diminution if necessary to
protect Germany's gold standard or as an offset to any future
reduction in the war debts owed by the creditor states to
their creditors — chiefly, the United States of America.   Already reparations and war debts were being tied together
into an elaborately interwoven knot in the hope that American generosity might solve all difficulties for debtors and
creditors alike.   If there were no such reduction, the Young
Plan contemplated a total reparations bill with a capital
value of about $8,500,000,000 plus interest at five and
one-half per cent.   Thirty-seven payments averaging about
$512,500,000 were to be followed by twenty-two payments
on a diminished scale, averaging about $391,250,000 a year.
A non-political Bank for International Settlements replaced
the existing agencies for the enforcement and collection of
reparations.

As a further concession, the remaining troops in the

Rhineland, mainly French, were withdrawn in 1930 and the whole of German soil freed from the presence of *The Rhine-* the conqueror. Under the strict wording of the *land evacu-* Treaty of Versailles troops might have been re- *ated* tained in Germany until 1935, the same year as the plebiscite in the Saar, but even the French now considered a garrison in western Germany a needless expense and a dangerous political irritation. In the first flush of victory the French had been guilty of great tactlessness in handling the whole question. While the British and American forces of occupation were small in number and kept as unobtrusively in the background as possible, the French maintained a large army and constantly lorded it over the civilians among whom the soldiers were billeted. Two French policies in particular roused irritation. The French, whose racial prejudices are not strong, maintained African colonial troops of many races in their regular army and used them in part to police the Rhineland; the Germans took this as a deliberate insult, the subjection of a cultured European folk to "African savages." The French encouraged political movements in the Rhineland which aimed at a separation of western Germany from the state of Prussia and, in some instances, from the German nation as a whole. This might have been a wise, if somewhat Machiavellian, policy if the movement had been a genuine and well-supported one; but it was never more than a flash in the pan, and France had taken counsel of her hopes rather than her reason in looking for advantage from it. The French found it hard to forget how recent had been the attainment of German unity, and the most common diplomatic delusion of this generally very level-headed nation was that Bavaria, the Rhineland or some other part of Germany might be induced to set up independently. Finally, the occupation of the Ruhr, which was east of the zone of occupation authorized directly by the Treaty of Versailles, made the Germans feel that the French were bound by no law but that of force in their dealings with Germany. So when the French turned to conciliation, to the policy of Herriot and Briand, and agreed to drastic reduction of reparations and other concessions to Germany, they agreed also to wind up the whole unhappy experiment of occupying German soil.

During the World War the belligerent governments borrowed freely from private citizens and from each other. The *Inter-Allied* largest loans between nations were those of Great *war debts* Britain to her continental Allies and those of the United States to Great Britain, France and several other nations. From the Peace Conference onwards the British government favored cancellation of all war debts except reparations, calculating that her paper loss in giving up claims against France, Italy and other continental states would be more than offset by the cancellation of American claims against her and by the general stimulus to business from the reduction of fixed international debts. In 1922, the British government announced that it would seek to collect from its debtors only such a sum as would offset its own payments to the United States. Therefore the whole question of war debts was made to pivot on American policy. During or immediately after the war the United States loaned $10,338,-000,000 at an interest rate of five per cent. Some of this went for relief, but most of it was spent for munitions, more than $7,000,000,000 being advanced prior to the armistice. In the interval before funding agreements were reached little either of principal or accrued interest had been paid by the debtors to the United States, so the aggregate debt owed the United States by 1924 amounted to more than $12,000,000,-000. The payment of so vast a sum created a problem in international credits second only to that of Germany's debt for reparations, and unfortunately caused about as much popular ill feeling. It is hard to forgive a debtor, and harder still to forgive a creditor!

There was a very good case for each side in this contro-

versy.   Each successive administration in the United States
held that the war debts were as valid as any other   *How Amer-*
business transactions and that any abatements   *ica viewed*
of principal or interest, made from motives of   *the question*
expediency or philanthropy, were acts of grace rather than of
right.   Whoever else had started the war, it was not the
United States!   The aid when granted had been very welcome; there had been no haggling over terms *then*; the money
had been raised by the American government from its taxpayers and bond buyers, and the latter would have to be re-
payed at an interest rate averaging four and one-fourth per
cent.   A general cancellation of credits would mean a war
indemnity of over ten billions levied on the American taxpayers for their share in contributing to victory.   The United
States had not gained an inch of territory from the war and
had made no claim to reparations,[1] although her war costs
had been very heavy.   Moreover, to cancel an international
debt was to set a dangerous precedent.   Who could borrow
in the future with such a monstrous example of repudiation
looming in the past?   Finally, there was every reason to
suppose that a large part of the debt so remitted would be
spent not on balancing European budgets but on increasing
European armaments; was it to the interest of the European
nations themselves to discover that they could escape the
international costs of one war and use the money preparing
for another?

America's debtors took quite another view.   To them the
war debts were no mere commercial transactions but contributions to a common cause; and sometimes they   *How Eu-*
hinted that the heavy losses in life or wealth   *rope viewed*
which they suffered while the United States was   *the question*
slowly getting ready for war might well be considered an off-

---

[1] A part of Germany's payments used to cover the cost of the small American
army of occupation maintained in the Rhineland after the war might be counted as
"reparations," but broadly speaking the statement is true.

set to the debt. The money was spent mainly in the United States for American goods and had notably stimulated American manufactures. Moreover the prospects of reparations from Germany were proving to be a will o' the wisp, and was it fair to exact war debts when the reparations which had been counted on to furnish the necessary funds could no longer be collected? As Ivy Lee, an American propagandist for revision, put the matter in 1932: "The victorious Allies, while receiving nothing whatever from defeated Germany, will yet be compelled to pay to the United States over a period of nearly two generations, the sum of approximately $250,000,000 annually. From a strictly financial point of view would this not place the Allies in exactly the same position... as if they had been defeated in the war and had been compelled to pay an annual indemnity of that amount?" The American contention that the war debts and reparations had nothing to do with each other might be legally sound, but it ignored economic realities and essential justice.

In view of this wide divergence on the merits of the case the practical thing to do was, as with German reparations, *Funding the* to seek an immediate compromise based on ex-
debts pediency rather than logic; but, again as in the case of reparations, such an adjustment was certain to require readjustment from time to time, and several "final settlements" might be made before real finality was reached. Great Britain funded principal and interest with her debtors, making large concessions. Over $10,000,000,000 was due her, but about a third of this debt was owed by Russia, and the Bolshevist revolution in that country had made it hopeless to collect any part of this; France had also lost heavily by the same revolution. The United States made similar agreements, based on the presumed "ability to pay" of the debtor states. Though the principal of nearly all the debts was left intact, the interest rate was reduced and the term of payment extended over sixty-two years. British obligations

amounting to more than $4,500,000,000 were reduced nearly twenty per cent by scaling the interest down to 3.3 per cent, leaving the funded debt at a present value of $3,788,000,000. The aggregate French debt was scaled down by more than half through interest reduction to $1,996,500,000. Italy was treated with still greater generosity, her interest rate being fixed at 0.4 per cent, thus reducing her obligation to $528,-000,000, a decrease of about three-fourths. The debts of the lesser states were treated in similar fashion. In all, the United States forgave about half of the total debt, including interest at the contracted rate, which was due to her.

Whether either the Young Plan reparations payments or the funded war debts would have been payable to the end if the comparative prosperity of the mid-'twenties *The Hoover* had continued will always remain a matter for *moratorium* debate. These adjustments were certainly based on such an expectation. In 1929, however, Europe and America sank together into an economic abyss.[1] In June, 1931, President Hoover, anxious to avert the threatened closure of the German banks and a general panic throughout central Europe, proposed a one-year moratorium on war debts and reparations to begin July 1, 1931. Though in theory the United States would have been the chief loser by the moratorium, within a fortnight the Wall Street market responded by an advance in stock values estimated to equal the whole face value of the war debts, clearly reflecting the opinion of the financial community that the United States would more than gain in commerce what it would lose in repayment of debts. But this advance was not sustained. It soon became clear that Germany would not only be unable for several years to make any substantial payment for reparations, but might even have difficulty in repaying her outstanding loans. France made difficulties on points of detail, fearing that the moratorium might be the first step to abandon reparations

[1] See below, pages 636–39.

entirely. The American Congress refused to consider any extension of the moratorium or even any further revision of the war debts. The Democratic party in the summer of 1932 inserted a plank into its platform opposing war debt cancellation, and in November defeated President Hoover. President Roosevelt's new administration was too busy handling a banking crisis and a program of internal reconstruction to resume negotiations where the ex-president had been forced to abandon them.

Under the weight of the world depression the Young Plan had broken down and the Hoover moratorium, though *The Lausanne agreement, 1932* limited in form to one year, made it almost impossible to revive payments. Representatives of the interested European states met at Lausanne in the summer of 1932 and agreed to reduce the balance of Germany's reparation debt to 3,000,000,000 gold marks ($714,000,000) with a complete moratorium for three years. This was less than a tenth of Germany's debt under the Young Plan and one forty-fourth of the amount originally established by the Reparations Commission only eleven years before! Of course, Germany had made important payments in the meantime, but it is difficult to ascertain their value since for the most part they consisted in deliveries in kind — coal, chemicals, etc. — whose value was differently estimated by debtors and creditors. The French contended that Germany had made total payments only up to $5,000,-000,000, or five times the war indemnity of 1871; the Germans insisted that they had already paid money or goods to a total value of $16,000,000,000.[1] To safeguard themselves, the British and French governments entered into an agreement to the effect that "ratification will not be effected before a

---

[1] Such payments as Germany did make were possible only because Germany had been sustained by loans made to her, and the difficulty of repaying these reconstruction loans became serious in 1934. In most years Germany had no favorable balance of trade with which to pay her creditors and had to "borrow from Peter to pay Paul."

satisfactory settlement is obtained between them and their own creditors." Thus the Lausanne agreement was still-born, since America refused to modify her stand that war debts and reparations were entirely separate transactions and must not be made dependent on each other.

Whether the Lausanne agreement would come legally into effect or not was generally recognized to be a minor question; the very fact of having negotiated such a revision made it practically impossible to restore the old scale of payments, no German government would last an hour that consented to do so.[1]   For prac- *The end of reparations and war debts?*
tical purposes reparations had been cancelled.   It proved equally impossible again to revive the interallied war debts. In December, 1932, France announced that the payment of the installment due the United States would be postponed until a new international conference had revised the whole system of war debts.   Belgium, Poland and several other debtor states followed the French example.   In June, 1933, Great Britain and Italy made only small "token payments" in acknowledgment of the debt, and even these payments were made in depreciated silver; France repeated her complete default.   By the Johnson Act of 1934 the American Congress attempted to put pressure on the defaulters through the prohibition of further loan flotations by defaulting governments in the American market.   Great Britain responded by abandoning even token payments until war debts could be adjusted on a new basis.   Finland alone of all the indebted nations continued to make payments in full. Apparently repudiation had become the accepted policy in most of the debtor nations of the world; Soviet Russia's re-

[1] One is tempted to find an analogy in the effect of Lincoln's Emancipation Proclamation.   Strictly speaking it did not free a single slave, for it applied only to those states which did not recognize President Lincoln's authority at all; yet it committed the nation in such a manner as to make impossible any further compromises with the institution of slavery.   So without altering the legal status of reparations, the abortive Lausanne agreement placed a revival of the old policy outside practical politics.

pudiation of all her foreign debts at the end of 1917 had created great consternation at the time but now found imitators among the most respectable capitalistic governments.

Nor were international obligations the only ones repudiated in part by the hard pressed governments. Prior to *Unbalanced* 1914 most European governments were on the *national* gold standard; their paper money was redeem- *budgets and* able at demand in gold coin or bullion at full face *inflation* value.[1] Most belligerents and even neutrals were forced to abandon gold payments by the extraordinary costs of wartime and reconstruction. Some, such as Great Britain, strove to restore the gold standard and succeeded for a time in doing so.[2] Some, such as France and Italy, stabilized their currency but not at face value. In 1926 the French franc was "pegged" at a fifth of its nominal value; exchanging for a little less than four cents in United States money instead of $0.193. The Italian lira was finally stabilized at a slightly higher rate, about a fourth of its pre-war value. A third group of nations, typified by Germany, practically repudiated their old currency and replaced it by a new issue. The depreciation of the currency had the fortunate effect of wiping out a large part of the fixed charges and obligations against the national budget and against private property as well, but the price for this relief was the partial confiscation of the property of credit holders, the buyers of government bonds, the holders of corporation bonds, the holders of mortgages on real property, the elderly folk living on pensions and annuities. Their losses did not in most countries go to the extreme lengths that we have noted in the case of Germany, but they were usually sufficient to sink a whole class of the thrifty and prosperous into relative poverty.

---

[1] Some governments, especially in parts of Asia, were on the silver standard.

[2] Great Britain restored the gold standard in 1925, but was forced to abandon it again in 1931.

If misery loves company, this class could at least console itself that it did not suffer alone. Even with the partial cancellation of war indebtedness brought about *The burden* by repudiation and inflation, the burden of the *of taxation* taxpayer in every country was several times heavier after 1919 than it had been before 1914. It was not merely a question of the cost of the war and its repayment to bondholders; the war left other obligations which only the future could discharge, such as care for wounded veterans, pensions, and unemployment doles for workingmen who were victims of falling export markets. Armament burdens decreased somewhat from wartime levels but rarely to the figures of 1913; the general sense of insecurity and the failure to find a satisfactory formula for limitation of armament kept Europe still keenly competitive "by land, by sea and from the air." The pressure of taxation tended to break up large estates, even where the government did not deliberately embark on a policy of land nationalization as in Soviet Russia or the creation of small peasant holdings as in the belt of little states from Finland to Bulgaria. Though the British government did not conduct a campaign against wealthy landlords, the advertisement columns of the London *Times* were crowded for years with announcements of country houses for sale. Alike from the tax burdened landlords and the middle-class men on fixed incomes, thousands sank to join the ranks of the "new poor," while a smaller group of war profiteers and successful speculators in the fluctuating currencies of Europe formed a rather unpleasant class of the "new rich."

International trade unquestionably suffered heavily from the direct and indirect effects of the World War in spite of the temporary "war prosperity" caused by the *Commerce* demand for munitions and other necessities of *after the* wartime. The great boom which this demand *war* produced continued by its own momentum for a few months after the armistice. Soon, however, the restricted buying power of an impoverished world made itself felt and the result was a sharp reaction, particularly acute in 1921 and 1922, the first "postwar depression." A second and more enduring depression began in 1929 and reached its nadir in 1932 when in most countries trade was most sluggish, stock values lowest and unemployment most general. Between the two depressions there was a "table land" of relative prosperity. Though these phenomena were almost world wide they differed in their intensity in different countries. The United States of America, where industrial technology and large-scale manufacture had been carried farthest, enjoyed a higher level of general prosperity during the period 1924–28 than at any time before the World War,[1] but in most European countries the recovery was only partial. Professor Clive Day has estimated that, allowing for the change in the purchasing power of money, the international trade of the world stood in 1924, a relatively prosperous year, a little below the level of 1913 and fully $17,000,000,000 below what it should have been if the normal increase of the years immediately preceding the World War had continued with no abatement.[2] Europe's share in the world's trade had declined relatively to that of every other continent. In 1913 Europe had over three-fifths of the world's trade; in 1924 little over one-half.

There are as many theories of the origins of the secondary postwar depression as there are of the origin of the war itself, and perhaps as little prospect of making peace among them. Certainly three factors were important: the excessive development of unstable credit, the political obstacles to economic expansion and the changes in industrial methods. A word may be

Genesis of the depression of 1929-34

---

[1] The farmers were an exception; they had not yet recovered from the agricultural collapse of 1921. The coal mining districts and the New England textile mills were also still depressed.

[2] Clive Day, *War Shocks to European Commerce*, *Foreign Affairs* (July 1927), pages 633–49.

said on each of these in turn.   Before the war the United
States balanced an excess of exports over imports by payments to European investors in American securities.   During the war so many of those securities were sold that the
country ceased to be a "debtor nation" in the *Over-*
field of private finance, while at the same time *strained*
the ten billion dollar war loans made the nation *credits*
a creditor in the field of public finance.   Yet the old excess
of exports over imports continued, partly because a high
protective tariff discouraged the foreign importer.   The result was a constant inflow of gold to the United States.   But
only a little of this was hoarded, most of it floated out again
in the form of loans and investments abroad, often made
with reckless optimism.   Within the United States, and in
lesser degree in the European nations as well, there was the
same inflation of credit.   Huge industrial combinations,
such as the Stinnes combines in Germany, the Insull properties in America, and Ivar Kreuger's monopoly of the
Swedish match trade, were pyramided to the skies.   Humbler
individuals learned by the million to purchase all their domestic furnishings on the installment plan instead of making
payment in full.   In the United States the financial fever
took the form of stock speculation, till in 1929 stocks were
sold at fantastic figures, far beyond any possible relation to
their profit yield, in the mere hope that they could be resold
as speedily as possible in an ever rising market.

But the world of 1929 which the stock buyers looked upon
as able to consume an unlimited amount of goods was really
handicapped in purchasing power as compared *Political*
with the world of 1913.   Debts were greater, *factors in*
taxes heavier, tariff barriers more numerous *the depres-*
and vexatious, and old economic units, such as *sion*
Austria-Hungary, were broken into new states that had not
yet adjusted themselves to the changed situation.   Soviet
Russia stood almost outside the circle of trading nations,

intent on developing her own economic system. Eighteen years of almost chronic civil war in China had disturbed the Oriental market; while Hindu nationalists threatened a boycott of British trade. Extreme radicals and reactionaries in Germany, threatening either a class war or a national war, seemed to be gaining at the expense of the moderate parties. Germany, Italy and France were all intriguing at cross purposes to bring Austria within their respective circles of friendly and dependent states. In spite of new security agreements, no one in Europe felt safe. After the depression had begun the political situation became rapidly worse, and this in turn reacted on the economic situation by freezing confidence and credit; a vicious circle indeed!

Changes in the nature of industry itself contributed to at least one phase of the depression, the growth of unemploy-

Industrial ment. When power-driven machines were first *factors* installed in the eighteenth century many dire prophecies were made that the new inventions would throw men out of work. In some particular cases they did have that effect, for example the new textile machines drove to destitution the hand weavers. But for every man whom labor saving machinery threw out of employment it sooner or later placed two or three others at new jobs which did not exist in the simpler life of the old régime. Some economists (the "technocrats") contended, however, that this process reached its limit about the time of the World War, when machinery overtook the supply of human needs it had to satisfy, and thereafter unemployment would increase with each new invention or improvement unless the problem were met by drastic reductions in the working week, so that decrease in work to be done need not mean decrease in the number of workers. Other economists asserted that "overproduction" merely meant the production of more goods than people could buy, not more than they needed, and declared that the whole difficulty arose from the failure to redistribute wealth so that the new goods could be purchased. Whichever theory be true, there is no question but that output, alike industrial and agricultural, overtook the market. Prices slumped to a point where profit was no longer possible. Factories discharged their hands, farmers let the fruit rot in the fields, and the tragic paradox of starving in the midst of plenty, even to all appearance *because* of plenty, perplexed a bewildered world.

The magnitude of the depression was first evident in the big Wall Street panic of October, 1929, although there had been apparent for some months before, alike in *Steps* western Europe and in the United States, a con- *downward* tracted market and an increase in unemployment. In two years about ten billion dollars worth of international trade disappeared. In such industrial nations as Britain, Germany and the United States there were millions of unemployed workingmen. Mainly agricultural nations such as France felt the reaction more slowly. Russia, with her self-contained economy, seemed busier than ever and with no particular problem of unemployment, but she had other and perhaps even more serious troubles of her own, especially in the hunger of her plundered peasants. In June, 1931, the Austrian *Kreditanstalt* threatened to collapse, and loss of confidence in the banks spread from Austria into Germany. As has been related, President Hoover intervened with his moratorium on reparations and war debts to bolster up Germany's falling credit. In September Great Britain was forced to protect her dwindling gold reserve by abandoning the gold standard. Other nations followed the British example. In 1933 banks closed all over the United States, and the richest nation on earth abandoned gold for a "managed" currency.

There were, however, many signs of recovery in 1933. Market values rose rapidly in the United States in response to President Franklin Roosevelt's program of regulating

industry and subsidizing employment. From 1932 onward
The World unemployment decreased in Great Britain. Much
Economic was hoped from an international economic con-
Conference ference, suggested by the Lausanne Conference
of 1932 that had virtually eliminated reparations. This
conference met in London in June, 1933. Unfortunately the
three chief problems of international finance — tariffs, war
debts and a stable exchange of currencies — were all left unsettled because of the domestic situation in the nations
represented at the conference. France and Italy desired to
restore the gold standard, Great Britain desired a fixed ratio
between the pound and the dollar, but the American government declared that the time had not yet come when the value
of the dollar could be stabilized. The United States also insisted that war debts be negotiated directly among the nations concerned, instead of being poured into any general
world melting pot. On the other hand Secretary Cordell
Hull, representing the American Department of State, was
unable to secure any agreement for the reduction of tariff
barriers because some European governments insisted that
no tariff reductions could be safely undertaken while currency and war debts were still unsettled. Only very minor
agreements were reached: a rather vague "tariff truce" or
understanding not to raise tariff rates competitively, and
concerted action among the silver-mining nations to keep up
the value of silver. A Wheat Conference, meeting in London
the same summer, reached a similar agreement to co-operate
in raising the price of wheat. The mountain had given birth
to a very small mouse indeed!

It was evident that the nations of the world would make
the attempt to find a way out of the depression by individual
Economic action rather than by concerted international
nationalism policy. Indeed, the whole period since 1914 has
been characterized by a tendency to make each nation a self-
contained economic unit — the policy called "autarchy."

Soviet Russia, though preaching internationalism, went farthest in that direction by placing all foreign trade in the hands of the government. The United States placed rigorous limits on foreign immigration after the war and raised high protective tariff barriers still higher. Great Britain, the one great nation without a protective tariff system, first adopted a policy of safeguarding "key industries" by tariffs, and then broadened the scope of this policy to meet competition from the countries with depreciated currency. Each nation followed a currency policy of its own; such prewar international systems as the "Latin monetary union" broke down as different countries adopted different degrees of inflation. Everywhere restrictions on foreign immigration increased. Passports, rarely required outside Russia and Turkey in 1913, became universal by 1919 and remained so thereafter, with the sole exception that a few countries suspended them to encourage the tourist trade. Extreme nationalists in Germany spoke of abandoning foreign trade altogether. Good patriots were everywhere urged to do their traveling and spending within their own countries; the slogan "buy British" kept millions of pounds within the United Kingdom. It is within bounds to say that every nation had by 1934 adopted measures of governmental regulation and control which would have been called "rank socialism" in 1913, but the socialism was national rather than international.

The usual political effect of "hard times" is to weaken the prestige of whatever government may be in power to the advantage of its opponents out of office. The *Political effects of the economic crisis* world depression after 1929 was no exception. In countries with a strong constitutional tradition, as Britain, France and the United States, it brought about a reversal of party fortunes, or at most compelled the formation of coalition ministries. In countries where the government was less surely established it produced violent revolution. In Spain a dictatorship fell and a republic rose on its ruins; in Germany and Austria the republic gave way to a dictatorship. These contrasting cases show that the revolutionary effects of economic hardship might be either radical or reactionary.

On the whole, however, the trend was toward the "right" rather than to the "left." There was just enough stirring of *Fascism* communist and socialist sentiment to stimulate *enters* governments to zealous repression, and parlia- *history* mentary democracy almost everywhere lost prestige. Yet the old-fashioned "legitimists" who looked backward with nostalgic longing to the good old days of hereditary monarchy, landowning aristocracy and established tradition, did not greatly profit from this reaction against liberalism. A new force was astir in the world, neither tradi- tionally conservative nor liberal. It resembled Bolshevism in its zeal for a "planned society" and its contemptuous in- difference to individual rights and liberties, but it differed from Bolshevism in admitting the principle of private prop- erty and in making national patriotism rather than class allegiance the mainspring of action. Till Mussolini's triumph in Italy this new force lacked a name. Since then it has been called "Fascism." In Italy, Germany and Austria it triumphed completely; in all the states of the Baltic, the Danube or the Balkans it had great political influence and widespread imitation; even in France, Britain and the other countries of western Europe it became a topic for everyone and an ideal for many. Let us therefore turn first to Italy, the country of its christening.

CHAPTER XXVI

FASCIST ITALY

ITALY emerged from the World War a victorious but disappointed nation. A large minority had opposed entrance into the war, and throughout the conflict Italy fought *The ashes of* with gallantry indeed but with something of a *" victory"* divided mind. To the average Italian the war was a "local issue," a quarrel between Austria-Hungary and Italy over the mastery of the Adriatic; it is significant that Italy waited to declare war on Germany for more than a year after she was at war with Austria-Hungary. At the Peace Conference Italy was preoccupied with her immediate territorial gains almost to the exclusion of the vaster issues of the peace, which were settled mainly by French, British and American diplomacy. Even in the limited field to which the Italian diplomats addressed themselves they were not very successful. Dalmatia (except Zara) was abandoned to the Yugoslavs and Fiume set up by the Treaty of Rapallo (1920) as an independent Free City.[1] Greece rather than Italy seemed likely to profit at Turkish expense in Asia Minor; and, while the Greeks later lost their Asiatic claims, Italy did not gain anything except the satisfaction of seeing a rival defeated. Italy obtained no colonial mandates in Africa or elsewhere. Nothing was done to promote Italy's hope for a protectorate over Albania. The national feeling roused by the war ended in disillusion, as in all other countries; but in the case of Italy, more than that of any other victor power, this was mingled with irritation.

Italian patriots said to themselves: "We have gained 9,000 square miles and about 1,600,000 new fellow citizens by the war. For this we paid over 600,000 lives and buried our im-

[1] For the Adriatic question at the Peace Conference, see Chapter XVIII.

poverished and overcrowded country under a load of debt. The unification of all Italy in the nineteenth century was bought at a much lower cost in blood and treasure! How have other nations fared, — the nations which begrudged us our small gains because some Germans live in our new Alpine territory of Alto-Adige and some Slavs in our new Adriatic territory of Venezia Giulia? Britain and France have divided the colonial spoils between them, and the United States has become the leader of world finance. Poland and Czechoslovakia, containing national minorities enormously greater than our own, have been created out of nothing; Yugoslavia and Rumania have doubled their area and population. It is evident that during the war we found not friends but rivals. It is evident also that our government has been weak and spineless; unable to secure our rights. Where may we look for a more zealous nationalism?"

Other Italians drew a different moral, dwelling not so much on the futility of the World War and the ingratitude *The swing* of Italy's allies as on the futility of all war and of *toward the* all "capitalist imperialism." Socialist and Com- *left* munist parties, though violently at odds with each other, alike made gains among the discontented workers. They did not confine their activity to parliament and the press, but shook the country with a disastrous series of political strikes. "A train might be held up because a judge who had dared to condemn a railwayman for criminal action was travelling by it... At Genoa a lightning railway strike was proclaimed because the government had dared to open a railway school for soldiers, as it was believed that troops might be employed to replace strikers." [1] Sailors, dock laborers, public utility workmen paralyzed all traffic and frightened away tourists by their frequent and unexpected strikes. In southern Italy, which was mainly rural, the peasants rose in violent insurrection against their landlords.

[1] L. Villari, *Italy* (1929), pages 151–52.

In 1920 the metal workers in the northern factory towns seized the factories and tried to run them without the participation of the owners and managers. The government let the movement run its course and fail without any forcible intervention. War veterans appearing in uniform were attacked and beaten up by gangs whose pacifism took the curious form of mob violence. In some extreme cases the red flag would be raised over a town hall by a small faction of communists, trades unionists or even anarchists. Men of property, badly frightened, were willing to join any party or any movement that would promise them peace and security.

To the government, conservatives looked in vain. All parties criticized it for weakness, but their factional wrangling made that weakness inevitable. Successive *The decline* ministries dared not crush sedition with a mailed *of parliamentary* fist, partly because it would mean the loss of *mentary* *democracy* votes and partly, to do them justice, because they thought it safer to let the fire of revolutionary sentiment burn itself out. Repression might mean revolution. So the unedifying game of party politics continued as though no great emergency confronted the nation. General disappointment at the peace treaty ousted Premier Orlando in 1919 and the pacifist Francesco Nitti succeeded him. Nitti gave way in turn to the veteran politician Giovanni Giolitti, who held office for a year. Both premiers followed a policy of renouncing foreign adventures and avoiding conflicts with radical groups within Italy, which may have been wise (for the question is arguable) but seemed to more impatient spirits sheer laziness and moral cowardice. The parliamentary scene shifted still further to the left under the mild socialism of Premier Bonomi in 1921, who was followed by Premier Facta, a rather feeble disciple of Giolitti, in 1922. Not one of these annual ministries, whatever its parliamentary majority, commanded any popular enthusiasm outside the legislative chambers. All real zeal and fire seemed to have departed from the traditional liberal groups and taken refuge with three relatively new parties: the Catholic Popular party, strong among the peasants of the south, the Communists, still inspired by the distant glow of the Russian revolution, and Benito Mussolini's nationalistic party of action, the Fascisti. By 1922 the future seemed certain to belong to some one of these parties, and the last named was already making the most rapid progress.

The new "savior of society" and restorer of authority in Italy rose from the ranks of labor and had been in his youth a *Mussolini* leader of radical socialism.[1] Benito Mussolini was born in central Italy in 1883, the son of a blacksmith father and a school-teacher mother. He was an ardent socialist of the "syndicalist" type, urging "direct action" by the workers and attracting the alarmed attention of the police in France, Switzerland, Austria and Italy. He was jailed for fomenting a strike in protest against the Tripolitan war of 1911. In 1912 he became editor of *Avanti!*, the official organ of the Socialist party. Had it not been for the war he might have remained a revolutionist "of the left" to the end of his career. But the prospect of a life-and-death struggle with Italy's ancient oppressor Austria-Hungary stirred him as the petty war with Turkey had not. He became an enthusiastic interventionist, broke with his party, left the *Avanti!* for a new personal journal *Il Popolo d'Italia*. In the war he served bravely and was wounded. After the armistice he turned his attention to organizing the war veterans for patriotic action. In March, 1919, he formed a League (*Fascio*) of combatants. Its program was still radical, with a tinge of socialism, but at the same time nationalistic; it advocated adult suffrage, proportional representation, aboli-

[1] This, though paradoxical, is not at all uncommon in history; the man whom "all the nation cannot rule" often becomes the man who rules all the nation. Several of the twentieth-century crop of dictators, such as Mussolini and Hitler, began in humble life with radical views, and in parliamentary governments the most resolute upholders of authority frequently began as socialists or extreme radicals — Clemenceau, Briand and Millerand in France are typical cases.

tion of the Senate, an eight-hour working day, heavy taxation of the wealthy, participation by the workers in the control of industry. Mussolini and his followers applauded the wild attempt of the poet D'Annunzio to seize Fiume from Yugoslavia by armed force, in defiance not only of the other powers of Europe but of the official Italian government itself.

To the impatient young veterans of the recent war Mussolini's Fascisti seemed the redemption of Italy. Whether they were classified as "radical" or "reactionary" *The "black shirts"* they did not seem to know — or care! Let the gray old men in parliament discuss such matters; this new movement stood outside all the old classifications and scorned them. The Fascisti were given a semimilitary organization, they wore a uniform (the famous black shirt),[1] were organized into "squads," saluted their leaders, and had for an emblem the *fasces* or rods which, bound about the lictor's ax, were the symbols of authority in ancient Rome. While rather vague as to what they did want, they were very clear as to what they did not want — cosmopolitan communism with its antinational tendencies. So Mussolini's *squadristi* fought communism, combating lawless anarchy by lawless repression. When the Communists beat up a war veteran, the Fascists replied by beating up a Communist; when the Communists burned a town hall, the Fascists burned the Communist headquarters. Sometimes they would seize a radical orator, shave his head and paint the bald spot with the national colors, or pretend that an opponent was "sick" and force him to swallow a bottle of castor oil. In this guerrilla warfare of the parties several hundred persons were killed on both sides.

The motives and elements that went to make up Fascism were extraordinarily complex. Some were *arditi* (shock

---

[1] Said to have been adapted from war veterans, who had followed D'Annunzio in his attack on Fiume, but they seem reminiscent, at least, of Garibaldi's "red shirt" volunteers.

troops) of the war, too restless to settle down to civilian life and genuinely horrified at the unpatriotic Communists. *Impulses behind Fascism* Some were ultra-nationalists who were disgusted at the meagerness of Italy's gains from the war. Some were Socialists who, like Mussolini himself, had deserted the party for opposing entrance into the war. Some were embittered and impoverished recruits from the lower middle classes, the men whose small salaries had been reduced in buying power by the inflated currency and extravagant expenditures of the government.[1] Some were hero worshipers, attracted away from the somewhat flighty and fanciful D'Annunzio by the sturdier personality of Mussolini. An increasing number as time went on were landowners, factory owners, conservatives and frightened bourgeoisie who had at first held aloof from Fascism, remembering Mussolini's radical antecedents, but eventually clung to it as the last barrier against Bolshevism. A very picturesque element was F. T. Marinetti's artistic clique, the "Futurists," who rejoiced in Fascism as "a box of dynamite for all the venerated ruins" and especially "archeology, academicism, senility, quietism, poltroonery, pacifism, pessimism, nostalgia, sentimentalism, erotic obsession and the tourist industry." [2] This was merely a rather hysterical way of saying that Italy had spent too much time dreaming of the past and should turn to a life of activity. A student song "Youth" (*Giovinezza*) became the party anthem. "All Italy is but twenty years old today" declared Mussolini.

The Fascisti organized as a political party, though their

---

[1] Some writers represent Fascism in Italy and National Socialism in Germany as merely a lower middle-class reaction against proletarian Communism and upper-class capitalism. This element is important but covers only one aspect of the movement.

[2] See H. W. Schneider, *Making the Fascist State* (1928), pages 233-34. Using American terminology, Professor Spencer has very aptly hit off certain aspects of the Fascist movement: "They were the methods of a vigilance committee, with here and there a touch of the Boy Scouts and of the Ku Klux Klan," H. R. Spencer, *Government and Politics of Italy* (1932), page 85.

most consistent principle was the repudiation of "Parliamentarianism" and the old party game. In *The "march*
1919 Mussolini's electoral list at Milan obtained *on Rome,"*
only four thousand votes, but in the elections of *1922*
1921 thirty-five Fascists were elected to the Chamber of
Deputies, though — a characteristic touch! — several could
not take their seats because they were not yet thirty years
old as the constitution prescribed. Though the Communist
outrages had subsided to some extent, the fear they caused
tended to increase and reached a climax when in August, 1922,
a general strike was proclaimed by the Labor Alliance with
the avowed object of forcing the government to suppress the
Fascisti. The Fascisti responded by ousting radical municipal administrations and themselves seizing all strategic
positions — government offices, postoffices, electric power
plants and railroad stations. Premier Facta after long weeks
of irresolution asked King Victor Emmanuel to proclaim
martial law against the Fascisti. But Mussolini had just repudiated republicanism, and the King hoped that "the
Leader" (*Il Duce*) in his new phase would be a bulwark of law
and order. Armies of black shirts converged on the capital.
It was no revolution but an orderly procession of victory, for
the King had given way and the terrified Chamber of Deputies dared do nothing. By the end of October the crisis
had ended. Mussolini was invited to become Prime Minister
at the head of a coalition government.

Those who expected Mussolini, like so many extreme
popular leaders, to become tame and conventional in office
were doomed to disappointment. It is true that *Premier*
he welcomed into his cabinet representatives of *against*
several other parties, the Nationalists, the clerical *Parliament*
Popular party, the Liberals and Democrats, even moderate
Socialists. But he himself took the key positions, the premiership and the portfolios of the Interior and Foreign Affairs. To the Chamber of Deputies he said defiantly, "Revo-

lution has its rights... I am not going — so far as I can help it — to govern against the Chamber, but the Chamber must understand the peculiar position it is in, which may entail its dissolution in two days or in two years." To the Senate he was more respectful; that appointed chamber of distinguished elderly men offered less potential opposition to his plans. Mussolini abandoned his earlier plan of abolishing the Senate and treated it with more consideration than any other part of the old political machinery. The Chamber of Deputies worried him; he was the head of the government and yet his party was in a minority. So one of his first tasks was to secure the passing of a new electoral law. Proportional representation, introduced after the war, was retained but with the new proviso that any party obtaining a *plurality*, even if not an absolute majority, provided it had at least a fourth of the entire vote of the nation, would automatically obtain two-thirds of the seats in the Chamber. The other third would be divided among the lesser parties. This was drastic medicine indeed for the disease of factionalism which had rendered ministries unstable in the past! Of course Mussolini was confident, and justly, that no other party would outvote his at the polls if a new election were held. To make assurance doubly sure he placed some friendly and co-operative men from other parties on his own list. The election of 1924 resulted as was expected; the Fascist "national list" with over four million popular votes rode triumphantly into power.

Only one serious check did Mussolini meet in his triumphant career after the march on Rome, and this came from *The Matteotti crisis, 1924* over-zealous fellow partisans. A bitter critic of the new régime, the Socialist Giacomo Matteotti, was murdered shortly after the new Chamber met. The murderers were certainly under the belief that they were doing *Il Duce* a service, and it was easy for embittered opponents to believe that they were acting under orders.[1] Mussolini, of course, disavowed the crime, and he took stern measures to put down the more lawless "squadrists" who were discrediting his party; he even dismissed from office Fascisti whom the murdered Matteotti had accused of graft. But the parliamentary opposition was not placated. Several of the more extreme parties withdrew from the Chamber and organized a meeting of protest on the Aventine Hill; hence the schismatic groups were called the "Aventine Secession." At first Mussolini treated the movement with contempt, then he became irritated and finally declared that by prolonged abstention the deputies had vacated their seats and no longer held any parliamentary mandate.

Step by step, with crafty deliberation, the forms of parliamentary democracy were now cast off. Non-Fascist members of the government were forced to resign and their places taken by Mussolini himself who at one time held eight cabinet offices. Later he *Evolution of the dictatorship* distributed the portfolios among his own partisans. The Catholic Popular party had to some extent worked in cooperation with the Fascist régime (though its radical left wing had approached the Socialists) but it was gradually stripped of power. The conservative Nationalists were absorbed by the more popular Fascists. The Liberals, Democrats and Socialists had been shipwrecked on the Aventine Hill. The Communists were openly outlawed. Soon Mussolini declared that "electionism" had come to an end; there was no need in Italy for any party save the Fascisti. Local self-government was completely eliminated in 1926 by legislation placing each municipality under an appointed city manager or *podestà*. After the Matteotti crisis all anti-Fascist newspapers were suppressed. Some were confiscated, some terrorized, some quietly bought up. To quote an ardent champion of Fascism, "There is no regular censorship

[1] In 1926 the murderers were tried and given light sentences.

of the press... but the editors do not publish attacks on the government because they know if they did the issue of the paper would be confiscated." [1] In 1925 a special law made the Premier independent of any parliamentary majority and responsible to the King alone. Public officials were forbidden to belong to secret societies; this law was directed against the Freemasons chiefly, who had been a great political power in Italy, and Freemasons, as well as Communists, suffered from Fascist mob violence. By a law of 1926, Italian emigrants might be deprived of citizenship and their property confiscated if guilty of any act which might bring "harm to Italian interests." This measure was aimed at the anti-Fascist exiles who were conducting a violent campaign of criticism beyond the frontier. By 1926 Italy was as absolutely under the rule of Mussolini as France had ever been under the rule of Napoleon Bonaparte or his nephew. [2]

One of the contentions of Fascism is that the nation must override not only all parties but also all classes. The class *The "Corporate State"* war must be brought to an end, not by a decisive victory for either employers or employed but by the subordination of both to the general welfare. For this purpose a modernization of a very successful medieval institution — the gild — was proposed. Local organizations recognized by the State are termed "syndicates"; these are united together into "confederations." Thirteen such confederations were recognized; an employers' and a workers' confederation respectively in industry, banking, commerce, agriculture, sea and air transport, and land transport, the thirteenth consisting of "independent artists, artisans and professional men." The syndicates can make binding contracts with each other and represent all workers and employers in their line of activity whether they are or wish

---

[1] Villari, *Italy*, page 200.

[2] Count Sforza, perhaps the ablest Italian critic of Fascism, declared that "Almost all the present laws of the Fascist régime are reproductions of measures invented by the government of Napoleon III between 1852 and 1867."

to be members of the syndicate or not.   Strikes and lockouts are forbidden, and if the syndicates and confederations fail to bring about a settlement Labor Courts of Appeal may give a final award.   Through the Ministry of Corporations and the National Council of Corporations the confederations are kept in close touch with the State.   The Fascist "corporate State" might in fact be termed "syndicalism turned inside out."   The old syndicalism preached by the French radical philosopher Georges Sorel, whom Mussolini had carefully studied and much admired, was a proposal for the capture of industry by large workingmen's gilds or syndicates, independent of the State; as "tamed" by Mussolini it became a method of subordinating labor organizations (and capitalist organizations as well) to the supreme authority of the State.

The "corporate State" was to be such on its political as well as its economic side.   For this purpose the extraordinary step was taken of making the Grand Council of *The Grand* Fascism, a sort of national committee of the *Council of* Fascist party, an organ of national government. *Fascism* Even Soviet Russia had not carried the Communist Political Bureau so directly and formally into the constitution.   In 1928 the Grand Council was definitely organized by law.   It was to contain three classes of members: (1) life members, including Mussolini himself, the four Fascisti who led the "march on Rome," cabinet members of long service and party secretaries; (2) members *ex officio*, including the current cabinet ministers and a variety of other high officials; (3) members appointed for meritorious services to the party or the State.   The Council was to guarantee the new constitution and consider questions relating to the succession to the throne, the still more important succession to the Premiership, the relations and powers of the organs of government, the relations between Church and State, and treaties involving a change of national territory.

The most extraordinary power conferred on this party

council was that of virtually designating the members of the

The new Chamber of Deputies, 1928 Chamber of Deputies! No longer were there to be any parties or real elections in Italy but there was still a Chamber, reduced to four hundred members, selected by a threefold process. First, the "confederations of syndicates" nominate 800 candidates, and certain other groups (schools, civil servants, war veterans, academies, etc.) 200 more. The Grand Council of Fascism then takes this list, reduces it to 400 and revises it at will, dropping names or even adding others. Finally, the whole list is placed before the electorate as a unit for complete acceptance or rejection. The electorate itself is limited, though not seriously, by a slight property qualification. In the most unlikely event of a complete rejection by the voters of the list prepared by the Grand Council of Fascism, and only in such an event, other lists might be presented to the voters. Over ninety-eight per cent of those who voted approved the Fascist list.[1]

Politically all Italy had become an army with Benito Mussolini as its commander-in-chief. To summarize the

The "totalitarian State" new constitution, everything centered around Mussolini, as Premier, Head of the State and Leader of the Fascist Party. He was legally responsible to the King alone. Directly or indirectly he selected the members of the Grand Council of Fascism. The Grand Council in turn selected (with some regard to the advice of the employers and workers in the Fascist syndicates) the Chamber of Deputies, subject to ratification by popular plebiscite. He filled vacancies as they arose in the Senate. He nominated, indirectly in some cases, practically every national, provincial and local official. Only the Fascist party was allowed to exist; no opposition press or organization was tolerated. The civil service was entirely Fascist — or discreetly silent! Trades unions had been merged into

[1] About ten per cent of those eligible failed to vote.

the new Fascist syndicates.   Outspoken opponents were imprisoned on certain small islands designated for the purpose,
or were refugees abroad.   Besides the army and the police,
both loyal to the new régime, there was a "militia" of about
a million black-shirted Fascisti, no longer so disorderly as to
be a danger or embarrassment to their leader.   New recruits
for that force were provided by organizations for children
and young people: the *Balilla* for boys under fourteen, the
Avanguardia for youths from fourteen to eighteen, and similar organizations for women and girls.   Italy, in a common
phrase, had become "totalitarian"; that is to say, no organization existed within it which had not been brought into
definite subordination to the government.

Fascism boasts of being a party of action rather than a
party of theory and Mussolini has never been worried by the
marked inconsistency of some of his speeches or *Fascist*
even of his policies.   He was a pragmatist and *principles*
opportunist, improvising his program to meet each new
emergency; in this respect his dictatorship differed from that
of Lenin and Stalin in Russia, whose absolute power was
qualified by the expectation of their followers that they would
never do anything in violation of the dogmas of Karl Marx.
So far as Fascism has had any consistent ideal, it is that of
Italian nationalism.   The nation must be lifted incomparably above all differences of class, party, creed or individual
interests.   The great mistake of the liberals, say the Fascists,
was in assuming that society was merely an aggregate of individuals whose "rights" were the chief concern of government; the great mistake of democracy was in substituting
the opinion of the common man for the expert leadership of
trained minds; the great mistake of the socialists was in ele-
vating class above national interests.   In its worship of authority, discipline and devotion to the State, Fascism deliberately copies ancient Rome; as Alfredo Rocco, Minister
of Justice, put the matter when accused of "going back to

the Middle Ages" of political despotism: "If Fascism can be said to look back at all it is rather in the direction of ancient Rome whose social and political traditions at the distance of fifteen centuries are being revived by Fascist Italy." In 1923 Mussolini flung defiance at his liberal critics in most uncompromising fashion: "Men are perhaps tired of liberty... For the youth that is intrepid, restless and hardy ... there are other words of greater power, order, hierarchy, discipline... Fascism knows no idols and worships no fetishes; it has already passed over and if necessary will once more pass over the more or less putrescent corpse of the Goddess of Liberty." Other Fascists, such as Giovanni Gentile, wincing from this blunt conclusion, assert that only in the subordination of the individual to the social organism can "true liberty" be found.[1]

Having no particular program of reforms to which they were irrevocably wedded, the Fascists devoted their main *Early Fas-* attention to a general "tidying up" of Italy. *cist achieve-* Law and order were restored, effectively if some*ments* times rather lawlessly. The Mafia of Sicily, the Camorra of Naples and other gangster associations of the south were crushed more completely than by any previous government. The train service was restored, not only to normal condition, but improved beyond the best standards of the past. Tourists were delighted to note the clean,

---

[1] Perhaps it is not very profitable to trace the theoretical roots of a non-theoretical movement, but Mussolini and other Fascists claim a varied parentage for Fascist ideas. Machiavelli, because he advocated Italian unity and elevated the welfare of the State above moral considerations, is the most frequently mentioned. Sorel, the French syndicalist, contributed to the theory of violent "direct action" and "corporate" economic organization. The American philosopher William James has been cited because of his "pragmatic" viewpoint: the truth is what proves true in practise. Mazzini's insistence on "duty" as a counterweight to "rights" is often commended. Nietzsche's exaltation of the strenuous life and the mystical virtues of war attracts some. Of course all famous Italian patriots and nationalists from Dante to D'Annunzio are praised, and even the liberals among them (as Cavour, Mazzini, Garibaldi) are usually forgiven. That some of these men would be rather surprised to find themselves in each other's company — or in Mussolini's — does not matter; Fascism is eclectic enough to take what it wants from each philosophy and discard the rest.

orderly streets, the absence of begging (now severely repressed) and the careful standardization of the tipping
system into a fixed service charge. Of course a nation cannot be run for the sake of casual foreign visitors, but Mussolini was mindful of the fact that tourism was for Italy one of
her major industries. The budget was severly trimmed,
though the economies obtained by dismissing superfluous
civil servants were counterbalanced by heavy expenditures
on public works and military defenses. The lira was stabilized at about nineteen to the dollar; a point rather above the
French franc and, in the opinion of some of Mussolini's critics, higher than Italian conditions warranted. A very advantageous debt settlement was negotiated with the United
States. Excavations of Roman ruins were undertaken on a
large scale, more from patriotic sentiment than scientific
curiosity. In the city of Rome the government launched a
truly magnificent building program, as if Mussolini (like another Augustus) would transform a city of brick into a city
of marble.

The Fascisti also turned their attention, pluckily if not
with complete success, to the deeper economic problems of
Italy. They discouraged both emigration and *Fascist*
birth control on the ground that Italy "needed *economic*
all her sons" and could support ten or twenty *policy*
million more even within her present too narrow boundaries.[1]
They reclaimed extensive marshlands around Rome. In so
doing they were only continuing a policy of land restoration
already well begun in the days of the liberal monarchy in
several parts of Italy, but to the task they brought a concentrated enthusiasm which produced striking results. They
fostered industrial expansion in much the same spirit as
the Russian Bolsheviki, to transform a mainly agricultural
country, dependent on foreign manufactures, into a self-de-

[1] In any case the limitation of immigration to the United States by postwar
legislation closed Italy's most important outlet.

pendent nation with farm and factory in due balance with each other. They claimed to have solved the labor problem by the incorporation of labor and capital into State-directed confederations of syndicates; but trades unionists in other countries viewed askance a system which forbade strikes and international labor unions and gave a small number of capitalists equal political power with a much larger number of workers, even assuming that the right to make recommendations to the Grand Fascist Council can be called "political power." [1]   The depression revived the old problem of unemployment, which the government tried to combat by tax-supported public works.   In nearly every way modern Italy is a brisker, more industrious country than before Mussolini took power, with fewer evidences of poverty on the surface, but there is a wide difference of opinion as to whether the general standard of living has actually risen.   Wages remained low and prices and taxes relatively high.   After all, nature has imposed severe limitations on Italy which no government can wholly overcome.

Mussolini was aware of these limits, but his answer was not that Italy should limit either her numbers or her ambi-*Fascist im-* tions but on the contrary she should expand.
perialism   He proclaimed that the new Italy, like ancient Rome, should be an imperialistic and conquering power, though his glittering speeches were usually vague on such essential points as whether Italy's conquests were to be commercial or political, whether they could be obtained peaceably or only through war, and in what directions they should lie.   His most concrete statement was that Italy must expand not towards western Europe but south and east, evidently with a view to northern Africa and western Asia. He declared that when Italy's forty millions had increased

---

[1] It is significant that the Grand Council further tipped the balance in favor of capital by selecting more candidates for the Chamber of Deputies from the employers' lists than from the workers'.   For statistics on this point, see Spencer, *Government and Politics of Italy*, pages 174–77.

to sixty millions the other powers would be forced to grant Italy an adequate colonial empire. His actual acquisitions were few enough. Fiume was acquired in 1924, a gain chiefly of sentimental importance. The Treaty of Tirana in 1926 strengthened Italian influence in Albania. Agreements with France and Britain slightly enlarged Libya (Tripoli) and Italian Somaliland.[1] Within Italy he resolutely repressed the Slavic and German minorities in the newly acquired provinces, thereby more than once almost coming to blows with Yugoslavia and Austria. Corfu, occupied in 1923 to punish Greek hostility, was abandoned under pressure of the League of Nations and the other Great Powers; but under the Treaty of Lausanne (1923) Italy still holds Greek-speaking islands conquered from Turkey.

Since the Fascisti came into office partly as a reaction from the conciliatory "good European" foreign policy of the Liberals, all the world expected Mussolini to as- *Italian foreign policy* sume a most truculent attitude in dealing with *eign policy* other nations. In his earlier phase he certainly lived up to Europe's fears, in words if not in deeds. Alone among the prominent postwar statesmen of Europe he openly praised war, conquest and military glory. Not even Wilhelm II in his palmiest days ever "rattled the saber" or "shook the mailed fist" so frequently. He adhered to the League of Nations, the Locarno Pact, the Peace Pact of Paris and took part in international economic and disarmament conferences, but in his speeches at home he professed good-natured contempt for all these scraps of paper. Most alarming of all were his frequent appeals to the "black shirts" to be prepared for anything that might happen, as though some vague but terrible emergency was in sight. These bellicose gestures, perhaps intended to please the chauvinists within his own following, did a great deal of harm. In particular they

[1] In 1935 France made still further concessions to Italy in Africa, in order to ensure Italian co-operation in European diplomatic problems.

alarmed France and led to a marked estrangement between the Latin powers. The French knew that "a new Rome, mistress of the Mediterranean" would find her chief rival in France, and there were further causes of friction in the hospitality granted on French soil to anti-Fascist refugees, French friendship for Yugoslavia and the French possession of Tunis, most coveted of north African colonies. With Yugoslavia relations were usually hostile, in spite of formal treaties of friendship. The forcible "Italianizing" of the 250,000 German-speaking inhabitants of Alto-Adige (the new name for southern Tirol) provoked protests not only from Austria but even from more distant Germany.

But Mussolini's actual policy was less alarming than his speeches. He accepted a peaceful solution of the Corfu crisis, he negotiated pacts of friendship and security with many European states, he came to a peaceful understanding with France in 1928 over the administration of Tangier, the "free city" of Morocco. In 1933 he made a contribution of his own to the network of security agreements in Europe by proposing the "Four Power Pact" for peaceful diplomatic co-operation of Germany, France, Britain and Italy over a ten-year period. He advocated a general reduction or cancellation of reparations and war debts and favored a limitation of armaments, though insisting on Italy's right to an army and navy comparable with that of other Great Powers, especially naval equality with France in the Mediterranean. Perhaps as a check on France, perhaps because of hostility to Yugoslavia, Mussolini cultivated the good will of Hungary, Bulgaria and Turkey, former enemy states, and advocated in general terms a moderate revision of the peace treaties. When Germany passed into the hands of the Nazis, he extended a protecting hand over Austria to prevent an *Anschluss* which would bring Germany down to the Italian frontier. On the whole, he followed a balance of power policy, sometimes siding with

Tendency towards conciliation

France and sometimes with Germany, so that neither country could safely ignore Italian friendship. With Britain, Italy has continued to have generally cordial relations.

Certainly Mussolini's most brilliant diplomatic triumph was the Lateran Accord of 1929, ending the "Roman question" which had plagued the Kingdom of Italy *Peace with* since 1870. The successive Popes, indignant at *the Papacy* the transformation of Rome from the Papal to the national capital, had steadfastly refused the guarantees of diplomatic freedom and the annual subsidy offered by the Kingdom, and demanded, if not the whole city of Rome, at least an international guarantee of Papal independence. Fear of foreign interference in what Italy regarded as a purely national question estranged Italy for many years from France and repeatedly embarrassed both the Papacy and the Kingdom during the World War. Mussolini hoped to strengthen his régime by consolidating behind it the moral authority of the Church and the political support of the former members of the clerical Popular party. Like Napoleon Bonaparte, Mussolini passed from a personal agnosticism to a political Catholicism. He no longer criticized the Church, as a creed or as an institution, he encouraged religious teaching in the schools, he prosecuted and finally dissolved the anti-clerical Freemasons. Finally, after many months of negotiation, an agreement was signed at the Lateran Palace on February 11, 1929. Pope Pius XI formally recognized the legality of the Kingdom of Italy with Rome as its capital and abandoned the attitude of protest which he and his predecessors had maintained. On the other hand, the immediate premises of the Papal palace were set aside as "Vatican City," an independent sovereign State, legally outside the bounds of Italy, empowered to coin money, issue stamps, give and receive ambassadors and live under its own laws. About one hundred acres in extent, with a population consisting mainly of Roman Catholic clergy and officials, Vatican City is the smallest sovereignty on earth.

Other parts of the agreement recognized the canon law, the official decrees of the Church, as binding in all matters ecclesiastical. Religious ceremony constituted a complete marriage; the civil ceremony was made optional. Religious instruction was introduced into public secondary schools. A financial indemnity was offered and accepted. Certain points of friction developed, as was inevitable. Mussolini forced the dissolution of the Catholic Boy Scouts, to merge them in his own Fascist organization the *Balilla*, and suppressed all Catholic societies which had a political color. Pius XI on several occasions denounced the exaltation of the State above the Church in terms that were clearly applicable to Fascist policy. But on the whole Mussolini seems to have handled religious susceptibilities much more tactfully than his fellow dictators, especially Stalin and Hitler.

The peculiar interest of the Fascist experiment in Italy lay not in its uniqueness but, on the contrary, as the clearest

The European trend to dictatorship

individual instance of a general trend of the times. There seems every probability that when the generation succeeding the World War has in the course of time dwindled to a paragraph in the textbooks, it will bear some such label as "The Age of Dictatorships," just as the period from 1740 to 1789 is often called "The Age of the Enlightened Despots." Before the World War hardly anyone seems to have anticipated this development;[1] the political fight in each country seemed to lie, as Thomas Jefferson had phrased it, between "liberals and serviles, Whigs and Tories, aristocrats and democrats." But the new dictators were as little to be identified with old-fashioned aristocracy as with democracy. The dictator may come from any walk of life with no passport except his energy and initiative. Moreover, he usually rides into power on the crest of a great wave of popular enthusiasm, and the

[1] A possible exception is Jack London's *The Iron Heel*, a Socialist's fantastic nightmare of a capitalist dictatorship.

"general will" can be as readily embodied in a single man
as in a group of representatives. Where dictatorship parts
company from democracy is less the way in which the dictator obtains power than in the way he retains it. Unlike a
mere elected magistrate, he need not keep within the limits
of a formal constitution or submit his claim to periodic free
elections. During and since the World War every government on earth has been termed a "dictatorship" by its enemies and its less judicious friends, and this is true if we mean
merely that every government has been compelled to assume
unusual powers to meet exceptional emergencies. But it is
more useful to reserve the term for those executives who
have placed themselves above the laws and beyond the control of the voters.

Even in this limited sense, dictatorships were established
at one time or another in the two decades following the outbreak of the war in Russia, Poland, Austria, *Forms of*
Hungary, Germany, Italy, Spain, Portugal, *dictatorship*
Turkey and all the Balkan and Baltic States, though in some
cases the régime was of brief duration. Outside Europe,
China and practically all the nations of Latin America have
had recent dictatorships. European dictatorships took
many forms, — radical in Soviet Russia, conservative or reactionary in many other countries. The dictator might be
a popular general, as in Turkey, Poland and Spain; or a civilian Prime Minister, as in Italy, Germany and Austria; or
a monarch, reviving absolutism for a temporary purpose, as
King Alexander of Yugoslavia; or a party leader, as in Russia. Title and office mattered nothing, the actual power
alone was significant. We cannot even say that the dictator
was always a single individual. Hungary was ruled for years
by a working alliance of Regent Horthy and Premier Bethlen, and in the short interval between the death of Lenin and
the supremacy of Stalin the Russian dictatorship was shared
by about half a dozen Communist party managers.

Perhaps the most useful classification of dictatorships is

not the conventional division into capitalist or socialist,
"Organic" radical or conservative, monarchist or republican,
dictator- and the like, but a discrimination between the
ships merely political controls, which left the social
life of the nation little changed, and the "organic" dictatorships which aimed to incorporate all activities and institutions of the nation.   The Bolsheviki in Russia, the Fascisti
in Italy and the Nazis in Germany were of the latter type.
In these organic dictatorships all parties were abolished except one, and that party was identified with the State itself;
and the symbols of party allegiance (the hammer and sickle
in Russia, the *fasces* in Italy, the swastika or hooked cross
in Germany) appeared on national banners.   In each case
the party established a semimilitary militia with special
privileges and a rigidly limited membership.   In each case
the government assumed complete control and direction —
not the mere negative censorship which all dictatorships
employ — of the press, the radio, the motion pictures, the
theater, public meetings and assemblies and all other agencies
of discussion and propaganda.   In each case the trades unions
and other voluntary economic associations were merged
into State-directed agencies; though Germany and Italy,
unlike Russia, did not abolish the private business unit —
shop, factory or farm.   In each case the schools and universities became agencies of party indoctrination, the church
was either enlisted or repressed, and special organizations
created to train the young for party service.   The State was
to be "corporate," "totalitarian," absolute, and the individual reduced to a mere cell in the social organism, and,
strangest of all, the force relied on to produce this result was
the devoted enthusiasm of very young men, the same sort of
young men who a hundred years ago would have been filled
with the new wine of romantic liberalism, shouting with
Victor Hugo and Heinrich Heine for free speech, a free press,
universal suffrage and personal liberty.   Has anything else
as strange happened in our strange time?

CHAPTER XXVII

GERMANY FROM DEMOCRACY TO NATIONAL SOCIALISM

NOTHING better has been said on the significance of the post-war developments in Germany than the comment of that alert, if often irritable, observer of world affairs, *Europe's* H. G. Wells: "War and disaster could not alter *central* the fact that the backbone of Europe, the most *problem* skilled, industrious, teachable and intelligent block of its population, spoke and thought German. What might happen to it, what would happen to it, should have been the primary preoccupation of every intelligent statesman. For if Germany had gone right everything would have gone right." [1] This was true from the time when Bismarck, by building and defending united Germany, became the diplomatic dictator of Europe; it was true when the World War raged and turned around Germany as a pivot; it remained none the less true after the war. Defeated and in part disarmed, Germany still numbered over sixty millions, still had the largest mineral wealth on the continent and still remained the geographical heart of Europe.

In Germany as in Italy the first effect of the war was to strengthen the forces of radicalism and socialism. Indeed, the leftward swing was much stronger in the *The demo-* former country because the people could reproach *cratic move-* their rulers with leading them not to a barren *ment in* victory but to a ruinous defeat. For months the *Germany* world waited in breathless anxiety lest a "Soviet Germany" bring Bolshevism westward to the Rhine. But the innate orderliness of the most docile of all European peoples, the strength and discipline of the propertied classes (much

[1] H. G. Wells, *The Shape of Things to Come* (1933), page 179.

larger and more competent than in prewar Russia) and the moderation of the majority of the Socialist leaders themselves averted this possibility.[1] Not communism but liberal democracy, tinged faintly pink with a very mild admixture of socialism, was the "ideal in office" when the new constitution was written at Weimar. The revolutionists of 1848 were about to be justified by their grandchildren.

Like so many of the liberal charters of new States written immediately after the World War, the German constitution *The Weimar* has faded into the past tense, and it is important *constitution* chiefly as an historical monument of Germany's solitary decade of democracy. The German Republic retained the old title of *Reich*, which is usually translated "Empire," but may with equal correctness be taken to signify "realm," "commonwealth" or simply "nation." The Reich was divided into *Länder* (Lands), successors of the old Kingdoms, Duchies, Principalities and Free Cities. In the main they retained their old boundaries; all the projects to divide the huge bulk of Prussia among several political units coming to nothing, though it was admittedly anomalous in a federal Republic for a single State to be larger than all the rest combined. The most important territorial change within the nation was the merging of the lesser Saxon Duchies into the single Land of Thuringia. The power of the Federal Government was greater than under the old Empire, a fact which caused much discontent in Bavaria, where many mourned the loss of the old special State privileges (*Sonderrechte*), and dismay in certain parties in France who vainly hoped for a revival of State particularism after the war. The Reich had exclusive authority over foreign and colonial affairs, immigration, national defense, currency, tariffs, posts, telegraphs and telephones. It shared with the Lands the right also to legislate respecting citizenship, the civil and criminal code, judicial procedure, poor relief, public health,

[1] For the German revolution prior to the Weimar constitution, see Chapter XVII.

protection of labor, socialization of industry and natural resources, commercial laws, insurance, industrial regulation, shipping, railways and traffic routes generally. Where laws conflicted, federal law prevailed over the local law.

The Reichstag was henceforth to be elected by equal suffrage of men and women on the principle of proportional representation each four years, or oftener if the *The legis-* President should dissolve it before the full term *lative power* expired. The Chancellor and other ministers were made responsible to it, and thus Germany became a "parliamentary" country. The upper house or Reichsrat represented the people, whereas the old Bundesrat had represented the ruling princes. Each Land had a vote in the Reichsrat, with an additional member for each million of population, save that no Land (a provision aimed at Prussia) might have more than two-fifths of the whole. The Lands were represented by members of their own governments, but they were not bound by diplomatic instructions nor forced to vote as a unit as in the old Bundesrat. Laws passed by the Reichstag and rejected by the upper house must be either repassed by a two-thirds majority or submitted to popular referendum. The referendum might also be invoked on the initiative of the President, or of one-third of the Reichstag together with a petition of one-twentieth of the voters, or by petition of one-tenth of the voters. Constitutional amendments might be carried by a two-thirds vote of both houses or by an absolute majority of those entitled to vote on referendum.

Unlike most of the new democracies, which followed the French system of legislative election of the President, Germany adopted the American plan of popular *The execu-* election without, however, the encumbrance of *tive power* an electoral college. The President was to hold office for seven years, and might be deposed by a vote of the Reichstag confirmed by a referendum. The President appointed

the Chancellor and other ministers but was required to select
men possessing the confidence of the Reichstag. On the
whole the German President had a less powerful position
than the American, because he was constrained to select the
cabinet desired by the Reichstag, but he was more powerful
than the French President, in fact if not in law, because in a
crisis he could appeal to his mandate directly from the people.

The bill of rights was very elaborate and inclusive, containing not only the conventional declarations of equal
Other fea- rights for all creeds and classes, freedom of
tures of the opinion in speech and press, and guarantees
constitution against judicial oppression, but laying down
general philosophical principles to guide legislation. Marriage was declared to be under the special protection of the
constitution, motherhood to have a claim on the care of the
State, youth to be protected against exploitation, illegitimate
children to have proper conditions for their upbringing.
There was to be no state church, each religious communion
might live freely under its own regulations, and religious
teaching was permitted to continue as an optional form of
instruction even in public schools (the attitude of the Catholic Center party made impossible any anti-clerical legislation). Economic freedom was proclaimed, subject to considerations of the social welfare. Land and industries might
be purchased by the government if due compensation were
paid. Landed estates might be subdivided, and entail was
forbidden. The government was required to maintain a
system of national insurance "against the economic effects
of age, debilities and the vicissitudes of life." The rights of
labor organizations were guaranteed, and representative
Workers' Councils provided. A National Economic Council
was constituted with somewhat vaguely defined powers; in
practise it became a mere advisory body on economic legislation. In place of the old bewildering variety of state constitutions, the eighteen Lands (later reduced to seventeen)

had a uniform system of single chambered legislatures elected in the same way as the national Reichstag. Each had a responsible ministry, but no ruler, governor or state president.

Considered in all its aspects, the Weimar constitution was probably the most liberal one in the world. It eliminated the Crown, Lords and established Church which *"The good colored, if they did not check, British democracy. die young"* It differed from the French constitution and most of the constitutions of the Baltic, Danubian and Balkan democracies in making frequent use of the popular referendum; in this respect it resembled the Swiss constitution, but it went beyond Swiss practise in according equal political rights to women. It was more easily amended and less complicated with "checks and balances" than the American constitution. The framework and theory of the document was due largely to the Democratic party, the most radical of the non-Socialist groups; [1] the provisions protecting church property and church schools show Catholic influence; the provisions for Workers' Councils and the right to socialize industry by legislative action were put in to please the Socialists. The machinery set up by the constitution was in itself simple and practical; the aspirations embodied in the bill of rights idealistic, almost millennial. Unfortunately the new democracy came to birth in an evil hour of poverty, unrest and national humiliation and it never became endeared to the people at large. Many of its provisions never really got off the paper on which they were written, and the clause most appealed to in practise was Article 48, empowering the President in case of national danger to suspend the rights of free speech, free press, public meeting, political organization and immunity from arbitrary arrest, search and seizure.

The so-called Weimar coalition of Democrats, Catholic "Centrists" and Social Democrats or moderate Socialists,

[1] Hugo Preuss was the most influential individual architect of the constitution.

who shared responsibility for the new constitution, had to
Enemies of face opposition from both right and left. Some
the young of these opponents were willing to enter the
republic constitutional arena and accept the republic pro-
visionally until they could convert the public to their own
views. Such were the radical or Independent Socialists, on
the one side, and the German People's and Nationalist
parties, on the other. The People's party, corresponding
in the main to the old National Liberal party, represented
chiefly conservative capitalism, relatively indifferent to political forms but always on guard against socialistic tendencies
in legislation. The Nationalists, the old Conservative party,
were monarchists, longing for the restoration of the German
Empire as it was before the war. Other opponents were
frankly revolutionary. The Communists repudiated "bourgeois democracy" and demanded the dictatorship of the proletariat in the Russian style. Various reactionary associations, of which Hitler's National-Socialist German Workers'
Party (conveniently shortened to "Nazi") was the most
enduring, also repudiated constitutional methods. They
would make no peace with a government which had "signed
away Germany's honor" by accepting the Peace of Versailles
and endeavoring to carry out its terms; "heads must roll on
the ground" to avenge such a disgrace. Outside professional politics the government had also many enemies. The
army officers, the civil service, the landed aristocracy and
"society" generally, even the schools and the universities,
were, in the main, still royalist in sentiment. Germany was
a republic; but many Germans had not yet become republicans. The greatest enemy of the republic, however, lay not
in men but in circumstances. Such events as the French
occupation of the Ruhr, the inflation and repudiation of the
currency, the prolonged disputes over reparations and disarmament, and the depression in world trade, acting upon
the discouraged and resentful state of mind which defeat in

a great war always induces, would have shaken any government and strengthened any opposition.

In March, 1920, the reactionaries ventured on an open rebellion (*Putsch*) against the republic. Dr. Wolfgang von Kapp proclaimed himself Chancellor with General von Lüttwitz as head of the national defense. The chief support of the movement came from certain military forces which refused to disband in accordance with the provisions of the Versailles Treaty limiting German armaments. Only a few of the royalist leaders joined the movement, which seemed to most of them premature. The would-be revolutionists seized Berlin without much difficulty, but the country at large was not with them. The deposed republican government fled to Dresden and Stuttgart; the working classes joined in a general strike. Most of the army and the propertied classes stood neutral waiting to see which way the cat would jump. Within a week the whole movement was at an end. Kapp fled the country. The factory towns of the Ruhr took advantage of the confusion to raise the red banner of Communism. The government was forced to drop its less popular members,— such as Noske who had crushed Communist revolts, and Erzberger, attacked as a financial adventurer, — and call elections for June.

The Kapp-Lüttwitz Putsch, 1920

The suppression of the Kapp revolt did not end the reactionary attempts to overthrow the republic. Matthias Erzberger, leader of the Catholic Center, was murdered in August, 1921, and Walter Rathenau, a Jewish financier and liberal politician, was assassinated the following June. The lives of many other radical leaders were attempted by reactionary conspirators who had sworn to punish by death all who had consented to the Treaty of Versailles or the subsequent agreements which grew out of it. Bavaria was a particularly promising field for intrigue, since monarchist sentiment had

The Hitler-Ludendorff Putsch, 1923

been peculiarly strong there ever since a brief and unhappy experience with a Communist dictatorship at Munich in 1919. States rights' feeling also operated to make the Bavarians disdain to yield too readily to orders from Berlin for securing the safety of the republic. In 1923 an Austrian agitator, Adolf Hitler, proclaimed himself Chancellor at Munich with the support of General von Ludendorff, who had shared supreme power (though scarcely popularity) with von Hindenburg during the war. The movement collided with another Bavarian attempt at counterrevolution led by Gustav von Kahr. The active conspirators were jailed. No one realized then that Hitler, the almost comic-opera figure of Munich's "beer hall rebellion," was to be Germany's Man of Destiny.

The election of 1920 had weakened the government by the loss of many "regular" Socialist seats to the critical opposition element in the party, the Independent Socialists. For a time Konstantin Fehrenbach, a Centrist leader, was Chancellor with the support of a coalition of all the moderate "bourgeois" parties with both Socialist factions in opposition. He was succeeded by Joseph Wirth and Wilhelm Cuno, who wrestled in vain with the financial problems presented by reparations payments and an inflated currency. The French occupation of the Ruhr and the final collapse of German credit brought the fortunes of Germany to the lowest ebb since the republic had been established. Chancellor Wilhelm Marx (Center party) and Foreign Minister Gustav Stresemann championed the Dawes Plan and carried through the Reichstag the necessary legislation to put it in force, but the position of the government had been much weakened by popular discontent. This was reflected in the Reichstag elections of May and December, 1924. The May elections ominously strengthened the Communists to the left and the Nationalists to the right and introduced a new group of irreconcilables, the followers

Reichstag elections of 1920 and 1924

of Ludendorff and Hitler. Though the regular and independent Socialists had united in 1922, disaffected radicals now simply voted Communist instead of Socialist tickets at the elections. Even the constitutional parties found it hard to act together, as the gulf was wide between the class conscious Socialists and the capitalistic People's party. The government had to appeal again to the electors half a year later, and at least had the consolation of seeing many Communists return to the Socialist fold and some of the Hitler-Ludendorff reactionaries decide to support the conservative Nationalists. Otherwise the political map was little changed. In 1925 Chancellor Hans Luther omitted the Socialists entirely from his government and for the first time included several of the royalist Nationalists. Germany had drifted far indeed toward the "right" since the winter of 1918–19, when the only question seemed to be whether Germany would go Socialist or Communist!

The double Reichstag election of 1924 was followed by a double presidential election in 1925. The first president of the Reich, Friedrich Ebert, had been chosen by *Hindenburg* the Weimar Assembly. Though a Socialist, he *chosen President, 1925* had made no attempt to impose his views on the nation but had loyally accepted whatever ministry the Reichstag desired. His kindliness and moderation made him personally liked even by those who rejected his political creed, and his death in February, 1925, was generally regretted. By German law the first election of a president was final only if a candidate obtained an absolute majority; otherwise a second or "run off" election must be held at which anyone obtaining a plurality would be considered elected. This gave a chance for each party to try out its separate strength on the first battle and then combine into coalitions for the final round. Dr. Karl Jarres, mayor of Duisburg, was the candidate of the conservative parties (Nationalists, People's and Economic), but the liberal and radical groups each ran an independent candidate. The March election resulted in no choice:

Karl Jarres (conservative coalition)..........	10,416,655
Otto Braun (Social Democrat)..............	7,802,496
Wilhelm Marx (Center).....................	3,887,734
Ernst Thälmann (Communist)..............	1,871,815
W. Hellpach (Democrat)...................	1,568,398
H. Held (Bavaria; "states' rights")..........	1,007,450
Erich von Ludendorff (extreme nationalist)....	285,793

The Socialists, Center party and Democrats, the old "Weimar coalition" agreed on the second ballot to combine on the Center candidate, ex-Chancellor Marx. The conservative parties decided to drop their candidate for the most popular of all German war heroes, Paul von Hindenburg "the victor of Tannenberg." The election which followed was so close that had the Communists joined with the other republican groups, Marx would have been elected; not for the first time in history the extreme radicals presented the conservatives with their victory! The April election, at which over thirty million votes were cast, resulted:

Paul von Hindenburg (conservative coalition) ...	14,655,766
Wilhelm Marx (liberal coalition)..............	13,751,615
Ernst Thälmann (Communist)................	1,931,151

The immediate consequences of the election were not so tragic as German liberals and foreign observers had feared. *Significance of the election* President Hindenburg was an "old Prussian" aristocrat, royalist in politics and sentimentally loyal to the name of Hohenzollern. But he was no fanatic like Ludendorff. During the war he had meddled much less with political matters than his more brilliant but less stable colleague, and after the war he had shown more dignity and discretion. Neither the Kapp nor the Hitler conspiracies knew him as participant. In one sense his election actually weakened the monarchists, for they could not attack the government without attacking their own candidate in the presidential chair. Yet when all allowance is made for

Hindenburg's estimable personal qualities and the quite unpolitical hero worship of many who voted for him, the fact that the German nation, voting freely by universal adult suffrage, chose a monarchist as president was no good omen for the republic. The nation had still to be converted to a belief in its own constitution!

For a brief time, indeed, affairs seemed to go tolerably well. Under the wise leadership of Gustav Stresemann as Foreign Minister, Germany emerged from iso- *The Strese-* lation and became a participant in the Locarno *mann era* Peace Pacts and the League of Nations. Stresemann, like Hindenburg, was a conservative, a strong nationalist and inclined to prefer the old monarchical constitution, but he also adapted himself to the new era. But Hindenburg was a soldier who could add nothing to the government except personal prestige and a certain heavy dignity; Stresemann was a keen, realistic politician, a leader of the capitalistic People's party, and possibly the best diplomat Germany had produced since the days of Bismarck. The Reichstag election of 1928 showed a liberal tendency, with a considerable strengthening of the Socialist vote. Parliamentary government did not work at all smoothly; there were too many parties and each clung too obstinately to its own program for any ministry to count on a well disciplined majority for its measures. Chancellors succeeded each other with kaleidoscopic rapidity. But few governments in continental Europe were free from that perplexity.

After the war Germany experienced a considerable industrial development. The inflation of the old currency, while ruining whole classes of the German people, *The new* brought a temporary "boom" to industry and for *capitalism* a time there was less unemployment in defeated *in Germany* and bankrupt Germany than in victorious and stable Great Britain. Even while Socialist ministries yet held political power, Germany was in the economic sphere becoming more than ever capitalistic.   Hugo Stinnes, multimillionaire, towered like a giant above the whole crowd of politicians. He exemplified the tendency to supplement the old "horizontal trusts" (combinations of separate units in a single industry) by "vertical trusts," uniting all stages and parts of an industrial process, such as coal mines, iron mines, steel mills, shipyards.   He was said to control a fifth of the total production of Germany and to have been engaged in 1388 undertakings in 1923, the last year of his life.[1]   He purchased lands, forests, summer resorts, paper mills, electric plants, oil fields, copper and aluminum mines, newspapers and many other productive properties.   Around the great central sun of the Stinnes trusts clustered many other fortunes only less great: Krupp, Thyssen,[2] Siemens, Rathenau. Bitterly the Socialists nicknamed Stinnes "the man for whom the war was fought."   More hated than the great captains of industry, who at least worked hard and lived simply, were the mere profiteers and currency gamblers who thronged the expensive Berlin hotels and by their reckless spending gave foreigners the impression that Germany was a prosperous nation which could well afford to pay her debts.

The general tone of German thought during the decade immediately following the war was very much like that of
Literary pessimism as a barometer   France during the similar period after 1871.   In both cases a defeated nation had turned against its rulers and established a more democratic system, but in both cases the new régime was insecure and the public mind dejected and pessimistic.   Literary history is not always appropriately related to political history, for an individual genius may write something not at all typical of his times, but it *is* significant when books of a certain type are widely read and admired.   Oswald Spengler's *Decline of the West* was actually written before and dur-

---

[1] G. P. Gooch, *Germany* (1925), page 279.
[2] Fritz Thyssen largely financed Hitler's political campaigns.

ing the World War, but it appeared at the end of the conflict and almost immediately attained widespread popularity though (or because) it held a message of doom.[1] A wide audience greeted also Count Keyserling, whose *Travel Diary* praised the dreamy mysticism of the Orient. A flood of justifications and explanations of the World War poured over the country, the ex-Kaiser and his eldest son being among the apologists. Several grimly realistic studies of the horrors of war, such as E. M. Remarque's *All Quiet on the Western Front* (*Im Westen Nichts Neues*), or of the dull and somber days of reconstruction, such as Remarque's *The Road Back* and Hans Fallada's *Little Man, What Now?*, exactly reflected the times. Strange cults of decadence bloomed briefly on the Berlin stage or startled the art galleries.

But a younger generation, infants or children during the war, looked on all this pessimism with a certain impatience. The German "youth movement" was protean *The youth* in character. Some groups were Catholic, some *movement* Protestant and some secular; some professed Communism and looked forward to the dawn of a new day of radicalism, others looked backwards to medieval Germany when life was (or was imagined to be) heroic and simple. Youths and maidens left the cities to wander as "birds of passage" (*Wandervögel*), wearing the simplest clothing and sometimes bathing naked in the sunshine, living on plain fare, scorning the trammels of convention. This passionate desire to simplify life to its essentials has often appeared in German history. One recalls Michael Geismayr's proposal in 1526 that "From now on, cities shall cease to exist and all shall live in villages"[2]; the "Leagues of Virtue," "Gymnastic

[1] The book is an interpretation of history couched in a ponderous philosophical jargon, largely of the author's own invention; the last book on earth, one would think, to attract the non-professional reader. Its central thesis is that "The future of the West is not a limitless tending upwards and onwards... but a single phenomenon of history, strictly limited and defined as to form and duration, which covers a few centuries." C. F. Atkinson's translation (1926), page 39.

[2] See J. S. Schapiro, *Social Reform and the Reformation* (1909).

Unions" and "General Student Fellowships" of the "young Germany" movement in the early nineteenth century, when the true patriot wore a bushy beard and dressed in homespun so that none might mistake him for the smooth shaven and foppishly dressed courtiers of the day. In foreign affairs the energetic spirit of youth tended too frequently, as it did in Italy, to chauvinism. The World War was not for most of them a bitter personal experience but an heroic tradition of the valor of a father or elder brother; the miseries of the reconstruction period were attributed not to the mistakes of the old monarchy but to the errors of the democratic republic or the oppressive conduct of foreign powers.

All this played into the hands of revolutionary agitators, both of the right and the left. Sometimes it was almost a *The rise of* matter of chance whether a spirited young man, *the Nazis* in revolt against tame and often cynical and corrupt parliamentary government, would become a Communist or a monarchist. The most successful of the revolutionary movements was that of the National Socialists, which appealed to ardent young patriots as widely as the Fascist movement in Italy. The leader,[1] Adolf Hitler, was, like Mussolini, himself a young man when the war ended. He was born in Austria in 1889, the son of a customs officer. On the eve of the war he moved to Bavaria, worked as a house painter, enlisted in the German army and fought bravely. With a group of other like-minded men he organized immediately after the war a National Socialist party with a platform of twenty-five points. This party program demanded the union of Austria with the rest of Greater Germany, the repudiation of the Treaty of Versailles, the limitation of citizenship to those of pure German blood ("No Jew can, therefore, be a member of the nation"), the expulsion of immigrants who had entered Germany since the war began (chiefly east European Jews), "the elimination of income which is

---

[1] "*Der Führer*," equivalent to the Fascist *Il Duce*.

acquired without labor or effort," confiscation of the wealth of war profiteers, elimination of big department stores and other concentrations of capital, land reform, social reform, elimination of the non-German (chiefly Jewish) newspapers, and the creation of a strong central authority over the whole Reich.

Even if Hitler had never lived there would certainly have been a strong reaction away from republicanism, democracy and socialism in Germany, but Hitler imposed on the reaction the particular form which it took. *Hitler* Much of his party tactics was borrowed from the Italian Fascisti. He also organized his party as a kind of uniformed volunteer militia. His brown-shirted "Storm Troops" (*Sturm-Abteilungen*) suggest Mussolini's black-shirted *squadristi*; the two armies rendered to their leaders a similar salute; the "hooked cross" or swastika satisfied the same love of symbolism as the Fascist ax and rods; both organizations conducted open street fights against the "reds" with many a deed of violence and many a political martyrdom on both sides. One is tempted at first to find in Nazi Germany nothing but a copy of Fascist Italy. But the parallelism though most striking is not complete. The difference lay partly in the personality of the leaders. Hitler lacked the cynical humor, the balanced common sense and practicality of the Italian dictator; he was narrower, more intense, more purely the fanatic. Probably he was an even greater orator; many foreign writers consider him the greatest orator who ever lived in Germany. But his power lay almost wholly in his white-hot sincerity and the fury of emotion he could work up in himself and his auditors. Another difference lay in the fact that while both the Fascisti and the Nazis exalted the Nation above class, creed, party, personal interest and the moral law itself, the Nazis laid even greater emphasis on the factor of race.

To the Nazis, race and nation were identical; those who

were not "of the blood" could never become true Germans.
"Aryan-ism"   Some Germans insisted that the tall blond "Nordics" were the only Teutons, the true aristocracy of mankind, but the Nazi movement, which was strong in south Germany and Austria,[1] could not make much use of this concept and so fell back on that triumph of the creative imagination the "Aryan race," [2] of which the Teutonic speaking peoples were the noblest branch. This echoed the doctrines of Count Gobineau half a century before, and Houston Stewart Chamberlain a generation later. The practical application of the Aryan concept was to rule out the Jews as a "Semitic people" from the national life. Unlike the Jewish persecutions of the Middle Ages, this modern anti-Semitism had little to do with religion; the converted Jew was often hated even more than the one who openly adhered to the religion of his fathers. In part it was a fanatical nationalism; the hatred of any alien element within the nation, very similar to the attitude of the Magyars to the Slavs and Rumanians in prewar Hungary. In part it was the result of economic competition; the Jews being an urban people, cut off from the land, thronged the paths of business and the professions and were often envied for their success. In part it was a political hatred; the Jews, as a cosmopolitan and often mistreated folk, tended in many cases to political radicalism, and were often prominent in the ranks of the various communistic and socialistic parties of Europe. The Jews in Germany numbered about 600,000, only one per cent of the population, but they had played a sufficiently conspicuous part in German commercial and political life to draw on themselves the hatred of the Nazis.

[1] Southern Germany and Austria are largely peopled by the broad-headed "Alpine" race.

[2] "Aryan" does not connote any racial type; it is, strictly speaking, merely a name applied to a group of languages. Neither the Germans nor the Jews are even approximately pure racial types, and the attempt to account for their antagonism on "racial" grounds is an ignorant misuse of words. Nor is the swastika, chosen as an emblem of the "Aryans," confined to the Aryan-speaking peoples; it may be found in many widely separated parts of the world.

One cause of the National Socialist success is expressed in its double name. The term "National" appealed to con- *Why the* servative Germans, hostile to cosmopolitan So- *Nazis grew* cialism of the Marxian brand, while the term "Socialist" attracted many who hoped that the new party would break up the great estates, put an end to the big stores and give the "little man," the peasant and the shopkeeper, a chance to live. The rather ambiguous platform had in it some attractions for all, or at least for all "Aryans." The most diverse motives led men to join it: unemployed army veterans, former Socialists disappointed with the ineffectiveness of their party leaders, bondholders ruined by currency inflation, underpaid clerks worried by the high cost of living, university graduates who found their education without value in the market,[1] small shopkeepers facing the stress of Jewish competition, poets and dreamers of an ideal Germany with all the stalwart virtues ascribed to the Teutons by Tacitus, anguished patriots anxious to reverse the verdict of the World War, and a sprinkling of jolly, reckless young fellows who just enjoyed the marching and singing and the fights with the republican *Reichsbanner* clubs. Other elements that were eventually to unite with the party held aloof as late as 1932 and only joined it as a last desperate resort against Bolshevism; the "solid men" of rank and property. They viewed the movement with a distrust similar to that which conservative Italians at first felt toward the Fascisti,— a feeling that the movement was a little crude, a little hysterical, perhaps a shade plebeian. It is significant that the royalist veterans' marching club, the "Stahlhelm" (steel helmet), held aloof from the Nazi party and even treated it as a rival organization. Though the Nazis opposed the democratic republic, they did not wish to restore the old Germany of 1913; they were rather indefinite on the question

[1] It is usually estimated that about half of the German university graduates in the postwar decade could find no positions open to them in any line for which they had been trained.

of putting the Hohenzollerns back on the throne,— the most vital of all issues to the conservative Nationalist party. Hitler and his friends spoke rather of a "Third Reich," which was to sum up but also transcend the glories of the "first Empire" (the Holy Roman Empire from Charlemagne's time to Napoleon's) and the "second Empire" (from 1871 to 1918).[1]

After the beginning of the world depression the republic was thrown altogether on the defensive. There were many *The last stand of the republic* causes for this,— the desperation of millions who had made a bare living ever since the war and now were deprived of even that margin, the impossibility of meeting further reparations payments, the coming to voting age of a new generation who knew little of the war and much of the hardships of the peace, the death of conciliatory statesmen such as Stresemann in Germany and Briand in France, and the cumulative effect of a decade of Nazi agitation. In the Reichstag elections of September, 1930, the Nazis increased their representation from twelve seats to 107. The Communists, at the opposite end of the political spectrum, also made striking gains; the moderate parties lost ground. Chancellor Heinrich Brüning of the Catholic Center was the last effective barrier to the Nazi revolution. In concert with President Hindenburg he governed by a series of emergency decrees without a true majority in the Reichstag. A new presidential election was due in 1932 and Brüning would like to have postponed it, but any such step would have been the signal for a Nazi outbreak. Hitler hoped to carry the presidency even in the face of Hindenburg's enormous personal popularity. Europe waited in anxiety, fearing lest a Hitler victory would be the signal for a new war between Germany and Poland or even between Germany and France. By a curious reversal of

[1] The republican government from 1918 to 1932 was treated as a mere transition period from the second to the third Empire.

rôles, Hindenburg whose election had caused so many misgivings in 1925 was now looked upon as the last hope of European peace.

Hindenburg had traded constituencies. In the March election he had the support of practically all who had supported his opponent Marx in 1925; the Center, *Hindenburg* the Democrats, the Socialists. On the other *re-elected,* hand he had lost the militarists, royalists and *1932* other reactionaries, who divided their vote between Hitler and Theodor Düsterberg, candidate of the Nationalists and the Steel Helmets. The Communists, uncompromising as always, ran their former candidate Ernst Thälmann on a separate ticket. Their refusal to support Hindenburg prevented him from obtaining an absolute majority:

P. von Hindenburg (liberal coalition) 18,651,497
A. Hitler (National Socialist) 11,339,446
E. Thälmann (Communist) 4,983,341
T. Düsterberg (Nationalist) 2,557,729

A second election was necessary. Düsterberg's followers divided between Hindenburg and Hitler; the Communists stood firm. The April election resulted:

Hindenburg 19,359,983
Hitler 13,418,547
Thälmann 3,706,759

The world at large rejoiced and hoped that Hindenburg's victory meant the beginning of the end of Hitler's movement. This breath of relief was assuredly premature. Not only were Hitler's thirteen millions a force to be reckoned with, but it was an ominous fact that the only way the republicans could stop Hitler's immediate advance to supreme power was by re-electing a Prussian royalist army officer, eighty-five years of age, whose war record could attract some needed votes.

Chancellor Brüning had resigned in May, partly in despair at sustaining the government in face of so much popular opposition, and partly because President Hindenburg refused

to sanction his plan of dividing the great estates of the
Death nobility into small peasant farms. Hindenburg
struggles of chose in his place Franz von Papen, a royalist and
the republic militarist who had been dismissed from a minor
diplomatic post in the United States for fomenting illegal
plots on neutral soil. He invoked a new Reichstag, but the
July election increased the Nazi membership from 107 to
230. Nothing could be done with so huge an opposition,
especially since the Communist vote had also largely increased. So in November Chancellor von Papen again appealed to the voters. The Communists gained again, winning 100 seats; the Nazi representation fell off somewhat, but
still no working majority could be obtained. Hitler refused
to enter or support any coalition ministry which he could
not control. Hindenburg, still unwilling to entrust Hitler
with supreme power, dropped von Papen and placed in office
another royalist reactionary, General Kurt von Schleicher.
Von Schleicher also found the task of government an insoluble riddle, and the reluctant president at last turned to
Hitler. In January, 1933, Hitler took office as Chancellor.
With the aid of the Nationalists he formed a coalition
ministry, but he lacked a parliamentary majority and resolved to appeal to the voters. In the meantime, with scant
regard for legality, the ministry forced out of office the Socialist state government of Prussia and appointed Nationalists or Nazis to every strategic post in the national or local
governments. Von Papen became Commissioner for Prussia with dictatorial powers.

On the eve of election a Dutch Communist, Martinus Van
der Lubbe, with accomplices who escaped detection, set fire
The Nazi to the Reichstag buildings. The Nazis hailed
revolution the incident as proof of a widespread Communist
of 1933 plot to "Bolshevize" Germany. Radicals on
their part accused the Nazis of having planned the fire in
order to discredit the Communists. Van der Lubbe was

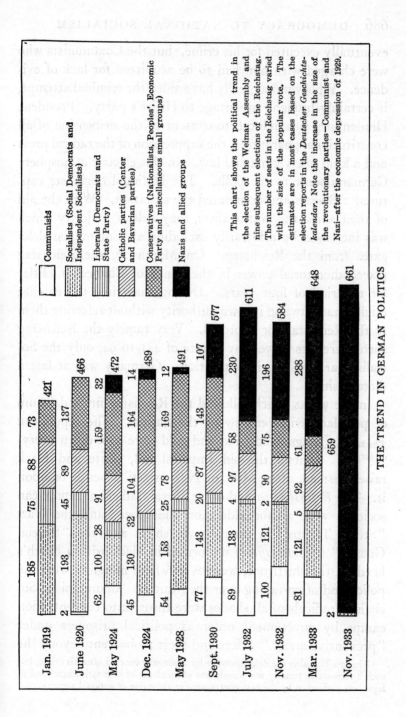

Communists

Socialists (Social Democrats and Independent Socialists)

Liberals (Democrats and State Party)

Catholic parties (Center and Bavarian parties)

Conservatives (Nationalists, Peoples', Economic Party and miscellaneous small groups)

Nazis and allied groups

This chart shows the political trend in the election of the Weimar Assembly and nine subsequent elections of the Reichstag. The number of seats in the Reichstag varied with the size of the popular vote. The estimates are in most cases based on the election reports in the *Deutscher Geschichts-kalendar.* Note the increase in the size of the revolutionary parties—Communist and Nazi—after the economic depression of 1929.

Jan. 1919 — 185 | 75 | 88 | 73 | 421

June 1920 — 2 | 193 | 45 | 89 | 137 | 466

May 1924 — 62 | 100 | 28 | 91 | 159 | 32 | 472

Dec. 1924 — 45 | 130 | 32 | 104 | 164 | 14 | 489

May 1928 — 54 | 153 | 25 | 78 | 169 | 12 | 491

Sept. 1930 — 77 | 143 | 20 | 87 | 143 | 107 | 577

July 1932 — 89 | 133 | 4 | 97 | 58 | 230 | 611

Nov. 1932 — 100 | 121 | 2 | 90 | 75 | 196 | 584

Mar. 1933 — 81 | 121 | 5 | 92 | 61 | 288 | 648

Nov. 1933 — 2 | 659 | 661

THE TREND IN GERMAN POLITICS

eventually executed for his crime,[1] but the Communists who were charged with him had to be acquitted for lack of evidence. Whoever may really have aided the criminal attempt, it certainly brought advantage to Hitler's party. President Hindenburg was induced to consent to the suspension of all constitutional guarantees, the suppression of the radical press and a kind of civic martial law. In this electric atmosphere Germany went to the polls. The National Socialists captured 288 seats and dominated the situation. With the aid of their allies, the Nationalists, they held a majority which was increased by arbitrarily excluding all Communist delegates from the Reichstag. On March 23, the Reichstag placed dictatorial power in the hands of Chancellor Hitler for a period of four years. During that time the cabinet might enact laws on its own authority without referring them to the Reichstag for approval. Very tamely the Reichstag surrendered its powers by a vote of 441 to 94, only the Socialist party voting in opposition. Germany was at last a dictatorship.

In the weeks which followed the Reichstag fire a delirium of popular excitement swept the nation. The republican *The reign* flags, black, red and gold were torn down every-*of terror* where; the old Imperial red, white and black raised instead, often with the Nazi swastika beside or upon it. The *Reichsbanner* and other liberal, radical or republican societies were all forbidden; on the other hand the Nazi "Storm Troops" in their brown shirts and the "Special Guards" (*Schutzstaffeln*) uniformed in black with a death's head on the shirtfront, were everywhere mingling with the police and often taking over their duties. Communists, Socialists, radicals of all shades were thrust into concentration camps by government order as political prisoners under "preventive arrest." Here and there mobs went beyond the

[1] The law imposing the death penalty for arson was enacted *after* his crime, but such a retroactive penalty was merely one of hundreds of unconstitutional and illegal acts performed by the new government in the name of national security.

official decrees and flogged or murdered scores of individuals unpopular on account of their race or politics. No accurate statistics exist on this early reign of terror and doubtless many reported atrocities were exaggerated. The government took no direct part in these mobbings but did little or nothing to discourage them; in fact, persons who dared complain to the police were usually thrown into concentration camps as suspicious characters. Captain Hermann Göring, Hitler's right-hand man, declared openly that if Jewish shops were looted by mobs the police were in no way bound to protect them. On April first Hitler decreed a general boycott of Jewish stores to punish their owners for spreading "atrocity stories" to the discredit of the government. The boycott was for one day only, but would be a convincing warning of what might happen in the future. The chief of the state secret police admitted that, from first to last, some thirty thousand persons had been arrested and held in detention camps, though most of them only for short periods. The Nazis insisted that the sum total of violence in their revolution was much less than that which accompanied most revolutions of history; but it must be added that few, if any, historic revolutions encountered so little resistance. All parties and institutions of the republican régime surrendered without a struggle.

Nazi Germany like Fascist Italy was to be a "corporate" and "totalitarian" State. All departments of human life were to be "correlated" or brought into due re- *"Gleich-* lationship (*Gleichschaltung*) with the new régime. *schaltung"* To this end all political parties were made illegal except the National Socialist, and it was forbidden under penalty of imprisonment to organize a new party. Appointed governors were placed over each state and the "state cabinets" were given law-making powers. The upper house or *Reichsrat*, representing the states, was eliminated from Germany as a mere encumbrance. Thus the proud federal states of Germany became nothing but administrative districts in a centralized Reich. The trades unions were dissolved, their leaders thrown out, their funds confiscated. Only National Socialist labor organizations were permitted. Capital was treated a little more tenderly than labor, but many Jewish or anti-Nazi directors of corporations or chambers of commerce were removed from their posts. All manner of social organizations, from the aristocratic student "corps" or university fraternities to the Boy Scouts, were dissolved and merged with Nazi organizations. Only the veterans' organization, the *Stahlhelm*, was spared, on condition that it accept the new order, and even this body was "purified" of non-Nazi leaders. Religious clubs generally were dissolved, much to the indignation of the Catholics. A ministry of "public enlightenment and propaganda" was created under Dr. Paul Joseph Goebbels with general control over all official publicity.

Hitler himself was nominally a Roman Catholic and most of his followers were either Catholics or Protestants. Indeed, the rescue of religion from "Communist atheists" was one of the telling election cries of the party. It is true that a few extremists of the party declared Christianity was accursed because of its Jewish origin and must be replaced by a true German national faith based on the ancient Teutonic myths; but these eccentrics were always a minority. The official program of the party was to create a German national church, Protestant and Christian but placed under the close control of the Nazi movement and officered by a wholly "Aryan" and patriotic clergy. Such a church was established, the German Evangelical Church, based on a merger of the Lutheran and Reformed establishments in the various German States, and a former army chaplain, Ludwig Müller, chosen as supreme national bishop. The Catholics and the smaller "free" Protestant denominations were assured that they would be left

Co-ordinating the Church

alone if they abstained from political activities. The attempted shackling of the Church met with more opposition than the elimination of the state governments, the political parties, the trades unions and the press all combined. Many pastors denounced Bishop Müller's policy of dismissing all clergymen of Jewish blood and boldly asserted that the Church "was built on the blood of Christ, not on the blood of the Aryans." Some of the more insistent clergy were dismissed from their livings, or even thrown into prison for taking this stand, but their remonstrances continued. Other voices, both Protestant and Catholic, were raised against the propaganda of the "heathen" minority within the Nazi ranks who would replace Christ by Wotan. The only effective criticism of the German government which existed under the Third Reich came from the pulpits.

The acts of mob violence against the Jews which marked the first phase of the Nazi revolution became less frequent as time went on, but were succeeded by a more for- *Repression* midable, because more systematic, policy of root- *of the Jews* ing the Jews out of the life of the nation. The law defined a "non-Aryan" as anyone "descended from non-Aryan, particularly Jewish, parents or grandparents." Thus to the 600,-000 Jews in the country were added two or three times that number of persons who had at least one Jewish grandparent. Public officials of non-Aryan descent were to be dismissed unless they were appointed before the World War or had served at the front in it or had fathers or sons killed in the conflict. Subject to similar exceptions, the number of Jews in law, medicine, teaching and other professions was limited to the proportion of Jews in the general population. From journalism the Jews were eliminated almost wholly. A racial quota principle was applied to the universities. Indeed, certain university students were more bitter and bigoted than anyone else; in one case a student association demanded that Jews be forbidden to write in German, a holy Aryan tongue, and be compelled to use Hebrew! Even the fine arts and pure sciences were not exempt. Jewish musicians and actors were removed from the stage and eminent Jewish scientists from the hospitals and universities. No quota was applied in commerce and Jewish businesses continued, but the popular prejudice against them drove many to ruin. Other Jewish firms camouflaged themselves by selecting a Gentile as the ostensible "leader" of the corporation. In despair of making a livelihood, over seventy thousand Jews left the country and hundreds committed suicide. The outlook for Judaism in Germany in 1934 was as dark as in the medieval ghettos or Tsarist Russia.

The case of the Jews awakened widest attention; indeed in many parts of the world the one fact that was known *Other* about the whole Nazi régime was that it perse-*repressions* cuted Jews. The popular boycott of German goods by Jews in other countries cut deeply and seriously into Germany's export trade, intensifying the economic crisis. But Jews were not the only victims. Among the exiles from Germany (including, by the way, several winners of the Nobel prizes in science and literature) were socialists, radicals and liberals of all shades, even anti-Nazi monarchists. In the name of economy the number of students admitted to all universities of the Reich was limited in 1934 to 15,000, and only one-tenth of these might be women! Not only was the national press placed under a censorship far more stringent than that of wartime, but foreign newspapers that had criticized the Nazi government were barred from circulation even if, as in the case of the English *Manchester Guardian*, they had shown the utmost sympathy with Germany's national aspirations in the field of diplomacy. The Nazis, like the Bolsheviki and the Fascisti, confiscated the property and imprisoned the families of those who succeeded in escaping from the country if they dared to "defame" it when abroad. Albert Einstein, the eminent Jewish mathe-

matician, was condemned to exile and confiscation of his
property in Germany because when in America he had criticized the Jewish persecutions. How the rest of the world
felt about it all is shown by the fact that almost immediately thereafter Einstein was showered with civic or university honors in Belgium, France, Spain, Great Britain and
the United States. Nazi mobs made a specialty of bonfires
of radical, "decadent" or "non-Aryan" books.

It would be wrong to represent the Nazi movement as exclusively concerned with repression, though that undoubtedly
absorbed most of its attention. The party had a *Nazi*
positive program of economic reconstruction, *economic*
though rather a vague one, perhaps more easily *policy*
stated as an ideal than as a platform. The ideal was not unlike that of Fascist Italy, an economic system based on private property but with strict national control in the public
interest. In place of the old class-conscious trades unions
there was to be a German Labor Front organized on the corporate or gild plan. In connection with the schools all
classes were to attend labor camps, drilled in military fashion,
and learn the realities of manual toil. A peasant class of
pure German blood was to be fixed on the soil and favored in
legislation. In a few cases large estates were voluntarily
offered for division into peasant freeholds. The government
undertook to furnish dowries to girls of pure German descent
who would leave business positions and marry, thus freeing
jobs for unemployed men. Work was to be spread out
within each business so far as feasible in order to combat unemployment. If the official statements are to be believed,
the number of unemployed which reached some 6,000,000 in
January, 1933, was reduced to less than 3,000,000 by April,
1934. Neither figure includes an uncertain number of "un-
registered" unemployed who escape the statistical tables,
and the increase in employment was in part a mere replacement of women workers, induced to marry, and of unrecorded

Jews or radicals, turned out of their places to make way for unemployed German men of orthodox politics; yet, with all deductions, the government had undoubtedly found or made work for many. The government took play as well as work under its benevolent supervision and in its youth organizations and its "Strength through Joy" association (similar to the *Dopo Lavoro*, "After Work," organization in Italy) tried to build sturdier bodies for the nation. "Race culture" was also attempted; eugenic boards being authorized to sterilize the degenerate and unfit, a policy denounced on religious grounds from many Catholic pulpits.

If the internal program of the Nazis was more ruthless and violent than the world at large had anticipated, their foreign *Nazi foreign* policy proved unexpectedly moderate. It is true *policy* that Hitler laid down before the Disarmament Conference and the League of Nations an ultimatum demanding equality of armaments with France and other Great Powers, and announced Germany's withdrawal from both organizations when the demand was refused. It is true that Vice-Chancellor von Papen and many others publicly rejoiced that pacifism was dead in Germany, and that every German prominently identified with pacifist or internationalist propaganda was exiled or imprisoned. Most significant of all, Hitler declared openly that since the Entente Allies had not disarmed to any appreciable degree, the disarmament clauses of the Treaty of Versailles were no longer legally or morally binding on Germany. But there was no sudden rush to seize Austria or the Polish corridor. In all his speeches, in sharp contrast with sundry warlike chapters of his autobiography *Mein Kampf* (1923), Hitler pleaded for European peace and asserted that all the new Germany wanted was to be let alone by other governments. In 1934 one of the party leaders, Rudolf Hess, went so far as to appeal to the French war veterans by their common memories of the horrors of the battlefield to work with Germany for continued peace.

With Poland, Germany voluntarily concluded a ten-year peace pact. With Italy, France and Britain, on Mussolini's initiative, Hitler consented in 1933 to a "Four Power Peace Pact" providing for direct diplomatic consultation on their mutual interests. Though Danzig went Nazi in its municipal government, no *coup d'état* followed. Though no one doubted or denied that the Nazis wished to unite the Saar, Danzig, Austria and the Polish corridor with the German Reich, they showed more patience in waiting for the fruit to fall from the tree than had been generally expected.

Europe was not, however, entirely reassured by the fair words of the Nazi government. France distrusted a Germany bent on rearming and turned her attention *Germany's* to increasing her own military defenses. The *isolation* British were less alarmed than the French but perhaps even more displeased; most Frenchmen had expected little pacifism even from the German Republic but the British had built great hopes on German liberalism. The changed attitude is reflected in Sir Austen Chamberlain's speech in Parliament on April 13, 1933, in which he said, "Are you going to discuss with such a government the Polish corridor... does the British government dare to put another Pole under the heel of such a government?" To get the full significance of this remark it must be remembered that Chamberlain was one of the authors of the Locarno Peace Pact and that the bulk of the English press had for a decade been much more in sympathy with Germany than with Poland. Russia was so incensed by the persecution of German Communists that she approached France in a friendly diplomatic manner for the first time since the Bolshevist revolution, and even joined the League of Nations. Italy viewed Nazi intrigues in Austria with some misgivings, and Austria, hitherto the friendliest state to Germany in Europe, swung over into close *entente* with Italy to prevent a German annexation. The moral and diplomatic isolation of Germany in 1933 was far more complete than it had been in 1914 or even 1919. Some Nazis rejoiced in this isolation and declared that the time had come for Germany to be a self-sufficing nation in no way dependent even on foreign trade. Others sought to reconstruct diplomatic friendships by conciliatory speeches.

A notable triumph for Nazi Germany in the sphere of foreign policy was the plebiscite of January 13, 1935 in the *The Saar* Saar District, a region detached from Germany *Plebiscite* by the Treaty of Versailles and ruled for fifteen years by the League of Nations.[1] The voters were offered three choices: return to Germany, union with France, or a continuance of the existing régime. Ordinarily there would have been little question of the result in view of the strong German sentiment of the inhabitants. But the district was mainly Catholic in faith and divided between the Catholic Center and the Socialists in politics, and on both grounds suspicious of Nazi rule; moreover, there were many refugees, Jewish or radical, who had fled from Hitler's Third Reich to the relative peace and tolerance of the Saar, and while, as recent immigrants, they could not vote in the plebiscite, they could and did carry on an active propaganda against union with Germany. Economically the region was closely dependent on the Lorraine iron fields, now on the French side of the frontier; it was more lightly taxed than either France or Germany, and it enjoyed more freedom of speech and of the press than any part of Germany. Hitler tried to secure the Saar by private bargain with France, to avert the risks of a plebiscite; when that failed he arranged to purchase the Saar coal mines from France for 900,000,000 francs (partly payable in coal) and to abstain from reprisals against minority groups in the Saar if the elections should go for Germany. To prevent disorders in so exciting an election, an international force of British, Italian, Swedish and Dutch contingents policed the district, establishing

---

[1] For the Saar question at the Paris Peace Conference, see Chapter XVIII.

an interesting and important precedent for possible "League of Nations armies" in the future. The result justified Germany's utmost hopes and proved once more that in modern times national sentiment tends to override all other considerations. The vote stood:

> For German rule.................477,119.
> For League of Nations rule ...... 46,513.
> For French rule................. 2,124.

Though the Nazis proclaimed dictatorship and repudiated democracy, they boasted of being a party of the masses and desired the prestige which might come from an *The nation* almost unanimous vote of approval at the polls. *endorses the* In November, 1933, all men and women of voting *party* age in Germany were required to vote for a new Reichstag at which only one party list, that of the Nazis, might be presented, and also vote by referendum to approve the general policy of the government with reference to foreign affairs and particularly the withdrawal of Germany from the League of Nations and the Disarmament Conference. The Nazi Reichstag list was endorsed by a popular vote of 39,655,212 (the 3,398,404 negative votes being listed as "void"), and the government policy was approved by 40,632,628 votes to 2,101,191 (over 757,000 other votes being counted "void").

Though on the surface the Nazi party had enlisted the virtually unanimous support of Germany, the party was itself torn by personal jealousies and wide discrepancies *Schism* of opinion. Former Nationalists, like von Papen *within the* and Alfred Hugenberg who had been tolerated *party ranks* for the conservative support they brought to the party, had to greet as comrades "beefsteak Nazis" ("reds" at heart under the brown shirt) who believed that the movement was primarily directed against "international capitalism." There was much rivalry between the brown-shirted "Storm Troops" and the black-shirted "Special Guards" and between both and the "Steel Helmets." Some of the more radical Nazis demanded the merger of the regular army (*Reichswehr*) with the party militia and the abolition of the "Steel Helmets." President Hindenburg resisted both demands, and on this issue Hitler himself sided with the conservatives. Those who wanted a national Protestant Church quarreled with those who wanted a national revival of paganism. Some thought that the persecution of the Jews had gone too far; others that it had halted half way under secret pressure from business interests. Von Papen, increasingly restive at the radical trend in the party, bitterly denounced "National Bolshevism" in the party ranks. His address caused wide protest and might have led to the loss of the Vice-Chancellorship had he not been protected by Hindenburg's personal friendship. Some royalists in 1933 had looked to National Socialism as a transition stage to a restoration of the Hohenzollerns, and the ex-Kaiser from his home of exile hopefully wrote that "Only under its Kaiser and the German federated princes can the Reich endure and regain its old might and glory," but the appeal received from most of the Nazis only contemptuous silence and Hitler declared that until more pressing matters had been settled the revival of monarchy would not even be considered. Only the leader's personality held together all these jarring elements. No one in Germany dared say a word against Hitler openly, but behind the scenes there was discontent and even furtive conspiracy.

Believing that he had sufficient evidence of conspiracy to justify ruthless "purging" of the party ranks Hitler, taking *The crisis of* into confidence Göring and a few other trusted *June, 1934* aides, ordered the arrest and summary execution of the chief malcontents. On June 30, 1934, seventy-seven of the rebels were killed in a sudden and completely successful raid. Whether all were guilty will never be known, as no adequate opportunity for self-defense was given to the men who were "executed," and some were killed in flight, or resisting arrest, or committed suicide. Chief among the victims were General Kurt von Schleicher, Hitler's immediate predecessor as German Chancellor, and Captain Ernst Roehm, a leader of the "Storm Troops" of the Nazi party. Hitler had struck out both right and left, for von Schleicher was a monarchist who did not like the radical trend in Nazi policy, while Roehm was an ardent extremist who had grumbled at Hitler's moderation. Some of the rebels were alleged to have plotted with a diplomat of an unnamed "foreign power," presumably France. Von Papen was protected by a military guard at the orders of Hindenburg, and Hitler continued to retain him in office, though some of his immediate subordinates had been killed in the raid. Though most of the slain were men of dubious character, there was much unfavorable comment in foreign countries at the summary execution of so many persons without trial and the refusal in several cases of Christian burial to the dead. Hitler listed and defended the killings in an address to the all-Nazi Reichstag, but he failed to submit detailed evidence of the plot. Though the incident terrorized all opposition and made Hitler more powerful, if possible, than before, it revealed ominous intrigues and divisions within the ranks of the dominant party which might have great significance for the future.

Three rapidly succeeding events in the summer of 1934 shook Europe with apprehension: the massacre of rebel Nazis in Germany, the uprising of the Nazis in Austria *The passing of Hindenburg* and the consequent murder of Chancellor Dollfuss,[1] and the death of President Paul von Hindenburg. The aged Field-Marshal President was the last tie which bound the old Germany to the new régime. Many a conservative German had shaken his head and consoled himself with the reflection, "These doings seem strange to me, but if Hindenburg is satisfied Hitler must be on the right track!" Hindenburg was believed to be a moderating influence be-

[1] See above, pages 580–82.

hind the scenes, though publicly he always endorsed the policies of his Chancellor. Some thought that when Hindenburg died the regular army might not show the same loyalty to his successor, Hitler or another, in the presidential office. But no serious crisis actually took place when the old war hero died and was buried on the battlefield of Tannenberg. Hitler combined the powers of President and Chancellor in his own person, but let the title of President die with its last possessor. He swore the army to personal allegiance to himself as though he were a reigning monarch, tactfully eulogized the late President to the Reichstag, and held another popular plebiscite to approve his new assumption of authority. He obtained a large majority, but the affirmative vote [1] showed a significant falling off from the plebiscite of the previous November.

The main contention of the National Socialists was that by their methods Germany would recover her original national *Did the Nazis represent German tradition?* character, too long varnished over by foreign influences. It is doubtful if this contention can be sustained. True enough, many old German institutions were revived out of a deliberate antiquarianism, especially the more barbarous ones, such as the executioner's ax and the duellist's sword,[2] but the atmosphere of the Third Reich was different from anything Germany had ever known. A centralized dictatorship was more Latin than Teutonic in actual historical tradition, and those features of it which were not borrowed from Fascist Italy might well have been taken from France under the first and third Napoleon. To a real German conservative, let us say Prince Metternich, Hitler would have seemed a mere upstart demagogue; to a real German liberal, such as the poet Schiller, a mere tyrant; but Louis Napoleon or Boulanger could have understood him at once! Nazi Germany would have seemed

---

[1] 38,362,760 for the government; 4,294,654 against; 872,296 "void."

[2] Duels were again sanctioned in the universities and the army.

too centralized and regimented to suit the very "rugged individualism" of a Teutonic viking or a medieval Rhenish baron; too narrow and nationalistic to please the Germans of the Enlightenment, such as Kant, Goethe or Lessing; too sentimental and hysterical to satisfy the cold practical realism of a Bismarck or a Frederick the Great. In fact, National Socialism was an attempt to base Germany's future on an almost wholly fictitious past, and it opened an utterly new act in the great drama of German history,— an act which bade fair to be a tragic one.

CHAPTER XXVIII

FRANCE AND HER NEIGHBORS

As COMPARED with Bolshevized Russia, Fascistized Italy, Nazified Germany and disrupted Austria-Hungary, France, *Stable* the other Great Power on the continent, had an *France* uneventful period of reconstruction after the war. Her problems were many and perplexing: the reconstruction of the devastated departments, the balancing of the budget, the stabilization of the franc, the collection of reparations and payment of war debts, the rule of new "mandated" dependencies such as Syria, the adjustment of Alsace-Lorraine to the rest of the nation, the diplomatic encirclement of Germany to prevent another "revanche." There were incessant parliamentary crises, the rise and fall of many ministries in accustomed French fashion, even minor outbreaks of violence, such as the Stavisky riots of 1934. But no revolutionary change took place; the Third Republic and all its institutions stood substantially as they had done in 1913. This exceptional stability can scarcely be laid to national temperament, for France has had many a revolution in her history. In part it seems to have been due to the prestige of victory; a defeated France might have turned to socialism or monarchy or, more probably, to some sort of nationalistic dictatorship. Perhaps another cause was the four-square structure of modern French society, the presence of a prosperous or, at all events, property-owning, peasantry and a cautious and unadventurous bourgeoisie; the two classes together placing at all times a substantial majority on the side of the *status quo*.

During the World War in France, as in most other European belligerent nations, party politics had been subordinated to the pressing need of national unity. But no more in

France than elsewhere did the "sacred union" outlast the war. In 1920 President Raymond Poincaré's seven-year term of office ended and the honor was awarded, not to Premier Clemenceau as he and the world at large had expected, but to Paul Deschanel, a man less famous and therefore less feared and envied. His health was poor, and before the year was out he resigned and Premier Alexandre Millerand, a former Socialist but now a conservative republican, became the new chief of state. The parliamentary elections of 1919, held under a modified system of proportional representation,[1] had returned a conservative or moderate Chamber of Deputies, the Socialists losing a few seats and the Radicals many. Ex-President Poincaré, instead of retiring gracefully from politics at the expiration of his presidential term in the usual French (and American) manner, became the strongest political force in the nation. It was his policy, primarily, that made France refuse compromise with Germany on the reparations question and sent a small army into the Ruhr in 1923.

The political scene in 1920

In 1924 a new Chamber of Deputies was elected. The Radicals regained the lost ground of 1919, partly because the bugbear of Russian Bolshevism which frightened many into conservatism just after the war had begun to lose its terrors, and partly because Poincaré's policy in the Ruhr seemed costly and futile. Edouard Herriot became Premier. He forced President Millerand to resign on the ground that the chief magistrate of the republic, whose duties are usually considered formal and nominal, had been playing politics too vigorously and usurping the powers which belonged to the ministry.

The swing towards radicalism, 1924

[1] The old *scrutin de liste*, or general ticket for a whole department, was restored in place of the single member district system (*scrutin d'arrondissement*), but with the new modification that if a ticket did not have an absolute majority of votes the seats in the Chamber representing that department should be divided proportionally among the party lists. Unlike Britain, Germany, the United States and many other nations, France did not at the end of the war adopt woman suffrage; the conservatism of the Senate standing in the way.

Gaston Doumergue (1924–31) was chosen in Millerand's place. Joseph Caillaux, imprisoned during the war as a pacifist "defeatist," was restored to civil rights and at once took an active part in the old game of parliamentary politics which he had played for so many years. He was regarded, even by those who thought him tricky, cynical and un-patriotic, as a financial genius; many hoped that he might stabilize the franc, balance the budget and yet refrain from adding to the already crushing burden of taxes. As finance minister, however, Caillaux could not work this miracle. Herriot, Paul Painlevé, and Aristide Briand in successive ministries tried in vain to meet the financial crisis. Evi-dently the give and take of party politics could find no solu-tion, and so an imposing coalition of parliamentary leaders was formed, with Poincaré at its head, to meet the emergency.

The essential trouble was that no government, radical or conservative, had dared face the unpleasant fact that France *Poincaré* would have to reconstruct the devastated depart-*saves the* ments largely at the cost of her own taxpayers. *franc* Hitherto reconstruction had been carried in a separate budget, as "recoverable expenditure," on the theory that Germany in the immediate future would repay all costs in the form of reparations. In the meantime the reconstruc-tion budget was met by loans and printed money instead of fresh taxation. The policy was not unlike that which Ger-many had pursued and threatened similar bankruptcy.[1] In 1924 the franc was worth about a quarter of its face value; by the summer of 1926 about a tenth. The coalition ministry under Poincaré simply faced the situation and stopped post-poning the obvious but painful solution. The reconstruction budget was merged with the ordinary budget; heavy taxes were added so that the combined budget might be balanced; current expenses were sharply cut; the franc was stabilized at about a fifth of its face value. Of course this meant a

---

[1] For the reparations question and German finance, see Chapter XXV.

heavy loss to the large "rentier" (bondholding) class and many other creditor groups; from wealth before the war many now found poverty, but at least something was saved from the wreck. The elections of 1928 returned a Chamber of Deputies generally favorably to the ministry, but Poincaré resigned because of ill health in 1929. The greatest service of a long and brilliant, but rather narrowly nationalistic, career had been the three years' ministry which saved the financial structure of the nation.

The reconstruction of the devastated regions of France is an inspiring story. No major country had suffered more heavily from the war. France had lost about one *The re-* and a half million lives and had more than four *building* million wounded. The principal battlefields of *of France* the west had been on French soil (with the exception of the corner of Belgium around Ypres) and the belt of devastation was much wider than in Belgium. Nearly 300,000 houses had been destroyed and a somewhat greater number damaged; as most of them were built of stone or brick they were not heaps of ashes, as American villages would have been, but varied from roofless ruins to mere heaps of tumbled stone. Refugees sometimes still tried to live in the cellars or under improvised canvas or corrugated iron roofing. Over 6000 public buildings and 20,000 workshops had been destroyed in whole or in part; about 1,360,000 head of livestock killed or confiscated; many coal mines deliberately flooded, and thousands of acres stripped of trees and crops by shell fire. Some two million refugees had to be returned to their homes and provided for until they could start life over again. Yet in 1921, little more than two years after the work of reconstruction was started, M. Briand was able to state that the population of the devastated districts, which had sunk to less than half during the war, was already about seven-eighths of the normal figure, and that nine-tenths of the land was under crops. About half of the injured factories were again at work, sometimes with better machinery, and nearly the whole of 2400 kilometers of railway destroyed in the war again in operation. By 1928 the work of construction was practically complete, at an estimated cost of some $7,000,-000,000 about six-sevenths of which had been advanced by France from her own resources.

Alsace and Lorraine had maintained a steady opposition to German rule from 1871 to 1918 and the majority of the *Alsace-* people welcomed reunion with France at the end *Lorraine* of the war, in spite of the fact that in Alsace German was more widely spoken than French. But cheers in the street and tricolors flying from the windows did not solve the practical problems of adapting the returned provinces to the changed France of the twentieth century. The Alsace-Lorrainers, whether under French or German rule or in the olden days of the nondescript Holy Roman Empire, had always been provincial and particularist, very fond of their local liberties and institutions. The Third Republic was centralized and recognized no "provinces." Difficulties arose chiefly with regard to the teaching of German in the schools and the legal position of the Catholic clergy. The language question was settled by a compromise making French the fundamental language of instruction in the schools, as elsewhere in France, but teaching German as a secondary language. More difficulty arose over the church question. At first the French retained the old system of government subsidies to the clergy and religious instruction in the public schools; but in 1924 the Radical (and therefore anti-clerical) Herriot ministry decided that the time had come to apply the uniform French system of the complete separation of Church and State. Here again compromise proved necessary. Secular instruction was offered to all children, but they might attend classes of their own choice during the hours reserved for religious instruction. In 1928 several German Alsatians were tried for sedition; it being alleged that the movement for "autonomy" was really a cloak for reunion with Germany. The disappearance of all local self-government in Germany in 1933, however, and the friction between the Nazis and the Catholic Church weakened what German attachments may have remained in federalistic, clerical Alsace-Lorraine.

The question of Alsace-Lorraine involved other aspects of the ever-vexing question of Church and State. On the whole, relations were much improved. In 1921 France *France and* again appointed an ambassador to the Vatican, *the Vatican* thus recognizing the Pope as a figure in European diplomacy. The Herriot ministry suggested the abolition of this post, but the suggestion aroused so much opposition that it was dropped. A more liberal spirit was shown towards the Catholic monastic orders after the war. In return for this friendly attitude, the Papacy condemned Charles Maurras and his paper *L'Action Française*, which advocated revolutionary action for the restoration of monarchy.

In 1932 Aristide Briand, the outstanding representative of French liberalism, retired from political life and shortly afterwards died. He differed perhaps more in *Briand the* spirit than in actual program from the men about *conciliator* him; though radical in domestic policy he had been one of the first French republican leaders to hold out the hand of friendship to the Catholic Church; though strongly patriotic in foreign policy, he had also been one of the first to make conciliatory approaches to Germany. A certain bluff geniality in his nature had captured Stresemann, and largely on the basis of their personal friendship negotiations had proceeded smoothly toward the Locarno Peace Pact. Similar tact and good will had impressed the Americans and led to the negotiation of the Paris Peace Pact,— often called, in recognition of its early negotiators, the Kellogg-Briand Pact. In several postwar ministries Briand had been Premier, in many others Foreign Minister. When President Doumergue's term of

office expired in 1931, the world expected Briand to be chosen
in his place; again, as when Clemenceau had been denied the
honor, the obvious choice was passed over for the sake of a
"safe" candidate without enemies. Paul Doumer, a popular
veteran of French politics who presided over the Senate and
had lost several sons in the World War, was selected instead.
Some argued against Briand that his health was failing,
others that he had conceded too much in his negotiations
with foreign governments, especially Germany. Both Herriot and Briand, though in a somewhat vague and inconclusive way, discussed the possibility of a "United States of
Europe,"— not a political federation after the pattern of the
United States of America, but a continent bound together by
commercial agreements and regional peace pacts so closely
that international war would be a very remote possibility.

The world depression struck France later and with less
force than more highly industrialized countries, yet it was

*Economic
depression
and political
tension*
serious enough to have important effects on
French political life. German reparations payments vanished, tourist spendings fell off, unemployment increased. The elections of 1932 revealed a pronounced trend towards radicalism. Herriot
again became premier, succeeding Clemenceau's disciple
Tardieu. Herriot's opposition to the suspension of debt payments to the United States brought about his downfall. A
series of more or less radical ministries followed, each wrestling in vain with the problem of an unbalanced budget. No
one wanted higher taxes, currency inflation revived memories
of the dangerous days before Poincaré had "pegged" the
franc and restored the gold basis of the currency; civil service
men were already complaining of their small salaries and
further budget cuts would put them into a discontented, even
perhaps a revolutionary, frame of mind. The most obvious
cut in the budget, a decrease in military and naval expenditure, was made impossible by the panic fear that swept the

country at the victories of Hitler and his followers and their demand for immediate military equality with France. The rapid succession of cabinet crises revealed a weakness of parliamentary life ominously similar to that which had immediately preceded the rise of dictatorships in Italy, Germany and Poland. In May, 1932, President Doumer was assassinated by a Russian refugee. Albert Lebrun was elected to succeed him, the fifth president since the World War.

Whenever during the course of the Third Republic French public life has become peculiarly weak and ineffective and impatient spirits have begun to talk dictatorship *The Stavisky affair* as a remedy, the bursting of a personal scandal has forced a crisis and cleared the air. So it had been with the many "affairs" of the nineteenth century, from Boulanger to Dreyfus, so it was again in the petty but notorious "Stavisky affair" of 1934. Alexandre Stavisky, an alien financier of criminal record, ruined a large number of credulous investors in a pawnbroker's enterprise at Bayonne. He was found dead shortly afterwards, probably by his own hand, but he had for a time cut such a dashing figure in society, including political society, that a rumor was started to the effect that the police had murdered him in order to silence the stories he might have told. In February, 1934, riotous demonstrations began from three sources: royalists who believed that the republic had revealed its rottenness and might be overthrown by a vigorous mass movement; Communists who conducted a counterdemonstration against "the Fascist peril"; and plain citizens, including in their ranks many army veterans, who desired in a rather confused way to register a protest against dishonesty and corruption in politics and also against the economic hardships of the time. Conflicts between soldiers and rioters took place on a scale unprecedented since the fall of the Paris Commune in 1871. Two mildly radical ministries wrestled in vain with

the situation. The Chautemps ministry had fallen because
of the scandal; the Deladier ministry fell because of the riots
which resulted. President Lebrun looked for a man with
reputation enough to save the hour, and recalled from retirement Ex-President Gaston Doumergue.

The seventy year old statesman accepted the premiership
and appointed the most remarkable coalition ministry which
The great the Third Republic had known. Besides its chief,
coalition the ministry contained five former premiers (Herriot, Tardieu, Barthou, Sarraut and Laval) and several other
members of comparable eminence, among them Marshal
Pétain, the hero of Verdun, as Minister of War. All the
principal parties and factions were represented except the
Socialists and Communists. The mere appointment of the
great coalition ministry quieted and reassured the nation
and ended the Stavisky crisis, but it contained so wide a
range of political opinion that almost from the first there was
friction between the nationalistic and conservative republicans, grouped around Tardieu, and the Radicals who followed Herriot. Only the pressure of a great emergency rendered such a combination possible; it resembled the coalition
of Conservatives, Liberals and Laborites in Great Britain
under Premier MacDonald at the same period. Premier
Doumergue urged constitutional reforms to strengthen the
executive, and especially to empower the Premier in certain
cases on his own authority to dissolve the Chamber of Deputies and order new elections. As he could not carry his
program he resigned in November, but his successor, Pierre-
Etienne Flandin, continued coalition government.

France in 1934 had still the strongest army and the best
balanced economic system in Europe. Though Germany's
The outlook rearmament alarmed the country and caused
for France enormous expenditure on an improved system of
frontier fortification, the new German militancy improved
France's diplomatic position by swinging Britain, Italy and

Russia nearer to the French point of view. Both the nation-alism of Clemenceau, Poincaré and Tardieu, and the inter-nationalism of Briand and Herriot, had the same object, the security of France, the difference being merely as to whether bayonets and alliances or the League of Nations and inter-national peace pacts represented the better road to that goal. There was little spirit left in France for great imperialistic ventures, such as the Napoleonic wars, or idealistic crusades, in the spirit of the French Revolution, for making the world (or any part of it except France) "safe for democracy"; or for revolutionary economic reconstructions either of the so-cialistic or the Fascist type. Disillusioned and "middle aged," engaged in a persistent but not too hopeful search for absolute security in an unsafe world, France faced the un-certain future.

Of the lesser states of western Europe, Spain had the most disturbed political career in the years immediately following the war. Though Spain was not a belligerent *Unrest in* nor in much danger of being drawn in, she could *Spain* not escape indirect economic influences of the war nor the general wave of political and social unrest which followed it. For many years before the war, indeed, the Spanish gov-ernment had been reputed one of the least stable in Europe. Alfonso XIII was a king of spirit and personally popular, but he had faced several attempts at assassination and knew that there were revolutionary factions among his subjects: republican doctrinaires who recalled that Spain had briefly experimented with a republic in the nineteenth century (1873–75) and that her immediate neighbors, France and Portugal, were both republics; socialists, communists, syndi-calists and even a formidable faction of anarchists; anti-cleri-cals who attributed all the woes of Spain, past and present, to the influence of the Roman Catholic Church; and Cata-lonian "regionalists" who demanded home rule for the Cata-lan-speaking districts on the eastern shore. The party politicians, conservative or liberal, were little solace to him; they were loyal enough, but often corrupt, cynical and incompetent, an easy target for the scorn of revolutionary extremists. The loss of colonial empire in 1898 had been humiliating to sensitive Spanish pride, and the prolonged bad fortune of the Spanish army in northern Morocco, where a small "zone of influence" had been allowed to Spain as compensation for the immensely greater gains of France, revived those unhappy memories. The revolutionary examples successively afforded by Portugal, Russia, Austria-Hungary and Germany, were anything but reassuring to a discontented monarchy.

In most of the twentieth century revolutions the active agent has been some civilian group or party (operating, to

The army takes a hand be sure, with the aid or the benevolent neutrality of the army); but Spain, like some of the Spanish-American republics, had a tradition of revolution by direct military action. In 1921 Abd-el-Krim, chief of the Mohammedan Riff tribesmen of northern Morocco, defeated a Spanish army superior in numbers. Shame burned in the soldiers' hearts and blame was freely cast on civilian ministers, incompetent generals and even on the monarch. Looking abroad at Mussolini's successful overturn of parliamentary government in Italy in 1922, many Spaniards began to whisper that it was time for the surgeon's knife to be applied to party politics in Spain as well. General Primo de Rivera, military governor of Barcelona, saw his chance to be a "savior of society." On September 13, 1923, he proclaimed a dictatorship and appointed a military directorate in place of the old parliament and ministry. The usual precautions were taken; the press was censored, opponents of the new government exiled, local governing bodies dismissed, obstinate civil servants discharged. Only King Alfonso was left undisturbed on his throne.

The new dictator undoubtedly meant well and conceived

himself to be performing a useful and necessary task. Indeed, Europe's twentieth century dictators seem *The dicta-*
to have been all men of genuine patriotism and *torship of*
sincere good intentions.[1] He strove to introduce *Primo de*
Rivera
efficiency and eliminate dishonesty from the
public services, to bring the Moroccan war to a victorious
conclusion, and to foster industry by subsidies and tariffs.
In December, 1925, he replaced the military directorate by a
civilian cabinet drawn from the new Patriotic Union party,
which he organized to sustain his régime. The change was
one of name rather than of substance, as "Premier Rivera"
had no more intention of conceding any parliamentary responsibility than "Rivera, Chief of the Military Directorate." Not until 1928 did he set about the making of a
permanent constitution to replace his personal rule. He,
like nearly all dictators, sought to win popularity by a
vigorous foreign policy and, like the others, sometimes
skated on thin ice. In 1926 he made a treaty with Italy
which was interpreted as directed against France, and he
announced Spain's intention to withdraw from the League
of Nations because the nation had not been granted a permanent seat on the League Council. This notification was,
however, withdrawn in 1928 and Spain continued to be a
Member State. In 1926 the Riff rebellion was finally crushed
by the joint efforts of Spain and France; at a total cost to
Spain of at least $150 for every rebel subject in Spanish
Morocco! The honors of war certainly rested with Abd-el-
Krim and the grim warriors of Islam who had for years held
at bay the scientific military machinery of Europe.

The tide of discontent rose in spite of all that the govern-
ment could do to terrorize opposition or bribe assent. The
Spanish "intellectuals," such as the philosopher Miguel de
Unamuno and the novelist Blasco Ibañez, were mainly

---

[1] But it is arguable that the paving system of the Infernal Regions has never been
more rapidly extended!

712 FRANCE AND HER NEIGHBORS

republican. Working-class discontent in no way lessened.

The fall of the dictatorship The Catalans continued to demand autonomy. Wearied by labor and sinking into illness, Primo de Rivera resigned power in January, 1930. King Alfonso appointed another officer, General Damaso Berenguer, in his place. The new dictator was personally popular because he had courageously denounced abuses in the army at the time of the first disastrous Moroccan campaigns. But the régime was not popular. A cry for the restoration of constitutional liberty arose from the university students, from the workingmen, from the Catalans, from some branches of the army itself. The promise to bring into force again the old constitution (1876–1923) no longer satisfied the crowd; nothing short of a new constituent assembly would suffice. Berenguer gave way to Admiral Juan Aznar. In April, 1931, local elections (for the towns and provinces) took place; they showed a sweeping republican victory.

The fall of the dictatorship brought down with it the monarchy, not only because it represented a swing towards

King Alfonso goes on his travels radicalism in general but because Alfonso was personally blamed for letting Primo de Rivera overturn the liberal constitution and make himself dictator. The ruler took things philosophically enough; not waiting for the national elections he quickly left the country, without any formal abdication but "suspending" his exercise of royal power. Many years before he was reported to have said: "Since 1914 thirty-nine dynasties have lost their thrones. One must always be ready for everything." [1] Quietly he traveled in France and England, seeming to be almost relieved at the loss of the burden of responsibility and danger which he had shrugged from his shoulders. A committee of republican leaders, headed by Niceto Alcalá Zamora, assumed the task of government which King Alfonso had laid down. The vengeance of the

[1] E. S. Bagger, *Eminent Europeans* (1922), page 43.

revolution pursued him even in exile; he was proclaimed a traitor and outlaw and his property in Spain confiscated.

In the midst of turmoil and popular excitement the general elections took place in June, 1931. A constituent Cortes was chosen, the moderate republican groups in control. Royalists and extreme revolutionists had alike been defeated. But the Cortes was sufficiently radical on the religious question to displease provisional President Zamora. In October it voted to abolish the Roman Catholic establishment, separating Church and State, to expel the Jesuit order and confiscate its property, and to limit the tolerated religious orders to their spiritual functions, forbidding them to maintain schools or engage in industry and commerce. Even Soviet Russia had not gone much further in anticlerical legislation! Zamora resigned in protest and his place was taken by Manuel Azaña. In December the constitution was adopted, — a purely democratic instrument, the culmination of more than a century of experiment with various paper constitutions and charters. Spain was declared a "democratic republic of workers of all classes" in which all political power rested on popular sovereignty. The legislative power was vested in a single-chamber Cortes, elected by universal suffrage without distinction of sex, holding office for four years. The President was to be chosen for a six-year term by an electoral college made up of the members of the Cortes and an equal number of specially chosen electors. He appointed the ministry, but it was made dependent on the support of the Cortes. The government was given power, if it wished, to undertake industrial enterprises and to buy up private land and industries, but the question of socialism was not prejudged but left for future legislation to determine. Education, marriage and divorce laws, and other matters of social policy were transferred entirely to secular jurisdiction and freed from control by the Church.

The Spanish Republic assumes its tasks

As a concession to the progressive but always turbulent and troublesome Catalans, the constitution permitted any

Home rule for Cata-lonia

region which desired home rule to frame a charter embodying the local liberties it desired and submit it to the Cortes for approval. In accordance with this provision, a special charter granted Catalonia the right to her own national language (akin to the Spanish but not identical with it) and flag, the right of raising local taxes and making local laws and controlling local executive officials; control over tariffs, immigration and military authority remaining with the central government. "Regionalists" in some other parts of Spain, notably Galicia and the Basque Provinces, agitated for similar privileges. Spain still remained hesitantly balanced between unitary government, like that of France, and complete federalism.

The constituent Cortes chose Zamora as the first president in spite of his protest against the anti-Catholic laws. Though

The swing towards conserva-tism

no formidable revolutionary movement developed, the government had to use martial force to put down a number of small insurrections of royalist army officers, communists and syndicalists who wanted a government in the Russian style, and violent anticlerical mobs that burned churches and convents.[1] A new election, the first under the terms of the constitution, took place near the end of 1933. It resulted in a complete defeat of the extreme revolutionary parties and the election of a considerable minority of royalists. The moderate republicans, however, continued to hold the balance of power. In the midst of disorders which every month threatened the republic with new revolutions and new dictatorships, the government had been able to do much useful work in the modernization of Spanish institutions. Education was zealously encouraged to reduce the heavy burden of il-

---

[1] The formation of a conservative ministry in October, 1934, caused a fresh revolutionary outbreak in several provinces.

literacy that had long handicapped the nation; a beginning was made in the breaking up of large estates into small farms; the army was reduced, and a repudiation of international war formally placed in the constitution.

Spain's western neighbor had shared in the World War among the victors but reaped no discernible fruits of victory, unless security for her African colonies against *Portugal* German ambition may be so counted. Since the revolution of 1910 the forms of government remained republican, but the substance was often a dictatorship. The most successful experiment in personal rule was that of General Antonio Carmona, who seized power in 1926 and held it with the aid of the army. In 1933 a new constitution was proclaimed and there was a partial return to parliamentary government, but General Carmona remained in power as President.

The Swiss Republic continued to be, on the whole, one of the happiest spots in Europe, though the difficulties inherent in being a neutral country entirely surrounded by *Switzerland* belligerent states had caused much anxiety during the war, and the influx of political refugees from Russia, Germany and the Danube nations often created difficult situations afterwards. As some compensation for these perplexities, the sessions of the League of Nations and of numerous international conferences of all sorts made the little country a sort of world capital and gave all nations a direct interest in maintaining Swiss independence and security.

The story of Belgium's reconstruction after the World War resembles that of France. On the whole, the smaller nation had the easier task. Although Belgium had *Belgium* suffered much from German exploitation during *and Luxem-* the occupation, yet the very completeness of this *burg* occupation diminished the area of military operations. Only the little western corner around Ypres was continuously in the battle zone. The devastated area was rebuilt, a new library rose at Louvain, and the chimes sounded again from the clock tower of Ypres. By drastic retrenchment and national self-denial Belgium restored stability to her currency. No fundamental change in the political life of the nation followed the war, though a tendency towards greater democracy appeared in the abolition of the plural vote and the establishment of equal manhood suffrage in 1921. The Socialist party was strong but unusually moderate in policy, and shared the tasks of government in a very conciliatory spirit with the Liberal and Catholic parties. A small Flemish "Front Party" caused some friction by demanding home rule for the Flemish-speaking districts. The Communist and Fascist groups were violent in tone but insignificant in number. King Albert (1909–34), the most heroic royal figure of the World War, died in a mountaineering accident and was succeeded by King Leopold III. After the war Belgium abandoned the "neutralization" which had failed to protect her in 1914 and assumed complete liberty of diplomatic action. In the main, her foreign policy has been one of the closest possible co-operation with France. Since 1922, Luxemburg, while retaining complete political independence, has been joined in a customs and currency union with Belgium.

The Netherlands, like Switzerland and the Scandinavian countries, maintained neutrality during the war in the face of *The* many difficulties. Since the war the Dutch have *Netherlands* maintained their traditional liberal institutions and have broadened the base of their democracy by the introduction of woman suffrage and proportional representation. The development of prosperity in the East Indies colonies and the new projects for draining the Zuyder Zee and thus building up a new province from the sea bottom have attracted national attention. The Dutch are "good Europeans" and have strongly supported internationalist and pacifist movements.

Denmark has been enlarged by the annexation of northern

Schleswig through plebiscite, but some of the more extreme chauvinists in Germany still conduct an active agitation against the new frontier in spite of the *Scandinavia* declared will of the people.   Denmark sold her West Indies possessions (the Virgin Islands) to the United States in 1917 and granted full home rule to her dependency of Iceland in 1918.   Norway gained the Spitsbergen (Svalbard) archipelago by international consent in 1919; barren and ice covered, but rich in coal.   Norway and Denmark had a friendly controversy over eastern Greenland, but the Danish claims prevailed; Sweden and Finland had a "case at law" over the Aaland Islands in the Baltic, in which Finland was victor.[1]   All the Scandinavian nations have been remarkably successful in maintaining substantial democracy under the forms of monarchy.   All are internationalist in sentiment and have a strong interest in upholding the League of Nations and the general peace of Europe, on which their own safety so greatly depends.

[1] See above, pages 496-97.

CHAPTER XXIX

THE BRITISH COMMONWEALTH
OF NATIONS

GREAT BRITAIN, like all the other victor powers, discovered after the war that victory in a great war, while doubtless

John Bull and a changed world
preferable to absolute defeat, afforded no guarantee of prosperity or security. At the cost of nearly a million lives, the direct expenditure of some $40,000,000,000, the loss of almost 8,000,000 tons of shipping, a ten-fold increase in the national debt, the Empire had been saved from a peace dictated by Germany. But the direct cost of the war was not the end of the matter. No other major nation was so dependent on foreign trade, and the close of the war found Germany bankrupt, Russia an "economic vacuum," France and Italy with reduced buying power, a series of "spite fence" tariffs surrounding the succession states to old Austria-Hungary, an American tariff higher than ever, anarchy in China, a native boycott of British goods in India, and everywhere a permanent dislocation of the old trade routes. The elation of armistice day did not long survive a study of the budget figures. Prime Minister David Lloyd George, who had succeeded Mr. Asquith at the head of the wartime coalition government in 1916, decided to hold an election in the first enthusiasm of victory, before a reaction of disillusionment might cut down his majority. He had an excellent pretext for doing so, in the fact that Parliament had already outlasted by three years the legal term of five years, it being reckoned inexpedient to hold general elections in the midst of war. He also desired a "mandate" from the voters, so that he could speak with confidence at Paris as the accredited representative of the British nation.

A new electoral law, passed earlier in the year, had made suffrage universal for men over twenty-one with a fixed residence qualification, and for the first time ad- *The election* mitted to the franchise a large number of women, *of 1918* those who were over thirty years of age and were qualified, or had husbands qualified, to vote in local elections. Thus about eight million new voters, some six million of them women, were added to the registry lists. At the same time parliamentary seats were redistributed to correspond with movements of the population, and plural voting (voting in more than one constituency) reduced to small proportions. Lloyd George headed a coalition of Conservatives, Liberals and Laborites without distinction of party, but it happened that many of the Liberals and most of the Labor men refused after the armistice to continue their support. So Premier Lloyd George was left in the difficult position of being the Liberal head of a mainly Conservative army. For the election, a mere appeal to patriotism sufficed. All opponents were dubbed "pacifists" or "pro-Germans" and the full costs of the war promised from the vanquished enemy. The coalition was overwhelmingly successful, winning 467 seats to 63 for the Labor party, the largest British opposition group.[1] But with the war ended could the ministry continue to count on the unfaltering allegiance of so composite a political army in the thorny days of reconstruction?

On his return from Paris, Lloyd George was faced with many tangled problems. In the first flush of generous enthusiasm at the end of the war, the British gov- *Troubles of* ernment had hoped to extend the scope of public *a coalition* education and by improved housing plans give the workingmen "homes fit for heroes to live in!" Instead the heavily burdened taxpayers revolted at any peace-time additions to the enormous load of debt which the war had left. As measures of relief, the government extended unemployment in-

[1] The Sinn Fein (republican) Irish party refused to enter Parliament.

surance on a liberal scale, agreed to a trade treaty with Russia in the faint hope of reviving commerce in eastern Europe, encouraged emigration to the colonies and imposed a duty of one-third on imports competing with certain "key industries" in Great Britain. In spite of every effort, unemployment rose to some two million in 1921. Unemployment insurance became a constant charge on the public purse, endured only because it was the alternative to starvation and revolution. The high cost of living caused labor discontent, reflected in numerous strikes.[1] Though Lloyd George stayed in office long enough to establish the Irish Free State, his handling of the Irish situation won him little credit, Conservatives regarding it as a surrender to sedition and Liberals wondering why it had taken years of miserable civil strife to open his eyes to the necessity of granting full "Dominion Home Rule." Liberals feared that the emergency tariff to protect industries essential in wartime might be the beginning of the end of free trade. The failure of the expected reparations payments from Germany brought the government foes on two flanks, those who laid blame on Germany and demanded stronger measures against the vanquished, and those who held that the Treaty of Versailles was impossible in its demands, and its authors — Lloyd George among them — were therefore to blame for the economic crisis. Finally, Lloyd George's support of Greece in the unsuccessful Turkish campaign displeased many Conservatives who feared lest British hostility to Turkey might rouse resentment among millions of Mohammedan subjects of the British crown in India.

Convinced by this accumulation of unpopularity that it was now safe to oust Lloyd George, the Conservatives in October, 1922, announced their withdrawal from the coalition. As this left the government without a majority, a

[1] "In 1919 we lost 34,000,000 working days through industrial disputes; in 1920 over 27,000,000; in 1921 nearly 90,000,000." C. F. G. Masterman, *England after War*, (1923), page 147.

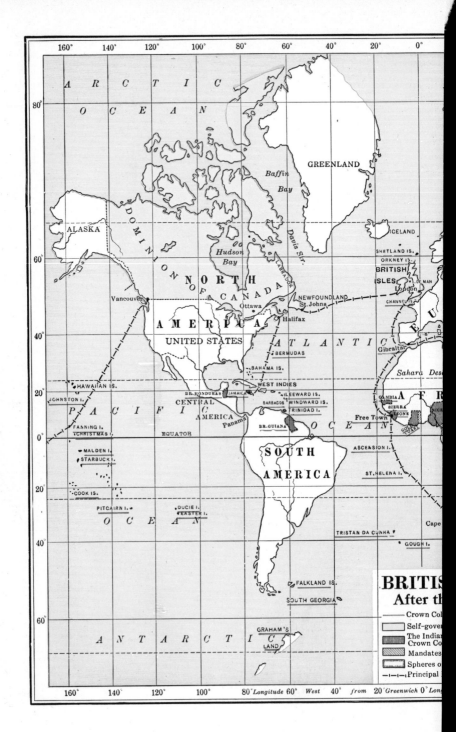

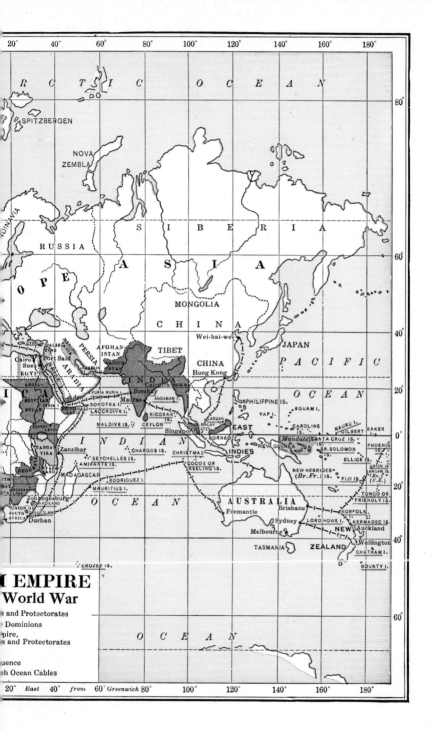

EMPIRE
World War

s and Protectorates
Dominions
pire,
s and Protectorates

uence
h Ocean Cables

new election was necessary. The Conservatives were completely successful, but the sensation of the election was the great increase in the Labor vote. *The Conservatives*
The Labor party polled over four million popu- *vault into*
the saddle
lar votes and seated 142 members of the House of
Commons. Andrew Bonar Law, as Conservative leader, became Prime Minister and Ramsay MacDonald, leader of the
Labor party, the head of "His Majesty's Opposition."
For the Liberals it was a day of disaster. Not only was the
party a poor third in the running, but it was split into mutually hostile factions. The followers of Mr. Asquith, the
"Independent Liberals," could not forgive Premier Lloyd
George for having forced his former chief from the premiership during the war and in many constituencies they ran
candidates against the "National Liberals." Had no new
issue been raised, the Conservatives might have had a long
tenure of office. But Premier Bonar Law was already in
poor health, and after a few months' tenure of office he relinquished the leadership to Stanley Baldwin. Mr. Baldwin
was a business man who had conducted the war debt negotiations with the United States on behalf of the government.
He bore an exceptionally high character as a man of honor
and integrity, but he was relatively a newcomer to politics
and his elevation to power caused some surprise in party
circles.[1] Rather suddenly he became convinced that a protective tariff system was necessary to meet the economic depression; he would consent neither to delay his remedy nor
to impose it on the country without a fresh mandate from
the voters. So in December, 1923, new elections were called.

The result was rather inconclusive. The Conservatives
still held a plurality but not a majority, for Britain no longer
enjoyed the conveniences of a two-party system. Any minis-

[1] Lord Birkenhead ridiculed Baldwin's "second-class brains" and Lord Curzon is
said to have wept on hearing of Baldwin's appointment, not only because he himself had been passed by, but because the honor had gone to a man whom he regarded
as of no political importance!

try which held office would have to do so in the continental
The first manner by seeking support from more than one
Labor min- group. The Conservatives could not join with
istry, 1924 anyone because both Liberals and Laborites
were opposed to the protective tariff policy on which the
election had just been fought. But Labor with 191 seats
was the second party in voting strength. So King George,
no doubt marveling much at this strange new world where
such things happened, summoned Ramsay MacDonald to
be the responsible head of the British government; the first
man ever called to that post since cabinet government began
who was neither Whig nor Tory, Liberal nor Conservative.
MacDonald, the son of a Scottish laborer, had been for many
years the most prominent Labor leader. He had flatly opposed Britain's entrance into the World War even after the
invasion of Belgium, and as a pacifist had suffered much
ostracism. But he was no radical firebrand; rather a suave,
moderate gentleman, strikingly handsome, an "old hand" at
the game of party politics and more criticized as a clever opportunist than as a stubborn extremist. No one who knew
him lost sleep for fear that a Labor ministry meant revolution. Moreover, the Labor ministry, though it contained only
a few Liberal (or formerly Liberal) members, depended on
Liberal votes. Any really socialistic measure would meet
with enough Liberal opposition to overthrow the ministry.
Though the Liberals were still only a third party and not
strong enough to form a ministry of their own, they had reunited their divided factions and held the balance of power
between Conservatism and Labor. The cabinet was a strong
one, though curiously composite, containing such leaders as
Philip Snowden, pacifist and Socialist; Arthur Henderson,
trades unionist and supporter of the wartime coalition government; Sidney Webb, social theorist and leader of the Fabian Socialists; and Lord Haldane, a liberal aristocrat.

Debarred from radical experiments in domestic affairs by

his parliamentary situation, MacDonald during his short first term of office devoted his attention mainly to problems of foreign policy, a field which had always interested him. He extended full recognition to Russia and negotiated a "most favored nation" commercial treaty with that country, though he failed to secure payment of Russia's debts to Great Britain. He was fortunate enough to find in Premier Herriot of France a kindred spirit and, paradoxically enough, he succeeded in establishing more cordial relations with France, in spite of his anti-war record, than any of his predecessors'in office who had supported the French alliance! Yet if his chief success was in the sphere of foreign policy it was on this point also that his ministry was wrecked. Rumors spread that Bolshevist propaganda, encouraged by British negotiations with Russia, was undermining the loyalty of the army. The Liberals withdrew their support and MacDonald appealed to the country in October, 1924; the third election in three years. Though the popular vote of the Labor party actually increased, many seats were lost; the Liberals suffered even more heavily, and the Conservative party returned to office with a secure majority over all opponents. As a matter of course, Baldwin again became Premier. This time he did not repeat his former mistake of an untimely revival of the tariff issue, and held office for five years. Many of his colleagues grumbled that Baldwin was not "doing anything," but he seems to have been of the opinion that the country wanted tranquillity from agitation more than any program of reform.

Among all the major British industries, with the possible exception of shipbuilding, none suffered more than coal mining in the years after the war. There were many causes for this: the lessened buying power of the continental European market, the increased use of oil fuel and water power, the burden of taxation and ground rents

Russia recognized and MacDonald defeated

The coal strike

("royalties"), the partial exhaustion of veins near the surface (for coal mining has been intensively carried on longer in Great Britain than anywhere else), competition with German coal delivered by way of reparations to France, the general depression in British industry. The coal operators threatened a cut in wages to maintain their profits in the face of falling prices. To avert a strike, the government agreed for a time to grant a subsidy to the depressed industry on condition that wage scales would be maintained from July, 1925, to May, 1926. The miners themselves demanded that the coal mines become national property, but the government was not ready for this step — or rather stride — towards socialism. In 1926 a royal commission which had investigated the situation recommended discontinuing the government subsidy, closing the less profitable mines, buying up royalty rights but permitting private operation and management under government lease. The suspension of the subsidy resulted in a decrease of wages and an increase of the working day from seven to eight hours. The miners' answer was "Not a minute on the day, not a penny off the pay" and a general strike.

This strike soon extended beyond the coal mines to include all unionized industry, and British industy is far more com-

The general pletely unionized than American or continental
strike, 1926 European. In May, 1926, the Trades Union Congress started a general strike, beginning with the railway, transport and printing trades, in aid of the coal miners. Nearly three million workmen, about half the trades unionists in the country, walked out. No attempt was made to stop gas or electric plants and other essential public utilities, and the transport tie-up was made less serious by the enlistment of hundreds of thousands of volunteer strikebreakers. Motor trucks took the place of railway trains to a great extent, as Britain is a small country with excellent highroads. Many trades unionists were frightened at their own temerity

and brought pressure on their leaders to call off the sympathetic strike. It ended in nine days, a complete failure. From first to last there was hardly an instance of serious disorder. With extraordinary good humor on both sides the strikers and strikebreakers alike refrained from violence. The coal strike dragged on until November and ended in surrender. In 1927 the government passed an important Trades Disputes Act which prohibited general sympathetic strikes and all "political" strikes designed to coerce the government and the general public rather than the employers, forbade intimidation of strikebreakers, prohibited civil servants from joining outside unions, and prevented the collection of party dues or political funds from any trades-union member except by his express permission.

Apart from the crushing of the general strike, there is not much of outstanding importance to chronicle during the second Baldwin ministry. Though the general *Conservative policies* question of a protective tariff had been postponed, certain industries were "safeguarded" by special legislation, among them the infant automobile and cinematograph industries which had to face heavy American competition. Industries were also helped by relieving them of three-fourths of their share of local taxes (the "rates"); most of the loss being made up by a gasoline tax. Old-age pensions were extended more widely and made to include benefits to widows and orphans. Women were granted suffrage in 1928 on the same terms as men, adding about five million more voters to the electorate.[1] A plan for the reform of the House of Lords, decreasing its membership and making it in part appointed by the Crown for life and in part elected by the whole peer-

---

[1] Sometimes called the "flapper vote bill" because the law lowered the age limit from thirty to twenty-one. The reason for the discrimination in the law of 1918 was that the war had increased the already marked excess of women over men in the British Isles and it was feared that equality would mean that the "women would outvote the men." The excess still existed ten years later, but it had been observed in the meantime that voting never followed sex lines, that the women divided their vote among all the parties very much as the men did.

age for fixed terms, was withdrawn because of the fierce opposition of the Liberals, Laborites and more progressive Conservatives, who pointed out that by depriving the Crown (in reality, the ministry) of the power to create an unlimited number of peers there would be no way of ending a serious deadlock between Lords and Commons and, in the words of a Liberal manifesto, "they might force the nation to choose between an uncontrolled hereditary Chamber and revolution." An attempt to revise the prayer book of the established Church of England, though it met with the approval of most of the church authorities, was rejected by Parliament on the ground that the changes slanted towards Roman Catholicism. In foreign affairs the ministry continued the internationalist and conciliatory policies of MacDonald and had the great credit of the Locarno Pact to place on its record. Indeed, there has been singularly little divergence in Conservative, Liberal or Labor foreign policy; all three parties being firmly convinced that peace was the greatest of British interests.

The elections of 1929 returned 289 Labor members, 259 Conservatives and only 58 Liberals. Though no party had an absolute majority, Labor for the first time held a plurality in the House of Commons. MacDonald was the only possible Prime Minister under the circumstances, and he had stronger support than for his first ministry. But he took office at an inauspicious moment. Trade was declining and unemployment rapidly increasing; from 1929 to 1931 the estimated number of those out of work increased from one to nearly three million. To effect drastic economies in order that the budget might be balanced, Premier MacDonald was forced to abandon party government and form a "national" or coalition cabinet, thereby virtually admitting that an economic crisis as serious as war confronted the nation. The Labor party split. Philip Snowden, the Chancellor of the Ex-

MacDonald's second ministry, 1929

chequer, stood with MacDonald, but the majority of the party repudiated his leadership, contending that the budget should have been balanced by increased taxation on the rich rather than by retrenchments in the social services that affected chiefly the poor. This dissident group chose Arthur Henderson as leader, and read MacDonald and all who stood with him out of the party. In September, 1931, Britain abandoned the gold standard and the pound sank to about two-thirds of its nominal value. New elections were ordered for October.

Ramsay MacDonald led to the polls an army as composite as that which formerly had followed David Lloyd George — a national coalition of Conservatives, Liberals and *Coalition* Laborites against those Liberals and Laborites *Government versus* who refused to, come into the fold. They de- *Economic* manded a blank check from the nation, the right *Depression* to take any essential steps, protective tariffs included, to meet the emergency. The representation of the Labor party was reduced to 52; Lloyd George's Liberal group was cut to four. The government had a majority over all opponents of nearly five hundred in a House of 615. It was a "famous victory," but it left Premier MacDonald in the very peculiar position of heading a mainly Conservative rank and file. At any moment the Conservatives could have turned him out, as they once had Lloyd George, and put at the head of the government a candidate of their own choice — Baldwin or another. That they did not do so may be attributed in part to fear of disturbing recovery and risking their majority by a new political crisis, and in part to a feeling that it would hardly be generous to overturn a statesman who had sacrificed his party ties and party program in order to establish national unity. At all events, if a Labor man headed the government, the Conservatives mainly dictated the program. They held a majority in the cabinet and their policy of a protective tariff was at last officially endorsed.

At an Imperial Economic Conference held at Ottawa in 1932 Great Britain and the Dominions embarked on a far-reaching policy of "Imperial preference" with a view to making the British Commonwealth a largely self-sustaining economic unit. No such plan was possible for the British Isles themselves, which *must* trade abroad or starve at home; but "abroad" might be made to mean "with the Dominions," to a very considerable extent. The commercial treaties resulting from the Ottawa Conference did not, indeed, go to the length advocated by Joseph Chamberlain at the opening of the century; there was no "Empire free trade," no customs union for the whole Commonwealth and no common tariff against the outside world. They amounted only to a series of reciprocity and preference agreements over a period of years by which British exports were given a favored position in the Dominion markets, and the British in return not only admitted Dominion produce on easy terms but erected new tariff barriers against foreign imports. Even tariffs on wheat and meat, denounced as "food taxes" ever since the eighteen-forties, were conceded to meet the wishes of the Dominions. The apparently complete transition from free trade to protection caused some schism in the large national majority which dominated Parliament. Philip Snowden (now Viscount Snowden) opposed the tariff legislation in the House of Lords, and Sir Herbert Samuel crossed the floor of the House of Commons to the opposition benches with a large section of the Liberals. There were no less than three Liberal parties now, — the followers of Sir John Simon, Foreign Secretary, who still supported the ministry; the Samuel Liberals who gave general support but refused to sanction protective tariffs; and the small Lloyd George faction which was at all points hostile!

Whether protective tariffs brought about the gradual economic recovery of Great Britain or impeded it is a matter

The Ottawa Conference and the protective tariff

of partisan debate; but, whatever the cause, in 1933 and 1934 signs of betterment were perceptible. The *The British* budget was balanced, though only by throwing *path to re-* overboard the debt to the United States. Unem- *covery* ployment decreased, though it still remained a major problem and perhaps an insoluble one. The internal debt was reduced by floating a conversion loan at three and one half per cent in place of an existing loan, now retired, at five per cent. If disastrous new shocks did not come to British trade from the unsettled political situation in central Europe, the road to recovery seemed clear. The political earthquakes of the continent, though they injured British prosperity, did not directly endanger British stability. The Communists were never able to capture more than one or two seats in the House of Commons, and Sir Oswald Mosley's attempts to emulate Mussolini and create an order of black-shirted British Fascists found even less support. In coalition government and a compromise program Great Britain had found an alternative solution to dictatorship for those moments of crisis when ordinary party government breaks down.

The end of the World War left the British Empire in a position comparable in many ways to that held on the eve of Waterloo. Once again the Empire had emerged *The British* intact, even augmented, from a struggle with the *Empire in* strongest continental European State; sea power *1919* had vanquished land power. The peril of 1914–18 had perhaps been greater than that of 1792–1815, for the invention of the Zeppelin, the airplane and the submarine robbed the command of the sea of its old guarantee of complete national security. But, at all events, the destruction of the German fleet had ended the greatest national peril since the battle of Trafalgar. Only the American navy remained as a serious rival to the British, and the United States was not generally reckoned a possible foe. As in the previous peace conferences of the eighteenth and nineteenth centuries, Britain sought territorial gains outside Europe, so that they could be protected by naval strength alone. By mandate from the League of Nations the British held Iraq, Palestine, Tanganyika (formerly German East Africa), parts of Togoland and Kamerun, and the Pacific island of Nauru. British South Africa held a similar mandate for German Southwest Africa; Australia for Kaiserwilhelmsland and the Bismarck Archipelago; New Zealand for German Samoa. Egypt and Cyprus had passed from nominal Turkish to British suzerainty, but without much actual change in administration. Few of these new acquisitions promised much immediate profit, but they at least relieved the fringes of the Empire from many strategic dangers to which they had been exposed in 1914.

The British were less interested in adding to the extent of their domains than in consolidating what they had al-

Nationalism within the Empire ready. During the war the press had constantly prophesied that a sense of common peril endured would make the British Isles truly a "United Kingdom," attach the Dominions more closely to the mother country, and cause the far-flung dependencies from Egypt to India to forget their ambitions for national independence. This prediction was in part justified, but in larger part falsified. No part of the Empire wholly broke away, but in many cases the bonds of union were loosened rather than tightened. The Dominions remained loyal but were cold to all plans for close Imperial federation; insisting, indeed, on separate representation in the League of Nations Assembly. British India was accorded increased home rule, but the independence movement remained as strong as before.[1] The definite protectorate over Egypt was abandoned for a veiled diplomatic control over a nominally independent Egyptian kingdom. In Ireland a sanguinary civil war terminated at long last in the creation of the Irish Free State with all the rights of a Dominion.

[1] For the problems of postwar India, see Chapter XXX.

Great Britain was not slow to recognize the local sentiment of the Dominions and find a formula which would reconcile complete autonomy with loyalty to that political entity which was now frequently termed "the British Commonwealth of Nations." At an Imperial Conference in 1926 the Dominions were ranked on a footing of entire legal equality with Great Britain as "autonomous communities within the British Empire, equal in status, in no way subordinate one to another in any respect of their domestic or external affairs, though united by a common allegiance to the Crown, and freely associated as members of the British Commonwealth of Nations." This declaration of constitutional principle was made concrete by the Statute of Westminster (1931) which declared that no law enacted by a Dominion was invalidated by reason of conflict with British legislation or might be vetoed by the King on the advice of his British ministers, that Parliament could not legislate for any Dominion without its express consent, and that no change in the law concerning the succession to the British throne might be made without the consent of the Dominions. The British Dominions, which had already chosen their own representatives to the League of Nations, appointed their own diplomatic agents to foreign countries and made treaties on their own responsibility. Though the British ministry still appointed governors-general for the Dominions, the custom became established of following the advice of Dominion ministries even in these appointments. What ties remained? The name of the King, the fact of the fleet, the consultations at Imperial Conferences, the carrying of certain legal cases involving constitutional issues to the judicial committee of the British Privy Council, a certain sentiment of common patriotism and a belief in common interests. Though some ties were invisible and others uncertain,[1] this did not diminish

From Empire to Commonwealth

___

[1] For example, legal experts were still divided as to whether the Dominions had the

the confidence of the average Briton that they would hold in time of stress as they had in 1914.

Ireland, the latest recruit to Dominion rank, won her position with much difficulty. Twice in Gladstone's day Home *Ireland in* Rule bills failed in Parliament; a third measure *the World* passed the Commons in 1912 and would have *War* been put into force in 1914 (after overpassing the veto of the House of Lords) if the coming of the World War had not delayed its operation. Acting on the old maxim "England's extremity is Ireland's opportunity," an extreme faction of Irish nationalists chose the spring of 1916, a dark moment of the war, for rebellion. The official Nationalist party of John Redmond held aloof, preferring parliamentary methods to insurrection. The driving force in the rebellion was the party of Sinn Fein ("Ourselves"), a group of ardent young supernationalists who had striven since 1905 to revive the Gaelic language and culture and sever Ireland from all contact with "the ways of the Saxon." During Easter week in 1916 an insurgent group captured public buildings in Dublin, proclaimed a republic and hailed Germany as one of their "gallant allies." The uprising was speedily put down and fifteen leaders executed, among them Sir Roger Casement who had made a distinguished record in the British colonial service. Resentment at the executions practically put an end to the already stagnant recruiting of soldiers in southern Ireland. Premier Lloyd George hoped to introduce conscription, already in force in Great Britain, but to sugarcoat the dose by an immediate introduction of home rule.

Evidently the old plan of 1914 would not serve; for one thing it would have meant civil war in Ulster, the Protestant *The "Irish* northeastern corner of the country which was *Republic"* strongly hostile to Irish independence or even to Irish autonomy. So Lloyd George invited a nominated

right to secede at will, whether any part of the Commonwealth could be neutral if the rest were at war, and sundry other matters.

convention of all shades of Irish opinion to elaborate a measure of compromise. Sir Horace Plunkett, whose activities on behalf of co-operative dairying had worked a veritable revolution in Irish agriculture, presided as a non-partisan chairman. The Convention failed, mainly because the Ulster members feared to be separated from Great Britain by a tariff wall, while the Nationalists insisted on control of the customs as an essential part of self-government. The failure of the Convention, the death of the moderate leader Redmond, and the fear of conscription worked together to revive Sinn Fein activity in 1918. In the general elections at the close of the year Sinn Fein captured 73 Irish seats to seven Nationalists and 25 Unionists (opposed to Home Rule). The Sinn Fein members treated the election as a plebiscite for an independent Irish Republic, which they duly proclaimed, and organized an Assembly (*Dail Eireann*) of their own. Eamonn De Valera, who had taken part in the rebellion but had survived its collapse, was chosen President. He was born in New York, the son of a Spanish father and an Irish mother, but had spent much of his life in Ireland. He was an intense, humorless idealist, full of the poetry rather than the prose of politics and revolted by the very idea of compromise. The presence of British forces prevented the Irish Republic from ever obtaining a *de facto* existence; many members of its government were in prison or exile, its revenues were largely "loans" (really gifts) from sympathetic Irish-Americans, and the Paris Peace Conference refused to receive its delegates.

Premier Lloyd George, though always a "Home Ruler," was in a difficult parliamentary position; he had to reckon not only with Sinn Fein but also with the moderate Irish Nationalists who did not demand complete independence, with the Ulstermen who had taken oath never to submit to an Irish government, and with the British public, — especially the Conservative or Unionist *The Home Rule Act of 1920* partisans who simply regarded the Sinn Feiners as "traitors" who had tried to wreck the Empire while it was in death struggle with Germany. Being as fond of compromise as De Valera was averse to it, Lloyd George hoped to please everybody by a new Home Rule bill which created two Irish parliaments, one for the South and one for Ulster, and a Council, chosen by the two parliaments, to arrange matters of common interest. As the general Parliament of the United Kingdom still held jurisdiction over matters of peace, war, national defense, foreign relations, tariffs and excise, both parts of Ireland were still to send representatives there, though in diminished numbers. Northern Ireland reluctantly accepted the new arrangements, but the Sinn Feiners would have nothing to do with any plan short of complete independence.

Something like anarchy ensued throughout Southern Ireland. The actual number killed was small in comparison *The Irish* with the death roll in some of the civil wars on *Civil War* the continent, as in Russia in 1918–20 or Austria in 1934, and the fighting did not come to a head in any large pitched battle; but there were on both sides village raids, reprisals, cottage burnings, assassinations from ambush and all the miserable characteristics of guerrilla warfare. The secret orders of the "Republic" were more readily obeyed than the public orders of the legal authorities. The old Irish constabulary failed to cope with the situation and had to be reorganized with a new auxiliary force, chiefly of World War veterans, who wore the army khaki and the black armband of the police and thus acquired the nickname of "black and tans." Weary of the inglorious strife, Lloyd George invited the leaders of the rebellion to a peace conference in the summer of 1921. Though an armistice was arranged, De Valera rejected the terms of settlement; but a second conference was called in October, and in December a treaty was at last signed.

By the terms of the treaty, subsequently approved as law

by the British Parliament and by the revolutionary Dail Eireann, Southern Ireland was given Dominion status as an Irish Free State. The Free State *The Irish Free State* was to have full control over her own finances and tariffs, complete legislative autonomy, and a responsible ministry. Northern Ireland (Ulster) was to be free to join the Free State or retain her status under the Act of 1920. No Free State representatives were to attend the British Parliament; just as none attend from Australia or Canada. No religious discrimination might be made. The Free State was to assume a proportionate share of the British national debt. Some of the Sinn Feiners balked at the oath of allegiance to King George V, so the explanation was inserted that this oath involved no subordination to Britain but was taken "in virtue of the common citizenship of Ireland with Great Britain and her adherence to and membership of the group of nations forming the British Commonwealth of Nations."

President De Valera refused to accept the treaty and civil war broke out afresh, this time between the Irish Free State and the irreconcilable minority who insisted on complete independence. Sinn Fein as an organi- *Civil War continues* zation split between the two parties. Arthur Griffith, head of the provisional government, died of heart failure brought on by overwork and anxiety; Michael Collins was murdered from ambush by rebels who a few months earlier had obeyed him as "Minister of War." In the elections of 1922 the Free Staters were victorious but the extremists continued their campaign of terror against the "traitors" who had compromised with England. William Cosgrave and Kevin O'Higgins took up the tasks which death had snatched from Griffith and Collins, and at last succeeded so thoroughly in stamping out insurrection that in 1923 De Valera at last ordered his followers to cease fighting. But individual acts of terrorism still took place; in 1927 O'Higgins was murdered to avenge his repression of the insurgents.

The Irish Free State was based on purely democratic principles. The Parliament or *Oireachtas* was divided into an
The Irish government Assembly (*Dail Eireann*), chosen by universal adult suffrage with proportional representation, and a Senate (after 1928 chosen by joint vote of the two houses). The *Dail Eireann* was much the more powerful house, not only because it initiated legislation and controlled finance, but because it directly elected the Executive Council or ministry. In 1922 the British government appointed an Irish Nationalist, Timothy Healy, as the first Governor General of the new Dominion. William Cosgrave became first President of the Council. De Valera changed his tactics but not his ultimate aim; he now strove to capture the Free State by election and then one by one sever the ties which still bound Ireland to the British Crown. Cosgrave's followers, better satisfied with the existing status of the Free State, turned their attention to the economic development of Ireland, advocating a policy of small land holdings, protective tariffs even against British goods, development of electric power, government subsidies for sugar beet culture, and a balanced budget.

Ulster, officially "Northern Ireland," not only refused to join the new Free State but clung to the frontiers fixed by the
The Ulster question Act of 1920. The British government was caught in a dilemma. To revise those boundaries, as the Free State expected, would be resisted by the Ulstermen as a violation of that Act, which Ulster had loyally accepted though not particularly desiring it. Not to revise them, would be treated in the Free State as disregard of the Treaty of 1921 which the moderates, at least, in Southern Ireland had accepted with equal loyalty. So in 1925 the British made a compromise agreement at their own expense; permitting Ulster to retain her old frontier, but compensating the Irish Free State by relieving her from her share in the public debts of the United Kingdom.

In 1927 the followers of De Valera, with the party designation of *Fianna Fail*, announced that they would swallow their scruples as to taking the oath of allegiance *De Valera* for the sake of entering political life. In 1932 *in power at* the elections turned in their favor and De Valera, *last* with the aid of a small Labor party which held the balance of power, became President of the Council. He held out three baits to the electors: the abolition of the oath to the King, the abolition of repayments to Great Britain of money loaned for land purchases, and an end to the repressive special acts and police measures under which Ireland had been governed since the assassination of O'Higgins. In office he endeavored to carry out this program but met with many obstacles. The British insisted that either to abolish the oath of allegiance or suspend land purchase annuities would break the treaty by virtue of which the Free State existed. Both sides offered to arbitrate the financial question, but the British insisted that since the controversy arose within the British Commonwealth no foreign or international tribunal could be chosen; De Valera insisted that, as Ireland was a sovereign nation, a non-British tribunal *must* be chosen! Because of the principle involved, neither side would give way and the result was a tariff war, the British levying a special import duty on Irish goods to cover the loss of the land annuities, Ireland imposing duties on British goods in retaliation. The tariff war was a heavier burden on Ireland than on Great Britain, since the British market bulks larger in Ireland's trade than the Irish market does in Britain's. De Valera, however, who wanted Ireland to become a self-sustaining nation, independent of Britain economically as well as politically, was not displeased. In 1933 a new election strengthened his party. Finding the Senate in opposition to his program, especially the abolition of the oath of allegiance, he added another plank to his platform, — the abolition of the Senate, — and introduced a measure to that effect in 1934.

The overseas Dominions of the British Commonwealth participated largely in the World War; Australian and New *The elder* Zealand forces ("Anzacs") mainly in the Turkish *Dominions:* war zone, Canadians and Newfoundlanders on *South* the Western front, and South Africans in "mop- *Africa* ping up" the German African colonies. Though some French Canadians, Irish Australians and Dutch South Africans showed indifference to the war, the only overt dis- loyalty was a small insurrection led by former Boer army officers in protest against the conquest of German Southwest Africa in 1914. Throughout the war and at the Paris Peace Conference the Union of South Africa was represented by two former Boer generals, loyal to the British Common- wealth, Louis Botha and Jan Smuts. Botha died in 1919, and in 1924 Smuts was forced from office by the more radical Dutch element headed by General J. B. M. Hertzog. Like De Valera in Ireland, Hertzog at first headed a coalition made up of republican separatists and socialistic Labor party allies; and in both cases it was the Labor element which acted as a brake to prevent an immediate secession crisis. But in office, as usually happens, General Hertzog proved to be more moderate than when in opposition. He dropped the secession issue and concentrated on some minor aspects of au- tonomy, — the right to fly a Dominion flag besides the Union Jack, the complete equality of Dutch [1] with English in all parts of the South African Union, and the like. The British colony of Rhodesia refused to enter the Union, but changed her chartered company government for the status of a British "crown colony." In all parts of southern and eastern Africa the overshadowing question is how to reconcile the rights of the native African with the settlement and development of the resources of the country by the European immigrant, be he Briton or Boer.

Canadian politics continued after the war very much

[1] In its local dialect, "Afrikaans."

along traditional lines: a Conservative party emphasizing the Imperial connection and advocating a pro- *Canada* tective tariff, and a Liberal party favoring home *and New-* rule, French Canadian interests and low tariffs, *foundland* and small radical labor and farmer groups. During the 'twenties the Liberals were long in office, but the return of hard times brought the Conservatives into power in 1930. The Imperial Economic Conference of 1932 for the promotion of trade within the limits of the British Commonwealth took place at Ottawa and enlisted much sympathy in the Dominion for a policy of "Imperial preference." Newfoundland felt so severely the effects of the depression that in 1933 she agreed to surrender her position as a Dominion and revert temporarily to the status of a "crown colony" governed by Great Britain until her financial entanglements could be straightened out.

The strain of the war told heavily on the young communities of Australia and New Zealand, which, like most newly settled regions, had been heavy borrowers even *Australasia* in time of peace, and their Pacific Island "mandates" added new responsibilities rather than new revenues. Yet in general their history was one of steady progress until the world depression, which was so severely felt that the local state government of New South Wales, in the hands of a radical Labor party group, threatened to suspend payment on the public debt, and the federal government of the Commonwealth of Australia had to straighten out the situation. In both Australasian Dominions the recent political tendency has been towards a grouping of all other parties into "national" coalitions against the trades-union dominated Labor parties.

CHAPTER XXX
EUROPE AND THE WIDER WORLD

AFTER the war a vast literature of pessimism appeared on both sides of the Atlantic whose burden was that Europe had

Has the sun of Europe set? lost both her moral and her material ascendancy in the world.[1] The prophets of woe differed only as to whether America or Asia would be the heir to the vacant throne or all the world collapse into a common anarchy. A more cheerful view has also been advanced: that Europe's apparent defeat is really only the completeness of her victory, that European civilization is no longer a monopoly of one continent but has broadened into a common world civilization. If Japan has become a formidable rival of the West, it is because she herself has become westernized; if China, India, Persia, Turkey and the Mohammedan states of North Africa show an intransigeant nationalism, it is because they have studied nationalism and democracy from European books and European example. On either theory it is universally admitted that colonial imperialism no longer stands where it did in the eighteen-nineties, and less is heard of "backward races," "subject peoples" and the "White Man's burden."

The two British dependencies outside Europe which have been most affected by native nationalism are Egypt and

Nationalism in Egypt India. Prior to 1914 Egypt was nominally tributary to Turkey, but in actual practise the British controlled the foreign policy, the administration, and (subject to certain rights of France) the finances of Egypt; they also held a controlling interest in the Suez Canal and, in form jointly with Egypt, ruled the Sudan on the upper Nile.

---

[1] Such as O. Spengler, *Decline of the West*; A. Demangeon, *Le Déclin de l'Europe*; F. Nitti, *The Decadence of Europe*; L. Stoddard, *The Rising Tide of Color*; M. Muret, *The Twilight of the White Races*, etc.

From 1914 to 1922 Egypt was a British protectorate, but in the latter year recognized as an independent monarchy under King Fuad. This independence, however, was very much qualified by treaty stipulations which guaranteed foreign financial interests, British control of the Suez Canal and rights in the Sudan, and general British direction of Egyptian foreign policy. Under the leadership of Zaghlul Pasha the extreme nationalists ("Wafd" party) continued their agitation against British interference in Egyptian affairs. In November, 1924, Sir Lee Stack, commanding the British forces in Egypt, was assassinated. The British government demanded an indemnity, repression of anti-British agitation, unrestricted military control over the Sudan and a free hand in managing Sudanese irrigation projects. The Egyptians appealed in vain to the League of Nations; the British replied that the issue was a "domestic" one — in other words that "independent Egypt" was still in reality a British dependency.

In the main British India remained astonishingly peaceful and loyal during the World War. In spite of disorders fomented by enemy agents, the natural sympathy *India after* of the Moslems of India with their fellow believers *the war* in Turkey, the general Asiatic unrest caused by the war and the Russian revolution, India contributed heavily both men and money towards the prosecution of the war and did little to distract British attention from the tasks in hand on European battlefields. Yet the articulate part of the Indian peoples were far from content with British rule and, with varying intensity, demanded self-government. In program they did not agree among themselves. At the extreme left were terrorists who were for driving out the British by a campaign of political assassination and open revolt. Next were the advocates of independence by passive resistance or "non-co-operation," who were in favor of a boycott of British goods, a revival of native handicrafts, "civil disobedience" to British laws and disregard of all alien authority. The leader of this group, Mohandas K. Gandhi, was generally revered as a "Mahatma" or saint. Next, an intermediate group of practical politicians found a useful formula in the phrase "Dominion Home Rule," with the implication that India might become an equal partner in the British Commonwealth like Australia or Canada. Still further toward the conservative side were the Mohammedan princes, the racial and religious minorities and the oppressed social classes or "castes" who feared that if British rule were wholly withdrawn the government of India would pass into the hands of the politically active upper class Hindus who would rule in their own interests — a view shared, it may be added, by nearly all British residents of the country.

The British government, recognizing that the spirit of nationalism and "self-determination" could not be merely repressed, decided to make some very far-reaching concessions. During the war a detailed report on political reform in India (known from its chief authors as the Montagu-Chelmsford report) had been prepared, and its chief recommendations were embodied in law by a Government of India Act in 1919. This provided for a two-chambered National Legislature, in part elected and in part appointed by the Viceroy. In each of the provinces a dual form of government or "dyarchy" was set up, certain subjects, such as military and police matters essential to public safety, being "reserved" to the Governor and his officials, and certain other matters being "transferred" to parliamentary ministries responsible to local legislatures.

The Montagu-Chelmsford reform program

These reforms satisfied only the most moderate sections of Indian opinion. Gandhi continued his policy of strikes, boycott and disregard of authority. The Rowlatt Acts for repressing sedition and the action of General Dyer at Amritsar in quelling a mob by repeated volleys of rifle fire (the "Amritsar massacre") made 1919 a

Nationalist agitation

year of tension and disturbance. The Mohammedans, who usually disdained the Hindu revolutionary movement, were increasingly uneasy at the prospect of a complete partition of Turkey and the degradation of the Sultan. Gandhi and other nationalist leaders were repeatedly arrested. The Act of 1919 had included a provision for its revision after a ten year's trial, but unrest had become so extensive that as early as 1927 the British government appointed a new commission under Sir John Simon to recommend revisions of the government of India. No Indians were appointed on the Simon Commission, so the radical nationalists continued their agitation. Gandhi introduced a picturesque novelty in his campaign by publicly making salt from evaporated sea water in order to defy the government salt monopoly.

Lord Irwin, the Viceroy, summoned a Round Table Conference in London, representing the three chief British parties (Conservative, Labor and Liberal) and *Indian* practically all shades of Indian opinion, except *Home Rule extended* the radical nationalists who refused to attend. Unsettled points of controversy led to new conferences in 1931 and 1932. Differences of opinion among the Indian delegates were found to be quite as wide as those between the Indians and the British. Burma wanted to be separated from India altogether and given a constitution of her own, a request which was granted. Minority groups, such as the Moslems, Parsis, depressed castes of Hindus (the so-called "untouchables"), desired special representation to protect their group interests. Gandhi, while hostile to caste discrimination, was opposed also to perpetuating those distinctions by having separate electorates along the lines of creed and caste; he wanted all India to be one nation with one body of voters. The native princes were watchful lest any innovation encroach on their sovereignty within their own domains. Serious Hindu-Moslem riots took place. In view of these dissensions, the British government presented its own project for a revised constitution, greatly extending Indian Home Rule but still falling far short of "Dominion status." The central legislative body was to be more largely elective and contain representatives of the native States as well as of British India, but the Viceroy had still extensive reserve powers and was not always bound by legislative action. The franchise for the provincial legislatures was to be widened, minorities to have their rights carefully safeguarded, and provincial powers extended. The whole plan was avowedly tentative and experimental, no one can tell whether it contained the answer to Indian aspirations or whether such an answer exists.

Through the whole Mohammedan world from Morocco to India, including French and Italian North Africa, Egypt, *The Middle* Turkey, Syria, Iraq, Arabia, Persia and Afghani-*East* stan, the repercussions of the World War caused unrest.[1] The Russian revolutionists took advantage of this ferment as a weapon against Western capitalism, and were as nationalistic in Asia as they were anti-national in Europe and America.[2] Russia played a strong card by withdrawing from her rights and claims in northern Persia and thus leaving Persian nationalism and British imperialism as the only antagonists in the field. Very important oil fields existed in Persia with a considerable investment of British capital, and in 1919 the British negotiated a treaty which gave them preference in foreign loans, railway concessions, and the appointment of civil and military advisers. The gradual establishment of a British economic protectorate over all Persia was prevented mainly by the rise of Riza Khan (a vigorous nationalist reformer, often nicknamed "the Mustapha Kemal of Persia"), who, like his Turkish contemporary, Europeanized his country to save it from Europe. In 1921 he assumed practically dictatorial powers as Minister of

---

[1] For tendencies in the Near East, see Chapter XXIV.
[2] For Bolshevist policy in Asia, see Chapter XXI.

War, in 1923 he forced the ruling Shah to leave the country, in 1925 he took the throne himself as Riza Shah Pahlevi. The army was reorganized, schools placed under national control, an American expert, Dr. A. C. Millspaugh, called in to adjust the budget, and, after a prolonged legal struggle with Great Britain, the concession to the Anglo-Persian Oil Company canceled and a new contract substituted much more favorable to Persia.   In 1919 Afghanistan waged a short and unsuccessful frontier war with British India. Peace was restored, and the rulers of this wild borderland, in the intervals of palace plots and intrigues, set themselves to the introduction of all manner of "Western improvements" in armies, roads and schools.

It is, however, in the Far East, and more especially in the vast territories of the Chinese Republic, that the new nationalism of the Orient has produced the most *The Far* significant changes.   The old Chinese Empire *East* was a dynasty, a bureaucracy, a race and a great civilization, but hardly a nation.   Japan, which was always a land of soldiers and patriots, found it easy in the nineteenth century to adopt Western fashions in engineering, sanitation, warfare and administration — perhaps the only four human activities in which the superiority of the West over all other civilizations was too obvious to be questioned.   But China, which lacked the national tradition, found the transition much more difficult.   Though a republic had been proclaimed in 1911, and though China had participated in the World War as one of the "Allied and Associated Powers" in 1917, no one of the presidents, party leaders, military chiefs or provincial dictators who grasped at power was long able to command the obedience of more than a portion of the country. Japan took advantage of the Chinese anarchy to impose demands which by the end of the war made her leaseholder of Germany's naval base at Kiao-chau, the successor to all Germany's economic concessions in the populous Shan-tung peninsula, the holder of an extensive "sphere of influence" in southern Manchuria, and the beneficiary of special treaty concessions in many parts of China.

The Washington Conference of 1921–22 was called not only to find a formula for the limitation of naval armament,[1] but *The Far Eastern question at the Washington Conference* also to solve the question of political security for China and for the powers — European, Asiatic and American — which might become involved in difficulties if China lost her independence, in whole or in part, or closed the "open door" to the trade of foreign nations. The Anglo-Japanese treaty of alliance was about to terminate; new security pacts must replace it if the "Pacific" were not to belie its name under the threat of a three-cornered naval race among the Americans, British and Japanese! The leasehold of Kiaochau on the coast of Shan-tung was still, by the terms of the Treaty of Versailles, in the hands of Japan; but there had at Paris been an unwritten understanding that it would be eventually restored to China. Chinese nationalists were demanding a relaxation of the treaties with foreign powers which limited China's right to fix her own tariffs and gave "extraterritorial rights" (chiefly exemption from the jurisdiction of the Chinese courts) to resident foreigners. The status of the myriad island groups of the Pacific was of interest to the British, the Japanese, the Americans, the French, the Dutch and the Portuguese.[2] All these questions were flung on the Conference table in the hope of a final solution.

A number of important international agreements resulted. The Pacific Ocean was made a partially demilitarized area, as in certain island groups no fortifications were to be erected or naval bases established. Two Four-Power trea-

---

[1] See Chapter XX for naval limitation at the Washington Conference.

[2] Italy and Belgium, though possessing no Pacific territory, were represented also because of their commercial interests; but Soviet Russia, though a Pacific power, and Germany, whose Pacific possessions had been lost by the World War, had no representation at the Washington Conference.

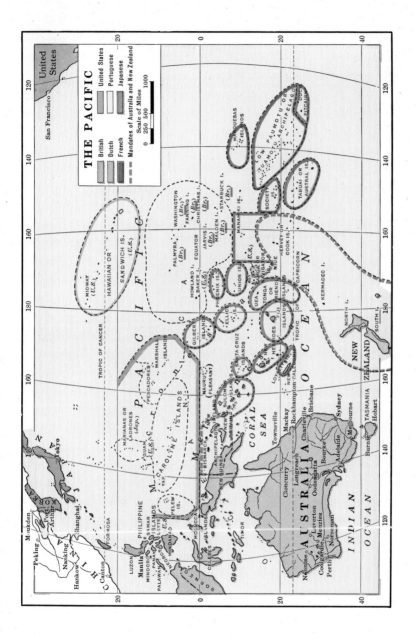

THE PACIFIC

British
Dutch
French
United States
Portuguese
Japanese
Mandates of Australia and New Zealand

Scale of Miles
0   250 500   1000

ties, signed by Great Britain, the United States, France and Japan, replaced the Anglo-Japanese alliance *Pacific and* by a mutual covenant to respect each other's is- *Far Eastern* land possessions and take counsel together in case *peace pacts* the peace were threatened. Two Nine-Power treaties, signed by all the states represented at the Conference,[1] asserted the independence and territorial integrity of China, permitted the Chinese to alter their tariff rates and pledged them to equal treatment of all foreigners on Chinese railways, and forbade exclusive agreements "designed to create spheres of influence or to provide for the enjoyment of mutually exclusive opportunities in designated parts of Chinese territories" — in other words, reaffirmed the principle of the Open Door. A Six-Power treaty, among Britain, the United States, France, China, Italy and Japan, divided the former German cable lines. A special Japanese-American agreement gave Americans the right to operate cables from the American island of Guam to the island of Yap, which had been awarded to Japan as a "mandate" at the Peace Conference. A direct agreement between China and Japan arranged the terms by which Kiao-chau and other former German holdings on the Shan-tung peninsula were transferred from Japan to China.

The more radical and democratic faction of the Chinese patriots were organized around the *Kuomintang* party and the personality of its leader, Dr. Sun Yat-sen. *The Chinese* They were particularly strong in southern China, *nationalist* and particularly at Canton. More conservative *movement* groups held power in the north around the capi- *war* tal of Peking. Between the two there was almost constant civil war, though waged in a curiously desultory and intermittent fashion. After Sun Yat-sen's death in 1925 the Kuomintang party split. General Chiang Kai-shek led the

---

[1] China, Britain, the United States, France, Japan, the Netherlands, Belgium, Italy and Portugal.

moderate wing and persecuted Chinese Communists; the Communists, hostile to all foreigners except the Russians, almost provoked intervention by antialien riots in Nanking in 1927.   In 1928 Chiang Kai-shek crushed the Peking government, changed the name of Peking to Peiping, and established a new capital at Nanking.   Though he enjoyed almost dictatorial power he was confronted with fresh rebellions from the radicals of his own party, and he failed altogether to establish effective authority over Manchuria, where General Chang Tso-lin and later his son Chang Hsueh-liang ruled almost as independent sovereigns.   The Chinese nationalists succeeded, however, in negotiating with foreign powers treaties restoring to China control over her own tariffs and relinquishing extraterritorial rights within the Republic. Even in the midst of famine and civil war much was done to promote popular education and introduce modern methods of administration.

China's northern dependency of Manchuria, the land of the old ruling Manchu dynasty, is a much coveted prize.   The

The Man-churian question

Russo-Japanese War of 1904–05 resulted largely from Russia's attempt to turn the region into a "sphere of influence" controlled by Russian capital and penetrated by Russian railways.   In 1929 a Russo-Chinese war almost occurred as a consequence of Chang Hsueh-liang's attempt to seize control of the Russian-built Chinese Eastern Railway.   In 1931 the Japanese sent an army into Manchuria "to restore order," and remained to establish the country as a nominally "independent" State — really as a dependency of Japan.   Manchuria is larger than the state of Texas, larger than all Japan (including Korea), and about a fourth as large as China proper.   It has a population estimated at over thirty millions; but this figure, large though it is, represents a density much less than that of either China or Japan, and the rapid growth in recent years has been due mainly to immigration from the more crowded parts of China.   The influx of Chinese has been so large as almost completely to absorb the rather scanty native Manchu element and impose an overwhelmingly Chinese character on the country.   Foreigners (Korean, Japanese and Russian chiefly) made up scarcely a twentieth part of the Manchurian population.   Yet though the Japanese did not emigrate to Manchuria in significant numbers, they had a large financial stake in the country.   Manchuria is no desert, like China's other outlying dependencies, Tibet, Mongolia and Turkestan, but a country wealthy in both mineral and agricultural resources; and the Japanese investment in mines, farms, factories, banks and railways has been estimated at close to a billion dollars.   Japan was the largest importer of Manchurian beans, grain, silk, coal and iron and controlled more than half of both the import and the export trade of Manchuria.   All this wealth seemed imperiled by the state of anarchy existing in the country.   The Chinese authorities had not been able to make their "writ run" effectively in Manchuria; and so far as life and property had been safeguarded at all, the credit was due rather to Japan than to China.

In 1931, on the pretext of certain bandit violences,[1] Japan decided to take forcible possession of Manchuria.   The Japanese seized the capital at Mukden, drove out *Japan intervenes in Manchuria* the forces of Marshal Chang and overthrew all Chinese authority.   To make the severance of Manchuria from China complete, Henry Pu Yi, the deposed Manchu Emperor of China, was recognized as Regent of Manchuria, now renamed Manchukuo.   In 1934 he was formally crowned as "Emperor Kang Teh" — the renamed sovereign of a renamed nation.   Unable to make adequate military resistance, the Chinese retorted by the only effective means in their power, the commercial boycott.   All over

---

[1] The murder of a Japanese officer and the alleged (though also denied) blowing up of a section of railway.

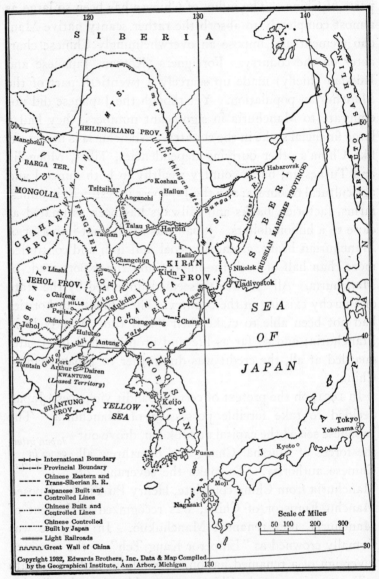

THE MANCHURIAN CRISIS

China, merchants were instructed to have no dealings with the Japanese, and those who persisted in their trade were often mobbed by excited young nationalists.

To coerce China into putting an end to this boycott, Japan decided to advance beyond Manchuria. In January, 1932, Japanese troops were landed at Shanghai, one of the chief centers of foreign commerce in China proper, where there had been several acts of violence against Japanese merchants and other residents. *Japan intervenes in Shanghai* Throughout February there was intense fighting — a "battle" certainly, though both sides for diplomatic reasons carefully avoided the admission that there was a "war" — in and around Shanghai. The Chinese under General Tsai Ting-kai held out for over a month in the face of better equipped Japanese forces with a creditable though hopeless valor before the city was abandoned. As the number of European and American residents of Shanghai was large, nothing but good fortune saved the world from some unfortunate "incident" which might have involved it in a Far Eastern war. In the north Japan also made conquests. Early in 1933 she seized the province of Jehol, lying between Manchuria and the Great Wall which surrounded China proper. The advance of Japan into northern Manchuria and into Mongolia created still another danger to world peace, the risk of an accidental collision between Japanese and Russian forces which might have led to a repetition of the Russo-Japanese War. Fear of this may possibly have contributed to the friendlier attitude shown by Russia to the United States and the powers of western Europe, and to her decision to join the League of Nations.[1]

Both Japan and China were members of the League of Nations and both had signed the Paris Peace Pact for renunciation of war. China, indeed, appealed to League, which appointed a committee of investigation under Lord Lytton.

[1] See Chapter XX.

The United States, though still outside the League, made
the significant declaration (sometimes called "the
Japan
versus the   Stimson doctrine" from the Secretary of State
League of   who sponsored it) that the United States would
Nations
not recognize the legal existence of "independent Manchukuo" or of any other state established in defiance
of the Paris Peace Pact.   Japan, however, "recognized" the
buffer state of her own creation without even waiting for the
Lytton report to be published, thus defying at once the
League of Nations and the United States.   In October, 1932,
the Lytton report appeared.   It reviewed the whole crisis in
minute historical detail, condemned the government of Manchukuo as an artificial sham, unsupported by the majority
of the population, recommended an end to the Chinese boycott of foreign goods, and suggested direct negotiations between China and Japan for new treaties of friendship, commerce and mutual security.   Japan contested the arguments
of the report and refused to be bound by its findings.   In
February, 1933, the Assembly of the League of Nations accepted a report from a committee of nineteen, following in
general the recommendations of the Lytton report, by a vote
of forty-two Member States to one, Japan alone voting in
the negative.[1]   Japan replied with open defiance and the
announced intention to withdraw from the League.   According to the implications in the Covenant, the League
Member States should have come to the rescue of China by
measures of coercion, at least economic; but they did not
feel sufficient confidence in themselves, or in each other, or
in the co-operation of Russia and the United States outside the League, to make the necessary sacrifice of trade
in the midst of the greatest of modern economic depressions.   Japan, unpunished, retained the actual control
over Manchukuo, and China's only consolation was the
moral support which other nations had given to her cause and

---

[1] Siam did not vote and some Latin-American delegates were absent.

their refusal to give legal recognition to the new Empire.[1]

The whole Far Eastern crisis revealed once more the weakening, almost crippling, effect on the League's machinery for peace enforcement resulting from the abstention of the world's greatest industrial nation. Had the United States acted alone against Japan, either with boycott or navy, Japan might have traded in European markets; had the League States acted, Japan could have bought nearly all she needed in America. Only constant assured co-operation of the United States with the League could give the latter real coercive authority when dealing with a Great Power. Although President Wilson and his advisers helped create the League of Nations, the United States remained a non-member, partly because of a general fear of "foreign entanglements" and partly because membership in the League became involved with the political fortunes of President Wilson; and thus the defeat of his party in the election of 1920, though due to many causes, could be interpreted as a national rejection of membership. For several months after President Harding's administration had begun the United States even refused to recognize the legal existence of the League and did not answer its correspondence. Later, under Presidents Coolidge, Hoover and Franklin Roosevelt, special "observers" were sent to attend meetings of interest, and the United States co-operated in nearly all the non-political activities of the League.[2] Though as private individuals Charles Dawes and Owen Young had been chairmen of the international committees which revised the plan for German reparations, official Washington preferred to transact all business relating to reparations, war debts,

Europe and the United States

---

[1] A minor case of the failure of the League of Nations to halt an extra-European war was the conflict between Bolivia and Paraguay over their ill-defined boundaries in a region of tropical jungle known as the Gran Chaco, where conflict broke out in 1928 and again in 1932. In 1935 the League was still trying to restore peace by negotiation and by a boycott on arms; naval blockade was out of the question as neither party to the conflict had a seacoast!

[2] In 1934 the United States adhered to the International Labor Organization.

currencies, tariffs and other international economic interests by old fashioned "foreign office diplomacy" rather than around the green table of an international conference. A similar timidity was shown with respect to the Court of International Justice. Though Elihu Root assisted at its organization and John Bassett Moore, Charles Evans Hughes and Frank Kellogg at various times served on its bench, the Senate persisted in making "reservations" which kept the nation from membership.

In other ways than those of diplomacy the United States endeavored to draw apart from Europe and the Old World *The closed* generally. The World War marked the turning *door to the* point in the American attitude toward immigra-*immigrant* tion. While there were still unclaimed but fertile farmlands on the frontier, immigrant labor was eagerly welcomed. Despite an increasing amount of restrictive legislation the gates still stood wide in 1914. The criminal, the contract laborer, the anarchist, the polygamist, the diseased, the pauper with no visible means of support, the Oriental coolie, were all debarred, but there was no fixed numerical barrier; immigrants might come in whatever numbers economic conditions would determine. In 1917, however, Congress at last passed a law over President Wilson's veto barring illiterates, and thus checking the flood of immigration from southern Italy and Slavic eastern Europe. In 1921 an emergency law limited annual immigration from any country (outside the Americas) to three per cent of its nationals already resident in the United States by the census of 1910, and in 1924 a more drastic measure reduced the quota from three to two per cent and based it on the census of 1890, choosing that date as the turning point when the old immigration from the British Isles, Germany and Scandinavia was beginning to be supplemented by the new immigration from southern and eastern Europe. Later limitations fixed the number of "quota immigrants" (excluding officials, students, temporary visitors, the immediate family of naturalized citizens, etc.) at about 150,000, the quota from each nation being based on the estimated proportion descended from that nationality in the whole population. The law of 1924 added Japanese laborers to Chinese on the totally excluded list, thus provoking a serious diplomatic controversy with Japan.

In at least two directions, however, American interest in the Old World was constant and positive: philanthropy and limitation of armament. The charitable services *America's* of the American Relief Administration, the Near *positive* East Relief, the Red Cross, the Rockefeller *contributions to* Foundation (specializing in the fight against *world welfare* epidemic diseases), the Y.M.C.A. and the missionary boards and colleges saved many millions of lives in China, Russia, Turkey, the Balkan States, Poland, Austria and other afflicted countries. American initiatives, either public or private, underlay to some extent the negotiations of the Covenant of the League of Nations, the Court of International Justice, the Geneva Protocol, the Washington Conference on Pacific Affairs, the Paris Peace Pact, the Dawes and Young reparations plans, and the disarmament conferences at Washington, Geneva and London. Many individuals have also undertaken the administrative responsibilities abroad which the government refused. To select a few names in addition to those already mentioned: Raymond Fosdick, sometime Undersecretary General of the League of Nations; George L. Beer, active in the early organization of the mandate system; Manley Hudson and Arthur Sweetser, on the legal staff of the League secretariat; Florence Wilson, librarian at Geneva; Royal Meeker, chief of the scientific division of the International Labor Office; James T. Shotwell, chairman of the American Committee on Intellectual Co-operation; Jeremiah Smith, who reorganized the finances of Hungary; Abram Elkus, commissioner to settle the Aaland

Islands dispute between Finland and Sweden; Norman Davis, chairman of the committee which established the rights of Lithuania in Memel; Charles Howland, Commissioner for Greek refugees, and James McDonald, Commissioner for German refugees.

Some two generations have elapsed since the Franco-Prussian War. The first of these generations saw changes, rapid *The choice ahead* and numerous indeed, especially in colonial development and industrial progress, but most of them were peaceful in character and constant in direction. The second generation witnessed such a shaking of the very foundations of civilization as had never occurred since the Fall of Rome. Swayed by this analogy many prophets of doom declared that "Europe is going back to the Middle Ages." From one point of view, indeed, the observer is tempted to cry, "No such good luck!" No medieval war approached in destructiveness the World War; no medieval Jacquerie was on as vast a scale as the Bolshevist revolution. If the Middle Ages saw men persecuted for religious heresies, the twentieth century has seen greater numbers persecuted on grounds of race, language and nationality. If medieval peasants starved, it was because of scarcity not because of "overproduction." Small wonder that many intelligent writers have urged that men were not only happier but more rational in the ordered feudalism of Saint Louis and the ordered universe of Saint Thomas Aquinas than in the revolutionary world of Lenin and Hitler and the dizzy, paradoxical universe of Einstein.

And yet, terrifying as may be the spectacle of these days of "change, alarm, surprise," there is something even in the very magnitude of our present disasters not without reassurance. Not love of peace but lack of invention made past wars less wholesale than the World War; not economic wisdom but lack of productive capacity prevented such worldwide industrial crises in bygone centuries. If power misused can cause such calamities, may not power well used build such a towering civilization as will dwarf even the noblest structures of the past?   We, and our fathers and grandfathers, have partially achieved one great task — the conquest of Nature; why may not we, and our children and grandchildren, achieve another task as great, the civilizing of Man?

BIBLIOGRAPHICAL NOTES

GUIDES TO READING: *A Guide to Historical Literature*, edited by W. H. Allison, S. B. Fay, A. H. Shearer and Henry R. Shipman (1931) is one of the most useful general bibliographical references. For the period since 1918 *Foreign Affairs Bibliography* (1933), prepared by the Council on Foreign Relations, should also be consulted. The annual *International Bibliography of Historical Sciences*, published since 1926, *The Encyclopædia Britannica* and other encyclopedic works such as the *Encyclopædia of the Social Sciences* and the *Catholic Encyclopædia*, *The Cambridge Modern History*, especially the later volumes, and Isaiah Bowman, *The New World* (1928 edition) contain valuable bibliographies.

SOURCES AND WORKS OF REFERENCE: Annuals such as *The Annual Register* (1758–); *The Statesman's Year-Book* (1864–); *The New International Year-Book* (1907–); *L'Année Politique* (1874–1905) continued as *La Vie Politique dans les deux Mondes* (1906–); Schulthess' *Europäischer Geschichtskalender* (1861–) are convenient guides to current events. Since 1928 the *Political Handbook of the World*, edited annually by Malcolm W. Davis and Walter H. Mallory, has been an accurate index to elections, parties and the press. The revised edition of *Ploetz' Manual of Universal History* (1925) is a useful compendium of dates.

DIPLOMATIC PUBLICATIONS IN SERIES: *British and Foreign State Papers; Archives Diplomatiques; Das Staatsarchiv; Die Grosse Politik der Europäischen Kabinette* (publications from the German archives for the period 1871–1914; a condensed four-volume edition was edited by A. M. Bartholdy and F. Thimme, 1928); G. P. Gooch and H. Temperley, *British Documents on the Origins of the War, 1898–1914.* Source books containing selected diplomatic papers are numerous; W. H. Cooke and E. F. Stickney, *Readings in European International Relations* (1931) is as good a one-volume selection as any. Attention should be called to the publications of the League of Nations and its various branches, to the series of monographs on the *Economic and Social History of the World War*, issued under the auspices of the Carnegie Endowment for International Peace, and the republication of official documents in the little pamphlets of the American Association for International Peace.

Constitutions and governmental methods for many countries are surveyed in Viscount James Bryce, *Modern Democracies* (2 v., 1921), F. A. Ogg, *Governments of Europe* (revised, 1920), A. L. Lowell, *Greater European Governments* (1925), H. L. McBain and L. Rogers, *New Constitutions of Europe* (1922), M. W. Graham and R. C. Binkley, *New Governments of Central Europe* (1924), M. W. Graham, *New Governments of Eastern Europe* (1927), R. L. Buell, *New Governments in Europe* (1934), and C. Seymour and D. P. Frary, *How the World Votes* (1918). F. M. Anderson and A. S. Hershey, *Handbook for the Diplomatic History of Europe, Asia and Africa, 1870–1914* (1918) is a "case-book" of diplomatic crises; A. Debidour,

Histoire diplomatique de l'Europe depuis le Congrès de Berlin jusqu'à Nos Jours (2 v., 1916) is a narrative account.

There are several good historical atlases, such as W. R. Shepherd, *Historical Atlas* (1929 edition), which may be supplemented by such analytical studies as Bowman, already cited, and L. Dominian, *The Frontiers of Language and Nationality* (1917). E. Hertslet's *Map of Europe by Treaty* (4 v., 1875–91) contains the text of treaties altering frontiers.

PERIODICAL LITERATURE: In dealing with contemporary history, even the best books are soon behind the march of events and must be supplemented by the current periodicals. Useful for European politics are such magazines as: *Foreign Affairs; Fortnightly Review; Contemporary Review; Nineteenth Century; Political Science Quarterly; Current History; Geographical Review; Slavonic Review*, etc. *The New Europe*, later discontinued, is useful for the war period. *The American Historical Review, The English Historical Review, The Journal of Modern History* and similar publications give timely notices of new books. For the newspaper reader the London *Times*, Manchester *Guardian* and New York *Times* have the fullest foreign news of any journals printed in English.

GENERAL HISTORIES AND TEXTBOOKS: C. J. H. Hayes, *A Social and Political History of Modern Europe* (2 v., 1927 edition) began the second volume with 1815, the current revision, *A Political and Cultural History of Modern Europe*, begins its second volume at 1830; no general textbook is fuller or more interesting. E. Achorn, *European Civilization and Politics since 1815* (1934) is also unusually full, especially on the side of cultural history. C. D. Hazen, *Europe since 1815* (2 v., 1923 edition) is strictly political. Other well-known texts are: F. Lee Benns, *Europe since 1914* (1934 edition), excellently proportioned; W. C. Langsam, *The World since 1914* (1933, with a supplementary chapter, 1934); J. W. Swain, *Beginning the Twentieth Century* (1933), a very thoughtful book, covering the period from 1890 to 1919; E. R. Turner, *Europe since 1870* (1927 edition); A. J. Grant and H. Temperley, *Europe in the Nineteenth Century* (1927); B. Croce, *History of Europe in the Nineteenth Century* (trans., 1933); C. P. Higby, *History of Modern Europe* (1932); G. Heard, *These Hurrying Years* (1934); J. A. R. Marriott, *History of Europe from 1815 to 1923* (1931); A. H. Noyes, *Europe, Its History and Its World Relationships, 1789–1933* (1934); F. C. Palm and F. E. Graham, *Europe since Napoleon* (1934); L. H. Holt and A. W. Chilton, *The History of Europe from 1862 to 1914* (1917) with emphasis on military events; J. S. Schapiro, *Modern and Contemporary History* (revised, 1929); P. Slosson, *Twentieth Century Europe* (1927). The economic history of the age is treated in the later chapters of M. Knight, H. E. Barnes, F. Flügel, *Economic History of Europe* (1928) and in F. A. Ogg, *Economic Development of Modern Europe* (1917). There are many studies in modern European diplomacy; perhaps the best and fullest being G. P. Gooch, *History of Modern Europe, 1878–1901* (1923). R. J. Sontag, *European Diplomatic History, 1871–1932* (1933) is very brief and somewhat elementary but easy reading. R. J. Mowat, *History of European Diplomacy, 1914–1925* (1927), and *History of European Diplomacy, 1815–1914* (1927) are intermediate in fullness between Gooch and Sontag.

Some interesting accounts of various personalities prominent in the world's news are: Count C. Sforza, *Makers of Modern Europe* (1930), W. Martin, *Statesmen of the War in Retrospect* (1928), E. S. Bagger, *Eminent Europeans* (1922), A. G. Gardiner, *Portraits and Portents* (1926), and S. Huddleston, *Those Europeans* (1924).

CHAPTER I
NATIONS ON THE ANVIL

The general texts listed above will give something of he background of the Europe of 1870. Other useful books of more special character are: C. J. H. Hayes, *The Historical Evolution of Modern Nationalism* (1931); J. H. Rose, *Nationality in Modern History* (1916); R. B. Mowat, *The States of Europe, 1815–1871* (1932); R. H. Lord, *The Origins of the War of 1870* (1924); H. Oncken, *Napoleon III and the Rhine* (trans., 1928); C. G. Robertson, *Bismarck* (1918); Bolton King, *History of Italian Unity* (2 v., 1899); W. R. Thayer, *The Life and Times of Cavour* (2 v., 1911); G. M. Trevelyan, *Garibaldi and the Making of Italy*, and the works on German, French and Italian history listed under chapters III, VI and VII. Certain interactions of economic and political forces may be studied in: J. A. Hobson, *The Evolution of Modern Capitalism* (1913); S. P. Orth, *Socialism and Democracy in Europe* (1913); Bertrand Russell, *Roads to Freedom* (1918), an examination of socialist, syndicalist and anarchist ideals, and his *Freedom versus Organization, 1814–1914* (1934); John Spargo, *Socialism* (1913); H. A. L. Fisher, *The Republican Tradition in Europe* (1911).

CHAPTER II
THE NEAR EASTERN QUESTION

The Balkan Wars of 1912–13 and the fact that the World War originated in the Balkans called forth an enormous, though very unequal, output of books on that hitherto neglected corner of Europe and of history. Among the better general surveys are:

J. A. R. Marriott, *The Eastern Question* (1930 edition); Ferdinand Schevill, *A History of the Balkan Peninsula from the Earliest Times to the Present Day* (1922); *The Balkans* (1915), a co-operative history by Nevill Forbes, Arnold J. Toynbee, D. Mitrany and D. G. Hogarth; N. Iorga, *Histoire des États Balcaniques jusqu'à 1924* (1925) by an eminent Rumanian historian; Mason Tyler, *European Powers and the Near East, 1875–1908* (1925); R. W. Seton-Watson, *The Rise of Nationality in the Balkans* (1917); W. M. Sloane, *The Balkans, a Laboratory of History* (1920 edition); M. I. Newbigin, *Geographical Aspects of Balkan Problems* (1915); J. F. Maurice, *Russo-Turkish War of 1877* (1905); A. C. Coolidge, *Claimants to Constantinople* (1917); T. E. Holland, *The European Concert in the Eastern Question* (1885); E. Driault, *La Question d'Orient* (1921 edition); S. P. Duggan, *The Eastern Question: a Study in Diplomacy* (1902); Hans Kohn, *A History of Nationalism in the East* (1929). Some references on later phases of the Near Eastern question are listed under chapters XI, XII, XIII and XXIV. R. J. Kerner's *Slavic Europe, a Select Bibliography in the Western European Languages* (1918) is an excellent guide to any study of the Slavic portions of eastern Europe.

For the Ottoman Empire in Particular: Geo. Eversley, *The Turkish Empire, its Growth and Decay* (1923 edition); W. E. D. Allen, *The Turks in Europe* (1920); E. G. Mears, *Modern Turkey* (1924); Wm. Miller, *The Ottoman Empire and Its Successors, 1801–1927* (1934); Sir C. N. E. Eliot, *Turkey in Europe* (1908); Sir Edwin Pears, *Turkey and Its People* (1912); S. L. Poole, *Story of Turkey* (1922 edition); Sir Edward S. Creasy, *History of the Ottoman Turks* (2 v., 1906 edition); Coleman Phillipson and Noel Buxton, *The Question of the Bosphorous and Dardanelles* (1917); P. P. Graves, *The Question of the Straits* (1931); J. T. Shotwell, *Constantinople and the Straits* (American International Conciliation pamphlet 180); E. M. Earle, *Turkey, the Great Powers and the Bagdad Railway* (1923).

Individual Nations: William Miller, *Greece* (1928), and *A History of the Greek People, 1821–1921* (1922); L. Sergeant, *Greece in the Nineteenth Century* (1897); H. A. Gibbons, *Venizelos* (1923 edition), sympathetic biography of the most eminent modern Greek statesman; P. F. Martin, *Greece of the Twentieth Century* (1913); E. Driault and M. Lhéritier, *Histoire diplomatique de la Grèce de 1821 à nos jours* (5 v., 1925–26); C. U. Clark, *Greater Roumania* (1922), and *Bessarabia, Russia and Roumania on the Black Sea* (1927); Oscar Brilliant, *Roumania* (1915); D. Mitrany, *Rumania, Her History and Politics* (1917); R. W. Seton-Watson, *A History of the Roumanians* (1934); H. W. V. Temperley, *History of Serbia* (1917); W. M. Petrovitch, *Serbia* (1915); F. S. Stevenson, *History of Montenegro* (1912); E. Dicey, *The Peasant State* (1894), an account of Bulgaria toward the end of the nineteenth century; A. H. Beaman, *Stambuloff* (1895), a biography of Bulgaria's national leader; W. S. Monroe, *Bulgaria and Her People* (1914); Lord Edward Gleichen, *Bulgaria and Roumania* (1924); H. N. Brailsford, *Macedonia, its Races and their Future* (1906).

Chapter III

Germany and the Triple Alliance

General Works on Germany especially in the modern period: E. F. Henderson, *A Short History of Germany* (2 v., 1916); J. A. R. Marriott and C. G. Robertson, *The Evolution of Prussia* (1917); W. H. Dawson, *The German Empire, 1867–1914* (2 v., 1919); G. M. Priest, *Germany since 1740* (1915); F. Schevill, *The Making of Modern Germany* (1916); Sir A. W. Ward and S. Wilkinson, *Germany, 1815–90* (3 v., 1916–18); R. H. Fife, *The German Empire between Two Wars* (1916); H. Lichtenberger, *Germany and its Evolution in Modern Times* (1913); G. P. Gooch, *Germany* (1925), mainly dealing with the postwar period but including a brief historical survey. The old Imperial constitution is discussed in B. E. Howard, *The German Empire* (1906), and Fritz-Konrad Krüger, *Government and Politics of the German Empire* (1915); H. G. James, *Principles of Prussian Administration* (1913) is also worth noting.

Economic and social developments are particularly stressed in many of the most valuable works on Imperial Germany, such as the highly important studies by W. H. Dawson: *Evolution of Modern Germany* (1919 edition), *Bismarck and State Socialism* (1891), *Social Insurance in Germany* (1911), *Municipal Life and Government in Germany* (1916). Other authors interested in these phases of German life include: J. H. Clapham, *Economic Development of France and Germany, 1815–1914* (1921); P. W. L. Ashley, *Modern Tariff History: Germany, United States, France* (1904); T. Veblen, *Imperial Germany and the Industrial Revolution* (1915); J. Ellis Barker, *Modern Germany* (1907); F. C. Howe, *Socialized Germany* (1915), with emphasis on social reforms; K. Helferrich, *Germany's Economic Progress and National Wealth, 1888–1913* (1915), a statistical study.

Bismarck's view of his own policies may be cautiously studied in his memoirs *Bismarck, the Man and the Statesman* (2 v., 1890), to which the close of the war made possible the publication of an additional volume, translated as *The Kaiser versus Bismarck* (1922). The best Bismarck biographies in English are by C. G. Robertson (1918) and by J. W. Headlam (1922 edition); the standard German biography by E. Marcks is still incomplete. Bismarck's diplomacy is analyzed in Wm. L. Langer's very able *European Alliances and Alignments, 1871–1890* (1931), Veit Valentin's *Bismarcks Aussenpolitik von 1871–1890* (1922), Joseph V. Fuller, *Bismarck's Diplomacy at Its Zenith* (1922), Count Julius Andrassy, *Bismarck, Andrassy and Their Successors* (1927), Munroe Smith, *Militarism and Statecraft* (1918), and A. C. Coolidge, *The Origins of the Triple Alliance* (1926 edition).

For German foreign policy after 1890, see Chapter X; for Germany during and after the World War, Chapters XVII and XXVII.

CHAPTER IV

The United Kingdom and Greater Britain

General British History: Of the dozen or more of good, recent single volume histories A. L. Cross, *Shorter History of England and Greater Britain* (1929 edition) is perhaps the most detailed. Of the longer co-operative histories, the very detailed twelve volume work edited by W. Hunt and R. L. Poole culminates in S. Low and L. C. Sanders, *Political History of England, 1837–1901* (1907), while the shorter seven volume work edited by Charles Oman terminates with J. A. R. Marriott, *England since Waterloo* (1913). G. M. Trevelyan, *British History in the Nineteenth Century, 1782–1901* (1922) is the most readable of books; Gilbert Slater, *Making of Modern England* (1915) emphasizes social and economic history; Sir Spencer Walpole, *History of Twenty-Five Years* (1856–1880) is a standard work; Sir Herbert Maxwell, *A Century of Empire, 1801–1900* (3 v., 1909–11) is a little pedestrian; H. W. Paul, *History of Modern England* (5 v., 1904–06), Justin McCarthy, *A Short History of Our Own Times* (1908), and R. H. Gretton, *Modern History of the English People, 1880–1910* (2 v., 1913) are interesting but somewhat "journalistic," E. C. Wingfield-Stratford, *History of British Civilization* (2 v., 1928) is philosophically treated.

Queen Victoria has had a very official biography from Sir Sidney Lee (1903), and a very unofficial and informal one by Lytton Strachey (1921). Her greatest ministers have been fortunate in their biographies, for both Viscount John Morley, *Life of William Ewart Gladstone* (3 v. in one, 1921 edition) and W. F. Monypenny and G. E. Buckle, *Life of Benjamin Disraeli, Earl of Beaconsfield* (6 v., 1910–20) are of the first rank, whether counted as history or as biography. A brief contrast is drawn between the two men in D. C. Somervell, *Disraeli and Gladstone* (1926). Other political studies: A. L. Lowell, *Government of England* (1912); Sidney J. M. Low, *Governance of England* (1915 edition); C. Seymour, *Electoral Reform in England and Wales, 1832–1885* (1915); L. Courtney, *The Working Constitution of the United Kingdom* (1910); Lord Hugh Cecil, *Conservatism* (1912); L. T. Hobhouse, *Liberalism* (1911); C. J. H. Hayes, *British Social Politics* (1913), a convenient compendium of Liberal social legislation during the period following 1905; J. H. Park, *English Reform Bill of 1867* (1920); Stephen Gwynn, *Ireland* (1924); Eleanor Hull, *A History of Ireland and Her People* (1931); Daniel D. Sheehan, *Ireland since Parnell* (1921); E. R. Turner, *Ireland and England in the Past and at Present* (1920); E. Barker, *Ireland in the Last Fifty Years, 1866–1916* (1919 edition); *Cambridge History of British Foreign Policy, 1783–1919* (3 v., 1922–23), by Sir A. W. Ward and G. P. Gooch. For the economic background to recent British politics see also: A. P. Usher, *The Industrial History of England* (1920); E. P. Cheyney, *Introduction to the Industrial and Social History of England* (1920 edition); C. R. Fay, *Great Britain from Adam Smith to the Present Day* (1928); G. H. Perris, *Industrial History of Modern England* (1914); Sidney and Beatrice Webb, *History of Trade Unionism* (1920 edition); G. J. Holyoake, *History of Coöperation in England* (2 v., 1906); M. Beer, *History of British Socialism* (2 v., 1919–20); P. Blanshard, *Outline of the British Labor Movement* (1923); G. D. H. Cole, *Short History of the British Working Class Movement* (3 v., 1927).

On the Empire as a whole there are two important descriptive series: Sir Charles Lucas, *A Historical Geography of the British Empire*, and the *Oxford Survey of the British Empire*. In briefer compass: Howard Robinson, *The Development of the British Empire* (1922); A. F. Pollard, *The British Empire* (1909); C. H. Currey, *British Colonial Policy, 1783–1915* (1916); H. E. Egerton, *Short History of British Colonial Policy* (1918); C. A. Bodelsen, *Studies in Mid-Victorian Imperialism* (1925); P. Knaplund, *Gladstone and Britain's Imperial Policy* (1927); A. B. Keith, *Responsible Government in the Dominions* (1928 edition) and *Imperial Unity and the Dominions* (1916); Viscount James Bryce, *Modern Democracies* (2 v., 1921) with useful chapters on the British Dominions; H. D. Hall, *British Commonwealth of Nations* (1920); Lionel Curtis, *Problem of the Commonwealth* (1916), a plea for Imperial federation; Richard Jebb, *Imperial Conference, a History and a Study* (2 v., 1911); Albert Demangeon, *The British Empire* (1925), a French view. For particular Dominions the following references may be selected: Carl Wittke, *A History of Canada* (1928); C. Martin, *Empire and Commonwealth* (1929); G. M. Wrong, *Canada* (1924); Edward Jenks, *History of the Australasian Colonies* (1912 edition); B. R. Wise, *Making of the Australian Commonwealth, 1889–1900* (1913); H. G. Turner, *First Decade of the Australian Commonwealth* (1911); G. H. Scholefield, *New Zealand in Evolution* (1909); R. I. Lovell, *The Struggle for South Africa, 1875–99* (1934); W. B. Worsfold, *Union of South Africa* (1912); H. Spender, *General Botha* (1916); B. Williams, *Cecil Rhodes* (1921).

For India and the tropical dependencies, see the following chapter; for postwar Imperial development, see Chapter XXIX.

CHAPTER V

THE PARTITION OF THE TROPICS

BACKGROUND STUDIES OF IMPERIALISM AND COLONIZATION: Parker Moon, *Imperialism and World Politics* (1926), hostile to imperialism but packed with facts; A. G. Keller, *Colonization* (1908); Paul S. Reinsch, *Colonial Government* (1902) and *Colonial Administration* (1905); Alleyne Ireland, *Tropical Colonization* (1899), imperialistic in outlook; J. A. Hobson, *Imperialism* (1902), anti-imperialist; H. C. Morris, *History of Colonization from the Earliest Times to the Present Day* (2 v., 1900), the later chapters; A. Zimmermann, *Die Europäischen Kolonien* (5 v., 1896–1903); Ramsay Muir, *Expansion of Modern Europe* (1923 edition). Paul Leroy-Beaulieu, *De la colonisation chez les peuples modernes* (2 v., 1908 edition). See also references for Chapters IV, IX, X, XI, XII and XXX.

THE PARTITION OF AFRICA: N. D. Harris, *Europe and Africa* (1927), a revision of his earlier *Intervention and Colonization in Africa*; Sir Charles Lucas, *The Partition and Colonization of Africa* (1922); Sir Harry Johnston, *A History of the Colonization of Africa by Alien Races* (1913 edition); H. A. Gibbons, *New Map of Africa* (1916); L. S. Woolf, *Empire and Commerce in Africa* (1919), anti-imperialistic; C. H. Stigand, *Administration in Tropical Africa* (1914); R. L. Buell, *The Native Problem in Africa* (2 v., 1928); Sir Edward Hertslet, *The Map of Europe by Treaty* (3 v., 1909), treaty texts and maps; Evans Lewin, *The Germans and Africa* (1915); Heinrich Schnee, *German Colonization Past and Present* (1926); Mary E. Townsend, *The Rise and Fall of Germany's Colonial Empire* (1930); A. Zimmermann, *Die Geschichte der deutschen Kolonialpolitik* (1914); W. M. Sloane, *Greater France in Africa* (1923); C. A. Julien, *Histoire de l'Afrique du Nord* (1931); S. H. Roberts, *History of French Colonial Policy, 1870–1925* (2 v., 1929); V. Piquet, *Histoire des Colonies Françaises* (1931); A. B. Keith, *The Belgian Congo and the Berlin Act* (1919); Sir Charles Bruce, *The Broad Stone of Empire* (2 v., 1910), the British Crown Colonies, especially in the tropics, considered; E. W. P. Newman, *Great Britain in Egypt* (1928); Sir Valentine Chirol, *The Egyptian Problem* (1920); Earl Cromer, *Modern Egypt* (2 v., 1908), a standard work by one of the great English "proconsuls"; George Young, *Egypt* (1927); A. A. H. Beaman, *The Dethronement of the Khedive* (1929), and Wilfrid S. Blunt, *Secret History of the English Occupation of Egypt* (1907), both very critical of British policy; Morrison B. Giffen, *Fashoda, the Incident and its Diplomatic Setting* (1930).

FOR INDIA AND THE FAR EASTERN TROPICS: Sir Valentine Chirol, *India* (1922); Marquis George Curzon, *British Government in India* (2 v., 1925); Vincent A. Smith, *The Oxford History of India* (1928 edition); H. H. Dodwell, *A Sketch of the History of India from 1858 to 1918* (1925); Alleyne Ireland, *The Far Eastern Tropics* (1905), conditions in Dutch, British and French Malaysia; Clive Day, *The Policy and Administration of the Dutch in Java* (1904); H. A. Torchiana, *Tropical Holland* (1921); A. Vandenbosch, *The Dutch East Indies* (1934); G. H. Blakeslee, *The Pacific Area* (1929); C. B. Fletcher, *The Problem of the Pacific* (1919); G. H. Scholefield, *The Pacific, its Past and Future* (1919).

Chapter VI

France and the Dual Alliance

Émile Bourgeois, *History of Modern France, 1815–1913* (2 v., 1919); C. H. C. Wright, *A History of the Third French Republic* (1916); E. A. Vizetelly, *Republican France* (1913), an informal narrative; J. C. Bracq, *France under the Republic* (1910); Gabriel Hanotaux, *Contemporary France* (4 v., 1903–09), covering only the period to 1882; M. Lhéritier, *La France depuis 1870* (1922); R. Recouly, *The Third Republic* (1928), R. H. Soltau, *French Parties and Politics, 1871–1930* (1930); L. Jacques, *Les Partis Politiques sous la Troisième République* (1913), a systematic survey of party platforms and programs; A. Tilley, *Modern France* (1922); A. Siegfried, *France: A Study in Nationality* (1930) and C. J. H. Hayes, *France: A Nation of Patriots* (1930), two able analyses of French nationalism; Charles Seignobos, *L'Évolution de la Troisième République, 1875–1914* (1921); Graham H. Stuart, *French Foreign Policy, 1898–1914* (1921); E. M. Carroll, *French Public Opinion and World Affairs, 1870–1914* (1931); William A. Langer, *The Franco-Russian Alliance, 1890–1894* (1929); L. Levine, *The Labor Movement in France* (1912); P. Moon, *The Labor Problem and the Social Catholic Movement in France* (1921); P. Sabatier, *Disestablishment in France* (1906); J. Reinach, *Histoire de l'affaire Dreyfus* (7 v., 1898–1911); J. H. Clapham, *Economic Development of France and Germany, 1815–1914* (1921). See also references for Chapter XXVIII.

Chapter VII

Other States of Western Europe

ITALY: In contrast to the abundance of books on Italy during the Risorgimento and since the Fascist revolution there is a relative paucity for the intervening years. Bendetto Croce's rather philosophical *History of Italy, 1871–1915* (1929) is perhaps the most important for the period. F. M. Underwood, *United Italy* (1915), W. K. Wallace, *Greater Italy* (1920), with emphasis on colonial expansion, B. King and T. Okey, *Italy Today* (1909), A. Pingaud, *L'Italie depuis 1870* (1915), Helen Zimmern and A. Agresti, *New Italy* (1920), and the Italian chapters in A. L. Lowell, *The Governments of France, Italy and Germany* (1915) and F. A. Ogg, *The Governments of Europe* (1913) may be used for the period also. Certain special aspects are interestingly treated in J. A. R. Marriott, *Makers of Modern Italy* (1931), E. A. Mowrer, *Immortal Italy* (1922), and T. Tittoni, *Modern Italy* (1922). For the postwar period, see references for Chapter XXVI.

SPAIN AND PORTUGAL: Charles Chapman, *History of Spain* (1918), based on Rafael Altamira's famous researches; Martin Hume, *Modern Spain* (1923); Henry D. Sedgwick, *Spain: a Short History of its Politics, Literature and Art* (1925); H. B. Clarke, *Modern Spain, 1815–1898* (1906); J. B. Trend, *The Origins of Modern Spain* (1934); Joseph A. Brandt, *Toward the New Spain* (1933); George Young, *Portugal, Old and Young* (1917); H. M. Stephens, *Portugal* (1908 edition); G. Diercks, *Das Moderne Portugal* (1913); A. Marvaud, *Le Portugal et ses colonies* (1912).

SWITZERLAND AND THE NETHERLANDISH NATIONS: W. Oechsli, *History of Switzerland* (1922); W. D. McCrackan, *Rise of the Swiss Republic* (1901); R. C. Brooks, *Government and Politics of Switzerland* (1918) and his *Civic Training in Switzerland* (1930); W. Martin, *History of Switzerland* (1931); E. Fueter, *Die Schweiz seit 1848* (1928); Ruth Putnam, *Luxemburg and Her Neighbors* (1918); P. J. Blok, *History of the People of the Netherlands* (Vol. V, 1912); Geo. Edmundson, *History of Holland* (1922); A. J. Barnouw, *Holland under Queen Wilhelmina* (1923); A. C. J. Jitta, *Holland's Modern Renascence* (1930); H. Pirenne, *Histoire de Belgique* (Vol. VII, 1932), the standard work; T. H. Reed, *The Government and Politics of Belgium* (1924); H. Van der Linden, *Belgium, the Making of a Nation* (1920); Emile Cammaerts, *Belgium* (1921); R. C. K. Ensor, *Belgium* (1915); L. Van der Essen, *Short History of Belgium* (1920); Comte L. de Lichtervelde, *Leopold of the Belgians* (1929), too eulogistic, but giving a useful picture of Leopold II's reign.

SCANDINAVIA: R. N. Bain, *Scandinavia* (1905), a general history; K. Gjerset, *History of the Norwegian People* (2 v., 1915) and *History of Iceland* (1924); G. Gathorne-Hardy, *Norway* (1925); C. Hallendorff and A. Schück, *History of Sweden* (1929); A. Stomberg, *History of Sweden* (1931); F. C. Howe, *Denmark, a Co-operative Commonwealth* (1921); J. Stefansson, *Denmark and Sweden, with Iceland and Finland* (1917).

CHAPTER VIII

RIVAL EMPIRES OF EASTERN EUROPE

AUSTRO-HUNGARIAN PROBLEMS: L. P. Léger, *Histoire de l'Autriche-Hongrie* (1920 edition); H. W. Steed, *The Habsburg Monarchy* (1919 edition); G. Drage, *Austria-Hungary* (1909); Wolf von Schierbrand, *Austria-Hungary* (1917); Joseph Redlich, *Emperor Francis Joseph of Austria* (1929); Eugene Bagger, *Francis Joseph, Emperor of Austria* (1927); L. Eisenmann, *Le Compromis austro-hongrois de 1867* (1904); B. Auerbach, *Les races et les nationalités en Autriche-Hongrie* (1917 edition); A. F. Pribram, *Austrian Foreign Policy, 1908–18* (1923); H. Friedjung, *Das Zeitalter des Imperialismus, 1884–1914* (3 v., 1919–22); C. M. Knatchbull-Hugesson, *Political Evolution of the Hungarian Nation* (2 v., 1908); Count Paul Teleki, *Evolution of Hungary* (1923); F. Eckhart, *A Short History of the Hungarian People* (1931); L. Eisenmann, *La Hongrie Contemporaine, 1867–1918* (1921); A. B. Yolland, *Hungary* (1917); R. W. Seton-Watson ably presents the case for the Slavs of the Dual Monarchy in *Racial Problems in Hungary* (1908), *German, Slav and Magyar* (1916), *The Southern Slav Question and the Habsburg Monarchy* (1911), and *Corruption and Reform in Hungary* (1911); B. Vosnjak, *A Bulwark against Germany* (1917) is a good account of the Slovenes. See also references for Chapters XVII and XXIII.

RUSSIA: R. Beazley, N. Forbes and G. A. Birkett, *Russia from the Varangians to the Bolsheviks* (1918); S. F. Platonov, *History of Russia* (1925); Geo. Vernadsky, *A History of Russia* (1929); Sir Bernard Pares, *History of Russia* (1930); V. O'Hara and N. Makeef, *Russia* (1925); G. Alexinsky, *Modern Russia* (1913); A. Kornilov, *Modern Russian History* (1924 edition); M. Kovalevsky, *Russian Political Institutions* (1902); T. G. Masaryk,

The Spirit of Russia (2 v., 1919), by the leading modern Czech statesman; A. Leroy-Beaulieu, *Empire of the Tsars and the Russians* (3 v., 1893–96); Sir D. M. Wallace, *Russia* (1912 edition); A. N. Rambaud, *Popular History of Russia* (3 v., trans. 1879–82; the French edition has been continued to 1904); V. O. Kliuchevsky, *History of Russia* (Part V, 1921); G. T. Robinson, *Rural Russia under the Old Régime* (1932); James Mavor, *An Economic History of Russia* (2 v., 1926 edition); Baron S. A. Korff, *Russia's Foreign Relations during the Last Half Century* (1922); F. H. Skrine, *Expansion of Russia, 1815–1900* (1915 edition), mainly concerned with territorial expansion; S. M. Dubnov, *History of the Jews in Russia and Poland* (3 v., 1916–20); A. Rambaud, *Expansion of Russia* (1904 edition); G. F. Wright, *Asiatic Russia* (2 v., 1902); M. P. Price, *Siberia* (1912).
See also references for Chapters XVI, XXI and XXII.

CHAPTER IX

EUROPE AND THE FAR EAST

GENERAL: N. D. Harris, *Europe and the East* (1926); H. H. Gowen, *Asia, A Short History* (1926), good for general background; H. B. Morse and H. F. MacNair, *Far Eastern International Relations* (1931); P. J. Treat, *The Far East, a Political and Diplomatic History* (1928); H. M. Vinacke, *A History of the Far East in Modern Times* (1928); R. K. Douglas, *Europe and the Far East, 1506–1912* (1913); G. M. Dutcher, *The Political Awakening of the East* (1925); T. F. Millard, *The New Far East* (1907); P. S. Reinsch, *Intellectual and Political Currents in the Far East* (1911); S. K. Hornbeck, *Contemporary Politics in the Far East* (1916).

THE CHINESE EMPIRE AND ITS DEPENDENCIES: Edward T. Williams, *A Short History of China* (1928) and *China Yesterday and Today* (1929 edition); K. S. Latourette, *The Development of China* (1929) and *History of Christian Missions in China* (1928); A. N. Holcombe, *The Chinese Revolution* (1930); W. W. Willoughby, *Foreign Rights and Interests in China* (2 v., 1927); P. H. Kent, *Passing of the Manchus* (1912) and, for the Boxer period, A. H. Smith, *China in Convulsion* (2 v., 1901), P. H. Clements, *Boxer Rebellion* (1915), J. O. P. Bland and E. Backhouse, *China under the Empress Dowager* (1910), and J. O. P. Bland, *Li Hung Chang* (1917).

JAPAN AND JAPANESE FOREIGN RELATIONS: F. Brinkley and D. Kikuchi, *History of the Japanese People* (1915); H. H. Gowen, *Outline History of Japan* (1927); J. H. Gubbins, *The Making of Modern Japan* (1922); A. S. Hershey and W. Susanne, *Modern Japan* (1919); W. W. McLaren, *Political History of Japan during the Meiji Era, 1867–1912* (1916); *The Secret Memoirs of Count Hayashi* (1915), good for origins of the Anglo-Japanese alliance; Chang C. Fu, *The Anglo-Japanese Alliance* (1931); A. L. P. Dennis, *The Anglo-Japanese Alliance* (1923); K. Asakawa, *The Russo-Japanese Conflict* (1904); A. S. Hershey, *International Law and Diplomacy of the Russo-Japanese War* (1906).

CHAPTER X

THE RISE OF THE TRIPLE ENTENTE

Bernadotte Schmitt's brief manual in the Berkshire Studies, *Triple Alliance and Triple Entente* (1934) is an excellent short introduction to the whole subject, which is more fully analyzed in such works as S. B. Fay, *Origins of the World War* (1928), Vol. I, G. P. Gooch, *History of Modern Europe, 1878–1919* (1923) and *Recent Revelations of European Diplomacy* (1930), E. Brandenburg, *From Bismarck to the World War* (trans. 1933), O. J. Hale, *Germany and the Diplomatic Revolution* (1931), M. Paléologue, *Un grand tournant de la politique mondiale, 1904–05* (1934), O. Hammann, *The World Policy of Germany, 1890–1912* (1927), V. Valentin, *Deutschlands Aussenpolitik von Bismarcks Abgang bis zum Ende des Weltkrieges* (1921) and F. Meinecke, *Geschichte des Deutsch-Englischen Bündnisproblems, 1890–1901* (1927).

The opening of long-sealed archives has outdated a number of books, equally excellent in their own day, such as Charles Seymour, *The Diplomatic Background of the War, 1870–1914* (1916), F. M. Anderson and A. S. Hershey, *Handbook for Diplomatic History* (1918), a "case book" of diplomatic crises, A. Tardieu, *France and the Alliances* (1908), B. E. Schmitt, *England and Germany, 1740–1914* (1916), C. Sarolea, *Anglo-German Problem* (1912), A. Bullard, *The Diplomacy of the Great War* (1916), running back to 1878 in its survey, W. M. Fullerton, *Problems of Power* (1915).

German authors take very divergent views of the course of foreign policy under Wilhelm II. In addition to the titles already listed, mention may be made of Chancellor Bülow's defenses of his administration, *Imperial Germany* (trans. 1914) and *Memoirs* (4 v., trans. 1931–32), K. Nowak, *Germany's Road to Ruin* (1932), H. Oncken, *Germany under Wilhelm II* (1913), J. Haller, *Die Aera Bülow* (1922), hostile to Bülow.

On some special aspects of diplomacy during the period, see also: Eugene N. Anderson, *The First Morocco Crisis, 1904–06* (1930); E. M. Earle, *Turkey, the Great Powers and the Bagdad Railway* (1923); A. F. Pribram, *England and the International Policy of the European Great Powers, 1871–1914* (1931); E. M. Carroll, *French Public Opinion and Foreign Affairs, 1870–1914* (1931); G. P. Gooch, *Franco-German Relations, 1871–1914* (1923); H. Bernstein, *Willy-Nicky Correspondence* (1918), documents; A. S. Hurd and H. Castle, *German Sea Power* (1913). Other references dealing with the general forces making for peace and war, but in part relevant to this chapter, are listed under Chapter XII.

CHAPTER XI

TRIPLE ALLIANCE VERSUS TRIPLE ENTENTE

For the Tripolitan and Balkan Wars see, in addition to the general works on the Near Eastern question listed for Chapter II: Sir T. Barclay, *Turco-Italian War* (1912); George Young, *Nationalism and War in the Near East* (1915), the best general account of the Balkan Wars in English; *Report* (1914) *of the International Commission to Inquire into the Causes and Con-*

duct of the Balkan Wars; Ivan Gueshov, *The Balkan League* (1915), a Bulgarian standpoint; Reginald Rankin, *The Inner History of the Balkan War* (1913), by a British War correspondent; J. G. Schurman, *The Balkan Wars* (1916). For a hostile view of French diplomacy in Morocco, see E. D. Morel, *Morocco in Diplomacy* (1912); for a favorable view, A. Tardieu, *Le Conférence d'Algésiras* (1909) and *Le Mystère d'Agadir* (1912). Other and more general phases of diplomacy during the period are listed for Chapters X and XII.

CHAPTERS XII AND XIII

CLOUDS OVER EUROPE AND THE STORM BREAKS

And now we come to the most discussed problem of modern times, the origins of the World War. A complete bibliography for this topic alone would fill volumes. Much of this vast war literature, however, never had any value, and much more, while useful and enlightening in its day, has been superseded by later studies. In any case, it must here suffice to enumerate a few representative examples of the more important books on the principal phases of the subject; the student who has time, patience and incentive sufficient to undertake a more intensive study will find good bibliographies in many of the works here listed.

SOURCE MATERIAL: This may for convenience be grouped into two classes: (1) official publications made by the belligerent nations from their archives in 1914 and 1915; (2) evidence which has since transpired, either as a result of the opening of foreign office archives after the war or from the personal testimony of diplomats and other informed persons. Documents of the first group, including the official British correspondence, the French Yellow Book, the Russian Orange Book, the Belgian Grey Book, the Serbian Blue Book, the German White Book, the Austro-Hungarian Red Book and a few subsequent publications by various powers, were published in *Diplomatic Documents* (1915) issued by the British government. There are innumerable other editions, one of the most convenient being the pamphlet republications by the American Association for International Conciliation. Of the many summaries of the evidence which appeared early in the war, perhaps the best is J. B. Scott, *Diplomatic Documents Relating to the Outbreak of the European War* (2 v., 1916).

The later wartime and postwar revelations have never been completely collected and summarized; indeed, new material is still sporadically coming to light. Perhaps the most important single series is the German *Die Grosse Politik der Europäischen Kabinette, 1871–1914*, edited by J. Lepsius, A. Mendelssohn Bartholdy and F. Thimme (40 v., 1922–27); a condensed translation was published in four volumes, 1928–31, and a translation of documents on the 1914 crisis (the so-called Kautsky documents) in 1924, *The Outbreak of the World War*, edited by M. Montgelas and W. Schücking. The *British Documents on the Origins of the War, 1898–1914*, edited by G. P. Gooch and Harold Temperley (11 v., 1926–   ) is also highly important. Many new French documents appear in the official *Documents diplomatiques français, 1871–1914* (1929–   ). A. F. Pribram, *The Secret Treaties of Austria-Hungary* (2 v., 1920) contains analysis as well as textual material from the Austrian archives; for fuller material, see *Österrich-Ungarns Aussenpolitik von der Bosnischen Krise 1908 bis zum Kriegsausbruch 1914* (8 v., 1930). Russian documents have been in part translated in *Un Livre noir* (3 v., 1922–27), edited by R. Marchand, *Der Diplomatische Schriftwechsel Iswolskis, 1911–14* (1924), edited by F. Stieve, and in *Entente Diplomacy and the World*, edited by B. de Siebert and G. A. Schreiner; the editing of some of these translations from the Russian is very unsatisfactory. W. H. Cooke and E. P. Stickney, *Readings in European International Relations since 1879* (1931) is a single-volume collection of some of the more interesting documents, old and new. See also G. B. Manhart, *Alliance and Entente, 1871–1914* (1932). G. P. Gooch, *Recent Revelations of European Diplomacy* (1930) is an excellent analysis of the later published material. Memoir literature is here listed under individual nations.

GENERAL STUDIES ON NATIONALISM, MILITARISM AND PACIFISM: C. J. Hayes, *Essays on Nationalism* (1926) and *The Historical Evolution of Modern Nationalism* (1931); Munroe Smith, *Militarism and Statecraft* (1918); H. H. Powers, *The Things Men Fight For* (1916); Edward Krehbiel, *Nationalism, War and Society* (1916); G. L. Dickinson, *The International Anarchy, 1904–14* (1926); R. B. Mowat, *The Concert of Europe* (1931); A. P. Higgins, *The Hague Peace Conferences and Other International Conferences* (1909); J. B. Scott, *The Hague Peace Conferences of 1899 and 1907* (2 v., 1909); Ramsay Muir, *Nationalism and Internationalism* (1916); P. T. Moon, *Imperialism and World Politics* (1926), the best book on the implications of colonial imperialism; Ralph Lane ("Norman Angell"), *The Great Illusion* (1914 ed.), a famous defense of pacifism on economic grounds; H. Feis, *Europe: the World's Banker, 1870–1914* (1930); Mildred Wertheimer, *The Pan-German League, 1890–1914* (1924), the best study of German expansionism, moderate expressions of which appear in P. Rohrbach, *German World Politics* (1915), by an advocate of "Berlin to Bagdad," and F. Neumann, *Central Europe* (trans. 1916), advocating "Mitteleuropa."

DIPLOMATIC STUDIES OF WAR ORIGINS: Decidedly the best of them all is S. B. Fay, *The Origins of the World War* (2 v., 1928), the first volume of which traces the remoter diplomatic causes and the second the immediate outbreak of the war. B. E. Schmitt, *The Coming of the War: 1914* (2 v., 1930) is as good for the immediate crisis of 1914, but needs to be supplemented by his *Triple Alliance and Triple Entente* (1934), and his other writings in books and periodicals to complete the picture of earlier events. Fay inclines a little towards the cause of the Central Powers and Schmitt to that of the Entente Allies, but both are before all else sound scholars seeking only the truth. G. P. Gooch, *History of Modern Europe, 1878–1919* (1923) is perhaps the best single volume study of diplomatic history in general, though E. Brandenburg's admirable *From Bismarck to the World War* (1933) rivals it in merit. The best book which definitely champions the cause of the Entente is the standard French work by Pierre Renouvin, *The Immediate Origins of the War* (1928), both moderate and weighty. Sir Charles Oman, *The Outbreak of the War of 1914–18* (1919) is a British contribution to the same side of the controversy. Favoring the German thesis, A. von Wegerer, *A Refutation of the Versailles War Guilt Thesis* (1930), and Count Max Montgelas, *The Case for the Central Powers* (1925) are the most important; H. E. Barnes, *The Genesis of the World War* (1926) is much more extreme.   J. F. Scott, *Five Weeks* (1927) surveys newspaper opinion during the crisis.

MEMOIRS AND STUDIES OF PARTICULAR NATIONS

AUSTRO-HUNGARIAN POLICY: J. Goricar and Lyman B. Stowe, *The Inside Story of the Austro-German Intrigue* (1920); A. F. Pribram, *Austrian Foreign Policy, 1908–18* (1923); Oswald Wedel, *Austro-German Diplomatic Relations, 1908–14* (1932); R. Gooss, *Das Wiener Kabinett und die Entstehung des Weltkrieges* (1919); Count J. Andrassy, *Diplomacy and the War* (1921); H. Friedjung, *Das Zeitalter des Imperialismus, 1884–1914* (3 v., 1919–22).

SERBIA AND THE SARAJEVO CRISIS: M. Bogichevich, *Causes of the War* (1919), though from a Serb, is hostile to the Serbian government; so is Mary Edith Durham, *The Serajevo Crime* (1925).   A more favorable view appears in R. W. Seton-Watson's *Sarajevo.   A Study in the Origins of the Great War* (1926).

RUSSIAN POLICY: *How the War began in 1914* (1925), from the diary of Baron Shilling of the Russian Foreign Office; Baron S. A. Korff, *Russia's Foreign Relations during the Last Half Century* (1922); F. Stieve, *Izvolsky and the World War* (1926), very hostile to Russian diplomacy; Baron Rosen, *Forty Years of Diplomacy* (2 v., 1922); S. D. Sazonov, *Fateful Years* (1928), by the Russian Foreign Minister.

GERMAN POLICY: In addition to the works of Brandenburg, Montgelas and von Wegerer already cited, mention may be made of B. von Bülow's *Memoirs* (4 v., 1931–32); Prince Lichnowsky, *Heading for the Abyss* (1928), an important criticism of Germany's Austrophil policy by the German Ambassador to London; Chancellor Theobald von Bethmann-Hollweg, *Reflections on the World War* (1920); F. von Pourtalès, *Meine Letzten Verhandlungen in St. Petersburg* (1927), by the German Ambassador to Russia; W. E. von Schoen, *The Memoirs of an Ambassador* (1922), by the German Ambassador to France; Karl Kautsky, *The Guilt of William Hohenzollern* (1920); the postwar writings of the Kaiser and the Crown Prince are singularly unilluminating.

FRENCH POLICY: R. Poincaré, *The Origins of the War* (1922) and *Memoirs* (4 v., 1926–28) by the war President; M. Paléologue, *An Ambassador's Memoirs* (3 v., 1924–25), by the French Ambassador to Russia; R. Viviani, *As We See It* (1923), by the French Premier of 1914; E. M. Carroll, *French Public Opinion and Foreign Affairs, 1871–1914* (1931); G. H. Stuart, *French Foreign Policy, 1898–1914* (1921); of the many French criticisms of national policy perhaps the best is A. Fabre-Luce, *The Limitations of Victory* (1926).

BRITISH POLICY: By far the most interesting official apologia is Viscount Edward Grey's account of his administration of the Foreign Office in *Twenty-Five Years* (2 v., 1925); the best of many criticisms of Grey's policy is H. Lutz, *Lord Grey and the World War* (1928).   Premier H. H. Asquith's *Genesis of the War* (1922) and *Memories and Reflections* (2 v., 1928) do not add much to our knowledge; more interesting are H. Nicolson, *Portrait of a Diplomatist* (1930), the life of his father Lord Carnock; Viscount Richard

Haldane, *Autobiography* (1929) and *Before the War* (1920); the reminiscences of Winston Churchill and David Lloyd George reveal more as to military than as to diplomatic history and will be later mentioned. *The Cambridge History of British Foreign Policy* (3 v., 1922–23); H. Kantrowicz, *The Spirit of British Policy and the Myth of the Encirclement of Germany* (1932), a very sympathetic German study; A. F. Pribram, *England and the International Policy of the European Great Powers, 1871–1914* (1931), by an able Austrian authority, may also be used to advantage.

OTHER COUNTRIES: A. Salandra, *Italy and the Great War. From Neutrality to Intervention* (1932); G. Giolitti, *Memoirs of My Life* (1923); H. A. Gibbons, *Venizelos* (1923), pro-Entente; P. Hibben, *Constantine I and the Greek People* (1920), anti-Entente; Djemal Pasha, *Memories of a Turkish Statesman* (1922). For American intervention, see Chapter XV.

CHAPTER XIV

THE WORLD WAR

The literature on the World War is but little less voluminous than that on its diplomatic origins. The principal belligerents have published official histories, such as the British *History of the Great War. Military Operations* (1922 ff.) and *Naval Operations* (1920–31), the French *Les Armées Françaises dans la Grande Guerre* (1922 ff.), the German *Der Weltkrieg* (1925 ff.). One of the best unofficial histories in English is J. Buchan, *A History of the Great War* (4 v., 1921–22), an abridgment of *Nelson's History of the War* (24 v., 1915–19). Another good history is F. H. Simonds, *History of the World War* (5 v., 1917–20). Some good single volume surveys are: C. J. H. Hayes, *A Brief History of the Great War* (1920); A. F. Pollard, *A Short History of the Great War* (1928); T. G. Frothingham, *A Guide to the Military History of the World War* (1920); B. H. Liddell Hart, *The Real War* (1930), iconoclastic and controversial; Sir G. G. Aston, *The Great War of 1914–18* (1930); W. L. McPherson, *The Strategy of the Great War* (1919).

Most statesmen and generals who took a leading part in the war have left us their impressions, e.g. Winston Churchill, *The World Crisis* (4 v., 1923–29), condensed into a one volume edition in 1931; David Lloyd George, *War Memoirs* (4 v. published, others in preparation, 1933–35); Ferdinand Foch, *Memoirs* (1931); J. J. C. Joffre, *Personal Memoirs* (2 v., 1932); E. Ludendorff, *Ludendorff's Own Story* (2 v., 1920); Paul von Hindenburg, *Out of My Life* (2 v., 1921); Sir William Robertson, *Soldiers and Statesmen, 1914–18* (2 v., 1926); Erich von Falkenhayn, *The German General Staff and Its Decisions, 1914–16* (1920); Liman von Sanders, *Five Years in Turkey* (1927); Charles Repington, *The First World War* (2 v., 1920).

SOME OTHER GENERAL STUDIES OF THE WAR: Sir Charles Lucas, *The Empire at War* (5 v., 1921–26); W. Martin, *Statesmen of the War in Retrospect* (1928); W. D. Puleston, *High Command in the World War* (1934), an analysis of civilian military control; J. de Pierrefeu, *Plutarch Lied* (1924), an attack on military reputations; W. S. Seaver, *Colossal Blunders of the War* (1930); Douglas Johnson, *Battlefields of the World War: A Study in Military Geography* (1921); B. H. Liddell Hart, *Reputations Ten Years After* (1928); H. D. Lasswell, *Propaganda Technique in the World War* (1927), the best of many books on the subject (for those who wish to study war propaganda in more detail R. H. Lutz has compiled a bibliography of over a hundred titles in the *Journal of Modern History*, Dec. 1933, pp. 496–516); E. L. Bogart, *Direct and Indirect Costs of the Great World War* (1919); C. R. Gibson, *War Inventions and How They Were Invented* (1917); L. Stallings, *The First World War* (1933), a photographic record; J. W. Garner, *International Law and the World War* (2 v., 1920).

STUDIES OF PARTICULAR CAMPAIGNS AND AREAS: Brand Whitlock, *Belgium* (2 v., 1919), by the American minister; Geo. I. Gay, *The Commission for Relief in Belgium* (1925), a statistical study; H. H. Sargent, *Strategy on the Western Front* (1920); A. von Kluck, *The March on Paris and the Battle of the Marne* (1920); G. H. Perris, *The Battle of the Marne* (1920); H. P. Pétain, *Verdun* (1930); H. Wendt, *Verdun, 1916* (1931); W. Churchill, *The Unknown War* (1931), a brilliant account of the eastern front; E. Dane, *British Campaigns in the Nearer East* (2 v., 1919) and *British Campaigns in Africa and the Pacific* (1919); G. Gordon-Smith, *From Serbia to Jugoslavia* (1920), on the Balkan campaign; Ahmed Emin, *Turkey in the World War* (1930); J. Masefield, *Gallipoli* (1916); L. Villari, *The War on the Italian Front* (1932) and *The Macedonian Campaign* (1922); T. E. Lawrence, *Revolt in the Desert* (1927), a picturesque study of the Arabian campaign; Paul Emil von Lettow-Vorbeck, *My Reminiscences of East Africa* (1920), by the German commander in that colony.

CHAPTER XV

AMERICA INTERVENES

NAVAL WARFARE: T. G. Frothingham, *The Naval History of the World War* (3 v., 1924–26); Sir Henry Newbolt, *Naval Operations* (4 v., 1920–25); Viscount J. R. Jellicoe, *The Grand Fleet, 1914–16* (1919) and *The Crisis of the Naval War* (1920); Alfred von Tirpitz, *My Memoirs* (2 v., 1919), by the famous German admiral; W. S. Sims and B. J. Hendrick, *Victory at Sea* (1920), an American contribution to the naval history of the war; Reinhardt Scheer, *Germany's High Sea Fleet in the World War* (1920); J. E. T. Harper, *The Truth about Jutland* (1927); G. von Hase, *Kiel and Jutland* (1926), a German view; Baron J. A. F. Fisher, *Memories and Records* (2 v., 1920), the original writings of a very original admiral; Lowell Thomas, *Count Luckner, the Sea Devil* (1927) and *Raiders of the Deep* (1928).

AMERICAN INTERVENTION: For the diplomatic steps leading to intervention, see J. B. Scott, *A Survey of International Relations between the United States and Germany, 1914–17* (1917); C. Seymour, *American Diplomacy during the World War* (*1934*), *Woodrow Wilson and the World War* (1922), a brief statement, and *The Intimate Papers of Colonel House* (4 v., 1926–28), an important study of Wilson's most trusted friend and diplomatic agent; B. J. Hendrick, *Life and Letters of Walter H. Page* (2 v., 1922); J. W. Gerard, *My Four Years in Germany* (1917), by the American Ambassador; Count J. von Bernstorff, *My Three Years in America* (1920), by the German Ambassador; Konstantin Dumba, *Memories of a Diplomat* (1932), by the Austrian Ambassador. For military aspects see J. S. Bassett, *Our War with Germany* (1919); T. G. Frothingham, *The*

American Reinforcement in the World War (1927); L. P. Ayres, *The War with Germany, a Statistical Summary* (1920); J. J. Pershing, *My Experiences in the World War* (2 v., 1931); J. B. McMaster, *The United States in the World War* (2 v., 1918–20); Shipley Thomas, *History of the A.E.F.* (1920); F. Palmer, *Newton D. Baker* (2 v., 1931), a biography of the American Secretary of War; Col. de Chambrun and Capt. de Marenches, *The American Army in the European Conflict*, A. Villate, *Les États-Unis d'Amerique et le Conflit Européen* (1919) and E. J. Réquin, *America's Race to Victory*, three French studies; P. C. March, *The Nation at War* (1932) by the American Chief of Staff. For Latin America see P. A. Martin, *Latin America and the War* (1925) and J. F. Rippy, *Latin America in World Politics* (1928).

CHAPTER XVI

THE COLLAPSE OF RUSSIA

J. Mavor, *The Russian Revolution* (1928), an excellent brief summary; V. I. Gurko, *War and Revolution in Russia* (1919), a study of the military collapse of the Tsar's empire; E. A. Ross, *The Russian Bolshevik Revolution* (1921); M. T. Florinsky, *The End of the Russian Empire* (1931); P. P. Gronsky and N. I. Astrov, *The War and the Russian Government* (1929); A. Bullard, *The Russian Pendulum* (1919); E. J. Dillon, *The Eclipse of Russia* (1918), with much firsthand material but many prejudices; Alexander Kerensky, *The Prelude to Bolshevism* (1919), *The Catastrophe* (1927) and *The Crucifixion of Liberty* (1934), three works by the anti-Bolshevist leader of moderate Russian Socialism; M. G. Hindus, *The Russian Peasant and the Revolution* (1920), an excellent study; L. Trotsky, *History of the Russian Revolution* (1932) by the famous Bolshevist leader after his exile; Frank A. Golder, *Documents of Russian History, 1914–17* (1927); Baron S. Korff, *Autocracy and Revolution in Russia* (1923); V. O'Hara and N. Makeef, *Russia* (1925); G. Vernadsky, *A History of Russia* (1929); G. G. Telberg and R. Wilton, *The Last Days of the Romanovs* (1920); V. Marcu, *Lenin* (1928); D. S. Mirski, *Lenin* (1931); G. Vernadsky, *Lenin, Red Dictator* (1931).

For the territorial disintegration of Russia see Judah L. Magnes, *Russia and Germany at Brest-Litovsk* (1919), a documented chronicle; Count Ottokar Czernin, *In the World War* (1919), the interesting memoirs of an Austrian diplomat; M. P. Price, *War and Revolution in Asiatic Russia* (1918); S. Rudnitsky, *Ukraine* (1918); H. J. Buxton, *Transcaucasia* (1926); Stephen Graham, *Russia in Division* (1925).

CHAPTER XVII

THE COLLAPSE OF THE CENTRAL POWERS

For the dissolution of Austria-Hungary and the rise of the succession states see: Karl F. Nowak, *The Collapse of Central Europe* (1924); J. Redlich, *Austrian War Government* (1929) and *Emperor Francis-Joseph of Austria* (1929); O. Jaszi, *The Dissolution of the Habsburg Monarchy* (1929); B. Auerbach, *L'Autriche et la Hongrie pendant la Guerre* (1925); F. von Kleinwachter, *Der Untergang des Osterreich-Ungarischen Monarchie* (1920);

Edmund Glaise von Horstenau, *The Collapse of the Austro-Hungarian Empire* (1930); E. Bagger, *Francis Joseph* (1927); O. Bauer, *The Austrian Revolution* (1925); Count S. Burian, *Austria in Dissolution* (1925); Polzer-Hoditz and A. Wolframitz, *Life of Emperor Karl* (1930); E. Benes, *My War Memories* (1928), by a famous Czech statesman; T. G. Masaryk, *The Making of a State* (1927), by the President of Czechoslovakia; V. Nosek, *Independent Bohemia* (1918); R. J. Kerner, *The Jugoslav Movement* (1918); H. Baerlein, *The Birth of Yugoslavia* (2 v., 1922); Arnold J. Zurcher, *The Experiment with Democracy in Central Europe* (1933); M. W. Graham, *New Governments of Central Europe* (1924). See also Chapter XXIII.

For the dissolution of the old Germany see: Ralph Lutz, *Fall of the German Empire, 1914-18* (1932), selected documents, and *The German Revolution of 1918-19* (1922); Arthur Rosenberg, *The Birth of the German Republic* (1931); George Young, *The New Germany* (1920), impressions of a sympathetic Englishman; Maurice Baumont, *The Fall of the Kaiser* (1931); H. Ströbel, *The German Revolution and After* (1923); G. P. Gooch, *Germany* (1925); M. P. Price, *Germany in Transition* (1924); Gustav Noske, *Von Kiel bis Kapp* (1920); Prince Maximilian of Baden, *Memoirs* (2 v., 1928). See also references for Chapter XXVII. The negotiations leading to the armistice are summarized in *Documents and Statements Relating to Peace Proposals and War Aims* (1919), edited by G. L. Dickinson.

CHAPTER XVIII

THE PEACE OF PARIS

The fullest general reference for the peace negotiations is H. W. V. Temperley (editor), *A History of the Peace Conference of Paris* (6 v., 1924). Other works worth attention include: C. H. Haskins and R. H. Lord, *Some Problems of the Peace Conference* (1920), dealing mainly with territorial questions; E. M. House and Charles Seymour (editors), *What Really Happened at Paris* (1921), a symposium by American experts; Ray Stannard Baker, *Woodrow Wilson and World Settlement* (3 v., 1922); A. P. Scott, *Introduction to the Peace Treaties* (1920); Bernard Baruch, *The Making of the Reparations and Economic Sections of the Treaty* (1920); J. M. Keynes, *The Economic Consequence of the Peace* (1920), the most important of the early attacks on the reparations settlement; A. Tardieu, *The Truth about the Treaty* (1921), the standard French defense of the peace of Versailles; Karl Nowak, *Versailles* (1929), a German viewpoint; H. W. Harris, *Peace in the Making* (1919); Winston Churchill, *The Aftermath* (1929); H. Nicolson, *Peacemaking, 1919* (1933); David Hunter Miller, *My Diary at the Conference of Paris* (20 v., 1928), a collection of source material which is, unfortunately, available only in a few libraries; Robert Lansing, *The Peace Negotiations, a Personal Narrative* (1921), very "anti-Wilson"; R. Martel, *The Eastern Frontiers of Germany* (1930), a study of the German-Polish frontier problem; Quincy Wright, *Mandates under the League of Nations* (1930); George L. Beer, *African Questions at the Paris Peace Conference* (1923); H. Howard, *The Partition of Turkey, 1913-23* (1931); L. P. Mair, *The Protection of Minorities* (1928); J. P. Chamberlain, *The Régime of the International Rivers* (1923).

Chapter XIX
The League of Nations

The League of Nations itself publishes an *Official Journal* and a monthly *Summary* besides many special reports on particular problems. For the negotiations which produced it, see especially David Hunter Miller, *The Drafting of the Covenant* (2 v., 1928) and Florence Wilson, *The Origins of the League Covenant* (1928). Other references on the League and its work: John S. Bassett, *The League of Nations: a Chapter in World Politics* (1928); P. J. N. Baker, *The League of Nations at Work* (1926); B. Bradfield, *A Little Book of the League of Nations, 1920–1927* (1927); C. Eagleton, *International Government* (1932); J. Epstein, *Ten Years Life of the League of Nations* (1929); H. R. G. Greaves, *The League Committees and World Order* (1931); Charles Howard-Ellis, *The Origin, Structure and Working of the League of Nations* (1928); R. Jones and S. S. Sherman, *The League of Nations: From Idea to Reality* (1927); F. Morley, *The Society of Nations* (1932); W. Rappard, *The Geneva Experiment* (1931) and *International Relations as Viewed from Geneva* (1925); A. Sweetser, *The League of Nations at Work* (1920); C. K. Webster, *The League of Nations in Theory and Practice* (1933).

FOR THE WORLD COURT AND INTERNATIONAL LABOR ORGANIZATION: Antonio de Bustamante, *The World Court* (1925); Manley O. Hudson, *The Permanent Court of International Justice* (1925) and *The World Court, 1921–31* (1931); A. P. Fachiri, *The Permanent Court of International Justice* (1925); P. C. Jessup, *The United States and the World Court* (1929); Edward Lindsey, *The International Court* (1931); John Wheeler-Bennett, *Information on the Permanent Court of International Justice* (1925); James T. Shotwell, *The Origins of the International Labor Organization* (2 v., 1934); G. N. Barnes, *History of the International Labour Office* (1926); *Labour as an International Problem*, by G. N. Barnes, J. T. Shotwell and others (1920); G. A. Johnston, *International Social Progress* (1924); Mrs. E. M. Oliver, *The World's Industrial Parliament* (1925); P. Périgord, *The International Labor Organization* (1926); World Peace Foundation, *The International Labour Organisation* (1931).

Chapter XX
The Search for Security

GENERAL STUDIES OF POSTWAR EUROPE: F. L. Benns, *Europe since 1914* (1934), excellent; W. C. Langsam, *The World since 1914* (1933, with supplementary chapter for 1934); I. Bowman, *The New World* (1928); J. H. Landman, *The World since 1914* (1934); R. L. Buell, *Europe: a History of Ten Years* (1928) and *International Relations* (1929 edition); C. Delisle Burns, *1918–1928. A Short History of the World* (1928); A. C. Coolidge, *Ten Years of War and Peace* (1927); A. J. Toynbee, *The World after the Peace Conference* (1925) and the periodic *Survey of International Affairs* (1925 ff.); A. E. Zimmern, *Europe in Convalescence* (1922); P. S. Mowrer, *Balkanized Europe* (1921); Ramsay Muir, *The Political Consequences of the Great War* (1930); C. A. Beard, *Cross Currents in Europe Today* (1922); Count Sforza, *Diplomatic Europe since the Treaty of Versailles* (1928); F. H.

Simonds, *How Europe Made Peace without America* (1927) and *Can Europe Keep the Peace?* (1931); Charles Hodges, *The Background of International Relations* (1931); R. B. Mowat, *A History of European Diplomacy, 1914–25* (1927); P. Gibbs, *Ten Years After* (1925); *These Eventful Years*, published by the Encyclopaedia Britannica (2 v., 1924). Many of these general references will be useful also for the later chapters and may be read in connection with them.

PACTS, ENTENTES AND PEACE PLANS: R. N. Coudenhove-Kalgeri, *Pan-Europe* (1926), a classic on its subject; É. Herriot, *The United States of Europe* (1930), a plea for economic federation by a French liberal; David Hunter Miller, *The Peace Pact of Paris* (1928), which may be supplemented by J. T. Shotwell, *War as an Instrument of National Policy* (1929), an analysis of the pact in detail; G. Glasgow, *From Dawes to Locarno* (1925); H. S. Quigley, *From Versailles to Locarno* (1927); D. P. Myers, *Origin and Conclusion of the Paris Pact* (1929); J. H. Ralston, *International Arbitration from Athens to Locarno* (1929); J. W. Wheeler-Bennett, *Information on the Renunciation of War* (1928) and *Information on the Problem of Security* (1927); P. J. N. Baker, *The Geneva Protocol* (1925); D. H. Miller, *The Geneva Protocol* (1925); J. O. Crane, *The Little Entente* (1931); F. Codresco, *La Petite Entente* (1930).

LIMITATION OF ARMAMENTS: H. N. Brailsford, *Olives of Endless Age* (1928); *Armaments Year Book* (1924 ff.) published by the League of Nations; P. J. N. Baker, *Disarmament* (1926); R. L. Buell, *The Washington Conference* (1922), perhaps the best account of its subject; S. de Madariaga, *Disarmament* (1929); D. P. Myers, *World Disarmament* (1932); G. Engely, *The Politics of Naval Disarmament* (1932); Y. Ichihashi, *The Washington Conference and After* (1928); J. W. Wheeler-Bennett, *Information on the Reduction of Armaments* (1925) and *Disarmament and Security since Locarno* (1932).

CHAPTER XXI
SOVIET RUSSIA

Wm. H. Chamberlin, *Soviet Russia* (1931), is perhaps the best all-round study in English; his later *Russia's Iron Age* (1934) emphasizes the grimmer side of Russian conditions. For the political structure of Russia, see especially W. R. Batsell, *Soviet Rule in Russia* (1929). The many studies by Maurice Hindus, such as *Humanity Uprooted* (1929), *The Great Offensive* (1933) and *Broken Earth* (1926) are admirable, especially for village and rural conditions. Other exceptionally useful references are: Calvin B. Hoover, *The Economic Life of Soviet Russia* (1931); P. Haensel, *The Economic Policy of Soviet Russia* (1930); James Mavor, *Economic History of Russia* (2 v., 1925 edition); G. F. Grinko, *The Five Year Plan of the Soviet Union* (1930), from official Soviet sources; Karl Borders, *Village Life under the Soviets* (1927); E. J. Dillon, *Russia Today and Yesterday* (1930); H. von Eckardt, *Russia* (1932); R. Fülöp-Miller, *The Mind and Face of Bolshevism* (1929); H. H. Fisher, *The Famine in Soviet Russia, 1919–23* (1927); W. T. Goode, *Bolshevism at Work* (1920); L. H. Guest, *The New Russia* (1926); S. N. Harper, *Making Bolsheviks* (1931), and *Civic Training in Soviet Rus-*

sia (1929); L. Lawton, *The Russian Revolution* (1927); and *An Economic History of Soviet Russia* (2 v., 1932); B. W. Maxwell, *The Soviet State* (1934); Arthur Rosenberg, *A History of Bolshevism* (1934); M. Ilin, *New Russia's Primer* (1931); A. Karlgren, *Bolshevist Russia* (1927); P. Miliukov, *Russia, Today and Tomorrow* (1922), by a moderate liberal; P. Scheffer, *Seven Years in Soviet Russia* (1931); E. Antonelli, *Bolshevik Russia* (1920); W. Gurian, *Bolshevism: Theory and Practice* (1932); R. W. Postgate, *The Bolshevik Theory* (1920); Bertrand Russell, *Bolshevism; Practice and Theory* (1920); H. N. Brailsford, *The Russian Workers' Republic* (1921); G. P. Fedotov, *The Russian Church since the Revolution* (1928); I. D. Levine, *Stalin* (1931).

INTERNATIONAL ASPECTS: A. L. P. Dennis, *The Foreign Policies of Soviet Russia* (1924); Louis Fischer, *The Soviets in World Affairs* (2 v., 1930); C. K. Cumming and W. H. Pettit, *Russian-American Relations, 1917–20* (1920); V. Iakhontov, *Russia and the Soviet Union in the Far East* (1931); L. Pasvolsky, *Russia in the Far East* (1922); A. Yarmolinsky, *The Jews and Other Minor Nationalities under the Soviets* (1929); R. P. Arnot, *Soviet Russia and Her Neighbors* (1927); B. C. Hopper, *Pan-Sovietism* (1931); H. J. Laski, *Communism* (1927); G. S. Counts, *The Soviet Challenge to America* (1931). See also references under Chapter XVI.

CHAPTER XXII

NATIONS OF THE BALTIC

IN GENERAL: M. W. Graham, *New Governments of Eastern Europe* (1927), constitutional studies of Russia, Poland and the Baltic States; J. Meuvert, *Histoire des pays baltiques* (1934), historical; Arthur Ruhl, *New Masters of the Baltic* (1921); Owen Rutter, *The New Baltic States and Their Future* (1926); A. M. Scott, *Beyond the Baltic* (1926); E. W. P. Newman, *Britain and the Baltic* (1930); and, as for all postwar nationalities, I. Bowman, *The New World* (1928).

IN PARTICULAR: T. W. Atchley, *Finland* (1931); F. Fox, *Finland Today* (1926); E. Van Cleef, *Finland — the Republic Farthest North* (1929); J. H. Wuorinen, *Nationalism in Modern Finland* (1931); H. Söderhjelm, *The Red Insurrection in Finland in 1918* (1919); K. N. Järvinen, *The Trade and Industry of Finland* (1922); A. Bihlmans, *Latvia in the Making, 1918–28* (1928); P. Meyer, *Latvia's Economic Life* (1925); A. Zalts, *Latvian Political Economy* (1928); F. J. Harrison, *Lithuania Past and Present* (1922) and *Lithuania* (1928); E. H. Lewinski-Corwin, *A Political History of Poland* (1917), for historical background; R. Dyboski, *Outlines of Polish History* (1931) and *Poland* (1933); R. Machray, *Poland, 1914–31* (1932); F. Bujak, *Poland's Economic Development* (1926); S. Karski, *Poland, Past and Present* (1927); C. Phillips, *The New Poland* (1923); W. E. Tennant, *Studies in Polish Life and History* (1924); N. O. Winter, *The New Poland* (1923); R. Martel, *The Eastern Frontiers of Germany* (1930), one of the fairest discussions of the "corridor question"; M. Felinski, *The Ukrainians in Poland* (1931); A. L. Goodhart, *Poland and the Minority Races* (1922).

Chapter XXIII
Nations of the Danube

GENERAL: M. W. Graham, *New Governments of Central Europe* (1927), valuable constitutional studies; M. H. H. Macartney, *Five Years of European Chaos* (1924); P. S. Maurer, *Balkanized Europe* (1921); H. L. McBain and L. Rogers, *New Constitutions of Europe* (1922); L. Pasvolsky, *Economic Nationalism of the Danubian States* (1929); G. E. R. Gedye, *Heirs to the Habsburgs* (1932); F. Codresco, *La Petite Entente* (1930); A. Mousset, *La Petite Entente* (1923); J. O. Crane, *The Little Entente* (1931); R. Machray, *The Little Entente* (1929).

AUSTRIA: Otto Bauer, *The Austrian Revolution* (1925); C. A. Macartney, *The Social Revolution in Austria* (1926); K. Hudeczek, *The Economic Resources of Austria* (1922); F. F. G. Kleinwächter, *Self-Determination for Austria* (1929) and F. Kleinwächter and H. von Paller, *Die Anschlussfrage* (1930), the best presentations of the case for union with Germany; P. Slosson, *The Problem of Austro-German Union* (1929).

HUNGARY: F. Eckhart, *A Short History of the Hungarian People* (1931), for background; O. Jaszi, *Revolution and Counter-Revolution in Hungary* (1924); Count P. Teleki, *The Evolution of Hungary and Its Place in European Politics* (1923); L. Buday, *Dismembered Hungary* (1923); E. Czekonacs, *Hungary New and Old* (1926); of a score or more published pleas for treaty revision in Hungary's interests perhaps the best is Count A. Apponyi, *Justice for Hungary* (1928).

CZECHOSLOVAKIA: T. G. Masaryk, *The Making of a State* (1927), by the President of Czechoslovakia; J. Opocensky, *The Collapse of the Austro-Hungarian Monarchy and the Rise of the Czechoslovak State* (1928); J. Papousek, *The Czechoslovak Nation's Struggle for Independence* (1928); J. Borovicka, *Ten Years of Czechoslovak Politics* (1929); J. Cisar and F. Pokorny, *The Czechoslovak Republic* (1922); L. Eisenmann, *La Tchécoslovaquie* (1921); J. Gruber, *Czechoslovakia* (1924); C. Holland, *Czechoslovakia* (1931); R. W. Seton-Watson, *Slovakia, Then and Now* (1931).

RUMANIA: J. S. Roucek, *Contemporary Roumania and Her Problems* (1932); D. Mitrany, *The Land and the Peasant in Roumania* (1930); J. Buchan, *Bulgaria and Romania* (1924); N. Iorga, *History of Roumania* (1926); C. U. Clark, *United Roumania* (1932) and *Bessarabia: Russia and Roumania on the Black Sea* (1927); S. Dragomir, *The Ethnical Minorities in Transylvania* (1927); Francis Deak, *The Hungarian-Rumanian Land Dispute* (1928), from the Hungarian angle; V. Madgearu, *Rumania's New Economic Policy* (1930); Marie (Dowager Queen), *The Country That I Love* (1925), lively court reminiscences.

YUGOSLAVIA: C. A. Beard and G. Radin, *The Balkan Pivot: Yugoslavia* (1929); H. Baerlein, *The Birth of Yugoslavia* (1922); J. Buchan, *Yugoslavia* (1923); K. S. Patton, *Kingdom of Serbs, Croats and Slovenes: Commercial and Industrial Handbook* (1928); A. Mousset, *La Royaume Serbe-Croate-Slovène* (1926).

Other references useful for this chapter have been listed under Chapters **XVII, XVIII and XX.**

CHAPTER XXIV

THE NEW NEAR EAST

BULGARIA: J. Buchan, *Bulgaria and Romania* (1924); L. Pasvolsky, *Bulgaria's Economic Position* (1930); G. C. Logio, *Bulgaria, Problems and Politics* (1919); L. Lamouche, *Le Bulgarie* (1922).

ALBANIA: C. A. Chekrezi, *Albania Past and Present* (1919); B. Bareilles, M. E. Durham and others, *Albania and the Albanians* (1920); J. Swire, *Albania. The Rise of a Kingdom* (1929); E. P. Stickney, *Southern Albania or Northern Epirus in European International Affairs* (1926).

GREECE: E. G. Mears, *Greece Today* (1929); J. Mavrogordato, *Modern Greece* (1931); William Miller, *Greece* (1928); B. Cunliffe-Owen, *Silhouettes of Republican Greece* (1928); Prince Andrew, *Towards Disaster* (1930); S. P. Ladas, *The Exchange of Minorities* (1932); C. B. Eddy, *Greece and the Greek Refugees* (1931).

TURKEY AND THE NEAR EASTERN QUESTION AFTER THE WAR: James L. Barton, *Story of Near East Relief* (1930); Hans Kohn, *A History of Nationalism in the East* (1929) and *Nationalism and Imperialism in the Hither East* (1932); W. M. Gewehr, *The Rise of Nationalism in the Balkans* (1931); J. A. R. Marriott, *The Eastern Question* (1930 edition); E. A. Powell, *The Struggle for Power in Moslem Asia* (1924), pro-Turkish; H. F. Armstrong, *The New Balkans* (1926) and *Where the East Begins* (1929), studies of Balkan boundaries; S. Panaretoff, *Near Eastern Affairs and Conditions* (1922); T. W. Arnold, *The Caliphate* (1924); L. Stoddard, *The New World of Islam* (1921); Baron G. J. S. Eversley and Sir Valentine Chirol, *The Turkish Empire* (1923); H. H. Howard, *The Partition of Turkey, 1913–23* (1931); E. G. Mears, *Modern Turkey* (1924); D. von Mikusch, *Mustapha Kemal* (1931); L. Ostrorog, *The Angora Reform* (1928); William Miller, *The Ottoman Empire and Its Successors* (1934); A. J. Toynbee, *The Western Question in Greece and Turkey* (1922), and *Turkey* (1927), with K. Kirkwood; C. Price, *The Rebirth of Turkey* (1923); Sir Telford Waugh, *Turkey: Yesterday, Today and Tomorrow* (1930); H. E. Wortham, *Mustapha Kemal of Turkey* (1931); K. Krüger, *Kemalist Turkey and the Middle East* (1932); F. Nansen, *Armenia and the Near East* (1928).

MANDATED TERRITORIES: Mrs. F. F. Andrews, *The Holy Land under Mandate* (2 v., 1931); N. Bentwich, *England in Palestine* (1932); A. Granovsky, *Land Problems in Palestine* (1926) and *Land Settlement in Palestine* (1930); M. Jastrow, *Zionism and the Future of Palestine* (1919); P. P. Graves, *Palestine — The Land of Three Faiths* (1923); H. M. Kallen, *Zionism and World Politics* (1921); J. Stoyanovsky, *The Mandate for Palestine* (1928); W. B. Worsfold, *Palestine of the Mandate* (1925); E. P. MacCallum, *The Nationalist Crusade in Syria* (1928); L. Stein, *Syria* (1926); John Loder, *The Truth about Mesopotamia, Palestine and Syria* (1923); R. Coke, *The Heart of the Middle East* (1925), on Mesopotamia; H. C. Luke, *Mosul and Its Minorities* (1925); T. Lyell, *The Ins and Outs of Mesopotamia* (1923). See also references for Chapters XVIII, XX, and XXX.

CHAPTER XXV
RECONSTRUCTION AND DEPRESSION IN WESTERN EUROPE

REPARATIONS AND WAR DEBTS: There is already a voluminous and mostly controversial literature on these vexed questions. A few of the more valuable references are: K. Bergmann, *The History of Reparations* (1927), a German view; J. M. Keynes, *A Revision of the Treaty* (1922), a sequel and vindication of his earlier *Economic Consequences of the Peace* (1920); H. G. Moulton and C. E. MacGuire, *Germany's Capacity to Pay* (1923); H. G. Moulton and L. Pasvolsky, *War Debts and World Prosperity* (1932) and *World War Debt Settlements* (1926); G. P. Auld, *The Dawes Plan and the New Economics* (1927); R. C. Dawes, *The Dawes Plan in the Making* (1925); H. G. Moulton, *The Reparation Plan* (1924); M. Sering, *Germany under the Dawes Plan* (1929); D. P. Myers, *The Reparation Settlement* (1929); J. W. Wheeler-Bennett and H. Latimer, *Information on the Reparation Settlement* (1930); W. R. Batsell, *The Debt Settlement and the Future* (1927).

OTHER ASPECTS OF ECONOMIC RECONSTRUCTION AND RELATED PROBLEMS: A. L. Bowley, *Some Economic Consequences of the War* (1930); Sir J. C. Stamp, *The Financial Aftermath of War* (1932); G. Cassel, *The Crisis in the World's Monetary System* (1932); H. C. Walter, *Foreign Exchange and Foreign Debts* (1926); H. T. Allen, *The Rhineland Occupation* (1927), by an American general; G. Greer, *The Ruhr-Lorraine Industrial Problem* (1925); H. Stegemann, *The Struggle for the Rhine* (1927); P. Wentzcke, *Ruhrkampf* (2 v., 1930–32); R. Recouly, *La Ruhr* (1923); H. Lichtenberger, *Relations between France and Germany* (1932); M. P. Price, *The Economic Problems of Europe* (1928); W. H. Pringle, *Economic Problems in Europe Today* (1928). See also the general references listed under Chapter XX and the references to particular countries under Chapters XXVI–XXX inclusive.

CHAPTER XXVI
FASCIST ITALY

POSTWAR ITALY: B. Croce, *A History of Italy, 1871–1915* (1929) is perhaps the best background study but it does not deal directly with postwar changes; J. A. R. Marriott, *The Makers of Modern Italy* (1931), and E. A. Mowrer, *Immortal Italy* (1922), overlap both periods. Most recent books on Italy are naturally concerned with Fascism. H. R. Spencer, *Government and Politics of Italy* (1932) analyzes the Fascist constitution; J. S. Barnes in *Fascism* (1931) and *The Universal Aspects of Fascism* (1927) eulogizes Fascist ideals; H. W. Schneider, *Making the Fascist State* (1928) and *Making Fascists* (1929), with S. B. Clough, traces the sources and roots of Fascism; L. Villari in *Italy* (1929) describes the new Italy as made over by the Fascisti. Other useful references in the same field include: Sir C. A. Petrie, *Mussolini* (1931); I. Bonomi, *From Socialism to Fascism* (1924), by a former Italian premier; G. Ferrero, *Four Years of Fascism* (1924), by an Italian liberal; H. N. Gay, *Strenuous Italy* (1927), sympathetic; H. E. Goad, *The Making of the Corporate State* (1932); P. Gorgolini, *The Fascist Movement in Italian Life* (1923), a good early work; Bolton

King, *Fascism in Italy* (1931), brief but good; G. Matteotti, *The Fascisti Exposed* (1924), an attack for which the author paid the penalty with his life; Odon Por, *Fascism* (1923); G. Prezzolini, *Fascism* (1927); G. Salve-mini, *The Fascist Dictatorship in Italy* (1927), on the whole the best an-tagonistic study of Fascism; L. Sturzo, *Italy and Fascismo* (1927); Sir F. Fox, *Italy Today* (1927); A. Pennachio, *The Corporative State* (1927); M. Currey, *Italian Foreign Policy, 1918–32* (1932), sympathetic; W. Parsons, *The Pope and Italy* (1929); B. Williamson, *The Treaty of the Lateran* (1929).

The best study of dictatorship in general is Count C. Sforza, *European Dictatorships* (1931); see also, A. J. Zurcher, *The Experiment with Democracy in Central Europe* (1933); *Dictatorship on Trial* (1930), by various authors; G. S. Counts, L. Villari and others, *Bolshevism, Fascism and Capitalism* (1932); K. Landauer and H. Honegger, *Internationaler Faschismus* (1928); F. Campo Battle, *Les Dictatures* (1930), and the references for particular countries.

Chapter XXVII

Germany from Democracy to National Socialism

Germany under the Republic: Besides the references given for Chapter XVII, see G. P. Gooch, *Germany* (1925), excellent; H. G. Daniels, *The Rise of the German Republic* (1927); G. H. Danton, *Germany Ten Years After* (1928); K. Francke, *German After-War Problems* (1927); E. Jäckh, *The New Germany* (1927); E. Luehr, *The New German Republic* (1929); M. P. Price, *Germany in Transition* (1924); H. Quigley and R. Clark, *Republican Germany* (1927); C. Horkenvach, *Das Deutsche Reich von 1918 bis Heute* (1931), an encyclopedic handbook; R. Brunet, *The New German Constitution* (1922); H. Oppenheimer, *The Constitution of the German Republic* (1923); J. W. Angell, *The Recovery of Germany* (1932 edition), an economic study; Sir P. Dawson, *Germany's Industrial Revival* (1926); W. Meakin, *The New Industrial Revolution* (1928); P. P. Reinhold, *The Economic, Financial and Political State of Germany since the War* (1928); H. Schacht, *The Stabiliza-tion of the Mark* (1927) by the head of the Reichsbank; R. K. Michels, *Cartels, Combines and Trusts in Postwar Germany* (1928); E. Koch-Weser, *Germany in the Post-War World* (1930); Count H. von Kessler, *Walther Rathenau* (1930); R. Olden, *Stresemann* (1930); A. Vallentin, *Stresemann* (1931).

Transition to the Dictatorship: K. Heiden, *A History of National Socialism* (1934); H. J. Heneman, *The Growth of Executive Power in Ger-many* (1934), stops short of the actual Hitler revolution; J. K. Pollock and H. J. Heneman, *The Hitler Decrees* (1934), translated texts of the new laws; C. B. Hoover, *Germany Enters the Third Reich* (1933), excellent survey; Hamilton F. Armstrong, *Hitler's Reich* (1933); A. Hitler, *My Battle* (1933), a rather naïve self-revelation by the German Leader; E. Lengyel, *Hitler* (1932); W. Lewis, *Hitler* (1931); "Nordicus," *Hitlerism* (1932); M. Florin-sky, *The Saar Struggle* (1935).

CHAPTER XXVIII

FRANCE AND HER NEIGHBORS

POSTWAR FRANCE: P. Vaucher, *Post-War France* (1934); J. Buchan, *France* (1923); Sisley Huddleston, *France* (1927); C. J. Hayes, *France: A Nation of Patriots* (1930), an able analysis of French nationalism; F. Sieburg, *Who Are These French?* (1932), a not unsympathetic German view; A. Siegfried, *France: a Study in Nationality* (1930); W. F. Ogburn and W. Jaffé, *The Economic Development of Post-War France* (1929); R. H. Soltau, *French Parties and Politics, 1871–1930* (1930); P. Renouvin, *Forms of War Government in France* (1927); A. Tilley, *Modern France* (1922); William MacDonald, *Reconstruction in France* (1922); R. M. Haig, *Public Finances of Post-War France* (1929); F. L. Schuman, *War and Diplomacy in the French Republic* (1931); S. H. Roberts, *History of French Colonial Policy, 1870–1925* (2 v., 1929); W. M. Sloane, *Greater France in Africa* (1924).

SPAIN AND THE REVOLUTION: S. de Madariaga, *Spain* (1930); J. A. Brandt, *Toward the New Spain* (1933); F. B. Deakin, *Spain Today* (1924); M. Hume, *Modern Spain* (1923); J. McCabe, *Spain in Revolt* (1931); R. Sencourt, *The Spanish Crown* (1932); E. Stewart, *Twenty-Nine Years* (1931), about Alfonso XIII; W. B. Harris, *France, Spain and the Rif* (1927).

MINOR POWERS OF WESTERN EUROPE: Geo. Young, *Portugal, Old and Young* (1917); G. Guyomard, *La Dictature Militaire au Portugal* (1927); William Martin, *History of Switzerland* (1931); R. C. Brooks, *Civic Training in Switzerland* (1930); E. Fueter, *Die Schweiz seit 1848* (1928); L. Pierard, *Belgian Problems since the War* (1929); T. H. Reed, *The Government and Politics of Belgium* (1924); S. B. Clough, *A History of the Flemish Movement in Belgium* (1930); A. C. J. Jitta, *Holland's Modern Renascence* (1930); A. J. Barnouw, *Holland under Queen Wilhelmina* (1923); E. C. Bellquist, *Some Aspects of the Recent Foreign Policy of Sweden* (1929); M. Blomstedt and F. Böök, *Sweden of Today* (1930); C. Hallendorff and A. Schück, *History of Sweden* (1929); A. Stomberg, *History of Sweden* (1931); G. Gathorne-Hardy, *Norway* (1925); K. Gjerset, *History of the Norwegian People* (2 v., 1915) and *History of Iceland* (1924); F. C. Howe, *Denmark, a Co-operative Commonwealth* (1921); M. F. Egan, *Ten Years Near the German Frontier* (1919), by the American minister to Denmark.

CHAPTER XXIX

THE BRITISH COMMONWEALTH OF NATIONS

IMPERIAL AFFAIRS IN GENERAL: Alfred Zimmern, *The Third British Empire* (1926); Ramsay Muir, *Short History of the British Commonwealth* (2 v., 1922–23); A. B. Keith, *Dominion Autonomy in Practice* (1930) and *The Sovereignty of the British Dominions* (1929); W. Y. Elliott, *The New British Empire* (1932); W. P. Hall, *Empire to Commonwealth* (1928); H. D. Hall, *The British Commonwealth of Nations* (1920); A. Demangeon, *The British Empire* (1925), a French view; H. E. Egerton, *British Colonial Policy in the Twentieth Century* (1922); A. J. Toynbee, *The Conduct of British Empire Foreign Relations since the Peace Settlement* (1928); P. J. N. Baker, *The Present Judicial Status of the British Dominions in International*

Law (1929); the chapters on the British Dominions in Lord Bryce, *Modern Democracies* (2 v., 1921).

GREAT BRITAIN: Gilbert Slater, *The Growth of Modern England* (1933 edition); C. F. G. Masterman, *England after War* (1923); E. C. Wingfield-Stratford, *History of British Civilization* (2 v., 1928); W. Dibelius, *England* (1930); W. R. Inge, *England* (1926), a highly individual view by a pessimistic ecclesiastic; A. Siegfried, *Post-War Britain* (1925) and *England's Crisis* (1931); F. W. Hirst, *The Consequences of the War to Great Britain* (1934); W. P. Maddox, *Foreign Relations in British Labour Politics* (1934).

IRELAND: Stephen Gwynn, *Ireland* (1925); D. R. Gwynn, *The Irish Free State* (1928); A. Phillips, *The Revolution in Ireland, 1906–23* (1926), hostile to the Irish movement; A. C. White, *The Irish Free State* (1923); R. M. Henry, *The Evolution of Sinn Fein* (1920); E. Hull, *A History of Ireland and Her People* (1931); J. D. Clarkson, *Labour and Nationalism in Ireland* (1925).

CHAPTER XXX

EUROPE AND THE WIDER WORLD

EGYPT, INDIA, AND THE MIDDLE EAST: Geo. Young, *Egypt* (1927); P. G. Elgood, *The Transit of Egypt* (1928); Sir Valentine Chirol, *The Egyptian Problem* (1920); Lord Lloyd, *Egypt since Cromer* (1933); Sir Wm. Goodenough, *Recent Constitutional Developments in Egypt* (1924); P. F. Martin, *Egypt, Old and New* (1923); E. W. P. Newman, *Great Britain in Egypt* (1928); M. T. Symons, *Britain and Egypt* (1925); Sir Valentine Chirol, *India* (1926); W. I. Hull, *India's Political Crisis* (1930); G. N. Singh, *Indian States and British India* (1930); E. Thompson, *Reconstructing India* (1930); C. H. Van Tyne, *India in Ferment* (1923); D. N. Banerjee, *The Indian Constitution and Its Actual Working* (1926); E. A. Horne, *The Political System of British India* (1922); C. F. Andrews, *Mahatma Gandhi's Ideas* (1930) and *Mahatma Gandhi, His Own Story* (1930); Mohandas K. Gandhi, *Young India, 1919–22* (1923) and *Young India, 1924–26* (1927), extracts from his speeches and writings; Sir H. Lovett, *History of the Indian Nationalist Movement* (1920); R. Rolland, *Mahatma Gandhi* (1924); Katherine Mayo, *Mother India* (1927), a violent and much debated attack on Hindu social organization and customs; S. Zimand, *Living India* (1928); Sir P. M. Sykes, *History of Persia* (2 v., 1930); Vincent Sheean, *The New Persia* (1927); Sir. G. F. MacMunn, *Afghanistan* (1929).

FAR EASTERN AFFAIRS: H. Kohn, *History of Nationalism in the East* (1929); G. M. Dutcher, *Political Awakening of the East* (1925); N. D. Harris, *Europe and the East* (1926); H. B. Morse and H. F. MacNair, *Far Eastern International Relations* (1928); P. J. Treat, *The Far East* (1928); H. M. Vinacke, *History of the Far East in Modern Times* (1928); Sir A. F. Whyte, *Asia in the Twentieth Century* (1926); S. G. Cheng, *Modern China* (1919); K. S. Latourette, *Development of China* (1929); Paul Monroe, *China. A Nation in Evolution* (1928); E. T. Williams, *China Yesterday and Today* (1927) and *Short History of China* (1928); A. N. Holcombe, *The Chinese Revolution* (1930); H. F. MacNair, *China's International Relations* (1926) and *China in Revolution* (1931); T. T. C. Woo, *The Kuomintang and the*

Future of the Chinese Revolution (1928); Hsü Shushi, *China and Her Political Entity* (1926); Sir A. F. Whyte, *China and the Foreign Powers* (1928); M. J. Bau, *The Foreign Relations of China* (1922); R. L. Buell, *The Washington Conference* (1922); Y. Ichihashi, *The Washington Conference and After* (1928); W. W. Willoughby, *Foreign Rights and Interests in China* (2 v., 1927); L. A. Lyall, *China* (1934); K. Adachi, *Manchuria* (1925); P. T. Etherton and H. H. Tiltman, *Manchuria, the Cockpit of Asia* (1932); P. H. Clyde, *International Rivalries in Manchuria* (1926); O. Lattimore, *Manchuria, Cradle of Conflict* (1932); Sir H. G. Parlett, *Brief Account of Diplomatic Events in Manchuria* (1929); Carl W. Young, *International Relations of Manchuria* (1929) and *Japan's Special Position in Manchuria* (3 v., 1931); W. L. Godshall, *International Aspects of the Shantung Problem* (1923); G. C. Allen, *Modern Japan and Its Problems* (1928); R. Fujisawa, *Recent Aims and Political Development of Japan* (1923); I. O. Nitobe, *Japan* (1931); Alleyne Ireland, *The New Korea* (1926).

AMERICAN RELATIONS WITH THE OLD WORLD: R. G. Adams, *History of the Foreign Policy of the United States* (1924); G. H. Blakeslee, *Recent Foreign Policy of the United States* (1925); L. M. Sears, *History of American Foreign Relations* (1927); C. P. Howland, *Survey of American Foreign Relations* (4 v., 1928–31); J. H. Latané, *History of American Foreign Policy* (1927); S. Brooks, *America and Germany, 1918–25* (1925); F. L. Schuman, *American Policy towards Russia since 1917* (1928); A. Tardieu, *France and America* (1927); J. D. Whelpley, *British-American Relations* (1924); F. R. Dulles, *America in the Pacific* (1932); P. J. Treat, *Japan and the United States* (1928); B. H. Williams, *Economic Foreign Policy of the United States* (1929); H. P. Fairchild, *Immigration: A World Movement and Its American Significance* (1928); Geo. Peel, *The Economic Impact of America* (1928). See also Chapters XV and XXV.

APPENDIX

RULERS AND GOVERNMENTS IN EUROPE
SINCE 1870

Albania. Turkish to 1913.
    Prince Wilhelm of Wied, 1913–14.
    Provisional governments to 1928.
    King Zog I, 1928–
Austria. Part of Austria-Hungary to 1918.
    Republic, 1918– ; dictatorship established in 1934.
Austria-Hungary.
    Emperor-King Francis Joseph, 1848–1916.
    Emperor-King Charles I (IV of Hungary), 1916–18.
Belgium.
    King Leopold II, 1865–1909.
    King Albert, 1909–34.
    King Leopold III, 1934–
Bulgaria. Part of Turkey to 1878.
    Prince Alexander, 1879–86.
    Prince Ferdinand, 1887–1908; King, 1908–18.
    King Boris III, 1918–
Czecho-Slovakia. Part of Austria-Hungary to 1918.
    Republic, 1918–
Denmark.
    King Christian IX, 1863–1906.
    King Frederick VIII, 1906–12.
    King Christian X, 1912–
Estonia. Part of Russia to 1918.
    Republic, 1918–
Finland. Part of Russia to 1918.
    Republic, 1918–
France.
    Emperor Napoleon III, 1852–70.
    Provisional Republic under Adolphe Thiers, 1871–73.
    Presidents of the Third Republic:
    Marshal MacMahon, 1873–79.
    Jules Grévy, 1879–87.
    F. Sadi Carnot, 1887–94.
    Casimir-Périer, 1894–95.
    Félix Faure, 1895–99.
    Émile Loubet, 1899–1906.
    Armand Fallières, 1906–13.
    Raymond Poincaré, 1913–20.
    Paul Deschanel, 1920.

Alexandre Millerand, 1920–24.
Gaston Doumergue, 1924–31.
Paul Doumer, 1931–32.
Albert Lebrun, 1932–

Germany.

Emperor (Kaiser) Wilhelm I, 1871–1888 (King of Prussia since 1861, head of the North German Confederation since 1867).
Emperor Friedrich III, 1888.
Emperor Wilhelm II, 1888–1918.

Republic, 1918–

Presidents Friedrich Ebert, 1919–25, and Paul von Hindenburg, 1925–34; *under dictatorship* of Chancellor Adolf Hitler, 1933–

Great Britain.

Queen Victoria, 1837–1901.
King Edward VII, 1901–10.
King George V, 1910–

Prime Ministers:

William E. Gladstone, 1868–74.
Benjamin Disraeli (Earl of Beaconsfield), 1874–80.
Gladstone, 1880–85.
Marquess of Salisbury, 1885–86.
Gladstone, 1886.
Salisbury, 1886–92.
Gladstone, 1892–94.
Earl of Rosebery, 1894–95.
Salisbury, 1895–1902.
Arthur James Balfour, 1902–05.
Sir Henry Campbell-Bannerman, 1905–08.
Herbert H. Asquith, 1908–16.
David Lloyd George, 1916–22.
Andrew Bonar Law, 1922–23.
Stanley Baldwin, 1923.
J. Ramsay MacDonald, 1923–24.
Baldwin, 1924–29.
MacDonald, 1929–1935 (coalition after 1931).
Baldwin, 1935–

Greece.

King George I, 1863–1913.
King Constantine, 1913–17.
King Alexander, 1917–20.
King Constantine (restored), 1920–22.
King George II, 1922–24.

Republic, 1924–

Hungary. Part of Austria-Hungary to 1918.
Republic under provisional governments, 1918–20.
Regent Nicholas Horthy, 1920–

Iceland. United with Denmark but enjoying home rule since 1918.

Irish Free State. United with Great Britain but enjoying home rule since 1922.

Italy.
> King Victor Emmanuel II, 1861–78 (King of Sardinia since 1849).
> King Humbert, 1878–1900.
> King Victor Emmanuel III, 1900–
> *Dictatorship* under Benito Mussolini since 1922.

Latvia. Part of Russia to 1918.
> *Republic, 1918–*

Lithuania. Part of Russia to 1918.
> *Republic, 1918–*

Montenegro.
> Prince Nicholas, 1860–1910; King, 1910–18.
> *Since 1918 part of Yugoslavia.*

Netherlands.
> King William III, 1849–90.
> Queen Wilhelmina, 1890–

Norway. United with Sweden to 1905.
> King Haakon VII, 1905–

Poland. Divided among Russia, Austria and Prussia to 1918.
> *Republic, 1918–* (virtually, though not formally, a dictatorship after 1926 under Marshal Pilsudski).

Portugal.
> King Louis, 1861–89.
> King Charles, 1889–1908.
> King Manuel II, 1908–10.
> *Republic, with frequent dictatorships, 1910–*

Rumania.
> Prince Charles (Carol) I, 1866–81; King, 1881–1914.
> King Ferdinand, 1914–27.
> Regency on behalf of King Michael, 1927–30.
> King Carol II, 1930–

Russia (and U.S.S.R.).
> Tsar Alexander II, 1855–81.
> Tsar Alexander III, 1881–94.
> Tsar Nicholas II, 1894–1917.
> *Provisional Republic, 1917.*
> *Soviet dictatorship, 1917–*

Serbia.
> Prince Milan, 1868–82; King, 1882–89.
> King Alexander, 1889–1903.
> King Peter, 1903–18; King of Yugoslavia, 1918–21.
> *Since 1918 part of Yugoslavia.*

Spain.
> King Amadeo of Savoy, 1870–73.
> *Provisional Republic, 1873–75.*
> Alfonso XII, 1875–85.
> Alfonso XIII, 1886–1931 (*Regency* to 1902; *dictatorship* of Primo de Rivera, 1923–30).
> *Republic, 1931–*

Sweden.
>   King Charles XV, 1859–72.
>   King Oscar II, 1872–1907.
>   King Gustavus V, 1907–

Switzerland.   Republic under federal constitution of 1848.

Turkey.
>   Sultan Abdul Aziz, 1861–76.
>   Sultan Murad V, 1876.
>   Sultan Abdul Hamid II, 1876–1909.
>   Sultan Mohammed V, 1909–18.
>   Sultan Mohammed VI, 1918–22.
>   *Republic under virtual dictatorship of Mustafa Kemal, 1922–*

Yugoslavia (Kingdom of Serbs, Croats and Slovenes).
>   King Peter I, 1918–21 (King of Serbia since 1903).
>   King Alexander, 1921–34.
>   Regency on behalf of King Peter II, 1934–

The Papacy (since 1929 rulers of *Vatican City* in Rome).
>   Pius IX, 1846–78.
>   Leo XIII, 1878–1903.
>   Pius X, 1903–14.
>   Benedict XV, 1914–22.
>   Pius XI, 1922–

Minor sovereignties in Europe:

Andorra — Republic under French and Spanish protection.

Danzig — Till 1919 German; city Republic under protection of the League of Nations.

Liechtenstein — Principality between Switzerland and Austria.

Luxemburg — Grand Duchy; independent since 1867 but attached to the German customs union till 1919 and to the Belgian since 1922.   In personal union with the Netherlands to 1890.

Monaco — Principality on Mediterranean coast of France.

Saar Valley — District administered by League of Nations, 1920–35; to Germany, 1935–

San Marino — Republic surrounded by Italian territory.

INDEX